Critical Terms for Literary Study

Critical Terms
for
Literary Study

Second Edition

Edited by Frank Lentricchia

and Thomas McLaughlin

The University of Chicago Press
Chicago and London

The University of Chicago Press, Chicago 60637
The University of Chicago Press, Ltd, London
© 1990, 1995 by The University of Chicago
All rights reserved. Published 1995
Printed in the United States of America
15 14 13 12 11 10 09 08 07 06   4 5 6 7 8

ISBN: 0-226-47203-5 (paper)

Library of Congress Cataloging-in-Publication Data

Critical terms for literary study / edited by Frank Lentricchia and
Thomas McLaughlin. — 2nd ed.
p.   cm.
Includes bibliographical references and index.
1. Criticism — Terminology.   2. Literature — Terminology.
3. English language — Terms and phrases.   I. Lentricchia, Frank.
II. McLaughlin, Thomas.
PN81.C84   1995
801'.95'014 — dc20   94-43640
                                                CIP

♾ *The paper used in this publication meets
the minimum requirements of the American National Standard for
Information Sciences — Permanence of
Paper for Printed Library Materials, ANSI Z39.48–1992.*

Contents

Preface to the Second Edition
ix

Introduction
Thomas McLaughlin
1

I. LITERATURE AS WRITING

1 Representation
W. J. T. Mitchell
11

2 Structure
John Carlos Rowe
23

3 Writing
Barbara Johnson
39

4 Discourse
Paul A. Bové
50

5 Narrative
J. Hillis Miller
66

6 Figurative Language
Thomas McLaughlin
80

7 Performance
Henry Sayre
91

8 Author
Donald E. Pease
105

II. INTERPRETATION

9 Interpretation
Steven Mailloux
121

10 Intention
Annabel Patterson
135

11 Unconscious
Françoise Meltzer
147

12 Determinacy/Indeterminacy
Gerald Graff
163

13 Value/Evaluation
Barbara Herrnstein Smith
177

14 Influence
Louis A. Renza
186

15 Rhetoric
Stanley Fish
203

III. Literature, Culture, Politics

16 Culture
Stephen Greenblatt
225

17 Canon
John Guillory
233

18 Literary History
Lee Patterson
250

19 Gender
Myra Jehlen
263

20 Race
Kwame Anthony Appiah
274

21 Ethnicity
Werner Sollors
288

22 Ideology
James H. Kavanagh
306

23 Popular Culture
John Fiske
321

24 Diversity
Louis Menand
336

25 Imperialism/Nationalism
Seamus Deane
354

26 Desire
Judith Butler
369

27 Ethics
Geoffrey Galt Harpham
387

28 Class
Daniel T. O'Hara
406

In Place of an Afterword — Someone Reading
Frank Lentricchia
429

References
447

List of Contributors
465

Index
469

Preface to the Second Edition

THE SECOND EDITION of *Critical Terms for Literary Study* adds six new essays to the collection: "Popular Culture," "Diversity," "Imperialism/Nationalism," "Desire," "Ethics," and "Class." All have been added to part three of the book: "Literature, Culture, Politics." We did not choose these terms with this part of the book in mind. Rather we added terms that we would like to have included in the first edition and terms that we thought reflected recent developments in literary study. But all of our new essays in fact belong in this section; they reflect the cultural turn in literary study, long ago predicted in the work of Kenneth Burke, for which literary works are cultural practices that relate in complex ways to other cultural practices, and many of those other cultural practices can be read effectively through terms that derive from literary interpretation. From this perspective, for example, sonnets on the beauty of the forest make a new kind of sense next to the language of timber legislation, and advertisements by timber and environmental lobbies are best understood in terms of their reliance on complex narratives of progress and conservation. Literary studies has learned from the versatility and passion of cultural studies, and cultural studies has much to learn from the commitment to textual analysis and aesthetic pleasure of literary studies.

We believe that these essays have at least two important messages for contemporary literary criticism in its cultural turn and for culture studies more generally. All interpretations of cultural practice rest upon powerful assumptions and commitments, many of which are carried in the specific terms of our critical language, and the goal of raising consciousness about everyday culture cannot be achieved unless these terms of interpretation themselves are examined critically. It is not self-evident what "desire" is, or what the "ethics" of reading are, and any interpretation that proceeds without examining such terms will reproduce cultural and political assumptions rather than question them. The sobering truth that even the most self-critical interpretations can't finally escape those enabling assumptions does not argue against theoretical reflection — absence of absolute interpretive freedom does not deny the existence of relative but crucial critical distance. Cultural studies must continue to theorize its own practice.

A number of these essays also demonstrate the necessity of intensive textual interpretation for the health of critical theory. Theory must always be learning from the act of reading, even as it can make finer and more powerful reading possible. Theoretical reflection itself derives from reading experiences that force us to question our own role in the making of meaning. And what's the good of theory if it doesn't make us better readers? It's as readers that we survive or fall in postmodern culture, and it's as readers that we experience the deepest textual pleasures and cultural illuminations. These days in English classes the text might as likely be Sonic Youth as *The Waste Land,* but there is nothing in the pleasure of one to deny pleasure in the other. And the ability to read both texts carefully and to reflect on the terms that enable those readings is one tactic that makes possible a critical consciousness in our cultural moment.

Introduction

Thomas McLaughlin

L ITERARY theory, which has a deserved reputation for its stylistic and conceptual difficulty, has escaped from the academy and become part of popular culture. "Deconstruction" is a word that gets used in *Newsweek*. A current British pop group, Scritti Pollitti, publishes its lyrics under the copyright of "Jouissance Music," adapting for their own purposes the term that the French critic Roland Barthes used to describe the pleasure of reading. "Jouissance," the French idiomatic equivalent of "coming," appealed to Barthes because he called for a reading without restraint, a reading that amounted to a creative act, fully as inspired as writing. The fact that this term finds its way into pop culture suggests how pervasive the mind-set of literary theory has become in our time. I have even heard a basketball coach say that his team had learned to deconstruct a zone defense. Literary theory has permeated our thinking to the point that it has defined for our times how discourse about literature, as well as about culture in general, shall proceed. Literary theory has arrived, and no student of literature can afford not to come to terms with it.

By "literary theory" I mean the debate over the nature and function of reading and writing that has followed on the heels of structuralist linguistics and cultural analysis. The basic premises of criticism have been interrogated, again and again, from perspectives as diverse as feminism, deconstruction, Marxism, psychoanalysis, semiotics, and reader-response theory. What holds these various and often combative programs and schools of thought together under the rubric of theory is a shared commitment to understanding how language and other systems of signs provide frameworks which determine how we read, and more generally, how we make sense of experience, construct our own identity, produce meaning in the world. Theory, then, gets at very basic questions that any serious reader must face.

And yet many serious readers do resist theory. They are troubled rather than challenged by it. Theory questions the assumptions by which readers read, and some readers feel that theory thereby draws unnecessary attention to a process that ought to be impulsive and emotional. Like a runner who has just had a coach analyze his stride and finds himself stumbling awkwardly, a reader might feel accosted by theory. Everything feels unnatural. What is an author? Should we care about the author's intentions? What is writing? How do (or should) readers proceed? What is at stake when we interpret literature? What is literature, and what isn't? How do we judge the value of a literary work? Questions. Too many questions.

And no lack of answers. Theory is contested territory. Every one of the questions I just raised, and a million more, elicits a complex array of answers, all engaged in rhetorical struggle. Theory is certainly not a place for readers to go for easy answers, for guides to good reading. Though every theorist offers an answer of one kind or another to such questions, the cumulative effect of the various answers is to leave readers with more complicated and more unsettling questions. And many readers—students and faculty, academics and other careful readers—feel that these questions come at the expense of their own response. Theory is cerebral. Even when it proclaims the Dionysian, its performance is always Appollonian. It doesn't let you just react emotionally and trust your intuition. It probes, asking, How did you do that? How did you make that sense of this text? Where are you coming from?

So the very project of theory is unsettling. It brings assumptions into question. It creates more problems than it solves. And, to top it off, it does so in what is often a forbidding and arcane style. Many readers are frightened off by the difficulty of theory, which they can then dismiss as an effort to cover up in an artificially difficult style the fact that it has nothing to say. This response seems to me valid as an emotional reaction to the often maddening difficulty of reading theory, but it is finally just defensive. Of course theory is difficult—sometimes for compelling reasons, sometimes because of offensive self-indulgence—but simply *assuming* that it is all empty rhetoric ultimately keeps you from confronting the real questions that theory raises.

Theory isn't difficult out of spite. It is difficult because it has proceeded on the premise that language itself ought to be its focus of attention; that ordinary language is an embodiment of an extremely powerful and usually unquestioned system of values and beliefs; and that using ordinary language catches you up in that system. Any discourse that was out to uncover and question that system had to find a language, a style, that broke from the constraints of common sense and ordinary language. Theory set out to produce texts that could not be processed successfully by the commonsensical assumptions that ordinary language puts into play. There are texts of theory that resist meaning so powerfully—say those of Lacan or Kristeva—that the very process of failing to comprehend the text is part of what it has to offer.

But legitimate as the difficulty of theory can be, one consequence of its stylistic commitment is that it has ghettoized itself, defining itself as an esoteric discipline for advanced critics in elite institutions. And, accordingly, the critical strategies that theory makes possible have had a limited political impact. The pop culture of our time shows signs, as I mentioned earlier, that students and general readers may be ready for theory, but until very recently theory has not been ready for them. Over the last five years there have been signs that theory could have a larger educational and cultural impact. Some curricula have been revised in the light of theory; some textbooks have begun to attempt to introduce theory to a more general audience. This text is part of that effort. Our aim is to present students and readers who want to learn about theory with some examples of theorists at work. We wanted to resist the tendency common to some introductions to theory to provide capsule summaries of "critical schools" or "approaches." Such essays might provide an abstract and conceptual framework for beginners, but they do not provide the *experience* of theory, which ought to engage the reader in a struggle over language and with language. What we asked theorists to do was to question the language of criticism—in other words, to *do* theory. Each theorist considered a different term prevalent in literary discourse, examining its history, the controversies it generates, the questions it raises, the reading strategies it permits. We also asked them to do so for an audience that was not conversant with recent theory. As a result, we are able to present essays in theory that demonstrate as well as articulate the basic issues that theory has raised.

Our concentration on the terms of criticism comes out of the conviction that the language we use in talking and writing about literature sets the boundaries within which we read. If we want to get at the assumptions that shape our reading practice, we should pay attention to the language we use as critical writers. In the terms of critical discourse, especially in the "ordinary language" of criticism, we can see at work the framing and shaping power of our particular brand of common sense. Almost all of the terms we chose are common and ordinary language, not technical terms or neologisms. They are terms that are particularly prone to the forgetfulness that comes with habitual use. We can put them into play as though they were neutral terms, exerting no particular pressure, commonly understood and beyond question. They do such good work for us that they make themselves invisible.

The essays in this volume pose problems for such an easy process. They insist that terms have a history, that they shape how we read, and that they engage larger social and political questions. They also assume that the meaning of the term is a matter of dispute, which is simply true in today's theoretical environment. The essays want to spotlight terms that function most efficiently when they are working behind the scenes. In some ways the model for our interest in the history of terms is the work of Raymond Williams, in such books as *Keywords* and *Marxism and Literature*. Williams's point is not simply that the meanings of terms change, but that their history impinges on their current use, and that the radical changes that terms undergo suggest that there is no stable and reliable meaning for any term. Terms cannot be used as though they were neutral instruments. Terms such as "culture" and "race" have been put to so many uses in so many different social and interpretive settings that no use of them can be innocent. Using a term commits you to a set of values and strategies that it has developed over the history of its use. It is possible to use a term in a new way, but it is not possible to escape the term's past.

A brief example can be seen in the history of the term "unity," which is often used in critical discourse as though it described a timeless and unquestionable value in the arts. Great art is unified, the theory goes, and the more diversity it includes and organizes, the greater the art. But even a brief look at the history of the term suggests that there is little agreement on the nature or even the desirability of unity. We need only think of the difference between the rather rigid concept of unity in some neoclassical critics like Boileau and Corneille—for whom unity meant following a set of rules about the arrangement of time, place, and action in a play—and the more fluid and organic notion of unity in the Romantics—for whom unity was achieved not by following rules but by infusing the materials of the work with the author's personality. In our century, the American New Critics transformed "unity" into a procedural principle which mandated that an interpretation of a work account for all its details as interrelated elements of a thematic or formal whole. More contemporary theorists, as a critique of this procedure, have tended to see "unity" as a coercive reading strategy, requiring us to impose unity on texts—like Blake's *Marriage of Heaven and Hell*—that seem to be blasting to smithereens. "Unity," from this perspective, can force us as readers who work under its auspices to accept it as a given and not question whether it is a necessary and inevitable quality of art.

In addition to emphasizing the historicity of terms, the essays in this volume also demonstrate that critical terms take part in larger social and cultural debates. Terms cannot simply be used and discarded—using them places you inside an argument, both in the sense that others might deny the importance of the term, and that they might disagree with your definition and deployment of the term. Furthermore, the argument is not a "purely literary" one; using a term engages you, whether you know it or not, in specific cultural and political arguments as well. If you read and interpret literature from the perspective that the term "gender" provides, you will cross with critics who see it as irrelevent to the study of literature (which, they might claim, transcends gender). You will also have to make clear exactly how the term functions for you, which will engage you in yet another debate with others who use the term differently. As a result, your use of the term had better be conscious and self-aware, taking account of the commitments that the term makes for you, because even without your awareness the term will make commitments—whether you like it or not. The term still exerts its power. But an unselfconscious use of a term can experience that power only as a limitation, a blindness that cannot be detected. A more critical use of the term allows a clearer sense of what it enables as well as what it neglects and, thereby, provides a degree of control for the reader at work. Of course, it is impossible to gain perfect control of terminology. We make commitments whenever we use language, and they are too many and too complex to be fully mastered. But using a term critically at least increases our awareness of the commitments we do make.

This text does not, however, attempt to cover the entire range of current critical terms. Recent theory has produced too many new terms, and these are in the process of sifting into an already broad spectrum of traditional terms. Since we wanted our essays to be substantial investigations of the terms, total coverage of the field was impossible. We chose not to deal with terms that function as a specialized vocabulary within a particular theoretical program—words like Derrida's "trace" or Foucault's "archaeology." Rather, we focused our attention on words widely used within critical discourse. Some of them, like "writing" and "author," are ordinary language words that have become centers of theoretical speculation and controversy. Others, like "culture" and "discourse," are terms whose relationship to literary study has changed in the light of recent theory. Traditional terms of literary analysis—those that might be included in a handbook of literature, such as "symbol" or "point of view"—are generally not included in this text, but only because of space limitations. These terms, which have now come almost to serve as the vernacular language of criticism, themselves deserve serious attention. They are on one level simply useful heuristic devices, yet they bring along with them commitments as complex as the terms we focus on here. Terms like "character" and "plot" will not be superseded, but they must be—and, indeed, are being—thought through in order to make sense of the assumptions they bring into play.

The terms in this volume, though, seem to us to call for immediate attention. They are used widely, often loosely, and with little agreement on their meaning. They are often deployed unselfconsciously, as a function of their common use. The selection of terms, however, is not based on a cool assessment of the needs of the current moment. It is, rather, a selection that suggests what we think should be the commitments of contemporary theory. Although the contributors to the volume bring to their tasks very different principles and practices, it is possible to discern some common, if not unanimous, themes.

I would suggest three important concerns around which the terms cluster. One set of terms, like "discourse," "structure," and "narrative," suggests that literature is best understood not as a self-contained entity but rather as a writing practice, a particular formation within the world of discourse. Terms such as "determinacy" and "intention" address the issue of interpretation directly, reflecting what many in the discipline see as a current crisis in our understanding of how meaning is produced. A third group of terms, like "race," "gender," and "ideology," places literature and its interpretation inside a larger cultural context, suggesting that there are political questions at issue in the reading process. The terms chosen for the text give, we feel, a rough overview of the current concerns of literary criticism and theory. They are the terms that seem to produce the most powerful interpretive questions at this moment, so they demand our attention in order to understand what they empower and what they constrain.

Examining the first group of terms, we see that they empower an inquiry into literature as writing not elevated into a realm of pure art but, rather, remaining open to the same social entanglements and limitations that condition all writing. This position contests the formalist or New Critical emphasis on the appreciation of literature in purely aesthetic terms, as writing that lifts us out of history—out of ourselves, finally—into a timeless and universal realm of beauty and truth. The essays in this text on such terms as "writing," "figurative language," and "narration" raise questions that apply to literature but also to other forms of writing as well, and therefore suggest that literary writing does not enjoy a privileged status within the arena of discourse. Figurative language does not happen only in poetry, and narrative does not happen only in novels. A philosophical text can be informed by a narrative structure; a political text can rest on a powerful figure of speech. And if these features of discourse do not respect any putative boundary between literature and other forms of writing, neither do the political and worldly concerns of writing. Thinking of literature as writing emphasizes a text's entanglement in language as a system of values: literature is part of the process by which the values of a culture are communicated. When we read, we encounter those values in a familiar form, so that they seem natural in their reliability, their power to make sense of experience.

Many critics have argued for the value of literature as a disruption of the very patterns that it employs. By its admittedly fictional status, the argument runs, literature reveals its own productive power. Literature draws attention to the value system, displaying it in operation. And once we attend to the fact that our frame of reference is socially produced, we can think through to the possibility of changing it. But this movement toward greater critical self-consciousness does not free readers from culture; rather, it situates them ever more finely. Readers always occupy a position from which they read.

Thinking of literature as writing also entails a commitment to the active and productive role of interpretation. As writing, literature is implicated in systems of language and culture that open it to the work of reading. Recent theory has emphasized the work of the reader who actuates the potential meanings made possible by the text and by the interpretive practices through which the reader works. Terms such as "evaluation" and "interpretation" in this text remind us that value and meaning are the outcomes of an active process, and that the process always occurs within a specific cultural and political context. It is the reader who produces meaning, but only by participating in a complex of socially constructed and enforced practices. Value and meaning do not transcend history and culture, just as literature itself does not. Interpretation—the process of producing textual meaning—is therefore rhetorical. It does not live in a realm of certain truths; it lives in a world where only constructions of the truth are possible, where competing interpretations argue for supremacy. Terms perform at least two functions within interpretation: they set the boundaries within which interpretation may proceed, and they help enforce the rhetoric of an interpretation by setting the terms of the debate. In a context in which we begin with the premise that no single "correct" interpretation is possible, since interpretation is always rhetorical, we find that terms serve the function of shaping our reading process and of enforcing the rhetorical power of the writing that comes out of that reading. Terms, that is, wield power in an open interpretive field.

The terms of the text also suggest, as I have emphasized, the participation of literature in culture and politics. Literature is a formation within language, which is the prime instance of the cultural system. The production of literature always occurs within a complex cultural situation, and its reception is similarly situated. Authors and readers are constituted by their cultural placement. They are defined inside systems of gender, class, and race. They operate inside specific institutions that shape their practice. They have been brought up inside powerful systems of value, especially powerful because these systems present values as inevitable rather than as ideological. As a result, acts of reading are always culturally placed, angled at the text from a specific point of view. Readers cannot legitimately claim to speak from outside or above the culture in some abstract and objective position that allows access to the hidden but authentic truth. Reading relies too much on the values and habits of mind that culture ratifies to claim an anthropological objectivity.

It is the purpose of this text to examine terms in order to discover the positions they provide for us as readers. These terms commit us to particular values, and if we are aware of those commitments, we can legitimately *take* the positions we inhabit. Every reading promotes the values that make it possible. A reading is a rhetorical act within a huge cultural debate; it is a matter of taking sides. Taking sides does not involve an apocalyptic moment of choice between two neatly opposed schools of thought—socialism or individualism, patriarchy or feminism, closed or open models of interpretation. Rather, taking sides develops over time, through a series of decisions and commitments in specific reading situations that develop into a cultural style, a way of negotiating experience. Terms remind us that reading is social and therefore political. Readers need to know how the use of a term enlists them into the debate.

After the three sections of terms in the text, there follows an essay by Frank Lentricchia which, as its title suggests, takes the place of an afterword. A traditional afterword sums up the points made by the book, providing a sense of closure. Instead, this essay dramatizes and demonstrates the issues the book raises by presenting a reading of a poem, Wallace Stevens's "Anecdote of the Jar."

Just as we chose not to present in these essays introductions to theory but rather instances of theory, Lentricchia offers a reading that is informed by the issues raised by current theory. His essay acts out the options and problems raised by various theoretical schools and approaches as they are encountered by "someone reading." He also demonstrates that no reading is, or should desire to be, innocent of political involvement. "Anecdote of the Jar" is not an otherworldly artifact, even if it seems to claim that status for itself; it sharpens our awareness of the structures of power that made it possible and make our reading of it possible.

The essays in this book are out to bring those structures to the surface. The terms by which reading proceeds are the instruments of those powerful structures, setting out the lines in which reading proceeds. It is therefore interesting to note that the etymology of "terminology" designates it as the study of boundaries. A "term" is a boundary line, a line of demarcation. It defines a field in which work can be done, within the limits of the term. But like all boundaries, even those meticulously surveyed, terms are social and arbitrary, not natural and inevitable. What divides my property from my neighbor's is not a natural boundary but a social system within which certain definitions of property prevail. It is important to remember that terms function in the same way. They limit and regulate our reading practices. But they do not do so by divine fiat. Their limitations can be brought to consciousness, their regulations can be overcome, as Lentricchia's essay suggests. It is not the job of this text to regulate those boundaries more carefully. Rather, these essays attempt to de-naturalize the limits that our critical system imposes.

If to define is to close off questions and meanings, then the essays in this collection are not definitions. They question the terms, searching for their powers and their weaknesses. Terms are inevitable—no discourse could go on without them. But they can be used in various ways, unselfconsciously, as though their meaning were self-evident, or consciously, with the awareness that using a term shapes reading and interpretation. Awareness is not freedom, but freedom from terminology is not the goal. A more modest and attainable goal is learning to negotiate the complexities of life in language. Learning how terms work is a part of learning how meaning is produced, and this, in turn, is part of the process of entering into that productive activity.

I
Literature as Writing

1

Representation

W. J. T. Mitchell

PROBABLY the most common and naive intuition about literature is that it
is a "representation of life." Unlike many of the terms in this collection,
"representation" has always played a central role in the understanding of literature. Indeed, one might say that it has played the definitive role insofar as the
founding fathers of literary theory, Plato and Aristotle, regarded literature as
simply one form of representation. Aristotle defined all the arts—verbal, visual,
and musical—as modes of representation, and went even further to make representation the definitively human activity:

> From childhood men have an instinct for representation, and in
> this respect man differs from the other animals that he is far more
> imitative and learns his first lessons by representing things.

Man, for many philosophers both ancient and modern, is the "representational
animal," *homo symbolicum,* the creature whose distinctive character is the creation
and manipulation of signs—things that "stand for" or "take the place of" something else.

Since antiquity, then, representation has been the foundational concept in aesthetics (the general theory of the arts) and semiotics (the general theory of
signs). In the modern era (i.e., in the last three hundred years) it has also become
a crucial concept in political theory, forming the cornerstone of representational
theories of sovereignty, legislative authority, and relations of individuals to the
state. We now think of "representative government" and the accountability of
representatives to their constituents as fundamental postulates of modern government. One obvious question that comes up in contemporary theories of representation, consequently, is the relationship between aesthetic or semiotic representation (things that "stand for" other things) and political representation
(persons who "act for" other persons). And one obvious place where these two
forms of representation come together is the theater, where persons (actors)
stand for or "impersonate" other (usually fictional) persons. There are vast differences, of course, between Laurence Olivier playing Hamlet and Ronald Rea-

gan playing the role of the president—the difference, say, between playing and real life; between a rigid script and an open, improvised performance; or between an aesthetic contract and a legal one—but these should not blind us to the structural similarities of the two forms of representation or to the complex interaction between playful fantasy and serious reality in all forms of representation. The fact that Ronald Reagan began his career as an actor and has continually exploited the symbolic, theatrical character of the presidency only makes the links between aesthetic/semiotic and political forms of representation more unavoidable.

What is the "structure" that is common to both the political and semiotic forms of representation? One way to think of it is as a triangular relationship: representation is always *of* something or someone, *by* something or someone, *to* someone. It seems that only the third angle of representation need be a person: we can represent stones with dabs of paint or letters or sounds, but we can represent things only *to* people. The other two angles can be occupied by people but need not be: I can represent a man with a stone, or a stone with a man; but it would seem very odd to speak of representing either a stone or a man *to* a stone. There also may be a fourth dimension to representation not captured by our triangle, and that would be the "intender" or "maker" of the representation, the one who says, "let this dab of paint stand for this stone to someone." This more complete picture of representation might be mapped as a quadrilateral with two diagonal axes, one connecting the representational object to that which it represents, the other connecting the maker of the representation to the beholder:

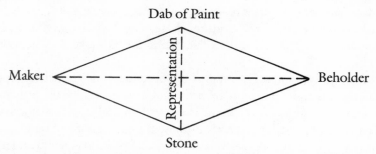

We might call these connecting lines the "axis of representation" (linking the dab of paint to the stone) and the "axis of communication" (linking the persons who understand the relation of paint to stone), respectively. The crossing of these axes suggests, I hope, one of the potential problems that comes up with representations: they present a barrier that "cuts across," as it were, our lines of communication with others, presenting the possibility of misunderstanding, error, or downright falsehood. As soon as we begin to *use* representations in any social situation—to claim, for instance, that this dab of paint represents *the fact that* this stone is in that place and looks like this—then representation begins to play a double role, as a means of communication which is also a potential obstacle to it.

So far I am speaking of simple, almost "atomistic" cases of representation, in which one thing stands for one other thing. But clearly the business of representation is much more complex than this. Representation is an extremely elastic notion which extends all the way from a stone representing a man to a novel representing a day in the life of several Dubliners. Sometimes one thing can stand for a whole group of things, as when the word "tree" stands for a concept that "covers" a multitude of individual things, or a political representative stands for a people, or a stick figure stands for the general concept of man, or a narrative represents a whole series of events. And the representational sign never seems to occur in isolation from a whole network of other signs: the dab of paint that stands for a stone will probably do so only in the context of a whole field of dabs of paint that represent other things adjacent to the stone—grass, earth, trees, sky, other stones. Take the dab of paint out of that context, and it ceases to represent, becomes merely a dab of paint. In a similar way, the word "tree" represents a certain class of objects only in the context of a language, just as a note or a musical phrase has meaning only in relation to a larger piece and familiar systems of tonality. These "systems" (tonality, language, representational schemes in painting) may be called "codes," by which I simply mean a body of rules for combining and deciphering representational signs. When something stands for something to somebody, it does so by virtue of a kind of social agreement—"let us agree that this will stand for that"—which, once understood, need not be restated on every occasion. In fact, the decision to let A stand for B may (and usually does) open up a whole new realm of possibilities for representation: B becomes a likely candidate to stand for C, and so on.

Aristotle says that representations differ from one another in three ways: in object, manner, and means. The "object" is that which is represented; the "manner" is the way in which it is represented; the "means" is the material that is used. What I am calling "codes" here are basically the same thing as Aristotle's "means"—that is, language, musical forms, paint. But the "manner" suggests yet another feature of representation, and that is the particular way a representational code is employed. The "means" of literary representation is language, but there are many ways of employing that means (dramatic recitation, narration, description) to achieve all sorts of effects (pity, admiration, laughter, scorn) and represent all sorts of things. Similarly, all paintings may employ shapes, shades, and colors on a two-dimensional surface (and this may be called the painter's "code"), but there are many ways of depicting a tree, many ways of applying paint to a surface. Some of them may become institutionalized as styles or genres, and these, like codes, are social agreements ("let us agree to represent this with that used in *this way*"), only of a more specialized nature. These "minicodes" associated with styles of representation are usually called "conventions."

The difference between a code and a convention may be illustrated by thinking of the difference between a medium and a genre: film is a medium, a material means of representation with a complex set of rules for combining and deciphering its signs; whereas the Hollywood Western is a particular kind of film, a genre that is recognized by the persistence of certain conventional elements (shootouts, wide open spaces, cowboys, Indians) from one example to another. In a similar way, we might think of language as one medium of representation, "literature" as the name of the aesthetic use of that medium, and things like poetry, the novel, and drama as very large genres within that medium.

One crucial consideration that enters into any analysis of representation is the *relationship* between the representational material and that which it represents. A stone may stand for a man, but how? By virtue of *what* "agreement" or understanding does representation occur? Semioticians generally differentiate three types of representational relationships under the names of icon, symbol, and index. An iconic account of the relation "stone-represents-man" would stress *resemblance:* a certain stone might stand for a man because it is upright, or because it is hard, or because its shape resembles that of a man. ("Mimesis" and "imitation" are thus iconic forms of representation that transcend the differences between media: I can imitate—i.e., mimic or produce a resemblance of—a sound, speech act, gesture, or facial expression and, thus, iconically reproduce it; icons are not just pictures.) Symbolic representations, by contrast, are not based on the resemblance of the sign to what it signifies but on arbitrary stipulation: the stone stands for a man because "we say so," because we have agreed to regard it this way. Representation in language is "symbolic," in that letters, words, and whole texts represent sounds and states of affairs without in the least resembling what they represent. Indexical representation, finally, explains "standing for" in terms of cause and effect or some "existential" relation like physical proximity or connectedness: the stone represents a man because a man set it up as a marker, to indicate (like a trace or footprint) the fact that he was here; a glove, a strand of hair, or a fingerprint are, to the skillful detective, all representations by "indication" of the person who left them behind. There is nothing, of course, to prevent any particular representation from employing more than one of these relationships: a written text may symbolically represent (describe or narrate or dramatize) an action, and it may also indexically represent (indicate the presence of) its author as the "cause" of which it is an "effect." Photographs are commonly thought to combine iconic and indexical representation, standing for visual objects by virtue of both resemblance and cause and effect.

Now it is important to realize that the long tradition of explaining literature and the other arts in terms of representation is matched by an equally long tradition of discomfort with this notion. Plato accepted the common view that literature is a representation of life, but for that very reason he thought it should be banished from the ideal state. Representations, Plato reasoned, are mere substitutes for the things themselves; even worse, they may be false or illusory substitutes that stir up antisocial emotions (violence or weakness), and they may represent bad persons and actions, encouraging imitation of evil. Only certain kinds of representations, carefully controlled by the state, were to be permitted into Plato's republic of rational virtue.

Although Plato's hostility to representation may seem extreme, we should recognize that some prohibitions or restrictions on representations have been practiced by every society that has produced them. Taboos against graven images, against writing or uttering the name of God, against the representation of the human form, against the representation of evil or ugly objects, against sex or violence, are an equally important part of the "social agreements" that constitute representation. The formula "let this stand for that to them" is regularly subjected to restrictions on subject matter ("let this stand for *anything but* that") or on the audience/spectator ("let this stand for that, but *not* to them"). Sometimes the prohibition may be directed at particular types of representational relationships: iconic representations, especially pictures and statues, are generally subjected to more stringent restrictions than symbolic or verbal representations. Greek dramatic conventions allowed the narrative, descriptive representation of violence but not its direct, visual portrayal on the stage. Pornography provides the most interesting examples of all these attempts to limit the triangle of representation, either by specifying the kind of persons who may witness the representation ("adults"; "18 and over"; "men only") or by restricting the kind of things that may be represented (no frontal nudity; no genitals; no actual sex acts), or by restricting the kind of representational signs that may be employed (dirty pictures and movies are usually subjected to more stringent prohibitions than dirty books).

It should be clear that representation, even purely "aesthetic" representation of fictional persons and events, can never be completely divorced from political and ideological questions; one might argue, in fact, that representation is precisely the point where these questions are most likely to enter the literary work. If literature is a "representation of life," then representation is exactly the place where "life," in all its social and subjective complexity, gets into the literary work.

There have been many other challenges to the notion of literary representation. Most of them, like prohibitions against idolatry or pornography, accept the basic model of the representational triangle but try to restrict or modify it in the service of some set of values. Thus, "idealist" theories of the arts will often posit some "higher nature" as the preferred object of representation and consign the representation of ordinary life to "lower" genres, such as caricature or satire, or some nonaesthetic genre, like "documentary" or "history." Realist theories of the arts tend to consign the idealist genres to the realm of "romance" and to see them as merely imaginary, fanciful representations. Both theories adopt the representational model of art: they simply disagree about what is to be represented (what Aristotle called the "object").

More strenuous challenges to representation come from the traditions of expressionism and formalism. Expressionism generally posits an unrepresentable essence (God, the soul, the author's intention) that is somehow manifested in a work. The "somehow" is the key: the unrepresentable is often construed as the invisible, the unpicturable, even the unspeakable—but not, generally, as the unwritable. Writing, arbitrary marks, hieroglyphics, and allegory are the signs that "encrypt" representation in a secret code. Thus, the cult of the artistic genius and the aura-laden artifact often accompany the expressive aesthetic. The aesthetic object does not "represent" something, except incidentally; it "is" something, an object with an indwelling spirit, a trace in matter of the activity of the immaterial. The anthropological model for the expressive aesthetic is fetishism, which does not treat its sacred objects as icons (i.e., representations by resemblance; pictures) or, in a sense, as representations at all (though they are frequently describable as indexes). The mimetic aesthetic, by contrast, finds its anthropological counterpart in the notion of idolatry, the worship of graven images that represent by resemblance.

Formalist or "abstract" theories of art have provided the most fundamental challenges to representational models in the modern era. Many of these theories take music (which, for obvious reasons, is hard to describe in representational terms) as the paradigm for all the arts. Formalism emphasizes the representational means and manner—the materiality and organization of the "signifier" or representational object—and de-emphasizes the other two angles of the representational triangle. The represented object may even disappear when the medium turns itself back on its own codes, engaging in self-reflexive play. The potential witnesses to the representational act are reduced finally to an elite of technical experts and connoisseurs who appreciate the ostensibly nonrepresentational object. Modernism frequently presents itself as having "grown out of" representational models of art, language, and mind, and it has, in the modern era, been very unfashionable to talk about literature or the other arts as representations of life. To the formalist, literature is about itself: novels are made out of other novels; all poems are about language. If representation sneaks back in, it is likely to be turned backward: life imitates art, reality (nature, society, the unconscious) is a text, and there is nothing outside the text.

Once this turn is made, then the opposition between "life" and "literature" which animates the traditional notion of literary representation begins to fall apart. But the structure of representation itself, as a relation of standing for, seems to come back with a vengeance. Postmodern culture is often characterized as an era of "hyper-representation," in which abstract, formalist painting has been replaced by experiments like photorealism, and reality itself begins to be experienced as an endless network of representations. The paradigm for the arts shifts from the pure nonrepresentational formalism of abstract painting and music to mass media and advertising, in which everything is indefinitely reproducible and representable as a commodity. Categories such as "the thing itself," the "authentic," and "the real" which were formerly considered the objects of representation (or as the presence achieved by formal purity) now become themselves representations, endlessly reduplicated and distributed.

A survey of postmodern experiments in literary representation would be outside the scope of this essay, which in any case is intended to raise the issue of representation as a problem that runs throughout the history of literary production. Suffice it to say that concepts such as the identity of the text, the determinacy of meaning, the integrity of the author, and the validity of interpretation all play a role in the representational (or antirepresentational) character of literary texts. The highly self-conscious fictive "labyrinths" of Jorge Luis Borges, with their pastiches of scholarly and historical documentation, deadpan realism, and bizarre fantasy, are often cited as paradigms of postmodern literary representation.

But it may be more useful to take as an example of literary representation a more traditional text, one that initiates a historic shift in conventions of literary representation and that takes the activity of representation itself as a theme. Robert Browning's "My Last Duchess" provides an especially interesting case study because it draws together so many different conventions of literary representation (lyric, dramatic, and narrative), and because it reflects as well on other modes of representation, including the pictorial and the political. Browning's text, to begin with, is a representation of a speech act, and thus of a speaker, a listener, and a specific setting. The Duke of Ferrara is "presented" to us (represented, that is, as if he were immediately present to us), describing a painting of his late wife ("my last duchess") to the agent of a certain count whose daughter is engaged to be married to the duke.

My Last Duchess

FERRARA

That's my last duchess painted on the wall,
Looking as if she were alive. I call
That piece a wonder, now: Frà Pandolf's hands
Worked busily a day, and there she stands.
Will't please you sit and look at her? I said
"Frà Pandolf" by design, for never read
Strangers like you that pictured countenance,
The depth and passion of its earnest glance,
But to myself they turned (since none puts by
The curtain I have drawn for you, but I)
And seemed as they would ask me, if they durst,
How such a glance came there; so, not the first
Are you to turn and ask thus. Sir, 'twas not
Her husband's presence only, called that spot
Of joy into the Duchess' cheek: perhaps

Frà Pandolf chanced to say "Her mantle laps
"Over my lady's wrist too much," or "Paint
"Must never hope to reproduce the faint
"Half-flush that dies along her throat": such stuff
Was courtesy, she thought, and cause enough
For calling up that spot of joy. She had
A heart—how shall I say?—too soon made glad,
Too easily impressed; she liked whate'er
She looked on, and her looks went everywhere.
Sir, 'twas all one! My favor at her breast,
The dropping of the daylight in the West,
The bough of cherries some officious fool
Broke in the orchard for her, the white mule
She rode with round the terrace—all and each
Would draw from her alike the approving speech,
Or blush, at least. She thanked men—good! but thanked
Somehow—I know not how—as if she ranked
My gift of a nine-hundred-years-old name
With anybody's gift. Who'd stoop to blame
This sort of trifling? Even had you skill
In speech—which I have not—to make your will
Quite clear to such an one, and say, "Just this
"Or that in you disgusts me; here you miss,
"Or there exceed the mark"—and if she let
Herself be lessoned so, nor plainly set
Her wits to yours, forsooth, and made excuse,
—E'en then would be some stooping; and I choose
Never to stoop. Oh sir, she smiled, no doubt,
Whene'er I passed her; but who passed without
Much the same smile? This grew; I gave commands;
Then all smiles stopped together. There she stands
As if alive. Will't please you rise? We'll meet
The company below, then. I repeat,
The Count your master's known munificence
Is ample warrant that no just pretense
Of mine for dowry will be disallowed;
Though his fair daughter's self, as I avowed
At starting, is my object. Nay, we'll go
Together down, sir. Notice Neptune, though,
Taming a sea-horse, thought a rarity,
Which Claus of Innsbruck cast in bronze for me!

The first thing that may strike us about this poem is the way that Browning
renounces any direct representation of his own views: the poet does not lyrically
describe the painting, or narrate any events in his own voice; he lets his invented

character, the duke, do all the talking, as if he were a character in a play. The second thing that may strike us is that this is not a play but something like a fragment or extract—a single speech or "monologue"—presented, however, as a whole poem. Browning has, in other words, deliberately collapsed the distinction between two kinds of literary representation—the brief, self-sufficient lyric utterance of the poet, and the dramatic speech that would conventionally belong in a more extended representation—in order to create a new hybrid genre, the dramatic monologue. This "collapse" of lyric and dramatic conventions is itself an act of representation in which what would have been a part or fragment (a dramatic speech) is allowed to "stand for" or take the place of the whole. And, indeed, one of the pleasures of reading this brief monologue is the unfolding of the whole drama that it represents in miniature. We quickly surmise that the duke is an obsessively jealous husband who had his last duchess killed because she was too free with her affections and approval—"she liked whate'er / She looked on, and her looks went everywhere."

The truly tantalizing mystery, however, is the meaning of the drama that this speech represents in little. Why is the duke telling this story to the agent of his bride-to-be's father? Is he trying to impress the emissary with his power and ruthlessness? Is he indirectly doing what he was unable to do with his last duchess, "stooping" to warn his next duchess that she had better be more discreet in her behavior? Is his speech better understood as a calculated threat in which signs of spontaneity are disguises for a deep plot or as an unwitting confession of the duke's inability to control the affections of women? What state of affairs (including "state of mind") does the duke's speech really represent? And (a rather different but related problem) what authorial intention or meaning is conveyed by Browning's *pre*sentation of the duke in just this way? What judgment are we being invited to make about the speaker and his words? It would seem clear enough that we are meant to disapprove, but what specific form does this disapproval take?

One way of getting at these questions is to reflect on the role of yet another character in the poem, that of the auditor, whose reactions are represented to us by the duke. The auditor is, of course, a representative of his "master" the count, a go-between who presumably is working out details about the dowry (the duke is evidently confident that the count's "known munificence" guarantees that he will make money on the marriage: "no just pretense / Of mine for dowry will be disallowed"), though the duke protests that he is really marrying for love ("his fair daughter's self, as I avowed / At starting, is my object"). But if the emissary represents the count to the duke in the implied drama of Browning's poem, he also represents the *reader* in its implied lyric address: like us, he is the auditor of the speech. What does this mean? What role are we, as readers, being coerced into by having ourselves represented within the poem?

One possibility is that Browning wants to place his reader in a position of

weakness and servitude, forced to hear a repugnant, menacing speech but deprived of any voice or power to counteract it. The count's representative, presumably, has the responsibility for seeing that negotiations go smoothly in a
marriage that will raise the count's daughter in the sociopolitical order (the difference between a duke and a count, exemplary representatives of feudal hierarchy, is crucial here). Should he warn the count that he's marrying his daughter
to a Bluebeard? Should he warn the daughter to watch her step? Neither of these
actions really opposes the duke's will; on the contrary, they are ways of carrying
out his will, of "stooping" on the duke's behalf to convey warnings the duke
would never "stoop" to make in person. If the duke represents the aristocratic,
feudal social order, understood here principally as a system giving some men
absolute power over others, and particularly over women in a system of exchange, the emissary represents a servant class or (as a representative of the
reader) the new bourgeois class of nineteenth-century readers who may hear this
speech as the echo of a bygone era, the "bad old days" of absolute power—a
power which may be deplored, but which still has a power to fascinate, and
which lies beyond our intervention.

The only representation in this poem that seems to have some power to intervene is the portrait of the duchess, which seems still to mock the duke with its
free looks from the wall. He may control who can see her by drawing aside or
closing the curtain that veils the painting, but he cannot control the way the
painting looks. He could, of course, destroy it, just as he destroyed its original,
the duchess herself; but he chooses not to. Is that because he wants it as a reminder that now he has her under his power? Or because he is, in some sense,
no more capable of destroying the duchess's smiling image than he is of destroying those galling, disgusting memories of her behavior that he pours out on the
envoy? If the painting functions as a representation of the duke's power, it also
seems to be a continual reminder of his weakness, his inability to "make [his]
will / Quite clear" to his wife. In a similar way, the duke's whole performance,
his boasting speech to the envoy, is an expression of a wish for absolute power
that has just the opposite effect, revealing the duke as someone who is so lacking
in confidence about his power that he needs constant reassurance. His final appeal to the envoy to "notice" his statue of Neptune "taming a sea horse" is a
transparent invitation to see the duke as a god "taming" nature, much as he
"tamed" his duchess by having her painted on his wall. The duke thinks of his
power as something that is certified by his control of representations—by his
painting of the duchess hidden behind a curtain that only he can draw, by the
statue of Neptune "cast in bronze for me," by his control over the envoy's attention (and those whom the envoy represents) with a strategic display of his gallery of representations. What Browning shows us, however, is the uncontrolla-
bility of representations, the way they take on a life of their own that escapes and
defies the will to determine their meaning. If the duke truly has his last duchess

(or himself) under control, why does he need to veil her image with a curtain? If he is so sure of his choosing "never to stoop" to make his will clear, why is he so conspicuously "stooping" to an underling, seducing a mere representative with this odd mixture of boasting and self-betrayal?

These, at any rate, are some of the questions that arise with respect to the duke's manipulation of representations within the mini-drama that makes up the poem. But what if we raised similar sorts of questions about the poem *as itself* a representation? Suppose, for instance, we think of this poem as itself a kind of dramatic portrait, a "speaking picture" in the gallery of Robert Browning's poetry? To what extent is Browning himself—or the commentator who claims to speak for Browning's intentions—playing a role like that of the duke, showing off his own power by displaying his mastery over representation? Should we think of Browning's poem, and the readings it evokes, as something we might call "My Last Duke"? Most readers of this poem have registered some version of Robert Langbaum's insight that "condemnation" is "the least interesting response" to the duke's outrageous display of evil. Just as the duke seems to hypnotize the envoy, Browning seems to paralyze the reader's normal moral judgment by his virtuosic representation of villainy. His poem holds us in its grip, condemning in advance all our attempts to control it by interpretation as mere repetitions of the duke's attempt to control his gallery of representations.

Browning's poem should make it clear why there would be a strong impulse in literature, and in literary criticism, to escape from representation and why such an escape can never succeed. Representation is that by which we make our will known and, simultaneously, that which alienates our will from ourselves in both the aesthetic and political spheres. The problem with representation might be summarized by reversing the traditional slogan of the American Revolution: instead of "No taxation without representation," no representation without taxation. Every representation exacts some cost, in the form of lost immediacy, presence, or truth, in the form of a gap between intention and realization, original and copy ("Paint / Must never hope to reproduce the faint / Half-flush that dies along her throat"). Sometimes the tax imposed by representation is so slight that we scarcely notice, as in the perfect copy provided by a laser disk recording ("Is it real or is it Memorex?"). Sometimes it is as ample as the gap between life and death: "That's my last Duchess painted on the wall, / Looking as if she were alive." But representation does give us something in return for the tax it demands, the gap it opens. One of the things it gives us is literature.

SUGGESTED READINGS

Aristotle. *Poetics*.
Auerbach, Erich. [1946]. 1953. *Mimesis: The Representation of Reality in Western Literature*.

Baudrillard, Jean. 1981. *For a Critique of the Political Economy of the Sign.*

Cavell, Stanley. 1979. *The World Viewed: Reflections on the Ontology of Film.*

Derrida, Jacques. 1978. "The Theater of Cruelty and the Closure of Representation." In *Writing and Difference.*

Eco, Umberto. 1976. *A Theory of Semiotics.*

Goodman, Nelson. 1976. *The Languages of Art.*

Langbaum, Robert. 1957. *The Poetry of Experience.*

Meltzer, Françoise. 1987. *Salome and the Dance of Writing.*

Mitchell, W. J. T. 1986. *Iconology: Image, Text, Ideology.*

Peirce, Charles Sanders. 1931–58. "The Icon, Index, and Symbol." In *Collected Works.*

Pitkin, Hanna. 1967. *The Concept of Representation.*

Plato. *Republic,* Book 10.

2

Structure

John Carlos Rowe

"STRUCTURE" derives from the Latin *structura,* the substantive formed from the past participle *structus,* out of the verb *struere,* "to heap together, arrange," or, as in the English cognate, *to strew.* The common meanings of "arrangement," "construction," and "building" are etymologically at some odds with the common meaning of "to strew." In its modern usage, "structure" more commonly suggests "to build up" than to "scatter, spread here and there as by scattering or sprinkling," in the conventional usage of the verb *strew.* The contrast in modern usage between the scientific connotations of *structure* and the decidedly less systematic implications of *strew* may not quite qualify as an instance of what Freud termed, after Karl Abel, "the antithetical sense of primal words," but it serves to introduce some of the chief issues in the use of the term "structure" in modern critical theories.

Structure and *strew* are not antithetical meanings of *struere,* because both demonstrate a common concern with *spatial extension.* In modern thought, after Kant and Einstein, it is impossible to think *space* apart from some form of *temporality.* Virtually every twentieth-century theorist to use "structure" as a key term recognizes the interrelation of time and space as fundamental to the concept of structurality. In practice, however, many of these same theorists tend to subordinate time to space. In fact, this tendency to treat time as governed by space might be said to be characteristic of most important modern uses of the term "structure."

Whether one scatters things here and there or "piles up" or "heaps" items in an "arrangement," both temporal *acts* depend upon the occupation of space, or *extension.* Yet the nature of the space involved in each act is considerably different. "To strew" suggests casting or scattering elements "here and there" over some preexisting space, such as the earth, in any case an a priori ground. These elements take their particular meaning, as in the meaning of a religious rite in which grain or wine is scattered over the earth, by virtue of the relation constituted between preexisting space (the soil) and what is scattered (grain or wine). To *structure* elements by heaping or piling them together suggests that the ele-

23

ments, in relation to each other, constitute their own self-subsisting space. Thus a "structure" is built upon a "foundation," which is an essential part of the structure and compatible with all the other elements, even in the case of a "foundation" that is perfectly *natural* (such as the soil itself, in cases where no other foundation is provided).

This abstract and elementary distinction helps distinguish the different temporalities at work in acts of strewing and structuring. The "form" of what is scattered or strewn is intimately involved in the performance of the act and depends upon the a priori ground that is essential to the meaning of the act. Even in a metaphor, such as "I scattered my thoughts to the wind," the *act* itself is stressed, and it determines the relation of "thoughts" to "wind." The form of what is structured is determined by the elements involved in construction, all of which are assumed to belong to the same set. Whereas "thoughts" and "wind" belong to different sets (mind and nature), the elements of a "structure" are assumed to belong to the same set, as in "the stones of this building." As a consequence, the *temporality* in the act of *structuring* may be said to subsist in the manifest form. Thus the constructive "acts" that made possible the structure of Chartres Cathedral, even though historically specific and determinate acts, are presumed *always*—for all time—to be discernible in the manifest object that is Chartres Cathedral. By the same token, the *act* of *strewing* or *scattering* even enduring materials, such as stones, is not self-evident and self-sufficiently discernible from the mere relation of those objects. This distinction encourages me to offer the further hypothesis that "structure" suggests an abstract conception of temporality, albeit capable of very specific applications to historical circumstances, whereas "strew" depends upon a specific temporal act that can be imitated but not *repeated*.

These hypothetical distinctions between the relation of space and time for the two modern words that have developed out of the Latin root *struere* help clarify why "structure" is commonly used (as both a noun and a verb) to describe a systematic activity subject to scientific analysis and reproduction whereas "strew" is commonly used (exclusively as a verb) to describe a more careless activity difficult to reproduce exactly and understandable primarily in historical terms. Having introduced the term "system," I want to add that "system" and "structure," as Raymond Williams has argued in *Keywords* (1983), are complexly related in usage and significance for twentieth-century theorists:

> A sense . . . overlaps with one sense of structural and is still close to it, down to details of procedure, in matters like *systems analysis*. But *system* also continued in its sense of a whole organization: a set of principles; an organized treatise; a *theory*. *Systematic* can then mean either orderly and complete inquiry and exposition, or that *structural* quality which pertains to the essential "constitutive" character of an organization. The shades of meaning are obviously

very difficult to distinguish. It is not as easy as it is often made to seem to distinguish one kind of procedure or one kind of definition of interest from another, by the use of terms as complex and variable as these.

As a "whole organization," a system presumes that total understanding or explanation is possible. As it is used by structuralists, "structuralist" means a set of *relations* among *elements* shaped by a *historical* situation. Properly understood, then, no structure could be *totalized* or understood in its entirety or essence. Changes in history, the elements, and/or their relations would change the explanatory structure required as well. Although this characterization of "structure" as historically specific is *theoretically* true for most structuralists, in practice many fail to live up to their own theoretical ideals. The commonest criticism of the structuralists is that they fail to take into account the historical conditions of their own explanatory models. In terms of the distinctions between "structure" and "system" that I have discussed above, we might conclude that such structuralists have employed *systems* rather than *structures* to understand complex historical relations.

The term "structure" replaces the venerable term "form" in many modern theories. Although Ernst Cassirer's *Philosophy of Symbolic Forms* was not translated into English and published in this country until the 1950s, Cassirer completed the third and final volume—translated as *The Phenomenology of Knowledge*—of this work in 1929. Cassirer's neo-Kantian argument regarding the ways that reality is shaped by symbolic forms of the mind is often considered a precursor to European structuralism. Cassirer's reliance on German idealist philosophy is also reflected in structuralism, which often draws upon idealist concepts even as it would reject fundamentally idealist assumptions and foundations. In the first decades of the twentieth century, the term "form" was the term much more commonly employed by philosophers, linguists, and literary critics to represent what later would be given the term "structure."

In philosophy, *form* refers primarily to mental capabilities and processes. Structuralists rejected the term "form," in order to distinguish their work from that of the philosopher, especially the idealist. In particular, the term "form" had two connotations that structuralists found objectionable. First, "form" connoted a transcendental essence, as in the Platonic *nous* (in Greek, "intelligence, mind"), commonly defined as the "primary form" or "principal form" governing phenomena. As we shall see, European structuralists were intent upon subordinating *mental* processes and substances—knowing and the objects of knowledge (thoughts)—to *linguistic* processes and substances (grammar and signs). Structuralists recognized that the word "form" carried with it certain undesirable *metaphysical* and *ontological* associations from Plato to Kant. They also recognized that the term "form" had a more recent history (from Kant to Cassirer) of "idealist" analyses of knowledge as a function of inherent mental processes and abilities. For such "formalists," *mind* precedes *language*, which becomes an *instrument* or *instrumentality* of mind. With that apparently commonsense assumption, formalists and idealists could focus on the individual *subjectivity* in which the properties of "mind" ought to be demonstrable. Thus twentieth-century *phenomenologists* from Edmund Husserl to Maurice Merleau-Ponty could claim to begin with the philosopher's own mind as the object of reflection and study, deducing thereby general characteristics of human cognition.

Shifting the focus from "mind" (and philosophical subject) to "language" had the strategic effect of turning that philosophical subject into a mere consequence of certain linguistic possibilities that could be demonstrated to exceed any individual user and even the specific historical moment. A direct line of historical descent is often traced from Russian formalism to structuralism, the former being a school of primarily literary critics that gained prominence in the first decade of the twentieth century and continued to operate as a "movement" well into the 1920s, until Soviet political pressures caused the group to break up. The demise of Russian formalism is often dated to the same year, 1924, that Trotsky's critical interpretation, "The Formalist School of Poetry and Marxism" in his *Literature and Revolution,* appeared, although Russian formalists like Mikhail Bakhtin continued to write, often pseudonymously and in a sort of cultural underground, well into the 1940s. The translation of many Russian formalist notions into European structuralism is often attributed to Roman Jakobson, a younger member of the Russian formalists, who helped found the Prague school of structural linguistics, which built primarily on the work of structural linguists like Ferdinand de Saussure. Noted primarily for its work on linguistics in the 1930s and 1940s, the Prague school also developed influential literary and aesthetic theories, notably in the work of Jakobson himself and Jan Mukařovský.

Although "structural linguistics" is traditionally traced to Saussure's pioneering lectures on structural linguistics, given in Geneva between 1906 and 1911, the term "structure" would not begin to achieve the multidisciplinary usage that it still enjoys today until the 1930s and 1940s, thanks in part to the centrality of Saussure's theory in the work of linguists like those of the Prague school. Saussure's lectures were not published in his lifetime and had to be compiled from various notes taken by his students (his *Course in General Linguistics* was first published in French in 1915), but they are generally considered to constitute as profound a revolution in modern thought as Galileo's theory of the solar system or Newton's theory of gravity were for their historical moments. Saussure's lectures established "structural linguistics" as a field of study and would be cited by virtually every major theorist of the various "structuralisms" of the next fifty years. Saussure himself does not give any special emphasis to the actual term "structure," but what he termed "synchronic linguistics" is the basis for structuralist investigations in virtually every humanistic discipline. By the mid-1970s,

Saussure's theories would be common assumptions of most literary critics as well, especially the theory of the arbitrariness of the sign and the basic division of the sign into "signifier" and "signified."

Synchronic linguistics studies the regularities of language in a relatively stable historical period. The linguist focuses on what Saussure terms a historical "slice," in which there are no significant changes in language use. Prior to Saussure, most linguists were philologists concerned with the etymologies and historical development of words and grammatical structures. This historical study, which Saussure called "diachronic linguistics," continued to play an important part in his linguistics—indeed, a role often ignored by subsequent structuralists—but Saussure argues that it could no longer be the basis of linguistic science. Philology is basically concerned with *meaning*, even though the study of historically different meanings for the same word (such as those given in the *Oxford English Dictionary*) made etymology a speculative venture at best. Structural linguists like Saussure are less interested in the meanings of words and more interested in *how* meaning is made possible.

Having selected a relatively stable historical period or slice, then, the linguist could study phonetics (the structural regularities of sounds), phonemics (the written transcription of sounds), syntagmatics (sentence structure), and morphology (the rhetorical organization of larger verbal units), among other distinctive features of language use. Relations in each of these and other linguistic categories cannot be studied independently but must be interrelated with the other categories. Thus phonetic analyses of relations between sibilants and fricatives, for example, would have to be correlated with written forms of those sounds in the particular language, as well as with such determinants as syntax and synonymity. On the basis of the study of these complex relations and interrelations in a particular historical moment, the linguist might determine certain regularities in the relations of sound, writing, syntax, and diction in the determination of a meaningful message. These regularities would have to be tested in relation to data gathered from yet other historical periods of relative linguistic stability. Synchronic linguistic evidence is always subject to the test of diachronic data. Relational regularities formulated on the basis of such linguistic study could then be elaborated into a basic "grammar" for the particular language. Such a "grammar," unlike the grammars used in school that dictate the rules of proper usage, would *describe* the elementary processes by which language functions to make meaning and achieve communication.

Such a "grammar" would describe the "structure" of a particular language. Proceeding from particular uses (*parole*) of language to the necessary regularities (*langue*) without which a language could not function, the linguist could provide a *structural model* for that language. Ambitious as Saussure's linguistic project was, it gave rise to a number of even more ambitious and in some cases fantastic linguistic goals. Subsequent structural linguists like Emile Benveniste,

Leonard Bloomfield, and Noam Chomsky variously attempted to formulate structural models that would *describe,* beyond any specific language, the grammar of the linguistic faculty of man. Chomsky's "transformational grammar," although now recognized as an impossible project for linguistics, attempted to theorize those elementary structures by which any communicative act could be generated in all the different languages of the world. The twentieth-century versions of the venerable dream of explaining man's elementary capability for language (*langage*) are all dependent upon Saussure's structural linguistics. Psychoanalytic adaptations of this structural model for linguistics, ranging from Jacques Lacan's revision of Freud along linguistic lines to Bruno Bettelheim's interpretation of folklore and fairy tales as verbal performances of basic human anxieties, would also rely on structural theories of language as basic to man's essential nature. In his famous formulation, Lacan would argue that "the Unconscious is structured like a language"; in effect, Lacan would treat the relation between the unconscious and consciousness *as equivalent to language.* Instead of deducing those a priori categories without which human *thought* would be impossible, structural linguists tried to describe and classify those linguistic structures without which communication and representation would be impossible.

In common usage, we think of a "structure" as an existing construction, whether mental or material, that has the status of a "thing" or "entity." Any architect or engineer can teach us, however, that a "structure" is defined by the *relations* of its parts, rather than by the parts themselves. Those relations in material construction may include the "forces" balanced in an arch or supported by a beam. Consideration of the materials to be used in a building always follows some design of the forces involved in the particular space to be defined. In an analogous manner, structural linguistics focuses on *relations*—the necessary "forces" of language. Whereas philologists had considered the chief variable in language to be history, structural linguists revealed a much more complicated system of relations even in the synchronic stability of a particular moment in the history of language. From the beginning of structural linguistics in the early years of the twentieth century, then, "structure" was a term that described relations among verbal elements, rather than the discrete elements themselves.

Although structural linguists from Saussure to the present increasingly have considered their work to be "scientific" and thus free of the "ontological" and "metaphysical" assumptions of philosophers, structural linguistics relies on several fundamentally ontological premises. Saussure claimed that linguistic science would dethrone philosophy as the "Queen of the Sciences." What he meant was that linguistics ought to become the foundational discipline for twentieth-century man as philosophy had been considered fundamental from Plato and Aristotle to Kant and Hegel. Once again, the rhetorical strategy of replacing the philosophically loaded term "form" with "structure" is particularly important in this regard. Whereas "form" traditionally related man (his mental forms) to some extrahuman realm of "nature" or "Being" (as in Plato's *nous*), "linguistic structure" stressed man's fabrication of a complex "tool" that structural linguists took considerable pains to dissociate from any natural or extrahuman origins. From the beginnings of its modern usage, then, the term "structure" was troublingly bound up with notions of technology.

Saussure's two most famous theses are often termed his "doctrines": of the "arbitrariness" of the sign and of the a priori status of language vis-à-vis thought. Redefining "word" not as the apparently solid entity that it is ordinarily considered to be but as composed, instead, of two elementary functions—the *signifier*, or "acoustic image," by which sound is transmitted from speaker to hearer; and the *signified*, or "conceptual image," by which the sound-image is translated into a mental concept—Saussure insists that the world's different languages teach us that there is no *necessary* relation (or "motivation") between signifier and signified. The relation between a sound and a concept is purely "conventional," based on a history of accepted usage and consensus, neither of which have any demonstrable natural basis. There is nothing inherent in the sound uttered that suggests the concept or the thing represented. Comparative linguistics teaches us that *arbor* in Latin, *Baum* in German, *arbre* in French, and *tree* in English all designate approximately the same concept but demonstrate no natural "regularity" or "structure" in the signifiers employed. Focusing on the relation between sound and concept, signifier and signified, Saussure relies on the basic Kantian assumption that "nature" as such cannot be known, except through the mediation of human thought and language. Like Kant, he does not exclude the possibility of some *natural origin* for words and language but declares such an origin to be utterly unknowable. Dramatically revising Kantian idealism, however, Saussure argues that language, rather than being a mere tool for expressing ideas, *precedes* all thought. If there were a priori categories distinctive to the human being, then for Saussure they would have to be understood as *linguistic* a priori categories (categories of *langage*).

The history of the shift from the use of "form" to "structure," irregular and full of exceptions as any such "history" must be, reflects the gradual shift from industrial and material Western economies to the postmodern economy of "information" and "service" that now governs productive and personal relations in the developed nations. In a material economy, such as Marx both criticized and analyzed, "nature" remains an important realm independent of "culture." Man's material production is most often justified by means of some appeal to "nature," according to the "use-value" of a product (the product is useful because it serves some undeniable natural "need," such as thirst, hunger, reproduction). The "exchange-value" produced by nineteenth-century capitalism generally justified itself by some appeal, often quite specious, to an increasingly vague category of natural "use." The gradual confusion of "use-value" and "exchange-value," resulting ultimately in what Jean Baudrillard has termed the "postmodern subordination of *all* use-value to exchange-value," may well have been the means by which industrial capitalism gave birth to its own best successor—our own economy of information and representation. "Nature" is no longer considered a foundation for judging the value of something produced in such an economy: "value" is entirely a measure of "exchange," the relation of one "product" to another as established by general market conditions. Without being cynical, we can say that the "value" of an "original" designer dress from some Parisian *haut couturier* is less a function of the materials and workmanship than of the "intelligence" and "creativity" of the designer or simply his or her knowledge of market conditions. Those nostalgic for an older, material world may condemn our postmodern economy for its disregard of the self-evident "values" of natural use. The fact remains, however, that we have entered an epoch in which "nature" is always a self-evident "fabrication," always the *effect* of certain human interests and social purposes. Even earthquakes and other unpredictable natural disasters "exist" for us only in their relation to social processes, in about the same fashion that we "go to nature" with guidebooks in our hands.

The shift from "form" to "structure" not only reflects but helped *effect* this transformation from a material to an immaterial economy. Platonic "form" could be approximated only by the most strenuous efforts of philosophical reflection and analysis; Saussurian "structure" is equally difficult to "comprehend"—but not because it belongs to a different (noumenal) order from our phenomenal experience. Linguistic "structure" is itself a human contrivance, a *heuristic* model constructed by the linguist to understand the operation of verbal phenomena that pervade every aspect of our experience. This postulation of "structure" as an abstract, constructed, even *fictional* model for understanding sociohistorical phenomena is consistent in virtually every structuralist use of the term. Even those rigorously scientific structural linguists who attempted to describe the "deep-structure" or "infrastructure" of language recognized that such hidden structures had no "real" or "natural" existence. No structural linguist would ever contend that the "deep-structure" of language (*langage,* for example) could take the place of language use (the relation of *parole* to *langue*), which is always and fundamentally social and historical.

It is not at all surprising, then, that structural linguistics should become the twentieth-century foundation for a wide range of investigations into the "elementary" structures of *human society.* Following Saussure's lead, linguistic anthropologists, like Bronislaw Malinowski, and later structural anthropologists, like Claude Lévi-Strauss, attempted to develop models that would describe the regularities of social interaction. Like Saussure, they considered the basic elements to be relational and the elementary *relations* to be *similarity* and *difference.* In practice, structural anthropologists focus on the relation of nature and culture. In purely theoretical terms, the relation of nature to culture was binary and a nominal tautology: culture's "other" is nature; nature's "other" is culture. The

self-evident character of structuralist models, when considered apart from specific historical investigations, explains several important aspects of structural
thinking in the twentieth century. First, "deep," "infra-," or "primary" structures
are in and of themselves merely abstract models for most structuralists; they are
purely heuristic models and possess no empirical reality. Much more important
than these models is the *system*—linguistic, sociological, behavioral—that operates temporally to organize diverse phenomena. "Structure" is not properly this
hypothetical and often openly *fictional* model but the systematic organization
that the model makes available for study. Thus Saussure's "discovery" of the fundamental linguistic relation of signifier and signified (a relation of *difference,* not
binarism, for Saussure) or Lévi-Strauss's "discovery" of the basic social relation
of "raw" and "cooked," for example, are not properly discoveries at all. They are,
in fact, methodological postulates that can be evaluated only in terms of the
linguistic or anthropological work they make possible.

Thus what constitutes "nature" for structural anthropologists never has any
transhistorical or pan-cultural validity. In Lévi-Strauss, when and how something edible is *cooked* establishes a social locus (a structural "site") that is
bounded by what is *not cooked*—that is, by what is "raw." The human act of
making either food or meaning has a double significance: it makes its world
(culture) by designating an "other" domain: nature, primitive, nonhuman. And
the "word" given that other realm is by no means incidental; that "word" involves a complex conceptual system, which when followed out reveals the governing terms of social reality.

Basic binaries—such as nature and culture for anthropologists, sound and
sense for linguists, private and public for sociologists—are thus less important
than the temporal functioning of the "structure"—that is, its *system*—and the
theoretical assumption of binarism itself. Poststructuralists turned Saussure
against the structuralists, reminding us that, for Saussure, "in language there are
only *differences* without positive terms." This understanding of "difference"—
that governing the relation of signifier and signified—is by no means the same
as what structuralists termed "binary differences," such as those employed by a
digital computer: on/off, 0/1, +/−. As the tool of structural classification, the
binary organized phonetic, phonemic, rhythmic, syntagmatic, and associative
aspects of language. In every case, however, such binary structures referred more
to the model than the system. What poststructuralists like Jacques Derrida recognize as a problem in structuralism is the tendency to transform the *regulative
function* of cultural signs into a totalizing explanatory system, such as those comprehensive approaches to cultural representation associated with *semiotics*.

Structuralism helped foster two disciplinary uses of the term "structure" in
twentieth-century thought. The more *systematic* approach to human structures
helped develop not only semiotics but new sciences that relied fundamentally on
explanatory and ultimately generational (or productive) models. Psychobiology,

cybernetics, systems analysis, and information theory all rely on the relation between "artificial intelligence" and some theory of human cognition. Cybernetics,
for example, compares computer functions with processes in the central nervous
system for the ostensible purpose of "understanding" the brain, thus relying on
essentially comparative and analogical modes of knowledge. As Anthony Wilden
has cogently described cybernetic methodology:

> The symptom, the ideology, the superstructure, or any equivalent
> "metastatement" is a "mapping" or a "transform" of some other
> proposition or communication. As communication, behavior im-
> plies an information-processing network in which messages,
> borne by energy, pass along mediated and unmediated channels
> disturbed by "noise." Information, in this technical sense, can be
> distinguished from both signification and meaning; we can define
> it as a "mapping between sets of structured variety." (Wilden
> 1972, 131)

Wilden's description agrees basically with the structuralist definition of structure, insofar as signification and meaning are less important than the informa-
tional function of establishing a relation among "sets of structured variety." That
such "relations" can be reproduced experimentally by way of certain models—
from computers to cyborgs—is quite obviously a methodological advantage offered by such an approach to knowledge as "communication" or "representation."

If the structuralist influence on sciences like biology and information theory
tended to challenge traditional science's claims to absolute knowledge, then the
structuralist influence on literature and the arts tended to *systematize* our approaches to aesthetics. I have said relatively little about the *literary* use of the
term "structure" until now, precisely because the incorporation of the structuralist version of the term into literary and artistic discussions occurred relatively
late in the twentieth century. The term "structure" had certainly been used with
great frequency prior to the advent of European structuralism to describe the
formal relation of the parts of a painting or narrative. The Anglo-American New
Critics of the 1930s and 1940s used "structure" often interchangeably with the
term "form" to describe the essential properties of the artwork and ultimately
the essence of aesthetic experience. When they did use "structure" with a precise
meaning, they often employed it in ways quite similar to those of the Russian
formalists. In Cleanth Brooks's famous essay "Irony as a Principle of Structure"
(1949), the rhetorical trope of irony is fundamental to literature, which uses the
trope to distinguish its own special language from that of ordinary experience.
As a principle of "structure," irony is thus quite similar to the *ostranenie* or strategic "estrangement of the familiar" that the Russian formalists considered essential to literary language. For most New Critics, literary "structure" was

achieved by the systematic *negation* of the empirical domain. By the same token, this cancellation of ordinary empirical experience or data allowed the artist to concentrate on the purely ideal determinations of our thought. The noted "autotelicism" or "self-reflexivity" of New-Critical art was based on the assumption that literature constituted a special verbal "model," in which thinking itself could be made an object of reflection. Such basic activities as signification, patterning, ordering, and imaginative reproduction or simulation were central to the "fiction-making" of the artist in the different fine arts.

Even so, "structure" in literature and the arts suggested for the New Critics something historically and psychologically transcendent or universal. In this regard, then, the New Critics are properly "neo-Kantian," as many of them have been termed, because the "aesthetic structures" they analyzed were assumed to escape the determinants conditioning linguistic and anthropological structures. W. K. Wimsatt's and Monroe C. Beardsley's conclusion to "The Affective Fallacy" (1949), although it expresses an extreme version of the New Criticism, succinctly expresses the abiding belief of many New Critics in the transcendent aesthetic "structure" of great literature: "A structure of emotive objects so complex and so reliable as to have been taken for great poetry by any past age will never, it seems safe to say, so wane with the waning of human culture as not to be recoverable at least by a willing student. . . . In short, though cultures have changed and will change, poems remain and explain" (Adams 1971, 1031).

For most European structuralists, literature and the arts remained relatively peripheral subjects, secondary to the more central disciplines of linguistics and anthropology. Lévi-Strauss and Jakobson both wrote influential essays on literature, including an essay they coauthored, "Charles Baudelaire's 'Les Chats'" (1962), and Prague linguists like Mukařovský turned their attention to literature and aesthetic functions as part of more encompassing theories of cultural representation. Jakobson and Lévi-Strauss's essay on Baudelaire's sonnet "Les Chats," however, was published in a French anthropological review, *L'Homme,* and was intended primarily for professional anthropologists. European structuralism was not very compatible with the exclusive aesthetic focus of Anglo-American New Criticism, even though the frequent use of the term "structure" in both movements has led many to assume that they share many theoretical assumptions.

On the other hand, structuralism did stress the ways in which a culture develops a stylistic and formal repertoire to express its needs, aims, and problems. Were European structuralism to be related closely to any single movement in twentieth-century literary criticism, then it would have to be with "myth criticism" of the sort practiced by C. L. Barber, R. W. B. Lewis, Lewis Mumford, Henry Nash Smith, and Leo Marx. Such historically specific studies of the myths informing a particular epoch—Barber's English Renaissance, Smith's America in the period of Manifest Destiny, Lewis Mumford's Modern Age—are much closer to the aims of European structuralism than those of Anglo-American New Criticism.

For both myth critics and structuralists, literary or artistic "structures" might be used to understand the boundaries of a particular culture's language, much in the manner that Lévi-Strauss had employed elementary kinship relations to describe the "rules" for the organizations of Amazonian tribal societies. Because literature stretches ordinary language to its virtual limits, the structuralist could find in surviving literary works some indication of the relative flexibility or conventionality of cultural language in the period studied. Even so, "literature" understood from a structuralist perspective became merely one of the many "human sciences," a view that could never be reconciled with the Russian formalists' and Anglo-American New Critics' special valorization of the distinctive forms and structures of literature.

Northrop Frye's *Anatomy of Criticism* (1957) was written before European structuralism had any significant impact on the humanities in England or America, and for that very reason it may be the only "native" version of structuralism that we have had (although Frye's Canadian citizenship argues against any theory of a *native* tradition of structuralism in the United States!). Frye's *Anatomy* is the triumph of myth criticism, or at least the most systematic statement of this theoretical approach produced in English. As Frank Lentricchia has argued in *After the New Criticism* (1980), Frye's monumental effort to provide a structural classification of the essential literary myths (or modes) concludes by claiming that psychology, anthropology, theology, history, law, and "everything else built out of words have been informed or constructed by the same kind of myths and metaphors that we find, in their original hypothetical form, in literature" (Frye 1957, 352). That quotation is from Frye's final essay, and it suggests for Lentricchia that Frye has mistaken "structural linguistics" for "literature," giving the latter priority where the former has shown Frye and his reader the way back to literature. As Lentricchia demonstrates, Frye's *Anatomy* challenged the very foundations of Anglo-American New Criticism, even as it made its own bid for the central authority of literature. What the *Anatomy* unwittingly accomplished was the bridge between *literary structure*—a term used narrowly to specify the uniqueness of literary language (or form)—and *linguistic structure*. The latter use of "structure" would require literary critics to abandon the separate "discipline" of literary study and to engage in some larger venture of what structuralists termed the study of "the sciences of man."

For some of these reasons, the integration of the structuralists' use of the term "structure" into literary criticism and aesthetics never occurred in its own "proper" time. There is no genuinely "structuralist" school of Anglo-American literary criticism, even though "poststructuralist" and "deconstructionist" approaches—all premised on some reaction to the narrow scientism of European structuralism—have had enormous popularity. And this "failure" of structuralism to influence the studies of literature and the arts is perfectly understandable when we comprehend the ultimately *semiotic* aims of structuralism as antithetical to the study of such separable disciplines as "literature" or "art." Yet, in its own definitions of structure as "model" and "simulation" of an ultimately unknowable reality, structuralism brought the "science" conveyed by its own best term, structure, into a precarious relation with art and the imaginary.

Founding knowledge on language, defining man according to his capability for language (*langage*), insisting upon the "arbitrary"—that is, historical rather than *natural*—character of the sign, structuralism helped legitimate the purely "man-made" character of postmodern social reality. This is nowhere better illustrated than by the expressly *fictional* status of "structure" in its modern usage. In "The Structural Activity," one of many essays Roland Barthes wrote in the 1960s to explain the movement's principles, Barthes defines *structure* as

> a *simulacrum* of the object, but a directed, *interested* simulacrum, since the imitated object makes something appear which remained invisible, or if one prefers, unintelligible in the natural object. Structural man takes the real, decomposes it, then recomposes it.

The result of this *activity* is that

> there occurs *something new,* and what is new is nothing less than the generally intelligible: the simulacrum is intellect added to the object, and this addition has an anthropological value, in that it is man himself, his history, his situation, his freedom and the very resistance which nature offers to his mind.

Barthes' formulation of "structure" virtually condenses all that I have to say about the ideological significance of the modern use of the term "structure." The structure is a simulacrum; it imitates a natural object in order to transform it. The purpose of this transformation is *intelligibility,* but in an interested, humanly *useful* manner. Barthes' conclusion is very metaphysical, but no more so than even the most technically narrow structuralism: man's "freedom" is demonstrated in his structural "transformation" of a nature that affirms human freedom by revealing its "resistance" "to his mind."

"The structuralist activity," Barthes continues, "involves two typical operations: dissection and articulation." My speculation about the ideological purposes served by structuralism should be clear enough in this context. "Structure" as a term increasingly referred to an *activity* of model building, which "dissected" what it imitated and reconstituted it in "human" terms. This is both the method and the subject of most structuralist works in various disciplines. Lévi-Strauss dissects Amazonian social organization in order to *articulate* it, and he does so by demonstrating how that very tribe "dissects" natural objects in order to articulate them in *cultural* practices.

"Structure" so understood involves an essential temporality, both in the making of models and in the system of organization to be studied. In the acts of "dissection and articulation," the structuralist is contributing to a particular historical moment, whose anthropological dimension is revealed clearly in Barthes' words: "It is man himself, his history, his situation, his freedom and the very resistance which nature offers his mind." On the one hand, "structure" seems to require that man understand himself only according to his particular historical moment and its unique relation to the past. This is generally defined as *historicism*. On the other hand, "structure" seems to rely on the postulation of a certain historical *necessity* by which man would transform an alien world of experience into his own property. Optimistically viewed, such necessity describes the process by which man *humanizes* the world, thus dissecting and articulating for the sake of *adding* intelligibility itself to the world. More pessimistically, we may judge such historical *necessity* as the human drive to conquer the alien and make it conform to a narrowly *human* understanding.

Above all, the term "structure" reflects the twentieth-century transformation from a material economy to an economy of immaterial production, from industrial to postindustrial societies in the West. Jean Baudrillard has argued that such societies are simply machines for the production and exchange of *simulations* that refer ultimately to illusory substances. The economy of simulation depends upon abstract models becoming *machines* that produce yet other models. Structuralism, as the movement that promised to relate the various disciplines of the "human sciences," lent a certain credibility to this new economy committed to the production and distribution of *representations*. It accomplished this work of accommodation in part by offering a certain ethical promise. Lévi-Strauss's anthropology was polemically directed against all ethnocentrism and consistently critical of our pretensions to "civilization" against the supposed backwardness of "primitive" peoples. The "savage" mind worked differently, Lévi-Strauss argued, even if the models on which it built its social systems could be analogized to those of Western, rational, civilized man. Saussure's approach to language fundamentally challenged most arguments favoring "proper" language use, insofar as verbal decorum and propriety were revealed to be matters of mere convention, of a consensus that had no other warrant than the social contract. Frye's conception of "verbal myth" broadened significantly the conventionally narrow focus of most literary criticism, requiring us to be attentive to the literary resources of everyday life, even though Frye himself did not provide such an analysis (or even theory) of everyday life in his own *Anatomy*. Frye still offered us the possibility of *redeeming myths*, just as his *Anatomy* warned us against myths of control and domination that could arrive in literary trappings. Barthes' "structuralist activity" appeared closely aligned with man's imaginative and creative faculties; the process of "dissection and articulation" sounds curiously like the Coleridgean powers of the imagination. And the essentially *relational* character of all human knowledge seemed to argue in favor of more open social and political systems based on the tolerance and even encouragement of differences, rather than their exclusion or repression.

Yet, I think that the term "structure" finally accomplishes quite contrary ends to these recognizably liberal and humane purposes. "Structure" becomes the referent for the ultimate *human* product—a representation that can be distinguished thoroughly from any *natural* use. The ability of that representation or "structure" to *explain* other systems of organization becomes its sole warrant, its "use" being nothing other than the exchange among systems of information that it facilitates. "Structure" thus becomes the medium of such exchanges in an economy no longer concerned with "natural use." Language is the perfect site for such a transformation, because the "use" of words is their exchange or communication. The prevalent use of the term "structure" in modern critical theories reflects the historical transformation of the so-called "developed" nations of the West from nineteenth-century industrial to our present postindustrial economies. In an industrial economy, the exchange value of a natural or manufactured object can be judged according to the ultimate *use* of that object. In our postindustrial economies, which are based on the production and distribution of information and related services, the *use* of an object is indistinguishable from its circulation or exchange-value. In this context, we must confront the possibility that our intellectual models, like our computer programs and media technologies, may have more functional *reality* than the "objects" they pretend to study or "represent."

"Structure" is one of the key terms of our postmodernity because it openly acknowledges its claim for scientific rigor as well as its fabricated character. Science and art discovered a certain shared interest in this term at precisely the historical moment in which science and art were needed to help effect what now appears to be an enormously successful social and economic transformation in the West. The success of the postmodern revolution, however, has not been accompanied by fundamental changes in class, gender, and minority relations for which many politically committed structuralists had worked and hoped. Perhaps this very failure is what has given deconstruction and other "poststructuralist" theories their special authority and appeal in this last quarter of the twentieth century.

SUGGESTED READINGS

Barthes, Roland. 1972. *Critical Essays.*

De George, Richard and Fernande, eds. 1972. *The Structuralists: From Marx to Lévi-Strauss.*

Jameson, Fredric. 1972. *The Prison-House of Language: A Critical Account of Structuralism and Russian Formalism.*

Lentricchia, Frank. 1980. *After the New Criticism.*

Saussure, Ferdinand de. 1966. *Course in General Linguistics.*
Wilden, Anthony. 1972. *System and Structure: Essays in Communication and Ex-change.*
Williams, Raymond. 1983. "Structural." In *Keywords: A Vocabulary of Culture and Society.*

3

Writing

Barbara Johnson

How is it that the word "writing" has come to be considered a critical term? Isn't "writing" simply one of those aspects of literature that can be taken for granted? Isn't it merely the medium through which a reader encounters words on a page—for example, these?

Every essay in this volume communicates to some extent *by means of* the very thing it is talking *about*. Nowhere is this more obvious than in the case of writing. An essay about writing, therefore, is an unclosable loop: it is an attempt to comprehend that which it is comprehended by. The non-Euclidean logic of such reciprocal inclusion has often itself been an object of attention in recent theoretical discussions of writing. That is only one of the consequences that the study of writing has entailed.

Writing about writing is hardly a new phenomenon, however. From Omar Khayyám's moving finger to Rousseau's trembling hand, from the broken tables of Moses to the purloined letters of Poe and Alice Walker, from Borges's encyclopedia to Wordsworth's lines left upon a seat in a yew tree, images of writing in writing testify to an enduring fascination with the mechanics and materiality of the written word. A comprehensive treatment of the question of writing is obviously beyond the scope of the present essay. I will therefore concentrate on a particular recent moment of reflection about writing—the theoretical "revolution" in France in 1967—which has had a decisive impact upon the shape of literary studies today.

Writing (*l'écriture*) came to philosophical, psychoanalytic, and literary prominence in France in the 1960s, primarily through the work of Jacques Derrida, Roland Barthes, and other writers who were at that time associated with the journal *Tel Quel*. Philippe Sollers, in a "Program" that heads the group's collective theoretical volume, proclaimed in 1967: "A comprehensive theory arising out of a thought about the practice of writing cries out for elaboration." Writing, it seemed, was to become the key to all mythologies. The sudden spectacular interest in writing sprang from many different sources, some of which I will outline quickly here.

As early as 1953, in *Writing Degree Zero,* Roland Barthes had investigated the paradoxical relationship that existed in the nineteenth century in France between the development of a concept of Literature (with a capital *L*) and the growing sense of a breakdown in the representational capacities of language. Literature was in some ways being exalted as a substitute religion, but it was a religion whose high priests seemed only to proclaim the obscurity, imperfection, or unreliability of their own medium. The proper names associated with the elaboration of *both* sides of this phenomenon are Flaubert and Mallarmé. These writers, says Barthes, *constructed* the object Literature in the very act of announcing its death. In later essays, Barthes lays out a theory of literature based on a split between the classic notion of a *work (oeuvre)*—considered as a closed, finished, reliable representational *object*—and the modern notion of a *text*—considered as an open, infinite *process* that is both meaning-generating and meaning-subverting. "Work" and "text" are thus not two different kinds of object but two different ways of viewing the written word. What interests Barthes is the *tension* between the concept of Literature and the concept of textuality. While Literature is seen as a series of discrete and highly meaningful Great Works, textuality is the manifestation of an open-ended, heterogeneous, disruptive force of signification and erasure that transgresses all closure—a force that is operative even within the Great Works themselves.

Closure versus subversion, product versus practice, meaning-containing object versus significance-scattering process: Barthes' theory of writing owes a great deal, as we shall see, both to Marxism and to psychoanalysis. But the *Tel Quel* writers' involvement with Marxism and psychoanalysis takes on its particular coloring, strangely enough, through the mediation of Saussurian linguistics. How does this happen?

In his *Course in General Linguistics* (first published by his students in 1916, with new editions in 1948 and 1966), Ferdinand de Saussure mapped out a science of linguistics based not on the historical ("diachronic") development of families of languages but on the structural ("synchronic") properties of language "as such," frozen in time as a *system.* This "structuralist" perspective, also developed in the 1950s in anthropology by Claude Lévi-Strauss, involves viewing the system as a set of relations among elements governed by rules. The favorite analogy for such systems is chess: whatever the particular properties of an individual "man" (ivory, wood, plastic), the "man" is involved in a system of moves and relations that can be known and manipulated in themselves. From the structural point of view, there is no difference between ivory and plastic. There is difference between king, queen, and knight, or between white and black.

Saussure's most enduring contribution has been his description of the *sign* as the unit of the language system. The sign is composed of two parts: a mental image or concept (the "signified"), and a phonic or graphic vehicle (the "signifier"). The sign is thus both conceptual and material, sense and sound, spirit and letter at once. The existence of numerous languages indicates that the relation between the signifier and the signified in any given sign is arbitrary (there is no natural resemblance between sound and idea), but once fixed, that relation becomes a convention that cannot be modified at will by any individual speaker. By thus deciding that what is relevant to a structural study of language is neither history ("diachrony") nor reality (the "referent") but rather the system of differential relations among signs, Saussure set up a tremendously enabling, as well as limiting, heuristic perspective for analysis. And by asserting that signs signify not as independently meaningful units corresponding to external objects but as elements whose value is generated by their difference from neighboring elements in the system, Saussure put forth a notion of *difference* (not identity) as the origin of meaning.

Saussure's suspension of interest in history and the external world would seem to place him at the farthest remove from Marxism. But theorists of writing saw a connection between the signifier/signified relation and the materialism/idealism relation. If the signifier was the material condition of the existence of ideas, then the privileging of the signified resembled the fetishization of commodities resulting from bourgeois idealism's blindness to labor and to the material conditions of economic existence. The liberation of the signifier, the rebellion against idealist repressions, and the unleashing of the forces of difference and desire against the law and order of identity were all part of the program for change that developed in France in the 1960s. Whether linguistic materiality and economic materiality are linked *only* by analogy, or whether there is some profound interimplication between them, is still a subject for debate today. But whatever the case, the repressive return to order that followed the strikes and demonstrations in France in May 1968 squelched the optimism of those who might have believed in any simple connection between liberating the signifier and changing the class structure of society.

The understanding of what it might mean to liberate the signifier also had roots in the psychoanalytic theory of Jacques Lacan. For many years prior to the 1966 publication of his *Ecrits* (*Writings*), Lacan had been conducting a seminar in which he attempted to work out a radically new way of reading Freud. What he emphasized in Freud's writing was the discovery that "the unconscious is structured like a language." The unconscious is *structured*. It is not a reservoir of amorphous drives and energies but a system of articulations through which repressed ideas return in displaced form. Freud's comparison of a dream to a rebus is extended as an analogy for all effects of the unconscious: just as each element in a rebus must be translated separately in order to decipher the total message, so each element in a dream is a knot of associations that must be explored without regard for the dream's surface coherence. Dreams, slips of the tongue, parapraxes, hysterical symptoms, and other expressions of the unconscious are for Lacan manifestations of a "signifying chain," a structure of associations that resembles an unconscious foreign language. Consciousness attempts to disregard this language in order to control and define the identity of the self, but the psychoanalyst's task is to attempt to hear that language despite the ego's efforts to scramble it. Using the terminology of Saussure, Lacan calls the units of unconscious expression "signifiers," linked to repressed "signifieds." But the search for the signified can only take the form of a sliding along the chain of signifiers. In other words, there is no one-to-one link between signifier and signified but rather an "effect of signified" generated by the movement from one signifier to another. Freud never comes to the end of his dream analyses, never "solves" their enigma, but it feels as though something like insight is achieved by following out the dreamer's chains of associations.

Lacan's troubling of Saussure's one-to-one link between signifiers and signifieds actually turns out to have its counterpart in Saussure's own work. Beginning in 1964, Jean Starobinski began publishing strange notebooks in which Saussure attempted to prove that certain late Latin poems contained hidden proper names anagrammatically dispersed throughout their texts. The poems, in other words, contained extra signifiers, readable only to those in the know. Whether or not these anagrams were a secret key to late Latin poetics, the notion that the signifier could take the lead in creating poetic effects appealed to students of poetry. Saussure's anagrams prompted Julia Kristeva, among others, to theorize an anagrammatic (or paragrammatic) functioning in poetic language as such.

The claim that signifiers can generate effects even when the signified is unknown serves as the basis for Lacan's famous reading of Poe's story "The Purloined Letter." In that story, an unscrupulous minister steals a compromising letter from the queen under the unsuspecting eyes of the king. An amateur detective, Dupin, is commissioned by the stymied prefect of police to get the letter back. Dupin suspects that the minister has hidden the letter in plain sight, just as it had been when he stole it. Dupin then repeats the minister's act and steals the letter back for the queen. Lacan emphasizes the way in which the characters' actions are determined by the position of the letter among them. Neither the letter's contents (the never-revealed "signified") nor the individual identities of the people (the psychological equivalent of Saussure's ivory and wood chessmen) determine the course of the plot. It is the movement of the letter that dictates the characters' actions.

The rebus, the anagram, and the letter are clearly all manifestations of *writing*. They are graphic, articulated, material instantiations of systems of marks that simultaneously obscure and convey meaning. They are also something other than mere transcriptions of the spoken word. In other words, they are not examples of *phonetic* writing. It is this "something other" that must be kept in mind as we now turn to the work of the most important French theorist of writing, Jacques Derrida.

It was in 1967 that Derrida published three major books devoted to the question of writing: *Writing and Difference, Of Grammatology,* and *Speech and Phenomena*. Derrida's project in these writings is to reevaluate the structuring principles of Western metaphysics. Western philosophy, writes Derrida, has analyzed the world in terms of binary oppositions: mind vs. body, good vs. evil, man vs. woman, presence vs. absence. Each of these pairs is organized hierarchically: the first term is seen as higher or better than the second. According to Derrida, the opposition between speech and writing has been structured similarly: speech is seen as immediacy, presence, life, and identity, whereas writing is seen as deferment, absence, death, and difference. Speech is primary; writing secondary. Derrida calls this privileging of speech as self-present meaning "logocentrism."

In his three volumes of 1967, Derrida gives rigorous attention to the paradox that the Western tradition (the "Great Books") is filled with *writings* that privilege *speech*. By closely analyzing those writings, Derrida attempts to uncover the ways in which the Great Books rebel against their own stated intention to say that speech is better than writing. What his analyses reveal is that even when a text *tries* to privilege speech as immediacy, it cannot completely eliminate the fact that speech, like writing, is based on a *différance* (a Derridean neologism meaning both "deferment" and "difference") between signifier and signified inherent in the sign. Speakers do not beam meanings directly from one mind to another. Immediacy is an illusion. Properties normally associated with writing inevitably creep into a discussion designed to privilege speech. Thus, for example, although Saussure wishes to treat speech as primary and writing as secondary for an understanding of language, he describes language as a "dictionary in the head" or as "linear"—a spatial term more applicable to writing than to speech. Or, to take another example, when Socrates tells Phaedrus that proper teaching must take place orally rather than in writing, he nevertheless ends up describing the truths such teaching is supposed to reach as being "*inscribed* in the soul." Because a gap of heterogeneity and distance is fundamental to the structure of language, Derrida sees "speech" as being ultimately structured like "writing." This emphasis on writing as the more originary category is designed to counter the history of logocentrism and to track the functioning of *différance* in structures of signification.

Many literary texts seem in fact to stage some version of this encounter between the search for spoken immediacy or identity and the recourse to writing and difference. The following poem by Edward Taylor (ca. 1642–1729), for example, does not seem to expect to end up talking about writing:

Meditation 6
Am I thy gold? Or purse, Lord, for thy wealth,
    Whether in mine or mint refined for thee?
I'm counted so, but count me o'er thyself,
    Lest gold washed face, and brass in heart I be.

> I fear my touchstone touches when I try
> Me and my counted gold too overly.

Am I new minted by thy stamp indeed?
> Mine eyes are dim; I cannot clearly see.
Be thou my spectacles that I may read
> Thine image and inscription stamped on me.
> If thy bright image do upon me stand,
> I am a golden angel in thy hand.

Lord, make my soul thy plate, thine image bright
> Within the circle of the same enfile.
And on its brims in golden letters write
> Thy superscription in an holy style.
> Then I shall be thy money, thou my horde:
> Let me thy angel be, be thou my Lord.

Written in a style of extended metaphor known as the metaphysical conceit, this poem sets out to express spiritual value in terms of material value (gold). The most obvious figure for the conjunction between the spiritual and the material is the word "angel," which means both a heavenly being and an old English coin. Through this spiritual/material alloy, the poem attempts to make human value both derive from and coincide with divine value, to eliminate the space of difference or distance between the human and the divine.

The poem is composed of a series of questions and imperatives addressed to God. While these aim to alleviate doubt, difference, and distance, they seem only to widen the gap they attempt to close. Am I gold or purse? value-object or container? the poet asks. He then pursues the first possibility, only to stumble upon a new inside/outside opposition: "Lest gold washed face, and brass in heart I be." The gold begins to resemble a sign, with no guaranteed correlation between face (signifier) and heart (signified). The becoming-sign process continues in the second stanza, where the speaker is "stamped" with an image and an inscription. The speaker is now a reader, and what he reads is himself. God has become an image, and a corrective lens. In the final stanza, the text ("inscription") that was dimly decipherable in the second stanza turns out not yet to have been written. While the poem still yearns for a perfectly reciprocal container/contained relation ("I shall be thy money, thou my horde"), this relation now requires the active intervention of writing ("in golden letters write / Thy superscription"). In his increasingly aggressive submissiveness, the speaker tries to order God to take his place as the writer.

From metal to image to letters, from touching to reading to writing, from counted to almost-read to not-yet-written, the speaker seems to be farther away from coincidence with God at the end than he was at the beginning. The mediating elements only increase the *différance*. Yet this *différance* is also the space of the poem's existence. The speaker cannot *write* his way into an immediacy that would eliminate writing. Nor can he write himself into a submissiveness great enough to overtake the fact that it is he, not God, who writes. His conceit will never succeed in erasing the "conceit" of writing itself.

The logic of writing is thus a double logic: writing is called upon as a necessary remedy for *différance*, but at the same time it *is* the very *différance* for which a remedy must be sought. In Derrida's analyses of writing, this logic is called the logic of the *supplément*. In French, the word *supplément* means both an "addition" and a "substitute." To say that "A is a *supplément* to B" is thus to say something ambiguous. Addition and substitution are not exactly contradictory, but neither can they be combined in the traditional logic of identity. In the poem, the inscriptions, images, and even spectacles function as *suppléments:* they are at once additions and substitutes simultaneously bridging and widening the gap between God and the speaker. Some sense of the way in which supplementary logic differs from the binary logic of identity (A = A) and noncontradiction (A ≠ not A) may be derived from the following list. In this list, all statements are to be taken as *simultaneously* equivalent to the statement "A is a *supplément* to B." (In terms of the Taylor poem, say B = the presence of, or coincidence with, God; and A = writing.)

> A is added to B.
> A substitutes for B.
> A is a superfluous addition to B.
> A makes up for the absence of B.
> A usurps the place of B.
> A makes up for B's deficiency.
> A corrupts the purity of B.
> A is necessary so that B can be restored.
> A is an accident alienating B from itself.
> A is that without which B would be lost.
> A is that through which B is lost.
> A is a danger to B.
> A is a remedy to B.
> A's fallacious charm seduces one away from B.
> A can never satisfy the desire for B.
> A protects against direct encounter with B.

Supplementary logic is not only the logic *of* writing—it is also a logic that can only really exist *in* writing. That is, it is a nonintuitive logic that inheres (Lacan would say, "in-sists") in a text as a system of traces. Like an algebraic equation with more than one unknown, supplementary logic cannot be held in the head but must be worked out in external form. It is no accident that the word "differential" is central both to calculus and to Derrida's theory of writing.

Derrida's theory of writing turns out to have been, in fact, a theory of reading. The epigraph to his *Writing and Difference* is a quotation from Mallarmé: "Le tout sans nouveauté qu'un espacement de la lecture" ("All without innovation except for a certain spacing-out of reading"). What does it mean to introduce "space" into reading? For Mallarmé, it means two things. It means giving a signifying function to the materiality—the blanks, the typefaces, the placement on the page, the punctuation—of writing. And it also means tracking syntactic and semantic ambiguities in such a way as to generate multiple, often conflicting, meanings out of a single utterance. The "meaning" of a Mallarmé text, like that of a dream, cannot be grasped intuitively as a whole but must be worked out rigorously by following each strand in a network of relations. What Derrida generalizes and analyzes in other writings is this "spacing" that Mallarmé attempts to maximize. In his reading of Plato's *Phaedrus,* for instance, Derrida follows the ambiguity of the word *pharmakon,* which Plato uses to describe writing itself. If *pharmakon* can mean both "poison" and "remedy," what does it mean to call writing a *pharmakon*? As Derrida points out, translators of Plato have rendered this word by choosing to favor one side or the other of the ambiguity according to the context. They have subordinated its ambiguity to their notion of what makes the most sense. They have thus subordinated "writing" as spacing and ambiguity to "speech" as single intention. The ambiguity of the poison / remedy relation is tamed thereby into something far less unsettling. "Sense" is achieved, however, at a cost. To know the difference between poison and remedy may be reassuring, but that reassurance may well make it difficult to come to grips with the meaning of Socrates' death.

Thus "reading," for Derrida, involves following the "other" logics of structures of signification inscribed in writing that may or may not be in conformity with traditional logics of meaning, identity, consciousness, or intention. It involves taking seriously the elements that a standard reading disregards, overlooks, or edits out. Just as Freud rendered dreams and slips of the tongue *readable* rather than dismissing them as mere nonsense or error, so Derrida sees signifying force in the gaps, margins, figures, echoes, digressions, discontinuities, contradictions, and ambiguities of a text. When one writes, one writes more than (or less than, or other than) one thinks. The reader's task is to read what is written rather than simply attempt to intuit what might have been meant.

The possibility of reading materiality, silence, space, and conflict within texts has opened up extremely productive ways of studying the politics of language. If each text is seen as presenting a major claim that attempts to dominate, erase, or distort various "other" claims (whose traces nevertheless remain detectable to a reader who goes against the grain of the dominant claim), then "reading" in its extended sense is deeply involved in questions of authority and power. One field of conflict and domination in discourse that has been fruitfully studied in this sense is the field of sexual politics. Alice Jardine, in *Gynesis* (1985), points out that since logocentric logic has been coded as "male," the "other" logics of spacing, ambiguity, figuration, and indirection are often coded as "female," and that a critique of logocentrism can enable a critique of "phallocentrism" as well. A theory and practice of female writing (*écriture féminine*) has been developed in France by such writers as Hélène Cixous and Luce Irigaray, who have attempted to write the specificity of female biological and ideological difference. While Cixous, Irigaray, and others work on the relations between writing and the body, many feminists on both sides of the Atlantic have been interested in the gender implications of the relations between writing and silence. In *The Madwoman in the Attic* (1979), Sandra Gilbert and Susan Gubar show how nineteenth-century women writers struggle for authorship against the silence that has already been prescribed for them by the patriarchal language they must both use and transform. Adrienne Rich also explores the traces of women's silence in a collection of essays entitled *On Lies, Secrets, and Silence* (1979). These and other works have as their project the attempt to read the suppressed, distorted, or disguised messages that women's writing has encoded. They require a reading strategy that goes beyond apparent intentions or surface meanings, a reading that takes full advantage of writing's capacity to preserve that which cannot yet, perhaps, be deciphered.

The writings of Western male authorities have often encoded the silence, denigration, or idealization not only of women but also of other "others." Edward Said, in *Orientalism* (1978), analyzes the discursive fields of scholarship, art, and politics in which the "Oriental" is projected as the "other" of the European. By reading against the grain of the writers' intentions, he shows how European men of reason and benevolence could inscribe a rationale for oppression and exploitation within their very discourse of Enlightenment.

While the critique of logocentrism undertaken by Derrida implies that Western patriarchal culture has always privileged the presence, immediacy, and ideality of speech over the distance and materiality of writing, this privilege has never, in fact, been unambiguous. An equal but more covert privileging of writing has also been operative. One of the ways in which colonial powers succeeded in imposing their domination over other peoples was precisely through writing. European civilization functioned with great effectiveness by remote control. And indeed, when comparing itself to other cultures, European culture has always seen its own form of literacy as a sign of superiority. The hidden but ineradicable importance of writing that Derrida uncovers in his readings of logocentric texts in fact reflects an unacknowledged, or "repressed," *grapho*centrism. It may well be that it is only in a text-centered culture that one can privilege speech in a logocentric way. The "speech" privileged in logocentrism is not literal but is a *figure* of speech: a figure, ultimately, of God.

Recent work by Henry Louis Gates, Jr., and others attempts to combine Derrida's critique of logocentrism with an equal critique of the way in which European graphocentrism has functioned historically to oppress and exploit non-European peoples. If European culture had ever unambiguously privileged speech and denigrated writing, there would have been no reason, for example, to forbid American slaves to read and write. The following passage from *The Narrative of the Life of Frederick Douglass, an American Slave, Written by Himself,* should be juxtaposed to Lévi-Strauss's suggestion in *Tristes Tropiques* that the function of writing is to enslave. Douglass agrees, in a sense, but he does not stop there:

> Very soon after I went to live with Mr. and Mrs. Auld, she very kindly commenced to teach me the A,B,C. After I had learned this, she assisted me in learning to spell words of three or four letters. Just at this point of my progress, Mr. Auld found out what was going on, and at once forbade Mrs. Auld to instruct me further, telling her, among other things, that it was unlawful, as well as unsafe, to teach a slave to read. To use his own words, further, he said, "If you give a nigger an inch, he will take an ell. A nigger should know nothing but to obey his master—to do as he is told to do. Learning would *spoil* the best nigger in the world. Now," said he, "if you teach that nigger (speaking of myself) how to read, there would be no keeping him. It would forever unfit him to be a slave. He would at once become unmanageable, and of no value to his master. As to himself it could do him no good, but a great deal of harm. It would make him discontented and unhappy." These words sank deep into my heart, stirred up sentiments within that lay slumbering, and called into existence an entirely new train of thought. It was a new and special revelation, explaining dark and mysterious things, with which my youthful understanding had struggled, but struggled in vain. I now understood what had been to me a most perplexing difficulty—to wit, the white man's power to enslave the black man. It was a grand achievement, and I prized it highly. From that moment, I understood the pathway from slavery to freedom. (Douglass, 1845, 49)

What enslaves is not writing per se but *control* of writing, and writing as control. What is needed is not less writing but more consciousness of how it works. If, as Derrida claims, the importance of writing has been "repressed" by the dominant culture of the Western tradition, it is because writing can always pass into the hands of the "other." The "other" can always learn to read the mechanism of his or her own oppression. The desire to repress writing is thus a desire to repress the fact of the repression of the "other."

What is at stake in writing is the very structure of authority itself. Whether writing is seen as the instance of the law, the loss of immediacy, or the subversion of the master, whether it opens up a stance of domination, a space of exile, or the pathway to freedom, one thing, at least, is clear: the story of the role and nature of writing in Western culture is still in the process of being written. And the future of that story may be quite unforeseeable, as we pass from the age of the book to the age of the byte.

SUGGESTED READINGS

Abel, Elizabeth, ed. 1982. *Writing and Sexual Difference*.
Barthes, Roland. [1953] 1967. *Writing Degree Zero*.
Derrida, Jacques. [1967a] 1978. *Of Grammatology*.
———. [1967b] 1973. *Speech and Phenomena*.
———. [1967c] 1973. *Writing and Difference*.
Gates, Henry Louis, Jr., ed. 1986. *"Race," Writing, and Difference*.
Ong, Walter. 1982. *Orality and Literacy*.

4

Discourse

Paul A. Bové

1

"**D**ISCOURSE**"** has been a key concept in modern literary criticism. The New Critics, for example, would speak of the "discourse of the novel" as opposed to "poetic discourse" as a way of identifying and separating genre. And, of course, for the New Critics, this distinction implied a hierarchy: poetry was always superior to prose, despite T. S. Eliot's description of the latter as "an unspeakably difficult art." Even the New Critics who wrote fiction and poetry called themselves primarily "poet-critics." Allen Tate, for example, thought of his fine novel, *The Fathers,* as a diversion, an experiment, and considered himself a poet.

To look, then, at the New Critics' use of "discourse" might be a good beginning to an understanding of certain changes that have taken place recently in this key critical term. For the New Critics, "discourse" marked differences and established identities. For example, it helped them set the limits of certain kinds of language use; and the New Critics and their heirs (including, in this case, Northrop Frye) tried to discover whatever it was that made for the identity of one sort of language as opposed to another. These are the sorts of distinctions critics came to think of as "genre differences." In other words, each "discourse," in itself, from this point of view, has an identity to be discovered, defined, and understood; in addition, each discourse established the limits of a particular genre: Tate, for example, could approve moments of *Finnegans Wake* because they were "poetic"; but he could not praise the entire novel, precisely because it exceeded the limits of any genre—that is, it was neither this nor that, neither purely poetry nor purely prose. Joyce's book, for Tate, was off the grid made up by the categories of discourse which, for him and many other modern critics, defined the identity of genre and marked the differences of one genre from another. Not incidentally, this categorization of "genre" was essentially ahistorical and resulted in the consideration of literature apart from the specifics of history and culture (many important contemporary critics have since tried to reverse this result; see, e.g., Jameson 1981). Indeed, one might say that the New Criticism's conservative political and cultural character appears most fully in its notion of genre: in opposition to what they saw as an unchanging "present" of capitalistic excess and the scientific dominance of culture, they counterposed the "memory" or "myth" of an equally unchanging agrarian or pastoral past. Only from this stable community of class relations, they believed, could there re-emerge the relatively fixed benevolent forms of tradition that capitalism destroyed (during the Civil War in the United States and globally in World War I) and that modern literature and criticism would fruitfully modify, replace, or restore.

Quite consciously, then, the New Critics (particularly the Southerners among them who passed through agrarian and regionalist moments in their development) linked these essentialist—and, thus, timeless—"genres" to specific modes of social existence, and they saw them as "expressive" of stable relations in a particular kind of rural or classical community. But paradoxically, they thought these genres still existed and that their recreation and use might help reestablish, in our world, the cultural values that had belonged to the societies that produced them. However, we should not forget that these idealistic and ahistorical notions developed in highly charged and specific political contexts (see Bové 1986). Another way to put this would be to say—with some contemporary poststructuralists like Michel Foucault and Gilles Deleuze—that the New Critics' idea of genre masked a specific link to power and desire. It obscured the New Critics' own historical needs and wants. It helped transform their real historical experiences of concrete political and cultural deprivation into a conservative expression of their mythic desire to recover a lost origin, a supposed premodern state of innocence best named by T. S. Eliot as "an undissociated sensibility."

It is worth pointing out, then, that, in effect, the New Critics put to *use* this term "discourse." Indeed, their case illustrates exactly how key terms are finally more important for their function, for their place within intellectual practices, than they are for what they may be said to "mean" in the abstract. In other words, we must try to see that while the New Critics were carrying on the post-Renaissance business of making distinctions and marking identities about such things as genre, their use of the term "discourse" powerfully shaped the field of literary critical understanding and contained an entire range of aesthetic, moral, and political value judgments which were often unacknowledged as such—although they were sometimes quite clearly understood.

To be more specific, we might say that "discourse," used in this New Critical sense, is itself an example of how we might now delineate the functioning of "discourse" as a category within contemporary critical practice: it helped to constitute and organize an entire field of knowledge about language; it helped discipline the judgment, and thereby the response, of students and teachers; and, in so doing, it revealed its links to forms of power—such as teaching—that have effects upon the actions of others. And in the case of New Criticism, we can, if we choose, easily trace this pattern, in which an intellectually specialized language of a professional discipline is constellated and made functional; we can see it extended both into a broader coherence with other discourses constituting other fields and into the processes which institutionalize discourses. When *their* "discourse" about language and criticism became institutionalized, it effectively produced the language of professional literary criticism and, accordingly, helped make up an academic discipline by giving it some of the characteristics of other intellectual fields already professionally organized. As a result, criticism joined in the general disciplinary project of producing and regulating the movement of knowledge, the forms of language, and the training of minds and bodies. Professionalized academic literary criticism came into being.

But a reader might ask: How can we arrive at such a far-flung set of conclusions? He or she might argue, for example, that Tate simply inherits the apparently self-evident distinction between "poetry" and "prose." It is part of "his discourse" as a man of letters, a literary critic, and poet-novelist; this traditional opposition makes possible, for example, Tate's quite remarkable discussions of Faulkner and Eliot. In other words, such a reader might say, this opposition is merely an accepted critical "tool" that allows Tate to produce essays and that makes possible the debate that surrounds them. Perhaps we would best respond to this respectable line of thought by saying that it is the very utility of the discourse that must be seen as functional and regulative. It hierarchizes not only poetry and prose but, implicitly, identity and difference, authority and subservience, taste and vulgarity, and continuity and discontinuity as well—that is, we might say, it shares in the operation of the generalized discourse of our society that constitutes its most basic categories of understanding and thought.

We might continue to answer this question by saying that *of course* this kind of "genre discourse" speaks through Tate and, indeed, from our point of view the very fact allows us to say that *in these terms* he too is a "function," that in doing his work, he helps maintain and extend the very hierarchies and disciplines we have already mentioned. The final poststructuralist attempt to convince such a questioner that these conclusions are legitimate (even if not fully demonstrated here) would be a quite simple argument: above all, what is noticeable about the way "discourse" functions in the New Criticism is that it draws attention away from itself, from its disciplinary operations and effects—with their promises of reward and assistance—and focuses the attention of the New Critics' apprentices on the need "to get the job done," to understand the "meaning" of texts and produce "new readings" of them. Like all successful discursive categories, in other words, the New Criticism became, for a time, transparent, naturalized, and self-evident. Its effects within the field of knowledge established by the discourse to which it belongs were not noticed or examined by those operating within, that is producing knowledge defined by, that field.

2

The work of Michel Foucault has given a special prominence to the concept of "discourse" in contemporary intellectual and political analysis. He used the term throughout most of his significant writing, but with *L'ordre du discours,* his inaugural lecture at the College de France (1970), and his methodological book *The Archaeology of Knowledge,* the idea gained a new rigor and a new significance that, one might say, has effectively changed the way in which we think of language and its relation to social institutions, systems of power, and the role of intellectuals in our society.

It must be said that in light of the new tenor given to "discourse," we can no longer easily ask such questions as, What is discourse? or, What does discourse mean? In other words, an essay like the present one not only does not but *cannot* provide definitions, nor can it answer what come down to essentializing questions about the "meaning" or "identity" of some "concept" named "discourse." To attempt to do so would be to contradict the logic of the structure of thought in which the term "discourse" now has a newly powerful critical function.

Of course, the reader of a book like this one may wonder why these questions about meaning cannot be answered and perhaps cannot even be asked. Do I not overstate my case? Do I not really mean that poststructuralists don't speak clearly and so cannot answer such commonsensical questions? To such remarks as these, I must reply that the original statement was correct: these essentialist, defining questions quite precisely *cannot* be asked of "discourse." But why not? Because to ask them and to force an answer would be, in advance, hopelessly to prejudice the case against understanding the function of "discourse" either in its poststructuralist context or in its existence as an institutionalized system for the production of knowledge in regulated language. To be more precise, poststructuralists hold that these essentializing questions emerge from the very interpretive models of thought which the new focus on "discourse" as a material practice aims to examine and trace.

Yet, without a doubt, these questions that I label illegitimate are absolutely "commonsensical" and "normal" within our disciplines' systems of knowledge and inquiry; but poststructuralists would argue that their very "normalcy" gives them a troubling power to shape thought and to hinder the posing of other questions. Indeed, poststructuralists would, I am sure, follow Gramsci in saying that it is their very place within the realm of "common sense" that should be questioned so that their effects—their "values" or "ideologies," if you prefer—can be brought into focus (Gramsci 1971, 323f.). Put yet another way, we can say that these questions imply a norm of judgment: meaning and essence are better and more important than a discussion of "how things work" or "where they come from." That is, within the normal procedures of our disciplines and the knowledge-producing system they make up, these "commonsensical" questions are more important than genealogical and functional questions. Such questions are "self-evident" because they are part of a particular network of powerful intellectual and disciplinary expectations. They are asked in all innocence, but their "anonymous" effect is directed and power-laden: to make a theory which "chooses" not to answer them appear to be naive, obfuscating, needlessly difficult, or simply wrong and confused. By obliging all to answer the "same" questions, the "discourse" of "truth" and "definition," of "understanding" and "meaning," to which these questions belong homogenizes critical practice and declares "invalid" whatever does not and *cannot* operate on its political and intellectual terrain. In other words, in this little exemplum, we can see something of what the new sense of "discourse" allows us to describe: the "self-evident" and "commonsensical" are what have the privilege of unnoticed power, and this power produces instruments of control. This matter of control is rather difficult; it does not mean, as it might in certain Freudian or Marxist theories, control by repression or by exclusion. It means, rather, control by the power of positive production: that is, a kind of power that generates certain kinds of questions, placed within systems that legitimate, support, and answer those questions; a kind of power that, in the process, includes within its systems all those it produces as agents capable of acting within them. For example, it produces psychiatrists who let people talk—"confess," as Foucault puts it (Foucault 1978, 58–67)—and so come to constitute themselves as a certain kind of subject who believes sexuality alone defines his or her identity. Indeed, from Foucault's point of view, all intellectuals, all teachers and students within the disciplines, are to some extent incorporated within these systems of control based upon the mode of knowledge and truth production that defines much of our social world. There is, in other words, no place for any of us to stand outside of it.

We should, then, ask another set of questions: How does discourse function? Where is it to be found? How does it get produced and regulated? What are its social effects? How does it exist—as, say, a set of isolated events hierarchically related or as a seemingly enduring flow of linguistic and institutional transformations? In effect, then, to understand the new sense of "discourse," one must try to position it, to see it in its own terms, to describe its place within a network of other analytic and theoretical concepts which are "weapons" for grappling with contemporary society and its history. For example, Foucault gives us a strong sense of discourse as an enduring flow by tracing the genealogy of "discipline" as a series of events existing as transformations of one another (see Foucault 1977a).

"Discourse" provides a privileged entry into the poststructuralist mode of analysis precisely because it is the organized and regulated, as well as the regulating and constituting, functions of language that it studies: its aim is to describe the surface linkages between power, knowledge, institutions, intellectuals, the control of populations, and the modern state as these intersect in the functions of systems of thought.

There is a broad political purpose to this project that develops out of a radical skepticism about "truth" and the correspondence of fact and concept. It is worth pointing out, however, that this skepticism is not nostalgic; that is, it does not regret the passing idealistic philosophies or empirical scientific certainties. On the contrary, it celebrates, if you will, the increasing impossibility of defending "truth" in any metaphysical way and welcomes the political possibilities for self-determination inherent in a recognition that "truth" is made by humans as the result of very specific material practices. A general source for this kind of thinking is in the writings of Giambattista Vico, who insisted upon seeing history and society as human productions. For poststructuralists, however, who are not historicists, a more important and immediate source for the development of this project is the philosophy and history of science developed in France, most notably by Gaston Bachelard and Georges Canguilhem—two important influences on Foucault (another is Georges Dumézil's study of ritual, while a fourth would be Kojève's, Koyré's, and Jean Hyppolite's critiques of Hegel [see Foucault 1976, 235–37]).

Canguilhem's influence was particularly important. His work showed that the history of systems of thought, of disciplines, and of sciences was not merely the chronology of concepts, ideas, and individual discoveries. He did at least two things that helped make possible certain characteristic poststructuralist efforts to rethink the functions of knowledge and truth in modern and postmodern societies. In a sense, he de-personalized science; that is, he showed that it did not have to be understood in terms of individual genius, even of individuals finding solutions and posing problems; he outlined the history of science as the workings of a number of material practices that make up a society. He traced how some of these practices and sciences extended—like "vectors," as it were—throughout a culture, and he showed how they opened new spaces for new forms of knowledge production. By so doing, Canguilhem also showed that science(s) "cohere"; this is a difficult notion. By saying that different sciences and systems of thought "cohere," he claimed that they share what Edward W. Said has called "adjacency" (Said 1975, 351–52), or what Wittgenstein and Chomsky let us call loosely "family resemblances." The order of business for the historian and philosopher of science, then, was to become a historian and philosopher of entire "systems of thought." This approach created unique problems as well as opportunities. Most important, it obliged Canguilhem and others after him to consider how, within the "systems of thought" they constituted, various "sciences" might be institutionally and even conceptually discontinuous; how they might be practiced, as it were, at disparate points within a culture and yet, given their "adjacencies," make up a coherent system of thought spread across a range of institutions and discourses whose family resemblances can be traced by the genealogist interested in their multiple origins, transformations, and their value for the present. (A similar problem for the literary critic might involve tracing the adjacencies between the rise of the realistic novel and, say, such pertinent discourses as anthropology or psychology.)

These three lines of inquiry intersect in poststructuralism and, joined with a certain understanding of Nietzsche (see Deleuze 1983; Foucault 1977b), make possible a skeptical and relativistic, or perspectival, view of the authority of scientific disciplines and, indeed, of all humanistic discourses. In effect, for poststructuralism, all "truths" are relative to the frame of reference which contains them; more radically, "truths" are a function of these frames; and even more radically, these discourses "constitute" the truths they claim to discover and transmit. In its thinking about discourse, then, poststructuralism offers us a kind of nominalism: all that exists are discrete historical events, and the propositions or concepts which claim to tell the truth about them have no reality beyond that acquired by being consistent within the logic of the system that makes them possible. This would seem to be a radical perspectivism, except as poststructuralism develops this idea, it has no psychologistic element; no given perspective depends upon the viewpoint of any actually existing person or even group of persons. The function of discourse and the realities it constructs are fundamentally anonymous. This does not mean that no individuals hold these perspectives nor that no individuals effect them. It means, rather, that their effective realities depend upon no particular subject in history. In opposition to certain kinds of Marxism, for example, this understanding of discourse does not make discourse the product of a particular class or set of class conflicts and conjunctions. There is no natural or necessary identity to the dispersed coherence of discourse; nonetheless, in their randomness the events form a coherence.

But how can this skepticism have a politics? A poststructuralist response would go something like this: Discourses produce knowledge about humans and their society. But since the "truths" of these discourses are relative to the disciplinary structures, the logical framework in which they are institutionalized, they can have no claim upon us except that derived from the authority and legitimacy, the power, granted to or acquired by the institutionalized discourses in question. This large fact turns us to an analysis of the history of discourses, or, more precisely, to their genealogies.

"Genealogy" complements the critical dimension of poststructuralism's radical skepticism. It aims to grasp the formative power of discourses and disciplines. This involves a double analysis, but one in which the two parts are not really separate. First, genealogy tracks down the ways in which discourses constitute "objects" and "classes of objects" which are available for study. Second, and more important, genealogy traces the way in which discourses constitute these objects as subjects of statements which can themselves be judged as "true" or "false" according to the logic, syntax, and semantics of the empowered discourse. Not unless a statement is about an "object" and can be judged in its truthfulness does it enter into a discourse; but once it does, it furthers the dispersal of that discourse and enlarges the realm of objects and statements which produce knowledge that can be judged legitimate or illegitimate. There is a relationship of constitutive reciprocity, then, between the "objects" and "statements" within any discourse. Neither can be studied without seeing it in its relation to the other.

For example (and this is a privileged example in poststructuralism), how did the human subject come to be that about which entire sets of psychological statements can be uttered that, in turn, as propositions, can be judged true or false? In effect what this kind of questioning supposes is that both the object of disciplinary study, in this case the subject as psyche, and the discipline which forms authenticated statements about the object are functions of discourses "about" the subject they constitute: for only within these discourses and the practices that grow from and depend upon them does the "psyche" exist as an object of a certain kind of knowledge ("a certain kind" is a necessary part of this formulation in light of Foucault's work in the second and third volumes of his history of sexuality; he showed there that sex can be and has been the "object" of many different kinds of knowledge and practice—see Foucault 1985, 1986). Genealogy tries to get hold of this power that crosses discourses and to show that it is, among other things, the power that makes possible and legitimate certain kinds of questions and statements. It is, in other words, the power to produce statements which alone can be judged "true" or "false" within the knowledge/power system that produces "truth" and its criteria within a culture. It is, in effect, recognizing that "truth" is produced in just this way as the "effect," so to speak, of systems-in-place to which are reserved the authorities of judgment—it is by recognizing this effect of power that genealogy does its work. Indeed, genealogy lets us confront how power constructs truth-producing systems in which propositions, concepts, and representations generally assign value and meaning to the objects of the various disciplines that treat them. Value, we might say, circulates along the paths or vectors these disciplines sketch. Within literary studies, for example, we might say that this power shapes the language that lets us speak about such creations of the discipline as "the author," while not easily letting us see the workings by which "the author" has come to be constituted by and for us when we "discourse" about literature and writing (Foucault 1977b).

But how, then, is "discourse" key to more than a politics of abstract language games? The answer lies in the materiality of discourse. That is, "discourse" makes possible disciplines and institutions which, in turn, sustain and distribute those discourses. Foucault has shown how this works in the case of prisons and medical clinics. In other words, these discourses are linked to social institutions which "have power" in the very ordinary sense we mean when we use that phrase: such institutions can control bodies and actions. But there is more to them than "having power" in the sense of being able to dominate others. And this is more slippery and strange as an idea, but it is central to grasping the utility of discourse for political intellectual analysis.

Discourses and their related disciplines and institutions are functions of power: they distribute the effects of power. They are power's relays throughout the modern social system. One of Foucault's late meditations usefully gets at this idea:

> In effect, what defines a relationship of power is that it is a mode of action which does not act directly and immediately on others. Instead it acts upon their actions: an action upon an action, on existing actions or on those which may arise in the present or the future. . . . A power relationship can only be articulated on the basis of two elements which are each indispensable if it is really to be a power relationship: that "the other" (the one over whom power is exercised) be thoroughly recognized and maintained to the very end as a person who acts; and that, faced with a relationship of power, a whole field of responses, reactions, results, and possible inventions may open up. (Foucault 1983, 220)

Power must not be thought of as negative, as repression, domination, or inhibition. On the contrary, it must always be seen as "a making possible," as an opening up of fields in which certain kinds of action and production are brought about. As power disperses itself, it opens up specific fields of possibility; it constitutes entire domains of action, knowledge, and social being by shaping the institutions and disciplines in which, for the most part, we largely make ourselves. In these domains we become the individuals, the subjects, that they make us. This phrasing, of course, makes things sound more deterministic than they are in fact, for there *is* no subject there to be determined in advance: the subject comes to be whatever or whoever he or she is only *within* this set of discursive and nondiscursive fields. What Foucault means when he says that power acts upon actions is precisely that it regulates our forming of ourselves. "Individuation," then, is the space in which we are most regulated by the ruling disciplines of language, sexuality, economics, culture, and psychology.

"Discourse" is one of the most empowered ways in modern and postmodern societies for the forming and shaping of humans as "subjects." In a now-famous play on words, we might say that "power" through its discursive and institutional relays "subjects" us: that is, it makes us into "subjects," and it "subjects" us to the rule of the dominant disciplines which are empowered in our society and which regulate its possibilities for human freedom—that is, it "subjugates" us. (The French have a set of words that gives them some punning insights into this whole matter: the poststructuralists have made much of the word "assujet-tir," which means to subject and to subjugate.) Indeed, we must even hypothesize that power affects the forms which our resistance to power can take. In other words, according to this notion there is no essential self somewhere else within power; consequently, resistance to any particular form of power—resistance to any discursive "truth"—depends upon power and not some abstract category of freedom or the self.

How does this happen? Recall that "true statements" are always relative to the authority of empowered discourses; recall, in addition, that what is constituted as "real" are only those objects of which statements can be judged true or false. As humans, we are the "subject" of these discourses and their crossings; if we are professional critics, literary criticism would be prominent among them. But before we had received our professional training, we would already have been the subject of other disciplines which criticism might enforce or, in part, subvert. Surely sexuality, law, and the psyche, embedded in fundamental institutions and discourses, would be the earliest means to "subject" us all within this culture. We would become, then, in very large measure, the objects who are the subjects of these (our own) discourses: readers and writers, subjects assessed by statistics, bodies available to punishment regulated by the helping services, psyches to be normalized, bodies to be "engendered," and so forth. A genealogical study of "discourse" would be a study of how these things have come about; even more, it would be a history of how the present has come about in part by virtue of the increasing ability of the power which forms such disciplines to arrange social and individual life.

The study of "discourse," then, leads inevitably to a study of institutions, disciplines, and intellectuals: poststructuralists like Foucault would argue that the research areas opened up by this concept of "discourse" are inherently restricted to matters of the local; other thinkers, especially those who might try to align some of these poststructuralist notions with certain forms of recent Marxist thinking—much of it derived from Gramsci—would argue that such study cannot stop at the local level but must be expanded to outline the relationship of these discursive institutions to the largest forms of power—civil society and the state (see Smart 1983, 119–20). In both cases, though, there seems to be a common concern: to understand how these material discursive realities act upon the actions of others, that is, of all of us, no matter where and how differently placed we are in the grid of identity and privilege these realities constitute.

Foucault argues that power is deeply rooted in social relations but that this fact should not be taken fatalistically:

> For to say that there cannot be a society without power relations is not to say either that those which are established are necessary, or, in any case, that power constitutes a fatality at the heart of societies, such that it cannot be undermined. Instead I would say that the analysis, elaboration, and bringing into question of power relations and the "agonism" between power relations and intran-

sitivity of freedom is a permanent political task inherent in all social relations. (Foucault 1983, 223)

"Genealogy" provides unique access to these relations and struggles: unlike
Marxism and whiggism, two major forms of historical explanation which it opposes, genealogy separates itself within the "will to truth" by trying to unmask
discourses' associations with power and materialities; also, it is not reductive,
that is, it alone allows for a full description of the complexly determined discursive practices it studies; and, finally, it describes and criticizes these practices with
an eye to revealing their "subjugating" effects in the present—it means always to
resist disciplining and speaking for others in their own struggles. (I should also
mention the relation of genealogy to certain forms of philosophical pragmatism
that are, in their own ways, prepared to admit a complicity between truth and
power, but this issue is too complex to explore briefly—for some sense of the
matter, see Rorty 1982, 136–37, 203–8; and Rorty 1986, 48.)

"Genealogy" aims not to trace causal influences among events, nor to follow
the evolution of the "Spirit of History"; it does not adhere to strict historical
laws, nor does it believe in the power of subjects, great or small, to act "originally," that is, to "change history." Rather it describes events as transformations
of other events which, from the vantage point of the present and its needs, seem
to be related by a family resemblance. It shows how these transformations have
no causal or historical necessity; they are not "natural." It shows how the adjacency of events, that is, their simultaneity within ostensibly different fields, can
transform entire domains of knowledge production: the rise of statistics and the
development of discipline within massed armies helped transform punishment
from torture to imprisonment with its rationale of rehabilitation. It also shows
that this new penal discipline makes the body's punishment the space wherein
the modern soul, the psyche, comes into being and is made available to the
"helping" (that is, the disciplining) professions of social work, teaching, and
medicine.

In the process of this description and criticism, genealogy also engages in intellectual struggle with the major forms of explanatory discourse in modernity,
with what are sometimes totalizing oppositional discourses—such as psychoanalysis and Marxism—which, from the point of view of poststructuralism, are
inescapably caught up in the same disciplining formations as penology, medicine, and law. This is not to say that genealogical work is simply "anti-Marxist"
or "anti-Freudian"; rather, it is interested in describing how these grand oppositional discourses have become authoritative and productive within the larger
field of humanistic discourse which defines modernity—and in trying to pose
other questions. Foucault would have it, for example, that everyone is a Marxist:
how can one not be? What this means, of course, is not just that the fundamental
Marxist analysis of class domination and struggle, as well as other basic Marxist

concepts, are uncontestable but also that we are all inscribed within the larger realm of discourse of subjectivity and struggle of which Marxism is, for certain intellectuals, a privileged part. Nevertheless, the centrality of discourse to poststructuralism requires understanding something more about its relation to Marxism, especially in France. In France, poststructuralism's questioning of Marxism has much to do with the student revolt of May 1968 and the so-called new politics that grew out of it. This questioning also grows out of a concern for socialism's weaknesses, of that kind now broadly (if wrongly) associated with Gorbachev's policy of *glasnost*. Intellectually, this concern has found its best voice in certain dissidents' objections to what one of their number calls "actually existing socialism" (Bahro 1978). It implies a conflict with Marxism's dialectical materialism and the principles of elite political leadership contained within it; for example, Foucault's experience of the events in Paris in 1968 led to his criticism of established forms of political leadership and representative institutions (see Foucault 1977b, 205–6). Just as genealogy can produce a critique of how liberal disciplines create the subjugated subjects differentiated, as such, within the regulated space of discourse, so Marxism—from this point of view—with its understanding of the proletariat as the subject of history, appears as a relay of power which acts upon the actions of the class it "constitutes" and the individuals disciplined by its institutions.

Foucault grew increasingly interested in what the rise of the modern disciplines had to do with modern state power—with what he called "governability"—and how it displaced sovereignty as the hegemonic figure of power and authority. A genealogical analysis of the discourses and practices that made for this transformation does not suggest that dialectics stands outside it. For example, a study of governability in an era of constitutive and regulative disciplines shows that actions always follow upon actions acting upon agents at a distance: liberal and Marxist discourses, by contrast always think of the actors as metaphysically constitutive subjects (for an example of how complex this notion can be, see Georg Lukács's discussion of "putative class consciousness" [Lukács 1971, 46–222]).

Politically, then, politics and democracy are the issues in poststructuralism's attempt to theorize power, action, agency, and resistance. In disciplinary societies, self-determination is nearly impossible, and political opposition must take the form of resistance to the systems of knowledge and their institutions that regulate the population into "individualities" who, as such, make themselves available for more discipline, to be actors acted upon. In this understanding of governability, truth produced by these knowledge systems blocks the possibility of sapping power; it speaks for—or, as we say in Western republics, it "represents"—others. But for poststructuralism, it is not self-evident, for example, that notions of oppositional leadership, such as Gramsci's conception of the "organic intellectual" (Gramsci 1973, 208–9), will be significant alternatives to the regulating ideal of "speaking for." Having emerged out of the events of 1968, post-structuralism remains politically suspicious of all rhetorics of leadership and all representational institutions. It gives priority to the politics of local struggles against defining forms of power and for marginalized identities; and it speaks for the difficulty (not the impossibility!) human beings face in trying to make their own "subjectivities" within the given sets of power relations.

The genealogical analysis of discourse, then, sets out with an eye on the present to criticize and trace the systems of power which have come to constitute human being in our world. It does this to stand in opposition to them and to provide the results of its work to whomever would like to use them in their struggles against the forms of power they are trying to resist.

3

The contemporary use of "discourse" turns literary critics away from questions of meaning; it also turns us from questions of "method" to the description of function. It suggests that a new set of questions should replace the interpretive ones that have come to constitute criticism and the normal practice of teachers and scholars. We might ask such things as, How does language work to produce knowledge? How is language organized in disciplines? Which institutions perform and which regulative principles direct this organization? With these questions and the turn from a discourse of "meaning," from hermeneutics, or from interpretive criticism as the grand humanistic practice, we turn to the question of the subject. We turn especially to the question of how the subject is produced within social discourses and institutions and how, also, the subject becomes the "subject-function." Within literary critical studies, this requires that we consider the function of the "author" in critical discourse and in the larger formation of the subject and the discourses of subjectivity within the modern and postmodern worlds.

Now with the question of the author, we come to an area heatedly debated and much misunderstood in recent criticism. Barthes, Derrida, and Foucault have variously proposed an apparently scandalous idea: the author is "dead"; language speaks, not the poet; the author is irrelevant. For the humanistic critic raised in the tradition of *belles lettres* or of American common sense or profitably invested in the defense of "traditional values," this sort of notion is either nonsensical, or, rather neurotically, taken to be a "threat to civilization," or not taken seriously, or, perhaps most commonly, simply dismissed as just too hard to understand.

One must try to clear up some of the confusion by recalling Foucault's assertion that no one is interested in denying the existence of the writer as a cause in the production of literature or any other form of written discourse. However, what Foucault and others interested in the material effect of writing intend to argue is that there are different ways to organize our considerations of writing—

that, indeed, we need first of all to describe and criticize the already institution-alized ways in which writing is conceptualized if we are to picture the principles which regulate the organization and which enable not only what we can *say* about writing but writing (and discourse) itself. In other words, when viewed as an element in a historical system of institutionalized discourse, the traditional idea of the "author," and the privileged value accorded to it in literary scholar-ship and criticism, is one of the two or three key concepts by means of which the critical disciplines organize their knowledge around questions of subjectivity and discipline both their practitioners and those they "teach."

The Foucauldian notion of discourse requires that we skeptically ask the ques-tion How did the category of 'the author' become so central to critical thinking about literature? This means "central" not only in theory but in practice: in the way single-figure studies dominate criticism; in the organization of texts in "complete editions"; in biographies; and, above all, in the idea of style, of a marked writing characteristically the "expression" of a person's "mind" or "psyche" whose essential identity scrawls across a page and declares its imagina-tive "ownership" of these self-revealing and self-constituting lines. (Even critics, after all, aspire to their own "style.") Carrying out this genealogy is beyond the scope of this essay. The attempt to do so, however, would, in itself, move critical analysis into a different realm and—if carried out in a nonreductive manner, one which did not simplify the complexities of discourse, one which did not newly reify certain "genealogical" categories—would exemplify a valuable new direc-tion for literary criticism. In the process, it suggests the privileged place "lit crit" has held in the construction of modern subjectivity—though it is by now a rap-idly retreating privilege. It also suggests to some, however, that literary criticism might assume a powerful oppositional political position within our society or that it might be of assistance to some people in their own forms of struggle elsewhere in the system. Were this possible, it would be very important. Since ours is a society which increasingly tries to ensure its political order through discursive systems that discipline our language and culture, any successful resist-ance to that order would seem to require strong weapons aimed to weaken that discipline. Hence the value of the poststructuralist idea that genealogical, discur-sive analysis can be politically valuable to others struggling against the estab-lished forms of power wherever they might be.

In other words, literary criticism, presumably always specially sensitive to the functions of language, and newly sensitive to its relationship to power on the site of institutionalized disciplines, can turn its tools to the critical examination of how, in relation to the state and its largest institutions, power operates in discourse and how discourse disciplines a population. How, in particular, dis-course helps to maintain a population as a set of actors always available for dis-cipline, to act to ends announced by agents themselves responding to (or even resisting) the distributed effects of power in this society.

In sum, then, discourse can turn literary studies into a full criticism, one which is skeptical, critical, oppositional, and—when appropriate—sustentative. It can help us to avoid reduction, either of the historical context of an event or of the rhetorically complex display of power within a textualized discourse or institutionalized discipline.

Of course, it is, in itself, no panacea of critical opposition; it is no talisman—although many newer critics chant its terms as if they were a magical charm. It, too, can become a new disciplinary technique—some would argue it already has—within our regulated society, one that enables the production of new texts, new discourses, whose "contents" may be different and whose politics may be oppositional but whose effects on given power relations may be either minimal or unpredictable and undesired. Criticism must always watchfully resist the promotional powers of the disciplined discourse in which it is placed. It can exploit the possibilities of that discourse to produce what Foucault calls a "counter-memory," but it needs to be careful not to assume the right of speaking for others in forming that memory. Above all, it needs to avoid becoming what R. P. Blackmur would have called a "new orthodoxy."

In his turn away from the very New Criticism that he had helped to establish, Blackmur explained that he was motivated by a commitment to criticism, to a process and position that Edward W. Said sums up as "critical negation" (see Bové 1986, 275–99), and that I am calling here "skepticism." When the tools of opposition, useful to a point and in a specific local struggle against a particular form of power, lose their negative edge—when their critical effect makes no difference and they simply permit the creation of new texts, new documents recording the successful placement of the previously "oppositional" within the considerably unchanged institutional structures of the discipline—at that point criticism must turn skeptical again and genealogically recall how the heretical became orthodox (perhaps the most powerful example of just this move is Blackmur's critique of Kenneth Burke [see Blackmur 1955]). This is a difficult chore of critical renewal: a perpetual measure of criticism's task in our society, one that must transcend both professional enticements and critical egoism. As Foucault says of Hegel's (that is, of philosophy's) encounters with his twentieth-century readers: it commits us to a task of "continuous recommencement, given over to the forms and paradoxes of repetition" (Foucault 1976, 236).

SUGGESTED READINGS

Arac, Jonathan. 1979. *Commissioned Spirits*.
———. 1987. *Critical Genealogies*.
———, ed. 1988. *After Foucault*.
Auerbach, Erich. 1953. *Mimesis*.
Bahro, Rudolph. 1978. *The Alternative in Eastern Europe*.
Bakhtin, M. M. 1981. *The Dialogic Imagination*.

Benjamin, Walter, 1977. *The Origin of German Tragic Drama*.

Blackmur, R. P. 1955. *The Lion and the Honeycomb*.

———. 1952. *Language as Gesture*.

Bové, Paul A. 1986. *Intellectuals in Power*.

———. 1986. "Agriculture and Academe: America's Southern Question."

———. 1988. "The Foucault Phenomenon."

Canguilhem, Georges. 1978. *On the Normal and the Pathological*.

Deleuze, Gilles. 1983. *Nietzsche and Philosophy*.

———. 1988. *Foucault*.

de Man, Paul. 1979. *Allegories of Reading*.

Dreyfus, Hubert L., and Paul Rabinow. 1983. *Michel Foucault*.

Foucault, Michel. 1976. "The Discourse on Language."

———. 1977a. *Discipline and Punish*.

———. 1977b. *Language, Counter-Memory, Practice*.

———. 1978. *The History of Sexuality*. Vol. 1.

———. 1980. *Power/Knowledge*.

———. 1983. "The Subject and Power."

———. 1985. *The Use of Pleasure*.

———. 1986. *The Care of the Self*.

———. 1988a. *Politics, Philosophy, Culture*.

———. 1988b. *Technologies of the Self: A Seminar with Michel Foucault*.

Gramsci, Antonio. 1971. *Selections from the Prison Notebooks*.

———. 1973. *Letters from Prison*.

Hoy, David Couzens, ed. 1986. *Foucault: A Critical Reader*.

Jameson, Fredric. 1981. *The Political Unconscious*.

Lentricchia, Frank. 1987. *Ariel and the Police*.

Lukács, George. 1971. *History and Class Consciousness*.

O'Hara, Daniel T. 1985. *The Romance of Interpretation*.

Robbins, Bruce. 1986. *The Servant's Hand*.

Rorty, Richard. 1982. *Consequences of Pragmatism*.

———. 1986. "Foucault and Epistemology."

Said, Edward W. 1975. *Beginnings*.

———. 1978. *Orientalism*.

———. 1983. *The World, the Text, and the Critic*.

Smart, Barry. 1983. *Foucault, Marxism, and Critique*.

Spivak, Gayatri. 1987. *In Other Worlds*.

Williams, Raymond. 1979. *Politics and Letters*.

5

Narrative

J. Hillis Miller

To My Colleagues in Lit. X

NOTHING seems more natural and universal to human beings than telling stories. Surely there is no human culture, however "primitive," without its stories and habits of storytelling, its myths of the origin of the world, its legends of the tribe or groups of stories about folk heroes. Linguists use the ability to narrate as a measure of advanced language competence. From our earliest childhood we hear stories and learn to repeat them. An example is the story my two-year-old granddaughter echoed from her mother, speaking of herself in the third person as the heroine of her own story: "Mama will carry baby up and down, and then baby will feel *much* better." As adults, we hear, read, see, and tell stories all day long—for example, in the newspaper, on television, in encounters with co-workers or family members. In a continuous silent internal activity, we tell stories to ourselves all day long. Jokes are one form of narration. Advertising is another: "Use this product, and then you will feel *much* better." At night we sleep, and our unconscious minds tell us more stories in our dreams, often exceedingly strange ones. Even within "literature proper" the range of narrative is wide and diverse. It includes not only short stories and novels but also dramas, epics, Platonic dialogues, narrative poems, and so on. Many, if not all, lyric poems have a narrative dimension. Quite a different result is obtained if one approaches Keats's "Ode to a Nightingale," say, as a miniature narrative rather than as an organically unified assembly of figures.

Narration, on the other hand, is so natural, so universal, and so easily mastered as hardly to seem a problematic region for literary theory. As Aristotle said long ago in the *Poetics,* plot is the most important feature of a narrative. A good story has a beginning, middle, and end, making a shapely whole with no extraneous elements. The other features of narrative—character, setting, diction, and so forth—are all subsidiary to the chief element of plot. That seems about all there is to say about it. The vast variety of different sorts of stories seems governed in one way or another by these simple laws of unity and economy.

A moment's reflection, however, will show that things are not quite so simple. For example, *why* is it that narration is so universal, present in all human beings everywhere? The fact that narrative is so universal, so "natural," may hide what is strange and problematic about it. Exactly what psychological or social functions do stories serve? Just why do we need stories, lots of them, all the time? The answers to those questions are not so easy to reach.

Aristotle's answer, again in the *Poetics,* was that narrative—for example, tragic drama, one form of narration dominant in the Greece of Aristotle's time—plays a fundamental social and psychological role. Plays effect what he called, using a medical term, *catharsis* of the undesirable emotions of pity and fear. Tragedy purges these emotions by first arousing them. It works as a kind of homeopathic medicine: tragedy cures the disease by administering a controlled dose of it and then clearing it away. Various other explanations of the nature and function of narrative have been proposed over the centuries since Aristotle. Moreover, the recent decades of this century have seen a tremendous development of diverse theories of narrative, so many and so diverse that it makes the mind ache to think of them all.

Among these are Russian formalist theories of narrative; Bakhtinian, or dialogical, theories; New Critical theories; Chicago school, or neo-Aristotelian, theories; psychoanalytic theories; hermeneutic and phenomenological theories; structuralist, semiotic, and tropological theories; Marxist and sociological theories; reader-response theories; and poststructuralist and deconstructionist theories. As the reader can see, each of these explanations of narrative tends to have a barbarous or jargonistic name that does not tell much about the theory itself. An enormous secondary literature has grown up around each of these approaches to narrative. It would require a book-length study to explain in detail any one of them, but each can be distinguished from the others by distinctive assumptions about narrative each tends to make.

Moreover, though there is much overlapping and contamination of one theory by adjacent ones in the actual practice of teaching and criticism, each of these theories tends to be associated with one or two major figures who either originated the theory or were exemplary practitioners of it: Vladimir Propp, Viktor Sklovskij, and Boris Eichenbaum, for example, for Slavic formalism; Mikhail Bakhtin for the dialogical theory of narrative he originated; R. P. Blackmur, among many others, for American New Criticism; R. S. Crane and Wayne Booth for the Chicago Aristotelians; Sigmund Freud himself, Kenneth Burke, Jacques Lacan, and Nicholas Abraham for psychoanalytic theories of narrative; Roman Ingarden, Paul Ricoeur, and Georges Poulet for hermeneutic and phenomenological theories; Claude Lévi-Strauss, Roland Barthes, Tzvetan Todorov, A. J. Greimas, Gérard Genette, and Hayden White for structuralist, semiotic, and tropological theories; Georg Lukács and Fredric Jameson for Marxist and sociological theories; Wolfgang Iser and Hans Robert Jauss for reader-response theories; Jacques Derrida and Paul de Man for deconstructionist theories.

The inclusion of Hayden White and Paul Ricoeur in my list is testimony to the fact that in recent years history writing as well as fictional narratives have been addressed by narrative theorists. My focus will be primarily on fictional narratives, but the recounting of events that "really occurred" on the stage of history is of course a form of narrative too. The two forms of narration are closely related forms of "order-giving" or "order-finding," in spite of the fact that fictional narratives are subject to referential restraints in a way very different from the way histories submit themselves to history and claim to represent things that really happened *exactly as* they really happened.

The interested reader can go for himself or herself to the vast literature by these authors and their followers. It is not my business here to attempt to summarize all these theories. What is most important for my purposes is the abundance and diversity of them. This swarming diversity of narrative theories is evidence that for us today the question of the nature and function of narrative is a challenging intellectual problem: narrative cannot by any means be taken for granted.

Just why is this? What's the problem? An approach to answering this question may be made by refining a little the question with which I began. I asked, Why do we need stories? To this may be added two more questions, Why do we need the "same" story over and over? Why is our need for more stories never satisifed?

Why do we need stories at all? Why do children listen so avidly to stories? Why do we never outgrow the need for stories and go on reading novels, mystery stories, seeing movies, or watching soap operas on television even as adults? Reading or watching fictive stories is, when one thinks of it, a strange activity. The reader of a novel detaches himself or herself from the immediately surrounding world of real-life obligations. With the help of those black marks on the page or images on the screen the reader or spectator comes to dwell in an imaginary world whose links to the real world are more or less indirect. One might have thought that by now the reality principle, growing more dominant as civilization grows, would have made storytelling obsolete. Nothing of the sort has happened. As Peter Brooks has observed, if man is the tool-using animal, *homo faber,* he is also inveterately the symbol-using animal, *homo significans,* the sense-making animal—and, as an essential part of the latter, the fiction-making animal. The word "fiction" comes from the Latin *fingere,* "to make" and "to make up." A fiction, as Brooks says, is made up in the double sense of being both fabricated and feigned. This make-believe is a fundamental human activity. It includes game playing, role-playing, daydreaming, and many other such activities, as well as literature proper.

Why do we need fictions and enjoy them so much? Aristotle's answer at the beginning of the *Poetics* was a double one. We enjoy imitation, *mimesis* (his word for roughly what I have been calling "fiction") for two reasons. For one thing, imitations are rhythmic, orderly, and it is natural to human beings to take pleasure in rhythmic forms. In addition, man learns by imitation, and it is natural to man to take pleasure in learning. What do we learn from fictions? We learn the nature of things as they are. We need fictions in order to experiment with possible selves and to learn to take our places in the real world, to play our parts there. Think how many works of fiction are stories of initiation, of growing up—fairy tales, for example, but also great novels like *Great Expectations* or *Huckleberry Finn*. A more modern formulation of what Aristotle asserts might be to say that in fictions we order or reorder the givens of experience. We give experience a form and a meaning, a linear order with a shapely beginning, middle, end, and central theme. The human capacity to tell stories is one way men and women collectively build a significant and orderly world around themselves. With fictions we investigate, perhaps invent, the meaning of human life.

Well, which is it, create or reveal? It makes a lot of difference which we choose. To say "reveal" presupposes that the world has one kind or another of preexisting order and that the business of fictions is in one way or another to imitate, copy, or represent accurately that order. In this case, the ultimate test of a good fiction is whether or not it corresponds to the way things are. To say "create," on the other hand, presupposes that the world may not be ordered in itself or, at any rate, that the social and psychological function of fictions is what speech-act theorists call "performative." A story is a way of doing things with words. It makes something happen in the real world: for example, it can propose modes of selfhood or ways of behaving that are then imitated in the real world. It has been said, along these lines, that we would not know we were in love if we had not read novels. Seen from this point of view, fictions may be said to have a tremendous importance not as the accurate reflectors of a culture but as the makers of that culture and as the unostentatious, but therefore all the more effective, policemen of that culture. Fictions keep us in line and tend to make us more like our neighbors. If this is true, then changes in the rise and fall in popularity of different genres over time or changes in the dominant medium—first from oral storytelling to print, then from printed books to cinema and television—will have an incalculable importance for the shape of that culture.

There is, however, another cultural function of narratives, one going counter to the "policing" function I have just noted. Narratives are a relatively safe or innocuous place in which the reigning assumptions of a given culture can be criticized. In a novel, alternative assumptions can be entertained or experimented with—not as in the real world, where such experimentations might have dangerous consequences, but in the imaginary world where, it is easy to assume, "nothing really happens" because it happens only in the feigned world of fiction. If novels coach us to believe that there is such a thing as "being in love," they also at the same time subject that idea to effective demystification, while perhaps at the end showing the triumph of love beyond or in spite of its demystification. Shakespeare's *As You Like It* is a splendid example of this, but many great novels, for example George Meredith's *The Egoist,* take the same form. There is reason to believe, then, that narratives reinforce the dominant culture and put it in question, both at the same time. The putting in question may be obliquely affirmative: we can ward off dangers to the reigning assumptions or ideologies of our culture by expressing our fears about their fragility or vulnerability in a safe realm of fiction. The officials of repressive regimes who have over the years censored or suppressed threatening novels may, however, have a shrewder sense of the political force a novel can have. It is not entirely an absurdity to say that the novels of Sir Walter Scott caused the Civil War in the United States and sent all those romantically infatuated plantation owners to their doom.

Second question: *Why do we need the "same" story over and over?* The answers to this question are more related to the affirmative, culture-making function of narrative than to its critical or subversive function. If we need narratives in order to give sense to our world, the shape of that sense is a fundamental carrier of the sense. Children know this when they insist on having familiar stories recited to them in exactly the same forms, not a word changed. If we need stories to make sense of our experience, we need the same stories over and over to reinforce that sense making. Such repetition perhaps reassures by the reencounter with the form that the narrative gives to life. Or perhaps the repetition of a rhythmic pattern is intrinsically pleasurable, whatever that pattern is. The repetitions within the pattern are pleasurable in themselves, and they give pleasure when they are repeated.

The quotation marks around the word "same" indicate another meaning for the sameness of the same story. If we, like children, want the same story over and over in exactly the same form, as though it were a magical charm that would lose its efficacy if a word were changed, we also need the same story over and over in another sense. We want repetition in the form of many stories that are recognizably variations on the same formula. If children want nursery rhymes and bedtime stories over and over in exact word-for-word order, they quickly learn even before the age of five or six the rules for proper storytelling. They learn the conventions of formulaic beginning and ending, "Once upon a time" and "They lived happily ever after." They learn the conformity to norm of a story that "works." Many kinds of narrative are demonstrably variations on a conventional form or formula: Greek tragedies, nursery rhymes, fairy tales, traditional ballads, Sherlock Holmes stories, James Bond novels, limericks, even such large genres as "the Victorian novel" or, within that, the forty-four novels of Anthony Trollope, all recognizably members of the same family. This repeatability is an intrinsic feature of many narrative forms. It is the whole point of limericks that there be lots of them and that they all have a family resemblance. The same thing can be said of mystery stories. Variations from the norm draw much of their meaning from the fact that they *are* deviations from the rules. An example would be a detective story in which the narrator is the murderer, for example Agatha Christie's *The Murder of Roger Ackroyd,* or a Victorian novel, such as Meredith's *The Ordeal of Richard Feverel,* that unexpectedly has an unhappy ending.

The universality of this form of "the same in the different" in narrative has two implications. It implies that we want stories for something they can do for us, something we inexhaustibly need. It implies that this function is not performed primarily by the characters, the true-to-life setting, or even by the "theme" or "message," the "moral," but by the sequential structure of events, the plot. Aristotle, it seems, was right to give plot primacy in narrative. The plot structure of a given narrative seems to be transferable from one story to another with perhaps very different characters and setting. Plot is detachable, translatable. Much recent analysis of narrative—by the Slavic formalists, by French structuralists, by semioticians, and by "narratologists" generally—has been based on this notion. Such theorists have sought in one way or another to find out the secrets of narrative form, its "deep structure." Vladimir Propp's influential *Morphology of the Folk Tale,* for example, one of the classics of Slavic formalism, attempts to demonstrate that one hundred Russian folk tales are all variants of the same structural form. The number of functional elements is limited. Though not all of the elements are present in every story, the sequence of such functions (plot elements such as "interdiction," "interrogation," "departure," "return") is always identical. Narratologists have thought of the laws of narrative as something like a code or a language with a grammar of its own, perhaps something on a larger scale like the grammar of a sentence. Aristotle, in the *Poetics,* the first great work of Western narrative theory, was already a structuralist before the fact, not only in according primacy to plot but in believing he could identify the essential structural features making a tragedy a tragedy and not some other thing.

Seen from this structuralist or semiotic perspective, narrative would be a process of ordering or reordering, recounting, telling again what has already happened or is taken to have already happened. This recounting takes place according to definite rules analogous to those rules by which we form sentences. This means that the secrets of storytelling are ascertainable by empirical or scientific investigation. This makes narrative theory part of "the human sciences." Hence, Propp's use of a term from biology as well as from linguistics: "morphology." The process of storytelling in a given culture or within a given genre at a particular place and time will be bound by certain unwritten but identifiable laws, so that a good story can be distinguished from a bad story, a story from a nonstory.

This structuring of events according to a certain design of beginning, end, and conventional trajectory connecting them is, it should be stressed, by no means innocent. It does not take things as they come. Reordering by narrative may therefore have as its function, as I have suggested, the affirmation and reinforcement, even the creation, of the most basic assumptions of a culture about human existence, about time, destiny, selfhood, where we come from, what we ought to do while we are here, where we go—the whole course of human life.

We need the "same" stories over and over, then, as one of the most powerful, perhaps *the* most powerful, of ways to assert the basic ideology of our culture.

Third question: *Why do we always need more stories?* This is the most difficult of my questions. It would seem that once a man or woman has reached adulthood, with the help of all the narratives with which a growing youth is surrounded, he or she would then be fully assimilated into the culture, with a definite self and a definite role in society and therefore with no more need for stories. This is obviously not the case. I can only hint at a possible explanation for this. But my discussion afterward of several examples may make the issue clearer. It could be that we always need more stories because in *some* way they do *not* satisfy. Stories, however perfectly conceived and powerfully written, however moving, do not accomplish successfully their allotted function. Each story and each repetition or variation of it leaves some uncertainty or contains some loose end unraveling its effect, according to an implacable law that is not so much psychological or social as linguistic. This necessary incompletion means that no story fulfills perfectly, once and for all, its functions of ordering and confirming. And so we need another story, and then another, and yet another, without ever coming to the end of our need for stories or without ever assuaging the hunger they are meant to satisfy.

One example of this might be that form of narration, almost always present among the myths, legends, and tales of any culture, that has as its purpose the explanation of mankind's origins, where man came from. Anthropologists call these "etiological myths." Rudyard Kipling's *Jungle Book,* with its stories of "How the Elephant Got His Trunk," and so on, is a collection of etiological legends. Sophocles' *Oedipus the King,* Aristotle's archetype of the perfect tragedy in the *Poetics,* has been interpreted by modern structural anthropologists as a narrative of this sort. A myth, that is, a fabulous narrative, may be necessary when no logical form of explanation will work, but the illogical premises will remain embedded in the story. The origin of man, his separation of himself from the beasts and from uncivilized nature, is a kind of chicken/egg problem. Whatever is chosen as the moment of origination always presupposes some earlier moment when man first appeared.

The story enacted with matchless power in *Oedipus the King* "solves" this apparently insoluble problem by presenting a narrative in which both incest and the taboo against incest are seen as simultaneously natural and cultural and in which Oedipus is both guilty and not guilty. Has he not murdered his father and slept with his mother? And yet he did not then know they were his father and mother, and so he has not intentionally committed the Oedipal crimes of parricide and incest. Like a beast he is innocent, since he did not know what he was doing. A beast cannot commit incest because it cannot understand the prohibition against incest. Incest exists only as the transgression of the taboo against it.

The taboo against incest, as the great structural anthropologist Claude Lévi-

Strauss has argued, is a basic trait distinguishing the human species from all other species of life. For a cat, a dog, or a bear, mother, daughter, brother, father may all be sexual objects, but all mankind everywhere at all times prohibits incest. This means that the taboo against incest occupies a peculiar position in human culture. It breaks down or transgresses the binary division between natural and cultural features of human life. Since the taboo against incest is absolutely universal, in the sense that there are no human cultures without it, it is natural to the human species, not cultural. On the other hand, it is a distinguishing feature of human, as against animal, societies, so it must be defined as cultural. The taboo against incest is neither cultural nor natural, or it is both, transgressing the barrier between the two, or, we could say, hovering on the border between them. The same thing might be said about Oedipus, who is like a beast in not recognizing that his mother is his mother and therefore someone he is prohibited from marrying. He recognizes that he has committed an abhorrent crime only when he discovers that she is his mother. Another way to put this is to say that the taboo against incest depends on kinship names; in other words, it depends on the distinctively human possession of language. Oedipus in his ignorance cannot name his mother as his mother and so, like an animal, can be said not to be guilty of incest. When he can name her his mother he knows he has committed incest.

On the other hand, Oedipus *has* in fact committed the horrible crimes of parricide and incest, whether he knew it at the time or not. Here too, it may be, ignorance of the law is no excuse. Certainly the power of the play depends on giving a striking example of that, an example arousing pity for Oedipus and fear that the same thing might happen to us. Oedipus accepts his guilt and punishes himself by blinding himself (a symbolic castration) and by exiling himself from the human community to wander the roads until he dies. On the other hand, again, how can Oedipus be held responsible for acts he did not intend to commit?

Nor is it even absolutely certain, as recent critics have argued, that he did in fact kill his father. There is a contradiction in the evidence about the massacre of Oedipus's father, Laius, at the crossroads. In one account, the murderer is said to have been one man. In another account, there were three murderers. As Creon observes, "One man and three men just does not jibe." Oedipus condemns himself by putting the somewhat ambiguous evidence together in a way that convicts him. He plays the roles of both detective and murderer in this aboriginal detective story.

But it may be this act of narration itself that creates the crime and points the finger of guilt at Oedipus. As Cynthia Chase has observed in a brilliant essay, the crime exists neither in the original acts, which were innocent, in the sense that Oedipus did not know that he was murdering his father and sleeping with his mother, nor in the "now" of the play, in which Oedipus bit by bit pieces together the data he is given and makes a story out of them. The crime exists somewhere in between, in the relation between the events of the past and the present recovery and highly motivated ordering of them.

It might be argued that *Oedipus the King* does not so much tell a story as dramatize a striking example of the way storytelling, the putting together of data to make a coherent tale, is performative. *Oedipus the King* is a story about the awful danger of storytelling. Storytelling in this case makes something happen with a vengeance. It leads the storyteller to condemn, blind, and exile himself, and it leads his mother-wife, Jocasta, to kill herself.

Oedipus the King, then, far from giving a clear answer to the question of man's origin, is a story about generational confusion, in which a son is also a husband of his mother, a mother a wife to her son, Oedipus the brother of his own children, and so on. Insofar as clear kinship names and identifications are necessary to a man's or a woman's sense of who he or she is and where he or she has come from, *Oedipus the King* presents a story in which the possibility of such clarity is questioned and suspended. The play, it is true, gives a narrative form to the logically insoluble problem of the origin of man. What cannot be expressed logically, one is tempted to say, we then tell stories about. The power of *Oedipus the King* through all the centuries since it was written is testimony to its success as a narrative. The play gave a name, for example, to Sigmund Freud's fundamental psychoanalytic discovery, the universality of the "Oedipus complex." All men, Freud claimed, want to kill their fathers and sleep with their mothers. Recent feminists have had much to say about the way Freud's formulation leaves out one-half of the human race, that is, all the women. Another way to put this is to say that a given story may have a function quite different for a female reader or spectator from the one it has for a male one.

But even if we put that problem aside, we would still need to say that the perennial success of the story of Oedipus may lie more in its powerful narrative presentation of the problem of narration than in any solution it presents to the question of man's origin and nature. At the end the problem remains, though the spectators no doubt understand better what the problem is. Nagging loose ends to the story, such as the ones I have identified, keep the narrative from reaching final clarity, and there remains at the end the fundamental enigma of why Oedipus should be so punished for crimes he has not knowingly committed. And so we need another narrative that will try in a different way to solve these problems, for example, Shakespeare's *Hamlet,* and after that another story, for example, William Faulkner's *Absalom, Absalom!*, and yet another, with never an end to our need for more stories.

A further approach to an answer to my questions may be made by looking at two extremely brief narratives in an attempt to identify the basic elements of a story. These are the elements that must be there if we are to say, yes, this is a narrative and not some other thing. What are those elements? I take as my min-

iature examples A. E. Housman's "The Grizzly Bear," and William Wordsworth's "A Slumber Did My Spirit Seal." Though they are "poems," they are
surely narratives too. Here they are:

The Grizzly Bear

The Grizzly Bear is huge and wild;
    He has devoured the infant child.
The infant child is not aware
He has been eaten by the bear.

A Slumber Did My Spirit Seal

A slumber did my spirit seal;
    I had no human fears.
She seemed a thing that could not feel
    The touch of earthly years.

No motion has she now, no force;
    She neither hears nor sees;
Rolled round in earth's diurnal course,
    With rocks, and stones, and trees.

Both of these minuscule narratives contain what I claim are the basic elements
of any narrative, even the longest and most elaborate, Tolstoy's *War and Peace,*
say, or George Eliot's *Middlemarch:* there must be, first of all, an initial situation,
a sequence leading to a change or reversal of that situation, and a revelation
made possible by the reversal of situation. Second, there must be some use of
personification whereby character is created out of signs—for example, the
words on the page in a written narrative, the modulated sounds in the air in an
oral narrative. However important plot may be, without personification there
can be no storytelling. The minimal personages necessary for a narrative are
three: a protagonist, an antagonist, and a witness who learns. Sometimes the
protagonist, the antagonist, or the reader may be the witness. Third, there must
be some patterning or repetition of key elements, for example, a trope or system
of tropes, or a complex word. To put this third requisite another way, there must
be some form of narrative rhythm modulating that trope or word. Any narrative,
then, to be a narrative, I claim, must have some version of these elements: beginning, sequence, reversal; personification; or, more accurately and technically
stated, *prosopopoeia,* bringing protagonist, antagonist, and witness "to life";
some patterning or repetition of elements surrounding a nuclear figure or complex word. Even narratives that do not fit this paradigm draw their meaning
from the way they play ironically against our deeply engrained expectations that
all narratives are going to be like that.

"The Grizzly Bear," for example, plays ironically against our assumption that
we learn from experience. The infant child learns nothing from experience. The
little story is an example of that version of narrative form in which the witnessing

narrator learns more than the protagonist does. In fact, it is a hyperbolic example, and that is part of the joke. No Oedipus, this child; nor does the "good guy," the infant child, have any chance at all against the "bad guy" in the form of the grizzly bear.

The pattern of rhythmic repetition with variation here takes the form of the reuse of the same grammatical pattern throughout the poem. The story is told in flat, declarative sentences, two of them turning on "is," two on "has." The last two lines can be read either as two sentences or as one. The fact that the first two lines are single end-stopped sentences prepares the reader to expect the third line to be the same, and then he discovers that the fourth line in fact continues the third. The patterning is what is called *chiasmus,* the crisscross reversal of elements. The grizzly bear is first at the beginning of a sentence, then at the end of a sentence. The infant child is first at the end, then at the beginning. The story begins with the bear and ends with the bear. The child is encompassed within the text, as indeed he is by the bear when he is eaten by him.

The basic trope in this minuscule narrative is also a prosopopoeia, the personification of the bear as a "he." This is repeated when the infant child is also called a "he," though neither the child nor the bear have the self-awareness and minimal mastery of language that justifies the use of the personal pronoun.

"A Slumber Did My Spirit Seal" is a much more complex narrative than "The Grizzly Bear," but, like "The Grizzly Bear," it tells the double story of an unaware protagonist, the "she" of the poem, and a knowing narrating witness, the "I" of the poem. Here the narrator speaks for himself rather than being present as an implication of ironic, laconic truth telling, as in Housman's poem. Now the "she" of the poem (usually assumed to be the Lucy of Wordsworth's so-called Lucy poems, of which this is one) "neither hears nor sees," but Wordsworth's narrator can say, in effect, "Before I was ignorant. Now I know. I am one of those, unlike Lucy, who has eyes and sees, ears to hear with and understand." The covert reference is to Matthew 13:12–13, Jesus' commentary on the parable of the sower he has just told: "For whosoever hath, to him shall be given, and he shall have more abundance: but whosoever hath not, from him shall be taken away even that he hath. Therefore speak I to them in parables: because they seeing see not; and hearing they hear not, neither do they understand."

According to Paul de Man, "The paradigm for all texts consists of a figure (or a system of figures) and its deconstruction. But since this model cannot be closed off by a final reading, it engenders, in its turn, a supplementary figural superposition which narrates the unreadability of the prior narration" (de Man 1979, 205). As de Man's use of "narrates" and "narration" here indicates, all "texts," for him, are narrations. To say that all narratives, including everything from "A Slumber Did My Spirit Seal" to big novels like Anthony Trollope's *He Knew He Was Right* or Henry James's *The Princess Casamassima,* are no more than the exploration of a single figure or system of figures is to make a large claim, to say the least. Nevertheless, it can be shown that Trollope's big novel is genetically programmed, as one might put it, by the question of what is figurative in the expression, "I know I am right," and that *The Princess Casamassima* turns on the question of what is figurative in the expression, "I pledge myself."

In de Man's model "deconstruction" is a name for learning from experience, and "unreadability" is a name for the impossibility of doing that once and for all. The "unreadability" is indicated by the reuse of the figure or some new version of it even when it has been shown to be illusory or deceptive.

Another way to put this would be to say that a narrative, even a long multi-plotted novel like *He Knew He Was Right,* with all its wealth and particularity of character, incident, realistic detail, may be an exploration of the resonances of a single "complex word," to borrow William Empson's term for such words. A complex word is in a special sense a figure. It is the locus of a set of perhaps incompatible meanings, bound together by figurative displacements, as "worth" may have both economic and ethical meanings, or as "right" may mean to have the right, or to be right, or simply to be "straight," as in "right angle." In a narrative such a word may be explored by being given contexts or situations in which it may be appropriately used. This is like that exercise in language classes, "Use the following words in sentences," or, in more difficult assignments, "Invent a story in which the following words are used." For Empson, a complex word may be the locus of ambiguities, but these are held together in a unified structure, however complicated. I suggest that a complex word may, on the contrary, be the crossroads of fundamentally incongruous meanings. This fact may be revealed—unrolled or unfurled, so to speak—by narrative disjunctions that can never be brought back to unity.

What these somewhat cryptic formulations might mean, "concretely," as one says, may be made clearer by way of a return to "A Slumber Did My Spirit Seal." The genetic, narrative-producing figure here is the trope calling a young girl a "thing." This trope is the symmetrical mirror image of calling a bear a "he." Wordsworth's figure is part of everyday speech, as in the refrain of the folk song: "She's a young thing and cannot leave her mother." "At first I thought she was a thing," says in effect the narrator of Wordsworth's little story, "therefore immortal, but now I know how wrong I was. Now I know she was mortal because she has literally become a thing, like a rock, or a stone, or a tree, though in another sense she shares the immortality of the earth, expressed in its eternal revolution. The earth goes round and round and round, and she moves with it. She neither hears nor sees, but I am one of those who has eyes and sees, ears to hear with and understand."

The second stanza, however, commits again the linguistic error that the blank space between the two stanzas demystifies by being the locus of Lucy's death. The death occurs in the blank, outside of language. Language begins again in the second stanza as the claim of a mastery over death, taking the form of the ability to say the truth about it. "Before I thought she was immortal. Now I know all human beings are mortal, even Lucy. All human beings become, at last, things." But this claim of knowledge and of the right to speak the truth may ironically be not all that different from the first illusory assertion of knowledge: "She seemed a thing that could not die." Let me explain how that is the case.

The symmetrical counterpart of the trope in "thing" is the trope of personification in "touch." The two together form a miniature example of the sort of "system of figures" which de Man claimed might be the nucleus of a narrative. If Lucy is a mere thing, then time, or, more precisely, "earthly years," is personified as an animate being who might try to "touch" Lucy but who cannot touch her because she is a thing. In the same way, the narrator is "sealed" from the knowledge of death by the "slumber" of his naiveté. The word "touch" has a strong sexual implication here. Far from vanishing when the narrator learns about the universality of death, the personification returns intact in the second stanza, though in muted or covert form. It returns in the phrase "rolled round." "Earthly years" are personified as a rapacious being, something like that grizzly bear in the Housman poem, a being that would touch Lucy, seize her, take her. Not the earth but "earthly years" is the antagonist in this poem. In the last stanza that figurative personification remains intact in the image of the earth's motion, measure of earthly days and years, rolling Lucy round. The narrator's formulation also contradicts in the moment of making it his own statement that she now has no motion and no force (the two basic elements in Newtonian physics). As part of the earth, incorporated in it with rocks and stones and trees, as the infant child is incorporated in the grizzly bear in Housman's poem, Lucy now shares in the "rolling," obscurely animate, motion and force of that earth, even though she no longer has the voluntary motion and force she had as a living child.

The narrator-witness's error and guilt may be not simply the claim of a knowledge that his own words ironically belie in his reuse of another version of the same figures he had at first mistakenly used. The performative as well as epistemological dimension of narrative may also be at stake. By "performative" I mean the power of a narrative to make something happen, as opposed to its power to give, or to appear to give, knowledge. Seen as patterned around knowledge, the poem says, "Before he was ignorant as a child. Now he thinks he knows, but his words show he is still as ignorant as a child." Seen as patterned around the performative power of narration, the little story dramatizes the terrifying possibility that figures of speech may have a tendency to realize themselves by a kind of linguistic magic. He thought she was a thing. Death, in the personified form of those half-animate earthly years, obligingly turned her into a thing. It is as if I were to transform someone literally into a turkey if I said, "You turkey," or as Gregor Samsa, in Franz Kafka's "The Metamorphosis," is turned into an enormous cockroach after having been treated by his family and by society as if he were a cockroach. In "A Slumber Did My Spirit Seal" it may be the poet's linguistic touch that has turned Lucy into a thing. Another of the Lucy poems would support this: "Oh mercy to myself I said, / If Lucy should be dead," and then she *does* die.

"A Slumber Did My Spirit Seal" is an example of the presence even in such a brief story of all those basic elements I identified. It is also an example both of the way a narrative depends on the trope of personification and of the way it may be a system of figures deconstructed and then blindly reaffirmed. It seems in this case that the narrator has not really learned what he claims to have learned. To put this another way, it seems as if personification, the fundamental trope of narrative, is so necessary a part of language as to be by no means effaced, not even by the clear recognition that it is illusory.

Suggested Readings

Aristotle. 1907. *Theory of Poetry and Fine Art,* translated by S. H. Butcher.

Bakhtin, M. M. 1981. *The Dialogic Imagination,* translated by Caryl Emerson and Michael Holquist.

Barthes, Roland. 1974. *S/Z,* translated by Richard Miller.

Booth, Wayne. 1961. *The Rhetoric of Fiction.*

Brooks, Peter. 1984. *Reading for the Plot.*

de Man, Paul. 1979. *Allegories of Reading.*

Empson, William. n.d. *The Structure of Complex Words.*

Freud, Sigmund. 1957. *The Interpretation of Dreams.*

Iser, Wolfgang. 1974. *The Implied Reader.*

Jameson, Fredric. 1981. *The Political Unconscious: Narrative as a Socially Symbolic Act.*

Propp, Vladimir. 1970. *The Morphology of the Folktale,* translated by Laurence Scott.

Ricoeur, Paul. 1984–88. *Time and Narrative,* Vols. 1–3, translated by Kathleen McLaughlin and David Pellauer.

6

Figurative Language

Thomas McLaughlin

Literary study teaches us to pay close attention to language. With poetry especially, we base our interpretive efforts on the assumption that the closer we look at a poem's language, the fuller it will come into its force. More specifically, many interpretations focus on figures of speech—similes and metaphors, metonymys and personifications. Understanding how such figures work allows us to bring out into the open what a poem suggests. In this way and in others we are involved in the process of producing the poem's meanings. The figurative process—that is, the mental work that interpreting figures requires—is complex, and it is not limited to poetry; so our analysis of it will take us far and wide within an emerging theory of language and culture. But let's begin with a familiar poem—William Blake's "The Lamb"—and look at the figures of speech.

The Lamb
LITTLE Lamb, who made thee?
    Dost thou know who made thee?
Gave thee life, & bid thee feed
By the stream & o'er the mead;
Gave thee clothing of delight,
Softest clothing, wooly, bright;
Gave thee such a tender voice,
Making all the vales rejoice?
    Little Lamb, who made thee?
    Dost thou know who made thee?

    Little Lamb, I'll tell thee,
    Little Lamb, I'll tell thee:
He is called by thy name,
For he calls himself a Lamb.
He is meek, & he is mild;
He became a little child.

I a child, & thou a lamb,
We are called by his name.
      Little Lamb, God bless thee!
      Little Lamb, God bless thee!

This poem is deceptively simple. As one of Blake's *Songs of Innocence,* it is both a celebration and a critique of the clear, naive thinking of children. The poem's speaker is a child talking to a lamb, giving it a lesson in theology. Both the lamb and the child, the speaker explains, are products of the creative power of Christ, the prime symbol of innocence. Christ and lamb and child share a moral quality; they are part of a structure of meaning which Christ verified by becoming a child and taking on the name of the lamb. The simple language of the poem reinforces the child's innocent insight. There are only basic sentence patterns and common words, appropriate to the age and attitude of the speaker. In fact, the poem's language is so simple that it is often included in anthologies of poems for children. I've even seen the poem in a religious gift shop, reprinted on a card tied by a ribbon to a little toy lamb. From this innocent view "The Lamb" is a reassuring reminder of God's goodness and of the simple innocence which God grants the child. But one way in which the poem is not simple is in its figurative language. The simple vocabulary of the poem is enmeshed in a system of figures of speech which complicate the poem and suggest meanings beyond those the child intends. But before I look closely at those figures, I want to examine briefly the process by which we make sense of figurative language in general.

The traditional meaning of "figurative" has always involved a contrast with the "proper" meaning of a word, its supposed rightful meaning, the idea which comes directly to mind when the word is used. The utterance "tiger," for example, evokes for English speakers the familiar image of a large, predatory cat. But the word is not always used in this "proper" sense. A sportscaster might call a football player a "tiger on defense." On hearing such a phrase, any user of the language will immediately realize that the proper meaning can't work—there is no real tiger with claws and sharp teeth on the field. Instead, we realize that the phrase is being used figuratively to suggest the player's aggressiveness and speed. All in a moment we work it out that the tiger and the player are both elements in a mental category, "aggressive things," so that it is appropriate to transfer a characteristic of the tiger to the player by means of the figurative phrase. Now if this analysis seems too obvious, that's because I'm trying to articulate the logical steps that we accomplish in an intuitive flash. Figures of speech twist the meaning of a word—the Greek word for figures is *trope,* which means "turn, twist"— but they are so common in everyday language that the process of interpreting them occurs almost unconsciously, like any frequently repeated skill.

In reading the first stanza of "The Lamb," we must perform this procedure repeatedly. Perhaps the most obvious example is the speaker's description of the lamb's wool as "clothing." The "proper" meaning of "clothing" clearly doesn't apply to the lamb. Wool is part of the lamb's body, not something added over it for warmth and beauty, as clothing is. And because this meaning obviously does not apply, we have to ask what elements of the meaning of "clothing" do apply to the lamb's wool. It keeps him warm; it gives him beauty. It makes the lamb seem almost human, as it does seem to the child, who doesn't think of the differences between himself and the lamb but, rather, of the category they share as god's creatures. And since they are both innocent, their god must also be innocent, Jesus the Lamb of God. What the child does not see is that it is his own figure of speech which has made the lamb seem human. The category he shares with the lamb is one that *he* has created. A similar process is going on in the lines "Gave thee such a tender voice, / Making all the vales rejoice?" In this figure, the echo of the lamb's call is said to "rejoice," thus describing the valleys and by extension the entire natural world as if they were capable of response. The speaker lives in a natural world which his figures have given a human dimension, a world which seems to reflect the innocence of the speaker.

The stanza also includes a less obvious set of figures which describe the god who created this innocent world. This god *gives* the lamb its life, its clothing, its "tender voice." He *bids* the lamb to feed on the gift of food he has provided for his creatures. It twists and stretches the "proper" meaning of these words to think of the lamb's wool as a gift or its food as a banquet set out as if for guests. But the speaker wants to suggest that god is a giver of gifts, a host, and that the lamb and the speaker are therefore in the hands of a benevolent power. The speaker uses these figures to construct an image of god which fits the poem's benign natural world.

But these figures reveal a much more complex and sophisticated theology at work than the speaker has in mind. Instead of the innocent and simple god that he seems to want, the figures of speech point to a powerful if benevolent being who allows the lamb and the child to continue in their innocence. Such a god is not as innocent as the child seems to think; the child's sense of god is not equal to the divine complexity. The speaker's own language seems to undo him, to suggest an image of god more complicated than the innocent child can grasp. Blake is taking us beyond the speaker's awareness into a realization that we create our own images of god. And the poem emphasizes this point by forcing the reader to share the creation of its meaning. In my own figurative process, the figures seem to me to point to a powerful god, which for me does not fit the image of innocence that the speaker desires. For me, any being who wields power has passed out of innocence, so that the speaker seems limited in his ability to perceive god. My construction of the poem's meaning is in excess of the "proper" meaning of the words and of the speaker's intentions. Any reader who engages in the figurative process will produce this excess. The full meaning of the figure cannot be kept within safe limits: it proliferates as a function of its implied invitation to the reader.

Because figures of speech are so important in poetry and in all forms of discourse, they have been studied and categorized frequently throughout our cultural history. One of the meanings of the word "rhetoric" is the study of figures. (One of the others, rhetoric as the study of persuasion, we will get to later.) Rhetorical systems have frequently been constructed, giving names to a bewildering array of "turns" that can be given to the "proper" meanings of words. I want to name and briefly define only a few of the most important of these *kinds* of figures.

The figure of speech that most closely resembles the general definition I've given is *metaphor*, which many critics think of as the master, or central, figure. A metaphor, such as the "clothing of delight" from "The Lamb," involves a transfer of meaning from the word that properly possesses it to another word which belongs to some shared category of meaning. A metaphor is therefore a compressed analogy. "Clothing" is to humans as wool is to lambs. And since there is an analogy here that we can accept, some of the meanings of "clothing" can transfer to the lamb's wool.

Another important kind of figure illustrated in this stanza is *personification*. In this figure the characteristics of a human subject are transferred to an inhuman object. The poem's description of the echo as the valley's rejoicing is an obvious example. For the child speaker of the poem this is a key figure, because it produces for him a harmonious and peaceful natural world, one which his loving god has created for him so that his innocence will be maintained.

In fact, the entire poem is built on a figure of speech, *apostrophe*. An apostrophe is a speech directed at an object or being which cannot respond to or even hear the speech. It fits our general definition of "figure" in that it creates an unreal speech situation, so that the very act of speech is twisted, taken out of its "proper" function. Apostrophe is a form of personification. It assumes for the imaginative moment that the object shares our human ability to respond to speech. When the child speaks to the lamb, he implies that the lamb can understand him.

Of course not all of the figures of speech that critics have identified appear in this poem. Some others of note are simile and metonymy. A *simile* is a comparison of terms. Unlike metaphor, which requires the reader to do the work of constructing a logic of categories and analogies, a simile states explicitly that two terms are comparable and often presents the basis for the comparison. "Her lips were red as wine" does not leave the reader with the work that a metaphor requires. The simile is therefore in general a more controlled figure than metaphor, producing less excess of meaning. *Metonymy* accomplishes its tranfer of meaning on the basis of associations that develop out of specific contexts rather than from participation in a structure of meaning. A metonymy such as referring to the king by the phrase "the crown" speaks of the king by means of an object frequently associated with him. It does not call for the magical sharing of meaning that a metaphor implies; instead, it relies on connections that build up over time and the associations of usage. It is therefore not surprising that there is no metonymy in this poem. The speaker is not simply claiming that the lamb and the child and Christ have come to be associated with one another by convention or by usage but, rather, that they share a deep identity. Metonymy places us in the historical world of events and situations, whereas metaphor asserts connections on the basis of a deep logic that underlies any use of words.

Returning now to "The Lamb," we might observe that if the first stanza of the poem is filled with vivid "figures of speech," the second seems starkly literal—all the words are used in their "proper" sense. It is as though the imaginative child of the first stanza had grown into a direct, truth-telling prophet who speaks "properly" in the name of god. This stanza does, after all, give the answers, the true answers, to the questions of the first stanza. It identifies the "maker" of the lamb as Jesus and tells the lamb that it shares this identity in that Jesus adopted the name of the lamb. The absence of obvious figures makes this stanza more direct, but there are still several complications. First of all, this "literal" stanza describes the creation of a figurative category. It tells the story of how Christ's deliberate actions—becoming a child, calling himself a lamb—establish the relationships that make the poem's metaphors possible. That is, even though the words of the stanza are used in their "proper" sense, they ask readers to think in terms of the figurative process. We are being taught to think, that is, by categories and analogies.

Furthermore, when examined once again, the stanza is not as free of figures as it seems. Its words could be called "primal." They are names for basic human actions and simple objects: "tell," "call," "become," "bless," "lamb," "child." But each of these words has a richness of implication that is produced by figures which occur within its "proper" meaning. (I know that's a contradiction in the terms I've set up, but I'll explain.) Each of these words has an interesting history which reveals that the words have figurative force. The most amazing example is "bless," which derives historically from the word "blood." To "bless" is to cleanse by a ritual sprinkling of blood. Now, surely, most of us are unaware of that aspect of the meaning when we use "bless," but the fact remains that the word is a figure of speech in which some of the meanings of "blood" are transferred to the purifying action. This is remarkably apt to the poem, in that one of the chief links between the lamb and Christ is that both are the victims of blood sacrifice.

Other simple words in the stanza reveal a figure within their "proper" meaning. "Meek" and "mild," for example, are words that now describe emotional states, personal characteristics. But both words have a history of reference to the tactile, sensory world—both at one time meant "soft, slippery." The modern meanings are a trope on these earlier meanings. What was once physical has been humanized, turned into the figurative terms of a psychology.

These passive, soft terms "meek" and "mild" create a complex image of Christ in combination with the more powerful figure of Christ the maker. Significantly, the history of "make" derives from the function of kneading, pressing; that is, what would be done to a meek and mild substance. Is Christ the maker of the figure or, is he the "meek and mild" material that gets shaped? The poem's figurative language here suggests both. He has the power to shape himself, to choose his own figure ("he calls himself a Lamb"). The powerful "maker" chooses to take on the name and the gentle quality of the innocent lamb. In this sense the poem becomes a story about the figurative process, in which Christ in an act of poetic creation produces the figurative link, Christ—Lamb—child, which the child takes to be natural and inevitable. To the child, the world simply *is* innocent. But when we attend to the figures of the poem, that innocence shows itself to be a function of the figures, a production of the child's language. Even the words that seem to be used in their "proper" sense exert a figurative force, shaping the world that the child perceives.

As a general principle, then, I would argue that the figurative history of a word is a part of its meaning and is therefore appropriate to a poetic interpretation whether or not the poet was aware of or intended it. These figures are the language's own contribution to the meaning of the poem. That is, if even the "proper" meaning of words are in this sense figurative, then the complexity of communication in a poem is not only a product of the poet's inventiveness but also a result of the interaction of tropes built into the language. These tropes bring out possibilities of meaning that preexist the poem in language, in the meaning structures that make tropes possible. The clearest example in "The Lamb" is the fact that the entire poem is based on the old personification of the lamb as innocent. This is a figure that Blake did not create but which has been part of our language for centuries. In this sense, the meaning of a poem is made possible by the systems of language by which whole cultures make sense of experience, and we now need to move to that level—from the poem to the systems which make it possible—if we are to understand the full impact of figurative language.

One consequence of our analysis is that the opposition between "proper" and "figurative" has come into question. Figures seem to be infiltrating the defenses of rightful meaning. If the "proper" meaning is itself a trope on an earlier meaning, then the poetic figure of speech is only a spectacular example of something all language does. Figures ask the reader to think in terms of a complex system of categories and analogies in order to make sense of them; but so does any use of language. How does any word make sense? It makes sense by being a part of a system of meanings, a set of contrasts and comparisons. No word has meaning in isolation but only insofar as it relates to and differs from other words in the language system. "Bless" is not "curse," but both are part of a system of words that refers to the act of calling on god. Each of these words makes sense because it is the opposite of the other and because both participate in a category of meaning. The word "bless" means "the act of purification" only because it is part of a system of sound and meaning. There is no natural connection (one might say "proper" connection) between the word and the idea but only an agreement among speakers of the English language that "bless" *shall refer* to that act in the world. Even when there is no strongly figurative etymology, meaning is figurative in the sense that it relies on categories and associations. Language is thus not a simple process of naming preexisting objects and states but a system through which we give meaning to the world. Instead of imagining "bless" as the name that is proper to the act, think of the act as what the word figures, gives form to, makes sense of. There is no "proper" meaning, only arbitrarily "assigned" meaning. And therefore all the complexities that "figures of speech" create in a poem are part of any use of language. Just as the figures of "The Lamb" construct the world that the speaker perceives, so language produces the set of meanings by which we shape reality.

Now if language gives meaning to experience, we have to think of it as the system in which our ideas become possible. Language is a conceptual grid, a system of values, through which we experience reality. In our culture both male and female children grow up learning, for example, that a girl fits into the same figurative category as chick, cat, bitch, and fox. And it is then very hard for any of us to think of the feminine outside these figurative categories. Some psychologists still talk about how women are essentially passive and soft unless their "femininity" is somehow denied and they turn, as a result, peevish and overaggressive. Clearly the psychological theory is in a sense a "reading" of this figurative category. It may be bolstered by studies and statistics, but the theory still depends on biases and value systems built into the language. Figurative systems of this kind are repeated so frequently that they cease to strike us as figures and take on, instead, some of the power of the "proper," as though the figurative system that surrounds the feminine were logical and natural. We come to think by means of figures worn smooth, made invisible. How hard it is to remember that the association female = chick, so casually used in our language, is an arbitrary assignment of meaning, one that has consequences for human behavior. Because of such forgetfulness, we put cultural biases and even cliches into play when we think, unless we reflect on the power of our language.

Figures play a powerful role even in areas of thought which are suspicious of figures, such as philosophy and science. Many philosophers and scientists hold very strongly to the proper/figurative distinction. For them, each idea should have a proper name, so that experience and data can be interpreted accurately. Yet figures of all kinds permeate philosophical and scientific thought. When philosophers talk about "congruence" or scientists praise the "elegance" of a theory, they are using tropes. Even such basic philosophical terms as "idea" have a figurative history—"idea" derives from the Greek word for "to see." As Paul de Man says, "As soon as one is willing to be made aware of their epistemological implications, concepts are tropes and tropes concepts" (in Sacks 1978, 21). The desire behind the idea of the concept, of course, is that concepts are derived from experience, but if concepts are tropes, then our categories create the shape of experience—they define what we agree to be true. The systems of meaning and value that make figures possible also produce our way of looking at the world.

Recent psychological theory also points to a powerful role for figures in the unconscious. Students of rhetoric have long realized that figures exert a more than rational influence on readers. One reason is that the unconscious processes material in a figurative manner. When Freud was trying to explain how the meaning of a dream was disguised or transformed, he described two functions—"identification" and "displacement"—which sound a lot like metaphor and metonymy. Because we cannot face unconscious material directly, dreams must transform that material into a form that we can accept. In "identification," an idea is associated with another in the same structure of meaning (as in metaphor); whereas, in "displacement," meaning is transferred to an idea or object related by association (as in metonymy). If in our dreams we are trying to come to terms with the death of a loved one, we might dream of being lost or of becoming separated from someone in a crowd. These are metaphorical transformations of grief, in that death is the ultimate form of loss or separation. All these experiences are part of the same meaning structure. On the other hand, we might dream of being in a church, or in a black car, or of wearing a black suit, all details experientially related to funerals and the rites of death. In this case we create a metonymy in which these details stand in for the fear of death that we cannot face directly. What these processes suggest is that figurative activity is deeply rooted in all our mental life and that poetic figures can bring us into contact with powerful psychological forces.

If all levels of thought are figurative, the power in the act of perception and understanding seems to lie in language. The image we've been developing seems to depict a passive world, to which humans give shape through language. But language is not an independent, all-powerful entity. It is part of the fabric of social and political life. It shapes our perceptions, but it also *is shaped by* its social context. That is, because of its strategic role in perception, language must be shaped to serve the needs of dominant groups. To return to an earlier example, the figurative system female = bitch = fox = chick = kitten = etc. is not the only possible way of thinking about women; but the associations force themselves on us because they serve a powerful interest, the interest of men who want to dominate women. This figurative system has rhetorical and political force.

Students of rhetoric as far back as the classical Greeks have realized that figures have force. They are the chief feature of eloquence, the ability to convince an audience of the truth of an argument. Figures convince, though, not by a strictly logical presentation but by an appeal to the irrational, the part of the mind that delights in their multiple meanings and deep reassurances. Figures reassure our belief in dominant systems of thought in that they rely on accepted categories and analogies. In this sense figures appeal to our desire to possess an untroubled, self-evident truth. We want to believe that our way of thinking is the only sensible one, and figures reassure us by taking the system for granted, as a field which allows free play within its secure boundaries.

A powerful example of eloquence in our culture is advertising, which uses figurative thinking very extensively. In TV advertising the figures are usually expressed visually rather than verbally, but the same mental function is called into action. Two images that belong to the same category are connected to each other so that emotional qualities of one will transfer to the other. An example: a series of commercials for a new McDonald's hamburger relies on very strong metaphorical associations. This new burger is packaged in such a way that the hot meat is kept separate from the crisp lettuce, tomato, and cheese. This modest improvement in package design is the focus of an incredibly intense set of figurative practices. The problem with the new design (and the reason there's a need for all this rhetorical effort) is that the eater has to put the sandwich together without making a mess. The crisp stuff has to be raised, turned over, and flipped on to the meat. What the commercials do is to associate by visual crosscutting this "coming together of what's been kept apart" with human, sentimental reunions—a kid and a dog, two staggering skaters, even Romeo and Juliet. Thus the warmth, humor, and emotion of the human contacts cross over to the act of assembling the sandwich. If this seems like heavy emotional freight for a new package design, the intensity of the ads suggests that something big is at stake. The viewer may shout, "Give us a break, it's just a new box," but the association is nevertheless a visual reality, a figure that we ourselves have helped to produce. The use of the figure makes us active participants in the meaning of the visual association. The ad is therefore more effective in appealing to our emotion. We have to compare the images, find the category they belong in (reunions), and work out the analogy that makes the metaphor possible. We do this, of course, very easily. The categories are right to hand, reassuringly reliable in constructing a sensible metaphor. This commercial therefore succeeds on two levels. It accomplishes the emotional association it sought, so that we feel positively toward the product. And more profoundly, it reinforces our reliance on culturally powerful systems of thought and feeling. It makes us use them, and they work smoothly for our comprehension.

More overtly political examples are rampant these days. Many commercials associate products with the Statue of Liberty or with the flag, giving the impression that the product delivers the kind of freedom that we associate with these political symbols. But even an apparently nonpolitical example like the Mc-Donald's ad serves political power in that it reinforces an accepting rather than critical attitude toward systems of meaning. Figures are therefore open to manipulation by those who have access to powerful forms of discourse.

But if figures of speech rely on an accepted system of thought, they also reveal to the critical reader that it *is* a system, that it is *not* a simple reflection of reality. Some figures of speech, particularly those in poetry, call attention to themselves, ask us to think very carefully about how they mean what they mean. Saying that an echo is a valley's joyful response to a lamb's voice risks making no sense unless the reader enters into a productive effort, thinking "echo" can be a "rejoicing" only if nature has a spirit capable of joy, a human quality that connects it to us, which is what the speaker wants to believe and communicate. We are relying here on a kind of mythic category, one which common sense would tell us is nonsensical—after all, echoes do not feel joy. A figure like this therefore reminds us that the system which makes it possible is itself the product of human thought. Figures of speech, especially spectacular ones, are potential weaknesses in the system, places where its workings are visible, places that remind us that our truths are not self-evident. Spectacular figures can attune us to the almost invisible figures at work throughout language and culture, and thus to the power of language over perception.

But what to do with that awareness? If our thinking always occurs within a system, are we condemned to repeat what the system imposes? Figures of speech, of course, are not the only way to bring systems of thought into question. Victims of political, economic, or sexual power often acquire by harsh experience the kind of skepticism I'm promoting. But the advantage of focusing on figures in this critical way is that it places language at the center of our attention, just as language plays a central role in the enforcement of all those forms of power. Language and culture provide us with ways of thinking about ourselves and our experiences. And any political or social program must come to terms with the power of language if it is to affect our lives deeply.

Figures and the systems they imply should not, however, be condemned as brainwashing techniques by which those in power control our thoughts and feelings. Figures and systems are inevitable in any use of language and are not the exclusive property of those in power. In fact, our culture is not one unified system but rather consists of competing systems of thought, each with its own set of possible figures. McDonald's associates constructing its new burger with the pleasures of human reunions; one could create a countermetaphor in which computer people consume integrated circuit sandwiches. Figurative language is a set of systems open to play. The possibilities for combination are not limited to those with which we're familiar, and the value systems they imply need not be those currently in power.

Let me conclude by returning to figures of speech in poetry. I've been calling them "spectacular" figures, using that word to suggest that they differ from ordinary language not because they are figurative but because they are visibly so. Two of the great benefits of poetry are the pleasure of meditating on these challenging, rich figures and the insight that they provide into the power of language itself. Of course, figures can be used to mislead or to enforce questionable values, but they can be—and are daily—used to question those values and to oppose them with new systems of thought and value. If figures tell us anything, it's that meaning is up for grabs, that the world can be shaped in an endless variety of forms, that language is a battleground of value systems. The challenge of figures is to make sure we are aware of their presence in discourse and their effects on our thought—but also to engage in the production of figures ourselves, in service of our own values.

Suggested Readings

Beardsley, Monroe. 1958. *Aesthetics: Problems in the Philosophy of Criticism.*
Derrida, Jacques. 1982. "White Mythology," in *Margins of Philosophy.*
Jakobson, Roman. 1971. "The Metaphoric and Metonymic Poles." In *Critical Theory Since Plato,* edited by Hazard Adams.
Lakoff, George, and Mark Johnson. 1980. *Metaphors We Live By.*
Sacks, Sheldon, ed., 1979. *On Metaphor.*

7

Performance

Henry Sayre

IN ORDINARY usage, a *performance* is a specific action or set of actions—dramatic, musical, athletic, and so on—which occurs on a given occasion, in a particular place. An artistic performance—as opposed, for instance, to an athlete's performance or a student's performance on an examination—is further defined by its status as the single occurrence of a repeatable and preexistent text or score. Thus there is *Hamlet*, and there are its many performances; the play itself, and its interpretations. Such a "commonsense" definition of performance contains within it one particularly important assumption, namely, that the work itself is not only distinct from its actual or possible realizations but in fact *transcends* them. That is, it anticipates, even *authorizes,* its many occurrences and somehow *contains* their variety.

Traditionally, then, the work of art itself possesses an a priori status in relation to its manifestations, and performance is itself an event of the second rank. It would be fair to say that in actual performance the audience expects to experience a range of possible imperfections, misreadings, or outright mistakes that in a hypothetical "perfect" performance would never occur. Each member of the audience, in other words, possesses some idea of what the "master" work ought to sound or look like, and each performance is measured against this theoretical standard. The analogy to performance in sports is useful in this regard. Each member of the audience judges a particular performance against his or her ideal of how the "master" work should be performed in a manner comparable to a gymnastics, skating, or diving judge measuring the performance of a given athlete against the standard of perfection represented by the score of 10.00.

The assumption, of course, is that the audience is in a position to make such judgments, that it somehow knows or understands what the "master" work is in its ideal realization, as distinct from its individual performances. There are two opposing ways an audience might "know" what it expects of a given performance. The *subjective* view is essentially a version of the famous phrase, "I don't know much about art, but I know what I like." Such a model can reach degrees of considerable sophistication, as it did, for instance, in Richard Wagner's famous interpretation of the opening of Beethoven's Fifth Symphony, an interpretation powerfully poetic in its own right but having little or nothing to do with what might be anticipated from a reading of Beethoven's score. As a conductor, Wagner impressed upon the Beethoven symphony his own wildly romantic sensibility. An *objective* point of view, on the other hand, would want to determine Beethoven's intentions and would reject Wagner's interpretation because, among other things, it holds the metronomic determinations of the score in complete disregard. A more objective interpreter of the Beethoven symphony—say, Toscanini—would thus maintain a more consistent tempo and a more even dynamic range than would Wagner, and he would imagine his rendition to be very close to the way Beethoven himself would have conducted the work.

There seems to be some justification for the objective point of view, at least insofar as Beethoven is concerned. In 1816, when Karl Czerny made indiscriminate use of the pedal, transposed certain sections from the first and second octaves above middle C to the third and fourth, and made other additions and emendations to a Beethoven chamber work, Beethoven, who was present at the performance, exploded in outrage. He quickly apologized in a letter to Czerny: "I burst out with that remark yesterday and I was very sorry after I had done so. But you must forgive a composer who would rather have heard a work performed exactly as written, however beautifully you played it in other respects." This dialectic between the *intentions* of the composer or author of a work and the *interpretations* to which it is submitted by its performers has traditionally been the critical crux around which the idea of performance has turned in literary, as well as musicological and art historical, studies. It is important to note that Beethoven does not himself state his intentions. Rather, he insists that his intentions are manifest in the score—he wants Czerny to play the piece as it is written.

In this model, then, a good performance will result from careful attention and scrupulous fidelity to the score or text. It presupposes that the artist's intentions are embodied in the work itself. The effort to determine the intentions of a work, in fact, accounts for a great deal of traditional literary history and criticism. The aim of *Endeavors of Art,* Madeleine Doran's classic study of Elizabethan drama, for example, is "to define and examine the problems of form that Shakespeare and his fellow dramatists had to face and try to solve." Her book, Doran says more precisely, is an effort "to reconstruct imaginatively some part of the context of artistic ideas, attitudes, tastes, and interests in which they worked, and to define their problems in light of these" (Doran 1963, 23). Literary history, in other words, is naturally disposed toward the objective interpretation of the work. It seeks to understand the work's intentions and provide the means for its performance with these intentions in mind.

In the work of the major modern avant-garde art movements, particularly in the public "manifestations" of the futurists in the 1910s and in the dada cabaret

in the 1920s, the idea of performance began to assume a different set of connotations, culminating in the rise, since the mid-1960s, of an interdisciplinary,
often multimedia kind of production which has come to be labeled "performance art." Some of the ways in which this new kind of performance can be distinguished from more traditional usages are directly addressed in a performance
work from the early seventies by Vito Acconci called *Learning Piece:*

> Playing, on tape, the first two phrases of a song (Leadbelly's
> "Black Betty"). Repeating the two phrases and singing along with
> them, until I have learned them and gotten the feel of the original
> performance.
> Playing the next two phrases; repeating four phrases until I
> have learned them. Continuing by adding, each time, two more
> phrases until the entire song is learned. (Meyer 1972, 6)

At first glance, *Learning Piece* seems an almost sublimely silly exercise, a tedious
rehearsal and rendition of a far superior original work by a conspicuously untal-
ented and amateur imitator. But it immediately raises a question about what the
"actual" work of art is here, Leadbelly's "Black Betty" or Acconci's *Learning
Piece?* In fact, the work seems to be defined in terms of the active relation between the two, as our attention is divided between the song as an art object in
its own right and Acconci's remaking of it. In the overt amateurishness of Acconci's efforts, interest in the work as product, as a "finished" whole, is de-
emphasized. It is the *process* of learning upon which we are forced to focus our
attention. This new work, *Learning Piece,* is the direct result of Acconci's engagement with a preexistent work, the Leadbelly song. But Acconci's performance is not merely a traditional performance, occurrence, or interpretation of the
prior work: a transformation of the original has taken place. The private, repetitive exercise of rehearsal has become the work of art itself.

"What I was doing," Acconci told an interviewer in 1979, "was making blatant what it seemed like any artwork does—private person doing work, putting
it into a public space" (White 1979, 20). Furthermore, the action, he has said,
"was done not as a private activity . . . but as an exemplar, a model" (Kirshner
1980, 10) for the potential activity of the audience. *Learning Piece,* in more precise terms, is a model for our relation to all art. Its difference from traditional
performance is comparable to the distinction made by Roland Barthes in *S/Z,*
his essay on Balzac's story "Sarrasine," between "readerly" and "writerly" texts.
Readerly texts, according to Barthes, "are products (and not productions)"
(Barthes 1974, 5). They represent "a kind of idleness" in which the reader becomes "intransitive," a passive receiver. The goal of the *writerly* text, on the other
hand, "is to make the reader no longer a consumer, but a producer of the text"
(Barthes 1974, 4).

Performance, then, has come to refer to a kind of work from which the authority of the text has been wrested. The concept of the "original," the self-contained and transcendent masterwork, containing certain discernible intentions, has been undermined, and a plurality of possible performative gestures has supplanted it. As a result, performance art often seems to be extraliterary or even antiliterary in nature. It seems to exist, that is, in domains other than the textual, or at best the texts that it produces seem incidental to a larger, more interdisciplinary kind of work. Acconci, for instance, began working in the late 1960s as a poet. He considered the page to be "a field of action," a phrase he borrowed from the poet William Carlos Williams. He soon realized, however, that "if I was using the page as a field for movement, there was no reason to limit that movement, there was no reason not to use a larger field (rather than move my hand over a page, I might as well be moving my body outside)" (Kirshner 1980, 6). Walls, galleries, public spaces soon began to function as pages for a form of "writing" that included not only the transcription of language but also the physical gestures of voice and body in space.

A good way to think of performance is to realize that in it the potentially disruptive forces of the "outside" (what is "outside" the text—the physical space in which it is presented, the other media it might engage or find itself among, the various frames of mind the diverse members of a given audience might bring to it, and, over time, the changing forces of history itself) are encouraged to assert themselves. This is different from traditional performance, in which, for instance, an unruly audience might completely wreck one's enjoyment of a symphony or in which, more subtly, bad acting might ruin *Hamlet*. It is, instead, upon the dynamics of such intrusions that performance has come to focus its attention.

This interest in an art which draws attention less to itself than to what is "outside" it can be traced to dada, and particularly to Marcel Duchamp's notorious 1917 "sculpture" entitled *Fountain*. Walking down the street one day, Duchamp spied, in the window of a plumbing fixture shop, a porcelain urinal. He purchased it, signed it "R. Mutt, 1917" and submitted it to the Independents Exhibition where, despite the "open" nature of the show, which technically allowed everyone to submit whatever they pleased, it was promptly refused. When rumors began to circulate that "R. Mutt" was actually Marcel Duchamp, it was circumspectly readmitted to the exhibition. Duchamp's point was simple and devastating: many things determined the relative artfulness (or artlessness) of *Fountain,* but few of them had much to do with anything inherent in the piece of porcelain itself, with its own formal properties. What made it a work of art rather than a urinal? Was it the fact that Duchamp selected it, recognized its aesthetic potential? Or was it that until Duchamp's name was attached to it, as long as it remained the work of R. Mutt, it remained a urinal as well? Or was it that in the context of the exhibition, the museum, it suddenly appropriated the aura of art, demanded that we approach it in a different light? One's judgment of the work could not be decontextualized. What it was depended on the "outside."

Dada poetry, such as Kurt Schwitters' *Ursonate* (*Primordial Sonata*) attacks natural language in the same manner that Duchamp's urinal attacks the norms of traditional sculpture:

> Fümms bö wö tää zää Uu,
> > pögiff,
> > > kwii Ee.
> Ooooooooooooooooooooooooooooooooooooo,
> > dll rrrrr beeeee bö,
> > dll rrrrr beeeee bö fümms bö,
> > > rrrrr beeeee bö fümms bö wö,
> > > > beeeee bö fümms bö wö tää (Motherwell 1951, 371)

And so on. This poem depends for its effect not only on the overt "noise poetry," or *bruitism,* but also on our immediate sense of its inadequacy as mere text, the absolute necessity for voicing it. The artist Moholy-Nagy recalls two Schwitters performances, including one of the *Ursonate:*

> In one of his demonstrations, he showed to the audience a poem containing only one letter on a sheet:

> Then he started to "recite" it with slowly rising voice. The consonant varied from a whisper to the wound of a wailing siren till at the end he barked with a shockingly loud tone. This was his answer not alone to the social situation but also to the degrading "cherry-mouthed"—"raven-haired"—"babbling-brook"—poetry.
>
> The only possible solution seemed to be a return to the elements of poetry, to noise and articulated sound, which are fundamental to all languages. . . . His *Ursonate* is a poem of thirty-five minutes duration, containing four movements, a prelude, and a cadenza in the fourth movement. The words used do not exist, rather they might exist in any language; they have no logical, only an emotional context; they affect the ear with their phonetic vibrations like music. Surprise and pleasure are derived from the structure and the inventive combinations of the parts. (Motherwell 1951, xxii)

The poem, then, is an entity so remote from its "score," so dependent upon its actual performance for its effects—effects largely unpredictable in a reading of the score in a way that music, for instance, is not—that it could be said to exist "outside" literature proper. And though one is tempted to call it music, as its structural terminology suggests, it exists outside the framework of traditional music as well. It is—and remains—noise, as Duchamp's *Fountain* remains a urinal, but it is transformed in performance into poetry.

This transformative potential of performance is one of its chief attributes and one of the primary reasons that so many contemporary artists and writers are intrigued by the dynamics of performance proper. One of the most interesting demonstrations of this potential is a short piece of "music" composed by John Cage and first performed by his colleague, the pianist David Tudor, in Woodstock, New York, in 1951. Called *4'33"*, the work consisted of Tudor sitting himself at a piano in front of an audience and raising and lowering the keyboard cover three times over the course of four minutes and thirty-three seconds in order to indicate the three separate "movements" of the work. Otherwise he remained motionless throughout, and he did not play a single note of music proper. The work, as it turned out, consisted completely of what was "outside" it—at Woodstock, the sound of the wind in the trees, raindrops on the roof, and, finally, the irritated and baffled musings of the audience itself. Our attention is drawn to such "noise" as music, not because it is inherently musical but because the performance situation transforms our attention, requires us to address it as music.

This eruption of the outside into the work, and the transformative potential such an intrusion possesses, becomes particularly interesting in light of the theatrical aspects of performance art. Performance artists distinguish themselves from actors and actresses, for instance, because the latter "pretend" to be someone else in a time different from the real time of the event. Sir Laurence Olivier, for instance, "becomes" Hamlet. But in a performance—as opposed to a production of *Hamlet*—performers maintain their own identities. In the words of Julian Beck, speaking of *Paradise Now,* a work by the late-1960s experimental group the Living Theater, the desire is "to make a play which would no longer be an enactment but the act itself[,] . . . an event in which we [the actors] would always be experiencing it [the play] not anew at all but something else each time" (Schechner 1969, 25). Ruth Maleczech, of Mabou Mines, another experimental performance group, puts it this way:

> It wasn't interesting to play parts in other people's plays anymore. Also, it probably wasn't interesting for directors to do new interpretations of often-done plays either. Something else had to happen. . . . It's not just due to performance art, but to [writer/director Jerzy] Grotowski's idea that it was no longer necessary for the actor to realize the author's intention when he wrote the part. Once that became clear, then a piece becomes the story of the lives of the performers. So the context is changing and within that

changing context, you see the life of the performer. We're
not really working with any material except ourselves. (Howell
1976, 11)

In this sense, *if* a performance group were to perform *Hamlet,* it would be as an
arena in which to discover themselves, and in fact several groups which exist on
the borderline between theater proper and performance art have tried just this,
notably Charles Ludlum's Theater of the Ridiculous in *Stage Blood* (1974), a play
about a family of actors performing *Hamlet* in a small town. Ludlum, who plays
the actor playing Hamlet in the Theater of the Ridiculous production, has explained his play this way: "My father in the play has recently died, and my
mother, who plays Gertrude, is marrying the guy who plays Claudius, and so
on. After a certain point, it's hard to tell which scenes are from *Hamlet* and
which aren't. The actors keep quoting from the play, so it's sort of open-ended"
(Tomkins 1976, 92). By the time one arrives at the famous "play-within-a-play"
scene, the levels of distinction between theater and reality, already at issue
in *Hamlet* itself, are so thoroughly confused that it is hard to tell which scenes
are from *Stage Blood*—let alone *Hamlet*—and which are, instead, "actual" in-
volvements among the members of the cast of the Theater of the Ridiculous.
Such framed actions allow Ludlum to ask questions about the world *outside* the
frame, because, metaphorically at least, they incorporate that world into the
world of the stage—they *admit,* that is, its possibility. *Hamlet* is no longer some
inviolable masterwork but, instead, a vehicle for investigating the lives of its
performers.

It is of course important to understand that in the late 1960s and early 1970s
this new idea of performance, this opening up of the work to forces outside it,
occurred within a broader politicization of art as a whole, tied to developments
such as the Vietnam War, Watergate, and the burgeoning feminist movement.
This politicization manifested itself in direct opposition to the predominantly
formalist inclinations of criticism at the time. The strongest statement of a formalist position had occurred in art criticism, with Clement Greenberg's insistence that each medium must discover the properties unique to itself and develop those properties to the exclusion of any others it might share with other
media. This had led to a kind of painting devoid of referentiality—that is, a
painting which deliberately eschewed "literary" elements—offering instead a
purely formal or nonobjective kind of art. In his book *The Performing Self,* Richard Poirier discovered the same sorts of tendencies at work in the fiction of such
writers as Jorge Luis Borges, John Barth, and Iris Murdoch, all of whom shared,
he felt, the "debilitating assumption" that "it is interesting, in and of itself, to
make the formal properties of fiction [or poetry] into the subject matter of fiction [or poetry]." For them, literature "creates a reality of its own," and it must

avoid, at all costs, "a confusion of realms"—that is, it must not confuse its own workings with "life, reality, and history" (Poirier 1971, 31, 28, 29). But there is, Poirier argues—and he is writing in 1971—a distinct confusion of realms:

> Where does Nixon's fictional self-creation end and the historical figure begin? Can such a distinction be made about a man who watches the movie Patton for the third or fourth time and then orders an invasion of Cambodia meant to destroy the Vietcong Pentagon, which he told us was there, but which has never been found?
>
> No wonder anyone who cares about politics now finds the claims made for literature by most critics ridiculously presumptuous. Why should literature be considered the primary source of fictions, when fictions are produced at every press conference; why should novelists or dramatists be called "creative" when we have Rusk and McNamara and Kissinger, the mothers of invention, "reporting" on the war in Vietnam? (Poirier 1971, 30)

For Poirier, performance always exceeds the formal and structural emphases of critical theory. Because performance is above all historical—that is, inevitably caught up in the social and political exigencies of the moment—the formal dimensions of an artist's particular medium might even be said to impede the action of performance. Faulkner, Poirier argues, "needed his structurings the way a child might need a jungle gym: as a support for exuberant, beautiful, and testing flights. . . . Structure may even be the element against which he is performing" (Poirier 1971, xv).

In the feminist movement, performance provided a way for its practitioners to express very personal, sometimes astonishingly aggressive feelings about women's place in society. It was a medium, that is, that allowed women to perform *against* the social structures and role models they felt were defined for them by society at large. Some of the earliest feminist performances occurred in Los Angeles at Womanhouse, an outgrowth of the Feminist Art Program at the California Institute of the Arts, a project begun in 1971 by Miriam Shapiro and Judy Chicago. Performance, as Chicago has explained in her autobiography *Through the Flower: My Struggle as a Woman Artist,* "seemed to provide the most direct means of expressing anger. . . . One of the reasons performance proved to be so important in the program is that it provided a release for debilitating, unexpressed anger, thereby opening up the whole range of emotions for creative work" (Chicago 1977, 125–26). Because it seemed, furthermore, a relatively "new" medium in the early 1970s, combining whatever aspects of any of several "competing" media it might wish to engage, performance also seemed uncontaminated by many of the formal expectations of more traditional, male-dominated art forms. It offered new territory for artistic exploration that helped women to establish and define their own identities, as artists and otherwise. "It is always a man," Chicago explains, "who embodies the human condition. From *Hamlet* to *Waiting for Godot,* the struggles of humanity are embodied in male characters, created by men, reflecting themselves and each other. . . . We told the truth about our feelings as women" (Chicago 1977, 128).

While the work of a performance artist like Laurie Anderson is not immediately recognizable as "feminist" in these terms, she chooses to work in a multimedia format precisely in order to avoid falling victim to the formal demands of any given single medium. Her work has been described as the combination of "a highly attenuated art-rock concert" and "a poetry reading writ very large indeed, with every aspect of the poetic concept amplified and counterpointed by aural and visual imagery," and she in fact invites each medium to collide with the others in her work, to disrupt and even distort one another. Her major work, *United States, Parts 1–4,* is a montage of instrumental compositions, songs—both full-scale production numbers and simpler tunes—narrative monologues, poems, dramatic skits, dances, carefully staged visual effects, films and multiscreen slide shows. It takes her roughly seven hours over two nights to perform it. Not only do the media themselves collide but so do the work's possible meanings. "In all the work I've ever done," Anderson explains, "my whole intention was not to map out meanings but to make a field situation. I'm interested in facts, images, and theories which resonate against each other, not in offering solutions" (Howell 1981, 6). This notion of the performance as a sort of "field situation" emphatically ties the audience into the problematics of the event itself, involves them in the dilemmas she presents. Anderson perpetually creates scenarios which baffle us or shows us how the landscape of our daily lives—a landscape so banal that we tend to take it for granted—can suddenly transform itself into a disorienting and mysterious terrain.

United States is framed, for instance, by the image of a Night Driver, windshield wipers monotonously moving back and forth before her, lost on the way home from work. Wearing goggles that light up like headlights, Anderson says, "I am in my body the way most people drive in their cars" (Anderson 1984, unpaginated). The body, that is, is a more or less mechanical conveyance for the mind that it hauls around—and yet most people drive in their cars mindlessly, or at least carelessly. At the outset we are introduced to this Night Driver in a piece called "Say Hello." It is accompanied by a drawing of a nude man and woman, the man's hand raised in a gesture of greeting, the same emblem that was drawn on the Pioneer spacecraft:

> Hello. Excuse me. Can you tell me where I am?
> *In our country, we send pictures of people speaking our sign language in Outer Space. We are speaking our sign language in these pictures.*
> Do you think that They will think his arm is permanently attached in this position?

> Or, do you think They will read our signs? In our country,
> Goodbye looks just like Hello.
> *SAY HELLO*.
> (Anderson 1984, unpaginated)

Anderson waves her violin bow like a windshield wiper and conducts this conversation with herself, but when she utters the text in italics she electronically manipulates her voice so that it sounds distinctly male, and to many ears distinctly like that of Richard Nixon. Though Anderson will only go so far as to say that "it's the Voice of Authority, an attempt to create a corporate voice, a kind of 'Newsweekese'" (Howell 1981, 8), this voice, authoritarian and, above all, male, helps us to understand the full resonance of the image from the Apollo 10 space capsule that is projected behind it. Not only are we confronted by an image which can be read in any of several contradictory ways—"In our country, Goodbye looks just like hello"—but the source of that contradictory message is male. The female is passive ("lost"), while the male takes the active, gestural role. *He* is the maker of signs, *he* is the artist. Anderson's strategy as a performer is to expose the mechanisms of authority and power in all manner of representation—visual, verbal, gestural, musical, and technological. If, as one critic put it in an analysis of the "Say Hello" segment of *United States,* "the woman is only represented; she is (as always) already spoken for" (Owens 1983, 61), then Anderson's discourse reverses that situation. She speaks for herself.

Anderson's "star" status—her successful career as a Warner Brothers recording artist and, more recently, as a filmmaker—raises important questions, of course, about her complicity with the very mechanisms of authority which she seeks to subvert. But such problematics are part and parcel of the terrain she seeks to explore, part of the "field situation" with which she confronts her audience. It could be said, in fact, that she is exploring, as much as anything else, questions about success and failure in American art and about the function of the audience—the community to whom the work is addressed—in determining a work's relative worth. Anderson's performances take place in a recognizably rock-concert format, for instance, in order to take advantage of the sense of community attendant to that form since at least the days of Woodstock and the concerts which occurred in connection with the Vietnam peace movement, a sense of community that militates against the cult of individuality—the idolatry—that so thoroughly defines the "star" system proper. Anderson has managed to recreate the sense that, as a performer, she is not speaking for us but with us.

Probably no other performance artist has so concentrated on creating just this spirit of dialogue—that is, a community of discourse between artist and audience—than David Antin. Antin calls himself a "poet," but his poems consist of improvised remarks, generally fifty to sixty minutes in duration, tape-recorded before live audiences and transcribed without margins left or right, without punctuation, and without capitalization. His form is meant to suggest the "live" voice as nearly as possible on the written page, its pauses and its pace, and the improvisatory nature of the address is meant not only to insure its liveliness but also its sense of "being in the present," its immediacy. For Antin, discourse is one of the fundamental—if not *the* fundamental—concept or activity upon which community is formed, and his relation to his audience is not unlike Anderson's. His poems create "field situations" in which we come to recognize that we face, as a group, a common dilemma. Like the performances at Womanhouse in the early 1970s, which could be seen as the focal point of a developing feminist community, Antin's talks are actions which help us to define both ourselves and our roles in the community proper. Furthermore, since this sort of performance is an integral part of—rather than apart from—the daily lives of both the performer and the audience, since it serves a catalytic or transformative function for them (helping them, for instance, to establish new roles and new identities), and since it helps to create a sense of collective celebration or accomplishment or to define a common task or goal, it could be said to be roughly equivalent to *ritual*.

Here is an excerpt from Antin's 1984 book of talk pieces entitled *tuning* which relates precisely such a ritual performance.

> when roys daughter died we held a memorial at
> the center for music experiment   the memorial
>   readings and performances by poets and artists
> and musicians   was an attempt to offer some
>   fellowship to roy and marie who were in a state
>   of shock over the terrible accident   it was held
> in the late afternoon in the long somber wooden
>   shed that had once housed a marine officers bowling
> alley   been refurbished with a black ceiling much
> redwood stripping and a mauve carpet to serve as the
>   university art gallery and then turned over to the
> music department in the middle 70s   the readings
>   proceeded quietly one after another without
> interruption for long introductions and the last piece
> on the program was a composition by pauline oliveros
>   pauline was working with a small performance
> group at the time and its young men and women were
>   scattered informally around the room   pauline
> came to the center of the gallery to tell us how to
>   perform the piece   we were all to rise and form
> a large single circle joining hands with our nearest
>   neighbors   to listen until we heard a tone we felt
> like tuning to   to try to tune to it and when we were
>   satisfied with our tuning we could fall silent and
> listen   choose another tone and try to tune to it

and go on like this listening and tuning and falling
silent as long as we wished   until we felt that we
were through   i was holding hands with a carefully
dressed young history professor and a smart looking
dark haired woman from a travel agency in la jolla
*   i listened for a while and could make out several*
humming tones coming from various places about
the room   i could hear the history professor clear
his throat and start to hum a tone in the middle of
the baritone register   i thought i would join him
there and my partner on the left opened a lovely
mezzo just above us   around the room soft surges
of sound floated up while others stayed suspended
or died away to be succeeded by still others in fifths
and octaves lightly spiked by onsets and decays that
underlined the simple harmonies that filled the
space   at one point a high clear soprano tone
floated out across the room and i saw the history
professor start to cry   i squeezed his hand and
tried to join a high tenor almost beyond my range
*   the history professor nodded and joined us there*
our dark haired neighbor to the left opened a flute
like tone a fifth above us   all around the room
people were crying and smiling and singing in
waves of sound that throbbed and swelled and ebbed
and climbed and peaked and dropped away into a
silence that lasted until pauline thanked everyone
because the piece was over

                                               (Antin 1984, 1–2)

What Antin describes here—it is the introductory piece to his book—is the kind of moment in which most all of us feel a certain measure of discomfort, ranging from our inadequacy in the face of death to our unwillingness to publicly perform or exercise our grief. And yet what Pauline Oliveros, a performance artist and musician herself, manages to do is allow the audience to overcome that discomfort. In fact, she transforms the group at the memorial service so that its relation to the event is no longer passive but active. It is no longer an audience but a community.

But this is by no means the only tranformation that takes place here. If "tuning" becomes Antin's metaphor for this common "coming together" of artist and audience in the activity of performance, Antin's text requires of itself a form of "tuning." Looking at Antin's writing, no one feels immediately at ease. And beginning to read, this discomfort increases, as one finds oneself longing for the traditional markers of written discourse—capitalization, commas, periods, quo-

tation marks, and so on. The point, of course, is that this is not written discourse. It is something else—the transcription of a voice, the voice of "a man up
on his feet talking," as Antin himself has put it. Antin's abnormal transcription,
especially the unjustified margins both left and right, announces this performative difference. One finds oneself disoriented on his page, and in longer pieces
(his normal "length" is somewhere between forty and fifty pages), unable to stop
because there are almost literally no places for the eye to rest. The effect of reading him, especially at length, is to find oneself going through a transformation
as a reader exactly analogous to the transformation Antin describes in the introduction to *tuning:* what begins in discomfort, even alienation, ends in a much
more intensive and productive relation to the text—the *event* of the text—than
normal. Antin's writing demands *attention*—an attention, incidentally, at odds
with the colloquial level of its diction—that forces its audience to *engage* it. It is
as if, in order to read Antin, one were forced to *voice* him. But one is not quite
sure just what it is that one is voicing. On the one hand, the writing looks a little
bit like poetry. It even reads, at moments, like a poem:

> around the room soft surges
> of sound floated up while others stayed suspended
> or died away to be succeeded by still others in fifths
> and octaves lightly spiked by onsets and decays that
> underlined the simple harmonies that filled the
> space   at one point a high clear soprano tone
> floated out across the room and i saw the history
> professor start to cry

We can detect poetic diction ("soft surges"), hard enjambments reminiscent of
the best free verse, caesuras (after "space," for instance) that imply meaningful
content. But, on the other hand, this seems to be prose. Whatever it is, the point
is that it defies generic designation. It cannot be so easily contained.

Gertrude Stein once said that "a long complicated sentence should force itself
upon you, make yourself know yourself knowing it" (Stein 1957, 221), and
Antin's texts are, in effect, very long sentences indeed. A whole network of transformations takes place here: in Oliveros's performance, Antin and the others are
transformed; Antin transforms the initial event into a narrative; the oral narrative is transformed into text; the typographical idiosyncracies of the page an-
nounce the text's own transformation, requiring a different sort of reading behavior from its audience; and reading itself becomes a sort of "listening" to
Antin's voice, though the "event" of his speaking is no longer present, and Antin's voice is transformed into our own. In these terms, finally, performance can
be defined as an activity which generates transformations, as the reintegration of
art with what is "outside" it, an "opening up" of the "field."

Suggested Readings

Benamou, Michel, and Charles Caramello, eds. 1977. *Performance in Postmodern Culture.*

Goldberg, RoseLee. 1979. *Performance: Live Art, 1909 to the Present.*

Loeffler, Carl E. 1980. *Performance Anthology: Source Book for a Decade of California Performance Art.*

Roth, Moira. 1983. *The Amazing Decade: Women and Performance Art in America, 1970–1980.*

Schechner, Richard. 1977. *Essays on Performance Theory, 1970–1976.*

Vincent, Stephen, and Ellen Zweig. 1981. *The Poetry Reading: A Contemporary Compendium on Language and Performance.*

8

Author

Donald E. Pease

IN COMMON usage the term "author" applies to a wide range of activities. It can refer to someone who starts up a game, or invents a machine, or asserts political freedom, or thinks up a formula, or writes a book. Depending on the activity and the application, the term can connote initiative, autonomy, inventiveness, creativity, authority, or originality. A common procedure whereby an anonymous agent turns into an individual binds the term to these different activities.

In turning anyone in general into someone in particular, the term "author" carries along with its common usage some long-standing debates over what is at stake in this transformation. These debates have continued over centuries and have taken place with different emphases in different fields. But certain questions, no matter whether they were asked by politicians, economists, theologians, philosophers, or artists, remained constant. Is an individual self-determined or determined by material and historical circumstances? Is the human self infinite or finite? Can an individual ground political authority on individual creativity? What is the basis for human freedom? Can any artist claim absolute originality?

These questions as well as different cultures' responses to them have accompanied the term from its inception. The variety of these responses constitutes the meaning of the term. Like other items that answer to a variety of applications, "author" will sometimes sanction utterly contradictory usages. At the time of its inception, for example, the word "author" was used interchangeably with its predecessor term "auctor," which did not entail verbal inventiveness, as "author" did but the reverse—adherence to the authority of cultural antecedent. A good way to sort out the various, sometimes contradictory, meanings of this term might be by way of historical narrative. Like most historical narratives, this one will cover an immense trajectory of time in a short space. Consequently, only the broad outlines of its historical development will become apparent. And only some of the questions which have shaped that development will be addressed.

Another question and the contemporary debate surrounding it will provide a conclusion to this brief narrative. Is the "author" dead? The question was asked by Roland Barthes in an essay "The Death of the Author," a title which presumes the answer. But Michel Foucault disagreed with this answer and wrote an essay "What Is an Author?" which raises in the terms of recent continental criticism some of the issues addressed in the following narrative. Because their debate recapitulates and advances those issues, a discussion of its implications for the continued usage of the term will conclude the history.

The idea of authorship has a lengthy and somewhat problematic genealogy. From the beginning this genealogy has been associated with that of a related figure, the individual "subject." Unlike other works referring to a writer's activity—such as essayist, or poet, or dramatist—the term "author" raises questions about authority and whether the individual is the source or the effect of that authority. The word "author" derives from the medieval term *auctor,* which denoted a writer whose words commanded respect and belief. The word *auctor* derived from four etymological sources: the Latin verbs *agere,* "to act or perform"; *auieo,* "to tie"; *augere,* "to grow"; and from the Greek noun *autentim,* "authority." In the Middle Ages every discipline in the *trivium* had *auctores* (Cicero in rhetoric, Aristotle in dialectic, the ancient poets in grammar) and similarly in the *quadrivium* (Ptolemy in astronomy, Constantine in medicine, the Bible in theology, Boethius in arithmetic) (see Minnis 1984, 1–73). *Auctores* established the founding rules and principles for these different disciplines and sanctioned the moral and political authority of medieval culture more generally. Over the centuries the continued authority of these founding figures derived from medieval scribes' ability to interpret, explain, and in most cases resolve historical problems by restating these problems in terms sanctioned by *auctores.*

Such restatements commanded authority because they organized otherwise accidental events into an established context capable of making them meaningful. The continued authority to make events meaningful in customary or traditional ways provided all the evidence necessary to sustain the *auctores'* power. In the Middle Ages, the relationship between these authoritative books and the everyday world was primarily an allegorical one. Worldly events took place in terms sanctioned by an authoritative book or were not acknowledged as having taken place at all. To experience an event in allegorical terms was to transpose the event out of the realm of one's personal life into the realm of the applicable authority. Following such a transposition, the event became impersonal—everyone's spiritual quest rather than one individual's personal biography. The benefit of this transposition for the individual was indeed a spiritual one—the ability to experience an event in one's life as a reenactment of a sacred custom. Any event, or thing, or emotion, or thought which made this transference into the realm of the *auctores* possible continued their cultural authority. Whereas individuals within medieval culture could interpret their lives in terms that elaborated or reenacted the sayings of the ancient *auctores,* only the monarch, as God's representative, could claim divine sanction for his everyday actions. By correlating the divine basis for his rule with auctorial precedents, the medieval ruler sanctioned the *auctores'* cultural authority. As the source, the beneficiary, and the agent of the culture's authoritative books, the monarch was the perfected cultural form of the *auctor*. His rule was his book, and his subjects were compelled to submit their world to the edicts of that book.

Auctorial sanction and monarchical rule remained more or less unquestioned until late in the fifteenth century, with the discovery of a New World whose inhabitants, language, customs and laws, geography, and plant and animal life did not correspond to referents in the *auctores'* books. Unlike events and persons in medieval Europe, the inhabitants and environment of the New World could *not* be explained in customary terms. Explorers could not find precedents in the work of *auctores* for what they discovered in the New World. Instead of returning to their culture's ancient books for allegorical prefigurations, many New World explorers described what they discovered by making up words of their own (or borrowing terms from the natives). One result of this breakdown was the addition to the English language of such words as hurricane, canoe, skunk; another was the loss of cultural authority for the *auctor*. A related effect was the appearance of what Renaissance historians now refer to as "new men," individuals within Renaissance culture who turned the "news" sent home from freshly discovered lands into forms of cultural empowerment for unprecedented political actions and their personification by new agents within the culture. Among these new cultural agents were "authors," writers whose claim to cultural authority did not depend on their adherence to cultural precedents but on a faculty of verbal inventiveness. Unlike the medieval *auctor* who based his authority on divine revelation, an author *himself* claimed authority for his words and based his individuality on the stories he composed.

More precisely, authors exploited the discontinuity between the things in the New World and the words in the ancient books to claim for their words an unprecedented cultural power, to represent the new. Authors rose to cultural prominence in alliance with other individuals who exploited this dissociation between worlds: explorers, merchants, colonists, traders, reformers, and adventurers. Like all these other "new" men, authors depended on what was newly discovered in the new lands as the basis for their cultural authority. The new lands were the source of news, and the news facilitated social mobility and cultural change. The recognition of what was new depended on an acknowledgment of the inadequacy of allegory as the source of cultural knowledge. Whereas medieval allegory subsumed a culture's persons and their actions—no matter how various or qualified—within its unchanging typologies, what was new asserted its difference from, rather than its correspondence with, these cultural typologies. By inventing new words to describe things in the New World, authors declared their right to be represented on their own terms rather than in the words of the ancient books. And their writings produced readers who also learned how to define themselves in their own terms.

From the fifteenth century through the first half of the twentieth century, the term "author" enjoyed a more or less constant rise in social prestige. The beneficiary of the esteem that cultures had previously bestowed on their *auctores,* the author and his work signified a break from the cultural constraints imposed by feudal kings. Authors maintained this affiliation with cultural freedom through the creation of alternative worlds wherein individual human subjects could experience the autonomy denied them in their cultural world.

This rise to cultural prominence of the author was correlated from the beginning with the *auctores'* fall. Like the autonomous human subject, the author was an emergent political and cultural category, which was initially differentiated from the culturally residual category of the *auctor* as an example of *self*-determination. The author guaranteed the individual's ability to determine his own identity and actions out of his own experiences in a culture he could reform rather than endorsing the auctorial aim of transcending culture.

The *auctor* based his authority on divine revelation; the author derived his authority from the discovery of new worlds whose native environments contradicted the *auctores'* mandates. The *auctores* produced a culture which reproduced their mandates; authors at first produced themselves out of the alternative world-pictures they used to explain (and imaginatively inhabit) other lands.

During the years when feudal Europe was undergoing a fundamental transformation, the author was never defined apart from this process of transformation. Once the work of cultural transformation was considered complete, however, the concept of the "author" underwent a fundamental change. Having helped effect the historic change from a feudal and predominantly agricultural society and through a variety of other political and economic arrangements to a democratic and predominantly industrial Europe, the author was no longer part of an emergent cultural process. Following the realization of an alternative culture he had earlier only envisioned, the author's work underwent a related change— from a reciprocal workaday relationship with other cultural activities into the realm of "genius," which transcended ordinary cultural work.

Like the medieval *auctor,* the "genius" identified the basis for his work with the laws of the Creator. Consequently, the realm of genius was defined as utterly autonomous. Free from determination by any cultural category other than the absolutely free constructions of his creative imagination, the genius broke down the reciprocal relationship between the author and the rest of culture.

But while the genius occupied a realm that transcended culture, he nevertheless served a cultural function. As an example of the perfection that could be achieved by an inhabitant of the culture, the genius sanctioned the political authority of the culture in which he appeared. But, like the medieval *auctor,* he defined this authority as the ability to transcend the entire cultural milieu.

Whereas the author developed within the culture he helped to develop, the genius claimed to be different from the rest of the culture. So defined, the work of genius provided a politically useful contrast to other forms of labor in an industrial culture. In producing his *own* work out of materials in his own imagination, the genius performed "cultural" as opposed to "industrial" labor. Industrial workers did not control the means and product of their labor but worked with materials and produced commodities owned by someone else. In correlating nonalienated labor with his work rather than with the work of an ordinary laborer, the genius provided a tacit justification for the class distinctions separating those individuals who owned their labor from those who did not. If nonalienated labor defined the category of genius, it became a cultural privilege, a benefit accrued in the cultural realm rather than in the ordinary workaday world.

The difference between the genius who creates other, "original" worlds and the author who cooperates in the emergence of an alternative culture underscores at least two contradictory impulses the author shared from the beginning with that other emergent cultural category, the "autonomous subject." Both the author and the individual collaborated with emergent collective processes in social life. The author and the individual shared a tendency to become alienated from society once these collective social processes were fully materialized. Although associated with the more inclusive social movements that led to revolution and civil war, the author's creative work was not separable from the collective work of these social movements. Only after an emancipatory social movement succeeded in establishing an alternative form of government with its own rules of law could an author's creative efforts be dissociated from a vital collective life—as the work of a "genius." As the authoritative source of the creative life, the genius marked the return of the role of the *auctor* to the postmedieval cultural world.

To understand how the *auctor* returned, we need to recall how the *auctor* was first overthrown. The *auctor* had formerly been supplanted when the Europeans, in confronting humans they believed to be of a nature other than their own, recognized their own capacity to be other. The basis for a successful transformation in a European's nature was the discovery in the New World of natural phenomena utterly inexplicable in terms of the *auctores*. These truly alien phenomena produced an "other nature" *within* the Renaissance men who discovered them.

This "other" within ultimately became the basis for the autonomous subject. But when it made its first appearance, this "other nature" was put into service by the new men of commerce, who were able to gratify its appetites with the foodstuffs, spices, and goods brought over from the New World. The qualities in this other nature not put to commercial use led to a different form of government in Europe. Using the New World as tacit backdrop for their arguments, political theorists like Hobbes and Locke argued that man in nature was like a "savage" in the New World. Prepolitical, protosocial, deprived of protection against an enemy, natural man required a social contract with the monarch to preserve "natural" rights and liberties.

These theories eventually led to civil wars and revolutions throughout Europe. But all of them traded on an identification within European individuals of another nature that was no longer subject to the rule of either feudal monarchs or their *auctores* but in need of an alternative European political system for its fulfillment. In its process of emergence, this new political system demanded accounts of its workings quite different from those of *auctores*.

As we have seen, the transformation of the *auctores'* models into alternative accounts of alternative worlds resulted in the appearance of authors. As long as the author was involved in the process of bringing new persons and new laws into existence, his creative powers were affiliated with a collective political imagination designed to realize a body politic that did not yet exist. It was through this collective imagination that the author addressed the other within the reading public. When the author addressed the collective imaginative capacity of Europeans to make the world they wanted out of the world they inherited, the result was revolution or civil war.

Once these civil wars succeeded in establishing alternative forms of government, the author underwent an unrelated transformation. When the author's work could no longer be correlated with an emancipatory social movement, it was defined as an emancipation from the political life. The term "genius" enabled this separation of the cultural from the political realm. As the legatee of a previous cultural identification, affiliating the *auctor's* creative power with a founder's power to establish a city-state, the genius established a cultural realm utterly dissociated from either the political or the economic realms. He called this realm a "Republic of Letters." In this realm the works of genius recovered the authority previously exercised by medieval *auctores* and were elevated into exemplars and sources of value for the entire culture.

With the installation of the genius as the *auctor* ruling over the Republic of Letters, the author's function shifted accordingly—from that of producing an alternative political world to that of producing a cultural alternative to the world of politics. After the cultural sphere distinguished its workings from those within the different worlds of politics and economics, the cultural realm became increasingly self-referential.

During the political and industrial revolutions of the eighteenth and nineteenth centuries the cultural realm could not be fully distinguished from the economic and political realms. But in the twentieth century the author's genius was invoked to explain the irrelevance of economic and political issues to questions of strictly cultural interest. The genius's putative freedom from material constraints authorized this separation of the cultural from the economic realm. Following this separation, the economic, political, psychological, and historical conditions that provided the material environment for an author's work were denied any determining relationship with it.

This separation of the cultural from the political and economic realms produced an even more fundamental division within the cultural realm, separating the author from his work. The cultural figure who supervised this division was neither the genius, nor the author, but the literary critic. Produced out of this division of labor within the cultural realm, the literary critic supervised further differentiation within the cultural realm and policed the boundaries distinguishing what was literary from what was not.

The division of cultural labor distinguishing the critic's function from the author's replicated the division of industrial labor within the economic realm. What alienated the author from his work's means of production, however, was not a factory owner but the literary critic who claimed a power to understand it greater than the author's own. The critic proved this power by interpreting the work in such a way that the author seemed an effect of the critic's interpretation rather than the cause of the work.

In an essay entitled "The Intentional Fallacy" (1954), Wimsatt and Beardsley, two American New Critics, turned the demotion of the author to a function of the critic's text into an explicit part of critical practice: "There is a gross body of life, of sensory and mental experience, which lies behind and in some sense causes every poem, but can never be and need not be known in the verbal and hence intellectual composition which is the poem." (See Wimsatt and Beardsley 1954, 12) In distinguishing the critic's text from the author's work, the New Critics successfully displaced the author's "genius" as the ruler within the cultural sphere. In the process the New Critics produced a cultural artifact, the "autotelic" or "autonomous" literary text that they defined as utterly separate from the surrounding environment. In separating the literary text from the control of the author, the New Critics only completed a movement that had begun in the cultural realm a century earlier, when the word "genius" separated the author's work from the socioeconomic world.

As the word "autotelic" text implies, the New Critics positioned their newly won texts in a realm apart from every limitation other than the rules, conventions, and constraints of a purely textual milieu. In the same postwar period in which the New Critics constructed the division separating a textual milieu from a social world, however, other critics located a critical dimension within the author's work. Instead of distinguishing the critic's work from the author, those critics using historicist, Marxist, Frankfurt school, and feminist frameworks have restored the critical dimension to the author's work, thereby linking the author and critic in a shared project. These critics returned the author's work to the social, economic, political, and gendered contexts which the New Critics separated off from their autotelic texts. In restoring the historical context to the author's works, these critics have rescinded the New Critics' claim that the genius's texts transcend historical contexts. Their criticism turns the genius back into an individual subject, determined by the social and economic forces whose shapes he reflected or altered in his work. In analyzing the complex relationship between the market economy and what was formerly described as the "free creative play" of genius, Marxist critics in particular have restored the explicit relationship between any author's work and the anticipated reception for it. Psychoanalytic, phenomenological, and feminist critics have likewise restored crucial psychosocial contexts. In thereby turning the transcendent genius back into a culturally situated human subject, these critics have attempted to reverse some of the effects of the divisions of labor within the cultural realm. Unlike the New Critics' approach, their criticism takes place at that moment within an author's work when the author becomes critically aware of determinant social, psychological, and political forces.

These critics have restored psychosocial relationships between the author and culturally committed critics by representing the author and the critic as participants in a still-emergent social process rather than as representative figures within a fully established culture or as partial selves within a textual environment.

But these revisionist efforts have more recently been opposed by still newer critics who construe the text as isolated from every context other than a purely textual one and consider the term "author" and the history of its cultural usages to be impediments to the workings of the textual environment. Since the controversy between two of the newer critics has resulted in a consideration of the cultural value of the term "author," it will function as a conclusion to this brief narrative genealogy.

In order to separate the text from contamination by an author, such newer critics as Roland Barthes have declared the author dead. By the "author," Barthes means the demands—for psychological consistency, meaning, unity—that an autonomous subject would exact from a textual environment. In the wake of the author's death, Barthes has proposed a new definition of literature: a discursive game always arriving at the limits of its own rule, without any author other than the reader (or "scriptor" as Barthes refers to him), who is defined as an effect of the writing game he activates.

Whereas Barthes declares that the author is dead, the text he thereby produces is not without an author. In Barthes' criticism the author returns—but in the displaced form of Barthes' metatextual account of the writing activity. In this view, then, the critic is the real beneficiary of the separation of an author from a text. It is the critic rather than the author or the reader who can render an authoritative account of the structure of the work, the internal relationships among the various textual strands and levels, and the shift from author to what Barthes names "scriptor." Without the author to demand the resolution of contradictory textual lines into an intended unity, the critic is free to reconstitute the text according to his own terms.

In an essay published one year after Barthes' "The Death of the Author," and contentiously entitled "What Is [rather than *was*] an Author," Michel Foucault reactivates the controversy between poststructuralists (who believed only in the environment of textuality) and historicists (who believed in a sociopolitical context for the literary work) over the cultural function of the author. Unlike Barthes, Foucault acknowledges the persistence of the author as a function within the commentary of poststructuralists who deny the author as agent.

To elucidate the crucial part the author continues to play in the material life of a culture, Foucault takes Barthes' "death of the author rule" as a literal ethical imperative and imagines what would happen if authors actually disappeared from culture. For one thing, there would then be no warrant for criticism. Critical language (its vocabulary of accusation, defense, judgment) depends on the legal system (and the cultural systems affiliated with it) for its warrant. Without Foucault's name to connect with the words in, say, *Les mots et les choses* there would be no one to be held accountable for them and, hence, no way to justify a critique of them (or any other commentary). The name of the author turns discourse into legal property, and the notion of legal property in turn supports and is supported by related discourses concerning entitlements, liberties, duties, rights, constraints, impediments, obligations, and punishment. The name of the author saturates the entire network of legal relations, thereby empowering the attribution of discourses to the procedures that result from them.

For Foucault, the author is finally neither an individual existing apart from a discursive practice, nor a subject acting within any specific practice, but what might be called a "subjecting" function. As the sanction for the rules within any specific practice, and as a function of the relations between them, the author for Foucault oversees and regulates all the diverse situations in which *any cultural subject* can act. Produced by the practices whose reproduction it guarantees, the name of the author turns otherwise unrelated discursive practices into a coherent cultural realm over which it maintains jurisdiction.

If the author disappeared, Foucault claims, so would the entire cultural realm under the author's jurisdiction. But Foucault postulates a different kind of author to explain figures (like Marx and Freud) whose work is discontinuous with the cultural realm. Such authors do not function within already existing discursive practices but are instead fundamental in a double sense: they found disciplines that are discontinuous with previous ones; and, unlike other cultural subjects, "fundamental" authors produce writing practices discontinuous with the practices that follow from them.

In ending his essay with a description of the fundamental author, Foucault gives his readers the appropriate way to understand his own authorship. More interestingly for our narrative, he gives them a way to put Barthes' text to strategic cultural use. The "fundamental" author, insofar as he begins a discipline that is discontinuous with its owns rules, gratifies what Barthes describes as the fundamental impulse of the writing practice. But, unlike Barthes, Foucault's "fundamental" author does not make the mistake of turning this impulse into the normative imperative that the author "die" into this discontinuity.

This controversy between Barthes and Foucault clarifies an important function that the author plays in contemporary culture. While they both write about the author as if the term has arrived at its limits as an enabling concept, their debate returns the "author" to its relationship with another term, the "autonomous subject." The author replicates the difficulties of the cultural subject who feels as much *ruled by* as *ruler of* the writing activity in which he is situated. Barthes' solution to the subject's dilemma is the radical one of situating the subject in a discourse (the text) that brings rules *and* their ruler (the authors) to an end. Foucault exposes the rule governing this discourse, then proposes a discursive practice—that of the "fundamental" author—that will enable every subject to experience the dilemma (of feeling ruled by the discourse he should be ruling) as its own solution. In the discourse inaugurated by a "fundamental" author, every apparently derivative position a later practitioner of that discourse occupies turns out to be originative.

Foucault's "fundamental" author opens up the cultural sphere by transforming the self-referential qualities underwritten by the author into a kind of planned heterogeneity. In a sense, the "fundamental" author conflates the cultural duties of the traditional author (who initiates a new cultural practice) and the critic (who exposes the limits, inconsistencies, and unwarranted assumptions of the new practice). Insofar as he initiates both his own practice as well as the revisionary (implicitly critical) practices discontinuous with it, however, the fundamental author simply incorporates an otherwise separate *critical* discourse into his means of elaborating the internal differentiations vital to this continued cultural life of new disciplines.

Foucault's redefinition of the author has not actually introduced a new form of cultural agency for the author; in fact, it has merely restored to the author a cultural power so general in its deployment (what ongoing cultural practices cannot claim to be an activation of function discontinuous with prior practice?) and so pervasive in its effect that the work of the "fundamental" author cannot be distinguished from any other exercise of power in the cultural sphere.

Whereas Foucault intended the "fundamental" author as an alternative to the traditional author, the practices of the fundamental author only reactivate what we have already recognized as the inescapable dilemma at work in the term. Foucault's reactivation of that dilemma gives me the occasion to recapitulate the historical narrative I have been writing.

The term "author" originally arose out of the sense of constraint experienced by the finite human subject. The authorial subject claimed the power at once to produce and to supersede those limitations. The historical result of this power was the autonomous cultural sphere. But here an imaginary scenario transpired in which the finite individual subject was instructed by the authorial subject to exclude as foreign to the cultural sphere any reminder of finitude in the form of economic, political, or material interests. When confronted with the alternative of being completely determined by material conditions, the authorial subject (as "genius") claimed the power to represent, and then find itself transparently represented in, the material conditions of human finitude. Producing in his work what previously had claimed to produce it, the authorial subject claimed the power to transcend these limitations to the subject's power and, then, along with the commentators who collaborated in the production, proved the effectiveness of this power by recognizing it in the unity, coherence, and regularity of the work of art.

The cost of the autonomy of the author's work was the separation of the socio-economic from the textual environment and the recognition, at the time of that separation, of the conditions of textual production (rules, conventions, generic assumptions) as the only rules applicable to the text. As historicist critics have reminded us, these textual rules were themselves rarefied versions of nontextual economic and political forces. And the division of the textual from the sociopolitical realm reproduced within the text the pervasive opposition between the determining and the determined subject informing the notion of the author.

Barthes suggests one way to resolve this opposition. By identifying with the critical subject (who can articulate the rules that determine the author's moves) until that subjectivity witnesses the disappearance of the author into the writing processes that determined his work, Barthes produced a subjectivity that was effected by the activity it engaged. Determined by the process it determined, the writing self is only a textual version of what historicist critics described as the emergent author, who was determined by the collective movement the author helped determine.

As Foucault pointed out, the expense of Barthes' vision was the recovery of the author as a function at the precise moment that the author was displaced by the writing process as a controlling force. But then instead of resituating the "author" within a socioeconomic (as opposed to purely textual) process, Foucault identifies the fundamental mechanism at work in the writing process—the "displacement with a difference" of what preceded it—with the political practice of the "fundamental" author.

In so doing, Foucault has not confronted the perennial dilemma of the author; instead, he defines the conditions of textual finitude—the revisionary activity of the writing process itself—as the determining cultural practice of the fundamental author. And the fundamental author then does, in Foucault's text what the genius had earlier done in the genealogy of the term "author"; that is, he claims a power to determine (in the form of a willed discontinuity from his practice) what otherwise would determine him.

Once transposed into the rarefied realm of revisionary discursive practices, Foucault's fundamental author can supervise a cultural domain organized like a textual or discursive milieu. His "fundamental" author, in other words, performs the historic role of the author as genius. He polices the boundary separating the cultural realm from contamination by those material and economic conditions no author can claim to have produced. It was this very separation of the cultural sphere from the political that produced the separation of the text from the author in the work of the New Critics. Insofar as he could be influenced by nontextual considerations (by the market economy, social movements, and such) the author had to be separated from the work (which by definition could not be influenced by nontextual matters). Following this *ultimate* separation of the work from its author (usually accompanied by a revolutionary rhetoric like Barthes' borrowed from social movements) a work no longer had to be addressed in anything other than textual terms.

The utterly textual milieu of the poststructuralists is ruled by the critic, or the authorless subject, as opposed to the author. In this domain the critic can do what the author cannot; that is, expose the rules that structure the language games productive of the textual environment. But at least one of these language games, the tendency of the textual environment to generalize its domain back into the political and economic spheres (as discourses), can reactivate the countermovement earlier described.

The authorless subject is not a fact of modern existence but only an effect of the discursive practices constitutive of subjectivity. Like every other discursive effect, the authorless subject depends on a critic's metatext for an elucidation of the operative rules of these practices. But if the critic's position has been identified with the rules of these discursive practices in the process of self-revision, the critic cannot transform these practices. Following the saturation of the cultural, economic, and political realms by the critic's text, only the return of an enabling concept of the author can facilitate a genuine transformation. In order to be enabling, the term "author" can no longer remain divided into partial subjects (the *auctor,* the author, the reader, the critic, the determining-determined subject). The controversy surrounding the term "author," however, may actually produce a material practice able to overcome the division in cultural realms that depends on such a partitioning of human subjectivity.

SUGGESTED READINGS

Abrams, M. H. [1953] 1977. *The Mirror and the Lamp*.
Althusser, L. 1971. *Lenin and Philosophy and Other Essays*.
Althusser, L., and Balibar, E. 1970. *Reading "Capital."*

Barthes, R., *S/Z* [1970] 1974.

———. [1973] 1975. *The Pleasure of the Text*.

———. 1977. *Image-Music-Text*.

Baudry, J-L. 1974. "Writing, Fiction, Ideology."

Benjamin, W. [1934] 1973. "The Author as Producer."

Coward, R., and Ellis, J. 1977. *Language and Materialism*.

Ducrot, O., and Todorov, T. 1972. *Dictionnaire encyclopédique des sciences du language*.

Ellis, J. 1978. "Art, Culture and Quality."

Foucault, M. [1956] 1977d. *The Order of Things*.

———. [1969] 1972. *The Archaeology of Knowledge*.

———. 1977c. *Language, Counter-Memory, Practice*.

Freud, S. 1977. "Fetishism." In *On Sexuality*.

Genette, G. 1972. *Figures III*.

Heath, S. 1972. *The Nouveau Roman*.

———. 1976. "Narrative Space."

Hirst, P. 1976. "Althusser and the Theory of Ideology."

Jakobson, R. 1971. *Selected Writings*.

Kristeva, J. 1975. "The Subject Insignifying Practice." In *Semiotext(e)*.

Lacan, J. 1977. *Ecrits: A Selection*.

———. 1977. *The Four Fundamental Concepts of Psychoanalysis*.

Laplanche, J. and J. B. Pontalis. 1973. *The Language of Psychoanalysis*.

Leavis, F. R. [1952] 1962. *The Common Pursuit*.

Lévi-Strauss, C. [1958] 1968. *Structural Anthropology*.

Macherey, P. [1966] 1978. *A Theory of Literary Production*.

Macksey, R., and E. Donato, eds. 1970. *The Structuralist Controversy*.

Metz, C. [1968] 1974. *Film Language*.

Williams, R. 1976. *Keywords*.

II

Interpretation

9

Interpretation

Steven Mailloux

When I think back on all the crap I learned
in high school,
It's a wonder I can think at all.
The lack of education hasn't hurt me none.
I can read the writing on the wall.
　　　　　　　—Paul Simon, "Kodachrome"

READING words on walls. Explicating poems in classrooms. Making sense
of treaties in Congress. Reading, explicating, making sense: these are
three names given to the activity of "interpretation," the topic of this essay. We
can begin to explore this topic by looking briefly at the word's etymology.

In English, "interpret" has most often meant, according to the *Oxford English
Dictionary,* "to expound the meaning of (something abstruse or mysterious); to
render (words, writings, an author) clear or explicit; to elucidate; to explain."
But an earlier sense of the verb was "to translate," and so "interpretation" is also
"the act of translating; a translation or rendering of a book, word, etc." (*OED*).
The word "interpretation" itself derives from the Latin, *interpretatio,* meaning
not only "the action of expounding, explaining" but also "a translation, a rendering." In Latin rhetoric, *interpretatio* referred to "the explanation of one word by
another, the use of synonyms." *Interpretatio* was formed on *interpres:* "an inter-
mediary, agent, go-between" and "an interpreter of foreign languages, a translator" (Glare 1982, 947). In its etymology, then, "interpretation" conveys the
sense of a translation pointed in two directions simultaneously: *toward* a text to
be interpreted and *for* an audience in need of the interpretation. That is, the
interpreter mediates between the translated text and its new rendering *and* between the translated text and the audience desiring the translation.

It is the heritage of these two etymological senses—translation *of* a text and
translation *for* an audience—that we might try to capture in a working definition: "interpretation" is "acceptable and approximating translation." Each term
here provokes additional questions: (1) Approximating *what?* (2) Translating

121

how? and (3) Acceptable *to whom?* For the next few pages, we can use these questions to organize our discussion of "interpretation."

1. Approximating *What?*

Translation is always an approximation, which is to say that interpretation is always directed. It is always an approximation of something; it is always directed *toward* something: situations, actions, gestures, graffiti, poems, treaties, novels, and so forth. Such objects of interpretation we can call "texts." Ultimately, anything can be viewed as a text, anything can be interpreted. Our focus here will be on written texts, like this poem by Emily Dickinson:

> Belshazzar had a letter—
> He never had but one—
> Belshazzar's Correspondent
> Concluded and begun
> In that Immortal Copy
> The Conscience of us all
> Can read without its Glasses
> On Revelation's Wall—

If we think of interpreting as the translation of texts, then this is clearly a text requiring translation. In fact, here we have two texts in need of interpreting: Dickinson's poem and the "letter . . . on Revelation's Wall" to which the poem refers. Just as the words of the "letter" are missing, so too are some of the usual texual markers in the poem, like traditional punctuation. Dickinson's idiosyncratic dashes do give us some guidance but not much.

The poem itself translates a biblical story. In chapter 5 of the Book of Daniel, Belshazzar, king of the Chaldeans, holds a feast using sacred vessels taken from the Jewish temple at Jerusalem. During the feast, a hand appears and writes on the wall the words "Mene, Mene, Tekel, Upharsin." The king cannot interpret the writing, nor can any of his advisors. The problem of reading, making sense of texts, thus becomes foregrounded in the story. Daniel is summoned for help, and he ends up interpreting the "letter" from the "Correspondent," God:

> This is the interpretation of the thing: Mene: God hath numbered thy kingdom, and finished it. Tekel: Thou art weighed in the balances, and art found wanting. Peres: Thy kingdom is divided, and given to the Medes and Persians.

The three words written on the wall refer literally to three measures of weight: a mina, a shekel, and two half-minas. Daniel interprets the message by punning off these words: the first resembles a Hebraic verb meaning "numbered"; the second, "weighed"; and the third, "to divide." He uses these verbal puns to interpret the message as an accusation and a prophecy. And in the chapter's final lines the prophecy of punishment is indeed fulfilled: "In that night was Belshazzar the king of the Chaldeans slain. And Darius the Mede took the kingdom . . ." Here we have an interpretation made in the context of political oppression and presented as a consequence of the oppressor's moral iniquity: Israel had been conquered, the Jews enslaved, and now their religious vessels were desecrated. The reading of the wall-writing both advertises the king's crime and announces his punishment (see Buttrick 1952, 418–33).

It is possible that Dickinson meant her poem to serve as a similar announcement. Adding the inscription, "Suggested by our Neighbor," she sent it to her brother probably after the 1879 Lothrop scandal in Amherst. This local incident involved newspaper reports of a father's physical cruelty to his daughter and resulted in a libel suit filed against the *Springfield Republican* by Reverend C. D. Lothrop, the accused father. The court found against Lothrop on 15 April, and Dickinson may have been commemorating the occasion with this poem. From this biographical perspective, the poem refers to the judgment made by the court, which found Lothrop guilty of patriarchal oppression (see Johnson 1955, 1008–9; Leyda 1960, 245–50, 257–59).

More generally, Dickinson's poem takes the biblical tale and makes it into an allegory for the conscience "of us all," through which God points out and warns us about our sins, giving each of us our own private "letter." This allegorizing of the poem translates the literary text, which itself translates a biblical story into a poem. Just as the poem approximates—is directed toward—the biblical story, so too does my interpretation approximate the poem.

Now, there are various ways to take the question, What does interpretation approximate? and develop it into a *theory* of interpretation, a general account of how readers make sense of texts. For example, we could say that the words of my reading approximately translate those of the poem and that Daniel's words approximately translate those on the wall. Such a *formalist* theory could go on to claim that what determines our interpretations is what they approximate, the words on the page. A different theoretical approach argues that what is approximately translated—for example, by Dickinson's reader and by Daniel—is, ultimately, the author's intention. Such an *intentionalist* theory could go on to claim that interpretations are constrained by the intention behind or in the words. Dickinson in the poem and God in the letter intended a meaning that the interpreter must decipher to read the text correctly. Both formalist and intentionalist theories attempt to provide a foundation for constraining the interpretive relationship between reader and text. Often, such theories not only claim to *describe* how interpretation takes place but to *prescribe* how it should take place. These *foundationalist* theories present themselves as both general accounts of making sense and specific guides to correct interpretations. Later we will take up the issue of whether such theoretical guarantees work in actual interpretive practice.

2. Translating *How?*

Our second question moves away from the *object* of interpretation—the text and
its sense—to the *activity* of interpreting—the process of sense-making. In reading the Dickinson poem above, I provided two kinds of interpretive approaches,
both grounded in a theory of the author's intention: historicizing and allegorizing. In the former approach, I suggested that Dickinson intended to refer specifically to Rev. Lothrop getting a well-deserved public humiliation. In the latter, I
suggested that Dickinson intended a more universal message about the conscience of us all. It is not necessary to choose between these two complementary
meanings, but it is important to recognize the contrasting *methods* used to arrive
at these different interpretations. In historicizing I used a strategy of placing the
text in the historical context of its production. In allegorizing I followed a strategy that assumes poetry can refer to a second, more universal level of meaning
beyond its particular historical reference. These reading strategies or *interpretive
conventions* provide a way of describing the process of interpretation rather than
its textual object. They are ways of characterizing how interpretive translation
takes place. They emphasize what the reader contributes to interpretation rather
than what the text gives the reader to interpret.

We have now seen displayed several different strategies for interpreting texts.
For example, Daniel uses puns or verbal resemblances to read the writing on the
king's wall, and I earlier used etymologies to explore meanings for "interpretation" itself. Methods or strategies of making sense are associated with various
theories of how interpretation does or should take place. Above, I connected
historicizing and allegorizing a text's meaning with intentionalist theories of interpretation. Punning and etymologizing are as often associated with formalist
theories of interpretation as they are with intentionalist approaches. All these
strategies—historicizing, allegorizing, punning, and using etymologies—can be
restated as rules for correct interpretation. That is, certain interpretive conventions become in certain contexts the privileged way of making sense of texts.
Identifying puns may be acceptable for interpreting ancient and contemporary
graffiti but not for reading constitutions. Allegorizing may be appropriate for
poetry and scripture but not for international treaties. For these supposedly
more straightforward legal texts, theories of *neutral principles* are often proposed
as ways to guarantee that interpreters resist more literary methods of making
sense. Theories of neutral principles posit rules for guaranteeing correct interpretations, e.g., formalist rules for looking at "the words on the page" or intentionalist rules for respecting authorial purposes. These rules or interpretive principles are presented as neutral in the sense that they are viewed as capable of
being applied in a disinterested manner safe from personal idiosyncrasy or political bias. We will return below to questions about whether treaties are in fact
inherently more straightforward than literary texts and whether interpretive

theories can actually constrain readings or avoid political entanglements. But for now let us turn to our third question.

3. Acceptable *To Whom*?

We can begin with an episode from the *Adventures of Huckleberry Finn:* In chapter 15 of Mark Twain's novel, Huck, the boy narrator, and Jim, the runaway slave, are separated in the fog while traveling down the Mississippi River. In despair after a night-long search, Jim gives Huck up for dead and, exhausted, falls into a troubled sleep. Meanwhile, Huck finds his way back to the raft, and, after Jim awakes, Huck plays a rather insensitive trick on his companion, convincing him that the pain and horrors of the night before never really happened. It was all just a dream. Jim then says "he must start in and ''terpret' it, because it was sent as a warning." After Jim presents a wild translation of the dream that wasn't a dream, Huck tries to clinch the joke by responding: "Oh, well, that's all interpreted well enough, as far as it goes, Jim . . . but what does *these* things stand for?" as he points to the leaves, rubbish, and smashed oar, all evidence of the previous night's catastrophe. Now one way to view Jim's dream interpretation is to see it as a rather laughable misreading. This is Huck's view and the view he wants his readers to share so that they get the joke on Jim.

But Huck's request for another interpretation, not of the dream but of the proof that there was no dream, produces a more serious response that makes Huck's joke backfire.

> Jim looked at the trash, and then looked at me, and back at the trash . . . [H]e looked at me steady, without ever smiling, and says:
> "What do dey stan' for? I's gwyne to tell you. When I got all wore out wid work, en wid de callin' for you, en went to sleep, my heart wuz mos' broke bekase you wuz los', en I didn' k'yer no mo' what become er me en de raf'. En when I wake up en fine you back agin, all safe en soun', de tears come en I could a got down on my knees en kiss' yo' foot I's so thankful. En all you wuz thinkin 'bout wuz how you could make a fool uv ole Jim wid a lie. Dat truck dah is *trash;* en trash is what people is dat puts dirt on de head er dey fren's en makes 'em ashamed."

If we saw Jim's dream interpretation as a misreading, we certainly see nothing wrong with his allegorical reading of the trash. We get the point and so does Huck, as he writes that Jim then "got up slow, and walked to the wigwam, and went in there, without saying anything but that. But that was enough. It made me feel so mean I could almost kissed *his* foot to get him to take it back." Twain turns the incident into another episode in Huck's struggle with his racist upbringing when he has the boy write further: "It was fifteen minutes before I could work myself up to go and humble myself to a nigger—but I done it, and

I warn't ever sorry for it afterwards, neither." Interpreting this passage, readers recognize how Huck's apology undercuts his continuing racial prejudice, how his respect and affection for Jim work to undermine his society's ideology of white supremacy.

If you agree that Jim misread the "dream" but convincingly interpreted the "trash," if you agree with my reading of these readings and with my interpretation of the final passage, then we are agreeing on what to count as a *correct interpretation* for these various texts. Correct interpretations are those that are considered accurate, valid, acceptable. But acceptable to whom? One answer is suggested by another Dickinson poem:

> Much Madness is divinest Sense—
> To a discerning Eye—
> Much Sense—the starkest Madness—
> 'Tis the Majority
> In this, as All, prevail—
> Assent—and you are sane—
> Demur—you're straightway dangerous—
> And handled with a Chain—

This poem is about how correct interpretations are established, how sense-making is defined as right or wrong, sense or nonsense, sanity or madness. Read literally, it simply states that sense or meaning is in the eye of the beholder, rather than in the object beheld. The poem suggests further that the majority of interpreters determine what counts as sense. Of course, the point of the poem does not end there. Dickinson is not simply describing the conditions of "correct" interpreting—majority rules—but is sarcastically protesting against that fact. Thus the poem rewrites the question—To whom are correct interpretations acceptable?—as a problem about the politics of interpretation, about a reading's status within the power relations of a historical community. These questions point us away from the exchange between interpreter and text and toward that between interpreter and interpreter—that is, from the hermeneutic question of how text and reader interact to the *rhetorical* question of how interpreters interact with other interpreters in trying to argue for or against different meanings.

4. The Politics of Interpretation

As we move from foundationalist theories about reading texts to the rhetorical politics of interpretive disputes, we will not completely abandon the questions dealt with in the first three sections. In one sense, we will simply be broadening our area of concern. When we focus only on the text, an author's intention, or a reader's interpretive conventions, as we did in the first two sections, there is a strong tendency to view interpretation as a private reading experience involving only an independent text (and author) and an individual reader. Many foundationalist theories give in to this temptation and compound the mistake by completely ignoring the sociopolitical context in which interpretation takes place. By focusing now on interpretive rhetoric, we will see how interpretation is always a politically-interested act of persuasion.

In the cases of reading discussed earlier, I hinted at this politics of interpretation whenever I noted how an interpretive act took place within the context of power relations in a historical community. For example in section 1, we saw how Daniel's reading of the wall-writing functioned within a national situation of political oppression and then how Dickinson's poem translated this biblical story into a new context involving the politics of family and gender. In section 3, Jim's dream interpretation and Huck's reactions play a part in Mark Twain's commentary on the politics of race in nineteenth-century America. In each of these cases, interpretation takes place in a political context and each interpretive act relates directly to the power relations (whether of nation, family, gender, class, or race) involved in that context.

However, what is not quite as clear in these examples is how interpretation itself can be politically interested, how claims for a reading are always direct attempts to affect power relations through coercion or persuasion. These effects can be subtle and microscopic, as in cases where students ask a teacher to explain a line of poetry and she convinces them to accept a particular reading. The effects become more obvious when there are radical disagreements over interpretations, when the correct reading is in actual dispute. At such times, the least persuasive interpretation loses out. Indeed, in some extreme cases of interpretive controversy, Dickinson seems to be right:

> 'Tis the Majority
> In this, as All, prevail—
> Assent—and you are sane—
> Demur—you're straightway dangerous—
> And handled with a Chain—

Most situations involving interpretive disagreement do not result in such blatant suppression of dissent. However, a poem protesting a majority's tyranny over an individual dissenter does foreground what is always the case: any interpretive dispute involves political interests and consequences.

In my final example of reading a text, I will focus on a treaty debated in Congress, but the interpretive rhetoric used by the disputants here relates directly to that used by interpreters in an academic classroom or a religious meetinghouse. In different ways, reading treaties, explicating poems, and interpreting scripture all involve arguments over such topics as textual meaning, authorial intention, past readings, historical contexts, and interpretive methods. All involve the rhetorical politics of interpretation.

The following rhetorical analysis will refer back to issues discussed earlier and deliver on various promissory notes. We will see, for example, how some of the interpretive theories described above work in actual disputes over meaning. What I hope to demonstrate is that theories of interpretation function not so much as constraints on reading as resources for arguing. That is, formalist, intentionalist, and objectivist theories do not provide guarantees of correct interpretation or algorithms for resolving interpretive disputes. They simply make available to the disputants some additional rhetorical tactics for continuing the arguments over meaning.

In 1972 the United States Senate ratified the Anti-Ballistic Missile Treaty with the Soviet Union. This treaty contained a crucial provision as Article V (1): "Each Party undertakes not to develop, test, or deploy ABM systems or components which are sea-based, air-based, space-based, or mobile land-based." For thirteen years, through three administrations, this short text was interpreted not only as outlawing the militarization of space but as prohibiting even the *development and testing* of space-based ABM systems.

On March 23, 1983, President Ronald Reagan announced his Strategic Defense Initiative, a research and development program leading to a space-based, anti-ballistic missile system using laser technology. The president promised that this program would be "consistent with our obligations" under the ABM Treaty, but it soon became clear that at some future date development of "Star Wars" would bump up against the explicit constraints of the treaty. Nevertheless, the Reagan administration continued to uphold the traditional interpretation of Article V (1). For example, its *Fiscal Year 1985 Arms Control Impact Statements* (1984, 252) declared: "The ABM Treaty prohibition on development, testing, and deployment of space-based ABM systems, or components for such systems, applies to directed energy technology (or any other technology) used for this purpose. Thus, when such directed energy programs enter the field testing phase they become constrained by these ABM Treaty obligations."

This interpretation held throughout 1984 and most of 1985. Then on October 6, National Security Advisor Robert McFarlane offered a new reading of Article V (1). On "Meet the Press," McFarlane claimed that the treaty "approved and authorized" development and testing of space-based ABM systems "involving new physical concepts" including lasers or directed energy. Such a radical reinterpretation provoked immediate controversy. As one newspaper put it: "This startling pronouncement by a high official, almost a 180-degree reversal of the longstanding U.S. position on the treaty, was a shock to the ABM Treaty's negotiators and other arms control advocates, to U.S. allies in Europe and arms control minded members of Congress" (Oberdorfer 1985, A10).

Eight days later, Secretary of State George Shultz took up this new interpretation in a speech to the North Atlantic Assembly, a speech which clearly set out to create an opening for the revised reading: "The treaty can be variously interpreted as to what kinds of development and testing are permitted, particularly

with respect to future systems and components based on new physical principles." The traditional interpretation, once so obvious, was thus declared problematic, and room was immediately established for a new, less restrictive interpretation that allowed what had previously been prohibited: "It is our view,
based on a careful analysis of the treaty text and the negotiating record, that a
broader interpretation of our authority is fully justified." Out-of-laboratory testing of SDI technology would now fall outside the constraints of the ABM
Treaty. Having asserted the validity of this new interpretation, Shultz then attempted to distance its consequences from actual policy: That the "broader interpretation" is "fully justified" is "however, a moot point" because "our SDI
research program has been structured and, as the President has reaffirmed last
Friday, will continue to be conducted in accordance with a restrictive interpretation of the treaty's obligations" (Shultz 1985, 23).

This attempt to depoliticize the new interpretation, to separate simply reading
the text from political policy-making, did not satisfy the critics. On October 22
the House Subcommittee on Arms Control, International Security, and Science
convened to discuss the "ABM Treaty Interpretation Dispute." The record of
this hearing provides a useful context for analyzing the arguments supporting
the old and new, the "restrictive" and "broader" interpretations of Article V(1)
of the ABM Treaty and thus for "explaining" its reinterpretation. Only when
such a rhetorical analysis is done within the historical narrative I have outlined
can the hermeneutics of the argument become clear. We will see how appeals to
foundationalist theory fail to resolve the dispute and how theoretical appeals
function rhetorically within a specific political controversy.

The most outspoken administration representative at the hearing was Abraham Sofaer, legal advisor to the secretary of state. Following the rhetorical strategy of his boss, Sofaer began by questioning the obviousness of the traditional
interpretation: "My study of the [ABM] treaty led me to conclude that its language is ambiguous and can more reasonably be read to support a broader interpretation" (*ABM Treaty* 1986, 5). Noting that the "restrictive interpretation
rests on the premise that article V (1) is clear on its face," Sofaer suggested that
such a view ignores the document's ambiguities and proceeded to argue that a
broader interpretation was just as plausible and in fact more reasonable (*ABM
Treaty* 1986, 5). To establish good reasons for the broader interpretation, Sofaer
appealed to several hermeneutic criteria: the language of the document, the intentions of the negotiators, relevant canons of construction, and, surprisingly,
the postnegotiation tradition of interpreting the treaty.

The rhetorical effectiveness of these appeals depends upon the acceptability of
the relevant hermeneutic theories that constitute these sources as guides for correct interpreting. Thus, a formalist theory undergirds the appeal to the language
in the text; an intentionalist theory supports the study of the negotiator's mental
purposes; and a theory of neutral principles provides a rationale for legal canons

of construction. Although these theories are often developed as foundationalist accounts of interpreting, here we will see how they are best viewed as rhetorical resources rather than hermeneutic foundations in debates over interpretation.

Sofaer began his arguments with a formalist appeal, but it was not only the advocates of the broad reinterpretation who pointed directly to the text. So did the advocates of the restrictive interpretation: John Rhinelander, former legal advisor to the ABM Treaty negotiators, stated emphatically that *"the prohibitions are clear from the text of the Treaty,* particularly Article V (1)" (*ABM Treaty* 1986, 58); and similarly Leonard Meeker and Peter Didisheim, both of the Union of Concerned Scientists, claimed in a statement submitted to the subcommittee: "The ordinary meaning of the treaty's terms are [sic] self-evident. The Administration's argument that the treaty permits the development and field testing of [space-based] ABM weapons and components based on new physical principles cannot qualify as an interpretation 'in good faith'" (*ABM Treaty* 1986, 117). In contrast, Sofaer rejected any clear or self-evident meaning in the language and in his formalist argument produced ambiguity by reading various parts of the text against each other. Thus, he claimed that Agreed Statement D (negotiated at the time of the original treaty) suggests that Article II (1)'s definition of "ABM system" refers only to technology current in 1972, and therefore the prohibitions in Article V (1) do not constrain development and testing of systems based on future technology, such as that involved in SDI. Congressman Henry Hyde found this formalist appeal persuasive, declaring that "the plain intent of those English words leaps out at you" and noting, "There isn't much of a conflict as I see it here between the English language and the interpretation [Sofaer] found that fits within the four corners of this document" (*ABM Treaty* 1986, 25, 43).

Others, of course, were not so easily convinced, and the rhetorical ground soon shifted from formalist claims about the text to intentionalist arguments about the negotiating history. Sofaer announced this shift early in his interpretive argument: "Under international law, as under U.S. domestic law, once an agreement has been found ambiguous, one must seek guidance in the circumstances surrounding the drafting of the agreement. Thus, in the present situation, once we concluded that the treaty is ambiguous, we turned to the negotiating record to see which of the possible constructions most accurately reflects the parties' intentions" (*ABM Treaty* 1986, 7). This move toward the broader interpretation was questioned in two ways by the advocates of the restrictive reading. First, the rule invoked for guidance in interpretation immediately became the new occasion for interpretive controversy: Rhinelander declared that Sofaer's interpretation rested "on a new canon of construction, never before heard of, that the *unambiguous* text of a treaty should be distorted to give an agreed interpretation [Agreed Statement D] an independent and amendatory role" (*ABM Treaty* 1986, 173). Second, when Sofaer began filling in the intention behind the text, the new source for guidance marked out still another area of interpretive controversy: even if the negotiator's past intentions do have priority over the present words on the page, it still remains an issue what those intentions actually were.

The argument over the negotiators' original intentions becomes especially interesting when the negotiators themselves turn up on both sides of the dispute. Gerard Smith, former chief of the U.S. delegation to the ABM negotiations, criticized the administration's revisionism and remembered the negotiators' intentions as supporting the restrictive interpretation of Article V (1). In contrast, Paul Nitze, also a member of the original negotiating team and President Reagan's special advisor on arms control, strongly endorsed the administration's new, broader interpretation. Certainly an appeal to a ground of intention fails to resolve the interpretive dispute when the appeal ends up supporting both sides of the argument. The thoroughly rhetorical nature of the intentionalist "ground" became even more obvious in an exchange between Nitze and Congressman Lee Hamilton at the hearing:

> MR. HAMILTON: Ambassador Nitze, I am curious about your interpretation of this treaty through this 13-year period. If I understood you correctly a moment ago, and I may not have, you suggested that you have been persuaded by recent legal interpretation that the agreement says something that you didn't think it said at the time you participated in the crafting of the treaty; is that correct?
>
> MR. NITZE: That is approximately correct. I think the facts of the matter are that it is hard to recollect exactly what one thought at the time 13 years ago. I know that some time thereafter I was asked a question about the treaty which differs from what I now understand to be the negotiating record.
>
> MR. HAMILTON: Well, what then comes through to me is that for 13 years you at least, by your silence on this important point, have given us all the impression that this treaty is to be interpreted restrictively, but now you say that the lawyers have persuaded you that you reached an agreement that you didn't know you reached? (*ABM Treaty* 1986, 41).

This exchange demonstrates how establishing past intention, like construing present meaning, can depend crucially on specific acts of persuasion. The example seems so striking because the person persuaded to a different view of the past is the same person whose original intention is at issue!

But if the rhetoric of interpretation cannot be permanently grounded in the text, intention, or interpretive rules, perhaps the history of interpretations will serve. Ralph Earle, former director of the U.S. Arms Control and Disarmament Agency, suggested just this option at the hearing in defense of the traditional, restrictive interpretation: "It would be a unique episode in international negotiations to have a completely unambiguous record, especially in a bargaining process requiring 2½ years. But be that as it may, the 13-year record for the parties holding the original version [the restrictive interpretation] should carry far greater weight than some statements reportedly inconsistent with the final language of the Treaty" (*ABM Treaty* 1986, 23). Rhinelander developed this reception argument further by citing still another guiding principle: "the Vienna Convention on the Law of Treaties and the A[merican] L[aw] I[nstitute] Restatement of the Foreign Relations Law of the United States . . . stress the importance of subsequent *practice* in interpreting a treaty," and "[s]ubsequent practice, including statements, of *both* the US and the Soviets *reinforce* the historic [restrictive] interpretation of the ABM Treaty" (*ABM Treaty* 1986, 173). The turn to interpretive history, then, would seem to decide the matter: The restrictive interpretation has been the traditionally accepted (and thus privileged) reading of the treaty. After all, isn't there at least agreement that the administration's interpretation is in fact a new one?

Not so, says Sofaer: "We do not accept the premise that this administration is departing from a consistent record of 13 years of statements of the restrictive view" (*ABM Treaty* 1986, 40). In fact, the broader interpretation was not new but old, and the administration's view was not so much a reinterpretation as the remembering of a forgotten tradition. Indeed, Sofaer concluded his lengthy narrative of the treaty's past readings with this moral: "[T]he 'broad' view of the Treaty has as strong a basis as the 'restrictive' view for being called 'traditional' or accepted" (*ABM Treaty* 1986, 212). Rhinelander provided a detailed critique of Sofaer's interpretive history, but this leaves untouched the fact that Sofaer was still able to make that history an effective part of his case (for Rhinelander's critique, see *ABM Treaty* 1986, 186–99).

After all the rhetorical exchanges, the congressional hearing ended somewhere close to where it began: in radical disagreement over the interpretation of the ABM Treaty. The text is clear, one side claims; no it's not, replies the other. If the text is ambiguous, both rhetorical lines of reasoning suggest, then we can turn to the negotiating record. Still no resolution. Since this record of intentions is ambiguous, we can turn to the treaty's thirteen-year interpretive history. But even here both sides are able to appeal to that "same" history to support their antagonistic cases. No appeal to theories or principles resolves the dispute, for the theories themselves become the new sources of controversy, either because of their theoretical claims or their practical applications. Which theories are relevant to the interpretive dispute? How should a relevant theory's principles be interpreted before being applied? Once interpreted, how should the principles be applied to govern this case? If the relevant theory is apparent (say, intentionalism), if its principles are clear (discover the negotiators' original intentions), if the principles can then be applied (ask the negotiators and check the negotiating record), we are still left with the problem of interpreting and arguing over texts, recollections, histories.

It is in this sense that I want to claim that interpretive theories are not foundational but rhetorical, establishing no permanent grounding or guiding principles guaranteeing correct interpretation but certainly providing much rhetorical substance for interpretive debate. That this debate is political through and through is perhaps too obvious to require further mention, but the "ABM Treaty Interpretation Dispute" does thematize its politics more emphatically than most interpretive arguments. In defending the Reagan administration's reinterpretation of the treaty, Congressman Hyde accused the critics of mixing politics with simply reading the text: "You are seeing a lot of people who have little use for the SDI, and they are going to assert an interpretation of the ABM Treaty which obstructs development of that system" (*ABM Treaty* 1986, 43). One of these "obstructionists," Gerard Smith, raised similar questions from the other side, asking: "Why did the administration decide to float this new treaty version just 6 weeks before a summit at which the ABM Treaty was expected to be an important part? Was it an exercise in playing hard ball? A gesture of machismo? . . . Or was it a bargaining ploy looking to a summit accommodation somewhere between the Soviet presummit position of no research at all and the Reagan new version of no limits on strategic defense development?" (*ABM Treaty* 1986, 22). It has been the argument of this final section that textual interpretation and rhetorical politics can *never* be separated. Indeed, the failure of foundationalist theory is just another instance of how interpretions can have no grounding outside of rhetorical exchanges taking place within institutional and cultural politics. The Reagan administration's emphasis on a clear "distinction between a legal interpretation and a [governmental] policy" (*ABM Treaty* 1986, 19) is another example of a theoretical attempt to separate a textual interpretation from its context of rhetorical power. In this case, it is not only bad hermeneutics; it is also dangerous politics.

I want, if I can, to avoid one possible misunderstanding of my argument here. I am certainly *not* saying that it is impossible to disagree effectively with the Reagan administration's absurd reinterpretation of the ABM treaty. One does not, however, have to become a foundationalist theorist in order to do so. Instead, one simply and rigorously argues a counterinterpretation making such rhetorical moves as pointing to the text, citing the authors' intentions, noting the traditional reading, and invoking the consensus—just as the supporters of the restrictive interpretation did at the congressional hearing. However, such moves are just as politically interested as those of the State Department in that they are interested attempts to persuade an audience to interpret the ABM Treaty in an antimilitaristic way. And the resulting interpretation is just as contingent and open to further debate as the militaristic reading. To admit this contingency, to recognize the rhetorical politics of every interpretation, is not to avoid taking a position. Taking a position, making an interpretation, cannot be avoided. Moreover, such historical contingency does not disable interpretive argument, because it is truly the only ground it can have. We are always arguing at particular moments in specific places to certain audiences. Our beliefs and commitments are no less real because they are historical, and the same holds for our interpretations. If no foundationalist theory will resolve disagreements over poems or treaties, we must always argue our cases. In fact, that is all we can ever do.

SUGGESTED READINGS

Levinson, Sanford, and Steven Mailloux, eds. 1988. *Interpreting Law and Literature: A Hermeneutic Reader.*

Mailloux, Steven. 1982. *Interpretive Conventions: The Reader in the Study of American Fiction.*

Mitchell, W. J. T., ed. 1983. *The Politics of Interpretation.*

———. 1985. *Against Theory: Literary Studies and the New Pragmatism.*

Palmer, Richard E. 1969. *Hermeneutics: Interpretation Theory in Schleiermacher, Dilthey, Heidegger, and Gadamer.*

Rabinow, Paul, and William M. Sullivan, eds. 1979. *Interpretive Social Science: A Reader.*

Tompkins, Jane P., ed. 1980. *Reader-Response Criticism: From Formalism to Post-Structuralism.*

10

Intention

Annabel Patterson

"INTENTION" is one of the most challenging terms in literary semantics, not least because it refuses to remain within the confines of literary discourse. Indeed, it might well be argued that its primary function today as a technical term is within legal theory and discourse, where it has always been operative in criminal law, has a special importance in cases of libel, and has recently acquired new political prominence in the debates on the United States Constitution and its amendments. In criminal law intention is a concept intended to distinguish one "degree" of crime from another, by focusing on the component of deliberation or premeditation; but it is also a concept central to legal interpretation, in ways that overlap significantly with "literary" concerns and analysis.

An early and somewhat special case of libel tried before the Star Chamber in seventeenth-century England exemplified the way in which authorial intention could not protect a writer from having his work interpreted invidiously. In 1633 the Presbyterian reformer William Prynne was charged with "seditious libel" in the form of an oblique attack on the monarchy, for having published a lengthy denunciation of the stage and all theatricals, including those enjoyed or participated in by rulers in the historical past, such as the Roman emperor Nero. Because the current royal family were notoriously interested in court theatricals, the book, *Histriomastix* (1633), was taken to argue, "thoughe not in expresse tearmes, yet by examples and other implicite means . . . that for acteinge or beinge spectatours of playes or maskes it is just and lawfull to laye violent handes upon kinges and princes." When Prynne declared that he meant nothing of the kind, his Star Chamber judges delivered their verdict in intentionalist language that was paradigmatic of, if not actually serving as a precedent for, many subsequent legal arguments in the history of censorship:

> Itt is said, hee had noe ill intencion, noe ill harte, but hee maye bee ill interpreted. That must not be allowed him in excuse, for he should not have written any thinge that would bear [that] construccion, for hee doth not accompanye his booke, to make his intencion knowne to all that reades it. (Gardiner, [1877] 1965)

Once released into public territory, in other words, the text is inevitably subject to whatever interpretation seems most plausible to its readers, who will determine its meaning in the light of local circumstances.

Increasingly since the nineteenth century, *intention* has become an issue in the interpretation of law itself, as lawyers wrestle with the imprecision of language, with the texts of preceding legislators who are no longer available to say what they meant, and, within their own profession, with divergent concepts of law's permanence or, conversely, historical evolution. The desire of common lawyers to establish the "meaning" of a law by attempting to determine its author's intentions, or of Attorney General Edwin Meese to define and fix the American Constitution by reference to the intentions of its framers in 1787, runs counter to the practice in civil law of assuming that the meaning and application of law can change over time. It also opposes the position of Supreme Court Justice William Brennan that social progress since 1787 must be taken into account, and that constitutional theory requires the "adaptation of overarching principles to changes of social circumstance" (Brennan 1985).

As in Prynne's case, the constitutional debate is rich in literary implications. Justice Brennan observed that the constitution is, above all, a text in the sense that literary studies have privileged, that is to say, enigmatic:

> Like every text worth reading, it is not crystalline. The phrasing is broad and the limitations of its provisions are not clearly marked. Its majestic generalities and ennobling pronouncements are both luminous and obscure. This ambiguity of course calls forth interpretation, the interaction of reader and text.

While the Constitution differs from the usual range of literary texts in being inescapably public in its implications and in demanding from its professional readers an eventual decision ("Unlike literary critics, judges cannot merely savor the tensions or revel in the ambiguities inhering in the text—judges must resolve them" [2]), the contemporary debate over its meaning is an exceptionally clear paradigm of the vexed relationship between intention and interpretation. Inherent in Justice Brennan's distrust of the intentionalist approach is his recognition of the sheer difficulty of recovering authorial intentions from the past. From the records of the ratification debates, "all that can be gleaned is that the Framers themselves did not agree about the application or meaning of particular constitutional provisions, and hid their differences in cloaks of generality." The very concept of intention is problematic when the text in question is clearly not only public but communal: "It is far from clear whose intention is relevant—that of the drafters, the congressional disputants, or the ratifiers in the states" (4). And the problem of perspective is summed up in language to which many a literary critic, though facing merely a single author from the past, would assent: "our distance of two [or more] centuries cannot but work as a prism refracting all we perceive."

Yet while firmly discarding a facile historicism and a crude intentionalism, Justice Brennan clearly believes that the American Constitution *as a text* reveals certain intentions—to change society for the better—which in turn are not fixed by the circumstances of 1787 but are principles capable of extension to later developments (including the abolition of slavery) whose occurrence could not have been anticipated at the time. This compromise, by no means free of internal contradictions, allows the historical circumstances of the Revolution to have a certain influence over interpretation, but by no means to fix or limit possible meanings. And Justice Brennan is clearly aware that his reading of the Constitution is also subjective, in the sense that it is shaped by values and beliefs *already* endorsed by the reader. The speech concludes with the claim that capital punishment is the greatest instance of the "cruel and unusual punishment to which the Eighth Amendment was directed, and that opposition to capital punishment is consistent with the amendment's "essential meaning"; yet this interpretation has been rejected by the majority in the Supreme Court and in the country at large. Justice Brennan knows himself, on this issue, to be in a quixotic minority; but his rhetoric balances the appeal to "essential meaning," with its implications of absolute or agreed-on truth, with the limiting and personal caveat: "As I interpret the Constitution" (Brennan 1985, 14–16).

Embedded in this contemporary legal controversy, then, are some of the central terms and contradictions that have structured the literary controversy over intention. But before turning to that cause célèbre, which became so confusing that many critics have abandoned it as an insoluble problem, we should take note of other arenas in which intention operates promiscuously as a technical term. These too, though they may initially deflect us, can equally illuminate literary practice by revealing the paternity of some of the ideas deployed in the literary arguments. There is, for instance, the philosophical tradition. A student who appeals to a library catalogue for assistance may find herself entangled in accounts of intention and intentionality that have become the province of logicians and analytic philosophers. There is, first, the highly specialized use of the term in phenomenology, or theories of perception, especially in the work of Edmund Husserl, who used "intention" to denote, roughly, the relation between an act of perception and the real object perceived. Although attempts are sometimes made to blend this usage with literary theories of intention, intelligibility is better served by simply observing that the two usages are quite distinct.

Philosophy also provides, however, an action-oriented account of intention. The deep and unanswerable question as to how human intentions are related to human actions, which in earlier cultures was considered under the auspices of metaphysics and religion, and gave rise to concepts of fate, providence, free will,

predestination, and the like, is now, as in Elizabeth Anscombe's classic mono-
graph *Intention* (1957), considered as a problem of how intentions to act are
expressed and whether they can be validated (by the rules of logic) by what follows their utterance. While distantly related to intentionalism in criminal justice,
an act-oriented approach has also established connections with a text-oriented
or interpretive one, in part by the intervention of speech-act theory, a branch of
logic that argued that certain utterances, whether written or spoken, are actually
acts, or possessed "illocutionary force." Speech act theory, introduced by J. L.
Austin's *How to Do Things with Words* (1962) was quite influential in the 1960s,
and made considerable incursions into literary theory. It reminded us, especially,
how vital to any successful act of communication are the interpretive conventions that govern it, and to which (to some degree intentionally) all parties to
the act of communication must agree. While Austin himself excluded literary
communications from the category of speech acts, as being non-serious or as
pretenses from which no action follows, others have subsequently felt that the
line between "real" and "literary" communications cannot be so sharply drawn.
It seems clear that the speech act of promising, for example, is logically indistinguishable from that of declaring one's intention, through the invocation of a
Muse, to deliver an epic poem.

Art history has its own considerable literature on intention, deriving more
immediately from classical problems in aesthetics. From the standpoint of aesthetics, the kind of questions that have been traditionally asked about intention
are those genially parodied by James Joyce in *A Portrait of the Artist as a Young
Man:* "If a man . . . hacking in fury at a block of wood . . . make there an image
of a cow, is that image a work of art? If not, why not?" (Joyce 1968, 214). In
other words, is it possible for a work of art to be created accidentally, without
the artist's intention to create it? One of the oldest art-history texts, Pliny's *Natural History,* approaches this problem empirically by recording several anecdotes
of artistic effects achieved by accident, as when the painter Protogenes, having
tried in vain to reproduce the effect of foam on the mouth of a hound, threw his
brush in rage at the picture, and achieved by a momentary lack of control what
hours of effort had failed to accomplish.

The non-empirical or theoretical version of this question focuses on the preconception or *idea* of the artefact that, for Plato and Aristotle and all subsequent
idealist aesthetics, exists in the artist's mind before he begins the physical act of
creativity; and the more idealist the aesthetics the more value is placed on the
intention (because spiritual or intellectual), as compared to the merely physical
product, which is conceived as inevitably an inadequate expression of its idea.
This concept too is represented in Stephen Dedalus's interest in "that mysterious
instant" of temporary incandescence ("like a fading coal") when "the esthetic
image is first conceived" (Joyce 1968, 213), a moment that Joyce found privi-

leged in Romantic aesthetics generally, and specifically in Shelley's *Defence of Poetry*.

An idealist aesthetics, whether classical or Romantic, usually presumes that the status of the artefact as art is self-evident. Such a view, by definition unexaminable, tends to be expressed in the language of tautology, as when Joyce, again, has Stephen discourse on the artefact's *quidditas* or "whatness," which he can only define by invoking additional learned abstractions—*integritas, consonantia,* and *claritas*. Precisely because art history, however, has as its primary task the description and assessment of a vast assembly of artefacts from various periods whose status as art is *not* self-evident, and whose differences speak rather to changing tastes and standards, the idealist conception of intention as preconception or inward form is often replaced by one that stresses the external conditions or terms of reference a particular artist would have used both to situate and to assert himself within the dominant artistic conventions of his time. These include the religious purposes presupposed by Byzantine mosaics or Gothic cathedral sculpture, the patronage structures of Renaissance Europe that both supported its artists and dictated the forms their work would take, the constraints of the physical media (such as stretched canvas) against which, by custom, an artist had to measure his skills, the differences between art designed for or appropriated by a community or private ownership, and the ideologies of particular "movements" or fashions such as Expressionism, Futurism, or Minimalism. Insofar as anyone, in the historical periods in which these conditions or conventions operated, entertained artistic intentions in the broadest sense (to be an artist) he must also have intended to operate within, or to push against, those conventions. It is theoretically possible, therefore, to recognize between the norms of artistic practice and its social evaluation (norms which are constantly changing) and the unique practice of any individual artist (unique in the limited sense of being specific to him) yet another category of intention, that which can after the event be recognized as the degree to which he *differs* from his contemporaries, as Manet from Monet, or Cézanne from van Gogh.

To raise the name of van Gogh is, of course, to raise another problem concerning intention with which art history does not usually concern itself; that is to say, subrational intentions that are subversive of or decisively alter the rational ones. After the event, it is impossible for viewers of van Gogh's late paintings not to feel that the sliced-off ear, the suicide, and the whirling landscapes are exceptionally strong instances of impulses that required expression at least as much as any Platonic preconception, and that, while certainly not equivalent to "hacking in fury at a block of wood," produced powerful works of art by a special form of inadvertence. Clearly, this aspect of artistic production is found equally in literary artefacts, with or without the benefit of clinical insanity. Since Sigmund Freud delivered the unconscious for rational analysis, and even more since the writings of Freud have themselves become texts to be interpreted, literary critics have been made uneasily or joyously aware that what we say is not always what we "really" mean, if reality is to be posited in the deep structure of the psyche rather than in explicit utterances.

Given the large issues, then, to which "intention" as a term and concept is related beyond the confines of literary criticism and theory, what has happened within those confines becomes more intelligible. It is best to begin not with what many believe to be the originating document in the controversy, the famous essay by W. K. Wimsatt and M. C. Beardsley on "The Intentional Fallacy," first published in 1946 in the *Sewanee Review,* but rather with a document that finely illustrates, by its similarity to the present project, our need for constant revision. The document in question is the 1965 essay on "Intention" written for the *Princeton Encyclopedia of Poetry and Poetics* (the article was written by R. W. Stallman, the author of several previous essays on intention, including a chapter in his *Critic's Notebook* [1950]); and it offers a manifesto, already at the moment of its appearance in danger of supplantation, for the New Criticism and for the theory of autonomous art:

> Once the work is produced it possesses objective status—it exists independently of the author and of his declared intention. It contains, insofar as it is a work of art, the reason why it is thus and not otherwise. The difference between art and its germinal event is absolute. The best artist constructs his work in such a way as to admit of no interpretation but the single intended one; its single intention being a single effect, one over-all meaning, one composite theme. All parts of the work of art are, *ideally,* relevant or functional to the whole. Irrelevant to the objective status of the work as art are criteria which dissolve the work back into the historical or psychological or creative process from which it came. . . . No judgement of intention has relevancy unless corroborated by the work itself, in which case it is supererogatory.

What defines this definition is, first, its own manifestly *regulatory* intentions, and, second, its idealist aesthetics (confirmed by the presence of *ideally*) which derive immediately from New Criticism's version of Modernist aesthetics but hark back in their tautological structure to the doctrine of artistic *quidditas* ("It contains, insofar as it is a work of art, the reason why it is thus and not otherwise").

It is striking to compare this document of American academic thought in the mid-1960s with the far more exploratory and, in its own terms, subversive essay produced by Wimsatt and Beardsley. Having themselves begun with a dictionary article on the subject of intention, but finding the genre constraining, they turned to the more expansive form of an essay to situate the problem in their own local culture. They needed, they felt, to formulate a theoretical opposition to the Romantic aesthetics that Modernist poetics had rendered obsolete. Somewhat oddly, they defined Romantic aesthetics by citing the positions of Goethe and Croce, and by focusing on the *evaluative* aspect of their thought, in which they claimed, intention was an overprivileged category. According to Wimsatt and Beardsley, Goethe and Croce had agreed that the value of an artefact was determined by, first, recovering the design or plan that preceded it and, second, by inquiring how far the artist had accomplished his design. While granting that a poem does not come into existence by accident, Wimsatt and Beardsley were not prepared to grant that the author's intention should serve as a *standard* by which to judge the performance. They wished, rather, to claim the evaluative function as a monopoly for the critic, whose role was currently being redefined and reemphasized as part of an emergent new discipline, the academic and professionalized study of English Literature.

But there was another, less spoken agenda in "The Intentional Fallacy." Without specifically addressing it, they were also reacting against the emphasis on subjectivity inherited from Romanticism. Wimsatt and Beardsley wished to establish a doctrine of critical impersonality, disassociating its procedures from those of literary biography, its concerns from those of psychology, and authorial voice from the notion of the *persona* or speaker in a lyric poem, which is therefore designated not an expression of its author's feelings but a dramatic utterance. In place of the concept of authorial responsibility for or ownership of a poem's meaning (a kind of intellectual copyright) Wimsatt and Beardsley claimed (like Prynne's judges) that any text, once published, is publicly owned; a statement that, when applied to poetry, in effect meant released into the custody of critics. The entire essay assumed that public and objective standards of evaluation were at least conceivable, and were more likely to be arrived at if the author's subjectivity was kept as far as possible out of the picture. The problem of the *critic's* subjectivity and how it might be substituted (or mistaken) for public standards (a question that Justice Brennan partially registered) went unconsidered.

There were other implications in the essay that were extremely influential: poetry was defined as "a feat of style by which a complex of meaning is handled all at once" (2). By "all at once" Wimsatt and Beardsley did not presumably mean simultaneity so much as coherence or unity, a concept as traditional in aesthetics as the emphasis on authorial design they rejected. But it was now connected to a second definition of the successful poem as one from which "what is irrelevant has been excluded" (2). And while the doctrine of relevance was initially posed as a semantic alternative, it seems, to the older vocabulary of unity, harmony, and so on, it came for admirers of "The Intentional Fallacy" to serve as a principle of exclusion of other interpretive methods. Thus, as a glance back will show, the *Princeton Encyclopedia* uses the term in two quite different senses, and designates as "[i]rrelevant to the objective status of the work as art criteria which dissolve [it] back into the historical or psychological or creative process from which it came."

In sum, Wimsatt and Beardsley were, despite beginning with a series of "axioms," somewhat less regulatory in their own intentions than some of their followers. It is important to remember that the initial focus of their argument was (a) evaluative and (b) specifically directed to poetry, especially lyric poetry, restrictions upon their theory which, while not stated as restrictions, gave their views as originally stated more plausibility than when they were extended to a general anti-intentionalism in literary studies. They were explicit about the relation of their endeavor to the poetry contemporary with themselves, whose allusiveness, epitomized by T. S. Eliot's *The Waste Land* and its authorial notes, seemed to require some rethinking of critical procedures, of the relation of what was internal to the text to what was outside or precedent to it. And they were certainly acute in recognizing that the concept of intention formed a crucial theoretical node in their discipline, entailing "many specific truths about inspiration, authenticity, biography, literary history and scholarship" (1). "There is hardly," they averred in their opening paragraph, "a problem of literary criticism in which the critic's approach will not be qualified by his view of 'intention'" (1). What they did *not* do, and what was subsequently done to their argument, with disastrous results for its intelligibility, was to extend their axioms about evaluation to interpretation. While the word "meaning" appears from time to time in their essay and its subsequent published clarifications, it is not central to the problematic they thought they faced; they defined it as a problem in aesthetics, not in hermeneutics.

That the shift occurred was perhaps inevitable, in view of the changed function of criticism itself. If evaluation was the primary task of the critic, as Alexander Pope understood it in his *Essay on Criticism* in the early eighteenth century, by the middle of the twentieth century, and largely thanks to the New Criticism, with its preference for *difficulty* in poetry, the critical task was primarily that of detailed exegesis. The question of intentionality was therefore transferred to the problem of whether authorial intention could or should be invoked as a tool in the task of meaning's excavation. One particularly aggressive critique of "The Intentional Fallacy" actually argued (with seemingly unintentional irony) that its authors had not meant what they said. Rather, "what they intended to say" was that "biographical data about an author, particularly concerning his intentions" is an undesirable ingredient of interpretation. But the most strenuous response to this shift in the application of anti-intentionalism was delivered by E. D. Hirsch, whose *Validity in Interpretation* appeared in 1967, just two years after the *Princeton Encyclopedia* had attempted to establish the Wimsatt/Beardsley position. While Hirsch distinguished between the evaluative focus of the original formulation, and the "popular version which consists in the false and facile dogma that what an author intended is irrelevant to the meaning of his text"

(11–12), he grasped that what was common to both the evaluative and the interpretive versions of anti-intentionalism was a depersonalization of literature, a program mounted initially by Eliot, Pound, and their followers. Against this agenda Hirsch mounted his own "Defense of the Author" (the title of his introductory remarks), as part of his commonsense conclusion that all interpretation "is the construction of *another's* meaning" (244). But he also took his stand for the possibility of *objective* interpretation, a notion that is subject to some of the same problems as Wimsatt's and Beardsley's belief in objective standards of evaluation. The self-contradictions inherent in Justice Brennan's account of constitutional exegesis were here writ large, large in the sense that what had been for Wimsatt and Beardsley an interesting problem in how to talk about certain types of modern poetry became, in *Validity in Interpretation,* a major exercise in literary *theory;* that is to say, an argument conducted as much by recourse to philosophers (Husserl and Heidegger as philosophers of consciousness, Saussure as a philosopher of language, Schleiermacher, Dilthey and Gadamer as hermeneuticists in the German tradition) as by discussions of how literary texts seem to work for and on their readers.

Hirsch's book was therefore transitional in more ways than one between Modernist and postmodernist views of critical method. In literary studies this phase has been most clearly marked by a destabilizing of the concept "literature," with the replacement of the ideal of criticism by that of "theory," of raising the problems of interpretation to a more philosophical level of abstraction. In this environment, the concept of authorial intention has come in for a new and potent form of disesteem, as a result of the convergence of a number of disparate attacks on the related ideas of human subjectivity, of selfhood, of the individual as a locus of subjectivity or an (even partially) free agent capable of having intentions, and hence on the very idea of authorship. Freud contributed to this undermining of the self by dividing it into different psychic functions, and Marx and his more structuralist followers such as Louis Althusser attacked the notion of the individual as a product of bourgeois false consciousness. But possibly the clearest statements of the new dogma in its postmodern form came from Michel Foucault, who devoted much of his *Archeology of Knowledge* to outlawing all approaches to texts that were ordered by any notion of an author, of an origin, of an *oeuvre,* of "another's meaning," to use Hirsch's phrase. In place of the idea of autonomous art promoted by Modernism and and the New Criticism, Foucault was central in promoting that of *anonymous discourse.* "Discourse," we are told, "is not the majestically unfolding manifestation of a thinking, knowing, speaking subject, but, on the contrary, a totality, in which the dispersion of the subject and his discontinuity with himself may be determined":

> The analysis of statements operates therefore without reference to
> a cogito. It does not pose the question of the speaking subject,

who reveals or who conceals himself in what he says, who, in speaking, exercises his sovereign freedom, or who, without realizing it, subjects himself to constraints of which he is only dimly aware. In fact, it is situated at the level of the "it is said" (*on dit*).

The *on dit* was clearly a stage further towards impersonality than the New Critical conception of the poetic speaker or persona; and lest he be taken to be reinstating the old discredited teleology of Hegel, in which history itself might be said to have intentions that are worked out through human behavior, Foucault adds that "we must not understand by it a great anonymous voice that must, of necessity, speak through the discourses of everyone" (Foucault 1972, 55, 122).

The *Archeology of Knowledge* was first published in France in 1969. It has obvious affiliations with the advent of deconstruction, inaugurated by Derrida's *De la grammatologie* (1967), whose complex attack on ideas of origin and certain or grounded meaning transferred the problem of intention to the territory of metaphysics. Between them, Foucault and Derrida gave anti-intentionalism a philosophical prestige that the literary-critical version never acquired, not least because of its own confused origins (in both aesthetics and hermeneutics) and the tendency of both its advocates and its antagonists to concentrate on counterexamples or flaws in the arguments of the opposing party. At least part of the attraction of Foucault's theory of anonymous discourse must have been that it disposed, in one fell swoop, of the problem of irony and parody, of authorial changes of mind or self-contradiction, of the endless distinctions between actual and implied authors, between persons, makers, masks, and mythologized self-representations, between verbal meaning and textual meaning, *langue* and *parole*, between meaning and significance, between conscious and unconscious, illocutionary and perlocutionary intentions, and between intentions, motives, and purposes. For along with its impersonality, Foucaultian analysis was resolutely anti-hermeneuticist, in the sense that it denied that the task of the cultural archeologist was to find the meanings that originating authors had hidden in their writings, an approach to reading that Foucault denoted allegorical.

But to eliminate problems is not to solve them. Iconoclasm, by virtue of its own extremism, makes visible the tendencies and consequences of related but less absolutely stated positions. Foucault was, also, more successful in doing the preliminary "negative work" he deemed necessary before reconstituting the study of language and culture than in devising more satisfactory procedures for such a study; while the logical conclusion to which he and other postmodern thinkers had brought the Modernist conception of "the text" runs counter, some might say, to the "natural" way to read. It is undeniable that literary critics and theorists do not publish their essays anonymously, and that their own intentions are part of the complex structure of professional practice that contributes to the meaning of the positions they take. It is difficult to see why Foucault's work should be read as an *oeuvre,* for instance, with the earlier work forgiven as only a preliminary and inadequate formulation (or ironically taken back by the author himself), when the same privilege is denied to a seventeenth-century poet or a nineteenth-century novelist.

And even among deconstructive critics the suspicion lurks that intention cannot so easily be banished, that it constantly defeats the most sophisticated attempts to bracket meaning, to "explode the myth of semantic correspondence between sign and referent," to free criticism from the task of paraphrase for the seemingly more "advanced" investigations of deconstruction, and to undermine the traditional value judgment of our critical discourse, "the metaphors of primacy, of genetic history, and . . . of the autonomous will to power of the self." Paul de Man, to whose *Allegories of Reading* these phrases are introductory, concluded an intricate reading of Proust with a still more intricate admission, that the deconstructive impulse is sometimes defeated by an intentionalism built into the very structure of our languages:

> Even if we free ourselves of all false questions of intent and rightfully reduce the narrator to the status of a mere grammatical pronoun, without which the narration could not come into being, the subject remains endowed with a function that is not grammatical but rhetorical, in that it gives voice, so to speak, to a grammatical syntagm. The term *voice,* even when used in a grammatical terminology . . . is, of course, a metaphor inferring by analogy the intent of the subject from the structure of the predicate. (de Man 1979, 6, 16, 18)

More profoundly, de Man here recognized that if deconstruction is "the recognition of the systematic character of a certain kind of error, then it would be fully dependent on the prior existence of this error." The concept of genesis or origin reappears at the end of the long circle of reasoning. "Philosophers of science like Bachelard or Wittgenstein are notoriously dependent on the aberrations of the poets," and by deconstructing Proust's text de Man was only, by his own admission, "trying to come closer to being as rigorous a reader as the author had to be in order to write the sentence in the first place" (17).

If, then, we have indeed come full circle, any attempt to define *intention* and its function for the literary studies of the near future should be no less humble than de Man's. While recognizing that our own conclusions are of less significance than those legal and constitutional issues to which they are related, we should take some comfort from the thought, not that we are not expected to make up our own minds, but that we are not required to be *regulatory* on the subject. It is surprising how often past discussions of intention have promulgated axioms, rules, and even prohibitions. Poets may or may not be the unacknowledged legislators of mankind; but critics and theorists are notoriously bad at drafting acceptable legislation. Common sense might argue that each literary case is different, as in art history a Jackson Pollock requires a different approach to intention than a Giotto or a van Gogh; and as even this brief essay has indicated, much of the heat generated by the intentionalist controversy could have been avoided if the participants had observed the semantic distinctions between different uses of "intention" as a term. Most important, we can now recognize how much of the anti-intentionalism of the past four decades had its origin in local circumstances, in response to changes in the cultural environment, and from the force of professional self-interest in the self-propagation of Modernism in the arts and of literary criticism as a professional discipline. Historical perspective alone would therefore suggest that positions on literary intention in the next decade will show the same degree of shift away from formalism and towards the history and theory of culture that is currently perceptible in literary studies in general. How long that shift will last will depend on the richness of the analysis—the quality and quantity of new insight into both the creative and the critical process—that deregulation may encourage.

SUGGESTED READING

Newton-de Molina, David. 1976. *On Literary Intention*.

11

Unconscious

Françoise Meltzer

THE DIFFICULTY with this term is so great that it is already in the title of this essay. If the title read "The Unconscious," then the term would be a noun—a substantive, a *thing*. But there is a good deal of controversy about this, and many argue that the unconscious is never a thing, nor a place, and that the term can therefore only be used as an adjective: for example, "unconscious activity" (but never "the activity of the unconscious").

Similarly complex is the fact that to be "unconscious" can mean all sorts of things—anything from being asleep, to being in ignorance of something, to being in a coma, to having a certain kind of innocence, and so on. The way that the term will interest us here, however, is in its psychological sense: the idea that an individual has within him activities of which he is not aware. But in this statement, too, we run up against the two central questions concerning any notion of "unconscious": (1) Is the unconscious a place or is it the activity of certain forces in the psyche and therefore not an "it" at all but rather a "how"? and (2) How can the existence of "unconscious" be ascertained in the first place since "it" is by definition something of which we are not aware? Both of these questions should be kept in mind as this essay progresses. At times we will be referring to "unconscious" as "it" (the word Freud actually uses in German to refer to unconscious means, in fact, "it"—*das Es*), but it must be stressed that such a usage stems from a syntactic difficulty and is not meant to imply that the unconscious is always a thing—or indeed, perhaps ever one.

Although we are proceeding here with the psychological sense of the term, that which is unconscious has been a problem for philosophy from the beginning. Human beings have always talked of "dark powers" forcing them to do things they did not intend; making them embark upon hopeless or incomprehensible missions in spite of themselves. Most religions are grounded in some notion of invisible powers in which one nevertheless believes, as are many myths. The idea of the unknown or unknowable in the mind of humankind is not a new one, and the concept of an unconscious can be made to dovetail nicely with certain theological beliefs.

147

Socrates had declared some knowledge hidden, "undetected by the soul," and his method itself is described as *maieutic*—a bringing forth, in the manner of a midwife, of latent ideas or memories into consciousness. Plato, Aristotle, Plotinus, Augustine, and Aquinas, to name a few, all concerned themselves with aspects of human thought that are dormant and cannnot be brought voluntarily to consciousness. But it was Descartes who made the statement against which what was to become psychoanalysis defined itself, for the French philosopher declared awareness to be one and the same as the mind: "By the term *conscious experience (cogitationis)* I understand everything that takes place within ourselves so that we are aware of it" (Ricoeur 1974, 101). This notion that everything mental is conscious, this certainty, is precisely what will be rejected by psychoanalysis, which will hold, on the contrary, that much that is mental remains hidden from us. But it should also be remembered that Descartes' famous dualism—the cleavage he makes between body and mind—will be inherited to a large degree by future methods of thought, including psychoanalysis. Psychology (the general science of the psyche which existed well before Freud invented what he called "psycho-analysis") takes this Cartesian dualism to posit a dual model of mind: the part which is known, and the part which is not. Descartes, in other words, is not as far removed from psychoanalysis as some would have us believe.

In the nineteenth century, then, there is a surge of renewed interest in that which is unknown in the mind, the "dark side." Rousseau, Goethe, Hegel, Schelling, Coleridge, the early German Romantics as a group, all refer to something "unconscious," although they do not necessarily use the term itself. As has often been pointed out, Schopenhauer's notion of the "Will" as an unbridled, ubiquitous, and ineluctable force, is similar to what we now call "the unconscious." Such a notion is found again in Nietzsche, who probably had more of an effect on Sigmund Freud than the latter was ever willing to admit.

The term "unconscious" already concerns philosophy, literature, psychology, and theology. It became a very popular concept in all of Western Europe with the publication, in 1868, of Eduard von Hartmann's *Philosophy of the Unconscious*. In the 1870s, there were at least a half-dozen books with the word "unconscious" in their titles. Freud certainly invented neither the term nor the concept(s) of the unconscious. He spoke of it at a time when every cultured European was familiar with the word and, to a large degree, accepted its validity as a concept. Why do we then sense, especially in Freud's early writings, the fear that the unconscious will be unacceptable to Freud's readers? The only answer can be that, at the height of a Victorian age, Freud took a popular idea and declared it to be an inherently *sexual* one. This was a particularly vulnerable stance to assume because of the very definition of "unconscious": that which, as the philosopher Paul Ricoeur puts it, cannot exist except in relation to some notion of what *consciousness* is. Ricoeur notes that the unconscious is something that cannot be pointed at; it can only be "diagnosed," since its existence cannot be empirically ascertained. That is, the unconscious is by definition unseeable; its existence is inferred (rather than empirically demonstrated) by occurrences in life which are not consciously motivated. The idea of the unconscious therefore partakes of a type of transcendental idealism in Kant's sense: it is one way in which we talk about that which we are not given to know. To declare this unknowable to be sexual at its foundations is a provocative statement which is doubly open for attack because it cannot be substantiated. Freud's trouble (his fears were justified) stemmed then from his characterization of an abstract notion as inherently sexual, an unpopular view which he was unable to support except by speculation and by the existence of elements in daily life that are unexplained by consciousness: dreams, slips of the tongue, puns, amnesia, compulsions to repeat, denials, and, most significantly here, literature. But before we embark upon the way in which literature works for Freud, and for psychoanalysis, let us look more closely at Freud's actual presentation of his favorite notion, the unconscious.

Ricoeur's comment cited above has pointed to another difficulty: no understanding of the unconscious can exist without a concomitant definition of what is meant by "conscious." In other words, the irony is that the unconscious can only be described in, or understood in, the realm and the rules of "consciousness." Or, to put it another way: the unknowable is forever condemned to being described in terms of the known. (It should be noted here that Freud's term for the unconscious is *das Unbewusste,* literally, "the unknown." The relation to knowledge is less explicit in the English term.) The importance of this fact, that the unknowable is condemned to being understood in terms of the known, is the point at which psychoanalysis meets literary theory. For Freud will be "condemned" to describe the unconscious rhetorically, through analogies, metaphors, similes, etymological play, and anecdotes. And the way that future critical theory will choose to read those rhetorical tropes employed by Freud will ultimately, it will argue, tell us as much about the "economy" of rhetorical structures and the inner workings of narration as it will about the psyche.

Freud will also describe the unconscious as making itself manifest through "gaps"—unintended lapses in memory, slips of the tongue, puns and dreams, as just noted. Already, we have the implication that the unconscious is alogical and nonlinear, while consciousness is the converse of these. Put another way, we might say that the existence of the unconscious is inferred from what emerges at times in speech as non-sensical or as unintentionally *too* sensical. Such "characterizations" are not without importance, it should be clear, to problems of narrative and story-telling. But we will return to these considerations.

When Freud begins to talk of the unconscious, as we have said, he is forced to discuss consciousness as well. His first important paper on the subject is "A Note on the Unconscious in Psycho-Analysis" (1912). There, Freud divides the unconscious into three types: the *descriptive,* the *dynamic,* and the *systematic.* The descriptive unconscious is presented in the following way: that which is present in our minds is *conscious* (having a conversation); that which is not present but retrievable in memory is *preconscious* (the date I was born); and that which is latent and not retrievable by any act of conscious will is *unconscious* (a childhood fear which has been repressed). It will be noted that the descriptive unconscious lends itself to notions of cartography, and is indeed based upon Freud's "topographical" model of the mind.

$$\frac{\text{CS}}{\text{UCS}} \longleftarrow \frac{\text{(consciousness)}}{\text{(unconscious)}} \text{ (repression barrier)}$$

This model will motivate the "topographic" metaphors found throughout Freud's writings: spatial notions of place and of "layers" in the mind. It is when Freud is alluding to the "descriptive" unconscious (which will henceforth in this essay be synonymous with the "topographic") that we get metaphors such as "regions of the mind," "map of the mind," "uncharted terrain," "unknown regions," the dream as the "royal road to the unconscious," and the unconscious itself as an antechamber leading to a sitting room (consciousness) which is carefully guarded by a sentry (the sentry is the personification of the repression barrier—the barrier that refuses unconscious thoughts entry into consciousness). In addition, it is in the discussion of this descriptive unconscious that Freud gives us a model such as the "mystic writing pad," a child's toy for writing and erasing which serves as an analogy for the mind and memory. In all of these metaphors and similes, the emphasis is on the spatial, almost as if there were a geography of the mind, with the unconscious lying as an area within it (indeed, in his earlier work, Freud tries to *locate* the unconscious in the psyche—see Freud 1951, 1:283–93). This notion of the unconscious, then, sees it as something close to being a "thing" or a "place." Here, the unconscious is a noun. The descriptive, or topographic unconscious, is the place of memories, thoughts, wishes, fears, and dreams. It can be defined as that which is absent from consciousness.

The *dynamic* unconscious is more of an energy flow than a "place." Freud, it should be kept in mind, began his work in the latter part of the nineteenth century and was very much a product of that period's notions of neurology and physiology. The reflex arc (for example: the involuntary jerk of the leg when the knee is struck) was Freud's model for human neurology: tension builds up and needs to be released, and this release is an involuntary action. Such a model has often been called "hydraulic" by critics, because the assumption is that stasis is pleasure and tension displeasure, which must find an outlet (so too, water seeks its own level, and will build up pressure if unable to find release). There are times, then, when Freud views the unconscious as a series of involuntary reflexes and an ebbing and flowing of energies. It is as if the unconscious were a throbbing energy center, active and busy, but hidden from the Subject's conscious mind. In other words, this model stresses that unconscious energy goes unperceived by the Subject; that just because the Subject is unaware that something exists does not mean that it doesn't (it is here that psychoanalysis refutes Descartes' assertion that all mental activity is conscious). Things can be going on in the psyche without the Subject having any knowledge of it. Freud's proof for this thesis is to point to what happens with a suggestion made to a Subject under hypnosis. The suggestion is carried out in a conscious, posthypnotic state, but without the Subject knowing why he is behaving as he is. For Freud, such posthypnotic behavior, for which the Subject has no conscious explanation, demonstrates the existence of an unconscious.

The major activity that characterizes the dynamic model is repression: the unconscious "contains" wishes and even information of which the Subject is unaware and which his "censor" (like the sentry at the door of the sitting room) strains to keep from the Subject's consciousness. Occasionally (like water exerting pressure against a weak wall) some of this unconscious energy will leak through the "repression barrier" and thrust its way into consciousness. But unconscious thoughts will always manifest themselves obliquely in consciousness: through dreams, slips of the tongue, puns, and so on. These are events that the Subject does not consciously "intend," and that he will assure any listener are coincidences or mere accidents. But for Freud, these "breakthroughs" into consciousness, disguised and distorted as they may be, are proof of the presence of unconscious activity. If the descriptive model for the unconscious is grounded in mapping metaphors, the dynamic model is couched in hydraulic metaphors: energy "flows," is "cathected" (attached to an object), and pulsates; repressed thoughts "build up the pressure," and at times put enough pressure on the repression barrier so as to "leak through"; drives "seek outlets"; desire is "displaced" or "transferred" to relieve the tension; traumas are relived over and over again (in dreams, even in daily life) to "relieve the tension" which the intrusion of the trauma into the unconscious has caused. To repeat, this model is hydraulic because it presupposes that tension is displeasure and will always find an avenue for release. The obverse side of this, again, is that stasis is pleasure. Freud's famous "death instinct" ("Thanatos" is the rather pretentious term used in English) is no more than a drive to return "to an earlier state of things," which in the case of the human organism is preorganic stasis. The dynamic model of the unconscious is an economic one, as it is often called, because it describes a system of control and exchanges: tension which builds up, seeking release into consciousness, in order to maintain a balance and stability, seen as "profitable."

The *systematic* unconscious is left rather vague in the early Freud (barely distinguished from the dynamic). In the 1930s, however, Freud will use this term to describe his "tripartite" model of the mind, which is a revision of the topographic model. The revised model, with its famous trio of *id*, *ego*, and *super-ego*, insists that the ego is both part of the unconscious (now called "id") and part of conscious perception as well ("super-ego"). It is this revision of the model of the mind that will, in the 1950s, divide American from French psychoanalysis; for the former will embrace the tripartite model and move toward "ego psychology," for which that model allows. The French, however, led primarily by the analyst Jacques Lacan, will see this revision as a repression in itself of the unconscious as a concept in dialectical opposition to consciousness. The French will insist upon a "return to the real Freud" of the topographic and dynamic models. Lacan will further claim that the proof of the accuracy of Freud's greatest discovery, the unconscious, is that Freud represses it in his later work. By Freud's own definition, in his early work, the unconscious is that which is always repressed once discovered. So in "repressing" his discovery of the unconscious, Freud (in Lacan's view) is merely acting according to the laws he himself described as governing conscious thought. Already, then, one can see that the choice of models for the mind, and therefore the choice of metaphors and rhetorical devices used to describe psychic activity, are highly politicized in subsequent psychoanalytic theory.

If things such as metaphors and other verbal or literary devices (puns, analogies, figures of speech, tropes in general) are ways in which the unconscious manifests itself for psychoanalysis, then it should not be surprising that many literary critics have called language in general, and literature in particular, the unconscious of psychoanalysis. The strength of this point can be seen immediately when we consider that Freud turned to literature to exemplify his most cherished theory: the Oedipal conflict.

The irony inherent in the notion of "unconscious" is that, because it is abstract, it can be represented only in concrete metaphors or analogies. Literature and its myths function as some of the analogies for psychoanalysis—as extended metaphors. Literature, in the eyes of psychoanalysis, is like a dream, uncovering deep, otherwise invisible workings of unconscious activity. The story of Oedipus—the king who is searching for the source of his city's plague, and who does not realize that he is that source—was for the Greeks the problem of destiny versus human freedom. After all, an oracle at the birth of Oedipus declares that the infant will become a man who will murder his father and marry his mother. The more Oedipus strains to avoid his fate, the more he is caught in its web. But for Freud, the story of Oedipus traces the unconscious wish of every (male) child: sexual union with the mother and a concomitant elimination of the father, so as to take his place.

Freud had a great deal of difficulty fitting little girls into this schema, as one can imagine. The situation of little girls vis-à-vis their unconscious desires and their parents was a problem which Freud never fully understood. In particular, his insistence upon penis envy as a necessary part of the development of the female child created, and has continued to create, a great deal of controversy.

Karen Horney and Melanie Klein, for example, produced important psychoanalytic studies questioning the universality of penis envy. But Freud rejected the work of these analysts, calling them everything from wrongheaded to repressed. Moreover, Freud's refusal to depart from his Oedipal paradigm in the case of the female child led him to other unacceptable pronouncements: because the girl has no penis, she is already castrated, according to Freud, and thus is impervious to the threat the father makes (castration) upon the boy child. As a result, Freud argues, the female emerges very slowly from the Oedipal phase and therefore has a less developed sense of justice and is less "civilized" (that is, less aware of the taboos and constrictions which make for civilized behavior) than is the boy child. In short, Freud's insistence on imposing male paradigms on female psychic life goes far to explain his self-avowed failure with most of his female patients. One of the great questions remaining to psychoanalysis, he once wrote to his friend Fliess, was "What does woman want?" (*Was will das Weib?*)

When Freud turns to Sophocles' great drama, then, that text becomes like the "manifest content" of a dream in psychoanalytic terms. Like the dream, *Oedipus Rex* is a disguise which both hides and reveals a "latent" psychoanalytic fact, in this case, what Freud will call the "Oedipus complex." Here, then, literature serves as the unconscious for psychoanalysis, representing mythically, through its plot and characters, that which is repressed in conscious life. It should be added that Freud's interpretation of the drama is not so removed from the Greek one as might appear at first glance. For the Greeks, as for Freud, the problem for Oedipus is one of knowledge of the most vital kind: knowledge of the self. For what Oedipus discovers is that the "other" he seeks (the cause of the plague) is in fact himself. That there is, in short, a part of himself that he does not recognize. Here we see more than the fact that psychoanalysis owes its own major myths to literature. We see as well that notions such as "destiny," "fate," "self-knowledge," and the "other" are all interconnected as partaking of what psychoanalysis calls the unconscious.

But Freud's use of literature can also be highly frustrating to literary critics, because a reductive, facile psychoanalytic approach to literature can be used like a cookie-cutter to mold great works of literature into the shapes of psychoanalytic axioms. Literature is then viewed as incomplete unless psychoanalysis "decodes" it and shows what it "really" means.

Another potential problem with a psychoanalytic approach to literature is the idea that a text is only a symptom of an author's psychological state. For example, psychoanalytic critics have been known to claim that Goethe's *Faust* was written because the great German writer had problems with sibling rivalry. At its best, such an approach will ultimately tell us something about the author (his neuroses, obsessions, traumas, and so on), but it will tell us little about the text itself. Furthermore, one would be left wondering what to do with texts whose authors' lives are essentially unknown to us—Homer's *Iliad,* for example, since

we know almost nothing about Homer himself. Here, a particularly useless un-
dertaking is often resorted to: the psychoanalysis of fictional characters. Fortunately, these reductive approaches are on the decline. As the philosopher Jacques
Derrida has pointed out, once psychoanalysis has invented itself, it proceeds to
"find" itself everywhere. Freud was a great student of literature, and would
doubtless have been horrified by a good deal of what has been done to literary
texts with what I am calling the "cookie-cutter" approach in psychoanalysis. But
it is, unfortunately, simply the case that Freud's understanding of the place of
literature for psychoanalysis encouraged such reductivism in the first place.

For an example of Freud's own contribution to such reductivism, let us consider his essay on "The Uncanny" (1917). This is a work that revolves around
"The Sandman," a short story by the German Romantic writer E. T. A. Hoffmann. The protagonist of the story, Nathanael, is a young student who is obsessed with the fear of losing his eyes. This fear was inspired by the terrifying
lawyer who worked for the family when Nathanael was a child. When the lawyer
came to the house, Nathanael was told to go to bed. If he resisted, he would be
told that the Sandman was going to come to snatch his eyes out and "feed them
to his children on the moon." Thus the traditionally kindly figure of the Sandman—who is said to throw sand into children's eyes to help them go to sleep—
comes to be identified with the ominous family lawyer in Nathanael's childish
mind. Nathanael will spend the rest of his life fearing (and continually being in
the presence of) "sandmen," men whose business is eyes in one way or another
(e.g., an oculist, and an eyeglass salesman who also sells instruments such as
telescopes and lenses). The hapless Nathanael will finally throw himself from a
high tower to his death, apparently because he sees one of the "sandmen" below
ordering him (or waiting for him?) to jump.

This story is "uncanny," says Freud, because Nathanael's fear of the "sandman"
is at once incomprehensible and strangely familiar: it partakes, in other words,
of the unconscious. Psychoanalysis will provide the explanation for this fear, says
Freud, and thus neutralize the uncanniness of the story. Nathanael, Freud tells
us, *thinks* that he fears losing his eyes; but that fear is the displacement (and
disguise) for another, more fundamental, fear: castration. For Freud, the eyes
are standing in for what they really represent: the male genitals. And why does
Freud believe this? Partly, he says, because his clinical work has established a
relationship between the eyes and the male genitals. But mostly, Freud believes
this equation because he is basing his reading of the Hoffmann tale on his own
psychoanalytic reading of Oedipus. For Freud, Oedipus performed the same
displacement as Nathanael: upon learning the truth about himself, Oedipus
gouged out his eyes. Freud sees this self-inflicted punishment as a substitute for
the "proper" one: castration. So the unconscious belief (that castration is the
necessary punishment) manifests itself (like all unconscious thoughts) indirectly
(displaced) in the gouging out of the eyes. Freud takes this literary text by Soph-

ocles as a manifestation which hides the unconscious wish that lies "beneath" it. This method, and the particular equation which the Oedipus myth yields for Freud, becomes in turn the model for "reading" the Hoffmann tale. Nathanael's obsession with his eyes is in fact castration anxiety, says Freud; just as Oedipus' gouging of his eyes is really a castration substitute. Because this substitution is universal (for males, at any rate), Freud continues, the reader of "The Sandman" experiences the "uncanny"—that which has been long familiar (here, castration anxiety) but repressed and thus displaced as a fear of losing one's eyes. Now that we know this, Freud claims, the uncanny in the story dissolves. In a sense, psychoanalysis has explained it away. The text's neurotic symptom, it would seem, has been "cured."

This way of viewing fictional texts—as essentially symptoms, disguised shapes of unconscious fears or wishes—is frequently inadequate and unconvincing for students of literature. Moreover, there is something in the reader-critic that would like to *keep* some texts uncanny, and that resists the notion that any discipline (especially one outside of literary studies) can claim to "decipher" the "real" meaning of a text. Where would Edgar Allan Poe's work stand, for example, if psychoanalysis claimed to explain the uncanniness of Poe's stories by showing them to be a neurotic symptom? These are some of the possessive fears of the literary critics. But there is also a counter-worry to consider here: if critics become self-righteous in such possessiveness, they may commit another crime of reductivism; for if they do not want their own turf invaded, they will have to decide upon difficult issues of boundaries between disciplines. Where, for example, does literature end and criticism begin? What topics are permitted for the literary critic to discuss, and what are off-limits? What is "inside" and what "outside"? Literary theory has, after all, been able to find itself in psychoanalytic theory, so why shouldn't psychoanalysis be allowed to find its unconscious inside literature?

Let us consider one specific way in which literary theory has been able to find itself in psychoanalysis: the telling of a tale. Psychoanalysis, let us not forget, is in fact a clinical procedure, not merely a theory. This procedure in Freud's day was called the "talking cure." The patient tells the analyst what comes to mind, through free association. This telling in turn becomes a story: the patient's story as he or she is able to reconstruct it from the fragments of childhood memories. The very process of psychoanalysis entails the construction of a linear, cogent narrative; the recounting and piecing together of a life. The goal of analysis is to have the patient reconstruct a "better," more cohesive story as the analysis progresses. The analysis is narrative, and the analysand is the narrator. The analyst, it follows, assumes the role of reader of this narrative, for he or she is obliged to interpret what is said; to retain images and facts which recur and to assess their value and function within the narrative; to "read" dreams as if they were texts; in short, to reconstruct in turn the "plot" of a life as it is itself being constructed.

And too, the analyst must "read" the "subplot" of this narrative: the unconscious as it may be itself reconstructed from the disguises and displacements it assumes in the tale the patient tells.

If we can say that the goal of the analytic experience is to create a coherent and logical narrative out of a life, then we may add that the analyst plays the role not only of reader but also of critic. For the analyst must first "read" or interpret the narrative. Then he or she must persuade the analysand of the accuracy of his or her own, corrected, version and interpretation. Finally, the analyst may write up a "case study," retelling the patient's story and the story of the analysis itself. The case study is then the narrative of a narrative which attempts to persuade readers (in this case, other psychoanalysts, for example) of the accuracy of the reading. Perhaps psychoanalysis is not "outside" of literary studies at all, then. . . .

The previous section concerned both the history of the term "unconscious" and some of the ways that its uses can, or should, involve literature and literary theory. Narrative structure; rhetorical devices such as metaphor and simile; verbal patterns such as slips of the tongue, puns, jokes and "gaps"; the prominent use in psychoanalysis of certain literary texts such as the Oedipus of Sophocles—all of these describe facets of the bond between literary theory and the unconscious of psychoanalysis.

But it is with the work of the French psychoanalyst and theoretician Jacques Lacan that literary theory and psychoanalysis cease being separate enterprises, only occasionally sharing the same ground. Lacan sees literature and psychoanalysis as two systems which are part of the same project, that of at once seeking and affording glimpses into the hidden workings of human thought. This is not to say that Lacanian theory avoids all the pitfalls mentioned earlier of more "traditional" psychoanalytic approaches to literature. But let us first look at what Lacan sees as the issues and at what the stakes are for him.

As we have already noted, Lacan believed that Freud's greatest discovery was the idea of the unconscious, as described by the descriptive, or topographic, model of the mind. The tripartite model, with its id, ego, and super-ego, is in Lacan's eyes already a repression by Freud of his own discovery. To repeat Lacan's view: since Freud's unconscious is by definition something which is repressed, always repeating its own discovery of itself only to repress it yet again, the tripartite model is the demonstration of the force and truth of Freud's intial discovery. This later model is revisionistic, in Lacan's view, because the third term (super-ego) that is introduced functions as a synthesis of what had first been seen as an eternal dialectic between conscious and unconscious. For Lacan, such a synthesis tries to cover up the tension that Freud's earlier model describes between the dynamic unconscious and consciousness. It is as if the sentry discussed earlier, standing between the antechamber of the unconscious and the sitting room of consciousness, had suddenly become a third, mitigating term—another architectural structure between those two "rooms" which combines the best of both while concealing the unknown wishes of the first and the "acting out" of the second. That, in any case, is how Lacan might be said to view the later Freud.

The tripartite view also, for Lacan, ushers in ego-psychology (the direction largely taken by American psychoanalysis and scorned by Lacan), because it fosters and even cultivates the illusion (as far as Lacan is concerned) of the ego, or Subject, as an unfragmented entity; or of an ego that can be made "whole" through the healing powers of ego-psychology and its various therapies. For Lacan, however, the Subject is always split, roughly along the same lines as the topographic model implies. The Subject is constituted by a conscious, accessible mind and an unconscious, inaccessible series of drives and forces. That which is unconscious for the Subject is that which is unknown, alien (although fundamental) to him or her. For Lacan, therefore, the notion "unconscious" lends itself at once, and in turn, to the idea of *otherness*. Hence Lacan's symbol for the Subject is S—that which is eternally split within itself. Linked to this idea in Lacan is his concomitant notion that the Subject is constituted by something missing, which in turn creates desire. Desire is experienced by the subject as a *lack,* which he or she will strain, of course, to eradicate. Already, we can read in this a "hydraulic" view of the Subject's mental activity, in the Freudian sense: Lacan's argument is that the Subject, constituted as he or she is by a lack, will try to overcome the tension of desire with the achievement of stasis (pleasure, or the absence of desire). It is desire that makes humankind different from animals, the latter experiencing biological *need* but not psychological *desire*. The unconscious manifests itself, among other ways, by insisting upon filling the "gap" left by that which the Subject feels is lacking in him or her.

In Lacan's firm view that the representation of the mind should remain the topographic one, we can see his insistence on a dialectical model: unconscious and conscious; Subject and object; desire and satisfaction; tension and stasis; and so on. The dialectic is important because it is here that we can see the great influence of Hegel on Lacan's thought. Indeed, the master-slave relationship as presented in Hegel's *Phenomenology* can be seen as the paradigm for Lacan's idea of the constitution of the Subject. For Hegel, the master-slave conflict is born of the confrontation between two consciousnesses, each seeking to be recognized as primary by the other. Obviously, one will win and one will lose. The winner will become the master of the loser. The master is the one who will be recognized, and the slave will be the unrecognized Other whose sole purpose is to feed and generally sustain the master. Ultimately, in Hegel, the roles will subtly reverse themselves: the slave, because he is working, is a maker and a producer of goods who has a purpose. The master, because his victory allows for it, basks in inactivity; his only purpose is to consume the goods provided by the slave. (The use of the masculine pronoun is Hegel's.) Thus the master is useless and must depend upon the slave for his existence. The slave, on the other hand, is only apparently suppressed: in fact, he is more independent and freer than the passive master. This very sketchy and reductive rendition of Hegel should none-theless give the reader an idea of how much Lacan depends on Hegel when rereading the Freudian unconscious.

In the situation just described, the term "consciousness" can easily replace that of "master"; and that of "unconscious" can stand in for "slave." Consciousness, in other words, appears to be the master of the psyche: it is that which is *recognized* and which seems to determine psychic activity. The unconscious, mean-time, like the slave, is repressed. But the unconscious works, while consciousness sleeps, and catches the latter unawares. The unconscious, further, will produce the materials which allow for the very existence and shape of consciousness. The unconscious, with its apparent repressed status, is in fact master, to which the conscious master is really slave. Without the material "goods" supplied to con-sciousness by the unconscious, the first has nothing by which—or with which—to function.

This Hegelian paradigm also applies, for Lacan, to the relationship between the Subject and the Other. As with master and slave, the dialectic between the two is not made up of discrete, noncontiguous parts. The Subject will (says La-can) project his own desire onto the Other, and the Other will see himself in the Subject. This is not the place to go into all of the complex permutations of La-can's theories of Otherness. Suffice to say that Lacan exteriorizes the internal dialectic of conscious/unconscious with a parallel (and even, at times, identical) Subject/Other. Lacan's famous maxim is that "the unconscious is the discourse of the Other." One of the ways of reading this statement is along the lines sug-gested here: the unconscious is that which the Subject does not recognize to be himself, and which he experiences as other from himself. The way the Subject views, and projects upon, an Other will yield a clue concerning the Subject's relationship to his unconscious wishes and desires. For Lacan, the unconscious is thus often in the place of the Other, the place where the Subject does not recognize himself. Thus the unconscious in Lacan becomes aligned with the problem of otherness: if the unconscious is that part of the Subject which he fails to recognize as one aspect of himself, the Other marks the place where the Subject refuses to recognize himself. Subject and Other, moreover, become mu-tually entangled; just as unconsciousness emerges as otherness within conscious-ness.

Another famous Lacan axiom is that "The unconscious is structured like a language." In this statement, we see Lacan's debt to linguistics. Here the two greatest influences on Lacan are the linguists Ferdinand de Saussure and Roman Jakobson. Freud was himself greatly interested in language—particularly in ety-mology and philology—and Lacan often contended that had Freud had the ben-efit of modern linguistics he would have come to the same conclusions as Lacan did about the close relationship between language and the unconscious. In any case, Lacan's first debt in this regard is to Saussure.

In his *Course on General Linguistics,* Saussure makes the famous statement that a linguistic *sign* unites, not a thing and a name, but a concept and a sound-image. The sound-image Saussure calls the *signifier,* and the concept he calls the *signified*. The example he gives is the sound-image "tree" (signifier) and the corresponding concept which is the idea, or picture, that the word conjures up in our minds when we think "tree" (the signified). Lacan will make constant use of these terms, even though he will alter the notion of the Saussurian sign a bit, as we shall see. Saussure claimed that meaning is generated by signifiers, not just in relation to their signifieds but also according to their position in the sentence in relation to other signifiers. So, too, Lacan will liken the unconscious to the movement of the signifier which generates meaning according to its place in the "signifying chain." It is this view which allows for Lacan's idea of the primacy of the signifier; what matters, in other words, is the meaning generated by the position of the signifier, not the usual meaning (signified) associated with it. We will return to this point a bit later in this essay.

Lacan combines the Saussurian sign and its parts with the work of the linguist Roman Jakobson. Jakobson (1956) had argued that there are two fundamental axes to language: metaphor and metonymy. Metaphor provides a word-*for*-word substitution, while metonymy is a contiguous chain, a word-*to*-word displacement. Metaphor is "semantic," says Jakobson, and metonymy is "syntactic." Lacan takes these axes to be the rhetoric of the unconscious. If we remember the Saussurian sign, it will be noted that it is a scheme which lends itself nicely to the Freudian topographic model of the mind:

$$\frac{\text{Signified}}{\text{Signifier}} \quad \frac{\text{Conscious}}{\text{Unconscious}}$$

Lacan will use Saussure's model (upside down) and say that the topography of the unconscious is defined by the algorithm:

$$\frac{S}{s} \text{ (signifier over signified)}.$$

Thus Lacan takes Freud's topographic model and puts it into linguistic terms. When Lacan says that the unconscious is structured like a language, he means that the unconscious is constituted in the same way as the Subject's innate capacity for language, which makes speech possible. There is an inherent structure in the mind which will allow for language acquisition, just as there is an inherent structure which will allow for the making of an unconscious. Metaphor and metonymy are such shared structures of language and the unconscious. Desire (unconscious desire) is never fulfilled; it is only displaced or substituted for, forming a "chain of signifiers," which always (like the unconscious) leaves traces of itself but eludes us. It should be clear too, that the bar Saussure placed between the signifier and the signified, demonstrating that the two are of separate orders, is very like the repression barrier separating consciousness from the unconscious in the topographic model. This is also an analogy that Lacan will insist upon.

If we now bear these two "maps" in mind, we can return to Lacan's application of Jakobson's theory. Metonymy, says Lacan (following the linguist) is a chain of signifiers that are horizontal, and do not cross the "bar" to the signified. Metonymy is the signifier of desire for Lacan. What is desired is always displaced, always deferred, and reappears endlessly in another guise. Desire, in other words, is the signifier that never changes, that can never cross the bar that marks the repression barrier. In spite of its apparent difference of meaning (the signifieds) in each case, each signifier in this chain has in fact the same meaning as the one before it: the lack which spells desire. Metaphor, on the other hand, is a vertical, noncontiguous structure, and is a system of substitution rather than displacement. For Lacan, who continues to use the Saussurian model, this can be shown by saying that one signifier can substitute as the signified for another signifier. The "bar" is not really crossed in this way, but it is overcome when the signifier (S) "drops down" into the position of the signified (s) for another signifier:

$$\frac{S}{s} \searrow \frac{S}{s}$$

The point of going (briefly) into all of this extremely complicated discussion of Lacan's ideas on metaphor, metonymy, and linguistics in general is to show that, for him, rhetorical figures provide the model for the way the unconscious works, and for the way it generates its signification.

It should be added that the structuralism of Lévi-Strauss, which is itself grounded in Saussurian terminology and method, equally affects the way Lacan understands the rhetoric of the unconscious: as "deep structures" which create meaning through certain patterns of repetition and exchange. The patterns, and not the "official" meaning of each term, are what make for meaning, along with their intrarelationships. So, too, Lacan says that the movement of the signifier—its position—is what creates meaning; not the signified.

To demonstrate this last point, Lacan "reads" a story by Edgar Allan Poe, "The Purloined Letter." The story concerns a certain letter which the queen has lost and which will incriminate her if it falls into the wrong hands. What Lacan points out is that the contents of the letter (its signified, official meaning) are never known to the reader. What matters rather is the *placement* of the letter—who has it, who doesn't, and where it is hidden. The movement of the letter from hand to hand is like the chain of signifiers discussed above as metonymy. Lacan shows that each individual in the story is determined by his or her relation to the presence of the letter, not by its contents. In a similar manner, says Lacan, the Subject is determined by a lack which engenders desire. The desire is forever displaced and disguised as something else (as is the missing letter), and this is evidence of repression. For Lacan, the Poe story shows us a "lesson" about the unconscious: the letter's itinerary, like the chain of signifiers, constitutes whatever subject is in its presence. When, at the end of the story, the letter has been returned to its rightful place and owner, the tension is relieved (to return to Freud's hydraulic language) and stasis (pleasure) is reachieved. The letter's circuit is then (for Lacan) like the displacement of the signifier; its return to its "sender" (the queen) is a fable of the notion that the unconscious always manifests its desire—frequently through displacement. "A letter," says Lacan, "always arrives at its destination." This can be interpreted to mean that the unconscious always attains its goal, even if by deferral. The unconscious is the "discourse of the Other" because the Subject does not know that he desires what the Other desires. That Other, as we have seen, is in Lacan the Oedipal drama (the father is the "real" Other); but it is also that part of himself which the Subject always fails to recognize (or misrecognizes, as Lacan says) because he does not know it is a part of himself: his own unconscious.

Lacan's views on literary texts have had great resonance in literary theory. His easy moves between linguistics, philosophy, psychoanalysis, literature, and anthropology, prefigure (and indeed, may have largely shaped) the similarly interdisciplinary turn taken by literary criticism today. Even critics who profess little if any interest in psychoanalytic theory apply, e.g., Saussurean terminology to literary texts much as Lacan did, or use certain words with a specifically Lacanian intent (words such as "symbolic" or "imaginary" or "mirror stage"). Lacan's impact on literary theory cannot be underestimated; nor his influence on such diverse thinkers as Jacques Derrida, Michel Foucault, Julia Kristeva, Roland Barthes, Paul de Man, Fredric Jameson, to name just a few. And yet it should also be remembered that Lacan was first and foremost a practicing psychoanalyst, a clinician for whom every manifestation of human thought could be another clue to understanding the psyche. In this, as in many other respects, he resembles Freud. And as with Freud, the unconscious for Lacan represents a clinical problem, a force underlying the behavior of real, living and breathing patients; it is not only an abstract concept to be imagined in differing ways. If the literary critic is ultimately faced with the text, the practicing analyst faces the patient and the difficulties of the very concrete manifestations of desire which that patient's unconscious generates. "Unconscious" at the moment of such confrontations begins to mean and to matter in fundamentally separate ways.

These, then, are some of the ways in which the notion of an unconscious has come to have an impact on literary theory, philosophy, anthropology, and linguistics. At least, these are some of the ways that psychoanalysis has chosen to use such disciplines as a way of describing what is by definition indescribable: the unknowable part of the psyche and its activities which the term "unconscious" stands in for. We have noted that, because the unconscious is an abstraction, an invisible "place" in the mind, or an unseeable system of energy flowing beyond consciousness, it is then condemned to being represented concretely through analogies and extended metaphors. But perhaps the converse is also true. Perhaps the unconscious is the way in which we imagine the unknowable and its hidden workings. Is it possible, then, that the "unconscious" is the twentieth-century version of the mythologies humankind always generates to explain the inexplicable, to chart the "unknown terrain" which ultimately remains mysterious in (and to) the psyche? It may be that when we discuss or describe the unconscious, we are revealing more about the human will to explore and explain precisely that which is unknowable and inexplicable than we are about any system or topography of the mind. To return to the idea which opened this essay, any discussion of the unknowable must perforce be born of the known, and therefore be nothing more than speculation. And yet, it may be that the way we speculate about the unknown will tell us in itself about the structures and patterns of the psyche, about its limitations and its prejudices.

Suggested Readings

Archard, David. 1984. *Consciousness and the Unconscious.*

Derrida, Jacques. 1978. "Freud and the Scene of Writing." In *Writing and Difference.*

Freud, Sigmund. [1895] 1951. "Project for a Scientific Psychology."

———. [1912] 1958. "A Note on the Unconscious in Psycho-Analysis."

———. [1915] 1957. "Repression."

———. [1919] 1957. "The Unconscious."

Jakobson, Roman. 1956. "Two Aspects of Language and Two Types of Aphasic Disturbances." In *Fundamentals of Language.*

Lacan, Jacques. 1977. "The Agency of the Letter in the Unconscious, or Reason since Freud" and "The Direction of Treatment and the Principles of Its Power." In *Ecrits: A Selection.*

———. 1978. "The Unconscious and Repetition." In *Four Fundamental Concepts of Psychoanalysis.*

Ricoeur, Paul. 1974. "Consciousness and the Unconscious." In *The Conflict of Interpretations: Essays in Hermeneutics.*

de Saussure, Ferdinand. 1959. *Course in General Linguistics.*

12

Determinacy/Indeterminacy

Gerald Graff

O NE OF THE most controversial ideas in recent literary theory is that literary texts possess a radical "indeterminacy" that makes the possibility of
a "right" or "wrong" interpretation of any work impossible. It is easy to see why
such an idea has alarmed many teachers of literature, who fear that if the possibility of correctness in interpretation is denied, the basis of their classroom and
research practices is undermined. The theorist E. D. Hirsch, for example, has
argued that "without the stable determinacy of meaning there can be no knowledge in interpretation, nor any knowledge in the many humanistic disciplines
based upon textual interpretation."

In reaction to various versions of the theory that literary meanings are indeterminate, Hirsch and others have attempted to define the grounds on which "determinate meanings" can at least sometimes be legitimately attributed to literary
works. Whichever side of the dispute one ends up favoring—and more than two
sides may be possible—one can learn something from understanding the dispute
itself, which poses fundamental questions about the nature of meaning and the
functions of literature.

Though the word "indeterminacy" has only recently become a frequent one
in literary criticism, the issue to which it points has preoccupied rhetoricians and
philosophers since the earliest antiquity. Since the earliest recorded times, it has
been felt that literature possesses a dimension that resists the grasp of everyday
rational understanding. (I am passing over the fact that the word "literature" did
not actually become a generic term until the later nineteenth century. Previously,
the word "poetry" tended to be used to denote what we now would call "imaginative writing.") Plato, in the dialogue called the *Ion,* depicts the typical poet as
a person who is "inspired and . . . out of his senses." In Plato's eyes, this trait
sheds no credit on the poet, but only proves his inferiority to the philosopher,
who follows a more reliable, rational path. Longinus's treatise on the "sublime,"
written by a rhetorician of the first century A.D., presents a more favorable view,
describing the emotional transport produced by great writing as an experience
beyond the level of ordinary reason. This view that a powerful nonrational ele-

ment marks literature has been strengthened by the affinity felt to exist between literature and religious experience. Like biblical parables, works of literature are thought to invite a variety of different interpretations.

Even the rationalistic neoclassical theorists of the seventeenth and eighteenth centuries acknowledged that any work of original genius was likely to possess a certain *je ne sais quoi* (literally, "I know not what") which could not be reduced to prescribed rules. It was not until the romantic period, however, that the non-rational became a central rather than a marginal component in definitions of literature. The argument then became common that the distinguishing feature of literature was its capacity to "suggest" meanings that could not be translated into the purely logical propositions of reason and science.

The growth of empirical science and the expansion of industrial, commercial, and technological forms of society after the mid-eighteenth century thus encouraged a way of thinking about the indeterminacy of literature that was different from earlier ways. As modern science and commerce identified themselves with the procedures of clear, distinct thought and practical efficiency, it seemed natural for poets and literary critics to claim a special affinity with the more shadowy, undefined, and elusive regions of consciousness that science and commerce tended to ignore or undervalue. The poetic or literary function thus came more and more to be defined as an alternative to the unambiguous clarity promoted by scientists, businessmen, and engineers.

In the criticism of the mid-twentieth century, this tendency to define literature as the opposite of science led to the theory that "ambiguity" of meaning is a distinguishing feature of good literature. The influential group which came to be called "New Critics" in America and England after World War II argued that whereas ambiguity may be a fatal defect in a laboratory report or an accounting ledger, it is a necessary and valuable attribute in a literary work. Whereas science speaks directly by means of propositional *statements* that aspire to have one and only one meaning, poetry speaks obliquely through *metaphors* or *images,* which multiply the number of meanings rather than restrict it. As one New Critic, Cleanth Brooks, put it, "the tendency of science is necessarily to stabilize terms, to freeze them into strict denotations [i.e., references to objects]; the poet's tendency is by contrast disruptive. The terms are continually modifying each other, and thus violating their dictionary meanings."

Is ambiguity really a feature of all good poetry, as the New Critics argued, or is it only a feature of *some* poetry that certain critics at a particular moment have happened to *like*? Is it the nature of poetry itself that led critics to see ambiguity as one of its primary features, or has it been something in the cultural situation of the critics that induces them to counter the claims of science by investing poetry with nonscientific characteristics? Over the long course of history, the words "poetry" and "literature" have been applied to a diverse range of forms of writing with a diverse range of purposes and goals. It is unlikely that any one set of attributes or purposes should have characterized *all* poetry and literature in all times and places.

As a general rule, it seems wise to maintain a cautious attitude toward any assertion that states, "All good literature (or poetry) possesses ingredient X," whether "ingredient X" be ambiguity, indeterminacy, or any other single trait. But though the New Critics may have exaggerated the importance of ambiguity as an element of all literature, their insistence on this trait did encourage readers to look at literary works in a new way and enabled them to see complexities in such works that previous readers had overlooked.

In the past two decades, critics wishing to emphasize that element in literature that resists clear-cut definition have tended to speak of "indeterminacy" rather than of "ambiguity." Whether the new term means something significantly different from the earlier one is still in dispute, and some observers have argued that new indeterminacy is only old ambiguity by another name. But the critics who have popularized the term "indeterminacy" insist that there are crucial differences. The most prominent of these critics are the so-called deconstructionists, who take their primary ideas from the French philosopher Jacques Derrida and the Belgian-American literary theorist Paul de Man.

Timothy Bahti, a commentator sympathetic to the deconstructionists, has offered a useful statement of the distinction between the New Critics' ambiguity and the deconstructionists' indeterminacy. Ambiguity, Bahti says, denoted a property of a text which, however elusive it might be, was assumed to be finally capable of being described by an interpretation of the text. By contrast, "indeterminacy" denotes a property of a text that enters into and infects the interpretation of the text, so that it is not just literature but also the *interpretation* of literature that is fraught with uncertainty. In other words, the concept of indeterminacy spreads the range of ambiguity by making interpretations of literature, as well as literature itself, uncertain. As Bahti writes, "for New Criticism texts were fundamentally ambiguous and interpretations were not. Today, texts are ambiguous and interpretations are indeterminate."

As these statements suggest, the concept of indeterminacy claims to threaten the authority of literature and literary interpretation in a way that the concept of ambiguity did not. Whereas "ambiguity" stood for a positive and valued attribute of richness in a literary text, "indeterminacy" bespeaks a limitation or failure of a text to fulfill its purpose, whether this be a literary work's purpose of expressing the truth about the human condition, or an interpreter's purpose of arresting the meaning of the literary work. The concept of indeterminacy proposes that a radical limitation is built into the activity of literary interpretation, whose very attempt to find a determinate meaning in literary works prevents it from succeeding in this enterprise. Whereas ambiguity was a quality that literature presumably mastered, indeterminacy is a quality which makes literature a victim.

Since these are difficult points, and for many teachers repellent ones, to understand them better it is best to try to start at an elementary level by asking how the concept of indeterminacy challenges the usual account of the way we make determinate sense of any verbal utterance. According to the usual account, we make sense of an utterance by inferring the *intention* of its speaker or author. Whether our intentions are actually knowable has itself long been a controversial issue among philosophers and linguists. At first thought, it may seem that because an intention is a private experience that happens in one's head, nobody but the person who was harboring an intention could know what it is. But a little further reflection and observation should suggest that we come to conclusions all the time about the intentions of other people, and we do so by using the various means we possess of drawing *inferences* about those intentions.

More specifically, we infer the intentions of speakers and writers from situational clues of various kinds—the form and features of the utterance itself, the circumstances in which the utterance is made, the information we already may possess about the speaker or writer. Such inferences about the circumstances of an utterance that help us infer a picture of the probable kind of utterance it is are what we call the "context" of the utterance.

When we learn a language, we not only learn the meanings of a great many words along with the basic forms of sentence construction. We also unconsciously acquire a set of codes for making inferences about the situations or contexts in which particular words and sentences tend to be used. Without these codes, which enable us to guess what the relevant context of any utterance may be, we would have no way of inferring any intention and thus no way of deciding what any utterance meant. Without the codes that enable us to determine the context, "the words on the page" of a text would tell us nothing.

To illustrate this last point, take the following expression:

Go jump in the lake.

If this expression were addressed to you by a friend, spoken in a certain tone of voice, you would probably take it as a more or less friendly rebuff to something you had just said or done. You would certainly not take the expression as a literal command to carry out the action proposed. Under a different set of circumstances, however, you might well take it just that way. Imagine these same words called out to you by a lifeguard at a moment when, right in front of you, several people are visibly on the verge of drowning and calling for assistance. Note that in these two instances, since the words themselves are the same, the words alone are not sufficient to determine their intention and hence their meaning. The difference in meaning in the two cases can be explained only by the different contexts in which the words are spoken, the one inviting you to infer a friendly rebuff, the other to infer a serious proposal for action. The different intentions, therefore the different meanings, are fixed by the differences in contexts.

Note that in both the hypothetical situations we just imagined, clues are available to us about what the relevant context is. But now let us imagine a situation in which we do not have enough clues to infer the relevant context. Imagine the words "go jump in the lake" painted on a sign encountered in the middle of the desert. What would the words mean then? The most likely inference might be that the sign must have been intended as a perverse joke, but it would be hard to decide for certain. Could "go jump in the lake" be a place-name, perhaps, which would mean the sign is a direction-pointer? Or could the phrase be a message in a code with which one is not familiar? Only further information about the context will help us resolve these uncertainties and make a more confident guess.

In other words, determining the relevant context of an utterance is a process just as dependent on inference as any other part of the interpretive process, and therefore just as open to dispute. We can always disagree about what the proper context is of any utterance, and this disagreement creates the possibility of indeterminacy. The point has some importance for literary interpretation, whose procedures depend on basically the same processes of inference that we use to interpret expressions like "go jump in the lake" and other everyday utterances. For a long time, the standard assumption was that, just as we can usually make good enough guesses about relevant contexts to interpret everyday utterances with reasonable assurance, we can also make good enough guesses about the relevant contexts of literature to attain a comparable level of assurance in that sphere. The various "approaches" to literature are essentially instruments for determining the contexts of literary works—e.g., consulting the biography of the author, examining the social and intellectual "background" of the period, looking more closely at the texture of the work's language, and so forth. As long as we have these ways of locating the context of a work, we presumably have a touchstone to appeal to when interpretive disagreements break out.

If, however, the contexts we appeal to in order to settle interpretive disagreements are themselves always subject to dispute, then there may be problems with this assumption. In some cases at least, the situation may be like the sign encountered in the desert.

The problem of indeterminacy becomes even more complicated when we note that it is always possible to look at any text in contexts other than the one its author may have intended. In this sense, a text takes on a new meaning every time we read it from a new angle. We can reinterpret the horrific elements in Shakespeare, for example, in the light of the experience of totalitarianism in World War II (as the Polish critic Jan Kott has done in his book, *Shakespeare Our Contemporary*). We can ask about the political effects of literary works which do not explicitly mention politics, as feminist critics do when they ask what a text assumes about gender even when it is not directly about issues of gender. We can read literary texts in philosophical terms or can read philosophical texts in terms of their figures of speech, and we can read both kinds of texts as forms of social or psychological behavior.

Some people object to such readings on the ground that literature should be read "as literature," not philosophy, politics, history, or psychology. But this objection raises the question of who has the right to define the application of these categories. Who is to say, for example, that "literature" is not already philosophical and political, or that philosophy and politics are not literary? Recent literary theorists have argued that our customary sharp distinctions among literature, philosophy, and politics derive not from anything in reality, but from the need to protect the established departmental definitions of universities. When these theorists assert the indeterminacy of textual meaning, then, they are often challenging these established departmental divisions and demanding the right to read texts in contexts that cross their boundaries.

One might argue, however, that the fact that a text can be read in contexts other than the official institutional ones does not necessarily make that text's meaning indeterminate. A critic who argues that *Hamlet* implies certain things about the way gender was conceived in the Renaissance is making a perfectly *determinate* claim about *Hamlet,* even if such a claim is not concerned with Shakespeare's intentions. A literary text can have a perfectly determinate relation to certain political or philosophical effects. Of course, debate about what that relation may *be* can never be closed off. The fact that we can never limit the number of contexts that can be legitimately applied to a text makes reading open-ended. But open-endedness need not be confused with indeterminacy.

An exemplary case of contextual indeterminacy in a work of literature is a poem by William Wordsworth, "A Slumber Did My Spirit Seal," which has recently become a focal point of critical dispute:

> A slumber did my spirit seal;
> I had no human fears:
> She seemed a thing that could not feel
> The touch of earthly years.
>
> No motion has she now, no force;
> She neither hears nor sees;
> Rolled round in earth's diurnal course
> With rocks, and stones, and trees.

Critics who have discussed this poem have divided between those who read it as the tragic lament we would normally expect to hear on its subject—the death of a girl or woman—and those who read the poem as the expression of a pantheistic religious outlook, in which the death of "she" is seen as a return to the living unity of nature and is thus to be regarded cheerfully. To settle a dispute between these two interpretations, we need some reason for choosing the tragic-lament context or the pantheistic context as the more probable. But the inability to settle this question is precisely what has led the meaning of this poem to be disputed.

One critic, James Phelan, has pointed out that the difficulty of determining the probable context comes from the poem's lack of any *explicit* signals of emotion. It would be easier to decide on the probable context if Wordsworth had written in one of the following more emotionally explicit ways:

(1) Rolled round in earth's *delightful* course
With *blessed* rocks and trees.

or, alternately:

(2) Rolled round in this earth's *dreary* course
With rocks, and stones, and trees.

Another critic, E. D. Hirsch, has argued that since Wordsworth is believed by biographers to have been a pantheist at the time he wrote this poem, it is more likely he intended the poem to be read in the benign mode of (1) than in the tragic-lament mode of (2). This is not a very very satisfactory argument, since it leaves unexplained why Wordsworth did not give the sorts of indications one would expect a pantheist to give of his beliefs when writing in a largely non-pantheist culture. Even the most cheerful pantheist would presumably be aware that nonpantheist readers do not see death as a delightful occurrence, and would therefore feel obliged to give them a clue to his unusual view of the subject. There seems to be no alternative except to regard this as a poem of indeterminate meaning. It supports the cheerful-pantheist context, but it supports the tragic-lament context equally well—or equally badly. Whether it is a better or worse poem for being indeterminate depends on the criteria for good poetry that are applied.

Some deconstructionist theorists argue that the indeterminacy of "A Slumber Did My Spirit Seal" is not merely an exceptional case, and that this same indeterminacy is inherent in every act of interpretation, by virtue of the inherent disputability of any appeal to the context of an utterance. If this were the only argument for it, the theory of the fundamental indeterminacy of literature would be a weak one, since it would ignore the fact that we can usually at least distinguish between relatively more defensible and less defensible guesses about contexts, and that is all we need to do in the practice of interpretation. The fact that we can never determine the context of any utterance beyond the possibility of dispute is not particularly worrisome, since the practical purposes of interpretation do not require indisputable proofs, only reasons and evidence that hold up against competing reasons and evidence. But there is a second argument for the indeterminacy of literary meanings, one that rests on the alleged instability of intentions themselves, and the often shadowy desires and attitudes that attach to intentions, quite apart from the contexts that enable us to infer intentions. Intentions may be complicated, conflicted, and ambiguous in ways that resist determinate formulation.

Again, it will help to start with an example drawn from everyday discourse.

Suppose someone says, "It goes without saying that our party will win tomorrow's election." The phrase "it goes without saying" is the kind of intensifier we conventionally use when we wish to indicate that our point is obvious. Yet if you think about the matter, there is something curiously contradictory about both the logic and the actual effect of this expression. If it really did "go without saying" that our party is likely to win the election, why did we bother to say it? If the statement literally went without saying, we could have left it unsaid.

If we look at the customary use of the phrase "it goes without saying," as well as similar phrases such as "needless to say" and "I need hardly say," we can see that such assurances of certainty tend to be used when we feel *uncertain* about what we are saying. One sees the same contradiction in our use of the phrase "I strongly believe. . . ." Take the sentence, "I strongly believe Jim stole the money." The prefix "I strongly believe" purports to strengthen the assertion's credibility, but the effect is rather to weaken its credibility by conceding that the assertion is made from an individual viewpoint: it is merely *my belief* that Jim stole the money—presumably I could be wrong. As in "it goes without saying," an expression that supposedly reinforces the assertion tends actually to weaken it.

We can see the bearing of these examples on the concept of indeterminacy if we ask what any of them *means* as a speech act. Does "It goes without saying that our party will win tomorrow's election" mean the speaker is confident his party will win? Or does the "it goes without saying" mean that he is uncertain about the victory—or even that he is bluffing, trying to convince himself of an outcome that he fears may not happen? Considered merely as an arrangement of words, the statement's meaning is determinate in that a native English-speaker would have no trouble understanding it. But considered with respect to the intentions, attitudes, and desires the statement conveys, the questions we have just raised suggest indeterminacy. The statement's confident prediction about the election is called into question by the form of the statement itself.

We could thus conclude that the statement's meaning lies neither in its confident prediction nor in the doubts it raises about the prediction; but neither does it lie in some synthesis of the two positions. The meaning is finally suspended between the two positions in an indeterminate space. Likewise, considered as an arrangement of words, "I strongly believe Jim stole the money" could hardly be more clear and unequivocal. But considered as an expression of intentions, attitudes, and desires, the meaning of these words is suspended in the space between the positive and negative implications of "I strongly believe."

The point here is that language attempts to build up positions of authority which language itself calls into question. We use phrases like "it goes without saying" or "I strongly believe" in the hope of gaining credibility for what we are saying, but, as we have just seen, the very expressions by which we claim that credibility betray how fragile and challengeable it is. This way of thinking about language challenges the traditional premises of literary study, since it takes the position that the authority claimed by any piece of writing derives not from any truth or validity in its vision of the world, but only from the coercive power of language and rhetoric. An expression such as "it goes without saying" is an act of rhetorical power, an attempt to sway a listener or reader by making one's position sound invulnerable. Yet if "it goes without saying" is merely a rhetorical move, a "trope" of language, then the state of obviousness it declares is certified not by anything in the real world or the nature of things, but only by the fiction-making power of language itself. It is in the nature of language to disguise this fiction-making power with claims of truth or sincerity, but once we see the disguise we can no longer accept the claims.

Note that what we have been concerned with is not only a certain theory of how texts mean, but also a certain method of reading texts. It is a method which does not take the texts' apparent contexts and intentions at face value, but looks at the doubts they repress or leave unsaid and how this repressed or "absent" element can undermine or undo what the text says. This method has been described as "reading against the grain." In many ways it resembles the interpretive method of psychoanalysis, which proceeds by going beyond the surface or "manifest content" of our dreams and actions, to the repressed or unconscious "latent content" that is presumed to lurk below.

In the classic instances of psychic repression, we become fixated on one subject in order to avoid thinking about something else, but what we repress is betrayed by our behavior (or our dreams) in a way that can be "read" by a trained analyst. According to recent literary theorists, something similar is built into the structure of all speaking and writing: in order to say something about any subject we presumably repress some of our thoughts and feelings about it, but what we are repressing is betrayed by our words in a way that will be readable by analysis. Such a view threatens the traditional humanistic belief that great literature expresses truths about the human condition which transcend language. For if the authority of the expressed "truths" depends not on their correspondence with some reality but only on the coercive power of language, then the traditional claim of the humanities to be a repository of universal wisdom is put in doubt.

Read against the grain, the most revered works of literature are like large-scale versions of "it goes without saying," expressions that, in the act of presenting themselves as representations of truth, call their own representational authority into question. Read against the grain, what these works prove to be about is not the truths and values that traditional interpretations have found in them, but rather the uncertain, indeterminate nature of their own status as representations.

To put it another way, for many recent theorists the problems of meaning and interpretation that we have been describing are not only features of works of literature, but are also what works of literature are *about*. Literary works "thematize" (or take as their theme) those conflicts that make them indeterminate—conflicts between the claims the works make to tell the truth, represent the

world, and present an authoritative picture of things, and the way their status as
language and fiction calls these claims into question. In other words, the theory
is not only that literary works are indeterminate, but that they are at some level
commentaries on their own indeterminacy.

The following text by John Keats will help illustrate this last proposition and
complete our discussion of the problem of indeterminacy:

> This living hand, now warm and capable
> Of earnest grasping, would, if it were cold
> And in the icy silence of the tomb,
> So haunt thy days and chill thy dreaming nights
> That thou would wish thine own heart dry of blood
> So in my veins red life might stream again,
> And thou be conscience-calm'd—see, here it is—
> I hold it towards you.

Much of the interest of this text lies in its seemingly poignant gesture of reaching out to the reader across the abyss of the centuries. Keats invites us to imagine
the speaker reaching to us, his imagined future readers, as if to annul the force
of time and his own mortality. One critic, Lawrence Lipking, has said "'This
living hand' goes as far as a poem can go toward encroaching on a reader's space,
or abrogating the distance between poet and reader." The poet's yearning to
touch us physically with his living hand ("I hold it towards you") provokes an
eerie sensation—we flinch uneasily as the disembodied hand moves toward us,
or perhaps we also feel a yearning to touch back. The eeriness may be reinforced
by the possible literary echoes of the gesture, Lady Macbeth's guilt-bespotted
hands, or the dagger which Macbeth imagines moving toward his hand ("come,
let me clutch thee. . .").

But all this is to assume a number of things about this text that cannot necessarily be assumed. In the first place—and this is not something that can be inferred from the text itself—it is not certain whether these lines were actually
written by Keats. The "'This living hand' fragment," as it has come to be known,
was found after Keats's death in 1821 scribbled in the margin of a manuscript of
a verse narrative Keats never finished. The fragment was never published in
Keats's lifetime, but only at the end of the nineteenth century.

Furthermore, Lipking has pointed out that the scholar who discovered the
lines, H. B. Forman, was subsequently revealed to be a forger and perpetrator of
hoaxes, as well as a would-be poet himself who felt that his poetic talent had not
been generally appreciated. Putting these circumstances together, Lipking speculates that Forman, not Keats, may be the author of the lines.

This speculation raises an intriguing question: do the lines *mean* something
different if we read them as the work of a forger rather than the work of Keats.
It seems that what a text means can depend on who is taken as saying it. Merely

by virtue of Keats's stature as a major poet, the lines take on a weight and pathos they would surely lose if we knew they were the product of a forgery. If we take the fragment to be enacting the gesture of reaching to us across the abyss of the centuries, such a gesture is clearly more impressive if made by a great poet than by an obscure forger.

But can we even be sure that the speech act of the fragment enacts a gesture of reaching across the abyss of the centuries? This interpretation assumes that the "thou" referred to in the fragment is meant to be the reader, or future generations of readers. Another fact, that Keats was writing plays at this time, creates the alternate possibility that "thou" refers not to the reader but to a character in a play, and that the lines themselves are a dramatic speech addressed to some situation internal to the play. Yet attempts to find a likely place for the speech in any existing play by Keats have not proved successful.

A further possibility is that "thou" refers neither to a character in a play nor to future readers, but to a particular reader, Fanny Brawne, with whom Keats is known to have been in love. Read in this personal context, as Lipking notes, the lines seem to accuse Fanny of "indifference or heartlessness toward her lover. When he is gone, he suggests half-gloatingly, she will be stricken with guilt and remorse." The apparently vindictive tenor of the lines, which say, in effect, "you're going to be sorry when I'm dead and gone," is difficult to account for on the assumption that the lines are addressed to readers in general—unless we take them as a somewhat grotesque expression of resentment at being neglected by readers.

As Lipking puts it, "the meaning and effect of 'This living hand' depend entirely on context," yet there are several possible contexts and it is not clear what basis we have for choosing one over the others. Acknowledging this fact, Lipking concludes that the fragment constitutes one of the best examples in literature of a "rabbit-duck"—a sketch that looks like a rabbit from one angle and a duck from another—"an artifact that can be read in two fully coherent yet mutually exclusive ways."

Suppose, however, we resolve the contextual indeterminacy by arbitrarily deciding to read the text in the context which probably makes it most interesting to most of us, as an expression of longing by a great poet for contact with posterity. Such a reading would make the meaning determinate in one way, but in the process of doing so it would produce another kind of indeterminacy. To see why, we need only think about what is implied in writing a text in which one professes to hold out one's "living hand" to one's reader. There is something inherently self-contradictory in such a gesture, since it goes without saying that one thing a piece of writing cannot do is establish *an immediate physical connection* with a reader.

A deconstructionist critic, Jonathan Culler, has thus observed that Keats's text "baldly asserts what is false: that a living hand, warm and capable, is being held towards us, that we can see it." Even if Keats were still alive, his assertion that he is extending his living hand towards us to see would be belied by the conditions which enable the gesture to be made, namely, the fact that the gesture is made in writing and writing can convey only a verbally described hand, an avowedly textualized hand, not a "living" one.

Like our earlier examples, then, this text is divided from its own intentions, suspended between irreconcilable desires. It expresses a powerful desire literally to "touch" the reader directly, yet the medium that enables the expression of this desire places the object of the desire out of reach. The poem cannot literally touch us by physical contact across the gulf of the centuries or the gulf between desire and language. It can only "touch" us in the secondhand, linguistically mediated way that literature touches us, a way that cannot help remind us of the distance between ourselves and what we would like to be touched by. The poem promises us the living hand of the poet while betraying its inability to fulfill this promise, and this discrepancy between desire and its frustration, which suspends the meaning in indeterminacy, is what finally (according to this interpretation) this poem is about.

The foregoing discussion has left a number of questions unanswered. Assuming that the kinds of indeterminacy we have been exploring are real rather than simply imposed on the texts by my interpretations, to what extent should we expect to find the same kinds of indeterminacy in other literary texts? Is all literary meaning (or all textual meaning) indeterminate, or is indeterminacy a feature of some kinds of texts but not necessarily all?

With respect to the "This living hand" fragment, nobody would claim that the indeterminacy here concerning the text's authorship is typical of all literary texts, or even of many. Indeterminacy concerning the identification of the relevant context may be more common (see the earlier example of "A Slumber Did My Spirit Seal"), but even in the most controversial instances, reasons can usually be given for preferring some contexts over others. Furthermore, even in the instances we have dealt with where a choice between contexts is radically uncertain, the uncertainty exists within a larger context that is less uncertain. For example, though it may be unclear whether Wordsworth's poem "A Slumber Did My Spirit Seal," is a lament or a pantheistic celebration, it is not uncertain that a death has occurred, that the "I" of the poem has been affected in some way by it, and that a number of other things are the case which we might list if they were not obvious, or at least have not so far been challenged and are therefore uninteresting. We tend naturally to be more aware of indeterminacy than of determinacy, because only the former poses itself as a problem we have to deal with. But indeterminacy could hardly pose itself as a problem unless it could be seen against a background of partial determinacy that makes it stand out. Wordsworth's indeterminacy makes sense only in contrast with all the things in the poem that are not indeterminate.

What about the kind of indeterminacy that arises from the discrepancy between a text's claims and its failure to fulfill them? Is all literature to some extent implicated in the deceptive gesture at the end of "This living hand"—a gesture that claims to deliver a living, breathing, human reality which, since it can only be an illusion created by language, must undermine this claim in the very act of the claim's being made? There is a sense in which literature (and any act of verbal communication) may be said to carry a false promise within its very nature. It does not follow, however, that this "false promise" is necessarily an interesting or significant phenomenon in every instance. To revert to our earlier example, the phrase "it goes without saying" in the statement "It goes without saying that our party will win tomorrow's election" *may* betray an interesting and significant conflict within the speech act in question, but it also may be insignificant.

One can imagine a situation in which it might *in fact* go without saying that a certain party is going to win the election, so that in saying so one would be open to no particular suspicion of ambiguity or indeterminacy. "It goes without saying" would still function as a rhetorical trope, but in this situation it would be justified by the facts of the case. Some theorists might concede this point while arguing that, in the case of literature, there is no possibility of any trope's being justified by "the facts of the case." But this seems a somewhat arbitrary assertion—one that is based less on the nature of literature than on the questionable view that literature has to have a wholly different status from science or logic.

In any case, with respect to the type of indeterminacy that stems from the self-deceit allegedly built into language, the point is that some instances of this indeterminacy are more interesting and plausible than others. The most interesting and plausible instances ("This living hand") would seem to be those in which the desire to transcend the condition of language is an explicit preoccupation of the text, as opposed to a theme that is attributed to the text on the ground that it is present in all language. To put it another way, this type of indeterminacy becomes more interesting the less one has to rely, in order to produce it, on something that is supposedly the case for all language.

Then, too, even the more certifiable cases of indeterminacy of this type are only partial, and depend on a prior background of determinacy. One cannot read a text "against the grain" unless one can determine the grain. Even to say that we cannot choose among interpretations A, B, and C is still to limit the field to the determinate possibilities A, B, and C. It is noteworthy that critics who insist on the indeterminacy of literature are usually just as sure of their interpretations, and write in just as confident a fashion, as critics who believe in determinate meanings and correct interpretations.

Suggested Readings

Bahti, Timothy. 1986. "Ambiguity and Indeterminacy: the Juncture."
Belsey, Catherine. 1980. *Critical Practice*.
de Man, Paul. 1979. "Semiology and Rhetoric." In *Allegories of Reading*.
Hirsch, E. D. 1967. "Objective Interpretation." In *Validity in Interpretation*.
Reichert, John. 1980. *Making Sense of Literature*.

13

Value/Evaluation

Barbara Herrnstein Smith

Introduction

Issues of value and evaluation tend to recur whenever literature, art, and other forms of cultural activity become a focus of discussion, whether in informal or institutional contexts. Some of those issues, moreover, though musty-sounding and unresolvable in their traditional formulations, retain considerable contemporary force: for example, the significance of such labels as "classic" and "masterpiece," the extent to which the value of literary works is "intrinsic" to them or a matter of "fashion," whether literary judgments can claim "objective validity" or are only "expressions of personal preference," whether there are underlying standards of taste based on universals of "human nature," and so forth. While such questions, formulated in one set of terms or another, have been central to Western critical theory for at least the past two hundred years, the past decade has witnessed the emergence of both significantly new perspectives on them and also dramatically transformed and expanded agendas for their exploration.

These new and changing interests and approaches arise from a number of sources, among them the increasing interaction between the theory of criticism and recent work in social, political and cultural studies. An important result of this interaction has been a recognition of the ways in which evaluation operates as a characteristic activity not only of individuals but of institutions and cultures, and also the extent to which value is itself a product of such activities. Reformulations of traditional questions in this general area also reflect important intellectual developments in philosophy and related fields: the growing dominance, for example, of various forms of skepticism, especially with respect to the ways in which beliefs and judgments, whether in science, political theory, ethics, or literary criticism, have traditionally been justified as "true" or "valid."

Within literary studies itself, these issues have been of particular concern to feminist and Marxist critics and to others who, from one perspective or another, have debated the structure—exclusions, inclusions, and priorities—of the standard academic canon and also its standard justifications. Also, the various concepts and methods developed by such contemporary critical approaches as reception-theory, psychoanalytic theory, and deconstruction have proved to be suggestive in relation to problems of value and evaluation as well as to those of meaning and interpretation.

VALUE

Like certain other terms, such as "meaning," "truth," and "reality," that have strong currency in everyday speech and also long histories as the focus of philosophical analysis, the term "value" seems to name an aspect of the world so fundamental to our thinking—so elementary and at the same time so general—as to be both irreducible and irreplaceable: it defies attempts to analyze it into simpler concepts, and efforts to explain, define or even paraphrase it seem obliged sooner or later to return to the term itself.

As can be seen from the following extracts, the *Oxford English Dictionary* solves the problem of recursive definition by defining "value" in terms of "worth" and vice versa:

> VALUE.
>   1. The equivalent (in material worth) of a specified sum or amount. . . .
>   2. Worth or worthiness (of persons) in respect of rank or personal qualities. *Obs[olete]* b. Worth or efficacy in combat or warfare; manliness, valor.
>   3. The relative status of a thing, or the estimate in which it is held, according to its supposed worth, usefulness or importance. . . .
>   WORTH.
>   1. Pecuniary value; price; money. b. The equivalent of a specified sum or amount.
>   2. The relative value of a thing in respect of its qualities or of the estimation in which it is held (1961, 12: 29–30, 326).

It appears that the English wordform "value" has always maintained two related but more or less distinct senses. One is the material or monetary *equivalence-in-exchange* of something: for example, an object's price in some market or, as it is sometimes said, its "exchange value." In the other broad sense, "value" is not monetary, and not obviously or necessarily material, but a more abstract matter of relative quantity or measure. Examples of the value of something (or someone) in this second and rather more elusive sense include its relative effectiveness in performing some function or meeting some need, the relative degree of satisfaction it gives someone, its comparative handiness or suitability for advancing some purpose, and the object's (or person's) rank on some scale: for example, a scale of strength and courage in battle, as in the now obsolete sense of value as "valor"; or a scale of duration of sound, as in the "value" of tones in music; or a scale of sheer abstract numerosity, as when we speak of the "value" of some variable in a mathematical equation. These examples suggest that what "value" in this second sense means is something like *relative* [*amount of*] *positivity*. Since both senses of the term involve two key ideas, namely *comparison* and *amount,* that relate to an exceptionally broad range of practices and domains of human life, it is not surprising that "value" seems to name so fundamental an aspect of the world.

The history of the term also indicates that, while it has long had, as one of its central senses, the extent to which something is "held in esteem" (presumably by *people*), "value" is nevertheless often conceived as something residing or embodied in *objects themselves:* some essential quality or inherent property of a thing, in other words, that is independent not only of what amount of money (or anything else) it might fetch in some market but also independent of its performing any functions, or giving satisfaction to anyone, or being esteemed (or, in effect, "valued" or found valuable) in any of these or other ways by anyone. Though increasingly problematic, these latter conceptions remain common, and much usage of the term continues to suggest that value is an inherent property of things (something like *weight* in a conception of the latter that we would now regard as naive), or that it is itself a kind of ineffable *thing.* Contemporary discussions of the concept of value, especially in disciplines such as aesthetics and ethics, are complicated by the related fact that denials and inversions of the senses discussed above are also current, as where the ("absolute," "essential," "intrinsic," "pure," and so on) value of something, such as an artwork or person, is said to be precisely that about it which (rather like its *soul*) is unique, immeasurable, and independent of anyone's experience of it.

In literary theory, further complications are introduced by the notion that there is a special kind of value that characterizes certain texts after all specifiable values or sources of interest—e.g., market value, use value, historical interest, personal interest, and political or ideological interest—have been subtracted. This special value, often referred to as the text's "essential *literary* value," or its "value *as* a work of literature," is sometimes said to reside in the text's purely "formal" as opposed to "material" qualities, or in its "structure" as opposed to its "meaning," or in its "underlying meaning" as opposed to any obvious "theme," "subject," or ostensible "message." This special kind of value, the possession of which is sometimes said to mark off genuine works of literature from all other texts (e.g., those that are "nonliterary" or "subliterary"), is also commonly associated with a text's inherent capacity to produce some purely sensory/perceptual gratification, independent of any other kind of interest, or some purely passive and intellectual gratification, independent of any practical, active, or material response to the text. (Such notions are comparable to, and typically derived from, the conception of pure aesthetic value, or "beauty," developed by Immanuel Kant in his *Critique of Judgment* [1790].) Notions of this special kind of value are, however, increasingly subject to skeptical scrutiny, with questions focusing largely on (a) whether anything *is* left over when all those other forms of value and sources of interest are subtracted, (b) whether any of those crucial distinctions can actually be drawn as clearly and firmly as is required, and (c) whether the various types of purity of response and experience posited by such notions are possible at all among human beings.

Although the term "value" is characteristically produced in singular and genitive constructions (that is, as *"the value of"* something), it does not seem possible to reduce the value of anything, including an artwork or work of literature, to a single, simple property or possession. It is sometimes useful, therefore, to think of "value" as a general name given to a variety of different positive *effects*. In relation to literature, "the-value-of" a particular text—say, Charlotte Brontë's novel, *Jane Eyre*—though any other text, "literary" or otherwise, would do here—may be thought of, accordingly, as any of the multiple, diverse kinds and forms of positivity that may have emerged out of various people's engagement with it at various times: the money its sale may have fetched in various markets, its effectiveness in implementing and sustaining various individual and communal projects, its occasioning of various sorts of sensory/perceptual pleasures and excitements, its communication to various people of various reassurances and/or revelations, its eliciting of both memories of such effects in the past and expectations of them in the future, and so forth. Any selection of these effects, or the abstract notion of all of them taken together, may be what someone indicates as the text's "value" in framing a judgment or assessment of it at some particular time.

EVALUATION

In relation to literature, evaluations are commonly thought of as the specific acts of individual people, either journalistic reviewers or others—primarily teachers and academically situated readers—in their role as critics of other people's writings. Acts of evaluation are also typically conceived as taking the form of overt verbal statements, such as "It is among the greatest lyrics in English" or "His first book was more forceful, though this one is perhaps more imaginatively realized." Such statements are usually thought to be of interest insofar as they are more or less valid, and valid insofar as they correctly identify the objective value of a piece of writing or accurately describe those features of it that are self-evidently related to its value. And the most valid judgments are commonly thought to be made by persons with certain appropriate qualifications, including acute literary sensitivities, wide literary experience, an adequate understanding of the meaning of the work, and freedom from the biases of personal interest or ideology. Just about every aspect of this familiar conception of literary evaluation has, however, been questioned in recent critical theory.

To begin with, literary evaluation is no longer thought of as confined to the discrete verbal statements of journalistic and academic "critics." The evaluation of a work is seen, rather, as a continuous process, operating though a wide variety of individual activities and social and institutional practices. Moreover, the relation between "value" and "evaluation" is itself understood differently, with the work's value seen not as something already fixed in it and *indicated* ("accurately" or not) by particular critical judgments but, rather, as numerous different effects continuously *produced and sustained* by those very evaluative activities and practices themselves.

Thus reconceived, literary evaluation would be seen as including the following:

(a) The initial *evaluations of a work by its author:* for example, in the case of *Jane Eyre,* the innumerable, unspoken acts of approval and rejection, preference and assessment, trial and revision, that constituted the entire process of Charlotte Brontë's writing—in the sense of conceiving, composing and editing—the text. This suggests, in turn, that literary "criticism" should be seen not as distinct from and opposed to literary "creation" but as a central and inevitable aspect of it.

(b) The countless *covert, usually nonverbal, evaluations* of a text that someone may make "for herself" when, for example, she chooses it (usually, of course, to read, but not necessarily) in preference to other texts (or other things), or when she continues to read it rather than setting it aside, or when she keeps it rather than discarding or selling it—or, of course, if some occasion elicits such an act, when she specifically articulates (that is, "gives verbal expression to") her general sense of its "value": either how the work figures for *her* in relation to other texts (or to anything else at all) and/or how she thinks it is likely to figure for other people.

(c) The many diverse acts of *implicit evaluation* of a work performed by the various people and institutions who, as may happen, publish it or purchase, preserve, display, quote, cite, translate, perform, parody, allude to, imitate, or, as in the case of *Jane Eyre,* make a film version of it, and so forth. All these acts are significant in staging—and, indeed, making possible—various positive effects of a work for numbers of people and, therefore, in producing, transmitting, and maintaining its value within some community or culture.

(d) The more explicit, but still relatively casual, *overt verbal judgments* of a work made, debated, and negotiated in informal social contexts by readers and by all those other people for whom, in some way, it may figure. Like the implicit and largely nonverbal acts mentioned above in (c), these informal "expressions of personal preference," tips and recommendations, and defenses and explanations of specific judgments are also part of the systems of cultural activity and social interaction through which the value of texts is continuously sustained— and, of course, also continuously challenged and transformed.

(e) The highly specialized *institutionalized forms of evaluation* exhibited in the more or less professional activities of scholars, teachers, and academic or jour- nalistic critics: not only their full-dress reviews and explicit rank-orderings, eval- uations, and revaluations, but also such activities as the awarding of literary prizes, the commissioning and publishing of articles *about* certain works, the compiling of anthologies, the writing of introductions, the construction of de- partment curricula, and the drawing up of class reading-lists.

Although our experience of the value—in the sense here of positive effects— of literary works is not a simple product of "social forces" or "cultural influ- ences," nevertheless texts, like all the other objects we engage with, bear the marks and signs of their prior valuings and evaluations by our fellow creatures and are thus, we might say, always to some extent pre-evaluated for us. *Classifi- cation* is itself a form of pre-evaluation, for the labels under which we encounter objects are very significant in shaping our experience of their value, often fore- grounding certain of their possible effects and operating as signs—in effect, as culturally certified endorsements—of their performance of certain functions.

The labels "art" and "literature" are, of course, commonly signs of member- ship in distinctly honorific categories. The particular functions those labels may endorse, however, are not readily specifiable but, on the contrary, exceptionally various, mutable, and elusive. To the extent—always limited—that the relation between a label such as "work of literature" and a particular set of expected and desired effects is stabilized within some community, it is largely through the sorts of *normative* (that is, value-maintaining and value-transmitting) activities described above. Although, as the list indicates, textual evaluation is by no means confined to academic criticism, nevertheless the normative practices of scholastic institutions form a central part of the transmission and indeed *defini- tion* of literary value within contemporary Western culture.

As indicated, "evaluation" can be understood as embracing a wide range of *forms* of practice, not all of them public or overt, not all of them individual, and certainly not all of them verbal. Once the range is granted, however, we may recognize the particular interest commonly directed toward those individual acts that *are* overt and verbal: that is, explicit value judgments. Current conceptions of literary evaluation emphasize two important features of those judgments ob- scured in traditional analyses. The first is that, when we offer a verbal judgment of a text, we are always doing so in some *social and/or institutional context*: for example, among family members, to a casual acquaintance, in a classroom, or in the columns of some newspaper or journal. The second is that the "force" of our judgments in every sense—that is, their meaning and interest for other people and their power to affect them—will always depend on, among other things, the nature of that context and *our relationship to the people we address*. Thus an explicit statement concerning the value of *Jane Eyre* will have a certain kind of interest and effect when delivered in the midst of a tense family conversation about the corruption of taste by the mass media, and a rather different interest and effect when affirmed at a meeting of the curriculum-review committee of the English department of some university; it will be different also when offered by a student to his or her teacher, or a teacher to his or her students, or by one student to another, perhaps his or her roommate; and whether it happens to be "his" or "her" may very well itself make a difference in such cases.

Current conceptions of evaluation also emphasize the significance of the *tacit assumptions* evaluators make when producing value judgments. Thus, when someone says "*Jane Eyre* is great," it is always possible for someone else to ask, "Great at doing what? . . . compared to what? . . . for whom?" If the answers to such questions were spelled out, the conditional nature both of the evaluation and also of the value of the work itself would be apparent: that is, it would be clear that the judgment implies (and could be rephrased as) "*Jane Eyre* is great, and certainly much better than many other texts, at doing certain things ("doing things" here includes having effects on people) for certain people," which, of course, also implies that it may not be as good as some *other* texts at doing *other* things and/or at doing them for *other* people.

In thus recognizing the tacit assumptions built into value judgments, we can also recognize that, when we frame an explicit verbal evaluation of a text, we are usually not expressing only how we feel about it "personally" but, rather, observing its effects on ourselves and estimating—in effect, predicting—its value for other people: not *all* other people, however, but a limited set of people with certain relevant characteristics—usually, though not necessarily, characteristics that they share with *us*. Though the limits of the set and the nature of those characteristics are usually only implicit, they may be obvious enough to all concerned from the context of the evaluation (as in the informal exchanges of value judgments among colleagues and companions, or in the book reviews published in such magazines as *Art News* or *Scientific American*) and may, in fact, be quite explicitly described, as in, "This is a challenging work for specialists in neuroanatomy, but is not recommended as an introductory text for first-year medical students."

It should be noted that, in describing, above, how any judgment *could* be rephrased to make explicit certain of its tacit assumptions, the conclusion was not drawn that that all judgments *should be* thus rephrased. Indeed, what follows from the preceding discussion is not that "critics should always make their criteria explicit" but, rather, a number of somewhat different points. One is that there is no reason for us to spell out our assumptions when we are pretty sure that they are understood in more or less the same ways by those whom we are addressing—which is why we usually do not spell them out. (By "criteria" in such formulas, what is usually meant, it seems, are the positive effects someone looks for and expects from works of that kind and/or the features of such works that he or she believes produce those effects.)

A second point is that someone's value judgment is likely to be interesting and useful to his or her audience precisely to the extent that the latter (a) *do* take its assumptions for granted in the same ways as the evaluator (that is, look for and want the same sorts of effects) and also (b) think that they are among the set of people for whom the judgment is implicitly framed and whose characteristics are implicitly defined in it—or, of course, are interested in being among such people.

An earlier allusion to the significance of gender for literary evaluation may, accordingly, be amplified here. The *appropriability* of one's judgments for other people (that is, how readily they can use those judgments for themselves) always depends on the extent to which they share one's particular perspective, which is itself always a function of one's relevant characteristics; and, of course, gender—like other characteristics such as age, economic class, and regional background—is sometimes highly relevant to one's perspective as a reader of literature. We may thus imagine the following sort of question as always implicitly put to a literary evaluator by his or her listeners: "Yes, given who you and various of your associates are (among other things, men/women), this work tends to be valuable for all of *you* the way you claim; but, given who *we* (e.g., the readers of your book review; your students) are, and that a number of us are, among other things, women/men, how well does that predict whether it will operate in just that way for *us?*"

It should also be noted here that, because literary authority, like any other normative authority, tends to be vested differentially along lines of general social and cultural dominance (that is, the people whose judgments have institutional power are usually those who have social and cultural power otherwise) and because, in our own communities, general social and cultural dominance follows, among other lines, gender lines, institutionalized literary norms (academic canons, high-culture critical standards, and so on) tend to have, among other biases, those of gender perspectives.

A third related point is that, to the extent that someone's predictions and recommendations of value reflect highly specialized, perhaps even idiosyncratic, assumptions and interests, the use and value of his or her judgments for other people will be limited accordingly. They may be informative to, and appropriable by, *some* people, but will obviously be pointless and useless to those with quite different assumptions, expectations, and interests—and, depending on the context of the evaluation and the evaluator's relation to those people, they may also be (as in exhibitions of class snobbery or acts of state censorship) socially and/or politically arrogant or oppressive.

It is sometimes suggested that, before we can evaluate a work, we must understand its meaning(s). The relation between interpretation and evaluation is, however, more complex than such a formulation indicates. Different aspects of a text—including such aspects as we call its "meaning(s)"—will become more visible and more significant for us in accord with our different interests and perspectives, and the value of the text will vary for us accordingly. But we are also more likely to engage with a text in ways that yield certain meanings—say, broadly philosophical or specifically historical or ideological ones—if its value has already been marked for us in certain ways (as, for example, "a masterpiece of world literature" or, differently, as "a document of English colonialism"), and our expectations of its effects are directed and limited accordingly. As this suggests, our interpretation of a text and our experience of its value are to some extent mutually dependent, and *both* depend upon the particular assumptions, expectations, and interests with which we approach the work.

For those who conceive of interpretation and evaluation as the identification of, respectively, determinate meaning and intrinsic value, the latter—that is, our individual interests, expectations, assumptions, and other personal tendencies and desires with regard to a work—would be seen as our "biases" or "prejudices" and, accordingly, as what would prevent us from being "ideal critics," the sort of people who can frame and deliver "objectively valid" interpretations and judgments of the work. To be sure, as already indicated above, a critic who judges out of narrowly specialized interests and highly idiosyncratic assumptions will not gain much of an audience, since his or her predictions and recommendations will be pointless and useless to most other people. It must be added, however, that, if we could exclude *all* assumptions, expectations, interests, and other individualizing characteristics from our engagements with texts, the result would not be that we would become perfect critics but, rather, that there would be no reason for us to approach any text to begin with and nothing in relation to which we could find any work of literature meaningful or valuable at all.

SUGGESTED READINGS

Bourdieu, Pierre. 1984. *Distinction: A Social Critique of the Judgement of Taste.*
Mukařovský, Jan. 1970. *Aesthetic Function, Norm, and Value as Social Facts.*
Smith, Barbara Herrnstein. 1988. *Contingencies of Value: Alternative Perspectives for Critical Theory.*
Tompkins, Jane. 1985. *Sensational Designs: The Cultural Work of American Fiction, 1790–1860.*

14

Influence

Louis A. Renza

A UBIQUITOUS term in literary criticism, "influence" can indicate the study of anything from religious myths to historical events—elements often understood as external to the supposed essence of "literature" itself—as they exert pressures on the production or reception of specific literary texts. The myth of Adonis, the "dying god," for example, haunts Milton's shaping of "Lycidas" (Frye 1963, 119), just as Joyce's *Ulysses* self-consciously traces and deviates from *The Odyssey*. The threat of Southern secession acts as a provocation for Whitman's unionizing style in the untitled, 1855 version of "Song of Myself." German Idealistic philosophy, say, or the theory of relativity—dominant intellectual paradigms—sponsor the construction, respectively, of Wordsworth's *The Prelude* and the fissioning plots of Thomas Pynchon's fiction. Nothing prevents us, in short, from construing "background" sources as essential rather than contingent influences on literature.

But after Harold Bloom's series of studies on "the anxiety of influence" in the 1970s, critics now most often use the term to designate the affiliative relations between past and present literary texts and/or their authors. Even before Bloom, influence-study generally entailed the practice of tracing a text's generic and thematic lineage, especially but not always as evidenced in established canonical works (including myths) from Western literary history. (The most extreme example of such practice is still John Livingston Lowes' *The Road to Xanadu*.) And in focusing on the ways literary works necessarily comprise revision or updating of their textual antecedents, this type of criticism performed a conservative cultural function. When a critic like Leo Spitzer explicates Whitman's "Out of the Cradle Endlessly Rocking" in terms of "motifs . . . elaborated through a period of 1500 years of Occidental poetry" (1962, 21), he effectively underwrites the homogeneity and continuity of the Western literary "tradition."

Grounded in nineteenth-century philological notions of historical scholarship (Mailloux 1985, 633), this tradition-bound position regards literary influence as a benign, even reverential, endorsement of humanism: the ongoing project to transform the world into the image and likeness of human beings. At the very

least, older views of literary influence officially upheld the ideal of textual relations espoused in Alexander Pope's critical exhortation to "modern" writers to
imitate as well as become chastened by the "celestial fire" of great classical works
("An Essay on Criticism" I.181–200). Writers should *seek* the influence of canonical masters. Indeed, these masters themselves often invoked the authority of
cultural *maiores* within their own work, if only as a strategy to legitimate the
work's potentially unorthodox or unreverential implications. Dante begins his
vernacular *Commedia* with the self-created genealogical blessing of Virgil. Milton's "protesting" epic invokes Dante's (by then) established work, classical
works too, and especially biblical Genesis. In the classical American grain, *Walden* conspicuously declares its "first-person" stance (Thoreau 1985, 325), alluding to the *self*-evident truths of Jefferson's "Declaration of Independence."

No matter the differences it discerns in textual relations after the fact, literary
criticism today still tends to focus on "influential" textual linkages and the traditionalist ideology they support. Spotting certain thematic likenesses or disclosing related verbal patterns between as well as within texts seems to inaugurate
the excitement fueling the critical act. Even Walter Jackson Bate, Bloom's main
critical precursor in examining influence as *dis*continuous relations between past
and present literary texts, concedes that the mimetic view of influence pertains
to the major portion of Western literary history. Only in the eighteenth century
does the poet first suffer "the burden of the past"; only then does he experience
a "loss of self-confidence" about what to write and how to write it "as he compares what he feels able to do with the rich heritage of past art and literature"
(Bate 1970, 7).

Although he focuses most of his attention on post-Enlightenment poetry,
Bloom roughly limits the origins of anxious poetic influence to the same period
as does Bate. But Bloom not only suggests that this anxiety affects the construction of novels and criticism as well as poems (for Bate, the Enlightenment novel
lacks a "rich heritage," and criticism devolves on the historical *accumulation* of
knowledge [1970, 8]), he rejects Bate's idea that writers of this period suddenly
experience poetic anxiety or "self-consciousness" primarily because of their
literary-historical situation, secondarily because of newly changed social circumstances (Bate 1970, 49–54). Instead, Bloom ascribes this sudden appearance to
a psychological imperative of the poetic imagination. At best, changed social or
literary-historical circumstances allow this imperative to come out of its idealistic
closet, i.e., the writer's operative illusion that he can choose at will the influential
precursor(s) of his particular imaginative acts. For Bloom, in short, the ephebe
or imaginatively ambitious Romantic poet cannot begin to write without wishing to "[have] named something first," hence to "sin against continuity" or traditionalist notions of influence (1973, 78). On the face of it, this task seems
impossible to effect since certain writers have always already named that "something." Yet Bloom's "strong" ephebe poet embraces this task whereas "weak" or

minor poets skirt the issue of their literary belatedness by accepting the influence of (read: inheritance from) prior canonical masters within the sanctioned literary tradition.

Formerly construed as ideals the new writer should imitate, these canonical masters now assume in Bloom's own sin against literary continuity the role of threatening Freudian fathers. A later writer, that is, cannot help but unconsciously perceive his precursor as a paternal figure who, through the power of imagination evinced in the latter's text, appears as if in the lubricious throes of verbal coitus with the maternal Muse (1973, 37). And so

> The poet, locked in Oedipal rivalry with his castrating "precursor," will seek to disarm [the latter's] strength by entering it from within, writing in a way which revises, displaces and recasts the precursor poem; in this sense, all poems can be read as rewritings of other poems, and as "misreadings" or "misprisions" of them, attempts to fend off their overwhelming force so that the poet can clear a space for his own imaginative originality. (Eagleton 1983, 183)

One needs to stress the unconscious as opposed to self-conscious aspect of this inescapable oedipal scenario. The ephebe poet encounters a precursor whom he can't choose at will (1975b, 12) except as a defense against an even more psychically immanent precursor. For example, Thoreau writes *Walden* in relation to an established or historically distanced Jeffersonian text that helps Thoreau ward off or repress the more influential proximity of Emerson's essays on nature and self-reliance. But this defense remains a fiction or "trope" of misreading which constitutes Thoreau's work. The textual locus of this work *is* its dynamic relation to the earlier Emersonian texts it exists in the process of repressing.

Though we must insist that they do occur, no "right readings" of a text *can* occur since its "meaning" always involves a motivated (mis)interpretation of other texts, and since we also misread the text insofar as it becomes the precursor to our own necessarily belated relation to it (Bloom 1975a, 107): "The interpretation of a poem necessarily is always interpretation of that poem's interpretation of other [precursor] poems" (1975b, 75). Moreover, such misreading threatens to surface *as* misreading. Thus, within its larger governing project of misreading, a post-Enlightenment poem or interpretation deploys a discrete series of tropological strategies to sustain its writer's paradoxically enabling act of repressing-alias-misreading his precursor. Bloom terms these strategies "ratios" or "relational events" (1975a, 28), limits them to six, and arbitrarily assigns them names from esoteric classical sources—clinamen, tessera, kenosis, daemonization, askesis, and apophrades. As "revisionary ratios" intended to measure "the relationship between two or more texts" (1975a, 65), each ratio interchangeably signifies both a psychic defense against and a formal mode of misreading the precursor text so as to facilitate the poet's illusion of naming his "something" as if for the first time.

"Clinamen" constitutes the poet's "reaction-formation" against and misprision of the precursor text through the trope of irony. The ephebe writer swerves from and attempts to void the earlier text's "intolerable presence" by exposing its relatively naive visionary limitations. He fastens on this text's inability to comprehend the negation of its own expressed vision, a negation which his work includes just as if it were implicitly "*there*" in the earlier work (1975a, 67). Deploying the trope of synecdoche and the Freudian defense of "turning-against-the-self" (1975b, 72), "tessera" allows the ephebe to go beyond the precursor's "truncated" because overidealized vision as disclosed by his initial use of clinamen (1973, 66, 69). In "a restituting movement," he proceeds to recover the transcendental implications of the earlier text's vision that were thwarted by its elided negation, its lack of irony, its inauthentic idealization, so that this vision now becomes a "part" of his work. His work, that is, here becomes a "whole" version or "belated completion" of the earlier work (1975b, 72).

Although Bloom restricts these inaugurating ratios to "strong" or "major" literature, they undoubtedly can occur in some works of so-called popular fiction. Permeated by the competitive ethos of the commercial marketplace, such fiction surely remains vulnerable to oedipalized scenes of writing. Thus, an Englishwoman writing a mystery novel such as Agatha Christie's *The Clocks* can also experience the anxiety of influence. Specifically, she unavoidably encounters the male English precursor of this fictional genre, Sir Arthur Conan Doyle. And so she attempts to swerve from his "classic" influence by, say, making her novel's surrogate author, Hercule Poirot, review and situate the precedent of "Sherlock Holmes" in the context of other mystery novels, most of them imaginary and the majority of which she regards as riddled with "fantastic," "unreal," "improbable," or "dull" plots (Christie 1963, 116–17). The sheer momentum of this associative strategy enables her to describe Doyle's *actual* fictional work as "far-fetched, full of fallacies and most artificially contrived" (119), i.e., as *not* influencing her work. Moreover, Poirot, a hero Christie explicitly renders as a figure comically aware of his pompous airs, serves to expose her precursor's nonironic, noncomical projection of his *un*self-consciously pompous hero of detection. Yet the sense of his precedent persists beyond her strategic reductions (clinamen) of Doyle's work. She is still forced to acknowledge Doyle's "art of writing" or the "pleasure of [his] language" (119). Tessera-like, then, she restitutes the genius of his work by displacing it into other works of "criminal fiction" which she allows her surrogate hero to admire, especially one work, " 'a masterpiece, and, I gather, almost forgotten nowadays,' " the fictional power of which remains "concealed with a careful and cunning use of words" (117)—a "forgotten" or repressed synecdoche of her own present work.

Not unlike clinamen, however, the revision effected by tessera posits the completion of the precursor's work as if it were still located in that forgotten master-piece: "still *in* the earlier poem" (Bloom 1975a, 68). And since an ephebe writer wants to recover this vision for his work alone, he next uses the ratio of "ken-osis," the psychic defense of "undoing" or "regression" effected by the trope of metonymy: "As a metonymy for influence, [kenosis] conveys an emptying-out of a prior fullness of language, even as the irony of influence was the voiding or absenting of a presence" (1975b, 72). In other words, he reduces the precursor's vision (and in the process, his own) to *non*visionary status. Its apparent synec-dochical resemblance to his own vision becomes merely accidental, contiguous, metonymical—as if no precursor existed at all. Kenosis therefore produces the illusion of the ephebe's ability to write as if from a preoedipal or noncompetitive childlike perspective, "when poetic experience seemed more an unmixed plea-sure" (1975b, 72).

A passage from Mark Twain's *Life on the Mississippi* provides a good illustration of this ratio. Traveling on a steamboat during his trip to the Mississippi River years after his experience as a cub pilot, Twain briefly refers to an event that occurred near "the Kentucky Bend country," the "scene of a strange and tragic accident in the old times" (Twain 1984, 229). Despite or rather because of its reportorial brevity, this "scene" clearly evokes a tale by a literary precursor from whom Twain seeks to disaffiliate himself. The event concerns a "Captain Poe" who "cut into his wife's stateroom from above with an ax; she was asleep in the upper berth, the roof a flimsier one than was supposed; the first blow crashed down through the rotten boards and clove her skull." Even as he encounters this precursor, Twain literally reduces his own writing about an event found in Edgar Allan Poe's "The Black Cat" *to* an "accident." Moreover, not only does Twain's shrunken or "realistic" version of Poe's tale undo the relation of his writing to Poe's more gothically sensational precedent, his local or regionalist ("Ken-tucky") topos also works to undo the universal claims of the solipsistic Romantic imagination evident in Poe's place-free tale.

Since such undoing again only results in the ephebe's "illusion of self-sufficiency and unity" (Bloom 1975a, 68–69), he adopts the ratio of "daemon-ization" and its trope of hyperbole to repress the "Sublime" vision he regards the precursor's work as communicating to him and others (1975b, 73). If the ephebe cannot fully sustain the illusion of the precursor's minor significance or even virtual nonexistence, he can at least transform the "high" transcendental intimations of the precursor's vision into the effect of "low" or merely human desires; and against this now repressively de-sublimed figure, he can propose his own "Counter-Sublime" vision, which expresses the imagination as an indepen-dent, solipsistic or virtually inhuman force (1973, 100–104; 1975a, 98). For example, Poe's previously mentioned *prose* tale about the arbitrary killing of a *black* cat itself exemplifies a daemonized misreading or forgetting of Coleridge's homicidal *poem* about an ultimately humanizing *white* albatross. In short, the

ephebe here situates the precursor's vision as if it were repressing the more extreme implications of his own (1975a, 69).

But the ephebe is also likely to become enervated by this struggle with the
precursor's sublime vision. In that case, he will sublimate this struggle by the
ratio of "askesis"; he will seek to turn his aggression against himself or withdraw
from the oedipal fray altogether in order to arrive at a state of poetic "solitude"
(1973, 115–16). Or what amounts to the same thing, this ratio induces the
ephebe's sense of resignation or "guilt of indebtedness" towards the precursor
(117), but only in the sense of puncturing the imaginative power of both ephebe
and precursor alike (119). Against a world impossible to overcome through visionary transformation, the ephebe's work as well as his precursor's (who by this
time has become a "composite figure" [121]) uses metaphor to set "inside
against outside" (1975a, 70), which in turn works to position their commitment
to the poetic pleasure-principle against the world's commitment to the reality-
principle. Through a pared-down because now resigned version of the precursor's more expansively self-centered vision, the ephebe here affectively identifies
with his precursor. He transfers, substitutes, and/or displaces the precursor's influence "to a series of inapplicable objects" of the world, to "substitutue gratification[s]" (1975b, 73) that bind rather than separate the two parties. Just as
Wallace Stevens writes poems tracing Romantic visionary precedents (especially
as represented by Emerson and Whitman [1973, 134–36]) in the face of a skeptical modernist sensibility, so the ephebe accepts the limited potency of his own
and the precursor's poetic efforts, although he still remains unconsciously (anxiously) motivated by his composite, imaginative double.

This sense of limitation, of course, can also revitalize the poet's quest for radical originality. In one last attempt to realize this quest, he can turn to the ratio of
"apophrades" or "the Return of the Dead." A more extreme version of tessera,
apophrades allows him to incorporate or absorb the precursor's past vision and,
through the trope of metalepsis or transumption, "the illusion of having fa-
thered one's own fathers" (1975a, 20), to project this vision as if it had not yet
occurred (1975b, 74–75). With this ratio, the ephebe's work appears to realize
what the precursor's vision longed to express but couldn't itself realize (1973,
147). Here the identification "with the poetry of the precursor" becomes complete; it blots out his otherness in an act of narcissistic appropriation (146–47).
Like Milton with Spenser, the ephebe makes "covert reference[s]" or allusions
to, even virtually plagiarizes, this precursor's imaginative work (1975b, 126).

Taken together, these "relational" strategies define a kind of self-propelling
cyclical turning (or repetition compulsion) from one ratio to the other, since
after apophrades "the whole cycle begins again with the first [ratio]" (1975a,
70–71). As we have seen, each ratio encounters its own limits, and so gives way
to the next one. Intended to disarm the ephebe's aversion to influence, these
ratios not only reveal poetry (and literary tradition) as a remorselessly discontin-

uous inter- and intra-textual event, they themselves exist in relation to each other, whether in dialectically paired sequences as in the case of Romantic "crisis-poems" (1975b, 96–97), or in an apparently hierarchical arrangement as to their ability to effect the illusion of radical originality. Nor does the poet ever achieve a vocational self-certitude that would free him from needing to resort to these ratios. Even after his sixfold "scene of Instruction," his experience of "what a poem *first was for him*," the vocationally "decisive initial encounter and response [to the precursor] that begat him" (1975b, 18) will continue to fuel a writer's struggle, however illusory, to wrest his radical independence, which is to say his visionary self-presence.

Bloom's depiction of literary influence thus turns personal as well as public literary history into a ceaselessly volatile or "murderous" zone of psychic warfare (1975a, 104). Simply wishing to write, the ephebe enters an endless "civil war" (63) in which he continually uses rhetorical weapons—the "[self-]persuasive system of tropes" changing within the ephebe's text (1976, 1)—to overcome or destroy the system of tropes defining his precursor's text. Indeed, this literary psychomachia also defines Bloom's own proposed system of tropes. Not only does his theory work to overthrow all idealistic or traditionalist notions of influence, it resists critical charges concerning its questionable addiction to the genetic fallacy, the impossibility of determining a literary work's particular causes, which plagues these other notions as well. Or rather, it willfully embraces this fallacy with a vengeance. Critical statements attributing the genetic fallacy to his position themselves cannot avoid defending against influence (1975a, 64). That is, they too unconsciously repress the desire to witness and dominate their own genesis, in this instance by diluting the critical value or influence of "other" origins.

In Bloom's vicious oedipal circle, then, this *operative* fallacy or fiction motivates *all* writing, poetic and critical alike. Even Bloom's own theory perforce metamorphoses into a trope ironically confirming the efficacy of his "machine for criticism" (1976, 21). At the same time, he himself clearly cannot control or foresee how this machine unconsciously applies to his own theory. For example, doesn't his self-interlocking, cyclical mobile of ratios, even his rhetorically aggressive postures and postulations, uncannily recall (and thus repress) aspects of Poe's *Eureka,* an American precursor text that also quests for "a perfect [theoretical] consistency" and seeks to construe itself as a "Poem" (Poe 1985, 1269, 1259)? But if Bloom himself defensively misreads his own theory of influence as a "severe poem" in relation to preferred precursors (1973, 13)—as an askesis, say, of Emerson's *Nature,* which in fact he elsewhere cites as the precursor of Poe's *Eureka*—such self-misreading again serves to demonstrate rather than restrict the virtually limitless and provocative range of his theoretical machine.

Why, then, does Bloom limit "the anxiety of influence" to post-Enlightenment literature in his own critically influential works of the 1970s? If in a much later work, *Ruin the Sacred Truths* (1989), he explicitly extends the literary historical scope of his theory to include pre-Enlightenment canonical texts, in these earlier works he effectively corroborates Bate's traditionalist view of literary influence as regards the greater portion of Western literary history. As noted earlier, canonical precursors stood as authoritative figures for pre-Enlightenment writers to emulate, especially since the ideology of "authority" itself, as Hannah Arendt has argued, devolved on the desire to preserve the very moment of a particular culture's ancestral founding. Continually reproducing "example[s] of greatness for each successive generation" (Arendt 1977, 119), "Tradition preserved the past by handing down from one generation to the next the testimony of the ancestors, who first had witnessed and created the sacred founding [of the culture] and then augmented it by their authority throughout the centuries" (124). But pre-Enlightenment literature hardly remains free from the genetic perils of anxious influence as traditionalist *or* early Bloomian schemas of literary history would lead us to assume.

Evidence exists, for example, that even "ancient" Alexandrian poems inscribe their resistance to what for them comprised a written tradition of "major" literary precedents (Zetzel 1984, 119). Similarly, a later canonical writer like Dante, as Ernst Curtius remarks, "intended to outdo Ovid" (1963, 18) as well as Lucan (164), and did so in the manner of other panegyric writers of the European Middle Ages who virtually made a genre out of interpoetic "outdoing." More generally, one could argue that pre-Enlightenment texts in "the great tradition" exhibit aggressive rather than benign misreadings of precursors understood as already misread by certain sociocultural institutions controlling the criteria for canonical greatness. Thus, the vernacular medium of Dante's Christian epic itself functions as a trope or politically anxious misreading of both classical and ecclesiastical "Latin" appropriations of Virgil. In the same vein, Shakespeare, that canonical writer par excellence whom Bloom briskly consigns to "the giant age . . . before the anxiety of influence became central to poetic consciousness" (1973, 11), writes *plays:* writes in an ideologically motivated "pop" genre or verbal space that eludes the Renaissance period's official criterion of "literature" as defined by other generic practices.

In fact, one could read *Hamlet* as internally staging Shakespeare's poetic ambition precisely in the throes of wishing to disrupt (even kill) a traditionalist notion of literary influence, not to mention the prevailing Renaissance literary ideology of mimesis which supports it. Hamlet's relation to his murdered father traces the story of an ephebe poet's repressed anxiety over his daimonized precursor—a ghost who "could a *tale* unfold whose lightest word/ Would harrow up [the ephebe's] soul, freeze [his] young blood . . ." (I.v. 14–16; my emphasis). The play proceeds to enact the ratio of askesis on a number of elusive registers, in the process thus imitating not reality but Shakespeare's *wish* to depict reality on his own terms. For example, Hamlet allies himself with his father to take revenge against his father's murderer, Claudius. From a Bloomian perspective, Claudius's murder of Hamlet's father, his fratricidal accession to the throne and his marriage to Hamlet's mother (or his father's wife) actually objectify an unconscious Shakespearian wish: Claudius as scapegoat for an alliance between the ephebe and his direct lineal precursor. Claudius, that is, Hamlet's uncle or metonymical father in the play, serves as a pretext enabling Hamlet, i.e., Shakespeare's ephebe poetic self, and the ghost of King Hamlet, i.e., Shakespeare's daimonized precursors in "tragedy," to seek revenge together (askesis) against a *substitute* authority figure: against a literary precursor whose demise would facilitate the ephebe's quest to recover the Muse whom this pseudo-legitimate precursor has claimed for himself.

Indeed, Claudius could easily represent the debased and politically disguised "Claudian" or Nero-like literary tradition (cf. III. ii. 419–20), which to Shakespeare egregiously dominates his own writing of *Hamlet,* and which his play aggressively exposes as having reductively misread the visionary, Muse-inspired significance of his daimonized precursor's work. In short, the theme of revenge that motivates Hamlet in the play becomes indistinguishable from the revenge Shakespeare seeks in writing the play against the Claudian precedent of *Seneca*'s revenge-tragedies. Or put another way, Shakespeare regards these Senecan precedents, translated into English in 1581 and depicted by Thomas Nashe in 1589 as the precursor of the "Ur-*Hamlet*" supposedly written by Thomas Kyd (Hoy 1963, viii), as having usurped or "killed" the visionary force of what *Hamlet* construes as its legitimate precursor: a composite of ancient Greek tragedies, among them, of course, that more likely "Ur-*Hamlet*" named *Oedipus Rex*. (These plays or progenitors of *Hamlet*'s desired literary origins and identity would have possessed a de facto ghostlike appearance to a playwright of Shakespeare's educated station. That is, they existed as hearsay or even as extant but for the most part untranslated texts—texts thus present through their absence—in Renaissance England as well as other countries of Western Europe [Highet 1957, 120–21].) Such a Bloomian allegorization helps us make particular sense of even a subordinate character like Polonius, who in this context represents an apparently benign version of the Claudian ideology that *Hamlet* vengefully seeks to expose. Hamlet's "accidental" killing of Polonius, the misreader of Hamlet's madness in the play, actually inscribes Shakespeare's denigration of sibling Claudian/Senecan supporters like Kyd who hide behind the "arras" of traditional literary authority, but whose visionary values Shakespeare anticipates as demonstrably fated to misread—or no less murderously reduce—both *Hamlet*'s and its pre-Claudian precursor's more ambitious expression of tragic "madness" as a matter of *mere* "play."

But Polonius's homicide also amounts to Hamlet's unconscious swerve or clinamen from killing Claudius. Why doesn't the ephebe poet seal his alliance with his desired precursor by effecting direct open war against this authoritarian representative of an envy-ridden literary traditionalism? *Hamlet,* in fact, all but confesses its desire to withdraw from this project. Already absent by virtue of the dramatic genre itself, Shakespeare actively proceeds to absent himself from the play when he assigns Horatio as its "real" author by having the dying Hamlet enjoin him, "Absent thee from felicity awhile . . . / To tell my story" (V. ii. 361–62). But the play also displaces Horatio as its author since, even when absent, Hamlet rather than the sporadically appearing Horatio dominates the play's effective point of view, both its action and its "Words, words, words" (II. ii. 196).

In Bloomian terms that themselves misread Ernest Jones's classic Freudian vision of *Hamlet* (Jones 1954, 90–102), *Hamlet*'s conspicuous staging of authorial disappearance, especially coupled with Hamlet's stuttering attempts at revenge, symptomatically reveals Hamlet-cum-Horatio-cum-Shakespeare's guilty but still enabling wish *to have killed the precursor first.* The ephebe's initial wish to ally himself with his legitimate precursor against a (Claudian) substitute thus conceals an ironic identification with this very substitute precursor, the latter's having all along substituted for *the ephebe* in denying *his* literary-parricidal wish. Even through the ratio of askesis, Hamlet/Shakespeare's legitimate precursor persists as the primary source of "his" anxiety, of Hamlet's inability to execute revenge in the play and Shakespeare's inability to write this play with the *sense* of total imaginative authority. By Act III, not only does this source take the form of a more demanding ghost (itself a figure of hellish afterlife that in Christian societies once served, as Arendt maintains, to reinforce "religious authority" in its "contest with secular power" [1977, 132]), this precursor compulsively reappears in Hamlet's verbally dispersed image of his father as "the dread of something after death,/ The undiscovered country . . ." (III. i. 78–79).

In short, already constrained by the very project of revenge to remain in explicit relation to his implacable, nonrepressible poetic father, *Hamlet* can never quite suppress its own parricidal wish. And this situation results in Shakespeare's overdetermined dilemma/wish about whether to be a genuine poet or not to be one at this moment, here, in the act of writing this play. Like its internalized ephebe, *Hamlet* cannot resolve this dilemma. It can only end up entrusting its anxious poetic predicament to the possible understanding of similarly situated readers, in other words to the "strong" interpretive "arm" of tradition—to "Fortinbras." But *Hamlet* itself abandons or virtually suicides its inscribed desire to confirm its own original authority to itself, and so Hamlet perforce dies as a mitigated tragic hero, Horatio becomes a minor character, and Shakespeare disappears into the role of author literally absent from the spectatorial aspect of his play.

However else one might wish to misread *Hamlet*'s internalized, intertextual tale of self-ambitious poetic woe, this play clearly demonstrates the applicability of Bloom's theory of influence to pre-Enlightenment scenes of writing. One could easily make a case for other pre-Enlightenment literary texts analogously caught in the anxious throes of desiring to repress and overcome established canonical traditions, if not individual precursors. At the very least, the Bloomian critic's enabling generalization about how Enlightenment literary works bear the self-evident signs of "depletion anxiety" or register "the burden of the past" in a more "onerous" way than works "in previous eras" (Sherwin 1977, 4) here turns into a historically relative matter which invites rather than dismisses further Bloomian speculation. Once again, we witness how Bloom's ratio-ridden machine of perpetual influence perhaps misreads its own implications. Even in his early critical works on influence, Bloom's recourse to the Kabbalah and Valentinian Gnosticism as precursors to even the "giant" literary tradition of postclassical and pre-Enlightenment times suggested his own effort to preempt this composite tradition, to defuse the anxiety *its* influence exerted over his critically enabling focus on post-Enlightenment literature.

Moreover, one can use other aspects of the Freudian "family romance" to depict a text's literary "influenza." Bloom himself suggests that a writer's work also exists in anxious relation to "the youth he was" (1975b, 107), in other words to *his own* prior works. In this context, Agatha Christie's *The Clocks,* we could say, occurs less in the force-field of Arthur Conan Doyle's precedent than in her own earlier work, as when she has Poirot belittle the " 'young' " work of a mystery writer, Ariadne Oliver (1963, 117), and then praise a repressed image of Christie's own "young" work in the (dis)guise of a current American woman writer's: " 'what excitement, what mounting apprehension she arouses in her reader'" (119). Or does such praise confess a different valence of Freudian anxiety, especially since Christie's text also takes pains to reduce its contemporary competition, the "American thriller," the macho detective protagonists of which "do not seem to [Poirot] interesting at all" (118)? As we saw in the more canonical case of *Hamlet,* the writer's precursor can also implicitly comprise the "secondary revision" of other contemporary writers or texts, thus permitting us to examine literary influence in terms of the scenario Freud described in *Totem and Taboo* of siblings in guilty strife over their common wish to assume the father-precursor's literary priority. Eruptions of such strife clearly occur in many past and present literary works: "What should I do to distinguish my 'self' from/ My confrere rattle-shakers in/ The wickiups of the outcast?" (Bullis 1986, 7). Bloom's own most motivating precursors on the issue of literary influence and its rhetorical subterfuges explicitly include critical contemporaries from the New Critics and Northrop Frye to Kenneth Burke, Paul de Man and Jacques Derrida (Lentricchia 1980, 326).

Here again, then, Bloom's theory promotes but seems conspicuously to desist from exploring the implications of its vision that the flight patterns of all texts are determined by the psychic crosswinds deriving from other texts. This hesitancy to assume a totalizing theoretical authority no doubt partly results from Bloom's self-fulfilling premise that influence mitigates the putative autonomy of theories as well as poems. Bloom's own "strong" misreading of literature, that is, must define itself as a sporadic fictive delusion within the history of criticism. But one also could ask whether this self-defining theoretical finitude isn't a strategy defending against the influence of bad social or ideological dreams. At the very least, he perversely refuses "to recognize . . . the constitutive role of extraliterary forces" on the question of literary self-identity (Lentricchia 1980, 326), for example in his failure to consider the possible political causes for the sudden breach of anxiety into Enlightenment and especially Romantic literary production. Besides isolating "literature" as a special "nonalienated" discourse in nineteenth-century Romantic culture (Eagleton 1983, 18, 19), the anti-aristocratic "bourgeois" milieu of this period surely frames the issue of literary authority *as* an issue—as an "aristocratic" or privileged position to overcome and yet competitively to strive to achieve for oneself.

Bloom's theory not only seems to displace the source of anxious literary production and reception from culture-specific ideological circumstances to the theater of timeless psychic forces, it also seems unwilling to purge its own ideological assumptions. Such sociohistorical unconsciousness exposes Bloom to accusations of bourgeois bias (poetry and the poetic self, he argues, are "property" [1973, 78]), and just as conspicuously, to patriarchal blindness. For surely his oedipal or father-son reformulation of textual relations presupposes a "sexist" or fixed Freudian paradigm of Western literary history that minimizes and misreads the situation of women writers in this same tradition (Gilbert and Gubar 1979, 47). Moreover, Bloom's claim for priority as the condition for anxious literary relations inversely points to his paradigm's modernist ideological inability to abide Hannah Arendt's sense of "authority." Even as her own before-and-after depiction of authority supports rather than contradicts Bloom's dubious attribution (Lentricchia 1980, 327–28; Donoghue 1984, 133) of anxious poetic influence to post-Enlightenment literary texts, Arendt isolates this issue and by extension "influence" itself as a historically relative critical concept. Unable to sustain the "predetermined aspect of the past" synonymous with any traditional sense of authority (Arendt 1977, 94), the modern age conflates authoritarianism with authority, hence tends to suspect the latter (and its poetic representatives) as in fact embodying the former. Only when the notion of authority becomes a pejorative social term can anxiety concerning it spread to other areas like literature and criticism. And to a "free world" American critic like Bloom, any view endorsing the continuity of tradition perforce endorses the authority of past writers or critics, which is to say connotes, ideologically, allegiance to an authoritarian regime of discourse.

Bloom's nationalist as well as modernist situation thus fuels what we could more accurately depict as his politically displaced "cold war" theory of literary anxiety. At the same time, this theory remains unconsciously concerned with the political alternative to its anti-authoritarian project: the increasing demands within Bloom's post-1970s academic scene of writing for canonical pluralism, in some cases even for a radically relative "noncanonical theory of [literary] value" (Smith 1983, 11). Such demands would clearly undermine the very tradition that his theory regards as paradoxically oppressing *and* enabling poets and critics like himself to produce "strong" works of their own. As a consequence, Bloom's theory works to reinforce as well as to de-idealize the traditionalist ideology of the literary canon (Lentricchia 1980, 330; see Leitch 1983, 132). In complicating the relations between past and present texts, "the anxiety of influence" clearly serves to *re*connect these texts by reemphasizing these relations. Or put another way, Bloom's theory effectively confesses its own anxiety over the *loss* of literary influence (cf. clinamen) resulting from the excision of authority in the modernist era, an excision notably exploited (cf. tessera) by early twentieth-century writers like T. S. Eliot and Ezra Pound.

But one cannot underestimate the wiliness of Bloom's formulations as they anticipate these same "political" deconstructions of his theory. After all, even as the effect of unconscious political causes, a writer's or critic's affective relation to authority through his or her work clearly manifests itself in psychic terms, hence still remains ripe for Bloomian studies of influence. Thus, against Bloom's gender-restrictive oedipal theory of literary relations, certain (themselves) influential forms of feminist criticism would posit a counterpatriarchal, noncombative, matriarchal tradition of women writers/precursors. This alliance allows women writers to waive, challenge, or acknowledge the ideological influence of the dominant patriarchal literary tradition—including theories like Bloom's which underwrite it (Abel 1981, 433–34; Kolodny 1980, 464–65; Gilbert and Gubar 1979, 50). But in the two senses of the word, Bloom's theory already "contains" this feminist revision. The latter's "preoedipal" claims and the "ideological" strategies used to effect them (1) ironically repeat the idealistic or traditionalist notion of influence (and thus remain subject to *this* influence), (2) devolve on the ratios of kenosis and askesis precisely to deny the influence of Bloomian notions of influence, and (3) promulgate a paradigm that could easily be said to substitute an ideological for an essential imaginative wish to have named something first, i.e., "a literature of their own."

Similarly, if Bloom's theory anxiously responds to the loss of literary influence in the modernist era, it does so by using a critical frame that unconsciously allows it to acknowledge this loss. In the process, it also effectively preempts sibling critical theories which repress such loss. With Bloomian bravado, for example, we could claim that the twentieth-century institution of literary studies intuits the ideological loss of "authority" in the specifically anxious terms of textual demographics: the subliminally perceived threat of textual anonymity promoted by the rapid "mechanical reproduction" of available texts; the sense of textual alienation produced by a socioeconomic proliferation of past as well as present texts. Framing the issue in this way, we can argue that formalist critical theories proffer methods to limit this modernist text-boom, especially by projecting the counterideal of uniquely autonomous poetic texts (clinamen). On the other hand, so-called postmodernist theories "beyond formalism" tend to endow this text-crowded environment with honorific significance, that is, transform it into a zone of textual liberation in the guise of "writing" or canonical heterogeneity (tessera). But despite *and* because of their self-consciously different theoretical or ideological orientations, criticisms both before and after the New Criticism (including criticism that would arrest Bloom's criticism for "extraliterary" negligence) willy-nilly evince the Bloomian desire to disclose "new" textual space for literary and/or *their own* critical labors. More, this project of disclosure ironically exacerbates the very demographic condition for modern textual anxiety these criticisms exist to repress. Thus, the New Criticism facilitates and even mandates an explosion of critical texts within the literary academy. And in the case of so-called postmodernist criticism, even as it disseminates "the" established literary canon as an operative source of anxious influence, such criticism reinstates a more amorphous and inescapable precursor, i.e., "textuality" itself, which at once converts *everything* into a text for "new" critical study and marks any disclosure of "new" critical space as "always already" a belated project.

The graffito "Bloom was here" thus also haunts Bloom's critical siblings and his sometime critics. Like theirs, his theory seeks to ward off the authoritarian implications of a still entrenched traditionalist view of literary influence. But in effect, Bloom also frames his would-be deconstructors as suppressing the anxiety he openly braves concerning the entropy of modern literary identity. This particular concern discloses yet another possible precursor for Bloom in American literary history. Bloom can only fail at banishing the influence of modernist textual multiplicity in ways that recall how Henry Adams could only fail at achieving "education" in the face of new modernist forces. Bloom's theoretical machine specifically misreads Adams's "dynamic theory of history," itself a theoretical machine constructed to comprehend all modernist "supersensual" forces in order to reach "the largest synthesis in its ultimate contradiction" (Adams 1973, 407). In the end, Bloom's kenosis of Adams, his "emptying" of Adams's prior modernist vision or self-contradictory "synthesis" even as he, Bloom, appears "to empty himself of his own" vision of radical independence (see Bloom 1973, 91), best explains the otherwise curiously self-delimited appearance of his theory of influence.

But Bloom's dynamo of tropes purports to do more than repetitively confirm its own theoretical validity or cognitive value at the expense of other (more repressed) critical misreadings of a modernist-textual environment. His theory clearly attempts to recover nothing less than the human pathos behind all critical acts, all textual relations, especially in the face of modernist reductions of the "self" to linguistic and/or ideological fictions. Yet far from proposing to put a defunct "humanism" back together, Bloom rhetorically positions other criti-

cisms into serving as tropes primarily working to confirm the self-centered poetic aspect of his critical project *as his alone*. Even criticisms of his theory are
machined into pretexts for grasping *his* critical act as in the process of becoming
a unique "severe poem." Self-consciously expecting and even inviting resistance
by his academic audience, Bloom's rhetorically perverse pronouncements (e.g.,
poetry as warfare, poetry as property) strategically serve to isolate his theory
from adherents of both traditionalist and antitraditionalist critical persuasions.

In other words, his praxis *actively* seeks to elude past, present, and future critical codes; thus to seem self-contained to itself; indeed to see its influence on
these other criticisms by turning them into latecomers or unconscious imitations
of its own precedent—in short, to name "influence" itself as if for the first time.
For example, Bloom's theory has the effect of transforming the historical priority
of even Bate's analogous view of influence into a position of post-Bloomian belatedness. As we saw, Bate regards the "literature of knowledge" or criticism as a
progressive project which supposedly differentiates its scene of writing from the
poet's. Bloom, on the other hand, maintains that critical texts like Bate's can
come into existence only as "strong" or "weak" misreadings of a prior poetic text
and its accrued critical interpretations: "Just as a poet must be found by the
opening in a precursor poet, so must the critic. The difference is that the critic
has more parents. His precursors are poets and critics" (1973, 95). From
Bloom's more comprehensive oedipal perspective, Bate's differentiation of poetry and criticism inevitably works as a trope to displace his own modernist burden of reading, his sense of *critical* influences, onto his perception of the Enlightenment poet's burden of writing texts.

But the final turn of Bloom's theory to get before or misread ahead of time its
possible critical revisions particularly defines his defense against the sibling critical position of poststructuralist thought. The notion of poetic selfhood on
which his theory of influence depends brazenly invites Derridean critiques of its
"self-present" or logocentric assumptions. Alternatively, by construing this selfhood not as a fixed empirical or psychological referent but as a linguistic strategy
or trope, Bloom's theory of influence, as Paul de Man argues, escapes the charge
of endorsing an idealized "subject" or thematic "meaning," and thus becomes
"even more subversive with regard to tradition than it claims to be" (de Man
1973, 274, 276). Bloom himself apparently accepts the notion of influence as a
relentlessly displaced affair of linguistic tropes that de-idealizes subject-centered
versions of literary history. No matter the poet's will, this history remains vulnerable to an intertextual shredding of the poet's self-identity into the destabilizing status of "interpoet" (Bloom, 1975a, 114).

Thus, if Bloom still insists on defining intertextual relations as constituted by
"supermimetic" influence "rather than [a Derridean] antimimetic" contagion of
"writing" (1975b, 80), he does so in spite of his own poststructuralist postula-

tions. Moreover, besides licensing arbitrary sources for a writer's experience of influence (Emerson, Poe, or Adams—which one for Bloom himself?), misreading—the pivotal master trope of his theory of influence—inevitably constitutes an undecidable term. As theoretician, Bloom can only construe "misreading" by positing a point where a willfully defensive misreading can become recognized as such. Yet according to his own system, misreading can occur only if the poet or critical reader does *not* recognize it *as* "misreading." Such recognition, after all, would clearly dilute the affective force of misreading's repressive but text-enabling function. Misreading, then, must misread itself as not "misreading." Bloom's notion of influence through misreading consequently becomes *his* story, another misreading which conceals the misreading carried on in another text, which his theory by definition purports to disclose.

From the poststructuralist perspective, Bloom's theory of influence and its machine of fluxing ratios thus only eventuates in a Freudian "science fiction": a repressed knowledge of its own fictionality, all the more repressed for giving itself room to entertain this self-fictionality. Yet even for Derrida, "writing" always already transpires through the desire for self-presence—or in Bloomian terms through the writer's (and reader's) quest for radical textual independence. And if "writing" disseminates this willfull desire, such desire also tends to re-claim or identify with this very act of dissemination, which act in turn becomes reducible as yet another "latecomer's defense, since it seeks to make of [writing] a perpetual earliness," or to repress "the shadows of anteriority" (Bloom, 1975a, 105).

But in the end, Bloom's theory of influence does more than preempt its own potential criticisms. It also provides its own antidote to its self-induced influenza or negative thesis that neither the ephebe poet or critic (including the theorist of influence), nor his singular or composite precursor, text, or even textual situation, can ever luxuriate in a determinate knowledge of who or what serves as an efficient agent of influence. Like Adams's dynamic theory of history, Bloom's dynamic theory of influence belies its vision of imaginative "failure," of literature and literary history wherein the modern ephebe's or critic's "quest-romance" for priority is always found "collapsing . . . into one tragic recognition" (Hartman 1975, 50). Rather, its built-in defenses against influence from future as well as past and present texts exist as inescapable fictions in the *process* of disclosing the only indeterminate (non)space remaining for the modern self to occupy: never, to borrow from Bloom's preferred precursor, "in the instant of repose," but always "in the moment of transition from a past to a new state, in the shooting of the gulf, in the darting to an aim" (Emerson 1957, 158). In this context, "influence" indeed becomes a term applicable to other voices—other texts—even to those other disciplines themselves supposedly influencing the study of literature.

Suggested Readings

Bate, W. Jackson. 1970. *The Burden of the Past and the English Poet*.

Bloom, Harold. 1973. *The Anxiety of Influence*.

———. 1975a. *Kabbalah and Criticism*.

———. 1975b. *A Map of Misreading*.

———. 1976. *Poetry and Repression*.

———. 1989. *Ruin the Sacred Truths*.

de Man, Paul. 1983. "Review of *Anxiety of Influence*."

Hartman, Geoffrey H. "War in Heaven."

Highet, Gilbert. 1957. *The Classical Tradition*.

Kolodny, Annette. 1980. "A Map for Rereading: Or, Gender and the Interpretation of Literary Texts."

Leitch, Vincent B. 1983. *Deconstructive Criticism*.

Lentricchia, Frank. 1980. *After the New Criticism*.

15

Rhetoric

Stanley Fish

> . . . up rose
> *Belial,* in act more graceful and humane;
> A fairer person lost not Heav'n; he seem'd
> For dignity compos'd and high exploit:
> But all was false and hollow; though his Tongue
> Dropt Manna, and could make the worse appear
> The better reason, to perplex and dash
> Maturest counsels: for his thoughts were low;. . . .
> . . . yet he pleas'd the ear,
> And with persuasive accent thus began.
> (*Paradise Lost,* II, 108–15, 117–18)

I

FOR Milton's seventeenth-century readers this passage would have been immediately recognizable as a brief but trenchant essay on the art and character of the rhetorician. Indeed in these few lines Milton has managed to gather and restate with great rhetorical force all of the traditional arguments against rhetoric. Even Belial's gesture of rising is to the (negative) point: he catches the eye even before he begins to speak, just as Satan will in Book IX when he too raises himself and moved so that "each part,/Motion, each act won audience ere the tongue" (673–74). That is, he draws attention to his appearance, to his surface, and the suggestion of superficiality (a word to be understood in its literal meaning) extends to the word "act"; i.e., that which can be seen. That act is said to be "graceful," the first in a succession of double meanings (one of the stigmatized attributes of rhetorical speech) we find in the passage. Belial is precisely *not* full of grace; that is simply his outward aspect, and the same is true for "humane" and "fairer." The verse's judgment on all of his apparent virtues is delivered in the last two words of line 110—"he seem'd"—and the shadow of "seeming" falls across the next line which in isolation might "seem" to be high praise. But under the pressure of what precedes it, the assertion of praise undoes itself with

203

every Janus-faced word (the verse now begins to imitate the object of its criticism by displaying a pervasive disjunction between its outer and inner meanings; indicting seeming, it itself repeatedly seems): "compos'd" now carries its pejorative meaning of "affected" or "made-up"; "high" at once refers to the favored style of bombastic orators and awaits its ironic and demeaning contrast with the lowness of his thoughts; "dignity" is an etymological joke, for Belial is anything but worthy; in fact, he is just what the next line says he is, "false and hollow," an accusation that repeats one of the perennial antirhetorical topoi, that rhetoric, the art of fine speaking, is all show, grounded in nothing but its own empty pretensions, unsupported by any relation to truth. "There is no need," declares Socrates in Plato's *Gorgias,* "for rhetoric to know the facts at all, for it has hit upon a means of persuasion that enables it to appear in the eyes of the ignorant to know more than those who really know" (459), and in the *Phaedrus* the title figure admits that the "man who plans to be an orator" need not "learn what is really just and true, but only what seems so to the crowd" (260).

This reference to the vulgar popular ear indicates that rhetoric's deficiencies are not only epistemological (sundered from truth and fact) and moral (sundered from true knowledge and sincerity) but social: it panders to the worst in people and moves them to base actions, exactly as Belial is said to do in the next famous run-on statement, "and could make the worse appear / The better reason." Behind Belial is the line of sophists—Protagoras, Hippias, Gorgias, shadowy figures known to us mostly through the writings of Plato where they appear always as relativist foils for the idealistic Socrates. The judgment made on them by a philosophic tradition dominated by Plato is the judgment here made on Belial; their thoughts were low, centered on the suspect skills they taught for hire; the danger they represented is the danger Belial represents: despite the lowness of their thoughts, perhaps *because* of the lowness of their thoughts, they pleased the ear, at least the ear of the promiscuous crowd (there is always just beneath the surface of the antirhetorical stance a powerful and corrosive elitism), and the explanation of their unfortunate success is the power Belial now begins to exercise, the power of "persuasive accent." "Accent" here is a resonant word, one of whose relevant meanings is "mode of utterance peculiar to an individual, locality or nation" (*OED*). He who speaks "in accent" speaks from a particular *angled* perspective into which he tries to draw his auditors; he also speaks in the rhythms of song (etymologically "accent" means "song added to speech") which as Milton will soon observe "*charms* the sense" (II, 556). "Persuasive accent" then is almost a redundancy: the two words mean the same thing and what they tell the reader is that he is about to be exposed to a force whose exercise is unconstrained by any sense of responsibility either to the Truth or to the Good. Indeed, so dangerous does Milton consider this force that he feels it necessary to provide a corrective gloss as soon as Belial stops speaking: "Thus *Belial* with words cloth'd in reason's garb/Counsell'd ignoble ease and peaceful sloth" (II, 226–27). Just in case you hadn't noticed.

I have lingered so long over this passage because we can extrapolate from it almost all of the binary oppositions in relation to which rhetoric has received its (largely negative) definition: inner/outer, deep/surface, essential/peripheral, unmediated/mediated, clear/colored, necessary/contingent, straightforward/angled, abiding/fleeting, reason/passion, things/words, realities/illusions, fact/opinion, neutral/partisan. Underlying this list, which is by no means exhaustive, are three basic oppositions: first, between a truth that exists independently of all perspectives and points of view and the many truths that emerge and seem perspicuous when a particular perspective or point of view has been established and is in force; second, an opposition between true knowledge, which is knowledge as it exists apart from any and all systems of belief, and the knowledge, which because it flows from some or other system of belief, is incomplete and partial (in the sense of biased); and third, an opposition between a self or consciousness that is turned outward in an effort to apprehend and attach itself to truth and true knowledge, and a self or consciousness that is turned inward in the direction of its own prejudices, which far from being transcended, continue to inform its every word and action. Each of these oppositions is attached in turn to an opposition between two kinds of language: on the one hand, language that faithfully reflects or reports on matters of fact uncolored by any personal or partisan agenda or desire; and on the other hand, language that is infected by partisan agendas and desires, and therefore colors and distorts the facts which it purports to reflect. It is use of the second kind of language that makes one a rhetorician, while adherence to the first kind makes one a seeker after truth and an objective observer of the way things are.

It is this understanding of linguistic possibilities and dangers that generates a succession of efforts to construct a language from which all perspectival bias (a redundant phrase) has been eliminated, efforts that have sometimes taken as a model the notations of mathematics, at other times the operations of logic, and more recently the purely formal calculations of a digital computer. Whether it issues in the elaborate linguistic machines of seventeenth-century "projectors" like Bishop Wilkins (*An Essay Towards a Real Character and a Philosophical Language*, 1668), or in the building (à la Chomsky) of a "competence" model of language abstracted from any particular performance, or in the project of Esperanto or some other artificial language claiming universality (see Large 1985), or in the fashioning of a Habermasian "ideal speech situation" in which all assertions express "a 'rational will' in relation to a common interest ascertained without deception" (Habermas 1975, 108), the impulse behind the effort is always the same: to establish a form of communication that escapes partiality and aids us in first determining and then affirming what is absolutely and objectively true, a form of communication that in its structure and operations is the very antithesis of rhetoric.

Although the transition from classical to Christian thought is marked by many changes, one thing that does not change is the status of rhetoric in relation to a foundational vision of truth and meaning. Whether the center of that vision is a personalized deity or an abstract geometric reason, rhetoric is the force that pulls us away from that center and into its own world of ever-shifting shapes and shimmering surfaces.

The quarrel between philosophy and rhetoric survives every sea change in the history of Western thought, continually presenting us with the (skewed) choice between the plain unvarnished truth straightforwardly presented and the powerful but insidious appeal of "fine language," language that has transgressed the limits of representation and substituted its own forms for the forms of reality (see Kennedy 1963, 23).

II

To this point my presentation has been as skewed as this choice, because it has suggested that rhetoric has received only negative characterizations. In fact, there have always been friends of rhetoric, from the Sophists to the antifoundationalists of the present day, and in response to the realist critique they have devised (and repeated) a number of standard defenses. Two of these defenses are offered by Aristotle in the *Rhetoric*. First, he defines rhetoric as a faculty or art whose practice will help us to observe "in any given case the available means of persuasion" (1355b) and points out that as a faculty is it not in and of itself inclined away from truth. Of course, bad men may abuse it, but that, after all, "is a charge which may be made in common against all good things." "What makes a man a 'sophist,'" he declares, "is not his faculty, but his moral purpose."

Aristotle's second defense is more aggressively positive and responds directly to one of the most damaging characterizations of rhetoric: "We must be able to employ persuasion . . . on opposite sides of a question, not in order that we may in practice employ it in both ways (for we must not make people believe what is wrong), but in order that we may see clearly what the facts are" (1355a). In short, properly used, rhetoric is a heuristic, helping us not to distort the facts but to discover them; the setting forth of contrary views of a matter will have the beneficial effect of showing us which of those views most accords with the truth. By this argument, as Peter Dixon has pointed out (1971, 14), Aristotle "removes rhetoric from the realm of the haphazard and the fanciful" and rejoins it to that very realm of which it was said to be the great subverter.

But if this is the strength of Aristotle's defense, it is also its weakness, for in making it he reinforces the very assumptions in relation to which rhetoric will always be suspect, assumptions of an independent reality whose outlines can be perceived by a sufficiently clear-eyed observer who can then represent them in a transparent verbal medium. The stronger defense, because it hits at the heart of the opposing tradition, is one that embraces the accusations of that tradition and makes of them a claim.

To the accusation that rhetoric deals only with the realms of the probable and contingent and forsake truth, the Sophists and their successors respond that truth itself is a contingent affair and assumes a different shape in the light of differing local urgencies and the convictions associated with them. "Truth was individual and temporary, not universal and lasting, for the truth for any man was . . . what he could be persuaded of" (Guthrie 1971, 193). Not only does this make rhetoric—the art of analyzing and presenting local exigencies—a form of discourse no one can afford to ignore, it renders the opposing discourse—formal philosophy—irrelevant and beside the point. This is precisely Isocrates' thesis in his *Antidosis*. Abstract studies like geometry and astronomy, he says, do not have any "useful application either to private or public affairs; . . . after they are learned . . . they do not attend us through life nor do they lend aid in what we do, but are wholly divorced from our necessities" (Isocrates 1962, 2:261–62).

What Isocrates does (at least rhetorically) is shift the balance of power between philosophy and rhetoric by putting philosophy on the defensive. This same strategy is pursued after him by Cicero and Quintilian, the most influential of the Roman rhetoricians. In the opening pages of his *De Inventione* Cicero elaborates the myth that will subsequently be invoked in every defense of humanism and belles lettres. There was a time, he says, when "men wandered at large in the field like animals," and there was "as yet no ordered system of religious worship nor of social duties" (Cicero, 1:2). It was then that a "great and wise" man "assembled and gathered" his uncivilized brothers and "introduced them to every useful and honorable occupation, though they cried out against it at first because of its novelty." Nevertheless, he gained their attention through "reason and eloquence" (*propter rationem atque orationem*) and by these means he "transformed them from wild savages into a kind and gentle folk." From that time on, "many cities have been founded, . . . the flames of a multitude of wars have been extinguished, and . . . the strongest alliances and most sacred friendships have been formed not only by the use of reason, but also more easily by the use of eloquence" (1:1). Whereas in the foundationalist story an original purity (of vision, purpose, procedure) is corrupted when rhetoric's siren song proves too sweet, in Cicero's story (later to be echoed by countless others) (see, for example, Lawson 1972, 27) all the human virtues, and indeed humanity itself, are wrested by the arts of eloquence from a primitive and violent state of nature. Significantly (and this is a point to which we shall return), both stories are stories of power, rhetoric's power; it is just that in one story that power must be resisted lest civilization fall, while in the other that power brings order and a genuine political process where before there was only the rule of "physical strength."

The contrast between the two stories can hardly be exaggerated because what is at stake is not simply a matter of emphasis or priority (as it seems to be in

Aristotle's effort to demonstrate an *alliance* between rhetoric and truth) but a difference in worldviews. The quarrel between rhetorical and foundational thought is itself foundational; its content is a disagreement about the basic constituents of human activity and about the nature of human nature itself. In Richard Lanham's helpful terms, it is a disagreement as to whether we are members of the species *homo seriosus* or *homo rhetoricus*. *Homo seriosus* or serious man

> possesses a central self, an irreducible identity. These selves combine into a single, homogeneously real society which constitutes a referent reality for the men living in it. This referent society is in turn contained in a physical nature itself referential, standing "out there" independent of man.

Homo rhetoricus or rhetorical man, on the other hand,

> is an actor; his reality public, dramatic. His sense of identity depends on the reassurance of daily histrionic reenactment. . . . The lowest common denominator of his life is a social situation. . . . He is thus committed to no single construction of the world; much rather, to prevailing in the game at hand. . . . Rhetorical man is trained not to discover reality but to manipulate it. Reality is what is accepted as reality, what is useful (Lanham 1976, 1, 4).

As rhetorical man manipulates reality, establishing through his words the imperatives and urgencies to which he and his fellows must respond, he manipulates or fabricates himself, simultaneously conceiving of and occupying the roles that become first possible and then mandatory given the social structure his rhetoric has put in place. By exploring the available means of persuasion in a particular situation, he tries them on, and as they begin to suit him, he becomes them (see Sloane 1985, 87: "Rhetoric succeeded in humanism's great desideratum, the artistic creation of adept personhood"; see also Greenblatt 1980). What serious man fears—the invasion of the fortress of essence by the contingent, the protean and the unpredictable—is what rhetorical man celebrates and incarnates.

Which of these views of human nature is the correct one? The question can be answered only from within one or the other, and the evidence of one party will be regarded by the other either as illusory or as grist for its own mill. When presented with the ever-changing panorama of history, serious man will see variation on a few basic themes; and when confronted with the persistence of essentialist questions and answers, rhetorical man will reply as Lanham does by asserting that serious man is himself a supremely fictional achievement; seriousness is just another style, not the state of having escaped style. That is to say, for rhetorical man the distinctions (between form and content, periphery and core, ephemeral and abiding) invoked by serious man are nothing more than the scaf-

folding of the theatre of seriousness, are themselves instances of what they oppose. And on the other side if serious man were to here *that* argument, he would
regard it as one more example of rhetorical manipulation and sleight of hand, an
outrageous assertion that flies in the face of common sense, the equivalent in
debate of "so's your old man." And so it would go, with no prospect of ever
reaching accord, an endless round of accusation and counteraccusation in which
turth, honesty, and linguistic responsibility are claimed by everyone: "from serious premises, all rhetorical language is suspect; from a rhetorical point of view,
transparent language seems dishonest, false to the world" (Lanham 1976, 28).

And so it *has* gone; the history of Western thought could be written as the
history of this quarrel. And indeed such histories have been written and with
predictably different emphases. In one version written many times, the mists of
religion, magic, and verbal incantation (all equivalently suspect forms of fantasy)
are dispelled by the Enlightenment rediscovery of reason and science; enthusiasm and metaphor alike are curbed by the refinement of method, and the effects
of difference (point of view) are bracketed and held in check by a procedural
rigor. In another version (told by a line stretching from Vico to Foucault) a
carnivalesque world of exuberance and possibility is drastically impoverished by
the ascendancy of a soulless reason, a brutally narrow perspective that claims to
be objective and proceeds in a repressive manner to enforce its claim. It is not
my intention here to endorse either history or to offer a third one or to argue as
some have for a nonhistory of discontinuous *episteme* innocent of either a progressive or lapsarian curve; I only wish to point out that the debate continues to
this very day and that its terms are exactly those one finds in the dialogues of
Plato and the orations of the Sophists.

III

As I write, the fortunes of rhetorical man are on the upswing, as in discipline
after discipline there is evidence of what has been called the interpretive turn,
the realization (at least for those it seizes) that the givens of any field of activity—including the facts it commands, the procedures it trusts in, and the values
it expresses and extends—are socially and politically constructed, are fashioned
by man rather than delivered by God or Nature. The most recent (and unlikely)
field to experience this revolution, or at least to hear of its possibility, is economics. The key text is Donald McCloskey's *The Rhetoric of Economics* (1985), a title
that is itself polemical since, as McCloskey points out, mainstream economists
don't like to think of themselves as employing a rhetoric; rather they regard
themselves as scientists whose methodology insulates them from the appeal of
special interests or points of view. They think, in other words, that the procedures of their discipline will produce "knowledge free from doubt, free from
metaphysics, morals, and personal conviction" (16). To this McCloskey responds by declaring (in good sophistic terms) that no such knowledge is avail-

able, and that while economic method promises to deliver it, "what it is able to deliver [and] renames as scientific methodology [are] the scientist's and especially the economic scientist's metaphysics, morals, and personal convictions" (16). Impersonal method then is both an illusion and a danger (as a kind of rhetoric it masks its rhetorical nature), and as an antidote to it McCloskey offers rhetoric, which he says, deals not with abstract truth, but with the truth that emerges in the context of distinctly human conversations (28–29). Within those conversations, there are always

> particular arguments good or bad. After making them there is no point in asking a last, summarizing question: "Well, is it True?" It's whatever it is—persuasive, interesting, useful, and so forth. . . . There is no reason to search for a general quality called Truth, which answers only the unanswerable question, "What is it in the mind of God?" (47)

The real truth, concludes McCloskey, is that "assertions are made for purposes of persuading some audience" and that given the unavailability of a God's-eye view, "this is not a shameful fact" but the bottom-line fact in a rhetorical world.

At the first conference called to consider McCloskey's arguments, the familiar antirhetorical objections were heard again in the land and the land might have been fifth-century B.C. Athens as well as Wellesley, Massachussets, in 1986. One participant spoke of "the primrose path to extreme relativism." Other voices proclaimed that nothing in McCloskey's position was new (an observation certainly true), that everyone already knew it, and that at any rate it didn't touch the core of the economists' practice. Still others invoked a set of related (and familiar) distinctions between empirical and interpretive activities, between demonstration and persuasion, between verifiable procedures and anarchic irrationalism. Of course, each of these objections had already been formulated (or reformulated) in those disciplines that had heard rhetoric's siren song long before it reached the belated ears of economists. The name that everyone always refers to (in praise or blame) is Thomas Kuhn. His *The Structure of Scientific Revolutions* (1962) is arguably the most frequently cited work in the humanities and social sciences in the past twenty-five years, and it is rhetorical through and through. Kuhn begins by rehearsing and challenging the orthodox model of scientific inquiry in which independent facts are first collected by objective methods and then built up into a picture of nature, a picture that nature herself either confirms or rejects in the context of controlled experiments. In this model, science is a "cumulative process" (3) in which each new discovery adds "one more item to the population of the scientist's world" (7). The shape of that world—of the scientist's professional activities—is determined by the shapes (of fact and structure) already existing in the larger world of nature, shapes that constrain and guide the scientist's work.

Kuhn challenges this story by introducing the notion of a paradigm, a set of tacit assumptions and beliefs within which research goes on, assumptions which rather than deriving from the observation of facts are determinative of the facts that could possibly be observed. It follows then that when observations made within different paradigms conflict, there is no principled (i.e., nonrhetorical) way to adjudicate the dispute. One cannot put the competing accounts to the test of fact, because the specification of fact is precisely what is at issue between them; a fact cited by one party would be seen as a mistake by the other. What this means is that science does not proceed by offering its descriptions to the independent judgment of nature; rather it proceeds when the proponents of one paradigm are able to present their case in a way that the adherents of other paradigms find compelling. In short, the "motor" by which science moves is not verification or falsification, but persuasion. In the case of disagreement, "each party must try, by persuasion, to convert the other" (198), and when one party succeeds there is no higher court to which the outcome might be referred: "there is no standard higher than the assent of the relevant community" (94). "What better criterion," asks Kuhn, "could there be?" (170).

The answer given by those who were horrified by Kuhn's rhetoricization of scientific procedure was predictable: a better criterion would be one that was not captive to a particular paradigm but provided a neutral space in which competing paradigms could be disinterestedly assessed. By denying such a criterion, Kuhn leaves us in a world of epistemological and moral anarchy. The words are Israel Scheffler's:

> Independent and public controls are no more, communication has failed, the common universe of things is a delusion, reality itself is made . . . rather than discovered. . . . In place of a community of rational men following objective procedures in the pursuit of truth, we have a set of isolated monads, within each of which belief forms without systematic constraints. (19)

Kuhn and those he has persuaded have, of course, responded to these accusations, but needless to say, the debate continues in terms readers of this essay could easily imagine; and the debate has been particularly acrimonious because the area of contest—science and its procedures—is so heavily invested-in as the one place where the apostles of rhetorical interpretivism would presumably fear to tread.

At one point in his argument, Kuhn remarks that, in the tradition he is critiquing, scientific research is "reputed to proceed" from "raw data" or "brute experience"; but, he points out, if that were truly the mode of proceeding, it would require a "neutral observation language" (125), a language that registers facts without any mediation by paradigm-specific assumptions. The problem is that "philosophical investigation has not yet provided even a hint of what a language able to do that would be like" (127). Even a specially devised language "embodies a host of expectations about nature," expectations that limit in advance what can be described. Just as one cannot (in Kuhn's view) have recourse to neutral facts in order to settle a dispute, so one cannot have recourse to a neutral language in which to report those facts or even to report on the configuration of the dispute. Whatever reports a particular language (natural or artificial) offers us will be the report on the world as it is seen from within some particular situation; there is no other aperspectival way to see and no language other than a situation-dependent language—an interested, rhetorical language—in which to report.

This same point was being made with all the force of philosophical authority by J. L. Austin in a book published, significantly, in the same year (1962) that saw the publication of *The Structure of Scientific Revolutions*. Austin begins *How to Do Things with Words* by observing that traditionally the center of the philosophy of language has been just the kind of utterance Kuhn declares unavailable, the context-independent statement that offers objective reports on an equally independent world in sentences of the form "He is running" and "Lord Raglan won the battle of Alma" (47, 142). Such utterances, which Austin calls "constative," are answerable to a requirement of truth and verisimilitude ("the truth of the constative . . . 'he is running' depends on his being running"); the words must match the world, and if they do not they can be criticized as false and inaccurate. There are, however, innumerable utterances that are not assessable in this way. If, for example, I say to you, "I promise to pay you five dollars" or "Leave the room," it would be odd were you to respond by saying "true" or "false"; rather you would say to the first "good" or "that's not enough" or "I won't hold my breath" and to the second "yes, sir" or "but I'm expecting a phone call" or "who do you think you are?" These and many other imaginable responses would not be judgments on the truth or accuracy of my utterance but on its appropriateness given our respective positions in some social structure of understanding (domestic, military, economic, etc.). Thus the very identity, and therefore the meaning, of this type of utterance—Austin names it "performative"—depends on the context in which it is produced and received. Nothing guarantees that "I promise to pay you five dollars" will be either intended or heard as a promise; in different circumstances it could be received as a threat or a joke (as when I utter it from debtor's prison) and in many circumstances it will be intended as one act and understood as another (as when your opinion of my trustworthiness is much lower than my own). When the criterion of verisimilitude has been replaced by the criterion of appropriateness, meaning becomes radically contextual, potentially as variable as the situated (and shifting) understandings of countless speakers and hearers.

It is, of course, precisely this property of performatives—their force is contingent and cannot be formally constrained—that is responsible for their being consigned by philosophers of language to the category of the "derived" or "parasitic," where, safely tucked away, they are prevented from contaminating the core category of the constative. But it is this act of segregation and quarantining that Austin undoes in the second half of his book when he extends the analysis of performatives to constatives and finds that they too mean differently in the light of differing contextual circumstances. Consider the exemplary constative, "Lord Raglan won the battle of Alma." Is it true, accurate, a faithful report? It depends, says Austin, on the context in which it is uttered and received (142–43). In a high-school textbook, it might be accepted as true because of the in-place assumptions as to what, exactly, a battle is, what constitutes winning, what the function of a general is, etc., while in a work of "serious" historical research all of these assumptions may have been replaced by others, with the result that the very notions "battle" and "won" would have a different shape. The properties that supposedly distinguish constatives from performatives—fidelity to preexisting facts, accountability to a criterion of truth—turn out to be as dependent on particular conditions of production and reception as performatives. "True" and "false," Austin concludes, are not names for the possible relationships between freestanding (constative) utterances and an equally freestanding state of affairs; rather they are situation-specific judgments on the relationship between contextually produced utterances and states of affairs that are themselves no less contextually produced. At the end of the book constatives are "discovered" to be a subset of performatives, and with this discovery the formal core of language disappears entirely and is replaced by a world of utterances vulnerable to the sea change of every circumstance—the world, in short, of rhetorical (situated) man.

This is a conclusion Austin himself resists when he attempts to isolate (and thereby contain) the rhetorical by invoking another distinction between serious and nonserious utterance. Serious utterances are utterances for which the speaker takes responsibility; he means what he says, and therefore you can infer his meaning by considering his words in context. A nonserious utterance is an utterance produced in circumstances that "abrogate" (21) the speaker's responsibility, and therefore one cannot with any confidence—that is, without the hazard of ungrounded conjecture—determine what he means:

> a performative utterance will, for example, be . . . hollow or void
> if said by an actor on the stage, or if introduced in a poem, or
> spoken in a soliloquy. . . . Language in such circumstances is in
> special ways . . . used not seriously, but in ways *parasitic* upon its
> normal use. . . . All this we are *excluding* from consideration. Our
> performative utterances . . . are to be understood as issued in or-
> dinary circumstances. (22)

The distinction then is between utterances that are, as Austin puts it later, "tethered to their origin" (61), anchored by a palpable intention, and utterances whose origin is hidden by the screen of a theatrical or literary stage-setting. This distinction and the passage in which it appears were taken up in 1967 by Jacques Derrida in a famous (and admiring) critique of Austin. Derrida finds Austin working against his own best insights and forgetting what he has just acknowledged, that "infelicity [communication going astray, in an unintended direction] is an ill to which *all* [speech] acts are heir" (Derrida 1977). Despite this acknowledgment, Austin continues to think of infelicity—of those cases in which the tethering origin of utterances is obscure and must be constructed by interpretive conjecture—as special, whereas, in Derrida's view, infelicity is itself the originary state in that any determination of meaning must always proceed within an interpretive construction of a speaker's intention. In short, there are no ordinary circumstances, merely those myriad and varied circumstances in which actors embedded in stage settings hazard interpretations of utterances produced by actors embedded in other stage situations. All the world, as Shakespeare says, is a stage, and on that stage "the quality of risk" admitted by Austin is not something one can avoid by sticking close to ordinary language in ordinary circumstances, but is rather "the internal and positive condition" of any act of communication (Derrida 1977, 190).

In the same publication in which the English translation of Derrida's essay appeared, John Searle, a student of Austin's, replied in terms that make clear the affiliation of this particular debate to the ancient debate whose configurations we have been tracing. Searle's strategy is basically to repeat Austin's points and declare that Derrida has missed them: "Austin's idea is simply this: if we want to know what it is to make a promise we had better not *start* our investigations with promises made by actors on stage . . . because in some fairly obvious ways such utterances are not standard cases of promises" (Searle 1977, 204). But in Derrida's argument, the category of the "obvious" is precisely what is being challenged or "deconstructed." Although it is true that we consider promises uttered in everyday contexts more direct—less etiolated—than promises made on a stage, this (Derrida would say) is only because the stage settings within which everyday life proceeds, are so powerfully—that is, rhetorically—in place that they are in effect invisible, and therefore the meanings they make possible are experienced as if they were direct and unmediated by any screens. The "obvious" cannot be opposed to the "staged," as Searle assumes, because it is simply the achievement of a staging that has been particularly successful. One does not escape the rhetorical by fleeing to the protected area of basic communication and common sense because common sense in whatever form it happens to take is always a rhetorical—partial, partisan, interested—construction. This does not mean, Derrida hastens to add, that all rhetorical constructions are equal, just that they are equally rhetorical, equally the effects and extensions of some limited and challengeable point of view. The "citationality"—the condition of being in quotes, of being *in*direct—of an utterance in a play is not the same as the citationality of a philosophical reference or a deposition before a court; it is just that no one of these performatives is more serious—more direct, less mediated, less rhetorical—than any other.

One recognizes in these assertions the familiar world of Rhetorical Man, teeming with roles, situations, strategies, interventions, but containing no master role, no situation of situations, no strategy for outflanking all strategies, no intervention in the arena of dispute that does not expand the arena of dispute, no neutral point of rationality from the vantage point of which the "merely rhetorical" can be identified and held in check. Indeed deconstructive or poststructuralist thought is in its operation a rhetorical machine: it systematically asserts and demonstrates the mediated, constructed, partial, socially constituted nature of all realities, whether they be phenomenal, linguistic, or psychological. To deconstruct a text, says Derrida, is to "work through the structured genealogy of its concepts in the most scrupulous and immanent fashion, but at the same time to determine from a certain external perspective that it cannot name or describe what this history may have concealed or excluded, constituting itself as history through this repression in which it has a stake" (1981, 6). The "external perspective" is the perspective from which the analyst knows in advance (by virtue of his commitment to the rhetorical or deconstructive worldview) that the coherence presented by a text (and an institution or an economy can in this sense be a text) rests on a contradiction it cannot acknowledge, rests on the suppression of the challengeable rhetoricity of its own standpoint. A deconstructive reading will surface those contradictions and expose those suppressions and thus "trouble" a unity that is achieved only by covering over all the excluded emphases and interests that might threaten it.

Nor is this act performed in the service of something beyond rhetoric. Derridean deconstruction does not uncover the operations of rhetoric in order to reach the Truth; rather it continually uncovers the truth of rhetorical operations, the truth that all operations, including the operation of deconstruction itself, are rhetorical. If, as Paul de Man asserts, "a deconstruction always has for its target to reveal the existence of hidden articulations and fragmentations within assumedly monadic totalities," care must be taken that a new monadic totality is not left as the legacy of the deconstructive gesture. Since the course of a deconstruction is to uncover a "fragmented stage that can be called natural with regard to the system that is being undone," there is always the danger that the "natural" pattern will "substitute *its* relational system for the one it helped to dissolve" (de Man 1979, 249). The only way to escape this danger is to perform the deconstructive act again and again, submitting each new emerging constellation to the same suspicious scrutiny that brought it to light, and resisting the temptation to put in place of the truths it rhetoricizes the truth that everything is rhetorical.

One cannot rest even in the insight that there is no place to rest. The rhetorical beat must by definition go on, endlessly repeating the sequence by which "the lure of solid ground" is succeeded by "the ensuing demystification" (Ray 1984, 195). When de Man approvingly quotes Nietzsche's identification of truth with "a moving army of metaphors, metonymies and anthropomorphisms," a rhetorical construction whose origin has been (and must be) forgotten, he does not exempt Nietzsche's text from its own corrosive effects. "A text like *On Truth and Lie,* although it presents itself legitimately as a demystification of literary rhetoric remains entirely literary, and deceptive itself" (113). The "rhetorical mode," the mode of deconstruction, is a mode of "endless reflection," since it is "unable ever to escape from the rhetorical deceit it announces" (115).

IV

That, however, is just what is wrong with deconstructive practice from the viewpoint of the intellectual left, many of whose members subscribe to Nietzsche's account of truth and reality as rhetorical, but find that much of poststructuralist discourse uses that account as a way of escaping into new versions of idealism and formalism. Frank Lentricchia, for example, sees in some of de Man's texts an intention to place "discourse in a realm where it can have no responsibility to historical life" and fears that we are being invited into "the realm of the thoroughly predictable linguistic transcendental," the "rarified region of the undecidable," where every text "speaks synchronically and endlessly the same tale . . . of its own duplicitous self-consciousness" (1980, 310, 317). Terry Eagleton's judgment is even harsher. Noting that in the wake of Nietzschean thought, rhetoric, "mocked and berated for centuries by an abrasive rationalism," takes its "terrible belated revenge" by finding itself in every rationalist project, Eagleton complains that many rhetoricians seem content to stop there, satisfied with the "Fool's function of unmasking all power as self-rationalization, all knowledge as a mere fumbling with metaphor" (1981, 108). Operating as a "vigorous demystifier of all ideology," rhetoric functions only as a form of thought and ends up by providing "the final ideological rationale for political inertia." In retreat "from market place to study, politics to philology, social practice to semiotics" deconstructive rhetoric turns the emancipatory promise of Nietzschean thought into "a gross failure of ideological nerve," allowing the liberal academic the elitist pleasure of repeatedly exposing "vulgar commercial and political hectorings" (108–9). In both his study of Benjamin and his influential *Literary Theory: An Introduction,* Eagleton urges a return to the Ciceronian-Isocratic tradition in which the rhetorical arts are inseparable from the practice of a politics, "techniques of persuasion indissociable from the substantive issues and audiences involved," techniques whose employment is "closely determined by the pragmatic situation at hand" (601). In short, he calls for a rhetoric that will do real work and cites as an example the slogan "black is beautiful" which he says is "paradigmatically rhetorical since it employs a figure of equivalence to produce particular discursive and extra-discursive effects without direct regard for truth" (112). That is, someone who says "black is beautiful" is not so much interested in the accuracy of the assertion (it is not constatively intended) as he is in the responses it may provoke—surprise, outrage, urgency, solidarity—responses that may in turn set in motion "practices that are deemed, in the light of a particular set of falsifiable hypotheses, to be desirable" (113). This confidence in his objectives makes Eagleton impatient with those for whom the rhetoricity of all discourse is something to be savored for itself, something to be lovingly and obsessively demonstrated again and again. It is not, he says, "a matter of starting from certain theoretical or methodological problems; it is a matter of starting from what we want to *do,* and then seeing which methods and theories will best help us to achieve these ends" (1983, 211). Theories, in short, are themselves rhetorics whose usefulness is a function of contingent circumstances. It is ends—specific goals in local contexts—that rule the invocation of theories, not theories that determine goals and the means by which they can be reached.

There are those on the left, however, for whom the direction is the other way around, from the theoretical realization of rhetoric's pervasiveness to a vision and a program for implementing it. In their view the discovery (or rediscovery) that all discourse and therefore all knowledge is rhetorical leads, or should lead, to the adoption of a *method* by which the dangers of rhetoric can be at least mitigated and perhaps extirpated. This method has two stages: the first is a stage of debunking, and it issues from the general suspicion in which all orthodoxies and arrangements of power are held once it is realized that their basis is not reason or nature but the success of some rhetorical/political agenda. Armed with this realization one proceeds to expose the contingent and therefore challengeable basis of whatever presents itself as natural and inevitable. So far this is precisely the procedure of deconstruction; but whereas deconstructive practice (at least of the Yale variety) seems to produce nothing but the occasion for its endless repetition, some cultural revolutionaries discern in it a more positive residue, the loosening or weakening of the structures of domination and oppression that now hold us captive. The reasoning is that by repeatedly uncovering the historical and ideological basis of established structures (both political and cognitive), one becomes sensitized to the effects of ideology and begins to clear a space in which those effects can be combatted; and as that sensitivity grows more acute, the area of combat will become larger until it encompasses the underlying structure of assumptions that confers a spurious legitimacy on the powers that currently be. The claim, in short, is that the radically rhetorical insight of Nietzschean/Derridean thought can do radical political work; becoming aware that everything is rhetorical is the first step in countering the power of rhetoric and liberating us from its force. Only if deeply entrenched ways of thinking are made the objects of suspicion will we be able "even to *imagine* that life could be different and better."

This last sentence is taken from an essay by Robert Gordon entitled "New Developments in Legal Theory" (1982, 287). Gordon is writing as a member of the Critical Legal Studies movement, a group of legal academics who have discovered the rhetorical nature of legal reasoning and are busily exposing as interested the supposedly disinterested operations of legal procedures. Gordon's pages are replete with the vocabulary of enclosure or prison; we are "locked-into" a system of belief we did not make; we are "demobilized" (that is, rendered less mobile); we must "break out" (291), we must "unfreeze the world as it appears to common sense" (289). What will help us to break out, to unfreeze, is the discovery "that the belief-structures that rule our lives are not found in nature but are historically contingent," for that discovery, says Gordon, "is extraordinarily liberating" (289). To the question, what is the *content* of that liberation, given a world that is rhetorical through and through, those who work Gordon's side of the street usually reply that emancipation will take the form of a strengthening and enlarging of a capacity of mind that stands to the side of, and is therefore able to resist, the appeal of the agenda that would enslave us. That capacity of mind has received many names, but the one most often proposed is "critical self-consciousness." Critical self-consciousness is the ability (stifled in some, developed in others) to discern in any "scheme of association," including those one finds attractive and compelling, the partisan aims it hides from view; and the claim is that as it performs this negative task critical self-consciousness participates in the positive task of formulating schemes of associations (structures of thought and government) that are in the service not of a particular party but of all mankind.

It need hardly be said that this claim veers back in the direction of the rationalism and universalism that the critical/deconstructive project sets out to demystify. That project begins by rejecting the rationalities of present life as rationalizations, and revealing the structure of reality to be rhetorical, that is, partial; but then it turns around and attempts to use the insight of partiality to build something that is less partial, less hostage to the urgencies of a particular vision and more responsive to the needs of men and women in general. Insofar as this "turn" is taken to its logical conclusion, it ends up reinventing at the conclusion of a rhetorically informed critique the entire array of antirhetorical gestures and exclusions. One sees this clearly in the work of Jürgen Habermas, a thinker whose widespread influence is testimony to the durability of the tradition that began (at least) with Plato. Habermas's goal is to bring about something he calls the "ideal speech situation," a situation in which all assertions proceed not from the perspective of individual desires and strategies, but from the perspective of a general rationality upon which all parties are agreed. In such a situation nothing would count except the claims to universal validity of all assertions. "No force except that of the better argument is exercised; and . . . as a result, all motives except that of the cooperative search for truth are excluded" (1975, 107–8). Of course, in the world we now inhabit, there is no such purity of motive, but nevertheless, says Habermas, even in the most distorted of communicative situations there remains something of the basic impulse behind all utterance, "the intention of communicating a true [*wahr*] proposition . . . so that the hearer can share the knowledge of the speaker" (1979, 2). If we could only eliminate from our discourse-performances those intentions that reflect baser goals—the intentions to deceive, to manipulate, to persuade—the ideal speech situation could be approximated.

This is the project Habermas names "Universal Pragmatics" and the name tells its own story. Habermas recognizes, as all modern and postmodern contextualists do, that language is a social and not a purely formal phenomenon, but he thinks that the social/pragmatic aspect of language use is itself "accessible to formal analysis" (6) and that therefore it is possible to construct a universal "communicative competence" (29) parallel to Chomsky's linguistic competence. Sentences produced according to the rules and norms of this communicative competence would be tied not to "particular epistemic presuppositions and changing contexts" (29), but to the unchanging context (the context of contexts) in which one finds the presuppositions underlying the general possibility of successful speech. "A *general* theory of speech acts would . . . describe . . . that fundamental system of rules that adult subjects master to the extent that they can fulfill *the conditions of happy employment of sentences in utterances* no matter to which particular language the sentences may belong and in which accidental contexts the utterances may be embedded" (26). If we can operate on the level of that fundamental system, the distorting potential of "accidental contexts" will be neutralized because we will always have one eye on what is essential, the establishing by rational cooperation of an interpersonal (nonaccidental) truth. Once speakers are oriented to this goal and away from others, oriented toward *general* understanding, they will be incapable of deception and manipulation. A company of transparent subjectivities will join together in the fashioning of a transparent truth and of a world in which the will to power has been eliminated.

In his recent book *Textual Power* (1985), Robert Scholes examines the rationalist epistemology in which a "complete self confronts a solid world, perceiving it directly and accurately, . . . capturing it perfectly in a transparent language" and declares it to be so thoroughly discredited that it now "is lying in ruins around us" (132–33). Perhaps so, in some circles, but the fact of Habermas's work and of the audience he commands suggests that even now those ruins are collecting themselves and rising again into the familiar antirhetorical structure. It would seem that any announcement of the death of either position will always be premature, slightly behind the institutional news that in some corner of the world supposedly abandoned questions are receiving what at least appear to be new answers. Only recently, the *public* fortunes of rationalist-foundationalist thought have taken a favorable turn with the publication of books like Alan Bloom's *The Closing of the American Mind* and E. D. Hirsch's *Cultural Literacy*, both of which (Bloom's more directly) challenge the "new Orthodoxy" of "extreme cultural relativism" and reassert, albeit in different ways, the existence of normative standards. In many quarters these books have been welcomed as a return to the common sense that is necessary if civilization is to avoid the dark night of anarchy. One can expect administrators and legislators to propose reforms (and perhaps even purges) based on Bloom's arguments (the rhetorical force of antirhetoricalism is always being revived) and one can expect too a host of voices raised in opposition to what will surely be called the "new positivism." Those voices will include some that have been recorded here and some others that certainly merit recording, but can only be noted in a list that is itself incomplete. The full story of rhetoric's twentieth-century resurgence would boast among its cast of characters: Kenneth Burke, whose "dramatism" anticipates so much of what is considered avant-garde today; Wayne Booth, whose *The Rhetoric of Fiction* was so important in legitimizing the rhetorical analysis of the novel; Mikhail Bahktin, whose contrast of monologic to dialogic and heteroglossic discourse sums up so many strands in the rhetorical tradition; Roland Barthes, who in the concept of "jouissance" makes a (non)constitutive principle of the tendency of rhetoric to resist closure and extend play; the ethnomethodologists (Harold Garfinkel and company), who discover in every supposedly rule-bound context the operation of a principle (exactly the wrong word) of "ad-hocing"; Chaim Perelman and L. Olbrechts-Tyteca, whose *The New Rhetoric: A Treatise on Argumentation* provides a sophisticated modern source-book for would-be rhetoricians weary of always citing Aristotle; Barbara Herrnstein Smith, who in the course of espousing an unashamed relativism directly confronts and argues down the objections of those who fear for their souls (and more) in a world without objective standards; Fredric Jameson and Hayden White, who teach us (among other things) that "history . . . is unaccessible to us except in textual form, and that our approach to it and to the Real itself necessarily passes through its prior textualization" (1981, 35); reader-oriented critics like Norman Holland, David Bleich, Wolfgang Iser, and H. R. Jauss, who by shifting the emphasis from the text to its reception open up the act of interpretation to the infinite variability of contextual circumstance; innumerable feminists who relentlessly unmask male hegemonic structures and expose as rhetorical the rational posturings of the legal and political systems; equally innumerable theorists of composition who, under the slogan "process, not product," insist on the rhetorical nature of communication and argue for far-reaching changes in the way writing is taught. The list is already formidable, but it could go on and on, providing support for Scholes's contention that the rival epistemology has been vanquished and for Clifford Geertz's announcement (and he too is a contributor to the shift he reports) that "Something is happening to the way we think about the way we think" (1980).

But it would seem, from the evidence marshalled in this essay, that something is always happening to the way we think, and that it is always the same something, a tug-of-war between two views of human life and its possibilities, no one of which can ever gain complete and lasting ascendancy because in the very moment of its triumphant articulation each turns back in the direction of the other. Thus Wayne Booth feels obliged in both *The Rhetoric of Fiction* and *A Rhetoric of Irony* to confine the force of rhetoric by sharply distinguishing its legitimate uses from two extreme limit cases (the "unreliable narrator" and "unstable irony"); some reader-response critics deconstruct the autonomy and self-sufficiency of the text, but in the process end up privileging the autonomous and self-sufficient subject; some feminists challenge the essentialist claims of "male reason" in the name of a female rationality or nonrationality apparently no less essential; Jameson opens up the narrativity of history in order to proclaim one narrative the true and unifying one. Here one might speak of the return of the repressed (and thereby invoke Freud, whose writings and influence would be still another chapter in the story I have not even begun to tell) were it not that the repressed— whether it be the fact of difference or the desire for its elimination—is always so close to the surface that it hardly need be unearthed. What we seem to have is a tale full of sound and fury, and signifying itself, signifying a durability rooted in inconclusiveness, in the impossibility of there being a last word.

In an essay, however, someone must have the last word and I give it to Richard Rorty. Rorty is himself a champion of the antiessentialism that underlies rhetorical thinking; his neopragmatism makes common cause with Kuhn and others who would turn us away from the search for transcendental absolutes and commend to us (although it would seem superfluous to do so) the imperatives and goals already informing our practices. It is however, not the polemicist Rorty whom I call upon to sum up, but the Rorty who is the brisk chronicler of our epistemological condition:

> There . . . are two ways of thinking about various things. . . . The first . . . thinks of truth as a vertical relationship between representations and what is represented. The second . . . thinks of truth horizontally—as the culminating reinterpretation of our predecessors' reinterpretation of their predecessors' reinterpretation. . . . It is the difference between regarding truth, goodness, and beauty as eternal objects which we try to locate and reveal, and regarding them as artifacts whose fundamental design we often have to alter (1982, 92).

It is the difference between serious and rhetorical man. It is the difference that remains.

SUGGESTED READINGS

Guthrie, W. 1971. *The Sophists.*

Howell, W. S. 1956. *Logic and Rhetoric in England 1500–1700.*

———. 1971. *Eighteenth-Century British Logic and Rhetoric.*

Kennedy, George. 1972. *The Art of Persuasion in the Roman World (300BC–AD300).*

———. 1963. *The Art of Persuasion in Greece.*

Murphy, J. J. 1966. *Rhetoric in the Middle Ages.*

Nelson, John S., Allan Megill, and Donald N. McCloskey. 1987. *The Rhetoric of the Human Sciences: Language and Argument in Scholarship and Public Affairs.*

Ong, W. J. 1958. *Ramus, Method, and the Decay of Dialogue.*

Perelman, Chaim, and Lucy Olbrechts-Tyteca. 1969. *The New Rhetoric: A Treatise on Argument.*

Puttenham, George. 1936; 1970. *The Arte of English Poesie* (London, 1589).

Quintilian. *Institutio Oratoria.*

Smith, Barbara Herrnstein. 1988. *Contingencies of Value: Alternative Perspectives for Critical Theory.*

Tuve, Rosemond. 1947. *Elizabethan and Metaphysical Imagery. Renaissance Poetic and Twentieth-Century Critics.*

Vickers, Brian. 1988. *In Defence of Rhetoric.*

White, Hayden. 1973. *Metahistory: The Historical Imagination in Nineteenth-Century Europe.*

III

Literature, Culture, Politics

16

Culture

Stephen Greenblatt

THE TERM "culture" has not always been used in literary studies, and indeed the very concept denoted by the term is fairly recent. "Culture or Civilization," wrote the influential anthropologist Edward B. Tylor in 1871, "taken in its wide ethnographic sense, is that complex whole which includes knowledge, belief, art, morals, law, custom, and any other capabilities and habits acquired by man as a member of society." Why should such a concept be useful to students of literature?

The answer may be that it is not. After all, the term as Tylor uses it is almost impossibly vague and encompassing, and the few things that seem excluded from it are almost immediately reincorporated in the actual use of the word. Hence we may think with a certain relief that at least "culture" does not refer to material objects—tables, or gold, or grain, or spinning wheels—but of course those objects, as used by men and women, are close to the center of any particular society, and we may accordingly speak of such a society's "material culture." Like "ideology" (to which, as a concept, it is closely allied), "culture" is a term that is repeatedly used without meaning much of anything at all, a vague gesture toward a dimly perceived ethos: aristocratic culture, youth culture, human culture. There is nothing especially wrong with such gestures—without them we wouldn't ordinarily be able to get through three consecutive sentences—but they are scarcely the backbone of an innovative critical practice.

How can we get the concept of culture to do more work for us? We might begin by reflecting on the fact that the concept gestures toward what appear to be opposite things: *constraint* and *mobility*. The ensemble of beliefs and practices that form a given culture function as a pervasive technology of control, a set of limits within which social behavior must be contained, a repertoire of models to which individuals must conform. The limits need not be narrow—in certain societies, such as that of the United States, they can seem quite vast—but they are not infinite, and the consequences for straying beyond them can be severe. The most effective disciplinary techniques practiced against those who stray beyond the limits of a given culture are probably not the spectacular punishments reserved for serious offenders—exile, imprisonment in an insane asylum, penal servitude, or execution—but seemingly innocuous responses: a condescending smile, laughter poised between the genial and the sarcastic, a small dose of indulgent pity laced with contempt, cool silence. And we should add that a culture's boundaries are enforced more positively as well: through the system of rewards that range again from the spectacular (grand public honors, glittering prizes) to the apparently modest (a gaze of admiration, a respectful nod, a few words of gratitude).

Here we can make our first tentative move toward the use of culture for the study of literature, for Western literature over a very long period of time has been one of the great institutions for the enforcement of cultural boundaries through praise and blame. This is most obvious in the kinds of literature that are explicitly engaged in attack and celebration: satire and panegyric. Works in these genres often seem immensely important when they first appear, but their power begins quickly to fade when the individuals to whom the works refer begin to fade, and the evaporation of literary power continues when the models and limits that the works articulated and enforced have themselves substantially changed. The footnotes in modern editions of these works can give us the names and dates that have been lost, but they cannot in themselves enable us to recover a sense of the stakes that once gave readers pleasure and pain. An awareness of culture as a complex whole can help us to recover that sense by leading us to reconstruct the boundaries upon whose existence the works were predicated.

We can begin to do so simply by a heightened attention to the beliefs and practices implicitly enforced by particular literary acts of praising or blaming. That is, we can ask ourselves a set of cultural questions about the work before us:

> What kinds of behavior, what models of practice, does this work seem to enforce?
> Why might readers at a particular time and place find this work compelling?
> Are there differences between my values and the values implicit in the work I am reading?
> Upon what social understandings does the work depend?
> Whose freedom of thought or movement might be constrained implicitly or explicitly by this work?
> What are the larger social structures with which these particular acts of praise or blame might be connected?

Such questions heighten our attention to features of the literary work that we might not have noticed, and, above all, to connections among elements within the work. Eventually, a full cultural analysis will need to push beyond the boundaries of the text, to establish links between the text and values, institutions, and practices elsewhere in the culture. But these links cannot be a substitute for close reading. Cultural analysis has much to learn from scrupulous formal analysis of literary texts because those texts are not merely cultural by virtue of reference to the world beyond themselves; they are cultural by virtue of social values and contexts that they have themselves successfully absorbed. The world is full of texts, most of which are virtually incomprehensible when they are removed from their immediate surroundings. To recover the meaning of such texts, to make any sense of them at all, we need to reconstruct the situation in which they were produced. Works of art by contrast contain directly or by implication much of this situation within themselves, and it is this sustained absorption that enables many literary works to survive the collapse of the conditions that led to their production.

Cultural analysis then is not by definition an extrinsic analysis, as opposed to an internal formal analysis of works of art. At the same time, cultural analysis must be opposed on principle to the rigid distinction between that which is within a text and that which lies outside. It is necessary to use whatever is available to construct a vision of the "complex whole" to which Tylor referred. And if an exploration of a particular culture will lead to a heightened understanding of a work of literature produced within that culture, so too a careful reading of a work of literature will lead to a heightened understanding of the culture within which it was produced. The organization of this volume makes it appear that the analysis of culture is the servant of literary study, but in a liberal education broadly conceived it is literary study that is the servant of cultural understanding.

I will return to the question of extrinsic as opposed to intrinsic analysis, but first we must continue to pursue the idea of culture as a system of constraints. The functioning of such a system is obvious in poems like Pope's "Epistle to Doctor Arbuthnot" or Marvell's "Horatian Ode" on Cromwell, works that undertake to excoriate dullness as embodied in certain hated individuals and celebrate civic or military virtue as embodied in certain admired individuals. Indeed culture here is close to its earlier sense of "cultivation"—the internalization and practice of a code of manners. And this sense extends well beyond the limits of satire and panegyric, particularly for those periods in which manners were a crucial sign of status difference.

Consider, for example, Shakespeare's *As You Like It,* where Orlando's bitter complaint is not that he has been excluded from his patrimony—Orlando accepts the custom of primogeniture by which his brother, as the eldest son, inherits virtually all the family property—but rather that he is being prevented from learning the manners of his class: "My father charged you in his will to give me a good education: you have train'd me like a peasant, obscuring and hiding from me all gentleman-like qualities." Shakespeare characteristically suggests that Orlando has within him an innate gentility that enables him to rise naturally above his boorish upbringing, but he equally characteristically suggests that Orlando's gentility needs to be shaped and brought to fruition through a series of difficult trials. When in the Forest of Arden the young man roughly demands food for his aged servant Adam, he receives a lesson in courtesy: "Your gentleness shall force/More than your force move us to gentleness." The lesson has a special authority conferred upon it by the fact that it is delivered by the exiled Duke, the figure at the pinnacle of the play's social order. But the entire world of *As You Like It* is engaged in articulating cultural codes of behavior, from the elaborate, ironic training in courtship presided over by Rosalind to the humble but dignified social order by which the shepherds live. Even the simple country wench Audrey receives a lesson in manners from the sophisticated clown Touchstone: "bear your body more seeming, Audrey." This instruction in the management of the body, played no doubt for comic effect, is an enactment in miniature of a process of acculturation occurring everywhere in the play, and occurring most powerfully perhaps on an almost subliminal level, such as the distance we automatically keep from others or the way we position our legs when we sit down. Shakespeare wittily parodies this process—for example, in Touchstone's elaborate rule-book for insults—but he also participates in it, for even as his plays represent characters engaged in negotiating the boundaries of their culture, the plays also help to establish and maintain those boundaries for their audiences.

Art is an important agent then in the transmission of culture. It is one of the ways in which the roles by which men and women are expected to pattern their lives are communicated and passed from generation to generation. Certain artists have been highly self-conscious about this function. The purpose of his vast romance epic, *The Faerie Queene,* writes the Renaissance poet Edmund Spenser, is "to fashion a gentleman or noble person in virtuous and gentle discipline." The depth of our understanding of such a project, extended over a complex plot involving hundreds of allegorical figures, depends upon the extent of our grasp of Spenser's entire culture, from its nuanced Aristotelian conception of moral hierarchies to its apocalyptic fantasies, from exquisite refinement at court to colonial violence in Ireland. More precisely, we need to grasp the way in which this culture of mixed motives and conflicting desires seemed to Spenser to generate an interlocking series of models, a moral order, a set of ethical constraints ranged against the threat of anarchy, rebellion, and chaos.

To speak of *The Faerie Queene* only in terms of the constraints imposed by culture is obviously inadequate, since the poem itself, with its knights and ladies endlessly roaming an imaginary landscape, is so insistent upon mobility. We return to the paradox with which we started: if culture functions as a structure of limits, it also functions as the regulator and guarantor of movement. Indeed the limits are virtually meaningless without movement; it is only through improvisation, experiment, and exchange that cultural boundaries can be established. Obviously, among different cultures there will be a great diversity in the ratio between mobility and constraint. Some cultures dream of imposing an absolute order, a perfect stasis, but even these, if they are to reproduce themselves from one generation to the next, will have to commit themselves, however tentatively or unwillingly, to some minimal measure of movement; conversely, some cultures dream of an absolute mobility, a perfect freedom, but these too have always been compelled, in the interest of survival, to accept some limits.

What is set up, under wildly varying circumstances and with radically divergent consequences, is a structure of improvisation, a set of patterns that have enough elasticity, enough scope for variation, to accommodate most of the participants in a given culture. A life that fails to conform at all, that violates absolutely all the available patterns, will have to be dealt with as an emergency—hence exiled, or killed, or declared a god. But most individuals are content to improvise, and, in the West at least, a great many works of art are centrally concerned with these improvisations. The novel has been particularly sensitive to the diverse ways in which individuals come to terms with the governing patterns of culture; works like Dickens' *Great Expectations* and Eliot's *Middlemarch* brilliantly explore the ironies and pain, as well as the inventiveness, of particular adjustments.

In representing this adjustment as a social, emotional, and intellectual education, these novels in effect thematize their own place in culture, for works of art are themselves educational tools. They do not merely passively reflect the prevailing ratio of mobility and constraint; they help to shape, articulate, and reproduce it through their own improvisatory intelligence. This means that, despite our romantic cult of originality, most artists are themselves gifted creators of variations upon received themes. Even those great writers whom we regard with special awe, and whom we celebrate for their refusal to parrot the clichés of their culture, tend to be particularly brilliant improvisers rather than absolute violaters or pure inventors. Thus Dickens crafted cunning adaptations of the melodramatic potboilers of his times; Shakespeare borrowed most of his plots, and many of his characters, from familiar tales or well-rehearsed historical narratives; and Spenser revised for his own culture stories first told, and told wonderfully, by the Italian poets Ariosto and Tasso.

Such borrowing is not evidence of imaginative parsimony, still less a symptom of creative exhaustion—I am using Dickens, Shakespeare, and Spenser precisely because they are among the most exuberant, generous, and creative literary imaginations in our language. It signals rather a further aspect of the cultural mobility to which I have already pointed. This mobility is not the expression of random motion but of *exchange*. A culture is a particular network of negotiations for the exchange of material goods, ideas, and—through institutions like enslavement, adoption, or marriage—people. Anthropologists are centrally concerned with a culture's kinship system—its conception of family relationships, its prohibitions of certain couplings, its marriage rules—and with its narratives—its myths, folktales, and sacred stories. The two concerns are linked, for a culture's narratives, like its kinship arrangements, are crucial indices of the prevailing codes governing human mobility and constraint. Great writers are precisely masters of these codes, specialists in cultural exchange. The works they create are structures for the accumulation, transformation, representation, and communication of social energies and practices.

In any culture there is a general symbolic economy made up of the myriad signs that excite human desire, fear, and aggression. Through their ability to construct resonant stories, their command of effective imagery, and above all their sensitivity to the greatest collective creation of any culture—language— literary artists are skilled at manipulating this economy. They take symbolic materials from one zone of the culture and move them to another, augmenting their emotional force, altering their significance, linking them with other materials taken from a different zone, changing their place in a larger social design. Take, for example, Shakespeare's *King Lear:* the dramatist borrows an often-told pseudo-historical account of an ancient British king, associates with it his society's most severe anxieties about kinship relations on the one hand and civil strife on the other, infuses a measure of apocalyptic religious expectation mingled paradoxically with an acute skepticism, and returns these materials to his audience, transformed into what is perhaps the most intense experience of tragic pleasure ever created. A nuanced cultural analysis will be concerned with the various matrices from which Shakespeare derives his materials, and hence will be drawn outside the formal boundary of the play—toward the legal arrangements, for example, that elderly parents in the Renaissance made with their children, or toward child-rearing practices in the period, or toward political debates about when, if ever, disobeying a legitimate ruler was justified, or toward predictions of the imminent end of the world.

The current structure of liberal arts education often places obstacles in the way of such an analysis by separating the study of history from the study of literature, as if the two were entirely distinct enterprises, but historians have become increasingly sensitive to the symbolic dimensions of social practice, while literary critics have in recent years turned with growing interest to the social and historical dimensions of symbolic practice. Hence it is more possible, both in terms of individual courses and of overall programs of study, for students to reach toward a sense of the complex whole of a particular culture. But there is much to be done in the way of cultural analysis even without an integrated structure of courses, much that depends primarily on asking fresh questions about the possible social functions of works of art. Indeed even if one begins to achieve a sophisticated historical sense of the cultural materials out of which a literary text is constructed, it remains essential to study the ways in which these materials are formally put together and articulated in order to understand the cultural work that the text accomplishes.

For great works of art are not neutral relay stations in the circulation of cultural materials. Something happens to objects, beliefs, and practices when they are represented, reimagined, and performed in literary texts, something often unpredictable and disturbing. That "something" is the sign both of the power of art and of the embeddedness of culture in the contingencies of history. I have written at moments as if art always reinforces the dominant beliefs and social structures of its culture, as if culture is always harmonious rather than shifting and conflict-ridden, and as if there necessarily is a mutually affirmative relation between artistic production and the other modes of production and reproduction that make up a society. At times there is precisely such an easy and comfortable conjunction, but it is by no means necessary. The ability of artists to assemble and shape the forces of their culture in novel ways so that elements powerfully interact that rarely have commerce with one another in the general economy has the potential to unsettle this affirmative relation. Indeed in our own time most students of literature reserve their highest admiration for those works that situate themselves on the very edges of what can be said at a particular place and time, that batter against the boundaries of their own culture.

Near the end of his career Shakespeare decided to take advantage of his contemporaries' lively interest in New World exploration. His play *The Tempest* contains many details drawn from the writings of adventurers and colonists, details that are skillfully displaced onto a mysterious Mediterranean island and interwoven with echoes from Virgil's *Aeneid,* from other art forms such as the court masque and pastoral tragicomedy, and from the lore of white magic. The play reiterates the arguments that Europeans made about the legitimacy and civilizing force of their presence in the newly discovered lands; indeed it intensifies those arguments by conferring upon Prospero the power not only of a great prince who has the right to command the forces of this world but of a wizard who has the ability—the "Art" as the play terms it—to command supernatural forces as well. But the intensification has an oddly discordant effect: the magical power is clearly impressive but its legitimacy is less clear.

As magician Prospero resembles no one in the play so much as Sycorax, the hated witch who had preceded him as the island's ruler. The play, to be sure, does not endorse a challenge to Prospero's rule, any more than Shakespeare's culture ever encouraged challenges to legitimate monarchs. And yet out of the uneasy matrix formed by the skillful interweaving of cultural materials comes an odd, discordant voice, the voice of the "salvage and deformed slave" Caliban:

> This island's mine, by Sycorax my mother,
> Which thou tak'st from me. When thou cam'st first
> Thou strok'st me, and made much of me; wouldst give me
> Water with berries in't; and teach me how
> To name the bigger light, and how the less,
> That burn by day and night: and then I lov'd thee,
> And show'd thee all the qualities o'th'isle,
> The fresh springs, brine-pits, barren place and fertile:

Curs'd be I that did so! All the charms
Of Sycorax, toads, beetles, bats, light on you!
For I am all the subjects that you have,
Which first was mine own King: and here you sty me
In this hard rock, whiles you do keep from me
The rest o'th'island.

Caliban, of course, does not triumph: it would take different artists from different cultures—the postcolonial Caribbean and African cultures of our own times—to rewrite Shakespeare's play and make good on Caliban's claim. But even within the powerful constraints of Shakespeare's Jacobean culture, the artist's imaginative mobility enables him to display cracks in the glacial front of princely power and to record a voice, the voice of the displaced and oppressed, that is heard scarcely anywhere else in his own time. If it is the task of cultural criticism to decipher the power of Prospero, it is equally its task to hear the accents of Caliban.

SUGGESTED READINGS

Bakhtin, Mikhail. 1968. *Rabelais and His World*.
Benjamin, Walter. 1968. *Illuminations*.
Elias, Norbert. 1978. *The Civilizing Process*.
Geertz, Clifford. 1973. *The Interpretation of Cultures*.
Williams, Raymond. 1958. *Culture and Society, 1780–1950*.

17

Canon

John Guillory

"CANON" descends from an ancient Greek word, *kanon,* meaning a "reed" or "rod" used as an instrument of measurement. In later times *kanon* developed the secondary sense of "rule" or "law," and this sense descends as its primary meaning into modern European languages. The sense of the word important to literary critics first appeared in the fourth century A.D., when "canon" was used to signify a list of texts or authors, specifically the books of the Bible and of the early theologians of Christianity. In this context "canon" suggested to its users a principle of selection by which some authors or texts were deemed worthier of preservation than others. It is easy to see in retrospect what this principle was: Those scriptural writings of the Hebrews which were excluded from the biblical canon—the Bible as we know it—were excluded for dogmatic reasons, because early Christianity had to decide what its "truths" were, what it was going to teach its followers. It may surprise us today that many writers who believed they were as Christian as Matthew or Paul (for example, the "gnostic" Christians of the first century A.D.) did not find their writings included in the final form of the New Testament. At a certain point the biblical canon became closed forever. In the same way a number of early Christian theologians were excluded from the final list of "Church Fathers," because they promulgated doctrines which were inconsistent with the emergent orthodoxy of Christianity. Hence the "canonizers" of early Christianity were not concerned with how beautiful texts were, nor with how universal their appeal might be. They acted with a very clear concept of how texts would "measure up" to the standards of their religious community, or conform to their "rule." They were concerned above all else with distinguishing the orthodox from the heretical.

In recent years many literary critics have become convinced that the selection of literary texts for "canonization" (the selection of what are conventionally called the "classics") operates in a way very like the formation of the biblical canon. These critics detect beneath the supposed objectivity of value judgments a political agenda: the exclusion of many groups of people from representation in the literary canon. The controversy erupting over this question has produced

233

a great volume of polemical writing, so much in fact that one must say that the controversy is one of the more important events in the history of twentieth-century criticism. It was certainly not the case before the last several decades that the question of canon-formation itself was controversial, even though critics have always argued about the relative merits of individual writers. The critics of canon-formation have based their case upon a disturbing and indisputable fact: If one were to glance at the entire list of "great" Western European authors—the canon—one would find very few women, even fewer writers who are non-white, and very few writers of lower-class origin. This is simply a fact. What are we to make of it?

Clearly some process of exclusion is at work—but what process? As soon as we begin to think about this question, we are forced to consider some surprising hypotheses. Could it be possible that all along good or great works have been written, but that they have not been preserved, or not canonized, because their authors were not upper-class, or white, or male? Is it possible now to recover these great works from their undeserved obscurity? Literary critics have long known that the reputations of many writers have risen or fallen through the ages, and for many complex reasons. Is it possible to correlate acts of judgment with the categories of gender, race, or class? If this were possible, then the history of canon-formation would appear as a kind of conspiracy, a tacit or deliberate attempt to repress the writing of those who do not belong to a socially or politically powerful group or whose writing does not in some overt or covert way express the "ideology" of the dominant groups. Consequent upon this hypothesis, many new research projects have been undertaken, which have indeed recovered a number of forgotten works. Yet these works are fewer than one might expect, if it really were the case that individuals of excluded groups had been producing good literary works throughout Western history alongside the works of the famous, canonical authors. I shall return to this puzzling question in a moment. At this point we need to consider a little more carefully the process of selection itself. How does a work become canonical? How does a work become a classic?

For many readers and critics, this question has not been difficult to answer at all, since they would say that some works just *are* great, and have simply been recognized as such. One might maintain this very simple position until the moment when two intelligent readers disagree about the greatness of a particular work or writer. At this point, how is one to decide about who is right in the matter of judgment? Several possibilities emerge. We can say that readers disagree about the relative value of works because works can never be judged on "aesthetic" grounds alone, simply as works of art, whatever that might mean. Here the contemporary critic of the canon would say that the process of canon-formation has always been determined by the interests of the more powerful, and that is why works by women, or blacks, or other subject groups do not appear in the canon. Now let us imagine, if you will, the scene of judgment as that scene is implied by the debate between those who believe that great literature only needs to be recognized as such, and those who believe that judgment is always interested, or prejudicial.

To take the latter group first, it would seem that these critics must argue that literary works are judged by a kind of secret and exclusive ballot, that a certain elite group gathers together in order to decide which works will be canonized, which not. It is immediately obvious from this imaginary scene that if the ones who decide are all male, or upper-class, or white, then the works they judge to be good will tend to reflect their social position and their beliefs, their ideology. But if other social groups participate in the process of selection, then the canon will become truly representative; it will represent the identities and interests of the different social groups that actually do constitute the society as a whole. According to this argument, then, one can never be sure about the actual goodness of literary works, but one can take measures to be certain that the canon is properly representative. Let us call this position, commonly known as the argument for "opening the canon," the liberal critique of the canon. It is based ultimately upon an appeal to the standards of representative democracy, where disagreements are supposed to be resolved by a communal decision-making process which always seeks to guarantee the rights of minorities to representation.

Out of this liberal critique many new programs and syllabi have been developed, familiar to us now as the curricular innovations of such minorities-studies programs as Women's Studies or Afro-American Studies. One can hardly underestimate the beneficial effects of this development, not the least of which is that students have been disabused of the notion that only certain people can produce good literature, or judge it. The critique of the canon has forced teachers to confront questions about the teaching of literature that were answered too simply, if asked at all. Nevertheless we can still wonder whether the liberal critique, by transforming a scene of conspiracy into a scene of representation, has accurately described the historical process by which works become canonical. Notice, for example, that though this critique might well explain disagreements about value judgments between social groups, it cannot explain disagreements *within* a homogeneous social group without falling back on a concept of aesthetic value it regards as irremediably suspect. This problem points us to the great contradiction of the liberal critique: it must smuggle in a concept of real literary value if it wants to claim that some works—formerly noncanonical works—are just as good as the canonical works. Otherwise the liberal critique is committed to the erection of separate canons for different social groups, and there is no reason to assume that these different canons will not replicate the hierarchical positions of the social groups in the society at large. It has indeed been the case that these separate canons have often been regarded as separate but *not equal*.

Here the defender of the canon might reenter the debate, and say that it must be true that some works are better than others, after all. Consider now how the conservative critic might imagine the scene of judgment: This critic will point to the fact that the great works do not achieve canonicity by a single "vote" of the audience contemporary with their production. On the contrary, for a work to be canonical must mean that over successive generations, preferably many generations, readers continue to affirm a judgment of greatness, almost as though each generation actually judged anew the quality of the work. Even if we factor into this situation the inertial effects of simply or lazily accepting the judgments of one's predecessors, some works do appear to have a tenacious prestige in Western history. These are nothing other than the canonical works, "from Homer to Joyce." Very few readers, even the strongest advocates of literature considered to be "noncanonical," would reject these works as *really* bad, as only an expression of the ideology of the dominant groups. Does this mean that there is an objective standard of valuation for works, and if so what can it be? Unfortunately, when we look over the history of aesthetics from Plato and Aristotle to the present, we discover many different and quite mutually exclusive standards of greatness. What is worse, the same works have been judged great for different and incompatible reasons. The defenders of the canon have not hesitated to put forward new criteria of greatness, which would account for the survival of canonical works without recourse to the conspiracy theory of the liberal critique. But these criteria may well become as obsolete as the ones they replaced.

In response to the apparent impossibility of establishing a permanent criterion of literary greatness or value, the conservative defense of the canon must finally rest upon a belief in the *intrinsic worth* of canonical works, regardless of how well or badly the essence of this value can be explained in conceptual terms. At this point we can begin to reconstruct a scene of judgment quite different from the one imagined by the liberal critic. How does the defender of the canon know that a work is great, if no criteria of greatness can be established beyond dispute? Here the defender must affirm by a bold tautology that the canonical work must be great whether or not any particular reader recognizes its greatness. It is as though one imagined that the work had been judged for all time by a supreme, transcendent court, which considered only the work itself, apart from the particular biases of historical periods, apart from the defects of judgment specific to individuals. In this way we can suppose that even when two readers disagree, one of the two must be right. Disagreements about value, then, tend not to be resolved but simply aborted by a secret appeal to this higher court of judgment, which knows no time or place, which judges for every time and place.

One must insist, of course, that this transcendent court is a fiction; there is no third party to whom one can appeal in the case of disagreement. Should we not then admit that the *condition* for a judgment about value is the very possibility of disagreement? The conservative defender of the canon, at any rate, cannot dispense with the fiction of a transcendent position of judgment without becoming vulnerable to the argument of the liberal critic, who is always there to remind the defender that despite the robe of objectivity, the judge must always belong to a group, a time, a place.

If we cannot get away with secretly invoking a transcendent court of judgment to ratify our merely human opinions, are we then obliged to return to the scene of conspiracy? Are we obliged to say that there is no domain of aesthetic value, or that the pleasure experienced in works of art can always and only be reduced to the pleasure of seeing our social identities or beliefs mirrored in the work? At this point we must leave to others the question of value, or the question of what kind of pleasure works of art give, and draw a provisional conclusion with respect to the problem of the canon. I would like to suggest that the question of judgment is the wrong question to raise in the context of canon-formation. The selection of texts for preservation certainly does presuppose acts of judgment, which are indeed complex psychic and social events; but these acts are necessary rather than sufficient to constitute a process of canon-formation. An individual's judgment that a work is great does nothing in itself to preserve that work, unless that judgment is made in a certain institutional context, a setting in which it is possible to insure the *reproduction* of the work, its continual reintroduction to generations of readers. The work of preservation has other more complex social contexts than the immediate responses of readers to texts.

In what social context or institution, then, does the process of canon-formation occur? We know that for the biblical canon that institution is the church. Given the character of the church as an institution to which one either does or does not belong, the process of canonical selection in this context must take the form of a rigorously final process of inclusion or exclusion (on dogmatic grounds). Every would-be scriptural text is included or excluded once and for all. But does this process work in the same way for the literary canon? In what sense did the literary canon ever become "closed" to additional texts? It is on the contrary a historical fact that works are continuously added to, as well as subtracted from, this canon. If this is so, the canon of literature must be a very different thing than the scriptural canon. We may conjecture on this basis that acts of judgment concerning literary works (whatever prejudices or defects characterize individual judges) have a different social agenda than the dogmatic or the ideological. It may be that the process of selection never was like that scene in which a privileged group undertook to include or exclude works by scrutinizing their social origins, or assessing their ideological purity.

Here I would like to return to a point I made earlier, but did not follow up. I suggested that if the history of canon-formation really were a rigorous process of exclusion, then one ought to find many works through history which were actively suppressed, actively excluded from the canon. And it should follow that we would find many of these works to be as good as the works we today consider canonical. Many feminist critics, for example, have noted that the vast majority of canonical authors are men, and that before the eighteenth century one finds almost no canonical women authors. The first edition of the *Norton Anthology of English Literature,* for example, included no works before 1750 by women at all. After two decades of research, however, only a few women authors have been recovered from that obscurity for inclusion in later editions. The reason for the absence of great works by women before the eighteenth century (not after) is in fact very easy to determine: there were few women *writers* before this time. Great works could hardly be produced by women, if by and large only men were taught to write, or only men were in social positions which made possible a life of literary production. Hence it would be historically anachronistic to claim that it was a general practice to exclude from the canon works by women before the eighteenth century. Conversely, when more and more women after the mid-eighteenth century were taught to read and write, works by women did begin to appear in the canon (for example, the novels of Jane Austen). This is not to say that male critics did not react with various repressive measures to the appearance of women writers but that these measures were more successful in preventing women from writing in the "serious" literary genres, or from writing at all, than in excluding literary works by women from the canon. If this were not the case, then one would be able to find other Jane Austens or other Emily Dickinsons undeservedly suppressed; but if these forgotten great writers exist, then how are we to explain the canonization of Austen or Dickinson?

Clearly the literary canon is not produced in the way it is assumed to be produced by both the critics and the defenders of the canon. It is time to dismiss both the liberal and the conservative imaginary scenes of judgment. The literary canon does not represent social constituencies in the manner of a pseudo-democratic legislature. Nor does it stand for a concept of absolute aesthetic value, beyond and above the social conditions of judgment. Let us try rather to reconstruct a *historical* picture of how literary works are produced, disseminated, reproduced, reread, and retaught over successive generations and eras. As soon as we begin to consider the question in this way, we can relate the fact just noted—the relative absence of women writers before the eighteenth century—to the whole question of how works become canonical. What the critics of the canon took to be exclusion from a final, immutable selection of great texts was really, in historical context, exclusion from the means of literary production, from *literacy itself.* In order to understand the historical circumstances determining the constitution of the literary canon, then, we must see its history as the history of both the production and the reception of texts. We must understand that the history of literature is not only a question of *what* we read but of *who* reads and *who* writes, and in what social circumstances; it is also a question of what kinds (or genres) of texts are written, and for what audiences. We must be able to ask and answer all of these questions in order to arrive at a historical understanding of the constitution of the canon.

The analogy between the biblical canon and the literary canon has proven to be misleading at best. But to reject this analogy is by no means to isolate literature from the domain of ideology, or from the larger field of social relations. It is rather to observe that writing and reading are social practices which are too intimately related for their histories to be entirely distinguished; hence one cannot simply speak about a history of reception, of canon-formation. Like any other social practices, reading and writing are subject to various forms of control or regulation, to institutional forms of organization. If at a certain time women are not taught to read, or discouraged by various social pressures from writing, this fact tells us something about the relation between men and women at that time, and also something about the society as a whole. This fact tells us that certain kinds of knowledge—the capacity to read or write—are unequally distributed in that society; and this unequal distribution is in some respects not unlike the unequal distribution of wealth. Human beings are not born with the ability to read or write; these skills must be acquired. And even when they are acquired, the capacity to produce works of literature is a function not only of "talent" but of what one's social position makes possible. Hence the middle-class women who acquired literacy in the earlier eighteenth century (an acquisition connected with changes in the structure of the family and in the social role of the woman) were allowed and encouraged to write letters, as a proof of refinement, but found little opportunity yet for composition in publishable forms of writing. Even by the end of the century it was still easier (that is, less socially proscribed) for women to compose in what was at that time a largely popular genre—the novel—than, for example, in the long poem or the philosophical essay. To acknowledge the importance of these facts is to recognize that in any given society, the social practices of reading and writing are systematically regulated. The social effects of this regulation are produced, therefore, by the concerted operation of social institutions, not only by acts of individual judgment.

Once this point has been given its due, it should be possible to shear away the philosophical problem of aesthetic value from the historical problem of canon-formation (which is not to say that one could not also give a historical account of what people have said about the philosophical problem). The problem of canon-formation is one aspect of a much larger history of the ways in which societies have organized and regulated practices of reading and writing (it is perhaps an illusion of our own age to believe that we are simply free to read and write whatever, whenever, and however we wish). We are now in a position to recognize the major social institution through which this regulation is exercised: the school. From a very early point in Western history, not long after writing itself began to be used as a means of preserving oral compositions, the task of disseminating and preserving written works came to define and to belong to the school. Judgments about the worth of individual works, their suitability for preservation, were thus always made in the institutional context of the school and its needs, its social function. Moreover, the school did not emerge merely as an institution for the preservation of works. On the contrary, the school was assigned the general social function of distributing various kinds of knowledge, including the knowledge of *how* to read and write as well as *what* to read and write.

It has long been known by historians of literature that the process we call canon-formation first appeared in ancient schools in connection with the social function of disseminating a knowledge of how to read and write. The selection of texts was a means to that end, not an end in itself. Thus it has always been in the interest of the scholar-teachers to discover and preserve the best works, wherever they might come from, precisely in order to fulfill their institutional function of disseminating that knowledge we call literacy. The process of selection and preservation had originally these explicitly institutional motives, and only much later was it possible to defend the institutional process by claims about the value of certain works for every time and place. As we shall see, these institutional motives remain much the same today. The problem of the canon is a problem of syllabus and curriculum, the institutional forms by which works are preserved as *great* works. One might contrast this institutional function of the school with the function of the library, where ideally *everything* is preserved and where the system of preservation makes no distinction at all between good books and bad.

Let us consider more fully now the matter of the school's social function, the distribution of knowledge. The great works of literature are defined by the institution as knowledge, but this knowledge is not immediately acessible to students upon entering the school. It is mediated by a more primary knowledge, which is simply the knowledge of how to read and write. Now the transition from the primary knowledge to the secondary knowledge of the great works themselves would be relatively easy, if the texts to be read were linguistically just like the spoken language. But in fact, these two languages are seldom alike, because the spoken language changes continually, and in some periods very quickly. In only a few generations, or a century or two, it may change to such an extent that reading the older literature of one's language might well be like reading another language (as every high-school student knows who reads Shakespeare for the first time). If we look at the long-term effects of linguistic change, a remarkable development comes into view. The school brings the written text into contact with the spoken language, and this contact produces friction. To the early teachers, the scholars of Hellenistic times, for example, who first set out to preserve the poems and plays of classical Greece, it appeared that the language of earlier ages was better, more refined, more *correct,* than the language spoken in their own time. They saw their spoken language as a degeneration from that original standard of purity and correctness. So they attempted to refine their contemporary language by extracting from the written texts they preserved, the classics, a standard of usage—a syntax, a vocabulary, an orthography, in short, a *grammar*. Learning to read, then, also came to mean in the Greek and Roman eras, as ever since, learning to speak a more correct, refined version of one's native tongue, a grammatical language. The process of preservation was thus governed from the beginning by the institutional project of disseminating not only literacy, but grammatical speech. Both projects were undertaken in the classroom by means of a syllabus of literary works.

This point was observed many years ago by the literary historian Ernst Robert Curtius, who observed in his study of *European Literature and the Latin Middle Ages,* that "In antiquity, the concept of a model author was oriented upon a grammatical criterion, the criterion of correct speech." Over a period of time, the contact between the written language, preserved in the canon, and the continually changing spoken language produced a kind of third language, a fusion of, or compromise between, the differences of the two languages. This third language, which was the "refined" version of the language everyone spoke, came to be the possession only of those who had access to the schools. Thus in ancient Rome, the upper classes came to speak a version of Latin less and less intelligible to the "vulgar" masses. This effect of social stratification in the realm of language was not produced immediately by the works of literature themselves, or by their ideological messages, but by the social functions to which they were subordinated in the school.

Remarkably, the social function of the literary curriculum within the institution of the school continues to operate in much the same way two thousand years later. What the Hellenistic scholars called "grammar" we still recognize by the same name, but also now by the name of "Standard English," which the modern school disseminates as a linguistic compromise between contemporary spoken English and the literary English of our canonical literature. The promotion of Standard English as an institutional project dates from the eighteenth century, when many different dialects of English were spoken in Britain and the colonies. When the emergent middle class began to acquire more education, as part of its gradual rise to power, it embraced a more refined, upper-class speech as one means of expressing its political and social aspirations. For the first time works of English literature were collected into anthologies comprising a selection of the best in each genre; and these anthologies, which looked very much like the Norton or Oxford anthologies of our day, were employed in the schools as a means of teaching and disseminating Standard English. It was not even the practice at the time for teachers to "interpret" these texts in the way that we do today; rather, literary texts were offered as paradigms for the speaking and writing of grammatical English.

The fact that in our time the teaching of how to read and write, and the teaching of how to interpret literary works, are divided between the lower and the higher levels of the educational system has perhaps blinded us to the real historical motives of canon-formation, and to the relations among literature, language, and the social structure. Most important, we have yet to acknowledge or explain fully the relation between literature and society, a relation mediated by the school, as the institution of linguistic control. Literature and language have marched through history in tandem with one another, and yesterday's literature has become today's grammar. The language of societies with written literatures has thus tended to become internally stratified according to which groups among the population have access to the school and how much access each has. Since the eighteenth century the social stratification of speech has corresponded roughly with the level of class, and less and less with gender—hence the growing number of canonical women authors over the last two centuries. (Again, this does not mean that the system for the regulation of reading and writing does not continue to impose particular constraints upon women who write, but that the process of canon-formation is remarkable for having failed to exclude women.) If the educational system has now become so complex that the historical relation between literature and grammar is easy to forget, one reason for this amnesia is the fact that grammar is now sufficiently codified and routinized at the lower levels so that it is no longer necessary to use canonical literary texts in order to teach it at all. But this situation has itself been necessitated by the fact that older works of English literature are too remote linguistically to serve as models of grammar, and thus our conception of "correct" English has come to be based upon the literary prose of the eighteenth and nineteenth centuries rather than the works of the Middle Ages or the Renaissance. One consequence of this circumstance is that, over the last hundred years the major canonical works have defined the syllabus at the *higher* levels of the system, while at the lower levels the canon itself has been gradually replaced by a range of children's and adolescent's works useful for disseminating basic literacy because of their relative verbal simplicity (one thinks in this connection of the short stories of O. Henry, of the poems of Edwin Arlington Robinson, or of J. D. Salinger's *Catcher in the Rye*). When students (not everyone, of course) come to study the major canonical works at the secondary or university levels of the system, they are then able to acquire a sophistication about language presumably greater than the simple literacy or Standard English of the lower levels. They learn a "literary" style of speaking or writing, which is more than merely correct, more than merely an accurate reproduction of such prose paradigms as are still used in "composition" courses. This more sophisticated linguistic facility is signaled in many ways—for example, by the capacity to recognize quotations from canonical literature, recognitions which subtly broadcast the level of educational acquisition. Whatever else an individual might do with the real knowledge conveyed

by the school, this linguistic facility is an example of what the school does socially *for* the individual. Now as always the school continues to function as a
social institution which reproduces the stratified structure of the social order.
And within this institutional structure the literary curriculum performs this
function in a very major way by producing distinctive forms of linguistic knowledge.

At this point one might fairly ask: Could the linguistic stratification that produces and reproduces social stratification really be the only function of the canonical curriculum in the schools? Do not many teachers believe that they serve
a liberalizing, progressive function in the society, *especially* through the teaching
of literary works? The argument I am proposing need not deny that teachers
have many other motives, nobler and emancipatory motives, for the teaching of
literature. I would insist only upon the relation between the institution of the
school and the social order that allows the former to exist only in such a way as
to meet the latter's demands. If the same general knowledge (as opposed to technical specializations) were acquired by everyone, the social effects of literary education would perhaps be quite different. But such equal distribution of educational capital is no more characteristic of our "democratized" educational system
than it was of ancient Rome's. We know, for example, that the rate of functional
illiteracy in the United States is still very high, and that we are as far away from
a truly democratized educational system as we are from an equitable health-care
system. Must we say that meanwhile, until the school acquires a new social function, the social effects of the literary curriculum are necessarily pernicious?

There are several reasons why I do not think such a conclusion is necessary. To
begin with, it is not impossible that teachers and students should become more
aware of the relation between the institution of the school and the texts they
read. And this awareness should produce a better understanding of certain pragmatic questions relating to the social effects of education. Here I would offer
one suggestion, which must suffice in lieu of a fuller discussion. It should no
longer be desirable or necessary to characterize the literary curriculum in any
one way, as though all canonical works shared some intrinsic property (that is,
anything other than the possible pleasure one might experience in reading
them). Teachers of literature have tended to react against the pressures of the
institution, and the social order within which it resides, by finding in every canonical work either the same message of emancipation, or the same evidence of
collaboration with forces of oppression (two versions of liberalism that we find
in the university). We must recognize now that both of these characterizations
mistake the social effects of the canonical form—the syllabus, the curriculum,
the classroom itself—for the effects of individual works. The reading of "great
works" is not in itself liberating, nor does it necessarily immerse one in the illusions of ideology. Literary works may say many different and contradictory
things relating to many different social issues, and it seems very unlikely that the

social effects of individual works can be simply established as progressive or regressive. It is perhaps more important to see how the things they say came to be said than it is to discover the secret of their canonicity. At this point in our social and institutional history, I believe it is crucially important to resist homogenizing canonical works in any way. And the alternative to homogenizing works is to historicize them. The literary canon is itself a considerable part of the matter of history, and that historicity is not really transcended by the immortality of the canonical work. The canon is itself a historical event; it belongs to the history of the school. If there is now a need to rethink and revise what we do with the curriculum of literature, this project will entail not only reading new works, or noncanonical works (both of which it should entail), but also reading in a better way, by which I mean reading works for what they say and do in their place and time, as well as reading the *difference* between those meanings and the meanings which have been imputed to them by virtue of their being canonical works.

The pedagogical agenda I am proposing here is certainly not unheard of in recent practice; it participates in a general movement to reinstate historical context as a ground of interpretation. The present argument participates in this movement by referring it specifically to classroom practice. Within the constraints of a brief essay such as this, however, it would be difficult to demonstrate fully the difference such a historicist method would make for the reading of any particular literary text. Nevertheless it will perhaps be worth making a gesture toward such a self-reflective critical practice by glancing at one text, Donne's "The Canonization," which has played a rather unique role in establishing the syllabus of literary study since at least the 1940s:

The Canonization

For Godsake hold your tongue, and let me love,
　　Or chide my palsie, or my gout,
My five gray haires, or ruin'd fortune flout,
With wealth your state, your minde with Arts improve,
　　　Take you a course, get you a place,
　　　Observe his honour, or his grace,
Or the Kings reall, or his stamped face
　　　Contemplate; what you will, approve,
　　　So you will let me love.

Alas, alas, who's injur'd by my love?
　　What merchants ships have my sighs drown'd?
Who saies my tears have overflow'd his ground?
When did my colds a forward spring remove?
　　　When did the heats which my veines fill
　　　Adde one more to the plaguie Bill?
Soldiers finde warres, and Lawyers finde out still
　　　Litigious men, which quarrels move,
　　　Though she and I do love.

Call us what you will, wee are made such by love;
    Call her one, mee another flye,
We'are Tapers too, and at our owne cost die,
And wee in us finde the'Eagle and the Dove.
    The Phoenix ridle hath more wit
    By us, we two being one, are it,
So, to one neutrall thing both sexes fit.
    Wee dye and rise the same, and prove
    Mysterious by this love.

Wee can dye by it, if not live by love,
    And if unfit for tombes and hearse
Our legend bee, it will be fit for verse;
And if no peece of Chronicle wee prove,
    We'll build in sonnets pretty roomes;
    As well a well wrought urne becomes
The greatest ashes, as halfe-acre tombes,
    And by these hymnes, all shall approve
    Us *Canoniz'd* for Love:

And thus invoke us; You whom reverend love
    Made one anothers hermitage;
You, to whom love was peace, that now is rage;
Who did the whole worlds soule contract, and drove
    Into the glasses of your eyes,
    (So made such mirrors, and such spies,
That they did all to you epitomize),
    Countries, Townes, Courts: Beg from above
    A patterne of your love!

I shall not attempt here an interpretation of the poem, but only a kind of historical contextualization, a reflection on its canonicity, which is offered as a preface
to interpretation. "The Canonization" is very familiar to generations of university students as the perfect example of what has been called the "metaphysical"
poem. The designation refers to a certain quality of interconnection between
abstruse philosophical or theological concepts and the domain of everyday lived
experience (usually erotic), ostensibly the subject of the poem. Hence the metaphor or "conceit" of "canonization," by which the lovers are conflated with saints
on the basis of sacrificing worldly pursuits to the "transcendent" objective of
love. The poetry associated with this school was produced in England from
about the 1590s to perhaps the 1650s at the latest. It was produced in a variety
of social contexts, and by writers who may not at the time have considered themselves to belong to a single "school" of verse writing. By the eighteenth century,
this writing style was represented as a "school" of poetry in order to compare its
principles unfavorably with a verse practice based upon clarity of syntax and
greater conceptual simplicity. (Such a practice in fact reflected an ongoing stan-

dardization of English grammatical norms which disallowed many liberties of Renaissance usage.) In the wake of this literary-critical revolution, the "metaphysical" poets were eclipsed, in a sense "decanonized." For reasons too complex to examine here (but relating to a turn away from eighteenth-century verse practice), these same poets began to be reread with great enthusiasm by the Romantics, particularly Coleridge. Nevertheless this positive revaluation was insufficient to restore them to canonical status because it was insufficient to effect their inclusion in school syllabi. Again in the twentieth century certain poets (primarily T. S. Eliot) championed the metaphysicals, but again this partisan campaign was insufficient in itself to reform the canonical syllabus of the schools. Not until Eliot himself (and the modernist poets with him) began to be taught in the universities did it become possible also to revise the status of the metaphysicals.

The reasons for both canonical transformations are many, to be sure, but let me emphasize once more that the judgments of the larger literary culture (the community of readers and writers) must be seconded by the teachers in order for one to speak of "canonicity." The resistance to the teaching of the modernist poets in the schools was in fact very great, and it derived in part from the linguistic circumstance of modernist poetry's difficulty, a difficulty incidentally shared by the metaphysical poetry itself. The syllabus of literary study had long since been established as the means of producing Standard English as the language of the literate, the educated. Why then should this syllabus yield to a poetry which is conceptually opaque, grammatically deformative, linguistically inaccessible? In order to understand why the syllabus did indeed yield in this way, one has only to observe that, by the Second World War, the program of disseminating Standard English was being successfully accomplished at the primary level of the educational system. At the moment of this success, the universities were also becoming accessible to a larger number of students. This is the *historical* moment in which it can be said that modernist (and metaphysical) poets become canonical.

This revision of the canon was successfully installed in the curriculum of university English departments by a movement which came to be known as the "New Criticism." This movement responded to the complex forces of democratization transforming the educational institution by discovering in the new canon a means both of teaching literature to large numbers of students who were not primarily interested in literary study, and of doing something more with this study than merely reproducing the "Standard English" produced by the primary and secondary schools. This "something more" involved an introduction to a literary language more complex and sophisticated than Standard English, a language whose complexity was teased out in the practice of "close reading." Students learned that the language of poetry could not be paraphrased in ordinary language because it was densely figurative, ironic, or "paradoxical." At the same time it may be argued that the New Critics presented literature itself, the embodiment of this extraordinary language, as a world apart from the world to which most of their students were destined to return. And there was no doubt that this world was a higher world, a finer one.

Here one may begin to understand how what we may call the "canonical reading" of Donne's "The Canonization" emerged, a reading which took exemplary form in Cleanth Brooks's immensely influential volume of close readings, *The Well Wrought Urn* (Donne's poem gives Brooks his title). For Brooks, the irony of Donne's speaker is directed wholly toward the grubby world of politics, economics, and the like. Hence Brooks takes literally, so to speak, the valuation of the lover's "world" over that from which the lovers have withdrawn: "The lovers in becoming hermits, find that they have not lost the world, but have gained the world in each other, now a more intense, more meaningful world." But this conclusion is only half of the story: Brooks goes on to equate *poetry itself* with the lovers' withdrawal, to read that withdrawal as a legitimation of the notion that poetry belongs to a finer and higher world than the world of ordinary language, or ordinary human pursuits:

> The poem is an instance of the doctrine which it asserts; it is both the assertion and the realization of the assertion. The poet has actually before our eyes built within the song the "pretty room" with which he says the lovers can be content. The *poem itself* is the well-wrought urn which can hold the lover's ashes and which will not suffer in comparison with the prince's "half-acre tomb."

The entrance of Donne into the canon thus authorized a pedagogic practice which valued poetic language over mere Standard English, and which at the same time confined access to this language to a course of study consisting exclusively of literary works. As many critics have now argued, the New Criticism implicitly uprooted literature from the necessary ground of its existence, from history itself, in order to homogenize canonical works as representative of a transcendent poetic language. Let us juxtapose to the Brooksian reading, which reads the lovers' withdrawal as transcendent and ideal, a recent attempt to rehistoricize the poem, Arthur Marotti's *John Donne, Coterie Poet*. Marotti argues that in order to read the poem properly at all, one must understand the social conditions within which it was produced. Donne's poems, like those of his contemporaries, circulated in manuscript within a literate culture of gentlemen-courtiers, who used poetry to communicate to each other and to their social superiors their desires, their ambitions, their disappointments. In this context Marotti shows that the language of erotic conquest was frequently used to express in an indirect fashion the complex political jockeying of the courtiers in the Elizabethan and Jacobean courts. (This is not to say that the poems are not about love at all, but that love affairs were also politically significant happenings in the hothouse atmosphere of the Renaissance court.) The later printing of these poems decontextualized them, stripped them of their real political resonance, and thus allowed what appeared to be the idealization of a world-transcending love to be read without irony. Hence Marotti argues specifically against Brooks in re-historicizing "The Canonization."

> In its original context, however, "The Canonization" communi-
> cated a very different message [than the one argued by Brooks].
> Donne's readers knew that he was expressing his personal longing
> for the public world he pretended to scorn in this lyric and they
> would have read the poem as a more ironic, hence more aestheti-
> cally complex, work than the one the formalist critics and scholars
> utilizing literary and intellectual history have interpreted.

Rereading Donne's poem in Marotti's rather than Brooks's fashion has no effect on the *fact* of the poem's canonicity, only on the meaning of its canonical status. The poem is not less interesting but, if one can say this, more interesting (*more ironic,* more aesthetically complex) when fully contextualized in a social as well as a purely literary history. And yet it is doubtful whether this complexity can be reduced to the same meaning in every canonical poem. Let us say that it is *real* complexity because it emerges from the irreducably complex grounds of history itself.

By thus insisting upon the historical specificity of works against the homogenizing pressure of the canon, by resisting the tendency of the canonical form to determine in advance the meanings of works, it may be possible to acquire not only the knowledge the school offers but a knowledge *of* this knowledge, a knowledge of how the practice of reading is regulated or constrained by the institution and its social functions. This does not mean that we can read canonical works as if they were not canonical, as if they had no relation to the school. On the contrary, our continuous awareness of just these facts means that we have a better chance, as social agents, as the ones who teach reading or the ones who learn how to read, of controlling the social effects of our practices.

Suggested Readings

Baym, Nina. 1978. *Women's Fiction: A Guide to Novels by and about Women.*
Brooks, Cleanth. 1947. *The Well Wrought Urn.*
Curtius, Ernst Robert. 1953. *European Literature and the Latin Middle Ages.*
Fiedler, Leslie, and Houston Baker, eds. 1981. *Opening Up the Canon: Selected Papers from the English Institute.*
von Hallberg, Robert. 1985. *Canons.*
Kermode, Frank. 1983. "The Institutional Control of Interpretation." In Kermode, *The Art of Telling: Essays in Fiction.*

Macherey, Pierre, and Etienne Balibar. 1981. "Literature as an Ideological Form: Some Marxist Propositions." In Young, ed., *Untying the Text: A Poststructuralist Reader.*

Marotti, Arthur. 1986. *John Donne, Coterie Poet.*

Showalter, Elaine, ed. 1985. *Feminist Criticism: Essays on Women, Literature, Theory.*

18

Literary History

Lee Patterson

Despite its familiarity, the term "literary history" harbors an often unrecognized ambiguity. On the one hand, its commonsense meaning refers it to an immanent or *intrinsic* history of literature, a narrative account of either literature as a whole or of specific modes (poetry, drama, fiction), genres (epic, comedy, pastoral), or forms (complaint, sonnet, ode), that covers either a broad sweep of historical time or confines itself to one of the chronological periods into which the cultural past has been typically divided. In this sense, literary history is simply the history of literature. Yet the term also describes a critical practice concerned not with the history of literature as a self-contained cultural activity but with the relation of literature, as a collection of writings, to history, as a series of events. The goal of this *extrinsic* approach is to specify the forces that caused, governed, entailed, or were expressed by literary texts—what made them what they were rather than something else—and the routes by which these forces exerted their influence upon literature. While virtually all literary study must participate in both kinds of activity, the distinction between intrinsic and extrinsic is nonetheless useful both theoretically and historically. For although each practice can be present in the same work of literary history, and while each approach has always had its adherents, the mainstream of literary studies over the last hundred years or so has tended to move first from the extrinsic to the intrinsic and then back again. It is in terms of this sense of the history of literary history that the topic will be discussed here.

As originally conceptualized in the nineteenth century, extrinsic historicism was burdened with programmatic difficulties that eventually became so intractable as to bring it into disrepute. Its central weakness—imported from the reigning scientific positivism of the time—was its reliance upon a mechanistic cause-and-effect mode of explanation. This weakness manifested itself in two ways. First, nineteenth-century literary historicism shared the widespread assumption that historiography was capable of achieving an objectivity and reliability that other forms of cultural understanding, like literary criticism, could not achieve. However subjective might be one's understanding of a literary text, so ran the argument, history provided the facts that could control interpretation. The discovery of America, the English Civil War, the French Revolution—these were historical events that had a facticity and objectivity, a presence in the world, that allowed of precise and accurate description. They existed "out there," as part of the historical record, and diligence and discipline could reconstruct them accurately. Such a reconstruction could in turn govern the interpretation of literary texts by defining the parameters of possible significance, showing what texts could and could not mean.

Second, and in line with the desire to use historical context to provide interpretive reliability, nineteenth-century literary historicism assumed that each part of a culture was governed by the values that informed the whole. Hence it searched for the spirit of the time or *Zeitgeist,* those values that governed the cultural activity of a period as a whole; and it tended to construct its determinative historical context in homogeneous and even monolithic terms. This homogenizing of the past was motivated both by patriotic nationalism and by a desire to silence dissident voices in the name of cultural unity: it is no accident that historical scholarship developed contemporaneously with the emergence of movements of national unification, especially in Germany (see Riell 1975). Yet quite apart from the political agenda that underwrote its commitment to cultural harmony, what made this enterprise possible was the methodological positivism that saw history as objective and literature as subjective. The construction of a totalized past, whether as global as Hippolyte Taine's *History of English Literature* (1864) or as specific as E. M. W. Tillyard's *Elizabethan World Picture* (1944), depended upon a method that relied upon "historical" materials to construct an account of period consciousness that was then read back onto the "literature." The effect was that "literature" could never say anything that "history" had not authorized, that the literary critic was subject to the prior ministrations of the historian before he could expound the significance of his text. And to repeat, what made this tyranny of the historical possible was the unexamined distinction between "objective" history and "subjective" literature.

The development of literary criticism as a discipline in the first half of the twentieth century brought an inevitable reaction against this privileging of the historical. Interestingly enough, however, the reaction challenged neither the legitimacy of the distinction itself nor the advantages (much less possibility) of objectivity. On the contrary, literary critics sought to authorize their activity by declaring literature to be as much an object of study as history and hence as liable to precise and accurate description as historical events. An early instance of this strategy was developed by Russian formalism. In 1921 Roman Jakobson (cited in Eichenbaum 1965, 107) compared the literary historian of his day to

> the policeman who, intending to arrest a certain person, would, at
> any opportunity, seize any and all persons who chanced into the

apartment, as well as those who passed along the street. The literary historians used everything—anthropology, psychology, politics, philosophy. Instead of a science of literature, they created a conglomeration of homespun disciplines. They seemed to have forgotten that their essays strayed into related disciplines—the history of philosophy, the history of culture, of psychology, etc.—and that these could rightly use literary masterpieces only as defective, secondary documents.

What motivated Jakobson's objections—as his metaphor implied—was the desire to rescue literature from abduction by ignorant functionaries who were unable to recognize the special qualities that made a literary text different from all other kinds of writing. In his view, current literary history reduced the text to something "defective" and "secondary," the mere effect of an anterior cause, an epiphenomenon. Far from having any value in and of itself, the text was simply a symptom of the larger object the historian was seeking to recover: as Taine had said, "literary monuments" are valuable because through them "we can retrace the way in which men felt and thought many centuries ago" (Taine 1900, 1:1; Taine unselfconsciously adds, "This method has been tried and found successful."). And despite its old-fashioned phrasing, Taine's governing assumption of the exemplary function of literature was in fact ubiquitous throughout literary studies in the first half of the twentieth century: according to such studies, Donne shows how the new philosophy of the Renaissance calls all in doubt; Byron epitomizes Romantic excess; Thoreau is the quintessential instance of the self-making of America. Moreover, since literary historians were unable to decide what in fact constituted a primary cause, they had recourse to analytic methods derived from other disciplines; because they lacked a method specific to their object of study—Jakobson's "science of literature"—they applied to the text inappropriate analyses that caused it to disappear as an object of study in its own right. Seeking to explain the existence of the text, these literary historians actually decomposed it into a range of effects disconnected each from the other but causally bound to a determinative historical context.

In seeking to establish a science of literature, formalism hoped to remedy what was otherwise, in the context of the professionalized world of the modern university, and especially in relation to its scientific rival, history, a scandalous deficiency. And to achieve this goal, it was necessary to delineate the defining characteristics of the "literature" that was the object of literary study. To this end formalism insisted that the literary text must be defined as above all an artwork, an intricately constructed object organized according to immanent rules of structure. Literary writing is set apart from other kinds because it uses language in a special, self-reflexive way: in Jakobson's terms, literature suppresses the other functions of language, such as the emotive or the referential, in favor of the poetic function, by which he meant the capacity of language to draw attention to itself. This self-reflexivity is accomplished by a variety of means: meter, rhyme, ambiguity, paranomasia, sound symbolism—by, in effect, the whole range of practices classified by rhetoricians as figures of speech. Nor is this self-referentiality confined to poetry, for literary prose also marks itself off from other kinds of writing not primarily by its fictiveness but by its manipulation of the vast resources of literary form to construct intricately balanced linguistic artifacts. For another of the Russian formalists, Victor Shklovsky, "the most typical novel in world literature" is the elaborately crafted *Tristram Shandy* because it so pervasively deploys—and lays bare—the rhetorical techniques that control the production of all novels (see Shklovsky 1965, 27–57). Put bluntly, formalism defined literature as a kind of writing primarily concerned with neither reference to the world nor communication with an audience but rather with the conventions—the forms—of writing itself. Any account, therefore, that did not place this concern at the center of its attention inevitably traduced the very literariness that was its subject.

From a formalist perspective, then, the disparate terms that constituted extrinsic literary history formed a paradox that resisted all efforts at resolution: "literature" and "history" designated two radically incommensurate modes of cultural production that require sharply different analytic procedures. As Jakobson (1960, 356) put it, the poetic function, "by promoting the palpability of signs, deepens the fundamental dichotomy of signs and objects"—deepens, that is, the split between writing and the world that it is the literary historian's task to traverse. Or in the words of W. K. Wimsatt (1954, 217), the leading theoretician of American New Criticism, "In most discourse we look right through th[e] disparity [between words and things]. But poetry by thickening the medium increases the disparity between itself and its referents. Iconicity enforces disparity." The historical text, on the other hand, far from being a free-standing literary artifact that can lay claim to transhistorical value, derives its significance from its specific historical moment and remains meaningful in terms of that moment. It is a witness to local processes and concerns, a *document* whose significance derives from the events to which it testifies. Moreover, and crucially, a historical text is controlled by its author's specific and determinate intention. Rather than seeking to produce a disinterested work of art, the writer of a historical document designs his product to do actual work in the world, to participate in and to shape the historical processes of his own time. Consequently, his text cannot be understood in terms of its own literary dynamic, as an internally consistent verbal artifact governed by the laws of literary production, but must at every point be referred to and understood in terms of the instrumental purpose it sought to fulfill.

Conversely, the formalist emphasis upon the self-referentiality of the literary artwork foreclosed any effort to understand literature in terms of the historically specific intentions of its author. For one thing, in entering into the system of literary discourse, every author takes upon him or herself highly traditional modes of signifying—through structures of narrative, modes of external organization (verse forms, dramatic structures, length, etc.), patterns of imagery, and so forth—that entail meanings inherent within the literary system itself. And for another, in creating an artwork the author—regardless of his or her own understanding of an author's task—is in the position of a disinterested observer who is more concerned with the needs of the text as an internally consistent object than as a vehicle for the promotion of certain historically determined views and values. It should nonetheless be added, however, and especially in reference to American New Criticism, that formalism never embraced the "art-for-art's sake" hedonism of which it has been conventionally accused. On the contrary, both Russian and American formalism insisted that literature was a humanizing force in the world, a mission that the New Critics understood in terms of a powerful if largely unexamined Arnoldian humanism that saw literature as the bearer of permanent truths about the human condition. And in consonance with the ahistoricism of formalism, these truths were understood as having no merely local historical relevance but were, on the contrary, true for all time.

Given the inherent ahistoricity of literary writing, then, any attempt to locate literature within the causal processes of historical explanation must fail. Since historical documents are inextricably dependent upon the events of their historical moment, they can be accounted for by the same covering laws that govern historical explanation per se. But literature evades explanation entirely. On the contrary, it both signifies in ways unique to itself and refers not to merely local historical process but to transhistorical values implicit within the human condition as a whole. Consequently, as a long tradition of cultural studies has insisted, the literary text is an object that can never be *explained* as the effect of local historical causes but only *interpreted* as a bearer of cultural significance. While literature necessarily arises from a historical matrix it can never be adequately understood in terms of that origin, no matter how carefully the scholar seeks to reconstruct it. As René Wellek said (1982, 72), expressing with admirable directness an opinion that few recent scholars would articulate but that has nonetheless silently governed a wide range of critical practices, "We must concede the final inexplicability of a great work of art, the exception of genius." In the largest sense, the insistence upon the specialness of literary writing (however its characteristics may be defined) serves to sever the originary link between the literary text and a context constituted of other sorts of events, and to replace the text within this context requires us to apply to it crude techniques of understanding that traduce its essential nature.

By establishing an impassable barrier between the literary and the historical, formalism in effect sought to foreclose the very possibility of writing extrinsic literary history. This did not mean, of course, that this kind of literary history ceased to be written. But it did lose its self-assurance. The result was works that sought to describe literary texts in relation to their "background." On the one hand was an account of a period's major works; on the other, usually huddled somewhat awkwardly at the beginning of the account, were cursory observations on intellectual and social trends. What connected these two groups of observations was by no means clear; the "rise of a new reading public" was a common ploy (an excellent example of the genre, in large part because of its intuitive awareness of the impossibility of the task, is Lewis 1954). But while impeaching literary history in its extrinsic mode, formalism simultaneously legitimized it as an intrinsic practice. The Russian formalists, for example, proposed that since literature is "a self-formed social phenomenon," its history must be written in terms of what Boris Eichenbaum called the "dynamics of literary form," which meant the ceaseless replacement of one exhausted literary device by a new one in an effort to sustain the "defamiliarization" of ordinary experience which literature sought to achieve. Similarly, in a quest for what he called "a genuine history of literature, and not simply the assimilating of literature to some other kind of history," Northrop Frye provided in his *Anatomy of Criticism* both a synchronic account of literary structure (as modes, symbols, myths, and genres) and a diachronic disposition of this structure into five Viconian phases (of myth, romance, high mimesis, low mimesis, and irony) that traced the history of Western culture as a downward spiral of repetition (see Frye 1971, 23).

Despite its massive ambitions, Frye's project was founded upon the same assumptions that have underwritten a wide range of more narrowly focused, less teleologically committed scholarly work. Arguably, intrinsic literary history— literary history as the history of literature—has been the major scholarly production of the postwar years. A representative list of notable instances might include, for example, Rosemary Woolf's *English Religious Lyric in the Middle Ages* (1968), Alvin Kernan's *The Cankered Muse: Satire of the English Renaissance* (1959), Martin Price's *To the Palace of Wisdom: Order and Energy in Eighteenth-Century Literature* (1964), Warner Berthoff's *The Ferment of Realism: American Literature, 1884–1919* (1981), and *The English Elegy* by Peter Sacks (1986). All of these books are founded on the assumption that there is a specific object called literature that has its own, intrinsic history, and their content and organization are determined by the material they seek to explicate. As a secondary form of writing dependent upon the primary texts of English and American literature, literary history must accommodate itself to the patterns (historical periods) and categories (modes, genres, and forms) into which the texts organize themselves. In other words, literary history is both validated as a truly historical, cognitive activity by its dependent relation to the historical entity (literature) that it seeks to know, and derives its organizing principles from that entity.

In defining literature as its object of study, literary historians provided themselves with a *Fach*—a subject matter—that was equivalent to that which legitimized the other academic disciplines. But in designating that object as by definition different from other forms of writing, they erected a barrier that prevented it from being situated within a total historical account. In fact, of course, the arbitrariness of the definition of literature has always been something of an embarrassment to the literary historian. Browne's *Religio Medici* has traditionally been taken to be a literary text, while Spratt's *History of the Royal Society* is accorded only "background" status; Carlyle's *Sartor Resartus* is literature, but Marx's *The Eighteenth Brumaire of Louis Napoleon* is not. Despite the difficulty of justifying these discriminations, any essentialist theory of literature must assert them as absolute. And if there is an unbridgeable gulf fixed between *these* classes of documents, then how can the literary historian negotiate the space between more disparate texts—between, say, Eliot's *The Waste Land,* which literary historians locate at the center of modernism, and the writings generated by the general strike of 1926, which they typically ignore? Moreover, and more seriously, the essentializing of literature makes it impossible to understand literary production as itself a form of social practice, to understand it as itself part of both the cultural and material activities of its historical moment.

If literary writings were to be relocated within a nonliterary context, what needed to be sacrificed was nothing less than the very idea of "literature" as a special kind of writing. And this change entailed another, larger critique, an attack on the distinction between subjective literary studies and objective historical science that had originally driven literary critics to erect "literature" into an object of study sequestered away from other forms of cultural practice. In the late 1960s and 1970s these changes were accomplished through the intersection of two very different kinds of interests. On the one hand was a deconstructive textual analysis that appeared at times to be simply formalism writ large but that in fact subverted formalism's most deeply held assumptions. And on the other was a politically committed criticism that insisted that literary scholars could not escape from social engagement by taking refuge in the realm of the aesthetic. The combined effect of these movements has been itself twofold. First, literary critics have come to realize that the distinction between objective and subjective forms of cultural study cannot be sustained, that every historical account is constructed only by recourse to practices that are themselves as thoroughly interpretive as those that characterize literary criticism. And second, the term "literature" has been revealed as functional rather than ontological, as designating a kind of writing whose difference from other kinds is a matter not of its essential being but of its cultural function. In other words, a piece of writing is "literature" not because it possesses certain characteristics that other pieces lack, but because its readers regard it—for a variety of reasons—*as* literature.

A first step in mounting this critique was taken with the entrance into literary studies of the debate about the nature of language initiated by Ferdinand de Saussure's *Course in General Linguistics* (1916) and brought to the attention of literary criticism by the structuralism of the 1960s. Saussure showed that the relation of language to the world cannot be construed as a process of reflection—each word referring to its appropriate thing, as common sense assumed and as rhetoric had taught—but is instead analogical: on the one hand is language, with its differential system of making meaning, on the other the object-world of things that becomes available to human agency only in terms of the network of signification that language casts upon it. What follows from this insight is the recognition that the relation between language and the world is not that of correspondence—a statement is true when it conforms to the way the world is—but of convention: a statement is true when it conforms to certain norms that govern what a particular way of writing takes to be true. Truth is produced, not discovered, and is a property not of the world but of statements. To put the matter another way, statements do not refer to but rather constitute facts: what counts as a fact is determined not by its existence in the world but by the discursive practices that make it possible for something in the world to serve as a fact within a certain discourse.

Since at least the Renaissance, the central assumption that had served to support the category "literature" was the opposition between fact and fiction: as Sidney had famously said (1965, 123), the poet is to be distinguished from both the historian and the philosopher because he "nothing affirms and therefore never lieth." But the "linguistic turn" initiated by Saussure subverted this assumption by challenging not the fictiveness of literature but the factuality claimed by other forms of writing. Hence Jacques Derrida showed that philosophy is less a way of thinking than a form of writing that has always, in the name of absolute reason, suppressed not merely its dependence upon the very rhetorical forms it condemns in "literature" but its own inescapable entanglement in language per se. Hayden White revealed that historical writing is similarly governed by "tropes," rhetorical forms that do not merely embellish but more profoundly constitute the structure of historical narrative. Thomas Kuhn showed that the history of the physical sciences is a story not of the progressive discovery of a truth lying in wait to be found but of the gradual shift from one explanatory paradigm to another under the pressure of a wide range of social forces. In sum, this deconstructive movement revealed all of the self-designated human "sciences"—their very name implying a claim to referentiality—to be discourses that not only relied upon the literary devices that literature had always taken for its own but that told a truth that was itself constituted by the discourse within which it was told. Suddenly, all forms of writing were revealed as being as distant from the real world, and as linguistically embedded, as literature had been thought to be.

But if it is the case that there is no absolute essence that defines one form of writing as literature and another as nonliterature, if there is, despite all efforts at discovery, no quintessential "literariness," the possession of which admits a text into the charmed circle of the literary canon, then why do we have the designation at all? If it does not refer to an object in the world, what is the point of the name? A number of cultural critics, led by Raymond Williams, have cogently argued that the term performs an essentially social function. Williams has shown that the crucial moment in the history of the concept "literature" is the late eighteenth and early nineteenth centuries. For it was then that the concept, along with its legitimizing philosophical parent, the idea of the aesthetic, established itself as the site where a disinterested concern for formal beauty and emotional authenticity could be protected from the relentless commodifications of consumer capitalism. In the course of time, to be sure, the idea of "literature" has served other, less liberating purposes, primary among them being the privileging of one kind of writing as the preserve of the well-educated and well-off while stigmatizing other kinds as "popular." "Literature" has become absorbed into the capitalist dynamic and has "led almost inevitably," as Williams has said (1977, 151), "to new kinds of privileged instrumentality and specialized commodity." In recent years critics have shown in abundant detail how the concept of "literature" has been used to stigmatize writings by the culturally marginalized and politically repressed—women, blacks, gays, and members of the Third World, among others. Moreover, and more tellingly, since "literature" served as the concept by which the entire institution of literary criticism (including literary history) legitimized itself, the subversion of its very raison d'être has removed the most powerful ideological barrier to the entrance into the critical profession of a whole range of new initiatives and interests—including film studies, general cultural criticism, gender studies, and many others—whose specifically "literary" character is in no sense obvious.

While this syncretism has at times been felt by English departments as threatening, the refiguring of the relation of literature to other kinds of writing has in fact made possible a return to the extrinsic literary historicism with which the professional study of literature first began. But this is a return with a difference—or at least it should be. As originally conceived, the defining feature of extrinsic literary historicism was not the particular historical formation that served as the privileged category of explanation, nor even (as Jakobson charged) the invocation of a confused congeries of categories. Rather, what was definitive of this brand of literary history was its pervasive reliance upon the notion of *explanation* itself, of a cause-and-effect model of cultural production: first history, then literature. Hence the shift in recent years away from the more "idealist" of these categories of explanation (biography, history of ideas, period consciousness) and toward more "materialist" formations, especially socially determined patterns of gender definition and economically based political oppositions, has not, in and of itself, brought about a significant redefinition of the practice of literary history.

What *has* brought about a change, however, is the philosophical revision entailed by deconstruction. By insisting that all modes of writing are located at an equal distance from reality, deconstruction has established, as Fredric Jameson (1976, 205) has succinctly said, the

> methodological hypothesis whereby the objects of study of the human sciences . . . are considered to constitute so many texts which we *decipher* and *interpret,* as distinguished from the older views of those objects as realities or existants or substances which we in one way or another attempt to *know.*

The deconstructive argument that all writing stands at a distance from that which it seeks to represent entails both the dethronement of historicism as an objectivist discipline and the recognition that every document, no matter how closely tied to the events from which it arises, is itself a text that requires interpretation. In other words, the traditional attitude that would set a historicism that deals with objective facts over against a literary criticism that must rely upon the subjective interpretation of texts can no longer be maintained. Similarly, it is no longer possible to believe that an objective realm of history can serve to measure the correctness of the interpretation of literary texts, since history is itself as much the product of interpretive practices as are the literary interpretations it is being used to check. Both literary history and history per se deal with materials whose undeniable differences are less important than their shared status as verbal artifacts, a similarity that renders the methodology of the two disciplines essentially the same. So that the quest after causal explanation that had traditionally been taken as the hallmark of historicism—and that had distinguished it from, set it against, and served to devalue literary criticism—is now replaced by interpretive practices applicable across the field of historical studies as a whole.

This is not to say that the deconstructive dogma of writing as absence can be fully accepted by the literary historian. The deconstructive claim that textuality entails what Derrida (1978, 298) has called "the horizontality of a pure surface, which represents itself from detour to detour," necessarily forecloses the effort to recover the world of events in which the extrinsic literary historian seeks to ground his criticism. But it is not the case that events, even those of a chronologically distant past, are sequestered into a realm of presence closed to an irreparably deficient textuality. In fact, we know the past not simply by interrogating the surviving texts that represent it but also by its determinative effects upon our own lives. *The Red Badge of Courage* may be palpable in a way that the American Civil War is not, but the Civil War is a persistent presence—as both myth and influence—in the contemporary world within which we read Crane's novel. Even scholars who are dealing with chronologically and geographically distant materials are in fact examining a cultural matrix within which they themselves stand, and the understandings at which they arrive are influenced not simply by contemporary interests but by the shaping past that they are engaged in recovering. Indeed, this continuity between past and present, far from impeaching literary historians' efforts, is what makes them possible. But it does impose upon them the stipulation that they raise it to consciousness and include it within their interpretive activity.

Perhaps more important than these methodological issues, the breaking down of the category of literature has made it possible for literary historians to see that literary writing is best understood not as a diacritical or disengaged activity but instead as one of the many forms of cultural production by which men and women have made their world. Far from being divorced from the world, literary production is itself a form of social practice: texts do not merely reflect social reality but create it. Under the influence of this essentially anthropological perspective, recent literary historians have sought to replace literary texts within the larger cultural formations of which they were originally a part. Salient cases in point include Stephen Greenblatt's analogy between the theater and religious exorcism in the Renaissance, two cultural forms whose apparent difference disguises a profound similarity—a dialectic of what Greenblatt (1986, 326–45) calls containment and subversion—that itself figures the central dynamic of Renaissance culture. Similarly, Louis Montrose (1983, 61–94) reads *A Midsummer Night's Dream* in terms of the complexities of gender and power that pervade a political world where the sovereign is a woman, complexities that are visible not just in literature but in contemporary reports of the psychic dreamworld of the Elizabethan subject. In *Desire and Domestic Fiction* (1987, 164), Nancy Armstrong explains how the eighteenth- and nineteenth-century novel was one among the many discursive formations that cooperated "to produce men and women fit to occupy the institutions of an industrialized society." And Walter Benn Michaels, in *The Gold Standard and the Logic of Naturalism* (1987), interprets the development of a specific literary style in terms of the ideology of capitalism but avoids privileging one element as primary ("base") while stigmatizing another as secondary ("superstructure"). Instead, he reads the terrain of turn-of-the-century American culture as a single, semiotic whole. In sum, then, this drawing together of literary criticism and historical study into a new formation is enabled by the assimilation of writing not merely to other forms of cultural production but rather to all forms of social actions. The making of books neither reflects nor lies parallel to the making of history; on the contrary, it is itself both constitutive and representative of material production. As Caroline Bynum says (1987, 299), in explaining the method that animates her profound and moving exploration of the *vitae* and mystical writings of late medieval religious women, "My approach clearly assumes that the practices and symbols of any culture are so embedded in that culture as to be inseparable from it."

The value of this essentially anthropological conception of culture to literary historians is undeniable, allowing them to locate their texts within a larger signifying context that constitutes nothing less than the culture as a whole. But this conception also has vulnerabilities—ones to which, not coincidentally, the work of Caroline Bynum (the one historian mentioned in this survey) is conspicuously less liable than that of her literary colleagues. Clearly, literary critics need to continue to ponder what is required of them when they become (as become they must) historians. For one thing, the anthropological conception of culture tends to encourage a view of social action that would allow material forces to be wholly absorbed by symbolic needs. While it is certainly true that, as Marshall Sahlins says (1976, 206–7) "material effects depend on their cultural encompassment," that "the practical interest of men in production is symbolically constituted," the focus on culture as semiosis can induce the literary mind to occlude the material entirely. The effect is to return to a wholly textualized history, in which acts have symbolic significance but no practical consequences, in which history consists of gestures rather than real actions. This impulse is also encouraged by the Foucauldian conception—of central importance to recent literary historians—of discursive formations, which are seen as organized according to structures of dominance and subordination that replicate the structures of society as a whole and so allow for no external purchase that might make possible a reformation or even reversal of power relations. The individual is always already inscribed within a discourse that prescribes its own continuation, and his entrapment. Indeed, even to speak of agency becomes problematic, since priority must be given to the social field within which actions are made possible rather than to the agent who enacts them. Further, since this conception of culture encourages a symbolic and merely representational relation to the empirical materials of both literature and history, certain debilitating methodological practices are encouraged. Given this model of historical value, any single item of cultural practice can serve to represent every other item, so that a *geistesgeschichtliche* probe at any point in the cultural matrix will reveal the principle that organizes the whole. This results not merely in large claims resting on very little evidence, but also in historical accounts that tend to drain the heterogeneity and conflict out of culture, and with them the possibility of change.

Finally, to conclude with a familiar but not to be forgotten caveat, the literary historian must continue to respect the persistent capacity of the past to be not merely different but stubbornly resistant to understanding. Literary historians know, perhaps too well, that there is no methodological elixir (least of all "theory") that will enable them to tell the truth about either literature or history. But they must also not ignore the scrupulousness and inclusiveness that attend a commitment to the theoretically problematic yet ethically indispensable desire to get it right. Over sixty years ago Johan Huizinga (1959, 61, 49) argued that "contemporary man is a traitor to the spirit of his own culture if he creates myths in the knowledge that they are, or rather pretend to be, myths." Hence: "The utterly sincere need to understand the past as well as possible without any admixture of one's own is the only thing that can make a work history." As literary historians move into a postmodern age, it is by no means clear that they can afford to jettison Huizinga's difficult imperative.

SUGGESTED READINGS

Baldick, Chris. 1983. *The Social Mission of English Criticism, 1848–1932.*
Newton, Judith. 1988. "History as Usual? Feminism and the 'New Historicism.'"
Norbrook, David. 1984. *Poetry and Politics in the English Renaissance.*
Patterson, Lee. 1987. *Negotiating the Past: The Historical Understanding of Medieval Literature.*
Sammons, Jeffrey L. 1977. *Literary Sociology and Practical Criticism.*
Simpson, David. 1988. "Literary Criticism and the Return to 'History.'"
Williams, Raymond. 1977. *Marxism and Literature.*

19

Gender

Myra Jehlen

L IKE Molière's bourgeois gentleman who discovered one day that all the
time he thought he was only talking he was in fact speaking prose, literary
critics have recently recognized that in their most ordinary expositions of character, plot, and style they speak the language of gender.*

The terms of critical analysis, its references and allusions, its very structure,
these critics now find, incorporate assumptions about the nature of sexual identity that organize and even suggest critical perception. When we describe certain
verse cadences as "virile" while naming some rhymes "feminine," when Boswell
explains judiciously that "Johnson's language . . . must be allowed to be too masculine for the delicate gentleness of female writing," the conventional meanings
of "masculine" and "feminine" shape the sense of literary phenomena that have
no intrinsic association with sex. Posited as analytical terms rather than the objects of analysis, these meanings go unexamined and with them aspects of literature that they seem to explain but actually only name. It would not have occurred to Boswell to reverse the direction of his definition and, instead of
invoking the conventional attributes of masculinity to define the limits of Johnson's language, cite Johnson's language to define the limits of conventional masculinity. But just such a reversal has been going on in recent critical practice
where literary analysis is reflexively querying its own sexual rhetoric. The terms
"masculine" and "feminine," which the eighteenth-century biographer assumed

*Webster's *New World Dictionary*, second college edition (World: New York, 1968), defines gender as follows: "The formal classification by which nouns and pronouns (and often accompanying
modifiers) are grouped and inflected, or changed in form, so as to control certain syntactic relationships: although gender is not a formal feature of English, some nouns and the third person singular
pronouns are distinguished according to sex or the lack of sex (*man* or *he,* masculine gender; *woman*
or *she,* feminine gender; *door* or *it,* neuter gender): in most Indo-European languages and in others,
gender is not necessarily correlated with sex." This last specification underlies the choice of "gender"
over "sex" as the critical term that designates sexual identity and its associated characteristics. For as
the discussion below will explain, the argument implicit in analyzing literature from a "gender"
perspective is that sexual identity is not "necessarily correlated with sex"; in other words, that biological sex does not directly or even at all generate the characteristics conventionally associated with it.
Culture, society, history define gender, not nature.

263

were standard measures, have become for twentieth-century readers the first objects of critical measurement.

Boswell taking masculinity as a given expressed a traditional conviction that
the differences between men and women arise from natural causes to organize
the cultural order. Himself "too masculine . . . [for] female writing," Johnson
declared women in turn too feminine for masculine pursuits; "'Sir,'" he famously addressed Boswell, "'a woman's preaching is like a dog's walking on his
hinder legs. It is not done well; but you are surprized to find it done at all'"
(Boswell, 327).

Perhaps because upright dogs remain relatively rare while more and more
women are taking the podium, Johnson's view that the appurtenances of sex are
as distinct as those of species and as surely rooted in biology has lately had to be
rethought. The insurgent view that gender is a cultural idea rather than a biological fact shares the ground that it has been gaining with parallel arguments about
other identities—of class, of race, of national or religious association. De-
naturalizing the character of women is part of a larger de-naturalization of all the
categories of human character, which emerges as both a social and a linguistic
construction.

Implicating literature in the making of society has a reciprocal implication *for*
literature. If gender is a matter of nurture and not nature, the character conventionally assigned men and women in novels reflects history and culture rather
than nature, and novels, poems and plays are neither timeless nor transcendent.
This reciprocal historicizing extends to criticism which comes to read in the
character of Hamlet, say, instead of a portrait of universal manhood, let alone of
universal humanity, an exceptionally resonant but still particular depiction of
aristocratic young manhood in Renaissance England (featuring among other
characteristic attitudes, the assumption that young men of the dominant class
are universally representative.) If literature speaks gender, along with class and
race, the critic has to read culture and ideology. It turns out that all the time
writers and critics thought they were just creating and explicating transcendingly
in a separate artistic language, willy nilly they were speaking the contemporary
cultural wisdom.

Not all critics have been as delighted as Molière's Monsieur Jourdain to learn
that the way of speaking they took for granted constituted a statement in itself.
The aspiring bourgeois thought his conversation much enhanced by its participation in the ambient culture, but some critics fear that talk of gender, as of class
and race, will rather diminish literature. They worry that reading literature in
relation to society will, by rendering literature's meaning more particular, reduce
it *to* the particular. But it is possible to argue just the opposite, that uncovering
the social and cultural assumptions of literary language actually complicates
reading. For when we take fictional characters to be universal, they subsume the
particular traits and attributes of different kinds of people—as a character like

Hamlet does when he is taken as embodying the general human condition. Ironically such transcendent characterization works reductively to submerge the complexities of human difference; while in order to explicate the particular, a critic needs to focus precisely on distinctions and qualifications, on the complexities of human difference. Against the fantasy of transcendence, a criticism conscious of literature's and its own sexual politics affirms the permanent complexity of engagements and interactions.

This should suggest what it is useful nonetheless to say explicitly: that speaking of gender does not mean speaking only of women. As a critical term "gender" invokes women only insofar as in its absence they are essentially invisible. And it brings them up not only for their own interest but to signal the sexed nature of men as well, and beyond that the way the sexed nature of both women and men is not natural but cultural. In this sense, gender may be opposed to sex as culture is to nature so that its relation to sexual nature is unknown and probably unknowable: how, after all, do we speak of human beings outside of culture? From the perspective of gender, identity is a role, character traits are not autonomous qualities but functions and ways of relating. Actions define actors rather than vice versa. Connoting history and not nature, gender is *not* a category of human nature.

Uncovering the contingencies of gender at the heart of even the most apparently universal writing has been a way of challenging the view that men embody the transcendent human norm, a view to which the first objection was that it was unjust to women. But in proposing gender as a basic problem and an essential category in cultural and historical analysis, feminists have recast the issue of women's relative identity as equally an issue for men, who, upon ceasing to be mankind, become, precisely, men. Thus gender has emerged as a problem that is always implicit in any work. It is a quality of the literary voice hitherto masked by the static of common assumptions. And as a critical category gender is an additional lens, or a way of lifting the curtain to an unseen recess of the self and of society. Simply put, the perspective of gender enhances the critical senses; let us try to see how.

The Adventures of Huckleberry Finn is a man's book about a boy, and just as likely an object of gender criticism as writing by or about women. Mark Twain's best-known work is a classic or, to use a term also defined in this volume, a canonical text. This story of an adolescent who undergoes a series of trials on the rocky road or the river voyage to adulthood is a central work in the American tradition, a work that articulates and helps define dominant values and ways of seeing the world. Such works and their central characters claim to represent the universal human condition. So one prevailing critical view that *Huckleberry Finn* is "a great book" because it champions "the autonomy of the individual," (Smith 1958, xxix) assumes that "the individual" is generically a self-sufficient being able to define himself autonomously, meaning apart from society. Note that in the preceding sentence one could not substitute "herself" and "her" nor indicate that the representative individual is black or Asian because specifying an alternative and subcategorical sex or race invokes limits on individual autonomy. On the other hand, not to specify alternative categories of identity subsumes them in the white male norm, when it does not exclude them from it altogether. Huck's individuality transcends all the particularities of his class and generation.

A little like Hamlet, except that Huck is no prince but in fact the antithesis of a prince, occupying the very bottom rung of his social ladder. It has been suggested that in Hannibal society Huck ranks below the slaves, who at least play a useful role in the community, whereas "poor white trash" like him are at best useless and most times a nuisance. The son of the town drunk, almost illiterate, dirt-poor and innocent of ambition for either education, property or shoes, Huck seems to lack all conventional worth, but this only makes him the better embodiment of individual values. For Huck's missing social attributes and graces dramatize his separation from society and make him an emblem of individualism. Huck personally transcends his abjection (as Hamlet, the unsuccessful prince, his loftiness). From the beginning of the story, he is headed out. He starts by leaving the home of the Widow Douglas and the village itself. This places him on the threshold of more radical departures, as Huck opposes his universal principles to the fundamental tenets of both his class and his race. He achieves heroism by renouncing genteel hypocrisies as Hamlet does by denouncing the rot at the Danish court.

For all its systematic extraction of its hero from social categories and roles, however, the novel actually reaffirms one category and role, paradoxically appropriating its terms to depict transcendence. By rejecting the false values of his society, Huck eventually becomes a man of integrity; and whatever else in our culture defines a man's integrity, not being feminine, being un- and even antifeminine is key. In fact Huck's first passage, once he leaves village society, takes him into a limbo of gender.

Huck's voyage out begins on the island in the middle of the Mississippi where he comes upon the runaway Jim. Having joined forces, the outcast boy and the escaped slave deem it prudent before proceeding with their journey to freedom to see whether they are being pursued. Huck will have to return to the shore to reconnoiter and, to avoid being recognized, he will need a disguise. A deep bonnet such as is worn by local girls seems ideal for the purpose. Dressed therefore in bonnet and gown, Huck sets off, concentrating hard on remembering that he is a girl. Fortunately the first house he comes to is inhabited by a stranger in town, a middle-aged woman to whom, introducing himself as Sarah Williams, he spins a tale about a sick mother for whom he is seeking help. As they sit comfortably chatting, the woman mentions that the entire neighborhood is astir with rumors about Huck Finn's disappearance and probable murder. At first, she reports, everyone assumed that the murderer was the runaway Jim but now folks are inclined to believe that it was Huck's own "white-trash" father, who has also disappeared. Still, a reward of $300 has been posted for the slave's capture and the woman herself has great hopes of earning it; for she has seen smoke rising on the island where in fact Huck and Jim are camping, and that very evening her husband is to row out there.

Agitated by this ominous news, Huck cannot keep still and, as an occupation appropriate to his disguise, attempts to thread a needle. His hostess, who is named Judith Loftus, watches his maneuvers with astonishment and a short time later, on the pretext that she has hurt her arm, asks him to throw a lead weight at a rat that has been poking its nose out of a hole in the wall. Naturally Huck throws brilliantly, whereupon she retrieves the weight and tosses it to the seated boy who claps his knees together to catch it. With this, Mrs. Loftus announces triumphantly that she has not been fooled: he is not a girl but a boy apprentice run away from his abusive master. Huck breaks down and confesses to this new identity and, giving him much good advice, Mrs. Loftus sends him on his way. In a panic, he hastens to the island, and arriving, calls out to Jim to hurry, they have to get off at once: " 'There ain't a minute to lose. They're after us!' "

This last exclamation deserves all the critical attention it has received. "They" Huck cries to Jim are "after us," but of course "they" are only after Jim. Indeed, in racial and even class terms, "they" include Huck, who at that moment disengages from all his kind to identify with a black man and a slave. Earlier, hearing about the magnificent sum to be had for turning Jim in, Huck was so far from being tempted that Judith Loftus had to explain to him that although her neighbors no longer thought the slave was a murderer, the money was incentive enough to continue the chase. " 'Well, you're innocent, ain't you!' " she teases Huck who at this moment has become literally innocent, redeeming himself in these passages from sins of racism and of greed.

This episode culminates Huck's moral and political ascension; he will not rise higher in the rest of the novel but rather slide back. There is an archetypal, typological dimension in this situation of a boy discarding his given identity and recreating himself more just and good. But what is the role in all this of the feminine disguise? Why and to what effect does Huck pass through the crisis of rejecting his born identity dressed as a girl?

We should note first that the plot does not require this costume. Since Mark Twain makes Judith Loftus a stranger, there is no reason why Huck cannot pretend to be a runaway apprentice in the first place. One explanation could be that turning Huck into a girl gives Twain the opportunity to ridicule femininity— something he does intermittently throughout the novel, making fun for instance of female sentimentality in the tear-filled story of Emmeline Grangerford, young poetess, deceased. But if this was the inspiration for the masquerade, it effectively backfired. For the ridiculous figure in the Loftus kitchen is Huck himself, while in lecturing him on his ineptitude in impersonating the feminine, Judith effects a temporary but nonetheless radical reversal of the very nature of gender. What should have been Huck's saving grace, that he is too boy-like to imitate a girl successfully, cannot redeem his discomfiture; when Mrs. Loftus dispatches him at the end of the scene she is clearly skeptical about his ability to get on even in masculine guise: "if you get into trouble you send word" she offers, "and I'll do what I can to get you out of it." On the strength of this short-lived turnabout, womanhood even develops a maternal aspect all but unknown in the rest of Mark Twain's writings. "Keep the river road, . . . and next time you tramp, take shoes and socks with you," must sound an unaccustomed note to a boy whose experience runs more commonly to scolding aunts than to nurturing mothers.

The motherly Judith Loftus is in command of the scene and of Huck; but most unexpectedly, she is in command of herself, making this explicit when she takes command of femininity itself. In explaining how she has penetrated Huck's disguise, through his inept rendering of girl-ness, she analyzes feminine behavior as if from outside, herself standing apart as much "the individual" as Huck is when he stands apart from his "white-trash" ignorance, or Jim, briefly, from his "black" superstition. For the interval from that speech to the end of the chapter a few paragraphs later, conventional femininity is a social construction equally with the novel's account of organized religion or the cavalier ethic.

As a social construction femininity has its standard parts. A girl, Judith Loftus tells Huck, can thread a needle, she spreads her lap to catch things which thus land in her skirt, and she cannot throw straight. The precision with which Mrs. Loftus describes how a girl does throw necessarily implies equal knowledge of how boys do it. She can detail femininity because she sees it as a role, which must mean that masculinity is also a role. The logic of this is that anyone who knows the rules can play, boy or girl, man or woman. For instance she has just been playing, pretending not to be able to hit the rat, thus *pretending* to be feminine in order to force Huck to reveal his masculinity. In her criticism of Huck's feminine acting, Judith Loftus labels it just that, acting.

The chapter's opening inaugurates the notion that femininity is a situation by placing us on its threshold: " 'Come in,' " says the woman, and I did." No sooner has Huck taken on the role with the name Sarah Williams than he gets his first lesson in how to act as a girl. For while he had meant just to gather information and leave, the good Mrs. Loftus will not hear of the ostensible Sarah's wandering the roads at night alone. To be a girl is to be unable to move about freely: Sarah-Huck will have to wait for a man, Judith Loftus's husband, to return and escort her-him. In this scene displaced to the wings, men wait to act out their parts. Although Mrs. Loftus is the one who has discovered Jim's hiding place, properly, she will send her husband, "him and another man," to effect the capture.

The culminating moment in the reversal of femininity from nature to nurture—from sex to gender—comes toward the end of the episode when after warning Huck not to go among women pretending to be one of them Judith adds kindly, "'You do a girl tolerable poor, but you might fool men, maybe.'" This is the final blow not to male authority but to the authority of gender itself, for if women recognize femininity better than men that can only mean that femininity is a performance and not a natural mode of being.

Sexual orthodoxy is not self-contained but dualistic, a matter of relations. This interdependence between self-definition and the definition of the opposite gender is especially true for women, whose more restricted horizon is entirely spanned by masculinity. Taken to be rooted in biological propensity, femininity reveals itself, as it refers, first or at least equally, to men, who represent its reason and its rationality and who possess the key to its code as an essential component of their masculinity. If women are born and not made women, men should be the best judges of femininity.

When Judith Loftus tells Huck that women will recognize his absence of femininity but that he may fool men, she posits, on the contrary, a femininity that, instead of reflecting order, generates it, whose original impulse is therefore not biology but ideology. The femininity Mrs. Loftus deploys in restricted travel, sewing, knitting, and maladroit pitching represents its oppositional relation to masculinity as a series of actions that are anything but spontaneous or natural. These actions enact a stance that is willful if not consciously willed. Bring the thread to the needle, she instructs Huck, not the needle to the thread; hold your arm "as awkward as you can" and above all "miss your rat about six or seven foot." Missing rats is what a girl *does*. Let us say the obvious: when it is an action rather than an accident, missing implies the theoretical ability to hit. Nor can we interpret this to mean that, as a boy, Huck can choose to hit the rat or miss him but that a girl could only miss, because all of it, the way to hit and to miss and above all the necessity of choosing between them, is being explained by a woman who controls the entire situation: "'I spotted you for a boy when you was threading the needle; and I contrived the other things just to make certain.'"

Femininity, as Judith Loftus has here defined it, is something women *do,* a composite activity made up of certain acts they perform well and others they as skillfully perform badly, or perhaps most skillfully not at all. Masculinity is the equal and opposite condition: she spots Huck for a boy when after lacking the skill of threading needles—threading is what men skillfully do-not-do—he reveals that he usually wears trousers by clapping his knees together to catch the ball. One suspects, it is true, that sharp-eyed Mrs. Loftus would spot a girl in boy's clothing more quickly than her husband would, but this does not negate the implication of her warning to Huck, that gender is nurture rather than nature. In part this is because the performance of femininity includes observing more shrewdly, especially the performance of gender.

But the other reason for her likely superiority at catching out fraudulent boys as well as girls lies precisely in her ideological stance. At the close of the preceding chapter, before the trip to the village, Jim criticizes Huck, who is practicing walking about in a dress: he "said I didn't walk like a girl; and he said I must quit pulling up my gown to get at my britches pocket." Jim's instructions are negative, as is the entire disguise, whose intent is to hide and not to project, to conceal "real" masculinity. What Huck learns from Judith Loftus, however, is that concealment is not the issue but projection: projection, meaning construction. Extrapolating, masculinity also becomes a construction and in renaming Huck a boy, Mrs. Loftus returns his masculinity to him not in the old absolute terms but as *his* way of performing.

It is this experience, effectively a revolution in the way Huck defines himself in the basic area of gender, that sets the stage for the revolution to come in his sense of himself in the equally basic area of race. The move involved in both transformations is the same, from essentialist to cultural and political definitions of gender and race, from nature to history. When Huck, in that epiphanic cry " 'They're after us!,' " casts himself as an object of his own race's persecution, he does not mean that he now considers himself black. Rather he has come to see that in the cavalier South the blackness of an enslaved black man refers not to a set of inherent attributes but to a situation, to an oppression such as can also torment a poor white boy.

The sequence—Huck and Jim on the island as white boy and escaped slave; Huck pretending to be a girl in the Loftus kitchen; Huck and Jim fleeing the island to escape white slavers—places the middle episode in the role not only of catalyst but of mediator. It is in the context of a temporary displacement of his gender identity, and of the questions Judith Loftus raises about gender identity as such, that Huck moves permanently into a new social identity in which, resuming an unquestioned maleness, he questions the other conventions of his culture far more radically than he ever has before. At the moment when he associates himself fully with Jim, Huck Finn and his story might be said to touch bottom in the contemporary culture and ideology and to spring back to an antipode that marks not transcendence but the outer limits of the culturally and ideologically imaginable.

Such moments are not easily sustained. Many students of Mark Twain and *Huckleberry Finn* have noted that after a dazzlingly iconoclastic first half or so, the novel retreats toward a disappointingly conventional conclusion; and that on the way, with Huck's complicity, the character of Jim is returned to a black stereotype. The subject here, however, is not *Huckleberry Finn,* but the uses of gender as a critical term that can illuminate not only the literary treatment of associated topics like romantic love and the family but thematic and formal concerns that are not obviously involved with sexual identity at all. We could have fruitfully examined the treatment of the Widow Douglas, for instance, or of Emmeline Grangerford and the contemporary tradition of women's writings which Twain mocks through her, and related these examinations to the novel as a whole. But the issue of gender arises in the Judith Loftus episode in a more generally paradigmatic way, at once overtly, in that Huck pretends to be a girl, and as a deep structure whose ramifications Twain himself may not have fully understood.

These ramifications have to do with the overall theme of the early part of the novel which traces Huck's passage out of his society into a liminal state in which not only his moral philosophy but his very identity is in flux. It is no coincidence that he enters into a state of aggravated mutability by stepping into the woman's sphere of Judith Loftus; nor that her exposition of the inessentiality of femininity immediately precedes his extraordinary identification with a black slave. In this process, race and sex are not wholly analogous: Huck emerges from the encounter with Judith Loftus, indubitably and forever, a boy, whom one cannot imagine actually identifying with a girl, only protecting her. Conversely, the final lesson he learns from Judith Loftus is not the one she means to teach him, since she herself is hell-bent on catching Jim and returning him to slavery. But these complications are precisely the point in manifesting the fundamental or axiomatic character of gender in the organization of thought and writing: by plunging Huck into the deepest possible limbo of identity, this very brief eclipse of his masculinity, even rectified by his inability to maintain the pretense, opens him and Mark Twain's imagination to rethinking the basic principles of personal identity and social ideology both. Through Judith Loftus, the novel speaks as it could not through Huck himself. It is as if the novel itself had found a female voice and the language to say things its male vocabulary could not articulate and therefore did not know, or did not know it knew. The term "gender" can empower criticism in the same way, enabling it to pose new questions and thus discover new levels of interpretation. In reading the Judith Loftus episode, raising gender as an issue affects one's interpretation in a widening circle that finally encompasses the whole novel. At the center of the circle, the very fact of Huck's female impersonation becomes charged with a new energy when it is seen not so much to conceal or erase his masculinity as to render it problematical. So long as masculinity is considered literally organic, Huck's calico gown and bonnet could at the extreme signify his castration without thereby raising questions about masculinity as such. Castration as we know, is the classic stuff of anxiety, but it also allows for total reassurance. In that regard, the episode is entirely reassuring: Huck fails at being a girl because he is so thoroughly a boy. When the issue, however, is not the possession of masculinity but, precisely, its provenance—whether biological or ideological—no such reassurance can be had. On the contrary, the more explicitly the characteristics of masculinity are described, directly or as the reverse of Mrs. Loftus's account of femininity, the more they become contingent, possibly arbitrary, and certainly disputable.

With Huck sitting in Mrs. Loftus's kitchen got up like a girl, nothing any longer is given, anyone can be anything. The certainty of gender provides for literature generally and for the rest of *Huckleberry Finn* an anchor for the kinetic self. Lifting that anchor even briefly accentuates all the instabilities of Huck's other identifications. The early part of the boy's journey out of town moves toward an indefinite horizon. How indefinite or infinite a horizon is dramatically evident in the explosion of his cry "They're after us!" Joining an escaped slave in the first person plural, he has traveled a cosmic distance which the additional critical perspective of gender helps both measure and explain by bridging the opening of the chapter, in which Huck passes into the world apart of women, and the close, which propels him right out of his culture and society. In the end, while discarding the accoutrements of "white-trash" ideology, he will certainly retain the panoply of conventional masculinity. But the fact that he has temporarily put off even that gauges the radical reach of his alienation, and plumbs the depths of its terrors.

In other words, gender is both an embedded assumption and functions as a touchstone for others. It is logically impossible to interrogate gender—to transform it from axiom to object of scrutiny and critical term—without also interrogating race and class. The introduction of gender into the critical discussion multiplies its concerns and categories by those of historiography to produce a newly encompassing account of cultural consciousness that is also newly self-conscious.

From the perspective of gender, then, a critic sees both deeper and more broadly. But the view may also appear more obstructed, exactly the enhancement of critical vision seeming to hinder it, or to interpose a new obstacle between critic and text. In analyzing the ways gender concepts complicate the Judith Loftus episode, this discussion has invoked some issues and ideas which Mark Twain probably did not consciously consider when he wrote it. In a much later story, describing a boy and girl each of whom behaves like the opposite, Twain expresses a clear understanding that gender is a matter of ideology. Or as he puts it more vividly: "Hellfire Hotchkiss [the girl] is the only genuwyne male man in this town and Thug Carpenter's [the boy] the only genuwyne female girl, if you leave out sex and just consider the business facts." (Cited in Gillman, 109–10.) Indeed "the business facts" of sexual identity is about as good a definition of gender as one could offer and Judith's exposition of how girls are made girls and boys boys can certainly be read as an early draft. But within *Huckleberry Finn* itself there is little to indicate such understanding and in fact evidence to the contrary. When the narrator describes women directly they seem rather the incarnation of femininity than its practitioners, innately either sentimental sillies like Emmeline Grangerford or, like the Widow Douglas, pious hypocrites. On the whole in this story, being a woman is not a proud thing.

That Judith Loftus is anomalously admirable is not a problem but that we have read her as defining herself and the scene she dominates in terms for which there seems to be no other reference in the book could be one. The apparent absence within the text of these critical terms suggests that the reading has introduced its own notions into the writer's world. One of the ways the term "gender" alters the entire enterprise of criticism is by responding positively to such suggestions, though in relation to a revised understanding of the interactions between reading and text. Because an ideology of gender is basic to virtually all thought while, by most thinkers, unrecognized as such, gender criticism often has a confrontational edge. One has to read for gender; unless it figures explicitly in story or poem, it will seldom read for itself. On the other hand "interpretation" is an ambiguous word meaning both to translate and to explain. Literary interpretation does both inextricably, and when critics limit themselves to the explicit terms of the texts they read their interpretations can be more congenial yet not less (re) or (de)constructive. They also interpret who only think to explicate. Literary criticism involves action as much as reflection, and reading for gender makes the deed explicit.

The exhilarating discovery of Molière's bourgeois gentleman, that when he talked he talked prose, has a counterpart in the rather inhibiting epigram that when you speak you have to use words. The term "gender" in literary criticism refers to a set of concerns and also to a vocabulary—what Mark Twain might have called a business vocabulary—that contributes its own meanings to everything that is said or written.

Suggested Readings

No short list of titles can do justice to the rich variety of recent works in gender criticism. Moreover, for an understanding of the general significance of the term it seems as important to develop a sense of its possibilities as to explore these individually in depth. The following are five anthologies that among them offer a wide survey of the field and can provide an excellent introduction to it.

Christian, Barbara, ed. 1985. *Black Feminist Criticism.*
de Lauretis, Theresa, ed. 1986. *Feminist Studies, Critical Studies.*
Hull, Gloria T., Patricia Bell Scott, Barbara Smith, eds. 1982. *All the Women Are White, All the Blacks Are Men, But Some of Us Are Brave: Black Women's Studies.*
Keohane, Nannerl O., Michelle Z. Rosaldo, Barbara G. Gelpi, eds. 1982. *Feminist Theory: A Critique of Ideology.*
Miller, Nancy, ed. 1987. *The Poetics of Gender.*

20

Race

Kwame Anthony Appiah

Stretch forth! stretch forth! from the south to the north,
From the east to the west,—stretch forth! stretch forth!
Strengthen thy stakes and lengthen thy cords,—
The world is a tent for the world's true lords!
Break forth and spread over every place
The world is a world for the Saxon race!
Martin Tupper, "The Anglo-Saxon Race"

THESE famous words were published in 1850 in a new journal called *The Anglo-Saxon*. The publication lasted only a year, but its tone was emblematic of an important development in the way educated Englishmen and women thought of themselves and of what it was that made them English. This development was itself part of a wider movement of ideas in Europe and North America. As heirs to the culture of the modern world, a culture so crucially shaped by the ideas that Tupper's poem represents, most twentieth-century readers, not merely in Europe and America but throughout the world, are able to take for granted a set of assumptions about what Tupper meant by "race." Those assumptions, which amounted to a new theory of race, inform our modern understanding of literature—indeed of most symbolic culture—in fundamental ways; and this despite the fact that, as we shall see, many of them have been officially discarded.

That the specific form race-theory took was new does not, of course, mean that it had no historical antecedents. Almost as far back as the earliest human writings, we can find more or less well articulated views about the differences between "our own kind" and the people of other cultures. These doctrines, like modern theories of race, have often placed a central emphasis on physical appearance in defining the "Other," and on common ancestry in explaining why groups of people display differences in their attitudes and aptitudes.

If we call any group of human beings of common descent living together in some sort of association, however loosely structured, a "people," we can say that every human culture that was aware of other peoples seems to have had views about what accounted for the differences—in appearance, in customs, in language—between peoples. This is certainly true of the two main ancient traditions to which Western thinkers look back—those of the classical Greeks and the ancient Hebrews. Thus, we find Hippocrates in the fifth century B.C.E. in Greece seeking to explain the (supposed) superiority of his own people to the peoples of (Western) Asia by arguing that the barren soils of Greece had forced the Greeks to become tougher and more independent. Such a view attributes the characteristics of a people to their environment, leaving open the possibility that their descendants could change if they moved to new conditions.

While the general opinion in Greece in the few centuries on either side of the beginning of the common era appears to have been that both the black "Ethiopians" to the south and the blonde "Scythians" to the north were inferior to the Hellenes, there was no general assumption that this inferiority was incorrigible. Educated Greeks, after all, knew that in the *Iliad* Homer had described Zeus and other Olympians feasting with the "blameless Ethiopians"; and there are arguments in the works of the pre-Socratic Sophists to the effect that it is individual character and not skin color that determines a person's worth.

In the Old Testament, on the other hand, what is thought to be distinctive about peoples is not so much appearance and custom as their relationship, through a common ancestor, to God. Thus, in the book of Genesis, Jehovah says to Abraham,

> Go your way out of your country and from your relatives and
> from the house of your father and to the country that I shall show
> you; and I shall make a great people of you and I will make your
> name great. (Gen. 12:1,2)

And from this founding moment—this covenant or agreement between Abraham and Jehovah—the descendants of Abraham have a special place in history. It is, of course, Abraham's grandson Jacob who takes the name of Israel: and his descendants thus become the "people of Israel."

The Old Testament is full of names of peoples. Some of them are still familiar—Syrians, Assyrians, and Persians; some of them are less so—Canaanites, Philistines, and Medes. Many of these groups are accounted for in the genealogies of the peoples of the earth and are explicitly seen as descending ultimately not only from the first human couple, Adam and Eve, but more particularly from Noah. Just as the Israelites are "sons of Shem," the children of Ham and of Japheth account for the rest of the human "family."

But while these different peoples are taken to have different specific characteristics and ancestries, the fundamentally theocentric perspective of the Old Testament requires that what *essentially* differentiates them all from the Hebrews is that they do not have the special relationship to Jehovah enjoyed by the children, the descendants, of Israel. There is very little hint that the early Jewish writers developed any theories about the relative importance of the biological and the cultural inheritances by which God made these different peoples distinct. Indeed, in the theocentric framework it is God's covenant that matters, and the very distinction between environmental and inherited characteristics is anachronistic.

Neither the Greeks' environmentalism nor the Hebrews' theocentric notion of the significance of being one people are ideas that we should naturally apply in understanding Tupper's use of the idea of race. To the extent that we think of Tupper's doggerel as modern, as involving ideas that *we* understand, we will suppose that he believed that the world was "a world for the Saxon race" because of that race's *inherited* capacities. For by Tupper's day a distinctively modern understanding of what it was to be a people—an understanding in terms of our modern notion of race—was beginning to be forged: that notion had at its heart a new scientific conception of biological heredity, even as it carried on some of the roles played in Greek and Hebraic thought by the idea of a people. But it was, also, as we shall see, interwoven with a new understanding of a people as a nation and of the role of culture—and, crucially for our purposes, of literature—in the life of nations.

In short, Tupper, unlike the Greeks and the Hebrews, was what I shall call a *racialist*. He believed, as did most educated Victorians by the mid-century, that we could divide human beings into a small number of groups, called "races," in such a way that all the members of these races shared certain fundamental, biologically heritable, moral and intellectual characteristics with each other that they did not share with members of any other race. The characteristics that each member of a race was supposed to share with every other were sometimes called the *essence* of that race; they were characteristics that were necessary and sufficient, taken together, for someone to be a member of the race.

Unlike the Greeks and the Hebrews, racialists believed that the racial essence accounted for more than the obvious visible characteristics—skin-color, hair—on the basis of which we decide whether people are, say, Asian-Americans or Afro-Americans. For a racialist, then, to say someone is "Negro" is not just to say that they have inherited a black skin or curly hair: it is to say that their skin color goes along with other important inherited characteristics. By the end of the nineteenth century most Western scientists (indeed, most educated Westerners) believed that racialism was correct and theorists sought to explain many characteristics—including, for example, literary "genius," intelligence, and honesty—by supposing that they were inherited along with (or were in fact part of) a person's racial essence.

The twentieth century inherited these conceptions; but it was the nineteenth century that was the heyday of appeals to race in literary study. For by our own day the idea that the concept of *race* should have any place—let alone an important one—in literary studies has been attacked from a good many directions.

Perhaps the most surprising has been an attack in the name of "science." In a society like ours, where most people take their race to be a significant aspect of their identity, it comes as a shock to many to learn that there is a fairly widespread consensus in the sciences of biology and anthropology that the word "race," at least as it is used in most unscientific discussions, refers to nothing that science should recognize as real.

And it is not just the claim that there is a racial essence that can explain a person's moral, intellectual, or literary aptitudes that scientists have rejected. They also believe that such classifications as *Negro, Caucasian* and *Mongoloid* are of no importance for biological purposes. First, because there are simply too many people who do not fit into any such category; and second because, even when you succeed in assigning someone to one of these categories—on the basis of skin-pigmentation and hair, say—that implies very little about most of their other biological characteristics. Even those scientists who still have a use for the term "race" agree that a good deal of what is popularly believed about races is false—often wildly false.

But, of course, a discussion of some of the literary ramifications of the idea of race can proceed while accepting the essential unreality of races and the falsehood of most of what is believed about them. For, at least in this respect, races are like witches: however unreal witches are, *belief* in witches, like belief in races, has had—and in many communities continues to have—profound consequences for human social life. The racialism we see in Tupper and his contemporaries is real enough to make up for the unreality of races.

We can see something of the long process of transition from the views of the ancient world to the racialism we find in Tupper, if we ask how we should interpret the handling of questions of difference between peoples in such plays as Shakespeare's *Othello* (c. 1603) and *The Merchant of Venice* (c. 1597) or in Christopher Marlowe's *The Jew of Malta* (c. 1592).

In each of these plays a central figure—Othello, Shylock, Barabas—plays out a role we can understand only in terms of a stereotype of a people, Moors or Jews; a stereotype we are likely, if we are hasty, to conceive of as simply racialist. So it is important to go carefully. We should begin by recognizing that in Shakespearean England both Jews and Moors were barely an empirical reality. And even though there were small numbers of Jews and black people in England in Shakespeare's day, attitudes to "the Moor" and "the Jew" do not seem to have been based on experience of these people. Furthermore, despite the fact that there was an increasing amount of information available about dark-skinned foreigners in this, the first great period of modern Western exploration, actual reports of black or Jewish foreigners did not play an important part in forming these images. Rather, it seems that the stereotypes were based on an essentially theological conception of the status of both Moors and Jews as non-Christians;

the former distinguished by their black skin, whose color was associated in Christian iconography with sin and the devil; the latter by their being, as Matthew's account of the crucifixion suggests, "Christ-killers."

There is good reason, then, to interpret these Elizabethan stereotypes, which *we* might naturally think of as what I have called "racialist," as rooted far less in notions of inherited dispositions and far more in the idea of the Moor and the Jew as infidels, unbelievers whose physical differences are signs (but not causes or effects) of their unbelief. Yet in some ways the most revealing of the plays for the purpose of underscoring the distance that was still to be traveled from Shakespeare's Moor of Venice or Marlowe's Maltese Jew to the imperializing race of Tupper's Anglo-Saxonist vision is a play that does not explicitly invoke either of these familiar "racial" stereotypes: and that is Shakespeare's *The Tempest*.

We are accustomed nowadays to interpretations that cast Caliban as the *colonial* subject; and that is not anachronistic, given the play's historical context. *The Tempest* was first performed in 1611 for the court of James I, during an era of extensive overseas expansion. From abundant interval evidence we know that Shakespeare's conception of the "savage and deformed slave" was informed by contemporary pamphlets and speculative essays about the nature of the "native," travelogues describing European encounters with the inhabitants of the New World.

Caliban, as Prospero asserts, is "a born devil" (literally, perhaps) "on whose nature/Nurture can never stick" (IV.i.188–89). And if Caliban is the representative colonial, the peculiar brutality of Prospero as colonizer can be justified only by Caliban's incorrigibly devilish nature. For, of course, it is more than just colonialism in general that needs to be justified. What needs to be justified is the especial brutality of the colonization of nonwhite peoples—Africans and Indians. It is only because Caliban is incorrigibly wicked that Prospero can maintain our sympathy while making Caliban's colonization into what is simply a form of slavery. Miranda makes the issue clear the first time she addresses Caliban.

> Abhorred slave,
> Which any print of goodness wilt not take,
> Being capable of all ill! I pitied thee,
> Took pains to make thee speak, taught thee each hour
> One thing or other. When thou didst not, savage,
> Know thine own meaning, but wouldst gabble like
> A thing most brutish, I endowed thy purposes
> With words that made them known. But thy vile race—
> Though thou didst learn—had that in't which good natures
> Cannot abide to be with; . . .
>
> (I.ii.350–59)

Echoes here of the later image of the colonized male subject—ungovernable in his lusts, intractable, learning the colonizer's language in order to articulate his own vile purposes—may lead us to read back into this passage the triumphalist racialism of "The Anglo-Saxon Race." Yet if it is clear enough how this ideology that will develop into racialism could serve already in the seventeenth century to license the domination of subject peoples, it is important to mark its differences.

The word "race" occurs only in this place in *The Tempest* and an unprepared modern reader risks misunderstanding it. For "race" here in its Elizabethan usage means—as the *Oxford English Dictionary* tells us—"natural or inherited disposition." Miranda's point in speaking of Caliban's "race" is only to restate her earlier insistence on his individual moral incorrigibility: he will not take any "print of goodness" because it is not in his nature. For Tupper, of course, "race" is also a natural or inherited disposition; but it is, by contrast, one that is shared with a whole people.

What is interesting is that the very possibility of reading *The Tempest* as an allegory of colonialism does not appear to occur to theatrical interpreters of the play until the nineteenth century; while from the mid-nineteenth century on— at the pinnacle of British imperial power—productions of *The Tempest* in Britain increasingly reflect ongoing disagreements about the nature of subject peoples and the justice of their colonization. And when a conception of "primitive" peoples became biologized during the later nineteenth century—especially under the influence of Darwin's *Origin of Species*—we find that productions of *The Tempest* mirrored current speculation. In the age of Social Darwinism, Caliban became quite literally the "missing link" of evolutionary theory (the English actor F. R. Benson, who played the part in a touring company all around Britain in the 1890s, spent time observing various apes in the zoo in order to perfect his movements!) If Caliban is the "missing link," his status as a proper object of the colonizer's control is not in doubt. The very fact that by the end of the nineteenth century the character can move back and forth between interpretations as subhuman and as the colonial human subject, shows the tendency of an increasingly biologized idea of race to allow an uneasy oscillation between thinking of the natives as of the *same* fundamental kind as the ruling race (and thus both capable of elevation and, at least potentially, of being *wrongly* subjected) and thinking of them as of a different kind (and thus perpetually the natural subjects of their rulers). The distance from Shakespeare's understanding of the issue of difference between peoples to the ideas that surrounded Tupper is evidenced in these new Victorian readings of Shakespeare's play.

For literary purposes, the developments that begin at the turn of the nineteenth century have another immediate consequence: race becomes important as the theme of a great body of writing in Europe and North America—and, indeed, in the rest of the world under the influence of "Western" cultures—and the concept often plays a crucial role in structuring plot.

In *Ivanhoe,* a novel published by the Scottish novelist and poet Sir Walter Scott in 1819, the theme of the story is the hatred between Anglo-Saxons, the "original" inhabitants of Britain, and the Norman rulers imposed upon them by the conquest of England in 1066 by William the Conqueror. The presupposition of the story (which seems to have little historical basis) is that there was a natural antipathy between the Anglo-Saxon race and their French-speaking Norman rulers; and our understanding of the plot depends, in part, on our recognition of the struggle between Anglo-Saxons and Normans not simply as a struggle of the poor and oppressed against their rich oppressors but as a struggle for Anglo-Saxon national (or, equivalently, racial) autonomy. The racial theme of the book is reinforced by the presence of the character "Isaac the Jew" and his daughter Rebecca; as the Norman aristocracy are stereotyped as lawless and corrupt, and the Anglo-Saxons as noble and downtrodden, Isaac is stereotyped as avaricious, torn between love of his daughter and love of money.

Ideas about race could, in principle, have developed without a commitment to the view that some races were superior to others; but they did not. While the Christian tradition insisted on the common ancestry of all human beings, and the Enlightenment, even when it was critical of official Christianity, emphasized the universality of reason, by the middle of the nineteenth century the notion that all races were equal in their capacities was a distinctly minority view. Even those who insisted that all human beings had the same rights largely acknowledged that nonwhite people lacked either the intelligence or the vigor of the white races: among which the highest, it was widely agreed, was the Indo-European stock from which the Germanic peoples emerged. In England and North America, there was a further narrowing of focus: the Anglo-Saxons were the favored offshoot of the Germanic stock.

Indeed, one of the central questions for nineteenth-century race-science became the question *why* it was that the white races were superior to the others; and there was an almost equal interest in how the others should be ranked below them. But though there was, therefore, an inevitable element of moral evaluation in most theories of race, it is important to be clear that the racial theme never required a simple identification of one race with evil and another with good. In *Ivanhoe,* the hero—son of Cedric, an Anglo-Saxon "nationalist" who wishes to see the reestablishment of the Saxon monarchy—cooperates as a loyal subject with the Norman king, Richard the Lionheart, to overthrow the corrupt Norman nobles who run the country while the king is taking part in the Crusades; and, at a crucial point in the plot, Rebecca, Isaac's daughter—despite the essentially anti-Semitic presuppositions of Scott's day—nurses Ivanhoe back to life and falls in love with him. Nevertheless, the book depends not only, as we have seen, on an assumption of the naturalness of racial feeling but also on the maintenance of certain racial boundaries: despite Rebecca's more substantial character, it is Rowena, the Anglo-Saxon heiress, that Ivanhoe marries, and Rebecca, who is, in a sense, ruled out by race as a spouse, disappears from England with her father at the end of the book.

Forty years after *Ivanhoe,* in *Salammbô,* published in 1862, the French novelist Gustave Flaubert created a similar racial romance, set in ancient Carthage. While the central contrast in the work is between civilized and barbarous peoples—the French word *barbares* (which is both noun and adjective) occurs 238 times, more often than any other noun or adjective—the novel is replete with references to Campanians, Garamantes, Gauls, Greeks, Iberians, Lusitanians, Libyans, Negroes, Numidians, Phoenicians, and Syssites; and these types are often identified with certain physical and moral characteristics.

Ivanhoe and *Salammbô* depend on projecting nineteenth-century racial concerns back into the past. But in the heyday of the European world empires, as the great European powers divided the world between them (and as Americans of European descent conquered Native Americans through superiority in military technologies) it was common to offer the racial superiority of the "white man" as an explanation for the contemporary successes of imperialism; and these successes became the theme of a substantial body of literature.

In the United States, for example, in James Fenimore Cooper's well-known "Leatherstocking Tales"—from *The Pioneers* (1823) to *The Deerslayer* (1841)—a celebration of the American frontier (itself a substantial literary theme) reveals the overarching theme of the decline of the "redman" and the triumph of the "white man." Cooper's style is in many ways reminiscent of Scott's and, in fact, Cooper could hardly have escaped the influence of Scott's romances: for these were amongst the most widely read and admired works of fiction in the United States in the first half of the nineteenth century. They were adapted over and over again for the American stage, and published in numerous editions (something which was easier in an age before copyright). Scott's interest for Americans must have been in part a consequence of the fact that much of his work, unlike *Ivanhoe,* was devoted to establishing not English but Scottish national feeling. In such adventures as *Rob Roy,* Scott celebrates the people and the life of the Scottish borders; a world whose romantically conceived landscape and rough "manly" manners were easily transferred in imagination to the rigors of North American pioneer life.

Like Scott's representation of the Jew, Cooper's image of the Indian, though stereotyped, was ambivalent: Natty Bumppo, Cooper's hero, distinguishes between "Good Indians"—like Chingachgook, Bumppo's Indian companion, who will fight with the white man against other red men—and "Bad Indians," who combine the lack of civilization, common to all Indians, with an absence of the natural nobility that Chingachgook displays. In Cooper's racial scheme (unlike Thomas Jefferson's), the Indian is below the "white man" but above the "Negro": Indians in Cooper are sometimes "Nature's gentlemen," blacks almost always evoke contempt. We could argue that the Negro, in Cooper, plays the same sort of role as the Jew in *Ivanhoe:* the main plot in each case pits one race (Anglo-Saxon, redman) against another (Norman, white man) that dominates it, and the third race (Jew, Negro) provides a point of contrast with each of the others; a point of contrast that allows us to understand the sympathies between the members of the first two races, even though their conflict is at the center of the plot. In this case, then, as I suggested, the hierarchy of races becomes an essential element in structuring the plot.

In a world whose politics were so dominated by racialism, it is hardly surprising that races became a central literary theme. What is, perhaps, more puzzling is the fact that many of those works that have been central to our understanding of what literature is are also thematically preoccupied with racial issues. But the reason for this is not far to seek: it lies in the dual connection made in eighteenth- and nineteenth-century thought between, on the one hand, race and nationality, and, on the other, nationality and literature. In short, the nation is the key middle term in understanding the relations between the concept of race and the idea of literature.

The first of these linkages, between nation and race, will surely be the less puzzling. In the Old World, where people were the hereditary subjects of monarchies, it was natural that the emergent European nations conceived of themselves in terms of descent. Eighteenth-century theorists of the nation had, of course, to make a sharp distinction between nations and states because in eighteenth-century Europe there was not even an approximate correlation between linguistic and political boundaries. (It is important to remember that the correlation remains in most parts of the world quite rough-and-ready.) The modern European nationalism, which produced, for example, the German and Italian states, involved trying to create states to correspond to nationalities: nationalities conceived of as sharing a civilization and, more particularly, a language and literature. And because political geography did not correspond to nationalities, eighteenth-century theorists were obliged to draw a distinction between the nation as a natural entity and the state as the product of culture, as a human artifice.

But with the increasing influence of the natural sciences in the nineteenth century, what is natural in human beings—"human nature"—came increasingly to be thought of in terms of the sciences of biology and anthropology. Inevitably, then, the nation comes more and more to be identified as a biological unit, defined by the shared essence that flows from a common descent.

Yet the increasing identification of race and nation in European—and more particularly in English—thought was a complex process. The Anglo-Saxonism of the nineteenth century in Britain had its roots deep in the soil of historical argument about the English constitution: in the fascinating process through which a rising commercial class transformed the monarchy in Britain from its feudal roots into the "constitutional monarchy" that was established at the Restoration of 1660. In the arguments that surround this development, a mythology took hold in the seventeenth century of a free Anglo-Saxon people, living under parliamentary government in the period before the Norman conquest of 1066. Increasingly Anglo-Saxon institutions were seen both to account for the Englishman's natural love of freedom and to underlie the immemorial rights of free men against the crown.

This mythology was counterposed against the mainstream historiography of the Middle Ages, which traced the *History of the Kings of Britain*—as Geoffrey of Monmouth's influential work of 1136 was called—to Brutus, grandson of Aeneas of Troy. It was Geoffrey who established the story of King Arthur, son of Utherpendragon, as forever part of British mythology; and his work played a significant part in providing a framework within which the different cultural streams—Roman, Saxon, Danish, and Norman—that had come together over the first millennium in Britain could be gathered into a single unifying history.

When Richard Verstegen published his influential *Restitution of Decayed Intelligence* in 1605, he claimed that England's Anglo-Saxon past was the past of a Germanic people, who shared their language and institutions with the Germanic tribes whose great courage and fierce independence Tacitus had described many centuries earlier. Verstegen argued that these tribes were also the ancestors of the Danes and the Normans, whose invasions of Britain had thus not essentially disturbed the unity of the English as a Germanic people. The effect of this argument, of course, was to provide for the seventeenth century what the *History of the Kings of England* had provided in the Middle Ages: a framework within which the peoples of England could be conceived as united.

By the eve of the American Revolution, Anglo-Saxon historiography and the study of the Anglo-Saxon law, language, and institutions, were established scholarly pursuits: and the notion of a free Anglo-Saxon past, whose reestablishment would be an escape from the monarchy's potential to develop into a tyranny, was one that appealed naturally to such figures as Thomas Jefferson. Anglo-Saxonism spread easily to a United States whose dominant culture imagined itself—even after the revolution—as British. And when Jefferson, himself no mean Anglo-Saxon scholar, designed a curriculum for the University of Virginia, he included the study of the Anglo-Saxon language, because, as he said, students reading the "histories and laws left [to] us in that . . . dialect," would "imbibe with the language their free principles of government."

But the deep-rooted character of the second linkage—between nation and literature—will probably be less naturally intelligible. And our starting point for understanding the role of the idea of a national literature in the development of the concept of a national culture must be in the work of the man who developed its first real theoretical articulation: Johann Gottfried Herder.

In his 1767 work, *On the New German Literature: Fragments,* Herder—who is, in some ways, the first important philosopher of modern nationalism—put forward the notion that language is not just "a tool of the arts and sciences" but "a part of them." Herder's notion of the *Sprachgeist*—literally, the "spirit" of the language—embodies the thought that language is not merely the medium through which speakers communicate but the sacred essence of a nationality. Herder himself identified the highest point of the nation's language in its poetry: both the popular lyrics of the folk song, which he collected, and the work of great poets. The emergence of nationalism, in the eighteenth and early nineteenth centuries, depended upon the imaginative recreation of a common cultural past that was, in no small part, crafted into a shared tradition by literary scholars like Herder and—to return to an earlier example—Sir Walter Scott, whose *Minstrelsy of the Scottish Border* was intended, as he said in the preface, to "contribute somewhat to the history of my native country; the peculiar features of whose manners and character are daily melting and dissolving into those of her sister and ally" (i.e., England). From its inception, literary history, like the collection of folk culture, served the ends of nation-building.

Imposing the post-Herderian identification of the core of the nation with its national literature on the racial conception of the nation, we arrive at the racial understanding of literature that flourished from the mid-nineteenth century in the work of the first modern literary historians. Thomas Carlyle, the great British essayist and man of letters, wrote in 1831: "The history of a nation's poetry is the essence of its history." It was only a step to the identification of that history with the history of the race. Hippolyte Taine's monumental *History of English Literature,* published in France in the 1860s—perhaps the first modern literary history of English—begins with the words: "History has been transformed, within a hundred years in Germany, within sixty in France, and that by the study of their literaures" (1897, 1). But he is soon telling us that:

> a race, like the Old Aryans, scattered from the Ganges as far as the Hebrides, settled in every clime, and every stage of civilization, transformed by thirty centuries of revolutions, nevertheless manifests in its languages, religions, literatures, philosophies, the community of blood and of intellect which to this day binds its offshoots together. (17)

What is revealed, in short, by the study of literature that has transformed the discipline of history, is the "moral state" of the race whose literature it is. It is because of this conception that Taine finds it proper to start his study of English literature with a chapter on the Saxons; so that Chapter 1, Book 1, of Taine's *History* begins not in England at all, but in Holland:

> As you coast the North Sea from Scheldt to Jutland, you will mark in the first place that the characteristic feature is the want of slope: marsh, water, shoal; the rivers hardly drag themselves along, swollen and sluggish, with long, black-looking waves . . .(37).

The "Saxons, Angles, Jutes, Frisians . . . [and] Danes" (39) who occupied this region of Holland at the beginning of the first millennium are, according to Taine, the ancestors of the English; but since they themselves are of German descent, Taine also refers, in describing this "race" a few pages later, to some of their traits reported in Tacitus.

It is the conception of the binding core of the English nation as the Anglo-Saxon race that accounts for Taine's decision to identify the origins of English literature not in its antecedents in the Greek and Roman classics that provided the models and themes of so many of the best-known works of English "poesy," not in the Italian models that influenced the drama of Marlowe and Shakespeare, but in *Beowulf,* a poem in the Anglo-Saxon tongue, a poem that was unknown to Chaucer and Spenser and Shakespeare.

Yet this decision was quite representative. When the teaching of English literature was institutionalized in the English universities in the nineteenth century, students were required to learn Anglo-Saxon in order to study *Beowulf.* Anglo-Saxonism thus plays a major role in the establishment of the canon of literary works that are to be studied in both British and American colleges; and the teachers who came from these colleges to the high schools brought the Anglo-Saxon canon with them.

We must examine one final role for questions of race in literary study, a role that is especially visible in much recent writing about American literature. And that is how American literature and literary study both reflect the existence of ethnic groups the very contours of which are, in a certain sense, the product of racism. For, however mythical the notion of race seems to be, we cannot deny the obvious fact that having one set of heritable characteristics—dark skin, say—rather than another—blonde hair, for example—can have profound psychological, economic, and other social consequences, especially in societies where many people are not only racialists but racists. Indeed, much of what is said about races nowadays in American social life, while literally false if understood as being about biological races, can be interpreted as reporting truths about social groups—Afro-Americans, Asian-Americans, Jewish Americans—whose experience of life and whose political relations are strongly determined by the existence of racist stereotypes.

The most prominent such reflection of racially understood ethnicity in literary studies in recent years is in the development of Afro-American literary criticism. Anyone who has followed the argument so far will anticipate that the persistent stream of Afro-American nationalist argument (whose beginnings we can trace well before Tupper) has been accompanied by appeals to an African cultural heritage expressed in black folk-music, poetry, and song. To the extent that Afro-Americans were thought of as a separate people—and with the rise of racialism, this became increasingly inevitable—nineteenth-century thought proposed nationalism as a reflection of that separate status. Once black nationalism takes on this form, it is equally inevitable that a national literature, consisting of the folk art of the race, should be seen as the highest expression of the black national spirit. Such intellectual pioneers as W. E. B. DuBois, from the late nineteenth century on, attempted to articulate a racial tradition of black letters as a natural expression of the Herderian view of the nation as identified above all else with its expression in "poesy."

But there is another reason why the identification of a history of black literary production has been central not merely to Afro-American literary criticism but to the culture of Afro-Americans: for almost the whole time that there have been people of African descent in the New World, a powerful European and American intellectual tradition has consistently denied that black people were capable of contributing to "the arts and letters." Starting before the fixing of race as a bio-logical concept, influential figures expressed their doubts about the inherited "capacity of the Negro" to produce literature. Even in the Enlightenment, which emphasized the universality of reason, philosophers such as Voltaire in France, David Hume in Scotland, and Immanuel Kant in Germany, like Jefferson in the New World, denied literary capacity to people of African descent. And, as we have seen, once race was conceptualized in biological terms, such low opinions of black people would lead easily to the belief that these incapacities were part of an inescapable racial essence.

In response to this long line of antiblack invective, black writers in the United States since the very first Afro-American poet—Phillis Wheatley, who lived in Boston in the late eighteenth century—have sought to establish the "capacity of the Negro" by writing and publishing literature. More than this, the major pro-portion of the published writing of Afro-Americans, even when not directed to countering racist mythology, has been concerned thematically with issues of race; a fact which is hardly surprising in a country where black people were subjected to racial slavery until the mid-nineteenth century and then treated le-gally as second-class citizens in many places until the 1960s.

The recognition, especially in recent years, of the role of Anglo-Saxonism in particular, and racism more generally, in the construction of the canon of litera-ture studied in American university departments of English, has led many scholars to argue for the inclusion of texts by Afro-Americans in that canon, in part because their initial exclusion was an expression of racism. But it has led others to argue for the recognition of an Afro-American tradition of writing, with its own major texts, which can be studied as a canon of its own. Some of those who make such claims—the critics in the Black Aesthetic movement, for example—have been motivated largely by a black nationalism that is, in part, a response to racism; others have argued for the recognition of a black canon be-cause they have identified formal features in the writings of black authors that derive from a self-conscious awareness of black literary predecessors and African or Afro-American folk traditions. Though the debates about the Afro-American literary traditon may be couched in terms of the existence of a tradition of aesthetically valuable texts that has been ignored, the issue of an Afro-American canon is inevitably a political one. The politics of Anglo-Saxonist nationalism excluded Afro-American culture from the official American canon, and the politics of American race relations inevitably structures discussion of their *in*clusion.

Differences among peoples, like differences among communities within a single society, play a central role in our thinking about who "we" are, in structuring our values, and in determining the identities through which we live. In the last century and a half racialism and nationalism, often so bound up together that one can hardly tell them apart, have played a central role in our thinking about these differences, and since one of the contributions of modern nationalism has been to see literature as central to national life, race has been central to literature and to thought about literature throughout this period. The racialism of Tupper's verse now seems merely ridiculous, even though such sentiments went with the reprehensible abuses of British imperialism; but racialism in our own century has produced lynchings in the American South, sustained the racist South African state, and led to the still unthinkable horrors of the Nazi holocaust. The almost universal revulsion against these moral disasters does not, unfortunately, mean that racism is over. And so long as it continues it is likely that race will continue to be a preoccupaton, not only of the literary history of the nineteenth and twentieth centuries, but also of future literary production and literary study.

SUGGESTED READINGS

Gates, Henry Louis, Jr. 1986. *"Race," Writing and Difference.*

Gayle, Addison, Jr. 1972. *The Black Aesthetic.*

Horsman, Reginald. 1981. *Race and Manifest Destiny: The Origins of American Racial Anglo-Saxonism.*

Hunter, George K. 1978. *Dramatic Identities and Cultural Tradition: Studies in Shakespeare and His Contemporaries.*

Kohn, Hans. 1967. *The Idea of Nationalism.*

MacDougall, Hugh B. 1982. *Racial Myth in English History: Trojans, Teutons, and Anglo-Saxons.*

Taine, Hippolyte A. 1897. *History of English Literature.*

21

Ethnicity

Werner Sollors

> If one is nothing but a Spartan, a capitalist, a proletarian, or a Buddhist, one is next door to being nothing and therefore even to not being at all.
>
> Georges Devereux

I

IT MAKES little sense to define "ethnicity-as-such," since it refers not to a thing-in-itself but to a relationship: ethnicity is typically based on a *contrast*. If all human beings belonged to one and the same ethnic group we would not need such terms as "ethnicity," though we might then stress other ways of differentiating ourselves such as age, sex, class, place of birth, or sign of the zodiac. Ethnic, racial, or national identifications rest on antitheses, on negativity, or on what the ethnopsychoanalyst Georges Devereux has termed their "dissociative" character. Ethnic identity, seen this way, "is logically and historically the product of the assertion that 'A is an X because he is not a Y'"—a proposition which makes it remarkably easy to identify Xness. By the same token, the definition of Xs as non-Ys threatens to exaggerate their differences in such a way that if the Xs think of themselves as human, they may therefore consider the Ys as somehow nonhuman. Unless the equation is offset by the positive acceptance of its opposite, "B is a Y by being a non-X," contrastive identification may overrule the shared humanity of different groups and erect symbolic boundaries that may resemble those between human beings and animals or between living beings and dead things (Devereux 1975, 67). "X ≠ [does not equal] Y" is the fundamental ethnic formula. The Greek word "ethnos"—from which the English terms "ethnic" and "ethnicity" are derived—significantly contains an ambivalence between the inclusive meaning, "people in general," and the dissociative sense, "other people," in particular "non-Jews" (to render "goyim," the Hebrew word for Gentiles), "non-Christians," "heathens," or "superstitious ones." In the modern world the distinction often rests on an antithesis between individuals (of the nonethnically conceived in-group) and ethnic collectivities (the out-groups).

"Race" (perhaps derived from "generation") is, in current American usage, sometimes perceived to be more intense, "objective," or real than ethnicity. As in the cases of "Irish race" or "Jewish race," the word was, however, the eighteenth- and nineteenth-century synonym for what is now, after the fascist abuses of "race" in the 1930s and 1940s, more frequently discussed as "ethnicity" (an obsolete English noun revitalized during World War II, that seems to have served as a more neutral term than the one in the name of which the National Socialists shaped their genocidal policies). "Race," too, can be used both in the inclusive sense of "human race" and in the dissociative sense of "our race" or "that race," meaning "us" or "not us." What is often called "race" in the modern United States is perhaps the country's most virulent ethnic factor. It is used to make distinctions on the basis of such generalized propositions as "black ≠ white" or "red ≠ white" which mark more dramatic fault lines in this specific cultural context than such oppositions as "Jew ≠ Gentile," which, especially since the late 1940s, may simply be subsumed under the common United States category "white," but formed *the* crucial distinction in Nazi "racial" theory.

Together with nationalism (a similar phenomenon which, however, stresses territoriality), ethnicity has spread with particular intensity since the times of the American and French Revolutions and remained a powerful force in political history ever since. Whereas the aristocracy organized its rule by direct and personal knowledge and family relationships that notably transcended national and linguistic boundaries, bourgeois power was dependent upon a shared interest among people who might never meet but who could feel connected through literature: hence newspapers, broadsides, manifestoes, popular songs, as well as plays, poems, epics, and novels have played important roles in sustaining feelings of belonging—the need for which the bourgeois era exported to the far corners of the earth (Anderson 1983). Ethnicity and ethnocentrism may thus be described as modern Europe's and North America's most successful export items. The processes of modernization and urbanization which weakened specific forms of familial, vocational, and local belonging strengthened the commitment to more abstract forms of generalizing identifications such as ethnic and national ones. The watershed between old aristocratic or colonial orders in which nationalism and ethnicity were still unknown (or played very minor roles) and new systems in which these forces proliferated and claimed exclusive allegiance, is typically marked by bourgeois revolutions or movements for national independence which may adopt their "ethnic" strategies, ironically in the name of purity, authenticity, and originality, from the very entity that they oppose, secede from, or define themselves against. "Yankee Doodle," for example, was the prototypical song associated with American independence from Britain, yet may have been British in origin (Sonneck 1909; Vail 1937; see Twain 1979, 201). Ethnicity may spread and become universal precisely through a process of—frequently more than justified—resistance, a phenomenon Devereux suggestively termed "antagonistic acculturation" (Devereux 1943).

Especially since Herder and the Grimms, the notion has gained dominance that a "people" is held together by a subliminal culture of fairy tales, songs, and folk beliefs—the orginal ethnic ("völkisch") subsoil of the common people's art forms that may culminate in the highest artistic achievements. As a result of this legacy "ethnicity" as a term for literary study largely evokes the accumulation of cultural bits that demonstrate the original creativity, emotive cohesion, and temporal depth of a particular collectivity, especially in a situation of emergence— be it from obscurity, suppression, embattlement, dependence, diaspora, or previous membership in a larger grouping. The tradition of "folk-ish" literary history, exemplified most comprehensively in the case of German literature by Josef Nadler's massive *Literaturgeschichte der deutschen Stämme und Landschaften* (1928), may be criticized for viewing language, race, and the spirit of the place as compelling, quasi-permanent forces and for exaggerating the Germanness of German literature, enclosed by profound boundaries, at a triple price. First, German originality is stressed and illustrated by German influences on others: thus "romanticism" is defined as "the Germanization of the East." Second, however, for purity's sake, influences from beyond the boundaries are either ignored (such as Henry Neville's *Isle of Pines,* the prototype for Johann Gottfried Schnabel's *Die Insel Felsenburg*) or portrayed merely as foreign obstacles to be overcome (such as Philipp von Zesen's French literary models). Third, many historical dissimilarities within German literature (for example, between Gottfried von Strassburg and Grimmelshausen) are flattened in order to permit the portrayal of relatively homogeneous literary "tribes" such as the Alsatians, Bavarians, or Silesians who make up Nadler's ethnic Germany. The discussion of literature in tribal isolation is thus dependent upon the concepts of "roots," "blood," "earth," and the "German race" (which is also what it is because it is, for example, "non-English," "non-French," and "non-Slavic"). The ethnic approach to writing, even when applied less systematically than Nadler's, is often in danger of making one generalization (the writer is an X, meaning not a Y) the central, if not the sole, avenue to a text; yet making this Xness central may be circular and tautological (X writes like an X, not like a Y) since it reveals first and foremost this very Xness, a quality which cumulatively achieves the status of a somewhat mystical, ahistorical, and even quasi-eternal essence. Literature plays a central part in naturalizing the modern process of ethnic dissociation and may help to create the illusion of a group's "natural" existence from "time immemorial."

II

Mark Twain's novel *A Connecticut Yankee in King Arthur's Court* ([1889] 1982: all page references without further information refer to this edition of *CY* and the secondary literature reprinted there; a summary of the plot of *CY* appears below at the end of this essay) offers many possibilities to consider "ethnicity" (in a broader sense than that of its author's ancestry) in the reading of a canonical American text. The book centers not on any currently practicing ethnic group but on medieval Arthurians; and precisely because of its apparent distance from any immediate ethnic sensitivities, *CY* may be useful in clarifying modern ethnic processes. Conversely, the concept of ethnicity may also be helpful to an understanding of a novel of formal contrasts and with themes which range from culture clash to assimilation and genocide. Mark Twain (MT) does not use the word "ethnicity," but his novel is full of ethnic matter. The very term "Yankee" receives substance through a series of symbolic oppositions to the English, to American Indians, and to Southerners. The word "race" occurs both in inclusive and dissociative ways: when Hank Morgan (HM), like Huck Finn, feels "ashamed of the human race" (103; cf. 41), he views himself and the Arthurians as part of one miserable mankind; when he speaks of the Arthurians as "that race" (193) or "an ignorant race" (123), he dissociates himself from them and implies that he is a non-Arthurian, a member of a less ignorant race.

The book has been embattled by interpreters: is it a satire of medieval Britain, of Victoria's England, or of MT's United States (363 and 393)? Is it a light and humorous praise of worthy progress and much-needed reform, or is it a bitter and gloomy anticipation of the century of nuclear holocausts and mass genocides? Are MT's readers expected to laugh along with the cheery HM (whom William Dean Howells called a "delightful hero" [324], who was portrayed on the screen by Will Rogers and Bing Crosby, and who inspired Rudy Vallee's crooning band, his "Connecticut Yankees"), or should they despair when contemplating the futility and extremely bloody results of modernization which the novel also portrays? (452, 389, 417, and 433).

MT wrote in 1886: "The story isn't a satire peculiarly, it is more especially a *contrast*. . . . [T]he bringing [the two periods] into this immediate juxtaposition emphasizes the salients of both" (296). Again and again in the novel, the narrator reflects upon the contrasts that separate his modern world of nineteenth-century Hartford from sixth-century Camelot. For example:

> Now what a radical reversal of things this was; what a jumbling together of extravagant incongruities; what a fantastic conjunction of opposites and irreconcilables—the home of the bogus miracle become the home of a real one, the den of a medieval hermit turned into a telephone office! (130)

This clash is not only a self-conscious thematic, but also a formal feature of the novel, in which incongruities and contrasts are both theme and structure—more so than any sustained plot development, formal organization, or point of view. HM's first-person singular "I" is strengthened and defined, if not constituted, by the encounter with the strangers.

CY starts from the premise of a temporal and class contrast: HM is foremost a solitary bourgeois anachronism, an individual in the social world of Arthur's feudal Britain. This opposition, however, also takes on a national, seemingly transhistorical form, as these contrasts often derive from modern, at times characteristically American (as opposed to British) culture patterns and have little to do with the sixth century. Widening (or narrowing) the temporal gap into an ethnic antithesis, *CY* also resorts to a number of boundary-constructing strategies which help to create the impression that the Arthurians as an ethnic group are not only the Yankee's precursors but also his absolute antithesis; and their contrast resembles racial polarization in the United States, while the time-traveler is also like an immigrant who cannot adjust to his host society. Their very antagonism, however, also assimilates the opponents to each other so that the Yankee has or acquires many of the very qualities that he resents in Arthurians.

A rhetorical giveaway of the dissociative strategy is the negative catalogue, with which countries or groups may be described. For example, the United States has typically been viewed, in "exceptionalist" opposition to the Old World, as a country without Middle Ages or the land without kings and bishops. In *CY*, HM's descriptions of Camelot follow and invert this pattern. "There was no soap, no matches, no looking-glass—except a metal one, about as powerful as a pail of water" (35). "There wasn't even a bell or a speaking-tube in the castle. . . . There were no books, pens, paper, or ink, and no glass in the openings they believed to be windows. . . . But perhaps worst of all was, that there wasn't any sugar, coffee, tea or tobacco" (36). The Yankee also complains somewhat whimsically that Camelot is a land without chromos and thinks of the tapestries as poor (and, literally, "darned") substitutes for his familiar colorful trade lithographs that say "God bless our home" over his door in East Hartford (36; see also 18, 116). HM's negative catalogue is one of mostly modern objects and inventions (among which reading and writing supplies and colonial luxury articles are particularly noteworthy); they function as markers which differentiate his familiar Yankee culture from the strange one of Britain. The Yankee is particularly attached to very recent innovations, and he wants to replicate them in his new enviroment. Herbert Gans termed a similar dependence upon symbols and objects "symbolic ethnicity," which helps immigrants and their descendants to sustain an illusion of "authentic" ethnic cohesion while assimilation is taking place (Gans 1979).

CY thrives upon the stylistic possibilities of the temporal clash between the chivalric language of medievalism (best embodied by lengthy excerpts from Thomas Malory's *Morte d'Arthur* [1470]) and HM's version of modern American vernacular. In his temporal displacement, the Yankee clings to the modern habit of nicknaming, calls Amyas le Poulet "Clarence" (68), Alisande "Sandy" (62), Sir Gareth "Garry" (48), and translates his own position at King Arthur's Court as "THE BOSS. Elected by the Nation" (44). MT did not tire of accumulating anachronistic discrepancies in the novel for the sake of comic effect: Sir Launcelot and the knights come to the rescue—on bicycles (217); Sandy names

their child "Hello Central" in honor of Hank's explanation of the telephone
(234, 77); HM, who indulges in baseball talk (39, 71, 72), also introduces the
teams Bessemers and Ulsters (232); he rejoices that "Merlin's stock was flat" (39,
227) and speaks stock exchange language (98, 109, 237–38); he is happy to see
that Queen Morgan le Fay knows nothing of photographing (though she pretends to) and tries to do it with an axe (96–97); he uses a lasso (223) and a
dragoon revolver (226) in a fight against Sir Sagramour and five hundred
knights; and he makes the sacred hermit St. Simeon Stylites, who bows his body
ceaselessly while standing on a pillar, move the pedal of a sewing-machine and
produce, immigrant sweat-shop fashion, ten tow-linen shirts per day (120;
cf. 266).

At times HM reveals that his humor is an explicit weapon for progress. He
writes, for example, that Sir Ozana le Cure Hardy

> was in the gentleman's furnishing line, and his missionarying spe-
> ciality was plug hats. He was clothed all in steel, in the beautifulest
> armor of the time—up to where his helmet ought to have been;
> but he hadn't any helmet, he wore a shiny stove-pipe hat, and was
> as ridiculous a spectacle as one might want to see. It was another
> of my surreptitious schemes for extinguishing knighthood by
> making it grotesque and absurd. (112)

Comedy may thus serve a destabilizing purpose and support the assault of the
modern Yankee's technology and weaponry on the "dark" ages—in the name of
progress and the (accelerated) march of time. The process of dissociation, even
in comic form, may be connected to a struggle for power, as HM well recognizes. Yet he usually phrases his quest for power (see Cohen 1974) merely as a
commonsense republican's struggle against the superstitious backwardness of an
ecclesiastical aristocracy.

His efforts repeat the historical development from Britain to America: Hank
is a new Tom Paine, a second Benjamin Franklin who uses technology, journalism, the promotion of independence, and folksy humor to invent America again.
HM is thus a Yankee by virtue of opposing Englishmen. At one point, his
scheme seems on the brink of success: "all men were created equal before the
law; taxation had been equalized. The telegraph, the telephone, the phono-
graph, the type-writer, the sewing machine, and all the thousand willing and
handy servants of steam and electricity were working their way into favor. We
had a steamboat or two on the Thames, we had steam war-ships, and the beginnings of a steam commercial marine; I was getting ready to send out an expedi-
tion to discover America" (228). The future of civilization is clearly tied up with
technology, with America, and with the Yankee's progress. When threatened to
be hanged with the King, Hank reflects; "Nothing in the world could save the
King of England; nor me, which was more important. More important, not
merely to me, but to the nation—the only nation on earth standing ready to

bloom into civilization" (216). The collective future seems to depend on this individual who stylizes himself as the social embodiment of the new deal (68; see 68n7 vs. 385), while the collectivity stands for a backward reluctance to accept the innovations (41). Aware that he is a lonely avantgardist among a people that may or may not be good "material for a republic" (173, 138), he is inspired by the Connecticut constitution, which summons the citizen when necessary to alter the form of government: "the citizen who thinks he sees that the commonwealth's political clothes are worn out, and yet holds his peace and does not agitate for a new suit, is disloyal; he is a traitor. That he may be the only one who thinks he sees this decay, does not excuse him" (67). In Camelot, HM does not become a traitor to the Connecticut constitution. Yet how can he singlehandedly change the worn-out political clothes of medieval England? The solitary Hank literally challenges the English knighthood as a class: "Here I stand, and dare the chivalry of England to come against me—not by individuals, but in mass!" (226).

The symbolic course HM steers does not only lead from England in the Dark Ages to the discovery of modern American civilization, or from colony to independence: recreating modern gadgets in the Middle Ages (in explicit analogy to Robinson Crusoe on his island [36]), challenging the knighthood, and promoting republicanism, HM also wants to repeat the French Revolution and end feudalism violently once again. In the characteristic opposition of "I" and "this folk," he believes that "all revolutions that will succeed, must *begin* in blood, whatever may answer afterward. What this folk needed, then, was a Reign of Terror and a guillotine, and I was the wrong man for them" (101). Whether or not he was the wrong man, he justifies the "minor Terror, the momentary Terror," the "brief Terror which we have all been so diligently taught to shiver at and mourn over" by comparing it with feudalism, the other Reign of Terror that "had lasted a thousand years" (66) before it was ended by the Revolution. He asks pointedly: "what is the horror of swift death by the axe, compared with lifelong death from hunger, cold, insult, cruelty and heart-break?" (66). This is of particular significance for "ethnicity" in light of the trajectory that has been drawn from aristocratic consciousness to race thinking and from Reign of Terror to Holocaust (Arendt 1944, 42–47; Adorno 1941, 129; Nolte 1987, 29).

Yet Hank is neither a class nor a party; he is not even a revolutionary directory, but simply one man. Apart from Clarence and Sandy (both of whom have limited political views), only the elite corps of boys can be counted on as followers because "all the others were born in an atmosphere of superstition and reared in it. It is in their blood and bones. . . . With boys it was different" (242). Only the small Yankee youth movement, after "training from seven to ten years," is reliable; otherwise the Yankee is not able to convince Arthurians of the desirability of his "Republic on the American plan" (50n) that he advocates like a hotel meal service. The feudal order of the Arthurians simply does not cave in. This is espe-

cially annoying since the temporal progress that utopians and modern revolutionaries only envision is already a historical fact for this time-traveler. After all,
MT has inverted not only Don Quixote's attempts to bring the modern world
back to chivalric ideals, but also the popular nineteenth-century time-travel
scheme of such utopian books as Edward Bellamy's *Looking Backward: 2000–
1887* (1888), which sent a man into the future (as did Mark Twain in his plans
for a work entitled "1988"). John Reed's slogan after the Russian Revolution
was, "I have seen the future, and it works." HM's motto might be, "I have seen
the past, and it does not work." For the Yankee, the past is not historical (connected to him), it is "backward" (unlike him). This attitude produces a deep
antagonism between the impatient modernizer and the people in whose name
and for whose ostensible benefit he agitates, but who maddeningly cling to their
backwardness.

If the contrast between the Arthurians and the Yankee were consistently
phrased as a temporal one, *CY* would be a simpler book. Ironically, however,
historical development is not of much concern to the author, who openly admits
in the preface (which only appeared in the American edition) that historical accuracy mattered little to him: "One is quite justified in inferring that wherever
one of these [ungentle] laws or customs was lacking in that remote time, its place
was competently filled by a worse one" (4). The 1485 edition of Malory's *Morte
d'Arthur,* printed by Caxton, could have been a landmark in the Yankee's view of
modern progress (in which Gutenberg and newsboys are greater than kings
[184, 148]), yet MT uses Malory simply as a "medieval" prototype. All rhetoric
of progress notwithstanding, history is simply not the development from the
Middle Ages to the modern period but a sharp and irreconcilable contrast. All
history prior to America or before 1879 collapses into a collage (or "palimpsest"
[10, 292, 394]) of diffuse pasts: the year 513, the Tower of London, the Crusades, *The Divine Comedy, Canterbury Tales,* the peasant wars, the prehistory of
the French Revolution, the English Georges, *A Tale of Two Cities, The Count of
Monte Cristo,* Thomas Carlyle, Matthew Arnold, and many more diverse elements go into the construction of MT's "6th century" (66n, 96, 107, 116, 184,
235).

Since what HM encounters is not "history" but "backwardness," it is a feature
that ancient and modern England have in common. For if the past is backward,
all sorts of "backwardness," including modern kinds, can be used to give it substance—at which moment any "historical" contrast vanishes. Thus Hank detests
Sandy's "deep reverence which the natives of her island, ancient *and modern,*
have always felt for rank, let its outward casket and the mental and moral contents be what they may" (105; my emphasis). It is not only medieval but also
modern England that is MT's target (see 411, 314). This subverts the fiction of
a time-traveler.

The fiction that HM traverses space and goes to Britain is also partly undone when what he finds in Camelot are not only pre-American and non-American phenomena, but also ethnic problems that are clearly of the United States. MT's sixth-century British aristocrats resemble American Indians. Hank tellingly refers to the Arthurians as "white Indians" (19), a phrasing Howells mentioned in his review of *CY* (324). The narrator is a second Columbus (29–30); and his prediction of an eclipse, which establishes his power among the Arthurians, an event that he calls, in the fashion of American immigrant autobiography, the "making" of himself (31), is taken from Washington Irving's account of Columbus (262–63). Hank furthermore remarks that before their journeys, during which Arthurians often had to go without food for a long time, they freighted up "against probable fasts before starting, after the style of the Indian and the anaconda" (64). One of Hank's phrasings appears only in the American edition of *CY*: "I was as glad as a person when he is scalped" (54; the English edition reads "disembowelled"). Stereotypes of American Indians are applied to the knights of the round table: "The fact is, it is just a sort of polished-up court of Comanches, and there isn't a squaw in it who doesn't stand ready at the dropping of a hat to desert to the buck with the biggest string of scalps at his belt" (73–74). The aristocrats' bad language "would have made a Comanche blush" (26); "the pow-wow and racket were prodigious" (198); a rival magician's "dress was the extreme of fantastic, as showy and foolish as the sort of thing an Indian medicine-man wears" (132). It was MT's obsession to identify Indians and aristocrats. There is a passage similar to his sketch "The French and the Comanches" in *CY* (65–66), and in his notebook of 1878 he wrote—as James D. Williams mentioned—that the English were a "very fine and pure and elevated people," but, up to the nineteenth century, had been "a small improvement upon the Shoshone Indians" (364n7). "Medieval England" is thus another Golden West for HM, who alludes to Horace Greeley's famous exhortation, "Go west, young man, and grow up with the country," when he says: "Look at the opportunities here for a man of knowledge, brains, pluck and enterprise to sail in and grow up with the country" (40). One is tempted to read the novel as a roman à clef about the white settlers' treatment of American aborigines, in which Hank plays the part of the whites—as benevolent modernizer and military destroyer—and the Arthurians are the Indians. Hank is also a Yankee in the sense of one speculative etymology of the word "Yankee" as an Indian pronunciation of "English" and a slur for "white man."

Contemporary readers shared MT's conflation of the temporal and the ethnic dimensions and were reminded of white-Indian encounters in the modern-medieval collision. For example, the *Boston Sunday Herald* wrote on December 15, 1889:

> [J]ust as the Connecticut Yankee went back into the days of King Arthur's court, so might he go out into the world today, into Cen-

tral Asia or Africa, or even into certain spots in this United States
of ours, find himself amidst social conditions very similar to those
of 1300 years ago, and even work his astonishing 19th century
miracles with like result. For it is a fact that, when Frank Hamilton Cushing astounded the Zuni Indians with an acoustic telephone constructed of two tomato cans and a string, they deemed
him a magician, and tried him for witchcraft.(322)

Commenting on MT's descriptions of the Arthurians' stupidity and stubborn-
ness, the reviewer suggested that such "characterizations might apply equally
well to a tribe of Dakota Indians, to their hardly more civilized foes, the cowboys
of the plains, to the mountaineers of Tennessee and Georgia, or even to the
savages in our great city slums" (323). The contrast between white technology
and Indians evokes such other ethnic oppositions as the ones between Americans
in a position of dominance and Appalachians; between Easterners and cowboys;
between native-born residents and immigrants; or between "developed" and
"underdeveloped" countries. The focus on the contrast thus invited readers to
superimpose nativist and colonialist readings (402; Placido 1978; Cunningham
1987, 157–71).

    For American ethnic writers in the age of modernism, the metaphor of medie-
valism has also served to signal an ethnic past better left behind. In *The Promised
Land* (1912), for example, the Russian Jewish autobiographer Mary Antin described immigration as time-traveling and focused on the paradox of a life that
symbolically spans centuries: "My age alone, my true age, would be reason
enough for my writing. I began life in the Middle Ages, as I shall prove, and
here I am still, your contemporary in the twentieth century, thrilling with your
latest thought" (Antin 1912, xxi). Afro-American intellectuals, too, used the distinction between the Middle Ages and the modern period to describe the history
of the race. Thus Alain Locke wrote in the introduction to the landmark anthology *The New Negro* (1925) that each wave of migration is "in the Negro's case a
deliberate flight not only from countryside to city, but from medieval America
to modern" (Locke 1925, 6). All of this is a bit surprising in a country "without
middle ages" (see also 304–5; Thomas 1973, 246; Cahan 1986, 53–54; and
Bourne 1977, 250).

    The ethnic fault line within the United States that MT most fully develops
marks the Yankee's symbolic confrontation with the antebellum South of slavery.
Arthurian tyranny is persistently imagined as the "enslavement" of multitudes,
and, to HM, "an aristocracy . . . is but a band of slaveholders under another
name. . . . The repulsive feature of slavery is the *thing*, not its name" (136). Yet
the analogy between feudalism and capitalist enslavement of a racial group, developed from the specific point of view of a nineteenth-century writer who grew
up in Missouri before the Civil War, gets culturally charged in such a way that

the Arthurian Middle Ages may just be the "name," and the slaveholding South the "thing." In the vein of Joel Chandler Harris' Uncle Remus tales, Hank Morgan calls the chief Arthurian magician "Brer Merlin." He furthermore remembers the American Civil War (174–75: if only to explain prices and wages), implies an analogy between Arthurian farmers and Southern sharecroppers (166), and explicitly compares the attitudes of the Arthurians with those of Southern "poor whites" (172).

Henry Nash Smith reminded readers that Southern-style slavery did not exist in medieval Britain (412). Yet there is a long section in *CY* which shows the King's and Hank's experience with slavery and their enslavement. MT is obviously thinking of nineteenth-century America rather than medieval England when he draws on abolitionist plot-lines and rhetoric: there is a chain gang (110), a maltreated mother (111), the indifference of bystanders (111), the separated family (111–12), the chase with bloodhounds (195), the auction (200–201), and the rhetorical opposition of "thing" and "man" (familiar from *Uncle Tom's Cabin*). The contrast between the brutality of slavery and the rhetoric of American liberty that was often represented in antislavery literature by a juxtaposition of slavery scenes (an auction or a violent chastisement) and national symbols (the flag, a political rally, or the Capitol), is also present, only adapted to apply to—*Britain*! "I could not take my eyes away from these worn and wasted wrecks of humanity. There they sat, grouped upon the ground, silent, uncomplaining, with bowed heads, a pathetic sight. And by hideous contrast, a redundant orator was making a speech to another gathering not thirty steps away, in fulsome laudation of 'our glorious British liberties!' " (199; see also 382; Ball 1836, 91–95; Stowe 1852, 1: 178; Brown 1853, 217; Child 1858, 122–23; and Twain 1979, 414, 501, 503, 506). What those "British liberties" might have been remains unclear in the context of *CY*. HM proclaims: "If I lived and prospered I would be the death of slavery, that I was resolved upon; but I would try to fix it so that when I became its executioner it should be by the command of the nation" (111). Hank also tries to persuade the King to abolish slavery (203), and the King experiences a dilemma similar to Huck Finn's (168), but resolves it aristocratically. His abolitionism makes Hank a "Yankee" in the sense that he is not a proslavery Confederate rebel.

"Medieval Britain" is eclipsed by images of American slavery, and the text of *CY* reveals it. Thus HM introduces the section about his and the King's enslavement—which is made possible because they cannot *prove* that they are freemen—with the comment: "This same infernal law had existed in our own South in my own time, more than thirteen hundred years later . . . " (200). The demand to prove one's free status comes—as James D. Williams has shown in detail (381–82)—from Charles Ball's slave narrative, *Slavery in the United States* (1836), which MT read (200n1), planned to use in an appendix to *CY* (381), and from which he incorporated plot elements (200) and descriptions (110–11). In these passages, HM literally speaks with what MT assumed was the voice of an Afro-American slave, thus giving *CY* a specifically polyethnic and multi-vocal quality (see Blassingame 1985, 81–82; Andrews 1986, 81–86).

Did HM, who supposedly traversed the Atlantic and 1,300 years, ever get further than south of the Mason-Dixon line of about 1850? What he criticizes most severely in Arthurian England was a feature of his own country and his own century, projected upon a distant past and continent. At least in this respect, he uses Arthurians as scapegoats for a historical problem of which they are quite innocent. The inhabitants of MT's medieval world might be termed "white man's Arthurians" who could stand not only for modern Englishmen but also for American Indians and slaveholders, while HM takes the double part of the white settler who tries to "civilize" Indians and of the latter-day Yankee aboli-tionist who attempts to end African slavery anew (see the *London Daily Telegraph* critique of *CY*: 330).

III

The stable element that emerges in *CY* is the existence of a dividing line between worlds, not any historically specific cultural content of "Yankeedom" or "Arthu-rians." In that respect, the book illuminates Fredrik Barth's thesis that ethnicity rests on the *boundary,* not on the "cultural stuff that it encloses" (Barth 1969, 15). The construction of the ethnic boundary is a *general* procedure and centers in attempts to override the basic fact that all human beings—though far from being alike—are similar at least insofar as they are human. Boundary-supporting verbal strategies may distance other human beings so far from the speaker that they seem closer to other species (which often results in animal imagery in writ-ing). They may be stereotyped as childlike, superstitious, savage, dirty, or igno-rant. In extreme cases, they are seen as dead *things* rather than living beings, which is a rhetorical strategy that may prepare genocidal confrontations. MT's novel is rich in many of these verbal strategies.

HM frequently uses animal imagery, either in the general case of "these ani-mals didn't reason" (29; see also 36, 46, 94) or in the ways in which various Arthurians are viewed as or compared with rabbits (41), asses (56), anacondas (64), clams (65), jackasses (76), rats (87), bats (96), horses (97), pigs (102ff), catfish (139), or spaniels (198). Hank often assumes the role of a grownup when he observes the "childlike" Arthurians (19, 20, 25, 40, 56–57, 70, 117, 179), or mocks the "poor juvenile sixth century way" (207)—obviously from the point of view of a better known "way." He makes the metaphor of paternalism almost literal when he describes the King as a child, and himself as the mother (154, 155).

The narrator views the Arthurians as savages (30, 36, 64); hence it is his task to make plans for "civilizing and uplifting" them (78). Hygiene always plays a particular part in such plans (as the modern metaphor of "racial hygiene" also suggests). For HM, not only are the "savages" dirt and muck (247), but the gospel of soap and toothbrush (an anticipation of Booker T. Washington's famous campaign) has to be spread among them (99–100), a purpose for which Hank employs missionary knights. La Cote Mail Taile, one of those missionaries, Hank writes, "had tried all the tricks of the trade, even to the washing of a hermit; but the hermit died. This was indeed a bad failure, for this animal would now be dubbed a martyr, and would take his place among the saints of the Roman calendar" (80).

Dehumanization reaches its peak in those boundary-constructing images which render the Arthurians as puppets, objects, or dead things. This does not only apply to their descent-based system of rule and advancement (142) but to the people themselves: they are seen as "assets" (71), "automata" (89), "automatic dolls" (201), "lubber" (100), "sausage-meat" (104), "a pavement of human heads" (124), "mollusks" (141), "fragments" (158), and they have "waffle-iron faces" (170). In the language of the marketplace, knight-errantry is compared with pork: "knight-errantry is *worse* than pork; for whatever happens, the pork's left, and so somebody's benefited, anyway; but when the market breaks, in a knight-errantry whirl, and every knight in the pool passes in his checks, what have you got for assets? Just a rubbish-pile of battered corpses and a barrel or two of busted hardware" (98). Hank thinks this way long before the ending.

Despite this impressive array of boundary-constructing devices which stereotype the Arthurians and separate them from the Yankee, there are telling indications of a pervasive similarity between the two. The Arthurians may have been invented as "non-Yankees," yet the Yankee is also like them in more ways than is immediately apparent. Throughout the book, MT gives much evidence that suggests the process of successful assimilation, by which some Arthurians adopt not only the Yankee's technological innovations but also his catchy idiom. "Paying the shot," HM thus states proudly, "soon came to be a common phrase" (193). Although the Yankee likes to play the superior one whom the Arthurians ought to follow, this assimilation process is, to some extent, mutual. Early on he criticizes Sandy's vocabulary that includes "usufruct" (75), yet he, too, uses the word later on (140). Of course, he also literally becomes wedded to Arthurianism through the intermarriage with Sandy, of whom he deliriously dreams in the novel's postscript.

More pervasive than this cooperative form of assimilation is the process of antagonistic acculturation, according to which, in an ethnic confrontation, means and ends may be adopted from the opponent. X, defined in contrast with Y, becomes somewhat like Y in the confrontation. MT especially shows the Yankee doing the same thing or using the same dehumanizing words he criticizes among the Arthurians. The church is a persistent source of evil in the book, yet HM models his enterprise precisely on the ways of the church: he works secretly, trains "missionaries" (147), and speaks of one of his men as a "colporteur," that is, a Bible salesman (80)—thus admitting in his language that he uses the church's means in order to spread his gospel. HM is the embodiment of Franklin's self-made man; yet he finds, makes fun of, and humiliates the "self-made man" Dowling, who amazingly is in existence in the sixth century. What HM despises in slavocracy and aristocracy is "the possessor's old and inbred custom of regarding himself as a superior being" (136): yet the Yankee unhesitatingly views himself as a "superior man" (28) who should take advantage of the superstitious Arthurians. In order to fight the hold of superstition (we remember that "ethnicity" once was a synonym for heathenish superstition) and establish a reformed republic based on political consent, he relies not on rational arguments and innovations but on spectacular fake miracles (one might say, tricknology) that satisfy his limitless modern need for entertainment and fool the Arthurians at the same time. In his struggle for change and domination Hank uses the very means of the opponent that he may otherwise criticize. Thus he mobilizes our disdain for medieval Britain by emphasizing that it was a culture that viewed human beings as animals—as if he did not regard the English in the same manner. In many of these examples, the Arthurians make themselves felt as mirror images of the Yankee's hidden self: whatever HM denies in himself he may call "Arthurian"—and try to destroy. In order to save "humanity" and "civilization" he prepares to kill people who are not unlike him, after having removed them rhetorically from shared human categories.

While he seemingly encounters little opposition of any note, his very activities slowly make some groups of Arthurians form their own power base in confrontation with the intruder. Church, knighthood, and Merlin successfully oppose the Yankee and force him into the final battle of the Sand-Belt. Fighting with their respective means—religious interdict, massive self-sacrifice, and successful magic—they, in fact, defeat the Yankee. HM may have modernized the Arthurians to the extent that they are now "non-Yankees"—Arthurian fundamentalists united in their resistance *against him*!

"Antagonistic acculturation" is worth considering when one returns to the question of the character of Hank's enterprise and the ending of the novel. Since the Yankee's opponents, the imaginary "Arthurians," are a blurred composite of such diverse ingredients as medieval and modern England, the French *ancien régime*, American Indians and Southern slaveholders, and since HM's own character has much in common with what he opposes, the confrontation has an absurd rather than hopefully utopian quality. The Yankee hardly seems the embodiment of a new system of republican justice. For example, when Queen Morgan le Fay has a composer hanged after dinner (83–84), Hank (whose last is the

queen's first name) does not indignantly invoke the antislavery plot-line of the
mistress who had her cook thrown in the oven after an unsatisfying dinner, but
agrees explicitly with the Queen and, more than that, gives her "permission to
hang the whole band" (85). If this seems like an exceptional bit of black humor
á la *Alice in Wonderland* (1865), Hank also reacts to Sir Dinadan the Humorist
(see 24–25) who included an old joke (48) in his book, the first book published
in Arthur's Britain; Hank's decision: "I suppressed the book and hanged the
author" (228). This is not exactly a landmark in the history that started with
Gutenberg and continued with Franklin! When Hank, out of the blue, wants to
"hang the whole human race" (174), this may then be more than a phrase,
whether or not the hangman is part of the "race." Hank, who is often hopeful
but at times ashamed of the whole human race (41 and 103), prefers loud spectacles to systematic reform programs, and P.T. Barnum-style circus events to politics—even at the risk of making any encores after his last "effect" (258) impossible.

Early on, Hank uses the word "holocaust," commenting on Sandy's prose
with a list of words (75); and in the miraculous tongue-twisters of Germanoid
phrases that he uses during one of his "miracles," one notices the persistently
violent theme and the phrase "Massenmenschenmoerder"(125, an awkward rendition of "mass murderer"), the ultimate fate of the speaker. When he gives the
pep speech to his fifty-two boys he concludes with the chilling proclamation:

> "English knights can be killed, but they cannot be conquered. We
> know what is before us. While one of these men remains alive, our
> task is not finished, the war is not ended. We will kill them all."
> [Loud and long continued applause.] (250)

HM, who started out as the emissary of the modern world to a temporally removed place, soon constructed boundaries between himself and that enviroment
which entitled him to stylize himself as the Prometheus of progress (402) and to
look at Arthurians as a backward ethnic group. This contrastive strategy also
made him become like the very worst things he believed he opposed. In order to
fight the "petrified" (87) system of feudalism he ended up transforming knights
into "statues"—by electrocution (253–54), after a glare "petrified them, you
may say" (254). These are actions that defy the rationalizations of self-defense,
of paying the price of modernization, or of confronting an overwhelming nu-
merical majority. Because of the symbolic affinities of the novel's "Arthurians"
with American Indians the violence of the final battle evokes images of
nineteenth-century massacres or accounts of Custer's last stand; because of the
metaphoric connections with Southern slaveholders, it evokes the Civil War.
Whether or not Mark Twain's intention was to justify the end as a second Reign
of Terror for a grand purpose, *A Connecticut Yankee in King Arthur's Court* is

also the case of an intensive boundary construction that becomes both literal and lethal at the end.

IV

A canonical text illuminates the symbolic processes that help to constitute ethnic contrasts. While ethnic matter is often associated only with works by writers whose descent makes them members of the respective ethnic groups, the processes of generating feelings of dissociative belonging inform (and are themselves supported by) many literary texts. Investigating "ethnicity" in literature may thus accomplish more than yielding evidence for the Xness of the Xs in texts by writers reputedly descended from Xs, or supporting nineteenth-century purist models of supposedly ethnically based whole cultures. While often phrased as attacks upon ethnically exclusive canons of the past, contemporary purist approaches may yet replicate their antagonists' focus on the authors' Xness as the basis of literary evaluation and of constructing literary traditions. The very notion of ethnic purity is a modern invention that never applied to many writers in the first place (see Ellis 1893). The critiques of a narrow group-approach to literature have such illustrious ancestors as Goethe, whose cosmopolitan concept of a "world literature" has, however, generated relatively few institutional results in modern academic life. Despite the establishment of some departments for general and comparative literature, the study of literature is still overwhelmingly organized within national and ethnic boundaries.

The invented character of modern ethnicity could become clearer through a variety of approaches to canonical as well as noncanonical texts. Investigations of motifs and themes could contribute to an understanding of the imaginative and symbolic structures that intensify (or, at times, even generate) group consciousness among dominant as well as suppressed collectivities or prepare hostile confrontations; at the same time, studies could reveal the extent to which various ethnic literatures that are now often studied in isolation share a repertoire of available literary language. Formal analyses might illustrate the compatibility of ethnic and ethnocentric sentiment and modern forms, thus helping to dispel the misconceptions that ethnic consciousness and modernism form an antithesis or that modernism weakens ethnicity; such studies could also delineate the multivocal polyethnic elements within given texts (of any ethnic provenance) rather than absorbing works wholesale to the ethnic group that an author "belongs" to. The new historical works that are in the making could avoid sealing certain sets of texts hermetically in various "pure" ethnic enclaves and depart from the pious fiction that authors from one ethnic group are only influenced by other authors from the same group; instead, comparative approaches could help to deepen our understanding of the boundary-defiance of the literary tradition and subvert the proprietary attitudes on the basis of race (or Nadler's ahistorical tribes) with which professional readers have sometimes staked out their current territories in the academic marketplace. Although ethnicity remains potentially one of the most interesting aspects of modern literature around the world and opens many new possibilities for examining great texts on a comparative basis, it is hardly an exaggeration to state that it may also bring out the worst in readers of literature.

OUTLINE OF *CY*

At the beginning of the novel the frame narrator meets Hank Morgan, a man from Connecticut, in Warwick Castle and is treated to the Yankee's story, first by narration and then in the purported manuscript which forms the bulk of the book. Hank Morgan, a supervisor in the Colt Arms Factory in Hartford, is magically transported from the Connecticut of 1879 to King Arthur's Britain of the year 513. The resourceful Yankee brings a whole host of modern political and economic reform ideas (such as the abolition of slavery, universal suffrage, and free trade) as well as technological inventions to medieval Britain. Much space is given to the contrast between the Yankee's modern gadgets (newspaper, telegraph, telephone, sewing-machine, advertisements, bicycles, toothbrush, etc.) and the unsuspecting world in which he lets them loose. He finds a devoted follower, "Clarence," and a companion and loving spouse, "Sandy"; he also trains fifty-two young boys who become an elite troupe; yet he makes enemies with the church and with the magician Merlin. After an interdict is imposed upon his England, Hank Morgan decides on an all-out battle against the whole knighthood of the country. Summoning the means of modern warfare—from electrified wires to dynamite and rapid-firing guns—he, Clarence, and the boys succeed in destroying virtually the whole British chivalry, but find themselves lethally trapped in the poisonous air bred by the corpses. The manuscript ends with Clarence's narration of Merlin's success in magically putting the Yankee to sleep for thirteen centuries. The novel concludes with a postscript by Mark Twain which reports the Yankee's delirium and death.

SUGGESTED READINGS

[Adorno, Theodor W., Max Horkheimer, et al.]. 1941. "Research Project on Anti-Semitism."
Anderson, Benedict. 1983. *Imagined Communities.*
Arendt, Hannah. 1944. "Race-Thinking before Racism."
Barth, Fredrik. 1969. *Ethnic Groups and Boundaries.*
Bourne, Randolph S. 1977. *The Radical Will.*
Cohen, Abner. 1974. *Urban Ethnicity.*
Devereux, George[s]. 1975. "Ethnic Identity: Its Logical Foundations and Its Dysfunctions."

Devereux, George[s], and Edwin M. Loeb. 1943. "Antagonistic Acculturation."
Ellis, Havelock. 1893. "The Ancestry of Genius."
Gans, Herbert J. 1979. "Symbolic Ethnicity: The Future of Ethnic Groups and
    Cultures in America."
Locke, Alain. 1925. *The New Negro*.

22

Ideology

James H. Kavanagh

"IDEOLOGY" is a term that embodies all the problems associated with the cultural complexity of language: it has a rich history, during which it has taken on various, sometimes contradictory, meanings. Furthermore, most of the changes and internal tensions in the word are obscured by the single, dominant meaning it has recently taken on in American political discourse. Thus, before discussing how "ideology" is used in contemporary criticism, it is necessary to recognize how the term is used in the much more widespread and influential language of the mass media.

We are most likely to encounter the word "ideology" in a newspaper or news-program piece of political analysis, where the term is used to designate some kind of especially coherent and rigidly held system of political ideas. In this sense, ideology is a distinctly pejorative term, usually identifying someone who wishes to impose an abstract, extremist, intellectual-political obsession on a "moderate," mainstream political system. Thus, there are a few people on the right and left (like Robert Bork or Fidel Castro) who "have" an ideology, and who are *therefore* likely to mess things up, and there are the great majority of sensible people (and politicians) who get along quite well because they do not "have" one. "Ideology," in this language, works as the opposite of "pragmatism," "common sense," or even of "reality."

An analogous understanding of ideology can be found in some versions of literary criticism, especially those influenced by Anglo-American New Criticism of the 1940s and 1950s, which tended to isolate and value the formal complexity of the literary text. This tendency has lost much of its influence in the academy but still remains quite strong in the culture at large, perhaps because of its comfortable fit with the assumptions of the dominant political language mentioned above. In this kind of criticism, the ideological aspects of a literary work will be felt as at best irrelevant to, and at worst detracting from, its aesthetic value. In the terms of this criticism, ideology is the unfortunate irruption of opinions and doctrine within what should be a fully "creative" or "imaginative" work. This critical perspective, then, is part of a general framework of assumptions that shapes both political and literary languages, a framework within which "ideology" is assigned a negative value, and is always seen in a zero-sum relation to some positively valued term like "common sense" or "creativity."

It would hardly be possible for American students to forget this dominant sense of the term "ideology," which will continue ceaselessly to be reinforced by enormous, powerful media institutions. And this conventional meaning of "ideology," as nearly synonymous with "politics," remains useful in the many situations where it is difficult to support the finer distinctions we will elaborate below. Yet, this is distinctly *not* the meaning of "ideology" in recent cultural criticism, so one must make an effort temporarily to put aside, as it were, the dominant sense of the term, in order to understand its rather more complicated history and usage in critical theory.

The word "ideology" was originally used by a French rationalist philosopher of the late eighteenth century to define a "science of ideas" or "philosophy of mind" that would be distinct from older metaphysical conceptions. In this philosophical tradition, it is related to terms like "epistemology." Yet the most influential development of "ideology" has surely been in the discourses of political theory, particularly in Marxist theory, through which it has taken a long and complicated journey before its unexpected arrival in the newer forms of American literary criticism. Perhaps "ideology" was most powerfully developed in Marxism because Marxism always sought to be not just narrowly "political" but a more comprehensive kind of theory that could understand the important relations among the political, economic, *and* cultural elements in specific societies. "Ideology," in fact, became the term through which Marxists tried to articulate, in various ways, the relation between the realm of culture (including, but not limited to "ideas") and the realm of political economy (including "production"). In *The German Ideology,* Karl Marx and Friedrich Engels elaborated a first, polemical definition and critique of ideology that still influences cultural analyses of the political left. In later writings, Marx and/or Engels gave more diverse, and less systematic, suggestions about how to understand ideology, thus creating a constitutive set of tensions in the use of the term that continued to mark its later development in both Marxist and non-Marxist discourses.

It might be helpful, then, to outline briefly a few of the major emphases that have been placed on ideology within the Marxist tradition, and within the tradition of sociological thought influenced by Marxism. This will require putting aside another construction of meaning that is continually reinforced in our culture, namely, the conveniently simple construction of "Marxism" as meaning essentially "the Soviet Union." We must remember, however, that Marxism is first of all a complex social theory that has motivated, and continues to motivate, a wide variety of political movements, in a wide variety of cultural and historical contexts, while remaining irreducible to any one of them. Marxism is not some kind of "Russian" or "un-American" phenomenon, despite constant proclamations to that effect by the mass media and the respectable North American intelligentsia; it is, rather, a fruitful outgrowth of the Western intellectual tradition, one that has had powerful and diverse influence in virtually every modern society, including—as this essay indicates—the United States. As with any other theory, we can begin to understand and evaluate Marxism by confronting its logic and argument, not by proclaiming its putative national characteristics.

For Marxist theory, every historical society is crucially defined by its class structure, a network of relations much wider and more fundamental than a "form of government." Every society, that is, embodies a specific relation between the dominant class, which owns and controls the major means of producing wealth (in our society, large industrial apparatuses), and the producing or working class, which depends for its survival on selling its labor power to the dominant class. It is on the basis of such historically specific class relations (in modern society, between capital and wage labor) that the production (and unequal distribution/appropriation) of all the goods and services constituting the wealth of a society takes place. Therefore, in order even to assure the continuity of its mode of producing material wealth, every society must first assure the reproduction of these class relations themselves. Production of goods and services in a plantation economy requires that there first of all be landholders and slaves, in a capitalist economy that there be capitalist investors and wage-workers, and the continued stability of a society requires that members of all classes tend to accept the given structure of class relations. (This does not preclude an individual social subject attempting to change his/her class position. Individual social mobility does not change the class structure of a society one bit.)

Obviously, any such class-divided social situation embodies an implicit tension that can at any time erupt into open conflict, and thus every class society has certain repressive mechanisms (police, armies, courts) that can be called upon to manage recurrent social tensions, to *force* social subjects to accept the relations of subordination and dominance between classes. But a constant reliance on force, on the power of "the government," is an expensive and inefficient way to assure the stable reproduction of class relations. This is the sign, in fact, of a weak social regime, one in which a lot of people from the subordinate classes (as well as some from the dominant classes) perceive themselves as being in an unjust situation, and are trying to do something to change it. Much better is a situation in which everyone—from dominant and subordinate class alike—understands and perceives the prevailing system of social relations as fundamentally fair on the whole (even if it hasn't done so well by them), and/or as better than any possible alternative, and/or as impossible to change anyway. This is a situation in which *ideology,* rather than force, is the primary means of managing social contradictions and reproducing class relations; if society uses apparatuses of force to confront overt rebellion, it uses apparatuses of ideology to form members of its various classes into social subjects who are unlikely ever to consider rebellion.

When ideology dominates social reproduction, the process becomes indeed much better for the dominant class: subordinate-class subjects will tend to resign themselves to their social weakness, trying to get what they can for themselves in any way possible, and to express dissatisfaction through relatively easy-to-control individual forms of ambition, violence, and self-destruction (including crime); meanwhile, dominant-class subjects themselves are freer to believe that their wealth and power are after all justified, that it really is the best of all possible worlds they manage, and that they can comfortably dismiss all those inconvenient and fanciful notions of how society and the social production of wealth might be organized differently, schemes that would only take away their power and wealth without actually helping anybody else. In such a situation, the social regime of class relations will remain stable, even if there is a lot of individual dissatisfaction. In such a situation, Imelda Marcos's private shoe collection will be universally deplored as obscene in the face of Philippine poverty and starvation, while Donald Trump's private real-estate collection will be widely admired as a sign of entrepreneurial zeal, even in the face of American poverty and homelessness. It is much more effective—and cheaper—to put "You can't fight City Hall," or "the poor will always be with us," or "every revolution just leads to worse tyranny" on everyone's lips than to put all the cops on all the corners that would be necessary to confront any determined struggle of the poor and homeless against the social system that produces poverty and homelessness. Or, as one radical literary critic put it, in a considerably less urgent context: "Ideology, after all, is more influential than laws. Imagine legislation forbidding professors of literature to get their noses out of their texts!" (Franklin 1972, 115).

This brings us to the question of how the concept of ideology can be useful in contemporary literary or cultural analysis. One writer on ideology has remarked: "A society is possible in the last analysis because the individuals in it carry around in their heads some sort of picture of that society" (Mannheim 1964, xxiii). This observation, with the important addition of "and of their place in it," might serve as a fair introduction to current ideology theory, which tries to understand the complex ways through which modern societies offer reciprocally reinforcing versions of "reality," "society," and "self" to social subjects. When Marx and Engels first developed a critique of ideology, the Anglo-European popular classes were largely illiterate agricultural or first-generation urban workers, there was no universal public education or political suffrage, no technology of mass entertainment, and one social institution—religion—that influenced every cultural practice and offered everyone—in discourses, rituals and images—an explanation/justification of the world and society. Thus, the first Marxist attempt to understand ideology was inevitably limited by a relatively simple psychology of the social subject and was dominated by closely intertwined philosophical and political criticisms of European religious ideology. This approach tended to conflate a critique of ideology with a criticism of idealism, so that "ideology" was seen as the form of thinking that mistakenly understood ideas as determining specific historical forms of society rather than vice versa. In this sense, "ideology" defined a widespread form of epistemological error that a new, more empirically based—sometimes called "scientific"—mode of thinking could avoid, if not eventually abolish. At other points in their work, Marx and/or Engels use "ideology" to talk about the specific "forms of consciousness" appropriate to specific kinds of society, or to specific class interests. In this latter use, "ideology" veers away from designating the opposite of "truth," and towards indicating those specific and indispensable "forms in which men become conscious of [social] conflict and fight it out," forms which promote particular sociohistorical interests as representing natural and universal human needs.

Contemporary Marxist theory, deriving largely from the work of Louis Althusser, has reworked the concept of ideology in the light of the more complex notion of subject-formation given by psychoanalysis, and the more elaborate system of ideological practices that have developed in late capitalist societies. In this framework, ideology designates a rich "system of representations," worked up in specific material practices, which helps form individuals into social subjects who "freely" internalize an appropriate "picture" of their social world and their place in it. Ideology offers the social subject not a set of narrowly "political" ideas but a fundamental framework of assumptions that defines the parameters of the real and the self; it constitutes what Althusser calls the social subject's "'lived' relation to the real."

We now understand this process of "subjection" as working largely through an address to unconscious fears and desires as well as rational interests, and we understand it as working through a multiplicity of disparate, complexly interconnected social apparatuses. Ideology is less tenacious as a "set of ideas" than as a system of representations, perceptions, and images that precisely encourages men and women to "see" their specific place in a historically peculiar social formation as inevitable, natural, a necessary function of the "real" itself. This "seeing" precedes and underlies any ways in which social subjects "think about" social reality, and this "seeing" is as likely to be shaped through a relaxed fascination with the page or the screen as through any serious attention to political theory. Ideological analysis in literary or cultural study, then, is concerned with the institutional and/or textual apparatuses that work on the reader's or spectator's imaginary conceptions of self and social order in order to call or *solicit* (or "interpellate," as Althusser puts it, using a quasi-legal term that combines the senses of "summons" and "hail") him/her into a specific form of social "reality" and social subjectivity.

Notwithstanding its roots in a class-based understanding of history, contemporary ideology theory also recognizes that perceived forms of social "reality" and subjectivity are constructed within more than one system of differences. In various socially specific ways, differences of sex, race, religion, region, education, and ethnicity, as well as class, form complex webs of determinations that affect how ideology works up a "lived" relation to the real. Any concrete society incorporates a spectrum of ideologies and social subjectivities, and this field tends to be worked into an asymmetrical whole that must be continually readjusted, a structure in which most ideological positions take up an unequal, subordinate relation to the dominant ideology. Influential ideological practices (literature, film, music, and so forth) in our society must therefore address this entire field of "differences," and usually do not explicitly emphasize questions of class (which is not to say they don't affect the reproduction of social class structures). Modern cultural texts are experienced as complex psychological and personal events, oriented around the provocation and pacification (or, in the more highbrow forms, the intellectual exploration) of thrill and/or anxiety. Recent forms of ideological analysis in the United States have thus tended to focus on the ideological work that texts do on gender differences, a kind of work that is usually central to such textual events.

In principle, ideological analysis is open to the full spectrum of socially significant differences within which the subject is constituted. Of course, in any real sociohistorical situation, some differences will be more socially significant than others. The widespread turn to gender analysis as ideological analysis in this country also partly derives, I think, from the precarious but real gains of feminist politics and discourse in contemporary North America, as opposed to the relative weakness of class-based politics and discourse. It is perhaps worth emphasizing that this weakness hardly marks the disappearance of class as an important social reality, just the success of a social ideology that has constructed a "lived relation to the real" in which "class" is indeed very difficult to "see" and to "grasp," and through which the prevailing structure of class difference is *therefore* all the more securely reproduced.

We can now remark the radical difference between this use of "ideology" and the more common use I described at the beginning of this chapter. In my specification of the term, "ideology" is not the opposite of "common sense" or "realism," and there is no such thing as a social discourse that is nonideological. Indeed, "realism" (whether in politics or literature) can now be understood as the paradigmatic form of ideology, and one's insistence that s/he (or a given text) is "nonideological" because s/he (or it) disavows any coherent political theory is as silly as would be one's insistence that s/he is "nonbiological" because s/he has no coherent theory of cell formation. Ideology is a social process that works on and through every social subject, that, like any other social process, everyone is "in," whether or not they "know" or understand it. It has the function of producing an *obvious* "reality" that social subjects can assume and accept, precisely as if it had not been socially produced and did not need to be "known" at all. The "nonideological" insistence does not mark one's freedom from ideology, but one's involvement in a specific, quite narrow ideology which has the exact social function of obscuring—even to the individual who inhabits it—the specificity and peculiarity of one's social and political position, and of preventing any knowledge of the real processes that found one's social life.

It is important to note, too, some differences between this use of "ideology" and some others that one might encounter, either in Marxist or in literary-critical discourses. Ideology here is a category analytically different from, although always related to, "politics." Ideology is an important dimension or "instance" of social practice that develops within and alongside of other important instances of social practice, including the political, in the way that publishing houses and movie studios flourish in the same social space alongside political parties. This is, in fact, not just an analogy but an example: movie studios and political parties are what contemporary Marxist theory would call, respectively, ideological and political apparatuses. There is certainly a widespread interconnection and interpenetration between the two kinds of institutions, but there is also enough recognizable relative autonomy and specificity to the kind of work done in each, and to the kind of social product or effect each produces, so that a rigorous social theory has to be able to make the important distinctions, precisely in order to draw out the important relations. In this regard, we might remark that, if older theories of ideology tended too easily to subsume the ideological under the political, newer versions sometimes tend to overcorrect by minimizing the relative autonomy of the political and/or by forgetting to specify the relationships between ideological and political effects. For this writer at least, ideological analysis maintains its edge—that which prevents it from becoming a form of social psychology—only by keeping our eyes on the relations of cultural texts to questions of politics, power, and/or class.

The difficulty, of course, is to be analytically and historically careful in specifying these relations. Ideological effects are not identical with, but are related or attached in specific, complex ways to political effects. These relations are sometimes explicit, and sometimes surreptitious; they can be quite close, or rather strained; they can operate at the level of a single text, or only through an accretion of similar textual strategies throughout the culture; they usually serve to reinforce, but can also help to disrupt, the subject's acceptance of a given sociopolitical order. The multiple, potentially contradictory political effect of ideological work is *another* expression or displacement—coexisting with, and often more acute than, those that occur in political practices—of the ongoing conflicts that constitute the class-divided social formation in which all these practices develop.

We live in a society with a constantly changing variety of social apparatuses which have a heavily ideological function: the family (in crisis), churches (now multiple and quasi-competitive), schools, sports, network TV, public TV, cable

TV, Hollywood (mass-audience) films, independent, foreign, and "art" (educated-audience) films, not to mention the various "literary" genres from "serious" fiction and drama to "popular" romances, science fiction, westerns, comic books, and so on. Most of these institutions make every effort emphatically to disavow "politics," to avoid thinking about who should control the power of the state, and it would be silly to treat them as if they were indistinguishable from those institutions that do directly address explicitly political questions. A horror film does not work in the same way as a campaign speech, though it is in fact the kind of address that works *better* and *for more people*. A declining percentage of the American population pays any attention to predominantly political institutions (only about 50 percent of the electorate voted in the 1988 election); every single American subject is addressed by, and pays attention to, some of these predominantly ideological apparatuses. This declining political interest does not mean the system is not working; to the contrary, it is a sign that the system is working quite well, thank you—only working for more people more of the time through apparatuses of ideological interpellation/subjection, rather than those of political persuasion.

Indeed, the depoliticization of the social subject is one of the major political effects that the work of American ideology as a whole helps to reinforce. The American political process is itself increasingly characterized—quite to the benefit of the stability of the social system—by the predominance of the ideological over the political, by contests between photo opportunities rather than choices between political programs, by the election of leaders based on the distinctively ideological address of the feel-good fast-food commercial. The relative autonomy of ideology and politics allows us to imagine that some of the ideological techniques of the American entertainment and public-relations industries *could* be used to quite different political effect—to reinforce political awareness, historical perspective, communal responsibility, and a sense of everyone's right to help determine one's own, and the nation's, economic and social destiny. This would require, of course, that the social apparatuses of ideology develop alongside, and in a different kind of articulation with, different kinds of political and economic apparatuses, in a different kind of society. As Althusser puts it:

> In a class society ideology is the relay whereby, and the element in which, the relation between men and their conditions of existence is settled to the profit of the ruling class. In a classless society ideology is the relay whereby, and the element in which, the relation between men and their conditions of existence is lived to the profit of all men. (1970, 235–36)

The implication of this quotation—that ideology would be a necessary aspect even of the kind of classless society that Marxism posits as possible and necessary—marks a clear difference between this theory and one which would define ideology as in a zero-sum relation to "truth" or "science." Most previous versions of Marxism understood "ideology" within the framework of "illusions" or "mystifications" that must and could be dispelled by promoting a more accurate knowledge of society. In many ways, these Marxisms accepted a quasi-Platonic epistemological standard of evaluating ideological practice that did not recognize the distinctive social effects it produces; analogously, our insistence on the insufficiency of this Platonism further develops, within a radical social theory, a kind of response that has reappeared frequently in the history of criticism: "the poet . . . he nothing affirms, and therefore never lieth. . . . What child is there, that, coming to a play, and seeing *Thebes* written in great letters upon an old door, doth believe that it is Thebes?" (Sir Philip Sidney, *The Defense of Poesie*).

In our framework, too, the primary point of ideology, that which defines its social function, is not to "give knowledge" or make an accurate "copy" of something, but to constitute, adjust, and/or transform social subjects. The distinctive effect of ideology is not theoretical but pragmatic, to enable various social subjects to feel at home, and to act (or not act), within the limits of a given social project. Ideological discourses and practices will always contain and transmit some "knowledges," but are not vehicles for producing knowledge, and should not be judged in those terms. There are, indeed, other, complexly related social practices—perhaps identifiable as "scientific" or "theoretical"—that have the production of knowledge as their primary purpose, but these different kinds of practices are not the opposite of, and cannot replace ideology. Ideology is a necessary element of "sociality" itself, "a structure essential to the historical life of societies . . . *indispensable in any society if men are to be formed, transformed and equipped to respond to the demands of their conditions of existence*" (Althusser 1970, 234–35; emphasis in original). From this perspective, then, the problem with specific ideological discourses and practices is not *that* they are ideological, but exactly *how*, and to exactly *which* "social conditions of existence," they "form, transform and equip" men and women to respond. The kind of question posed by an ideological analysis is less: "Does a given ideological discourse or practice accurately represent Thebes, or New York, or Managua?"; it is more: "What is the effect on social subjects of a given ideological practice, in a given situation, transformatively (mis)representing Thebes, or New York, or Managua, in precisely the way it does?"

There can, of course, be more than one answer to this kind of question, depending on context, audience, and the ways that framing discourses such as literary criticism prepare and re-present texts, and associate them with other texts and social practices. It is probably easiest to grasp the point of contemporary ideology theory by looking at what it might do with a concrete cultural text, the recent film *Kiss of the Spider Woman*. This film demonstrates, first of all, the complexity of that ideological apparatus called "Hollywood"—a word that now designates not a town but a multinational industry. The severe financial constraints on current film-making have given rise to increasingly complicated prefilm credits, which both indicate the various sources of money and demonstrate our social "subjection" to a specific ideological apparatus that always (even in the case of relatively "progressve" entertainment) requires us to wait on the contractual agreement of capital sources for our entertainment. For this film, we have three separate credit screens, whose syntactical incoherence probably reflects an imbalance of financial clout; these images credit as follows (slashes indicate line breaks): "Island Alive/presents"; "In Association With/FILMDALLAS/Investment Fund I"; "HB Films/presents." These credits seem to indicate a true multinational conglomeration of capital backing the film: British (Island Pictures, an offshoot of Island Records, a British company that has produced a lot of reggae), American (FILMDALLAS a Texas-based investment group), and Brazilian (HB Films, presumably a venture of Hector Babenco, the film's Brazilian director). In addition, the film is based on a novel by an Argentine writer, Manuel Puig, and is carefully casted with hot, "bankable" young American actors who can establish its appeal to the financially crucial American mass market. Thus, this film was successful in part because it shrewdly negotiated the complicated economic preconditions of any contemporary ideological practice that wants to have a mass effect.

These factors describe crucial determinations on the film as the product of an ideological apparatus within a specific mode of production; but they do not yet explain its ideological effects as a cultural "text"—that is, as a system of representations perceived as a plenitude of "meaning" and/or "experience." For this is, after all, a film that strives for, and I think largely achieves, politically "progressive" *and* aesthetically "interesting" (avant-garde or "postmodern") effects. It is the product of a leftist Latin American writer, and a perhaps even more definitely leftist Latin American director. Manuel Puig is a professed homosexual writer who had to leave Argentina during the years of military repression. One of his earlier novels, the semiautobiographical *Betrayed by Rita Hayworth,* tells the story of a little boy who develops a fascination with the beautiful feminine screen image as a result of his weekend trips to the movies with his mother. Hector Babenco's previous film, *Pixote,* depicted the life of a homeless, abandoned Brazilian street kid, who eventually takes up male prostitution. The title character was played by a real child of the streets, one of the millions in the Latin American sector of the free world, who recently, at the approximate age of sixteen, met his unsurprising fate—death by gunfire. The previous work of both, in other words, showed a willingness to confront social issues in original and provocative forms; both have sought cultural languages to help deepen the political challenges that have recently broken up some of the more grotesque subfascist regimes in Latin America. The film is in part, then, a product of the historical process of Latin American revolution. In this context, in fact, *Kiss of the Spider Woman* explicitly explores the different ways in which ideology works on social subjectivity, and attempts to open the viewer (even as it presents the reciprocal opening of the characters) to the manifold, curious, and unforeseen relations that can obtain between ideology and politics.

The film portrays the jail-cell relation between Valentina, a Latin-American revolutionary, and Molina, who has been imprisoned for his homosexuality. This relation is mediated by Molina's "telling" of a film, a secondhand narrative that helps to "pass the time," and to distract Valentina from the pain of the beatings and poisoning to which he is subjected. Molina's favorite film, which in fact constitutes much of the film that we see, turns out to be a crude Nazi propaganda film about greedy and treacherous Jews versus heroic German officers in occupied Paris. While Molina's identification with such a film seems ludicrous, even shocking, to Valentina and the viewer, we quickly understand that he literally does not "see" the film in this way. Molina sees the Jews with yarmulkes as "Turks" with "fezzes," and the German officers as dashing young soldiers in sleek uniforms. When Valentina points out that it is actually a Nazi film, Molina responds (repeating a typical complaint about "criticism" from those who find intense pleasure in the way a text addresses and constitutes their subjectivity): "Look, I don't explain my movies. It just ruins the emotion. . . . That's just the background. *This* is where the important part begins—the part about the lovers." Molina sees and enjoys the film only as "romance," as a kind of ideological address that confirms and reconstitutes an identity and reality in which love, beauty, and finding the perfect mate (which for him has the conventionally "feminine" inflection of "getting the man") are what is "really" important.

This situation has all the trappings, then, of a typical division between the politically "serious" Marxist revolutionary, and the willfully naive, "decadent" homosexual/"romantic," a structure that seems confirmed when we learn that Molina's kindness to Valentina was instigated by the warden as a ruse to get information from Valentina about his comrades; in exchange for acting as an informer, Molina is promised an early release. After all, for Molina, the politics and history of Valentina's struggle are "just the background."

But the effects of ideology and ideological work can be surprising. Precisely because of Molina's romantic ideology, and his telling of the romantic film stories, he and Valentina grow closer, and each learns to respect and open himself to the other's ideology. Drawing Valentina into the romantic fantasies inevitably precipitates Molina's falling in love with him; Valentina, in turn, is actually helped and strengthened by Molina's emotional and physical support (whatever its original motivation), and takes it as (what it increasingly is) a genuine openness and sensitivity that expresses Molina's own different kind of strength. Their mutual ideological complicity is finally confirmed when Molina agrees to act as a messenger to Valentina's revolutionary group, and Valentina agrees to enter Molina's romantic imaginary by allowing the latter to enter his body. Both subject positions are transformed, without either being denied. Molina takes a new kind of political commitment into his life, which survives even his being shot by Valentina's comrades, prompting the police to suspect—correctly, though not quite in the way intended—that "he was more deeply involved than we suspected." (The police think that Molina "had agreed if necessary to be eliminated by them [the revolutionaries]," though it seems to the viewer that the revolutionaries shot him because they mistakenly but understandably thought he had led the police to them.)

For his part, Valentina, brutally tortured again, appropriates the strength of romantic fantasy in his own terms, entering the "spider woman" film-within-the-film as a means to avoid the pain of his fresh wounds, and the even more politically debilitating despair that might be inflicted with them. And the viewer finds him/herself enmeshed in a tale showing some surprising interpenetrations of ideology and politics, wherein one social subject's romantic ideology is detached from its original reactionary political associations and worked into a catalyst for revolutionary policital commitment, and another social subject's revolutionary ideology opens itself to the hopes embodied in romantic fantasy, and to the revolutionary possibilities of another kind of "lived relation to the real."

As I suggested above, a complex network of factors—including context, audience, and the influence of framing discourses and practices—helps to determine the "meaning" of any text, and it is unlikely, under current ideological conditions in the United States, that most viewers would spontaneously perceive *Kiss of the Spider Woman* as I just have. Indeed, the present state of American cultural ideology is perfectly epitomized by the following conversation that took place recently in a Brooklyn apartment, while a Puerto Rican family, their guest, and several mice were watching a video of *Demons II:*

> YOUNG MAN: This is a good movie, but it's not as good as *Demons I.*
>
> GUEST: I never saw *Demons I.*
>
> YOUNG MAN: Well, it's like *Halloween.* You've seen *Halloween,* haven't you?
>
> GUEST: No, I haven't seen *Halloween.*
>
> YOUNG MAN: Oh, well, it's like *Nightmare on Elm Street,* you've seen that haven't you?
>
> GUEST: No, I never saw that movie.
>
> YOUNG MAN: You never saw *Nightmare on Elm Street?* You don't know Freddy Kruger? Well, it's like *Friday the 13th.* You must have seen *Friday the 13th,* with Jason. If you don't know Freddy, you must know Jason!
>
> GUEST: No, I never saw *Friday the 13th,* either.
>
> YOUNG MAN: What are you, a communist?

Such reactions certainly indicate the conservative thrust of the "normal" American mode of perceiving or interpreting cultural texts, and its perverse, tenacious hold on the most disparate social subjects; they also indicate that this "normal" mode of perception is in fact no more "natural," "spontaneous," or "obvious"—and no *less* politicized—than what I have done with *Kiss of the Spider Woman*. *Any* mode of perceiving the film would be determined by a prior ideological construction of audience and context, and by the film's immediate entry into a network of framing discourses that compete to "clarify" and "elucidate"—actually to *produce*—its meaning and/or value, and to do that in politically significant ways. Academic literary and cultural criticism is only one such framing practice, within which contestatory theories—like the self-conscious ideology theory that underlies this essay—have somewhat more space to assert themselves than they do in the dominant Siskel-and-Ebert kind of critical discourse. The dominant discourse produces an audience, context, and text in which the reigning political framework appears as "normality" itself; any other sociopolitical nuances of a text are rendered either imperceptible—"just the background"—or impossible to take seriously—the effects of a demon ideology. The discourse of this essay attempts to make such nuances "obvious" in their own right; the encounter between these discourses marks an ideological struggle over whether a pleasurable/beautiful/fascinating cultural text will be used to reaffirm or to challenge the prevailing sense of self and social order—always a struggle over what is "obvious."

To give another brief, more direct, and even more "mass-cultural" example of the relation between ideological and political struggle, of how the power to define what is "obvious" helps to determine who rules, and of the relative strength of insurgent versus dominant ideological frameworks, we can offer the widely publicized tussle during the 1984 presidential campaign over the "meaning" of Bruce Springsteen. This began with a column by George Will, America's favorite reactionary nerd, lauding Springsteen as a shining example of the American dream—of how hard work, ambition, and the unfettered ability to accumulate wealth can give hope, if not ensure success, to working-class Americans. This version of Springsteen was then worked into a Reagan speech in Springsteen's home state of New Jersey, attempting to appropriate Springsteen, the cultural icon, as a Reaganite kind of guy. The national media soon followed, with full segments on the network nightly news, interviewing fans at Springsteen concerts, who proclaimed that, indeed, Springsteen appeared to them as another proof of the obvious American social fact that if he could make it, anybody can. All of the hoopla eventually prompted Springsteen himself to remind his concert audiences that the words of his songs (like "My Hometown") hardly proclaim the durability of the American dream; to donate concert proceeds to union welfare funds; and to speak to workers rallying against plant closures, telling them: "What goes unmeasured is the price that unemployment inflicts on people's families, on their marriages, on the single mothers out there trying to raise their kids on their own."

At stake here was how the vast appeal of an attractive cultural icon, and the wildly popular and pleasing cultural texts (rock songs) he produced, could be appropriated to support specific political and socioeconomic programs. Do Bruce Springsteen and his work obviously reaffirm or obviously challenge the American Dream according to Reagan and Will? Do he and his songs show an America that is a land of opportunity for everyone, or a land of broken hopes for too many? In this case, the repeated, if somewhat less-publicized, direct interventions of the "author" led right-wing propagandists to back off somewhat on their attempts to appropriate his work, and the result can be described as a kind of stand-off. For even such a rich and prominent "author's" explicit remarks cannot entirely efface the effects of an even richer and more influential ideological apparatus, which continually prepares audience and context to receive any cultural message as always-already confirming the obvious superiority of North American capitalism. Bruce Springsteen is, after all, a product of that ideological apparatus, and the various industries that constitute it; he is a beneficiary of a socioeconomic system whose fundamental project is to allow the unlimited private accumulation of wealth and unimpeded private discretion over its investment—a project that inevitably produces a pole of unemployment, poverty, and misery; he is an icon of an American dream that is not exclusively Republican or Reaganite but a bipartisan pillar of United States capitalist ideology, a dream that is at the present moment (the presidential election of 1988) being enthusiastically endorsed and promoted by liberal Democrats like Michael Dukakis and even Jesse Jackson. And to say this is not to issue some kind of ultraleftist criticism of Bruce Springsteen, who has been forthrightly and refreshingly progressive, but to recognize a sociocultural fact—namely, that he and his work are enmeshed in ideological apparatuses and ideological struggles that determine its "meaning" in ways he can (and does) affect but cannot entirely control. It is also to recognize that progressive ideological struggle inevitably confronts tenacious structures of social and class power, and can overcome their resistance only in conjunction with a progressive political struggle that is equally forthright and tenacious. Obvious, isn't it?

To conclude, "ideology" designates the indispensable practice—including the "systems of representation" that are its products and supports—through which individuals of different class, race, and sex are worked into a particular "lived relation" to a sociohistorical project. Ideological analysis studies the ways in which those "lived relations" and systems of representation are constituted, transformed, and affiliated with various specific political programs. More committed forms of ideological analysis also attempt to change the association of influential ideological ensembles and particular political programs. For there can be no successful political program that is not driven by powerful and comprehensive forms of ideological address. Thus, literary and cultural texts of all kinds constitute a society's ideological practice, and literary and cultural criticism constitutes an activity that, in its own rather meager way, either submits to, or self-consciously attempts to transform, the political effects of that indispensable social practice.

SUGGESTED READINGS

Althusser, Louis. 1970. "Marxism and Humanism." In *For Marx*.

———. 1971. "Ideology and Ideological State Apparatuses." In *Lenin and Philosophy*.

Belsey, Catherine. 1980. *Critical Practice*.

Eagleton, Terry. 1976a. *Criticism and Ideology*.

———. 1976b. *Marxism and Literary Criticism*.

Jameson, Fredric. 1981. *The Political Unconscious*.

Kavanagh, James H. 1985. "Shakespeare in Ideology." In *Alternative Shakespeares*.

———. 1982. "Marxism's Althusser: Toward a Politics of Literary Theory."

Marx, Karl. *The Eighteenth Brumaire of Louis Bonaparte*.

Marx, Karl, and Friedrich Engels. *The German Ideology*.

23

Popular Culture

John Fiske

"**A**ND WHAT," asked the emcee of the *New Newlywed Game,* "would you say best describes your wife's attitude to your romantic needs?" His voice put the last two words into heavy inverted commas. "'Yes, Master', 'No way, Jose' or 'Get serious, man'?" The four husbands in front of him duly answered "Yes, Master," some glossing it with comments like "I wear the pants," "She's very accommodating," or "She always does what I want," though one was slightly hesitant and was teased for being so. In the next segment of the show the wives were asked to guess their husbands' responses. Two dutifully guessed right and were rewarded with hugs from their men, points from the emcee, and applause from the studio audience. The wife of the hesitant one replied, "No way, Jose," and, embarrassedly, the husband admitted that she was actually correct, but only because of a "little operation" he had recently undergone. No hugs nor points for them, but a lot of studio laughter. The fourth wife's guess was "Get serious, man," which provoked a mock argument between the two about who was in control of their bedroom life. Again, no points, no hugs, but roars of laughter and prolonged applause from the studio audience.

The *New Newlywed Game* rewards the couple who best conforms to our ideological norms, for the winner is the couple who understands each other best as measured by their ability to guess each other's responses. Their prize commodifies their domesticity—it is usually an expensive kitchen appliance, a new bedroom suite, or a second honeymoon. These norms situate mutual understanding within a framework of male dominance and female submissiveness; the winners embody and underscore the naturalness of our socially produced normality.

But the popular winners differ from the official winners: it is the couples who challenge or fail to live up to the norms that provide the popular pleasure of the show—they provoke the most laughter from the studio audience, and the emcee dwells on their disagreements while passing quickly over the consensual couples. The ideological norms of the heterosexual couple and the gender roles appropriate to it are simultaneously rewarded and undermined, and it is in the contradictions between these lines of force that we may trace some of the key characteristics of popular culture.

Let us define those two slippery words before exploring further their meaning. (I must explain first that I am limiting my account of popular culture to its textual forms, for those are the most appropriate to literary studies, and am not considering its more performative and embodied forms such as sport, fashion, or dancing, which are more appropriate to anthropology than literature.) By "culture" we refer to the social circulation of meanings, values, and pleasures, to the processes of forming social identities and social relationships, and to entering into relation with the larger social order in a particular way and from a particular position. Social relationships are personal, social relations are structural, and the former turn the latter into the lived experience of everyday life. Thus, in a patriarchal society such as ours, the social relations between the genders grant masculinity the position of power, but actual relationships between individual men and women may conform closely to the gender relations or may oppose, modify, or struggle against them: relationships are not totally determined by social relations but they can never be free of them either. Similarly, the social identities that people struggle to produce for themselves can never be free of determining social relations as expressed through categorizations such as gender, race, class, age, and so on; yet they are never totally determined by those relations, either. We can take this argument a little further by recognizing that the structuring social relations provide us with preformed frameworks of meaning or ways of making sense of our social experience, that they equip us with value systems by which to orient ourselves toward the events of our everyday lives, and that they teach us to distinguish between legitimate and illegitimate pleasures. All this is the work of culture, but it is only part of its work, it is only the ideological part by which dominant norms are produced, circulated, and maintained. But, as the wives on the *New Newlywed Game* showed us, people sometimes comply with these norms and sometimes challenge them. There is a space between social norms and their application in particular circumstances, a space where compliance or contestation is negotiated, and a space between determining social relations and people's attempts to control their own identities and relationships; and these spaces constitute the terrain where popular culture is most active.

"Popular" is a more elusive term even than "culture." One meaning of the word, a widespread but debased one, is statistical — what is most popular is what appeals to the most people. Another, a more productive one, is that "the popular" serves the interests of "the people." "The people" as we use the term here, is not a class or social category, but rather a shifting set of social interests and positions that are defined by their subordinate relations to the dominant society. In this definition, the "complaint" wives were not behaving as members of "the people" for they were promoting the power relations and maintaining the norms of the dominant society — they were performing the roles and identities provided for them, they were making sense of their experience in a predetermined way, using the provided value system to evaluate their experience and to enjoy only the pleasures that it legitimated. They were producing nothing for themselves, and, insofar as they were members of a gender subordinated by the norms to which they conformed, they were acting against their gender interests and in the dominant ones. The noncompliant wives, however, particularly the one who answered, "Get serious, man," were trying to promote their gender interests against those of the dominating normality, and, in so doing, were acting as members of the people. "The people," then, are better recognized by what they *do* than by who they *are,* and popular culture, by analogy, is better recognized by what it *does* than by what it *is.* Popular culture is more a culture of process than of products.

This understanding of the word "popular" is both recent and a reversal of its earlier uses in cultural theory. As Europe and America industrialized themselves during the nineteenth century, their populations moved from rural areas to the cities that were built at high speed to house the workforce needed by the new mills and factories. This urbanized, highly concentrated mass of people was a new social phenomenon that traditional concepts of the people as rural peasantry or folk could not describe. As the development of a society's language and its ways of thinking is shaped primarily by its ruling classes (though this is less the case in today's multicultural, market driven societies), so the ways of talking and thinking about this new "people" reflected ruling class interests — they were either elitist and anxious, or patronizing and nostalgic.

The anxious elite used the word "popular" synonymously with ones like gross, base, vile, riffraff, common, low, vulgar, plebeian and cheap. In the same mindset, "democracy" was something to be feared, for it connoted mob rule. From this point of view, the people were seen as a cultureless, lawless timebomb that might explode at any moment into anarchy and social disorder. The danger lay less in the people themselves, however, than in their gullibility, for, paradoxically, besides being dangerous, they were also motiveless and sheeplike, following blindly whoever could win them over. Matthew Arnold, then, in his influential book *Culture and Anarchy* argued that the crucial issue facing nineteenth century society was the leadership of this mass of people. The culture wars of the time were fought between the properly cultured (that is, those maintaining the values of the best that had been thought and said in the world [read "Europe"]), and the new, emerging middle class who were materialist and uncultured but wealthy and increasingly powerful politically. He called them Philistines and worried that their influence over the masses would lead to social degradation, vulgarization (and ultimately), anarchy, and the destruction of civilization. The cultural elite for whom he spoke saw many parallels between Britain and ancient Rome, with the important difference that the modern equivalent of the Goths and Vandals who overthrew the Roman Empire and sank Europe into the Dark Ages were already inside the walls: the people were the enemy within. The direct descendants of this view of culture are still with us and show every sign of living on into the next century. It is still, unfortunately, necessary to remind ourselves not only of their elitism but also of their Eurocentricity.

The patronizingly nostalgic view of the people was also formed in reaction to the forces of industrialization and urbanization, but in this case the point of critical comparison was not a civilized culture threatened by the future but a pastoral folk culture lost in the past. The Romantics, who were the main proponents of this view, were genuine, if sentimental, in their criticism of the bad social conditions of the new working class, but, like the cultural elitists, they did not believe that this class had the ability to produce a culture of its own and to make its own contribution to the complex industrial society that was emerging. It was not until the second half of this century that cultural analysts began to discover how active the lower classes had been in shaping their own culture and to recognize the influence they could exert over the culture as a whole.

There is another way of conceptualizing the people in industrial societies that share certain features with both anxious elitism and patronizing nostalgia. This was most comprehensively proposed by the Frankfurt School, a group of Marxist social theorists who fled Nazi Germany to the United States. In their view, the industrialization of culture and the development of the mass media had destroyed all traces of authentic popular or folk culture and was rapidly eroding high culture. The culture industries ensured that capitalism could colonize people's leisure time as fully as their work time. They were crucial in enabling capitalism to saturate people's experiences and consciousness so thoroughly as to leave no space in which to experience a noncapitalist identity or consciousness, or to establish non- (let alone anti-) capitalist relations. The culture industries, then, were the means by which capitalism could erase any possibility of opposition and thus of social change. They alienated people from their social relations, whether with local communities or with their own class, and they turned the people into a mass of atomized individuals who had no sense of collectivity and were thus denied the social power that derives only from collective action. They commodified people by erasing their consciousness of all needs or desires except those that could be satisfied by commodities, and they produced one dimensional people who were incapable of criticizing capitalism because they had no experience of anything outside it. For the Frankfurt School, the universal human values of high culture provided the sole remaining noncommodified system of values, and they traced how capitalism set to work to extinguish this area of potential opposition as well. It commodified high art by using cheap reproductions of paintings in advertisements and by turning the products of human greatness into plastic souvenirs; it played classical music in elevators and packaged it for mass consumption; great books had their greatness taken out of them by being condensed and predigested for easy consumption. The result was what was later called a "middle-brow," conformist culture that seemed expressly designed for Matthew Arnold's Philistines. The industrialization of culture, then, destroyed both popular and high culture, the two possible sources of an authentic sense of being human from which to criticize the inhumanity of capitalist society. This critical pessimism was ultimately elitist because it saw the people as the helpless, passive victims of the system, and denied them any agency of their own. It did not allow them any ability to devise means of coping with, or exerting influence upon, the socio-economic forces that were ranged against them.

The idea that the people in industrial societies had no culture also drove the nineteenth century science of anthropology. To discover the universal truths of human society and culture, anthropologists went into "primitive" or non-European societies where they found that myth, ritual and religion did for them what elite culture did in the West — they kept the social order and its highest, traditionally tested values alive and in good shape. Anthropology has had a good influence in extending the notion of culture to encompass far more than elite works of art and has helped open up the space where popular culture could be studied. Its influence, for example, underlay Raymond Williams's richly simple, and in its day, highly provocative, proposition that "culture is ordinary." But it has been less positive when it has influenced cultural theorists to treat complex industrial societies as oversized tribes and their mass culture as the equivalent of rituals that give their society cohesion. Watching *Dallas,* the Superbowl, or the Gulf War on television serves, in this view, the same social function as a ritual in a tribal society. The problem with this view is that it subsumes the people into society as a whole and thus denies them their distinct cultures or social identities; it also denies any sense of conflict of interest between the elites and the people, and the only beneficiary of the denial of conflict of interest is the status quo and its power structure.

The theory of popular culture that underlies this essay derives from the tradition of cultural studies. This school of thought agrees with all the criticisms of industrial capitalism sketched above but disagrees with the claimed totality of their effectiveness. It accepts the accuracy of the diagnosis of the forces with which popular culture has to cope but rejects the assumption that the people have no resources of their own from which to derive their coping strategies, their resistances, and their own culture. Popular culture in industrial societies does exist, even though it may never be pure and authentic, for it is always made from cultural resources that are opposed to it, it is always contradictory and inscribed with traces of that to which it is opposed. It is always, then, a culture of struggle, a culture of making do rather than one of making. Popular culture is typically bound up with the products and technology of mass culture, but its creativity consists in its ways of using these products and technologies, not in producing them.

Three of the works that are often claimed to form the foundation of cultural studies are *The Making of the English Working Class* by the historian E. P. Thompson (published in 1963) and two books published in 1958 by literary critics and cultural theorists, *The Uses of Literacy,* by Richard Hoggart, and *Culture and Society,* by Raymond Williams. The German playwright Brecht was also influential, though less centrally. In essays such as "The Popular and the Realistic," he was one of the first to argue that "the people" and "the popular" could be "fighting" concepts. He understood that the people were the driving force of social change and that popular art had not only to appeal to them but that it had to represent and validate the progressive section of the people in such a way that it could take over the leadership. He tried to produce such a popular culture in his plays, but, unfortunately, apart from a brief period in pre-Nazi Germany, his work has been more popular with the left-wing intelligentsia than with the people. His attempt to produce a popular culture for the progressive section of the people was ultimately misguided, for it misunderstood the culture of the people as a culture of products or texts rather than a culture of process by which texts are used for popular purposes. Of course, some texts have greater potential for such uses than others, and Brecht's attempts to produce a popular theater were not entirely misguided. He did, however, attempt to direct and control the political uses to which his plays should be put, and, despite his best intentions, ended up didactically talking down to the people he was trying to talk with. Popular culture rejects preachiness and insists on determining its own uses of texts, for that is where the creativity of the people lies.

Mass culture, like high culture and like Brecht's putative popular culture, is a culture of products for products are readily sold. Mass culture produces cultural commodities, high culture produces artworks or texts. The cultural commodities of mass culture — films, TV shows, CDs, etc. — are produced and distributed by an industrialized system whose aim is to maximize profit for the producers and distributors by appealing to as many consumers as possible. This industrialized mass culture is not popular culture, though it does produce many of the resources out of which popular culture is made, and its market centered approach means that it is often more effective in producing texts that the people can use for their progressive purposes than was Brecht with his explicit progressive intentions. The marketplace has always been a site of negotiation rather than one of economic exploitation, and the market places of capitalism are, in this respect, no different from those of other economic systems. In industrialized societies the people make their culture out of resources that are not of their making and are not under their control. Popular culture typically involves the art of making do with what is available.

Crucial to the art of making do is the selection of what to use. Roughly 80 percent of the products of mass culture are rejected by the people: eight out of ten Hollywood films fail to make a profit at the box office (this is their main target market, though now many make more money in secondary markets such as home video or export); four out of five new television shows fail to survive their first season, and the music and print industries show similar patterns of rejection.

But popular discrimination does not stop at the selection of the commodity or text, it then selects the functional elements within it. Homeless Native Americans, for instance, chose to watch old westerns on the VCR in their shelter, but they selected only the first half of them, and switched off the movie at the point when the wagon train had been successfully attacked, the fort captured — they chose not to watch the reassertion of white empire. Aboriginal people watching the Rambo movies in Australia chose to ignore the conflict between the free west and the communist east and focused instead on the conflict between Rambo, whom they saw, by a selection of physical and behavioral characteristics, as a member of the third world like them, and the white officer class that systematically and mistakenly underestimated his abilities.

Popular selection, then, is performed not by universal aesthetic criteria of quality, but by socially located criteria of relevance. Rambo was a cultural resource that Australian Aboriginals could use in making their own sense of their identities in a white society; they saw similarities between the white officer class in the movie and the Australian government officials who regulated so much of their lives, so the movie was useful to them in making their sense, as opposed to the white sense, of the paternalist and demeaning bureaucracy with which they had to deal. Similar creative, functional, and selective processes can be observed in the way people watch the *New Newlywed Game*. When I showed students the episode that contained the exchange at the opening of this chapter I could detect three recurrent patterns in their widely varying responses. Some women, often those who explicitly aligned themselves with feminism, were so offended by the sexism of the question and its built-in assumption that women's sexuality exists only to respond to men's that they rejected the show altogether; they did not watch it at home and did not make it part of their popular culture. When asked to watch it in class, some of them, however, did recognize a wry pleasure in seeing just how awful patriarchy could be, as one put it, "You couldn't ask for a clearer example of what we're up against!" Other women, however, laughed delightedly at the noncompliant wives, and many of them chose occasionally to watch the show at home. They chose to attend to the popular winners rather than the official ones, and did make the show into part of their popular culture. We will trace some of the implications of this choice in a moment.

One other, possibly more surprising, pattern of response occurred among the men in my classes. Many of them commented that the husbands were put on the spot by the question. Patriarchy's construction of masculinity made it almost impossible for a man, in public, to reply in any way other than "Yes, master," for one of the requirements of this masculinity is public performance. So even those men who, in private, might relate to their wives or girlfriends very differently would, in public or on television, be under strong pressure to conform to the norms of mastery: they were placed at a point of acute and anxious contradiction between the social relations of gender and their own personal relationships. These particular husbands, if they experienced this contradiction, were less able or willing than their wives to stand up for personal relationships over ideological relations. We may speculate, on the basis of this slender evidence, that the ideology of patriarchy may work more effectively upon men than women, maybe because men have less to gain by resisting it, or, at least, less experience of resisting. For the men in my classes, however, who did recognize the contradiction, the question was so excessively patriarchal that instead of naturalizing patriarchal norms into common sense, it actually exposed those norms to questioning and criticism. In this respect their response was similar to that of the feminist women.

Popular culture is often excessive, and is frequently criticized by those who do not understand it for being "sensational." Excessiveness, sensationalism, and exaggeration are stylistic devices of contradiction, and, as I have argued, the contradictory is characteristic of popular culture. Each of these devices takes ideological norms and then exceeds them, magnifies them so that their normality is brought to our attention and is not allowed to continue its ideological work unseen: its powerful position of "the taken-for-granted" is thus disturbed. They promote a norm and then exceed it, spilling over beyond its ideological containment. This excess meaning then becomes a resource that people can use to interrogate or contradict the normal, the excessive is meaning that has escaped the control of the norm.

Intrigued and heartened by my students' responses to the *New Newlywed Game,* I then advertised locally asking for "real life" fans of the show to write or telephone me their accounts of why they enjoyed it. Twenty-two bothered to do so. Across their varied responses I was able to trace four recurrent similarities. The first was that twenty-one of the respondents were women, and the lone male called me only at his girlfriend's insistence because she was too shy to do so herself. This 100 percent female response does not indicate that the show was watched only by women, but it does indicate, I believe, that those to whom the show is important enough for them to want to describe their pleasures in it to a strange professor were disproportionately, if not exclusively, female. The show *matters* to women. This is an intriguing observation if the show is as patriarchal as it first appears.

It was common for these women not only to watch the show with their husbands or boyfriends but also to play it. But the genders did not watch in the same way—in almost every case the woman reported that the man only watched at her insistence: men typically expressed reluctance to watching it and even greater reluctance to playing it.

Almost as obvious as the gender of the respondents was the use of one particular concept, which appeared explicitly or implicitly in almost every response—

"embarrassment." This embarrassment took three forms, embarrassment at admitting to watching the show, the embarrassment of the couples, particularly the men, on the show, and a similar embarrassment experienced by the "real life" couples in front of the screen when they played the game themselves.

The final common pattern was the functional relevance of the show in the everyday lives of the women. They could use it actively in constructing their own sexual relationships and, more passively, but still usefully, as a point around which to organize their daily routines.

All of these typical responses come together in one of the letters, which is worth considering in some detail. Here it is:

> Dear Mr. Fiske,
>
> Although I'm not sure exactly what you want to know, I can tell you, with some embarrassment, that I have become an avid viewer of *The Newlywed Game*. I don't know if I can really explain why, but I know I started watching it over three months ago, mostly because the time it comes on fits my schedule well. After I come home from work, I make dinner while watching the evening news, then at 7:00 it's ready, and I can sit down and eat dinner while watching *The Newlywed Game*.
>
> Probably the thing I like about it is that I can relate a lot of that trivial domestic stuff to my relationship with my own husband, and it's a little uncomfortable realizing how much we are like those couples on the show. In fact, I will usually answer the questions and then guess how my husband would respond. If he's home at that time and watches the show with me, I urge him to answer the questions so we can compare our answers. Actually, we do learn something about one another, not always what we want to know. So, for that reason I enjoy the show. Another reason might be that I like to see people making fools of themselves. Well, maybe not fools, but just being themselves with all their peculiar idiosyncrasies. It makes for good comedy, in my opinion. . . .
>
> I just thought of something else: it has to do with the MC of the show. He definitely goads the contestants to get them going. Stirring up conflict between husband and wife does seem like part of the show's appeal.
>
> That about covers it, Mr. Fiske. For what it's worth, I also watch *The New Dating Game* which follows *The Newlywed Game,* but I don't enjoy that as much. If I were single, I probably would prefer that one more.

Let us explore the significance of embarrassment. Embarrassment occurs, I suggest, at the point of conflict between the prescriptive norm and the desire to challenge it, between the conventional and the subversive, the dominant and the subordinate. Embarrassment occurs when what we feel is in our interests or for our pleasure conflicts with the dominant norms that we have internalized. So men are embarrassed when the repressed disagreements between the couple are brought out into the open, but women find this pleasurable and liberating. The norm that is subverted here results in our ideological practice of laying the responsibility for emotional management upon femininity rather than masculinity. Failures or strains in a relationship are more likely to be judged the fault of the woman than the man, and consequently the woman is more likely than her partner to feel guilt when their relationship is under pressure. Making disagreements fun and turning them into the stuff of public comedy takes them out of the guilt-producing realm of feminine responsibility, and thus can be both a liberating and a norm-subverting process. This letter writer enjoys learning what she and her husband may not always want to know about each other, and in her letter this pleasure is associated with that of seeing people make fools of themselves. Being foolish subverts the norms of good sense, and her comment implies that living normally involves a form of masquerade, but that occasionally the mask slips to reveal the "real" people underneath: this show provides many occasions when the "real" person is embarrassingly revealed under the mask of social normality. This occurs both on the screen and in front of it.

The writer was also embarrassed to admit that she watched the show. She knows that the show is socially judged to be of low status that its appeal is only to those of low taste. She knows, in other words, that she "ought" not to watch and enjoy it, but she does. She is embarrassed to refuse to conform to the social hierarchy of taste, but she finds pleasure in that refusal. The hierarchy of cultural tastes corresponds precisely with the hierarchy of social positions, so that the cultural forms that appeal to the tastes of those lowest in the social hierarchy are always denigrated and critically evaluated as "bad art." In a patriarchy women are lower in the hierarchy than men, so the cultural forms that appeal to them are judged to be aesthetically inferior to those that appeal to men. If we wish, for instance, to denigrate any chain of events, we call it a "soap opera" or a "romance," but to call something a "detective story" is to accord it at least a degree of dignity. The difference in the evaluation stems from the gender of the cultural tastes not from the aesthetic values of the genres. To give another example, the pop music that appeals to teenage or pre-teen girls, who are subordinated by both age and gender, is commonly considered the lowest musical form.

These three forms of embarrassment are popular among the women because they are sites of recognition that what they ought to do and like is not what it is in their interests to do and like. Recognizing and overcoming embarrassment, then, is one way in which women can change the meanings of femininity as they operate in their own relationships. I sense a growing experience of empowerment and self worth in the first five sentences of the second paragraph of the letter — from "probably," "trivial," "a little" (first sentence), through "in fact" (second sentence) and "I urge him" (third sentence) to "Actually, we do" in the fourth sentence to the culmination in the confident assertion of the fifth: "So, for that reason I enjoy the show." This discursive increase in self-confidence is the linguistic equivalent of her behavior in her marital relationship, and is typical of the way that popular culture operates in the micropolitics of everyday life.

These gendered micropolitics permeate the letter. Despite the fact that both she and her husband work outside the home, it is the wife who cooks dinner, but she times it so that watching her game show rewards her for performing her feminine duty, and if she can embarrass her husband at the same time her reward is even greater. In cooking dinner she subjects herself to patriarchal norms, in watching the *New Newlywed Game* she challenges them. That's her popular culture in process.

Popular culture, then, is not mass culture, though it is typically made from it. The relationship between the commercial interests of mass culture and popular interests is always antagonistic and unstable. The people constantly scan the repertoire produced by the cultural industries to find resources that they can use for their own cultural purposes. The industry similarly constantly scans the tastes and interests of the people to discover ones that it can commodify and turn to its own profit. The industry always tries to incorporate the culture of the people and the people always try to excorporate the products of the industry — the to and fro between incorporation and excorporation, or between appropriation and expropriation, is a constant feature of the relations between mass and popular culture, and the boundary between the two is always on the move, never fixed in analytical certainty. While popular culture is never mass culture, it is always closely bound up with it.

The same may be said of the relations between high culture and popular culture, for popular culture is also defined in part by its difference from the high brow. High culture is recognized better by its texts or artworks than by its processes, though the cultural processes performed by these texts are now much more central in literary studies than at times they have been. Many argue that in postmodernity the distinctions among high, mass, and popular culture are rapidly disappearing. I think that this is overstating the case, though there is evidence that the boundaries are blurring and becoming more permeable. But some differences remain. While individual texts may move more rapidly and freely around the cultural geography, the ways in which they are evaluated and used still differ significantly, and still perform the function of distinguishing between high and popular culture.

Many of these differences are clustered around the status and use of the text. In popular culture the text is a cultural resource to be plundered or used in ways that are determined by the social interests of the reader/user not by the structure of the text itself, nor by the intentions (however we may discern them) of its author. Indeed, the text typically originates from a social position that differs markedly from that of its popular readers/users. To the extent that its conditions of origin are inscribed more or less explicitly within its structure, the text works in ways that can oppose the interests of its readers — the relations between reader and text contain strong elements of antagonism. In this light the text may be compared to the terrain of a landowner and the reader to a poacher: so the women who enjoyed the *New Newlywed Game* poached meanings that promoted their interests while avoiding capture by an ideological gamekeeper who controlled the overall structure of the text itself. The reading relations of high culture are not typically seen as antagonistic.

Analyzing texts that have been made popular involves, then, searching for their contradictions, their rough edges that have not been authorially smoothed out into organic coherence, for these abrasive bits that open a text up to popular uses, and enable it to be seen not as a complete and unified whole, but as a terrain upon which people can engage in the struggle for meanings. In popular culture the text is not an object of reverence to be understood in all its coherence and completeness, but a resource to be used. Indeed, the text that is made into popular culture is always incomplete until it is used, it remains at the level of cultural potential until it is selectively taken up and inserted into the social circulation of meanings. In popular culture, the film *Rambo* is a text that is not completed until it is taken up and used by socially situated readers. Australian Aboriginals used it one way, and Ronald Reagan, who claimed it was one of his favorite movies because it demonstrated the effectiveness of the free, self-motivated individual, in quite another. For some readers the character of Rambo embodied third world resilience, for others Reaganist yuppiedom.

The meanings that are made at the point of intersection of the text and the social position of the reader cannot then be determined by, nor even analytically predicted from, the structure of the text alone. At least an equal participant in the negotiation of meaning is the relevance of the text to the reader, and relevance is produced by the social interests of the reader not by the text or its author. In studying popular culture the textual analyst, then, has to identify the different lines of force in a text and to trace how those which promote the interests of the socially dominant may be contradicted by others. The textual analyst must also be a social analyst, for he or she must be able to speculate in a disciplined manner how different elements in the text may be taken up by differently situated readers. This is the analysis of potential rather than of a completed art object.

Selecting some of the potential meanings of the text entails rejecting others, and there is often as much for the critic to analyze in what is not used in a text as in what is. Absence and rejection can signify as importantly as presence and selection. In my collection of cultural uses of the *New Newlywed Game,* for example, racial meanings were significantly absent, though the text offered their potential. Two of the couples playing the game were white, one was Latino/a, and one African American. The women of color were the noncompliant wives, the white women the compliant ones. Each of the responses in the menu offered by the emcee encoded racial relations in its words of address — "man," "master," and "Jose" are words whose history of use by whites in relation to nonwhites cannot be entirely erased. Yet very few of my students and none of the respondents to my advertisement activated this potential set of meanings. And the few who did were almost always students of color. The show usually has at least one nonwhite couple (but never a mixed race one), though race relations are not always as clearly encoded into its questions and answers as in my chosen example. Not activating racial meanings is, then, a signifying rejection that produces a significant absence. And in this case the absence appeared to be a sign of whiteness. One explanation may be that racial identity is not a problem for whites in our society but can be taken for granted. If this is the case, then the racial dimension of their social identities and social relations would not be relevant to them in the way that the dimension of gender clearly was. This is not the case for people of color whose everyday experience in a white-dominated society is permeated with their racial identities. Ignoring race is a white privilege.

The analysis of which potential meanings of a text are activated and which rejected and of the social position in which this activation/rejection process occurs may be more speculative than the formalist analysis of the text in and of itself, but it is richer because the object of analysis extends beyond the text to its conditions of use. It is also more engaging in the classroom, because the students' ways of reading the text are just as valid as those of the critic or professor; indeed, they are necessary to the analytical process for they provide material that can be studied to answer questions about how meanings are made. These "how" questions are particularly appropriate to a culture of process.

Traditional ways of studying high culture give high value to the concept of "distance." One dimension of this is the critical distance between text and reader which is claimed to be essential if the critic is to analyze the text objectively. To be objective, critical readers have to distance themselves from their specific social identities and become ideal, or universal readers. In the analysis of popular culture this approach works well in uncovering the ideological norms embedded in the text, and in identifying its unrealized potentials, but it needs complementing by "insider" readings that are not distanced, but that trace the intimacy between a reading and the social conditions in which it is performed. I chose to take an episode of the *New Newlywed Game* into my classes, for example, because at the time the show was part of my popular culture. My first marriage had not long ended and I was in the early stages of the relationship that eventually became my second. The gender relationships of my first marriage were more "traditional" than those of my second, and I was thus, when well into middle age, involved in renegotiating my gender identity. It struck me that these conditions must have accounted for some, at least, of the pleasure I derived from watching the show. Now, happily married, I no longer experience the same need to renegotiate my gender identity, so the show is no longer a useful cultural resource and I rarely watch it. This nonobjective, "insider" reading is, I believe, significant because it provides an instance of culture in process, an instance that is not unique or eccentric, but that is culturally typical and thus a valid part of the object of cultural analysis. Such instances of culture in process are often brought into the classroom by students from their own popular culture. They provide educationally rich material not only because they break some of the barriers between the academy and everyday life, but also because they can open up the relations between teacher and students — they can absolve the professor-critic from the responsibility of holding the key to the true meaning of the text and of being the arbiter of its readings. They can help make the classroom into a place of collaboration rather than of dictation.

Another dimension of distance is that between a text and its conditions of production and reception. High culture texts are valued for their ability to transcend their immediate and therefore limiting social conditions. They are thus moved toward the universal and their values are claimed to be those of humanity rather than those of historically and socially situated human beings. Aesthetics is one way of theorizing and identifying these supposedly universal human values. Because these values transcend social conditions they are unchanging and can thus serve as a benchmark by which to measure the success of any one text in embodying them. The critical practice associated with them is that of valuing and ranking texts in which they can be found and of rejecting those where they cannot. By extension, then, the readings of a text, particularly those produced by students, can be ranked according to their approximation to the ideal reading. The popularity of a text, however, consists only in its relations with its immediate social and historical conditions: popular texts cannot be transcendent. Neither the texts nor their readings can be evaluated against universal values and are thus not subject to hierarchization. Those who denigrate popular culture because its texts "do not last" fail to understand that it is the transcience of the text which often links it so closely to its social conditions and that its transcience is often most active in ensuring its popularity. Popular culture is the culture of the here and now, not of the always and forever. Popular texts, therefore, are evaluated according to their social values, not their universal or aesthetic ones. If there are universal human values they enter popular culture only in forms that are peculiar to those immediate social conditions from which popular culture cannot be distanced. The critical evaluation of the *New Newlywed Game,* for instance, involves the social values that are promoted by the ways it is used: a value that we might like to consider universal, such as equality between human beings, comes into play only in the specific conditions in which it is denied and fought for. (Incidentally, both history and anthropology might lead us to question just how universal a value equality actually is.) Critically evaluating the *New Newlywed Game* involves evaluating the women and the men who use it progressively or reactionarily, and the socio-political values activated in that use. It can also, quite legitimately, involve criticizing its critics: members of the contemporary religious right, for example, might criticize the show for its bad effect upon women, its mockery of men and its undermining of so-called "family values." Such opposition to the show would quite properly form part of the object of cultural analysis, and its critical evaluation would extend to judging the so-called "traditional family values" against the values of the women who made it part of their popular culture.

Popular critical analysis and evaluation must recognize that a text cannot be distanced from its uses and users. Texts that once have been made into popular culture are occasionally treated as high culture and hung in galleries or exhibited at film festivals: these exhibitions distance the text from its conditions of popularity and move it toward the transcendent and the universal. The movement *toward* the transcendent is *away from* the people, who do not, in general, seek their culture in art galleries, film festivals, and similar sites that are set apart from the mundanity of the everyday; for them, the mundane is the crucial site of cultural significance, for the mundane is the only terrain upon which popular culture can be made and can be made to matter. Culture is ordinary, and the ordinary is highly significant.

SUGGESTED READINGS

de Certeau, Michel. 1984. *The Practice of Everyday Life.*
Dyson, Michael Eric. 1993. *Reflecting Black.*
Fiske, John. 1989. *Understanding Popular Culture.*
———. 1993. *Power Plays Power Works.*
———. 1994. *Media Matters.*
Grossberg, Lawrence. 1992. *We Gotta Get Out of This Place.*
Radway, Janice. 1984. *Reading the Romance.*
Storey, John. 1993. *An Introductory Guide to Cultural Theory and Popular Culture.*
Turner, Graeme. 1990. *British Cultural Studies: An Introduction.*
Williamson, Judith. 1986. *Consuming Passions.*

24

Diversity

Louis Menand

"**D**IVERSITY**"** is a term with no essential philosophical, political, or aesthetic content. It simply names a fact, which is that people who write works of literature are different from one another, and so are people who read works of literature. The population of writers is composed of individuals, each with a particular history and a particular identity, and the population of readers is similarly heterogeneous.

No one disputes this. What people dispute is the extent to which it matters to criticism. The burden on the people who think that it doesn't matter, or that it matters in only marginally interesting ways, is to explain how so blatant a fact can possibly be irrelevant to the interpretation, description, and evaluation of literature. This burden has been met by a series of elegant and powerful arguments. The burden on the people who think it does matter is to explain how so mundane a fact can be central to the analysis of an aesthetic form. This burden has not been met so successfully.

Since the demise of the Cold War, toward the end of the 1980s, "diversity" has become a slogan in a movement known as "multiculturalism," and in this context, the term has acquired a content: it is taken to name a good in itself. For multiculturalists, diversity is a condition to be recognized, encouraged, celebrated. Criticism that ignores diversity, or that regards literature as something which, by its nature, "overcomes" diversity, is suspect.

There is nothing about the mere fact of diversity that requires this view. People are different. So what? Grains of sand are different, too. That doesn't mean there's no such thing as a beach. But proponents of "diversity" believe that to say that the differences among writers and readers of literature are less important than the similarities is tantamount to suppressing the differences. They think that beach-talk is basically a way of keeping the sand in its place. Critics of multiculturalism don't disagree; they just think that belonging to a beach is better for the sand.

It's important to understand two things about this state of affairs. The first is that multiculturalism is only one of the ways in which the fact of diversity can be represented and accounted for in literary studies. Multiculturalism is a particular set of views arising at a particular time. There have been other responses to "the problem of diversity," with social and political implications different from those of multiculturalism. The second is that the belief that diversity is *not* a central category in the interpretation, description, and evaluation of literature is itself one of those responses. The conception of literature multiculturalism challenges did not develop (although you wouldn't always know it from reading some of its champions) in a historical vacuum. It was quite self-consciously an attempt to define the status of literature under conditions of diversity and change; and as Western societies have diversified and changed, it has been continually reargued, reformulated, and relegitimated. Multiculturalism is not an assault on a monolith.

Diversity is one of the problems of modernity. *"Was die Mode streng geteilt,"* Schiller says in the "Ode to Joy," naming what it is that only joy can bring together: "all that custom has divided." But the problem is a razor with two blades. Since the eighteenth century, people have complained that modern societies are acid to cohesion and continuity: market economies, the division of labor, democratic governance, religious dissent, and the whole progressive "disenchantment of the world" (a phrase Max Weber attributed to Schiller) have been accused of thriving on the dissolution of traditional bonds. But it has also been complained, for nearly as long, that modern societies bureaucratize the routines of daily existence, that they pasteurize and homogenize difference and dissent, that they colonize alien forms of life, and that they are generally relentless in the business of converting people everywhere to what are presented as "universal" behavioral and intellectual norms. On the first view, diversity atomizes. On the second view, unity asphyxiates. The first blade pulls them out, and the second blade cuts them off.

Not everyone who has written about literature since the eighteenth century has imagined that this situation (whichever way it is described) is one in which literature ought to play, or even could play, a meliorating role. T. S. Eliot, for example, although he has a reputation for being a champion of high literary culture, thought that the belief that literature can minister to the sickness of modern society not only was mistaken but was itself good evidence of just how sick modern society is. He saw no promise in regarding literature as something more than "a means of refined and intellectual pleasure"—a view not notably different, at bottom, from the view of Jeremy Bentham, who was one of the original theorists of the secular society Eliot despised, and who does not have a reputation for being a champion of high literary anything: "Poetry," said Bentham, "is as good as push-pin."

Eliot's sincere admirer I. A. Richards held another view. Richards regarded the modern condition as afflicted in both of the classic senses. He thought modern societies were responsible for a general dispersion of values and beliefs (too much mere diversity), and he thought they were responsible for a shallow and programmed reflexiveness in people's responses to life (too much mere conformity). To this extent, he and Eliot were essentially in agreement. But Richards believed, as Eliot did not, that literature could be enlisted in the battle against both tendencies: reading poetry was, he argued, "a perfectly possible means of overcoming chaos," and it was also "a powerful weapon for breaking up unreal ideas and responses." Richards endorsed a hope Matthew Arnold had expressed fifty years before — that "what now passes for religion and philosophy will be replaced by poetry" — and he was echoing Arnold when he insisted that poetry "is capable of saving us." ("It is like saying that the wallpaper will save us when the walls have crumbled down," was Eliot's comment.)

The dispute between Eliot and Richards took place in England in the 1920s and 1930s. Its context includes one of the first university programs in which literature was taught and studied critically, the Cambridge School of English, which Richards had helped to establish and which he once invited Eliot to join. (Eliot told him he preferred working in a bank.) And it includes Eliot's own poetry, which he had taken elaborate care to define in terms that would distinguish it from the sort of diffusely didactic poetry he associated with nineteenth-century liberalism, and with the views of Matthew Arnold in particular. Universal secular education is one of the principal legacies of nineteenth-century liberalism; it was for universal secular education that Richards hoped to secure the services of poetry. In the end, Richards's hopes prevailed; literature assumed a significant role in education; and Eliot, thanks to his success in defining literature as something whose value does not depend on its social utility or its "message," became a presiding authority in academic literary studies — and thus acquired a reputation for being a champion of high literary culture.

The story is likely to seem a little remote from the debate about multiculturalism in the 1990s. It *should* seem a little remote; for the question of the relation of literature to social goods is something that is always being reargued in the light of fresh circumstances. But arguments have institutional consequences which survive the circumstances that gave rise to them, and in which ideas that were once contested become transformed into assumptions everyone takes for granted.

The institution Eliot, Richards, and their contemporaries helped to bring into being was the modern English department, a place where it is taken for granted that literature is something that can usefully be taught, and that literary criticism is something that can usefully be practiced, in an academic setting. The English department is not part of the history department or the philosophy department or the department of social work because Eliot and Richards (and many other writers) persuaded people inclined to doubt it that literature is a field of instruction and inquiry that has its own integrity, its own boundaries, and its own intellectual value. They found a place within the university for something that was not the study of language, not the editing of texts, not the history of ideas, but the appreciation and analysis of what Eliot called "literature as literature." The case took a long time to make. The Modern Language Association, which is the professional association of language and literature specialists, was founded in 1883, but it did not add the word "criticism" to its constitutional statement of purpose until 1950.

The crucial element in the argument about literature Richards's and Eliot's academic interpreters advanced is universality. If reading literature is a good in itself, then it must entail an intellectual process that can be experienced in roughly the same way, or to roughly the same effect, by everyone. This does not mean that everyone should understand individual poems in the same way, but that everyone should understand *poetry* in the same way.

Richards didn't want students to come away from literature classes with firmer political or moral beliefs. He (like Eliot) was writing in a period, between the wars, of multiple competing orthodoxies, none particularly partial to the life of the mind, and the last thing he wished was to claim literature for the service of one of them. Richards wanted students to have an intellectual experience that transcended beliefs, that put beliefs in perspective. And this was an experience he thought poetry could provide. Understanding poetry, in Richards's view, was (to put it a little crudely) a kind of mental calisthenics: everyone with a body can profit from doing jumping jacks, and everyone with a mind can profit from reading poems.

This is one argument. There have been many others since the study of literature was established as something that properly goes on in universities. But the point of them all has been to define the literary experience generally enough and abstractly enough for it to be accessible and beneficial to any student who might choose to sign up for it. You can study literature historically without making this abstraction; you can study it philologically. But you cannot teach "literature as literature" without believing that there exists some experience essential to literature from which everyone can learn and in which everyone can participate.

In 1939, the ideological situation changed, and assumed a shape in which it would remain virtually frozen for fifty years. The spectrum of belief came to seem starkly bipolar: at one end was the open society; at the other was the totalitarian state. By 1945, with the defeat of the fascist powers and the opening of the nuclear age, the two alternatives had become identified with two nations, the United States and the Soviet Union; and in the Cold War that followed, the ideological difference was repeatedly figured as Manichean: American democracy tended to define itself in strict point-by-point contrast to Soviet communism.

That the Cold War led to the suppression and demonizing of difference and dissent in American life is a thesis that has been argued many times. But the

Cold War is also responsible, to a considerable degree, for the liberalization of American life since 1945. For if the existence of the communist threat could be used (as it certainly was used) as a standing argument for requiring people to conform to the mores of "the American way of life," it could also serve as a standing argument for taking the principles of freedom and equality seriously. If the recognition of individual liberties was what distinguished the United States from totalitarian societies, then individual liberties ought to be recognized as fully as possible — to the very letter of the Constitutional promise. Alarm over the communist juggernaut chilled criticism of American society from the left, but it also chilled criticism from the right.

By 1939, I. A. Richards had settled at Harvard, where he would remain for the rest of his career. The president of Harvard when Richards arrived there was James B. Conant, who had been appointed in 1933. Conant was, in many respects, a classic Cold Warrior. He had been trained as a scientist, and served as the chief civilian administrator of American nuclear research during World War II, which made him a principal figure in the decision to drop the bomb on Hiroshima and Nagasaki. In the early 1950s, he founded the Committee on the Present Danger, a group of prominent citizens dedicated to keeping the American public alert to the imminence of the communist threat; and he argued publicly that (although membership in the Communist Party was not illegal) Communists should not be allowed in the teaching profession. When he left Harvard, in 1953, it was to become Eisenhower's high commissioner, later ambassador, to Germany.

But Conant was also a great educational modernizer. He imposed a strict tenure system at Harvard, which required that professors be hired solely on the basis of national professional reputation and scholarly merit. He campaigned successfully for the use of standardized tests in the undergraduate and graduate admissions process, which led to the formation, in 1946, of the Educational Testing Service, headed by a former Harvard dean. And he established a scholarship program for students outside Harvard's traditional geographic and socioeconomic areas of recruitment.

Conant was, in short, one of the creators of the American meritocracy. He opposed any sort of class system in which wealth and position could be handed on unearned from one generation to the next, and he conceived of education as the mechanism by which talented people in a democratic society would be selected and raised to the positions their abilities entitled them to. The system he helped to build is the one we have today: students are admitted to college on the basis of aptitude (measured by, among other things, College Board scores), where they are instructed in a freely elected academic specialty by experts who have been hired on the basis of professional merit (something that is also "standardized," since it is measured against the national average in the discipline). Students who are successful in this arena take another series of standardized tests for admission to graduate or professional school, where they are ranked and certified all over again.

The reward for the individual is a career it is impossible to buy or to be born into: even the daughter of the president of the American Bar Association has to take the LSAT if she wants to become a lawyer. The reward for society is the enhancement in productivity that comes from matching talents more accurately with careers: if the daughter of the president of the ABA can't cut it in law school, she is required to make way for someone who can, and society is spared the expense of an incompetent practitioner.

Conant's educational philosophy and his political philosophy were a joint enterprise. He believed that a society stratified by class is a society in which communism can take root. The best domestic defense against communism, he thought, is social mobility, and the best way to insure social mobility is to make education the only key to economic success, and to give everyone equal access to it. Conant saw the Second World War as an opportunity to realize this vision, since mass conscription had already created social disruption on a national scale. When the 11 million Americans in military service came home, he argued, they could be placed on the career ladders appropriate to each, and a meritocracy would be achieved overnight. (In the end, the GI Bill allowed millions of people to attend college who otherwise could not have, and essentially created the postwar American middle class.)

There is a difficulty. When the talented tenth goes off to law school, it leaves behind the nine other tenths, who become office managers and civil servants and cab drivers. The cab drivers are, in theory, just as "selected" for the jobs they end up in as the lawyers are; but they are not as likely to take consolation in the thought, and a gap opens up into which resentment can seep. This divergence in life paths is inevitable (*someone* has to drive the lawyers to their meetings), and it raises what is known as the problem of "general education." In a system designed to separate students by tracking them into the specializations appropriate to their talents, which is how education funnels the right people into the right slots, there has to be some common core of learning appropriate to all, or class antagonisms will simply get reproduced in every generation. Shortly after the attack on Pearl Harbor, Conant appointed a committee of twelve professors to examine this problem, and after several years of cogitation they produced a volume called *General Education in a Free Society* (1945), sometimes referred to as the Red Book. Richards was one of the twelve professors, and the report's attempt at a "theory of general education" bears the impress of his thought pretty clearly.

The Harvard authors identify two dangers to social stability which they believe education must address. The first is the familiar corrosive of modernity itself. The more urban and secular — the more "modern" — a society becomes, they argue, the weaker the influence enjoyed by the traditional sources of acculturation. Nature, church, the community, and the family all diminish in formative moral power. Social life becomes impersonal, atomized; mental life withers under the onslaught of commercial culture, which acquires increasing, though increasingly inchoate, moral influence. "One need be no soft paternalist," the professors note, "to believe that never in the history of the world have vulgarity and debilitation beat so insistently on the mind as they now do from screen, radio, and newsstand."

The second matter of concern is what the report refers to as the "Problems of Diversity." Americans like to imagine themselves as a people yoked to a common destiny, but the American way of life depends on a pronounced diversification of career paths. By organizing knowledge according to specialization, and by placing students on vocational tracks according to their aptitudes, education serves the second of these conditions, but it undermines the first. If (as the authors think it must) education becomes the principal mechanism of acculturation in American life, it needs to balance specialized education (for careers) with general education (for citizenship).

This somewhat bird's-eye sociological analysis is the prolegomenon to a curricular recommendation which a certain parochialism seems to have led the Harvard team to regard as more novel than it actually was. What the report proposes is the "great books" solution: nonspecialized courses (courses not designed to be taught within the domain of any particular discipline) which use a common set of texts and which all students follow throughout their educational careers (though the authors think that the brighter students might have their own sections). These courses, the report suggests, would fall into three general areas: the humanities, social sciences, and natural sciences. The humanities requirement would be called "Great Texts of Literature."

"The root argument for using, wherever possible, great works in literature courses," the authors explain, "is briefly this: ours is at present a centrifugal culture in extreme need of unifying forces." Why do Americans need unifying? The answer is not only to prevent the irruption of group antagonisms, but because (as the report states) "open-mindedness without belief is apt to lead to the opposite extreme of fanaticism." People with no common core of beliefs are vulnerable to ideologues peddling, if nothing else, coherence. In the case of literature, this common culture is represented by the "great texts."

The Harvard report is not notable for its originality. Columbia had instituted its famous core requirements in literature ("Humanities") and political philosophy ("Contemporary Civilization") long before 1945 (and also in response to a "foreign threat": The requirements grew out of a course developed at the time of the First World War called "War Aims"). The University of Chicago, too, had already developed a general education curriculum, which was centered on philosophy. These programs go unnamed. But the Harvard report was, after all, the *Harvard* report, and it fixed a seal of approval on the theory of general education, and, as an element of that theory, on the idea that the study of certain literary works can provide what the committee refers to as "a binding experience."

Until very recently, then, the academic literary canon could be defined as the product of two institutional imperatives. Within the speciality of literary studies, the canon consisted of those works that repay investigation under the aegis of "literature as literature"—those works that exhibit (however it is defined) the essential abstract "literary" quality. And within the broader socializing mission of the university, the canon consisted of the books that can be regarded as cultural glue—the books that articulate the common assumptions of our way of life, and thereby speak to all future citizens.

In the first context, literature is not associated with a particular set of beliefs. In the second, it explicitly is: "As the transmitter of the canon," as one defender of the "great books" has recently put it, ". . . the humanities have traditionally instilled a sense of the value of the democratic traditions we have inherited." But in either context, literature, since it is installed within a meritocratic educational system, is understood to be formative for everyone. For the only differences meritocratic theory allows among students of literature (or any other subject) are differences of aptitude. You can say that English courses are for students with "high verbal aptitude" (whatever that may be); but you cannot say that English courses are for male students, or for students of Western European origin, or for Christian students, or for students with left-wing political views.

This system, and the views of literature embedded within it, dominated American higher education for almost fifty years. It is easy to see why it was so attractive. It is also easy to see why it would eventually be challenged, for it was clearly fated to become the victim of its own success. The greater the variety of people it accommodated—and accommodating the greatest possible variety of people was one of its chief social purposes—the greater the strain on the notions of "merit," "aptitude," and "greatness" that underwrite it.

The striking feature of the Harvard report is that despite its concern for "the problems of diversity," race, religion, ethnicity, and gender are never mentioned. The authors consider diversity exclusively as a socio-economic phenomenon, a consequence of the natural inequalities of aptitude, and therefore of attainment, among people in a mobile society. Diversity is never, to their way of thinking, a cultural problem. And for more than twenty years it did not become a cultural problem in higher education, because for more than twenty years the American university remained, demographically, extremely homogenous. When that homogeneity started to erode, with it the authority of the whole system began to erode.

In 1960, fifteen years after *General Education in a Free Society,* 94 percent of American college students were white; at private institutions, the figure was a little over 96 percent. Of the students making up the remaining 6 percent, one-third attended all-black or predominately black schools. Sixty-three percent of college students were men. Almost nine out of every ten doctoral degrees were awarded to men. Nearly 80 percent of college faculty were men. Many distinguished private colleges did not admit women, and there were several public universities — not to mention private institutions, including Duke — that did not admit African-Americans. In 1961, Charlayne Hunter (now Charlayne Hunter-Gault, the television newscaster) entered the University of Georgia after a federal judge had compelled the university to admit her; a week after she enrolled, state officials returned to the court to ask whether they were also compelled to allow her to eat in the campus dining hall.

Thirty-five years ago, in other words, a white man lecturing to a room filled with young white men was closer to the typical than to the anomalous classroom scene. The question that arises is obvious: Is it conceivable that, even assuming all the good will in the world, what was taught and how it was talked about did not reflect the interests and perspectives of the people who were not there? If you think that skin color, ethnic background, and gender make a difference to interest and perspective, then you think it is conceivable — and "diversity" has raised its head.

Since 1960, the demographics of American higher education have been transformed. Today, 55 percent of college students are women (against 37 percent in 1960), and over a third of doctoral degrees (in the humanities, nearly half) are awarded to women. Almost 20 percent of college students identify themselves as nonwhite or Hispanic. Most formerly single-sex institutions are coeducational, and, apart from traditionally all-black colleges and (a more ambiguous case) a few "historically black" campuses of state universities, virtually all colleges are integrated to some degree. Top-tier schools now actively recruit nonwhite students and faculty. Total enrollment in higher education has risen from a little over three and a half million in 1960 to more than 14 million in 1992. On many American campuses, white men are just one of several minorities.

This doesn't mean that every student body is equally integrated; but the skewing that exists makes very little difference to the curriculum, because curricula are designed by the disciplines, and the disciplines — thanks to the tenure system, which makes professional merit, rather than local service, the criterion for employment — are national. Students at state schools are taught by professors who, in training and outlook, are more or less interchangeable with professors in the same disciplines at Ivy League schools.

People calling themselves meritocrats have complained that the integration of American higher education has been achieved in violation of the spirit of meritocracy; but they're mistaken. This is precisely the way, in meritocratic theory, higher education is supposed to look: a faithful mirror of social diversity. For if students are admitted to college on the basis of aptitude rather than income, then every group should be represented proportionately, since there is no reason to assume that one group's average native intelligence is greater than another's.

But once these formerly excluded, or underrepresented, groups arrived on campus, it was inevitable that questions should arise about the "universality" of the curricula and the academic culture that had prospered happily for so long without them. "Multiculturalism" is one response to those questions. Blind to race and gender, and culturally tone deaf, meritocracy is the egg from which multiculturalism has been hatched.

In its current usage, "multiculturalism" has been around only since the mid-1980s. But following the demise of Soviet hegemony, in 1989, the term caught on quickly in the United States, and for two reasons. The first is that after 1989, the entire globe suddenly started looking strikingly multicultural — the ethnic and nationalist struggles that fissured Eastern Europe and the former Soviet Union almost immediately upon the eclipse of communism making a particularly vivid illustration. It became apparent that there are group passions Cold War consensus thinking considered it safe to ignore, but which have persisted nonetheless, and which seem to demand attention.

The second reason is that the external threat which served as a kind of background justification for the emphasis on consensus and national unity in the Cold War period has apparently vanished. And this has unshackled, in effect, both left-wing and right-wing social critics in the United States — the former to inveigh against efforts to make everyone conform to some single idea of what it means to be "an American," and the latter to inveigh against the danger to majority norms represented by the former. The failure of the Marxist state is the luckiest thing that ever happened to American radicalism.

Why should this make for a crisis? Because there is something else that had become heavily dependent on the Cold War dispensation, and that is the university itself. The university profited from an enormous investment of public funds after 1945 because Americans believed that the sort of pure knowledge universities were understood to produce and to purvey was essential to the business of surviving in a bipolar, nuclearized world. It's not irrelevant that Conant was once the leader of the atomic scientists, for the arms race was a key element in the public investment in universities — and the natural science disciplines, where the notion of culture-blind aptitude carries the greatest conviction, benefited disproportionately from that investment. It's like putting your biggest football players on the front line: you don't care who they are, so long as they're big. Science doesn't care who you are, so long as you're smart. Cutting-edge technology is precisely what meritocratic systems are designed to produce.

But if the knowledge universities produce and purvey is neither "pure" nor "universal," and if the meritocratic selection system is not "objective," but simply perpetuates racial and sexual inequalities, then the social status of higher education is in jeopardy. The problem can't be solved simply by moving diversity indoors, by splitting up learning according to group interest or cultural identity rather than according to aptitude; for there would then be no overriding social benefit to subsidizing universities. Higher education is supposed to make these differences irrelevant to achievement, not integral to it.

Multiculturalism proposes to replace the universalist conception of culture it associates with the Cold War university with a circumscribed number of categories. These are ordinarily enumerated as race, class, gender, and sexual orientation. What gives these categories (as opposed to, say, religion or age) bite is the assumption that they name cultural formations that can be defined in contrast to a "dominant" formation, which is usually characterized as patriarchal, heterosexual, and Eurocentric — or, in more strident versions, as racist, sexist, and homophobic.

You can take this train any distance you like. In its centrist version, multiculturalism simply means emphasizing the contributions every group has made to American culture, and insisting that each group's particular interests and perspectives be represented in every facet of the associated life — the military, the Supreme Court, the English department. In its more radical editions, multiculturalism embraces strong versions of "identity politics," which assumes the ultimate incommensurability of group values and interests, and "standpoint epistemology," which assumes that our beliefs and judgments can only be a function of who we are — of our "subject positions."

Radical multiculturalism is sometimes accused of "cultural relativism," which is the view that there is no basis for judging the values of other people's cultures. But radical multiculturalists are almost never relativists in this sense, since they encounter no difficulty in judging the values of Eurocentric culture, and since a large part of the point of multicultural criticism is the elucidation of the virtues of "deviant" or "alien" cultural values — of "otherness". What makes radical multiculturalism radical, and rouses the opposition of centrist multiculturalists, is the incommensurability thesis.

The concept of a common culture is a feature of most forms of pluralist social theory, dating back to the discussions between Horace M. Kallen (who invented the term "cultural pluralism"), John Dewey, Randolph Bourne, and Alain Locke in the early decades of this century. In a pluralist model, groups maintain their traditional folkways immune from the interference of other groups; but there is also a shared public space, where people engage with one another in the terms of a common culture. The notion of "civic culture" is one version of this idea; the educational program of "cultural literacy" recently promoted by E. D. Hirsch is another. The "great books" curriculum is a third.

Multiculturalism challenges these notions because it takes phrases like "the common culture" to be, essentially, beach-talk. "The common culture," in the multiculturalist view, just enshrines the norms of the dominant group, and thus functions as an enforcer of existing inequalities. This is why multiculturalist criti-

cism of canonical texts sometimes resembles a witch hunt: the demons of prejudice are being stripped of their "universalist" masks.

But how well does multiculturalism square the problem of diversity? If the
concept of a "common culture" suppresses differences, why doesn't the concept
of an "African-American culture," or a "gay culture," or a "women's culture" —
or, for that matter, a "Eurocentric culture"? In disposing of the big monolithic
abstraction "literature" — the notion that literature is something that transcends
the differences between people — multiculturalism seems to offer just a lot of
little monolithic abstractions instead. The logic of multiculturalism is that the
fact of diversity renders notions like "the common culture" meaningless; but the
logic is self-defeating, for the simple reason that diversity goes all the way down.
In the end, there are only grains of sand.

It has been observed, for example, that "class" is a category seldom used in
multicultural critical practice — even though for the authors of the Harvard
report on general education, in 1945, diversity *was* class difference, and even
though widening disparities among income groups constitute the most empirical evidence of increasing diversity in American life since the 1970s. There are
probably several reasons for the slighting of class, among them the vagueness of
class distinctions in the structure of American identity. But one reason is surely
that class cuts too strongly against two other multiculturalist categories, gender
and sexual orientation. To the extent that "class" is the determinant of identity,
an upper-middle-class woman must be assumed to have different interests and
perspectives from a woman living in poverty. To the extent, on the other hand,
that "gender" is the operative category in such a case, "class" loses its analytic
force. Once we open the door to "intercultural" definitions, though, we are lost.
Assume, at a minimum, four races, three social classes, two genders, and two
sexual orientations; then go down to the computer center and ask a mathemati-
cian to calculate the combinations.

The deeper difficulty is that diversity is a paradox: the more attention you pay
it, the more quickly it disappears. A society like the United States can be sliced
up into any number of "identity groups." Its government can decide to identify
certain of these groups as culturally distinct, to develop curricula around each
group, and to require schoolchildren to study these curricula and to respect the
differences among the groups. That would be a "multicultural" educational policy, and it is, in fact, the policy in some public school districts in the United
States. But what distinguishes "diversity," in such a society, from conformity?
Recognition of and respect for officially designated and defined subcultures has
simply become the enforced cultural norm.

This is a paradox with considerable application to American life since the end
of the Cold War. Many people have argued that American society is today rapidly
becoming more diverse, that it is experiencing a fragmentation unknown in the

past. "Since 1909 the Melting Pot has itself suffered a certain meltdown," as the editors of a volume called *The Faber Book of America* put it recently. "Assimilation has felt less and less distinguishable from a simulation." The assertion is unexamined. Statistically, the belief that the United States is becoming more racially and culturally diversified, more like a mosaic and less like a can of mixed paint, is unsupported. A much smaller percentage of the population is foreign-born than was the case earlier in the century: in 1930, 13.2 percent of Americans were born elsewhere; by 1980, the figure was down to 6.2 percent. The rate of interracial marriage has increased dramatically: there were one million in 1990, triple the number in 1970. Half of all marriages involving Asian-Americans are now interracial. A majority of Americans no longer define themselves by their ethnicity. Among descendants of the original European immigrant groups, only eleven percent live in neighborhoods with a significant concentration of people of similar ethnicity, only four percent believe they are discriminated against because of their ethnicity, and almost none are fluent in their group's original language. The Census Bureau projects that the country will maintain roughly its present racial proportions (about 80 percent of Americans identify themselves as "white") well into the next century. Ninety-three percent of the Americans who say they are religious are Christians — and (although "religion" is not a category in most multiculturalist criticism) 90 percent of Americans say they are religious.

What has happened in American life since the mid-1980s is a cultural phenomenon which is the consequence of group mixing, not group separation. In the commercial mass media (which is as plausible a "common culture" in the United States as anything), race, gender, and sexual orientation are the categories in which almost everything is defined and debated: Anita Hill and Clarence Thomas, Louis Farrakhan, the AIDS crisis, the Mapplethorpe controversy, the Los Angeles riots, Tawana Brawley, the Bobbitt trials, the Tyson trial, the William Kennedy Smith trial, the Simpson case. Polymorphous sexuality has been the dominant theme of American pop performance (Madonna); the most honored films have been about the oppression of minority groups (*Dances with Wolves, Schindler's List*); many of the most successful entertainers of the 1980s and 1990s were African-Americans (Michael Jackson, Michael Jordan, Magic Johnson, Eddie Murphy, Bill Cosby, Oprah Winfrey). Americans have been saturated with images of diversity.

But the consequence is that insofar as "multiculturalism" means *genuine* diversity — insofar as it refers to functionally autonomous subcultures within a dominant culture — the United States is becoming not more multicultural, but less. For when the whole culture is self-consciously "diverse" — when college campuses are self-consciously "diverse," when *television* is self-consciously "diverse" — real diversity has disappeared. Real diversity is what the United States used to have, when women and men, gays and straights, black and white Americans,

Christians and Jews, and the various ethnic communities of recent immigrant groups led, culturally, largely segregated lives. The notion that this means that the melting pot once really melted, and that it no longer does, is perverse. Assimilation does not come from suppressing difference (as people living in the former Yugoslavia can attest); it comes from mainstreaming it. Being "an American" now means wearing your particular "difference" on your sleeve. If you didn't, then you really *would* be different. A whole society cannot think "It's cool to be culturally diverse" and actually be culturally diverse at the same time.

This has been a schematic account of both multiculturalism and the view of literature multiculturalism is intended to displace. How literature actually gets talked and written about in the academy doesn't always correlate very precisely with the prescriptions of educational theorists and university presidents; and even where an educational philosophy is shared, it is not likely to be understood or applied in the same way in any two cases. These somewhat doctrinaire views of literature are important principally in the legitimation of institutional arrangements — the College Boards, the English major, the Modern Language Association, the research university. People whose work requires them to negotiate these arrangements daily can sometimes mistake engagement with institutional ideology for engagement with literature. They can assume that because a good deal of literature once got officially packaged as "the literary tradition" or "the common culture," and because a good deal of literature now gets officially packaged as "multicultural," these terms refer to something intrinsic to the works themselves, rather than to the face the institution is seeking to put on its enterprise.

What the modern academy has always thought it necessary to claim is that "culture" is something that can be organized and marshalled into the service of social and personal betterment. This presumption is at the core of both the multiculturalist and the "universalist" views. Culture formed you, they both suggest, and culture can reform you. The term is taken to name an entity whose lineaments are so discriminable, whose agency is so powerful, and whose effects are so diagnosable that we can write prescriptions for it. "These texts transmit our democratic heritage"; "these texts enhance this group's self-esteem"; "these texts deconstruct patriarchal discourse." Take two of each.

These views bank on a notion of culture that dates back to the eighteenth century — the notion that culture (high culture, or indigenous culture, or folk culture, depending on the theory) is the element of continuity and coherence in a social formation characterized precisely by its lack of respect for continuity and coherence. It is a wishful faith. Modern societies are socially mobile; but they are also, and equally, culturally mobile. Nietzsche thought the modern condition was one of "weightlessness," in which the ties to a moral and communal ground have all been cut away. Weber thought modern society was an iron cage, in which life goes on under a grid of bureaucratic rationality. The pictures are very different, but there is no place in either of them for an organic, uniform, and formative thing called "culture." Culture in modern life is like everything else in modern life: it's polymorphous, a Rubik's Cube of combinations, a kind of gene pool of possibilities. Social problems haven't been caused by the failure to teach everyone the correct combination. They have been caused by the failure to give everyone equal access to the Cube.

Ralph Ellison was born and raised in Oklahoma, a state which was segregated but had no history of black slavery. In 1933, he entered Tuskegee Institute, an all-black college in Alabama. Ellison had hoped to become a classical composer, and went to study music; but he was also introduced at Tuskegee to modern literature — to Gertrude Stein, Ernest Hemingway, Ezra Pound, T. S. Eliot. The most important of these writers for him was Eliot: he read *The Waste Land*, and then he went to the college library and read all the works cited in the notes to *The Waste Land*. Eliot's footnotes were Ellison's great books syllabus.

Tuskegee is the college whose founder, Booker T. Washington, and whose philosophy of subservience are pilloried so mercilessly in the opening chapters of *Invisible Man*. But Ellison's trope for the college, which gets figured as a mirage of fertility in a desert of futility, is quite clearly drawn from the poem Tuskegee introduced him to; and the influence is, in one place, played on quite explicitly, as a jazz performer might work a passage from a familiar tune into an improvisation. "I'm convinced it was the product of a subtle magic, the alchemy of moonlight," the unnamed narrator says of the college and its Northern white donors; "the school a flower-studded wasteland, the rocks sunken [Eliot: "Here is no water but only rock"; "Ganga had sunken"], the dry winds hidden ["And the dry grass singing"], the lost crickets chirping to the yellow butterflies ["And the dead tree gives no shelter, and the cricket no relief"]. And oh, oh, oh, those multimillionaires! ["But/O O O O that Shakespeherian rag—"]."

But *Invisible Man* is not designed in imitation of *The Waste Land*, or of any other work of modern literature. Its structural principle is the principle of two artistic forms associated with African Americans, jazz and the blues, in which effects are achieved not through a sequence of utterances, but through the repetition of a single utterance. There is no climax in the blues; there is only one more way of saying it. And each time it gets said, the whole piece is colored a deeper shade.

So that when Mr. Norton, one of the college's white donors, is driven by the ingenuous young narrator to the cottage of Trueblood, the black sharecropper who has managed to impregnate both his wife and his daughter, where he is made to listen to Trueblood's tale, and the narrator remarks, *a propos* of nothing in particular, "I stared at the two pairs of shoe before me. Mr. Norton's were white, trimmed with black," we are likely to feel that the point is possibly being pressed a little too firmly. Like the local whites, who come to Trueblood's aid, and unlike the African Americans at the college, who try to run Trueblood out of town, Mr. Norton requires an alien culture to define the limits of his own idea of civilization. The shoes are intended to offer a tiny lesson in diversity, which is that difference — that which is not us — is what makes identity possible. Do we need shoe symbolism to tell us this?

We do, because the relation of white to black is picked up again a few chapters later, in the section set in the Liberty Paint factory, where it has become the narrator's job to make white paint even whiter by mixing in ten drops of black. The paint is being prepared, we are told, for use on government buildings. Again, the allegory is obvious enough: the ten drops, of course, are the African-American 10 percent, now made, for white Americans, "just like us." But the point is complicated by, and it complicates in turn, the allegory of the shoes. For in the Trueblood episode, it is separation that creates the illusion; in the Liberty Paint section, it is integration.

It was Ellison's belief that American culture was thoroughly miscegenated, and that neither the insistence on difference nor the insistence on likeness did justice to the complexity of the phenomenon. It must have tickled him to see Eliot integrating Shakespeare and ragtime, and then to have tried his own hand at integrating Eliot and Booker T. Washington. But he didn't think these were unusual cultural conjunctions. He thought that whether or not America is, for an African American, socially mobile, it is, inescapably, and for everybody, culturally mobile.

In 1936, Ellison left Tuskegee and went to New York City (though not for the reasons the protagonist of *Invisible Man* does), where he met Richard Wright, who became his friend and one of his literary mentors. Wright had not yet published *Native Son,* which appeared in 1940. He had been born in Mississippi and raised in extreme poverty and under apartheid conditions. He eventually made it to Chicago, where he took a job in the post office — and, he later said, was thus able to go to sleep every night on a full stomach for the first time in his life. He began to read Stein, Eliot, and Hemingway; he also read two novelists whose influence on *Native Son* is obvious, Dreiser and Dostoevsky. He became active in literary circles, and wrote short stories, some of which were published in *Uncle Tom's Children,* and a novel, which remained unpublished until after his death. The novel's original title was *Cesspool.* It is the story of a black postal worker who is both a victim of bigotry and a bigot himself, a man who works at a job he despises, spends his time after work drinking and carousing, and beats his wife when he gets home.

The world of *Cesspool* represents Wright's conception of African-American culture: an endless cycle of demeaning drudgery and cheap thrills. He believed that white Americans had dehumanized black Americans (as Bigger Thomas has already been dehumanized when we meet him in *Native Son*), and had succeeded in stripping African Americans of a genuine culture. The only alternatives to the cesspool he knew were the fanatical religious belief and the suicidal resistance to

Jim Crow which he wrote about in his autobiography, *Black Boy,* and which he rejected in his own life. If it had not been for white writers, he says in the essay "How Bigger Was Born," he would not have been able to write his fiction: "for my race possessed no fictional works dealing with such problems, had no background in such sharp and critical testing of experience, no novels that went with a deep and fearless will down to the dark roots of life." It was his ambition to be thought of in the tradition of Poe, Hawthorne, and Henry James.

Culture in modern life is only a medium. It is the form through which my experience can be made available to you, and so become a part of your experience. And in the end, culture means something different for everyone, because everyone's experience is different. Some people are at home in the culture they encounter, as Ellison seems to have been. Some people borrow or adopt their culture, as Eliot did when he transformed himself from a Missouri Unitarian into a British Anglo-Catholic. A few people have to steal it. Wright was living in Memphis when his interest in writing began, and in order to get books to read, he asked a sympathetic white man to lend him his library card. He forged a note to present to the librarian, which read: "Dear Madam: Will you please let this nigger boy have some books by H. L. Mencken?" He had discovered a literary tradition from which the world had tried to exclude him, and he saw in that tradition a way to express his own sense of the world. Through persistence, he succeeded, and so made his experience a part of the experience of other people.

SUGGESTED READINGS

Bourne, Randolph. [1916] 1964. "Transnational America." In *War and the Intellectuals: Collected Essays 1915–1919.*

Brenkman, John. 1993. "Multiculturalism and Criticism." In *English Inside and Out: The Places of Literary Criticism,* edited by Susan Gubar and Jonathan Kamholtz.

Bromwich, David. 1992. *Politics by Other Means: Higher Education and Group Thinking.*

Buck, Paul H., et al. 1945. *General Education in a Free Society: Report of the Harvard Committee.*

Carnochan, W. B. 1993. *The Battleground of the Curriculum: Liberal Education and American Experience.*

Ellison, Ralph. 1952. *Invisible Man.*

———. 1964. *Shadow and Act.*

———. 1986. *Going to the Territory.*

Kallen, Horace M. 1924. *Culture and Democracy in the United States: Studies in the Group Psychology of the American Peoples.*

Locke, Alain. 1942. *When Peoples Meet: A Study in Race and Culture Contacts.*

Said, Edward W. 1991. "Identity, Authority, and Freedom: The Potentate and the Traveler." *Transition.*

Schlesinger, Arthur M., Jr. 1992. *The Disuniting of America: Reflections on a Multicultural Society.*

Sollors, Werner. 1986. *Beyond Ethnicity: Consent and Descent in American Culture.*

Taylor, Charles, et al. 1994. *Multiculturalism Examining the Politics of Recognition.* Expanded edition.

Todorov, Tzvetan. 1993. *On Human Diversity: Nationalism, Racism, and Exoticism in French Thought.*

Wright, Richard. 1991. *Works.*

25

Imperialism/Nationalism

Seamus Deane

THE MANY FORMS of imperialism have in common an expansionist economic system — capitalist or communist — that claims to have its roots in a universal human nature. They also boast of possessing a wondrous cultural system that is either the inevitable consequence of the triumph of that economic system or one of the preconditions of its emergence. As a system, imperialism is distinct from colonialism by virtue of its more coherent organizational form and its more fully articulated characterization of itself as a missionary project to the world at large. To disguise its essentially rapacious nature, colonialism has been represented in literary, historical, and political discourses as a species of adventure tale, dominated by an ethic of personal heroism that is embedded in a specific national-religious formation. Imperialism transmogrified economic rapacity into a consolidated crusade for civilization and development, with all its attendant bureaucracies, technologies, and controls (Arendt 1951, 185–221). In all its forms, it is immensely flexible in its internal structures, global in its homogenizing ambitions and range. It is also — with the exception in modern times of the Japanese and Ottoman Empires — a peculiarly Western form of domination, extending from the sixteenth century to the present day. Portuguese, Spanish, Dutch, Russian/Soviet, French, British, and American empires have succeeded or overlapped with one another in a series of military-ideological rivalries ever since the development of European science and technology made the prospect of world dominance an achievable reality.

Imperialism was and is successful for a wide variety of reasons. As Alfred W. Crosby has explained in *Ecological Imperialism* (1986), the migration of fifty million Europeans between 1820 and 1930 to the "neo-Europes" of the world — that is the temperate zones, north and south — led to the propagation and spread of what he calls "the portmanteau biota" (270), the collective name he gives to the Europeans and all the organisms they brought with them in their unprecedented exodus. Yet the European success was not exclusively biological or ecological. It was achieved over nature, but a nature inhabited by peoples whose defeat, expropriation, enslavement, or extermination had to be justified in a series of theoretical formulations that relied on categories paraded as fundamental and universal. Among these were the categories of history and of race. In the nineteenth century, the period in which European imperialism attained its fullest expansion, geographically and ideologically, a Hegelian philosophy of history was invoked to demonstrate that the task of completing human history had been passed on to the European nations. All others had fulfilled their historical destinies and now belonged to the past. Present and future were the temporal territories of white Europeans. This version of historical destiny was blended with later neo-Darwinian concepts of evolution in a mutually reinforcing alliance. History as a concept was enfolded with race; racial evolution and historical destiny were envisaged as ineluctable forces that marched together in the name of Progress toward the triumph of "civilization." Progress itself was identified with technological advance, which in turn produced modernization and development. Where these agencies were introduced, empire was performing its world-historical obligation to its destiny. Colonialism was the early, amateur form of imperialism. In its ramshackle, personal way it had inaugurated the rise of empire; but it was insufficiently global in its vision. By the late nineteenth century, most especially in the era of the "scramble for Africa" that succeeded the Berlin Conference of 1885, empire, or the New Imperialism as it came to be called, had assumed to itself the mantle of "responsibility" for the globe.

Joseph Conrad's novels have long been regarded as among the most memorable representations of the passage from colonialism to imperialism, especially because they register the co-ordination between this particular transition and the modernist experience of the dissolution of the individual self into a nullity, a condition of ghostliness. Despite or perhaps because of the Eurocentric bias of Conrad's fiction, works such as *Heart of Darkness* (1899), or *Lord Jim* (1900) question the assumption that the spectacle of a European individual imposing his will upon a whole non-European people could be represented as a moral triumph for him or for European civilization. Instead, the tragic distortions involved in such an enterprise make a nonsense of the ethical and cultural system that sanctioned such "heroism" as a form of duty. In novels such as *The Secret Agent* (1907), *Under Western Eyes* (1911), and *Nostromo* (1902), the political systems represented — British, Russian, American — are so systemic in their operation that the belief in the autonomous individual subject has to be surrendered. In effect, imperialism's success as an impersonal system reveals the illusory status of the bourgeois-humanist "subject" and, in so doing, manifests the historical nature both of that construct and of its own expansion. In Conrad, the revelation of the criminal nature of imperialism and the destruction of the idea of the self are intimately related experiences. The arrival of imperialism put an end to "the project of exoticism" (Bongie 1991, 270), the hope that the Romantic version of the individual self might find, in some remote part of the globe, an escape from the alienating conditions of modernity. Conrad's fiction, especially *No-*

stromo, had anticipated the weakening of the European rhetoric of destiny and world civilization and its exposure as a disguise for the realities of political and economic power. But it had also reproduced it. The emergence of a westernized Sulaco from the original country of Costaguana in that work is an emblematic instance of the new means by which self-determination would itself, as a political principle, become incorporated into a new imperialism. Conrad subverts *and* reproduces imperialism (Said 1993, xix). In a similar manner, so too does nationalism.

Conrad's work also creates and subverts one of the canonical oppositions of postcolonial and postmodernist discourse—that between Self and Other, between a cultural formation that is finely and intricately articulated and one that is inchoate and amorphous. The tragic form of this opposition in Conrad derives from the conviction that the definition of the self is produced in and through the appalling recognition of the Other's delinquent and savage formlessness. By now, that tragic dimension has been lost and has been replaced by a ludic pleasure in the capacity of discourse to shuttle between forms of determinacy and indeterminacy that are grounded in the nature of language and produced by it rather than in the experience of catastrophe. The catastrophe was, of course, experienced by those peoples—or, in the given terms of imperialism, by those races—subjected to violence and exploitation. It was, on that account, a mediated experience for Europe, at least until the Nazi extermination of Jews and others during the Second World War. In the light of that particular holocaust, Europe has undergone a series of crises about the possibility of representing such horror, the morality of attempting to do so, the complicity with it that any rendering of apocalypse as discourse might involve. There has been no comparable anxiety about the representation of imperialism's crimes. Instead, the West has discovered in postcoloniality a form of discourse that is irrepressibly given to misrepresentation of the Other. Such misrepresentation has been accorded an ontological status. The claim that representation is always misrepresentation can lead to a depoliticized celebration of heterogeneity that ignores or subdues the cultural power and political purposes of racial stereotypes, caricatures, and other, subtler, rhetorical strategies.

But this view can be contested by the reminder that postmodern theory does not merely celebrate plurality but also disturbs and disperses the sediments of prejudice and assumptions that operate in texts. Culture, when it is propagated as a canonical system, always asserts its "monogenealogy," repressing its internal differences and hybrid origins, proclaiming itself xenophobically, ethnocentrically, in clamant and mystificatory ways as unitary. Part of the postmodern/deconstructionist project is to expose these repressions and disestablish the standard texts as sites on which such assertions, ideologically closed within an established system of representation, can be made. Is deconstruction, then, the historical companion of decolonization? Even if language is thought of as identical with power, or thought of as the effect of power, is any space left for the production of representations of and by those who do not wield it? To make a fetish of difference, of otherness, may be an emancipatory gesture in itself. But equally, the determination of what is "difference" or "otherness" might itself be a ruse of power. An established structure of representation cannot produce an alternative to itself, no matter how severely it is put under question. The alternative is already established within and by those structures. So postmodern and deconstruction theories, although they do take their historical bearings from the process of decolonization, may be no more than contemporary forms of a western liberalism that can pride itself on its openness but cannot escape from being western. Even in their most radical formulations, they still see the world under western eyes.

Nevertheless, even if it is granted that the West has imperially constructed the world in its own image, that image itself is, obviously, a construction. One way of recognizing the power of imperialism is by acknowledging how effectively it naturalizes its own history, how it claims precedence for its own culture by identifying that culture with nature. But, then, this also reveals something about representation itself, namely that it is a process in which the relationship between a representation and that which is represented inevitably involves what Adorno and Horkheimer called the "organized control of mimesis" (Adorno and Horkheimer [1944] 1972, 180). Repression, both in the political and psychological sense, is central to it. That which is foreign to an established structure of representation, its other, is demonized and thereby laid open to extinction. As in anti-Semitism, the Jews are "declared guilty of something which they . . . were the first to overcome: the lure of base instincts, reversion to animality and to the ground, the service of images. Because they invented the concept of kosher meat, they are persecuted as swine" (186). Such an analysis led to an outright attack on the European Enlightenment as such, with its faith in reason and its central practice of abstraction. "The distance between subject and object, a presupposition of abstraction, is grounded in the distance from the thing itself which the master achieved through the mastered" (13). Further, the abstraction of reason led to the liquidation of the sensory, sensuous world of the primitive (or natural); this too fed into imperial theory since the occupants of colonized territories were taken to be immersed in such a world and therefore incapable of, or at least insufficiently evolved toward, the rational condition of the European. This division between the rational and other nonrational categories (myth, magic, superstition, rituals involving the body, animality, and such) has undergone many inversions, with the consequence that the totalitarian impulse in Enlightenment rationality and the totalitarianism of Fascist Germany have been read as disastrous attempts to repress those mimetic forms that so-called primitive societies have continued to nourish. In the imperial-colonial encounter between Europe and non-Europe, the role of the repressed primitive in modernism was illuminated and the possibility of the West escaping from its own imposed systems of rational domination became possible. The world of the other would reeducate the West into a reimmersion in the concrete, the specific, the heterogeneous and thus emancipate it from the practices of abstraction that had made it destructive both of itself and of the world (Jameson 1981, 227–30; Taussig 1993, 254–55).

This attack from the left on western rationality and its degeneration into the "culture industry" (Adorno and Horkheimer, 121) and pervasive commodification is, of course, an extension of the Marxist critique of capitalism. But it was preceded, in the era of High Modernism (c. 1880–1930) by an even more influential right-wing critique, most memorably embodied in the English speaking world in the work of poets like T. S. Eliot, Ezra Pound, and W. B. Yeats and in the novels of D. H. Lawrence, Wyndham Lewis, Ford Madox Ford, and many others. In effect, this critique was founded on the belief that the experience of the individual subject in the modern world was one of fragmentation and anxiety; that such an experience had itself been produced by a loss of the coherent unity of the civilized world and its canonical achievements (most of them in literature) along with its replacement by a culture of excess, of kaleidoscopic variety offered to an undiscriminating and uneducated, even ineducable, public. In a strange sense, it was the sensory overload of such a culture that indicated its barbaric state. In other words, rather than suffering from abstraction only, the modern world also suffered from abstraction's "other"—immersion in the inchoate and the sensory. London is the capital of the imperial crisis. It is the metropolitan world, surfeited with the spoils of success and excess, from which an escape into an authentically national tradition must be made. This project has a particular resonance in the Irish poet Yeats because it consorts so happily with his program of cultural nationalism for Ireland. But the whole modernist project depends upon a tensed relationship between the metropolitan and the national, between the universal and the local, between heterogeneity and specific national (and personal) identity. In trying to rescue the stability of the individual self from modernist dispersals, it attempts to relocate that version of the self in a rearticulated version of the cultural and the national. The three poets I have mentioned here are all well known for the forbidding range of arcane and esoteric reference which they deploy in their work. The whole world culture is ransacked by them for representative images that are deliberately displaced and relocated in the foreign environment of modernity. This procedure is akin to that of the great American collectors of the nineteenth and early twentieth centuries who scoured the world—particularly the European world—in a mania for "culture" and its artifacts and who then relocated those artifacts in collections that eventually became the core of America's great museums. The museum and its commercial cousin, the supermarket, are two of the most characteristic institutions of postmodernism; but they were initially two of the most characteristic images and emblems of modernism. Access to the products of the whole world, incapacity to absorb these effectively into a canonical version of the specific tradition of the "West," the rewriting of excess as fragmentation—these are the ills of modernism and part of the inheritance of imperialism for culture.

Nevertheless, strategies of Western representation have been and continue to be awesomely effective in affirming the propriety and order of the West in contrast to the chaos and disorder of all that is non-Western. Imperialism deploys a number of specific binary distinctions to effect a coherence between what it takes to be natural and what it takes to be cultural (Said 1978, 227). Darwinism and humanism, the processes of natural selection and survival and the operation of western, enlightened humanist ideals are so conjoined that imperialism is regarded as the agency that effects a suture between them. One of the paradoxes of this enterprise is that the various imperial powers have promoted the idea of a universal civilization that has the power and duty to overcome barbarity, backwardness, and savagery in highly specific national terms. Thus the British Empire produces a complicated discourse of chivalric, gentlemanly behavior towards inferior races as an extension of and substitute for its christianizing mission throughout the world; the French Empire relies more on the discourse of "culture," the reactivation of the French Revolutionary mission to humankind as a conferral of the benefits of French culture to peoples otherwise not inferior; the American empire combines the discourses of moral and material improvement. In all cases, a version of national identity and destiny is translated into a civilizing mission for humanity at large (Spurr 1993, 109–24). These rhetorics are not merely rationales for domination, they are narcissistic repetitions, part of what Derrida calls the "fundamental culpability" (1976, 165–66) of writing through which the subject subordinates the world by idealizing itself. Specific instances of such narcissism and idealization are readily visible in travel writing, most especially in those European visions of tracts of territory that seem to desire to be made over in the image of the traveler's homeland. Such "promontory views" of the foreign landscape are endemic in the writings of the nineteenth-century explorers of "Darkest Africa" (Pratt 1992, 201–27).

The sense of a common European destiny that shaped and rationalized the continent's various imperial enterprises and ambitions (including Belgian, Dutch, German, and Italian as well as the British and the French) was disrupted by the First World War. Nevertheless, by 1918, the French and British Empires were stronger than ever in the Middle East; the old Austro-Hungarian, the Russian, and the Ottoman empires were at the point of collapse. In the Arab world, Turkey emerged as the most remarkable example of the modernized and secular nation-state, gravitating toward Europe and away from its imperial and Arab past (Hourani 1991, 318–19). This was one of the earliest examples of twentieth-century colonial nationalism, defining itself as the alternative to an earlier imperialism, although the Turkish example was a complex one since it had itself been both an imperial and a subject nation. Nevertheless, some of the constituent ingredients of the afterimage of imperialism were present in Turkey — the drive toward a European-style modernization, secularity, a form of national solidarity based on ethnic identity, a controlling bourgeois westernized elite and a repudiation of much that was held to be "traditional" in favor of "modernity." A later and more famous example, the achievement of Algerian independence from France in 1962 after eight years of war, has become exemplary because of the historically important debates it generated and the reputations of those involved in them, particularly Frantz Fanon (1966; 1967), Albert Camus (1958), and Pierre Bourdieu (1958; 1963). Fanon called for decolonization through violent revolution as the only way to effect a psychic transformation in peoples traumatized by imperialism. Camus argued, in his *Chroniques Algériennes* (1958) for a liberal and democratic Algérie française. Bourdieu concentrated on "the breakdown of social structures caused by the colonial situation and the influx of European civilization" (Robbins 1991, 14) during the war and after independence had been achieved. All of these writers shared, amidst many differences, the recognition that the attritional relationship between modernizing imperialism and traditional attitudes and habits would not end but would enter a new phase in the aftermath of a successful revolution. Algeria had been Europeanized but could never be, nor wish to be, European. But in what sense could it remain Algerian? Could Algerian nationalism absorb the experience of imperialism and emerge the richer thereby, or would it suffer the double impoverishment of neither realizing its own ambitions for the future nor overcoming or profiting from its past?

Nationalism's opposition to imperialism is, in some perspectives, nothing more than a continuation of imperialism by other means. It secedes from imperialism in its earlier form in order to rejoin it more enthusiastically in its later form. In effect, most critiques of nationalism claim that, as an ideology, it merely reproduces the very discourses by which it had been subjected. It asserts its presence and identity through precisely those categories that had denied them — through race, essence, destiny, language, history — merely adapting these categories to its own purposes. It also accepts the requirements of "civilization" — modernization, development, and class and gender divisions, which are integral to the system from which it ostensibly seeks to liberate itself. In brief, in the name of emancipation for itself, it joins with the global system of late capitalism and the multinational companies, becoming economically subservient while endlessly asserting cultural independence.

Whatever the merits or demerits of this description of nationalism in relation to imperialism, it allows us to focus more closely on the role of "culture" within such ideologies and systems. Precisely because culture has been given or has gained within both a comparative degree of autonomy, it is more susceptible to forms of analysis predicated on the assumption that there, in culture, features of these systems, not otherwise sanctioned or even visible, will be made manifest. This is itself an intricate and insecure assumption but it is sufficiently widespread, in a variety of forms and emphases, to demand scrutiny. It is particularly important to recognize the relationship between nationalism and culture, generally known as "cultural nationalism," in order to adjudicate on nationalism's historical role in combating imperialism or in ultimate compliance with it. As Aijaz Ahmad puts it:

> Theoretical debates as well as global historical accounts are rendered all the more opaque when the category of "nationalism" is yoked together with the category of "culture" to produce the composite category of "cultural nationalism." Unlike the political category of the state, the regulatory and coercive category of law, institutional mechanisms such as political parties or class organizations like trade unions, "culture" generally and the literary/aesthetic realm in particular are situated at a great remove from the economy and are therefore, among all the superstructures, the most easily available for idealization and theoretical slippage (1992, 7–8).

Culture is, indeed, an amorphous term, especially when it is routinely and with every appearance of benignity locked in with its comparably ill-defined cousin "tradition" in the ideological cell of nationalism. The subsequent isolation is deceptively pure for it breeds all sorts of promiscuous fantasies that are as formless as the natal pairing might lead us to expect. The consequence is that such enclosed and hermetic national formations actually become caricatures of the unawakened communal consciousness they replace. An intellectual proletariat, with bourgeois pretensions, that claims it has achieved national consciousness is substituted for a nonintellectual subproletariat that once *was* the national consciousness. In such a situation, many forms of reaction are justified on the grounds that they are "national." External domination has been introjected to the point that a nation, so construed, may be said to have learned nothing from oppression but oppression itself.

The separation of culture from power that is so often found in cultural nationalism is itself a legacy of the fact that educated native intelligentsia in colonial systems were themselves kept away from the exercise of real control. Instead they were assigned the role of bureaucratic functionaries. But the diagnoses of nationalism as "the pathology of modern developmental history" (Nairn 1977, 359) derive for the most part from the examination of European nationalisms that, in the aftermath of the French Revolution, transformed the dynastic polities of Europe into a number of nation states. Yet nationalism was not, in its origins, a European phenomenon at all. The first great nationalist revolutions took place in the late eighteenth and early nineteenth centuries in South

America, partly in response to the American Revolution and partly as a consequence of the crumbling of the Spanish colonial structure there. By 1825, Spanish America had achieved independence. This was quickly succeeded by an influx
of North European capital into the continent, so that the complex processes
whereby South American elites reimagined themselves as national communities
and European capital reinvented South America as a "new" space for development produced a situation in which cultural independence and economic subservience were paradigmatically combined into an image of nationalist liberation
nestled within economic, imperial domination (Pratt 1992, 112–14).

The later developments of European nationalism in the nineteenth century
were structurally similar to the South American revolutions in that they too were
led by bourgeois elites, they too declared a cultural-national independence and
they too were flawed as emancipatory movements for the people by the fact that
their proletariats were not released from economic impoverishment by independence.

European nationalism did, however, have an alternative in Marxist socialism.
Because of this, it was in Europe first that imperialism found, in socialism, its
true international or transnational other. This, in turn, has led many thinkers on
the left to equate nationalism with various forms of reaction, to see it as a barrier
to socialism because of its emphasis on the particularities of territory, language,
and race and its consequent failure to transcend these fervent localisms for a
broader vision of human community in which the primacy of liberation from an
unjust economic system would be recognized. It is also significant that the New
Imperialism of the late nineteenth century drew heavily on nineteenth-century
nationalism for ideological resource and sustenance. Imperial countries, such as
Britain and France, took the lead in producing for themselves nationalist ideologies, replete with newly created versions of tradition, antiquity, national essence,
literary tradition, and the like, all of which were exported to their empires
through various educational agencies — such as the British Council — that had as
their aim the replication throughout the world of the homegrown national
ethos. In this form, nationalism and imperialism were not adversarial movements at all. They were interlinked elements within a system that was culturally
distinct in its British or French manifestations, but identical in its economic ideology — capitalism. In addition, the various totalitarian movements in twentieth-
century Europe — and in Japan — had such clear and damaging associations with
nationalism and with that post–World War I "breakdown of classes and their
transformation into masses" (Arendt 1951, 321) that the pathological critique
of nationalism was inevitable.

Yet it has been applied with little discrimination to nationalist resurgences and
revolutions in the imperial domains themselves. This is in part to be explained
by the resistance of such movements to modernization as a process destructive
of their integrity as separate cultures and their apparently retrograde refusal to

join in the global community. Of course it is also the case that such refusal could be defended and even glamorized as a dismissal of the desolate alienation of the developed world and an admirable adherence to "traditional" values. Such disputes about nationalism were often as internally crucial to imperializing countries themselves as they were to those territories in subjection to them. Nationalism was thus susceptible to many varieties of use and assault. The protean nature of the term is inevitable given nationalism's complex history as an ideology that both liberates and immures, that conspires with imperialism and resists it, that is imported into Europe in one form and re-exported from Europe in another, that is culturally literate in inverse proportion to its economic illiteracy, that is, as a political formation, historically defunct, transitional, or an inescapable reality for the foreseeable future.

Since nationalism and imperialism are so intimate and conflictual, it may help to look at an exemplary instance of their dialectical relationship to each other as it manifested itself at the very heart of the British Empire — in Ireland. Ireland is especially useful because its national independence movement was, from the beginning, closely involved with the production and recovery of a national literature and the question of a revival of the national language. In the process, Ireland also produced some of the masterpieces of literary modernism, thereby clarifying in a previously unprecedented manner the nature of the relationships between imperialism, nationalism, and modernism.

Two authors dominate the history of Irish cultural nationalism — W. B. Yeats and James Joyce. They had many famous contemporaries — Oscar Wilde, George Bernard Shaw, George Moore, John Millington Synge. But it is Yeats and Joyce who, between them, most potently rehearse the positions available at a foundational moment for a nation that was not only part of an empire but was also constitutionally bound up in that empire's central political formation — the United Kingdom of Great Britain and Ireland, an entity that had come into being in the year 1800. In that year, Ireland, long a disputed colony of the British State, was finally incorporated into it. As such, it became integral to the imperial power and yet remained a problematic element within it.

In the course of the nineteenth century, Ireland underwent two kinds of experience that between them summarized the condition of a country under imperialism. It was modernized and Anglicized; it was also devastated by famine and repression to such a degree that its population was halved and its old Gaelic culture, already in retreat since the seventeenth century, was rendered almost extinct. In addition, the Protestant/Catholic religious divisions, introduced by English invasion in earlier centuries, were coincident with complicity with British power on the one hand and resentment of it on the other. It was a bourgeois intelligentsia, predominantly Protestant in its early developments, that attempted to resolve the sectarian problem as a means toward resolving or modifying the political relationship between the two islands. To that end, it reinvented an idea of Ireland as an antique nation that had known in pre-Christian and in early Christian times a unity that English colonialism had shattered and had since then known only a disunity that the same colonialism had fostered. The characteristics assigned to the Irish by their conquerors — rebelliousness, backwardness, barbarism, fecklessness — were all features of that racial propaganda that gained such a pseudoscientific status in the nineteenth century. In response, Irish nationalists converted the racial ideology into one that reinforced their claim to independence and reformulated the British version of irremediable Irish difference. The Irish became Celts or Gaels, the British Anglo-Saxons, and each racial grouping was depicted as inalterably opposed to one another in the drama of world-historical conflict. The Celt was given to culture — imaginative intensity, poetry, story, mysticism; the Saxon was given to power — empire, pragmatic politics, commercial greed.

Here we see at once the problem raised earlier. Given such a form of cultural nationalism, how could such a racially based concept of culture ever be reconciled with an equally racial theory of power? Clearly, culture so conceived could only envisage power in terms of a refusal of the global modernization of the Empire, rendering this refusal as an Irish or Celtic virtue that ratified the reversal of the old tradition/modernity contrast. Ireland would become a nation by recovering its traditions and refusing both modernization and modernity. The irony is that such a refusal, variously formulated by many writers, was itself one of the critical features of modernity. Tradition, once conceptualized in this fashion, was already lost; modernity, once refused and dismissed, was already in place. Nationalism could not abolish imperialism; it could only redraft for its own purposes the double narrative that was at the heart of the imperialist enterprise — the narrative of a world civilization and that of a national civilization, one enfolding the other. The Celtic version of Irish nationalism had its own world-civilization narrative, the discourse of culture as a peculiarly Celtic "country," as a territory rescued from the dominance of an impoverishing modernity.

In Yeats and Joyce these paradoxes and anomalies are fundamental to the development of their very different discourses. Yeats's poetry and plays, along with his various prose writings, attempt to resituate in and through Ireland and through his version of the Irish national character and destiny a reconstituted ideal of the heroic individual at bay in the modern world. Such an individual belongs to a specifically invoked cultural form — Irish national culture, the culture of the occult and occluded orders of theosophy, Anglo-Irish aristocratic culture. All of these have suffered marginalization at the hands of an imperial modernity. Now, in the words of one of his most famous poems, "The Second Coming is at hand," the modern world is free-falling into violence and disintegration and the alternative and opposite world of tradition, ceremony, and the mage is emerging to take its place and usher in another era in world history. Ireland is the site for such an emergence. In claiming this role, Yeats reverses the relationship between Ireland and England, but, since this is a role that has yet to be, that is in a future guaranteed by nothing more than his own quixotic version of national and world history, the reversal is phantasmal. The inevitability of a vertically hierarchical distinction between Britain and Ireland is preserved. Edward Said regards this position as characteristic of one, early phase of nationalist resistance, what he calls the "*nativist* phenomenon" (1993, 228).

It is certainly the case that the alternating centrifugal and centripetal movements in Yeats's writing, the disinterring from the past of traditional stable sociopolitical formations and their reinterment in modernity are symptomatic of his ambivalent position between oppositions that cannot be resolved but at least can be exploited. The velocity with which he conducts his constant migrations from world arena to local place, from a specific historical event to its vertical symbolic role in what Walter Benjamin calls "Messianic time, a simultaneity of past and future in an instantaneous present" (1973, 265; Anderson 1983, 22–26) is so great at times that the reader can only perceive the passage as the blur of apocalypse, destruction, and creation identical with one another. Yeats's cultural nationalism is created out of a series of marginalized discourses that almost vengefully become, in their combination, a central discourse. But then that central discourse is itself marginalized as the actual Irish Revolution begins with the Rising of 1916 and proceeds to what Yeats deems to be a very pallid and bourgeois version of the nation-state, catholic rather than celtic, seeking a compromise with the modernity it had (or he had) initially spurned. In this, Yeats exemplifies the experience of disillusion and disenchantment often repeated in later postcolonial countries. For, although cultural nationalism is one of the foundational moments of a nation-state under imperialism, once the nation-state has emerged it forsakes culture as an originating energy and commodifies it as the logo of its subsequent identity (Lloyd 1993, 71–72).

Joyce was free of the Yeatsian nostalgia for the heroic individual in whom the nation's essence was embodied and through whom its destiny was articulated. This was the vocabulary of a belated romantic, although it should be said that colonial belatedness was recognized by Joyce as one of the inescapable heritages of imperialism. The time lag between the metropolitan center and its outlying provinces always ensured within those territories a certain outmodedness that stimulated their desire to keep up, to be in the fashion, and at the same time allowed them to pride themselves on remaining more faithful to the traditional values than the center itself. This had been one of the thematic preoccupations of Irish drama since the eighteenth century. It was renewed in the drama of Shaw and Wilde in the nineteenth century. But it was in Joyce's fiction that it underwent a thorough transformation.

Joyce's work introduces modernism to postmodernism. The Ireland of which he writes is a place, previously marginalized, that is now assigned a central position in world literature, history, and myth. This is not done without irony. But for the present purpose, only two main points need be made. First, Joyce finds a means of producing a modern narrative of the dissolving self; second, he finds a means of producing a modern narrative of the system or systems in which that apprehension of the self is being eroded. In *Ulysses* (1922) and *Finnegans Wake* (1939), his day- and night-fictions respectively, everything is subject to dissolution, including language itself; yet it is also the case that everything in these works is subject to enormously powerful forms of consolidation and organization. The story of Dublin or of Ireland is the story of the world, the story of humankind, a generic parable. At the same time, it is, through all its repetitions, also a story of repression, breakdown, disenchantment. It is the Fall and it is Redemption, not in serial but in dialectical relation to one another. World civilization and a national culture are brought into an allegorical relation to one another. The story of the nation is the story of the Empire and vice-versa. Power relations are reversed. This Irish discourse demonstrates the Babel out of which English emerged and to which it will return. It refuses privilege to all established order and grants primacy to its originating confusion. From Joyce, especially the Joyce of the *Wake,* it is but a short step to postmodernist celebration of difference, otherness, and the refusal of the grand imperial narratives that effect their ideological aims by erasure or diminution of these primary conditions of heterogeneity.

Yet the *Wake* is indeed, like *Ulysses* a great narrative. It exploits the miscellaneous for the sake of an ultimate ordering. So too, in Yeats, the lament for the disintegration of traditional society is part of a historical vision in which that sorrow and loss have a function and significance. These are both nationalist writers who have imperial ambitions and who recognize that this apparent anomaly, which is also a dialectic, is historically inescapable. The fact that they both write in English is also inescapable for them, but has its anomalous force too. The Irish Literary Revival was contemporaneous with the movement for the revival of the Irish language. Yeats's friend, the dramatist J. M. Synge, refashioned English through the Irish language in his plays, thereby reproducing in drama what the Irish people had done in history. Yet for all the extravagant assaults on and extensions of the English language carried out by the most renowned Irish writers, they wrote in the imperial language, English. There is a naive view that in doing so they made English their own language. There is the more complex view that a minor literature, written in a minor language like Irish-English, involves a true liberation from a major language. The major language is already established; the minor language is in a state of becoming.

> All becoming is minoritarian. Women, regardless of their numbers, are a minority, definable as a state or a subset; but they create only by making possible a becoming over which they do not have ownership, into which they themselves must enter; this is

a becoming-woman affecting all of humankind, men and women both. The same goes for minor languages; they are not simply sublanguages, idiolects or dialects, but potential agents of the major language's entering into a becoming-minoritarian of all its dimensions and elements. We should distinguish between minor languages, the major language, and the becoming-minor of the major language (Deleuze and Guattari [1988] 1992, 106).

In Irish writing of the Revival period, English entered into the state of becoming minor, a state since repeated for it in Indian, African, West Indian, Australian and other literatures where English was subject to such liberation from its majoritarian status. There is a certain attraction to this argument, but it may be no more than an ingenious attempt to deny what is true of Irish and all other writing that has emerged from former colonies, English, French, or other, namely that their reception and acceptance depends upon the metropolitan cultures against which they are in some ways directed but towards which equally they are aimed.

Joyce was one of the earliest in a long list of modern writers who have either chosen or suffered exile. Their distance from and disaffection with their home territories has almost always been understood as a paradigmatic refusal of the writer to surrender his or her radical freedom to the demands of an oppressive state or system. There is, indeed, a great deal of truth in this. The exile of the modernist writer was taken to be analogous to the loss of home, of somewhere to belong to; it was certainly a painful condition. But in the postmodernist era this has been significantly re-read. Exile is (in certain circumstances) only the loss of one possible home; it can lead from belonging nowhere to becoming at home everywhere, a migrant condition that owes something to the old Enlightenment ideal of the Citizen of the World, but also owes much to the contemporary belief that there is an essential virtue and gain in escaping from the singularity of one culture into the multiplicity of all, or of all that are available. In such a turn we witness the rejection of nationalism brought to an apparently liberating extreme and the hostility to the world system of imperialism and capitalism achieving a new definition. Voiced within such postmodernist acclaim is a profoundly political or politicized version of culture and power.

Still, there is also an equally strong tendency towards depoliticization within this acclaim. The reception of Joyce, especially of *Finnegans Wake,* makes this plain. Joyce is celebrated to the degree that he is (mis) understood as an antinationalist writer and *therefore* as both a modernist and an internationalist. In short, through a curious reading of his work, first by unfashionable second-rate critics then by fashionable second-rate critics, Joyce is depoliticized as an Irish writer involved in his country's anti-imperialist struggle and ostensibly repoliticized as a cult figure first of the modernist then of the postcolonial world. The writers of South American "magic narrative" have suffered the same fate, albeit with a remarkable equanimity. But the Ireland of Joyce and the South America of Garcia Marquez, Vargas Llosa and others are still disputed and colonized territories, are still economically and politically marginalized while being granted a canonical or semicanonical place in culture. This bespeaks no emancipation from an oppressive situation; it merely indicates how competently the imperial world, now rechristened the First World, can incorporate cultural material from the Third World and process it for worldwide consumption—just as it does with raw material for industrial and commercial purposes. Within postmodern and postcolonial celebrations of difference, within its anxious interrogations of migrancy, hybridity, and a number of other concepts of the interstitial that refuse to be hijacked within or into a larger global conceptual system, (Bhabha 1994, 236–56) there is a fading consciousness of the unshaken, even extended, global power of capitalist imperialism. The question of culture and power—their alliances, their separations, their phantom divorces, their separate upbringings—remains unanswered and increasingly unasked. It is arguable that postcolonialism has taken the harm out of nationalism by celebrating its inexhaustible capacity for minoritarian difference and that nationalism, by its endless plying of culture as a sufficient counteragency to power, has found in postcolonialism the future that it deserves.

Suggested Readings

Ahmad, Aijaz. 1992. *In Theory: Nations, Classes, Literatures.*
Anderson, Benedict. rev. ed. 1991. *Imagined Communities: Reflections on the Origin and Spread of Nationalism.*
Arendt, Hannah. 1951. *The Burden of Our Time.*
Crosby, Alfred W. 1986. *Ecological Imperialism: The Biological Expansion of Europe 900–1900.*
Pratt, Mary Louise. 1992. *Imperial Eyes: Travel Writing and Transculturation.*
Said, Edward W. 1978. *Orientalism.*
———. 1993. *Culture and Imperialism.*
Spurr, David. 1993. *The Rhetoric of Empire: Colonial Discourse in Journalism, Travel Writing, and Imperial Administration.*

26

Desire

Judith Butler

The body which is moved from without is soulless; but that which is
moved from within has a soul, for such is the nature of the soul . . . of
the nature of the soul, let me speak briefly and in a figure.
— Plato, *Phaedrus*, 286

ALTHOUGH MICHEL FOUCAULT has argued that desire has become within
modern times a preoccupation of discourse, it is not always clear what
a discourse on desire might be. The notion of an essay on desire is by definition beset by the very problem it seeks to explain. The expectation that we
might trust language to make something clear about desire presupposes that
language itself has no vested interests in desire. But if we consider the discourse
on desire since Plato, it seems that language is bound up with desire in such a
way that no exposition of desire can escape becoming implicated in that which
it seeks to clarify. This means that language is always less than "clarifying" when
it comes to desire. Desire will be that which guarantees a certain opacity in language, an opacity that language can enact and display, but without which it cannot operate.

Since Plato, desire has been thought of in many ways: in terms of its *origins*
in the body or in a more expansive set of passions; in terms of its *ends,* those that
are considered more sensuous, those considered more spiritual, and an ambiguous range in between. Under the pressure of philosophy, we might well ask in
what desire consists, whether desire is singular or plural, whether it is distinctively human. But there is a question that appears to be prior to those sorts of
questions: How is it that desire becomes an object of speech, of writing, or of
discourse in general? What is desire such that it becomes that of which we speak
but also, perhaps of equal importance, that which impels us to speech, which
establishes our rhetorical bearing in the world?

Plato will claim that he will only speak briefly and in a figure, and what he
offers us is an allegory that he never fully transcribes into more conventional
philosophical argumentation. If allegory is in its most general formulation a way
of giving a narrative form to something which cannot be directly narrativized,

then what does it mean that desire is approached through allegory? Is it that desire cannot make itself plain through a more direct linguistic representation? What is elusive about this referent? In what follows, I hope to show that language is bound to founder on the question of desire, that it is forced to seek modes of indirection, and that the writings of and on desire that we might consider are ones which seek, in the end, to cancel themselves as writing in order better to approximate the desire they seek to know.

If language cannot deliver desire in its transparency, and if desire is always to some degree displaced in (and by) language, it remains to be understood why precisely this is the case. In the positions we will consider here, a tension emerges between a conception of language that is said to form or produce desire — and without which desire itself cannot exist — and a conception of language that is the vehicle through which desire is displaced, that founders in every effort to present and communicate desire. It may seem at first that these are contradictory views, but I would suggest instead that the relation of language to desire is one that has assumed the status of an apparently necessary ambivalence.

I write "apparently" because the accounts of desire influenced by the Western metaphysical tradition from Plato through Lacan tend to assume an invariant structure to desire. Is all desire a desire to return to an impossible origin, as Plato insisted and Lacan reasserted? Can the various aims of desire be understood through recourse to a metaphysical trajectory of desire? Or are these very metaphysical tales cultural formations that have achieved the status of the metaphysical? Is heterosexuality presumed in the founding scenario of desire, and what happens to the account of language and desire if we trouble that founding presumption? What narratives are available for desire, and how might such narratives contest cultural presumptions about sexual difference and heterosexuality? These are some of the contemporary questions that have emerged in recent feminist and gay and lesbian theory, as well as in poststructuralist and cultural theory that takes aim at traditional metaphysical postulates. These questions have opened up new terrain for literary studies, for the question of what it means to read, and for ways we might think about "the readable" as such. To what extent, for instance, do narratives driven by desire presume heterosexuality and its patterns of rivalry and displacement? Is there, presupposed by such narratives, a complicating homoeroticism that calls into question the explicit direction of the narrative itself? Is desire itself metaphysically conditioned, or are there given social arrangements that lay claim to a metaphysical status in order to elaborate and justify their own authority? Does language give rise to desire and does it also set limits on the representability of desire? How are we to understand these dimensions of language and how is our notion of desire altered in the course of that understanding?

Let us, then, turn to Plato to interrogate the metaphysical scene of desire, and then move to modern fiction and to psychoanalytic theory, especially its adaptation of the metaphysics of desire. Last, we will consider the contemporary rejoinders to this particular legacy in order to reconsider the language of desire as well as the desires that language brings.

DESIRE ENGENDERS THE BODY: PLATO AND THE GREEKS

For Plato, to desire is to be moved, but desires differ according to their origins. If one is moved by oneself, one remains a disembodied soul, immortal, in communion with other souls. If one is moved by what is outside oneself, one acquires body and a human form. Plato concedes the difficulty of telling a story about how, in this second instance, desire acquires a body and how one makes the passage from the first to the second state, from disembodied to embodied desire. He seeks indulgence for seeking recourse to a figure, that of a charioteer and his two horses:

> The human charioteer drives his in a pair; and one of them is noble and of noble breed, and the other is ignoble and of ignoble breed; and the driving of them of necessity gives a great deal of trouble to him. I will endeavor to explain to you in what way the mortal differs from the immortal creature. The soul in her totality has the care of inanimate being everywhere, and traverses the whole heaven in diverse forms appearing; — when perfect and fully winged she soars upward, and orders the whole world; whereas the imperfect soul, losing her wings and drooping in her flight, at last settles on the solid ground — there, finding a home, she receives an earthly frame which appears to be self-moved, but is really moved by her power; and this composition of soul and body is called a living and mortal creature. For immortal no such union can be reasonably believed to be; although fancy, not having seen nor surely known the nature of God, may imagine an immortal creature having both a body and a soul which are united throughout all time, Let that, however, be as God wills, and be spoken of acceptably to him. And now let us ask the reason why the soul loses her wings!
>
> The wing is the corporeal element which is most akin to the divine, and which by nature tends to soar aloft and carry that which gravitates downwards into the upper region, which is the habitation of the gods. The divine is beauty, wisdom, goodness, and the like; and by these the wing of the soul is nourished, and grows apace; but when fed upon evil and foulness and the opposite of the good, wastes and falls away. (286–87)

The loss of the wings is the condition for the acquisition of the human bodily form. The wings fall to the ground, and the form descends, grounded and weighty. The acquisition of the body is, paradoxically, the effect of "evil and foul" desire. This appetitive desire exists first, and it implies that the soul is moved by what is outside itself, by the external sensuous world. The human body, that "earthly form," only *appears* to be self-moved but is really moved through a reaction to what is not itself. For Plato, this being moved by what is other than oneself is the sign of a fall into embodiment. Only that which moves itself is radically incorporeal (or corporeal in a divine sense). The body emerges or, rather, is acquired by virtue of the "imperfection" of the soul, which is, in turn, defined by the appetitive character of its desire. The appetite does not come from the body but is that which forms or figures that body and, then, literalizes that figure, acquires or materializes that bodily form. Plato thus needs his figure not merely to illustrate this philosophical truth; he needs it also because the human bodily form only comes into being through being figured in and by its appetitive desire.

For Plato, then, it is not that a desire emerges from a body, but that a body emerges *from* a desire. This contention is not so far afield from psychoanalytic reflections on the way in which a libidinal investment gives rise to an imaginary body, what Freud in *The Ego and the Id* calls "the bodily ego." Here desire is projected and takes a visual form, becoming, as it were, a figure, and it is only on the basis of this projection that the body emerges as an individuated object of perception. Thus, desire transfigured through projection gives rise to the idealized contour or morphology of the body. In Lacan, the body will emerge from the transfiguration of desire into an imaginary visual field, one which establishes the body first as a function of a specular imaginary reflection.

The sense in which desire might be said to be formative or creative is the explicit theme of Diotima's famous speech on love in Plato's *Symposium*. After all the members at that party have spoken, Socrates rises and cites verbatim a speech that he claims Diotima made to him. According to Socrates, she distinguishes between the two interrelated ends that govern human longing: procreation and creation in a more expansive sense. The first appears to be natural, and the latter spiritual or psychic. In the course of the speech, however, this distinction loses its stability. Consider her pedagogical address to Socrates, which Socrates cites to Phaedrus in the *Symposium*:

> All men bring to birth [begetting] in their bodies and in their souls. There is a certain age at which human nature is desirous of procreation—procreation which must be in beauty and not in deformity; and this procreation is the union of man and woman, and is a divine thing; for conception and generation are an immortal principle in the mortal creature, and in the inharmonious they can never be. But the deformed is always inharmonious with the divine, and the beautiful harmonious." (*Symposium*, 373)

For Plato, it appears that conception takes place in the union of man and woman, but the object of longing or desire is not "woman" as much as it is the expression and creation of "the beautiful." And "the beautiful" is not an object to be possessed but the character of a certain kind of creation. "Love," for instance, is defined in terms of a longing for the beautiful, but the beautiful is importantly only a condition for the possibility of conception and creation: "not the love for the beautiful only . . . but the love of generation and of birth in beauty" (374). This conception and generation, which appears at first to be defined by its ends, turns out to be an end in itself, an activity that is a good in itself.

Is this conception and generation natural and procreative, or spiritual and psychic? Diotima explains that there is a procreancy of the body which leads to the conception of children, but that there is a procreancy of the spirit "which conceive[s] and bear[s] things of the spirit" where these "things of the spirit" constitute the domain of "wisdom and all her sister virtues." Further, "it is the office of every poet to beget them, and of every artist whom we may call creative." Although Diotima appears to distinguish between the begetting of children and the begetting of things spiritual and, implicitly, philosophical, the term "begetting" continues to describe both activities, confounding the distinction through its repetition in both contexts. Indeed, she describes men with "pregnant souls." How are we to read this procreation, as literal — in the case of reproduction — or figurative — in the case of "things spiritual"?

These two apparently different forms of begetting or procreation appear to be interrelated in paradoxical ways. Through the speech of Diotima, Socrates characterizes the domain of ideal forms as a "an eternal oneness" that *cannot* "take the form of a face, or of hands, or of anything that is of the flesh . . . [and] will be neither words, nor knowledge." On the other hand, Diotima will insist that "it is only when he discerns beauty itself through what makes it visible that a man will be quickened with the true, and not the seeming, virtue." Here it is the visible that necessarily conditions the insight into the true, even as the true will be distinguished ultimately from both the visible and "the seeming."

As with the "soul" in *The Phaedrus,* the "ideal" and the "true" in the *Symposium* precede and form the phenomenal conditions of their knowability. This "forming" is the action of a domain which precedes the human knower, but which constitutes the desiring activity of that knower and makes of knowing a desirous and creative activity. Although Plato writes that this eternal oneness designated by the domain of forms "will be neither words nor knowledge," he also *writes* this disclaimer through the invocation of the figure of Diotima, through whom love is said to speak. So who speaks here? Plato, Socrates, Diotima, the gods? Is there a singular speaker at all? What has love done to the singularity of the subject of speech?

If we can only know the love of the beautiful through what appears, even as that beauty exceeds the apparent, what does that make of Plato's writing on love as an activity that appears on the page for us to read? Is this invariably a figuring, which turns out not only to embody but to facilitate this very insight into what exceeds the apparent world? Desire of the beautiful requires that writing seek to exceed its own constraints, to present what is "beyond" the word by and through the word.

The predicament that emerges in the writing of desire in Plato prefigures a set of difficulties that emerge within psychoanalytic and contemporary critical discourses on desire. If, for Plato, desire is for what is beyond writing itself, then the writing of desire will seek to cancel itself as writing and will always also fail to cancel itself completely. And yet, if the relation between writing and desire is strangely necessary, then the very effort of writing to present what is beyond itself, to capture or present a referent, will constitute the very trajectory of desire as the push toward necessary failure. And to the extent that writing cannot reach beyond itself, it is condemned to figure that beyond again and again within its own terms. Later this will become the problematic of the sublime within the domain of literary criticism and aesthetics.

Considering Plato's notion of the soul as that which precedes, occasions, and inspires the human form, it appears that what moves him and his writing is not merely his own invention. Indeed, Socrates receives his wisdom from Diotima, who also insists that her wisdom is received. The authorship of love is distributed through time. That which moves Plato's writing will of necessity precede his writing and, in that sense, be before and beyond him in some fundamental sense. Is this an ek-stasis (a standing outside oneself) of sorts that offers another view of desire, one that may be self-moved, but one in which the "self" or "soul" that moves precedes the individual author in whom the movement occurs?

SEXUAL DIFFERENCE, HOMOEROTICISM, AND THE LOSS OF MASTERY

In *Death in Venice,* Thomas Mann underscores this ecstatic and excessive character of conception and creativity in Plato. To the extent that Plato is understood to counsel philosophical detachment rather than ecstasy, he is seriously misunderstood. Aschenbach enacts this misunderstanding, pursuing a detachment from his desire for the young boy, Tadzio, only to find himself in the midst of excessive desire. Toward the end of the story, Aschenbach seeks to relieve himself of his "abysmal" desire through a return to aesthetic form and simplicity, but finds that the return is impossible:

> There he sat, the master: this was he who found a way to reconcile art and honours; who had written *The Abject,* and in a style of classic purity renounced bohemianism and all its works, all sympathy with the abyss and the troubled depths of the outcast human soul. This was he who had put knowledge underfoot to climb so high; who had outgrown the ironic pose and adjusted himself to the burdens and obligations of fame; whose renown had been officially recognized and his name ennobled, whose style was set

for a model in the schools. There he sat. His eyelids were closed, there was only a swift, sidelong glint of the eyeballs now and again, something between a question and a leer; while the rouged and flabby mouth uttered single words of the sentences shaped in the disordered brain by the fantastic logic that governs our dreams.

The master of detachment is thus undone by "the fantastic logic" of desire by which he is moved. And the apparent "detachment" of the Platonist is not a simple self-abnegation but a radical dissolution of the subject through desire, for the sake of desire. Thus, Mann's text proceeds without a break to cite directly (and translate freely) from Plato's *Phaedrus* for a full, free-standing paragraph. The paragraph consists in an address from Socrates to Phaedrus in which the return to detachment is invoked only to be undermined. The final lines are these:

> By beauty we mean simplicity, largeness, and renewed severity of discipline; we mean a return to detachment and to form. But detachment, Phaedrus, and preoccupation with form lead to intoxication and desire, they may lead the noblest among us to frightful emotional excesses, which his own stern cult of the beautiful would make him the first to condemn. So they too, they too, lead to the bottomless pit. Yes, they lead us thither, I say, us who are poets — who by our natures are prone not to excellence but to excess. (*Death in Venice*, 73)

Where Mann figures Platonic desire as that which promises mastery but culminates in ecstatic self-loss, the French feminist philosopher Luce Irigaray will insist that the homoerotic impulse toward self-duplication at work in Plato's discourse on desire and love implicates him in yet a different order of mastery. The homoerotic scene in which these elaborations of desire take place suggest that "spiritual desire" is that which takes place between men, not exactly a homosexuality, but a *hommo*sexuality, a spiritualized and desexualized desire for the form or reflection of a masculine self in another (the *de*sexualization of this desire suggests that it may be in the service of a homophobia rather than its counter). This returns us to the redoubling of the term "begetting" in Plato to describe both reproductive and spiritual forms of conception with a different interpretation: the transposition of the term onto the hommosexual or homoerotic scene between men suggests that it may well be an appropriation of the scene of "reproduction" for a fantasy of masculine autogenesis. Indeed, this fantasy might be read in Irigarayan terms as a peculiar twist on Mann's notion of "the fantastic logic that governs our dreams." A fantastic logic whereby men beget other men, reproducing and mirroring themselves at the expense of women and of their own reproductive origins in women/mothers. According to this fantastic logic, women are the token of a despiritualized materiality excluded from this higher

function of desire, but a materiality that persists as the unspoken and perhaps
unspeakable condition of its possibility. For Irigaray, the philosophical desire
associated with Plato and his tradition is one based on the repudiation of sexual
difference, one which elevates a desexualized homosexuality into the condition
of philosophical knowledge itself. Of this hommosexuality, Irigaray writes,

> The only men who love each other are, in truth, those who are
> impatient to find the same over and over again. And, in order to
> do this, they must not turn or direct their quest toward some
> other part of man or any object whatsoever, but only toward that
> very thing in which they see themselves: that *mirror of vision* in
> which they can look at themselves in the very gaze of the other,
> perceiving, in one and the same glance, their view and them-
> selves." (*Speculum,* 327)

This mirroring, however, depends on a medium — a third term — which does
not, may not, explicitly appear in the circuit of self-reflection: the girl, considered
as the flawed copy, or the mother, the medium through which procreation becomes possible and who physicalizes and, hence, demeans that higher form of
the spiritual reduplication of "man" that is philosophy. Hence, the feminine is
excluded from this circuit of masculine auto-erotic desire, but that exclusion
constitutes the very condition of its possibility. For Irigaray, then, there can be
no feminine desire inside this economy and certainly no parallel possibility of
feminine self-reflection: "She herself knows nothing (of herself). And remembers nothing. Providing the basis for the wise man's auto-logical speculations,
she lives in darkness." (345)

The Platonic tradition thus leaves us with a quandary: Does desire seek and
find a reflection of the subject who desires, and is that subject invariably figured
as masculine? Or does desire unsettle the mastery and subvert the intentionality
of the subject who desires? Ought desire to be understood as the undoing of the
subject or as its specular self-confirmation, and is this subject invariably masculine? Is the apparent division between a spiritual and a physical desire marked as
a division between masculine and feminine spheres? And how are we to understand the relation of desire to figuration as such? Is it related to the drama of
sexual difference in which the discourse of desire plays itself out?

To reconsider these questions, let us turn briefly to Aristotle and to a competing set of enduring metaphors for desire. In Aristotle, desire is figured as that
which persists between the natural and the psychic domains, mediated by an
ethos or a domain of regularly practiced habits. To a certain degree, desire is the
effect of deliberate choice. This is not a choice performed at an instrumental
distance from desire, but one embedded in habits which, over time, form dispositions to perform certain kinds of action. Whereas the rationally governed desire, determined by deliberate (i.e., rational) choice, is active, irrational and arbi-

trary desire is considered passive, merely undergone, suffered, but not structured or determined by the subject as a rational agent (not "self-moved" in a sense taken over from Plato).

The distinction between active and passive desire persists throughout neo-Aristotelian philosophy through nineteenth-century materialism, reemerging in the work of Freud. One question that emerges in relation to this distinction is whether active and passive forms of desire are correlated with masculine and feminine. The question becomes all the more plausible when one recognizes that, for Aristotle, the "rational" capacities of women are inherently diminished.

The kind of desire governed by a subject would appear to be both masculine and active, whereas the kind of desire ungovernable by a subject would appear to be both feminine and passive. A number of feminist scholars have made this case, and their positions would seem to be in line with the above-mentioned analysis of Plato offered by Irigaray. Indeed, Irigaray, in relation to Aristotle's *Physics,* will argue that the feminine is reduced to passive matter, deprived of the principle of rationality, and that the very activity of reproduction will be redescribed as "an act more passive than passivity" (*An Ethics of Sexual Difference,* 43). Of this imagining of the "passivity" of women, and the reduction of women to this "passive" notion of reproduction, Irigaray queries, "Hasn't woman been imagined as passive only because man would fear to lose mastery in that particular act [the act of reproduction]?" (44) For Irigaray, Aristotle, like Plato, elaborates desire not only as masculine but as the pursuit of masculine mastery through the appropriation and spiritualization of the power of reproduction as the philosophical fantasy of masculine autogenesis.

This feminist paradigm for thinking about desire and gender in classical Greek texts has come under question by classicists such as David Halperin and John J. Winkler. By virtue of this recent scholarship, it has become more difficult to draw a strict correspondence between masculinity, rationality, active desire, and mastery, on the one hand, and femininity, matter, passive desire (or desirelessness), and masterability, on the other.

Perhaps Irigaray overstates the distinction between rationality and matter, between, on the one hand, a culturally habituated desire and, on the other, a physical or natural state excluded from (and conditioning) the domain of vitalizing cultural norms. *De Anima* is the text which established the inseparability of matter and form. But if we consider the further proposition in *The Ethics* that the "form" of desire is produced through cultural norms, then it appears that the distinction between what is natural and what is conventional in desire becomes importantly undecidable. Indeed, it appears that in relation to desire, *phusis* (nature), defined as the self-motion of life, incessantly makes itself available to a formation by or through *ethos*. In this sense, the question of the separability of a natural and conventional desire remains a difficult one in Aristotelian terms. John Winkler cites the Twenty-sixth Problem in the fourth book of Aristotle's

Problemata as the "text [which] contains the most complex and many-sided theory of 'natural' sexual desire known to me from ancient sources" (*Constraints of Desire,* 67). The determinants of desire are to be found not only in physical (or nutritional) and psychic sources, but also in *ethos* or habit (habituation) which may appear as a kind of second nature. Oddly enough, "nature" (*phusis*) does not determine desire in Aristotle; it not only vies with *ethos* as a determinant, and is itself formed by *ethos* over time, thus becoming altered in its very character in the process. The notion that nature is formed over time by habit, and that habit is more or less encoded in norms conveyed rhetorically by moral pedagogies, leads Winkler to the conclusion that "'Nature' in that usage, though it can be made to sound impressively absolute, refers precisely to convention: *it is norm-enforcing language*" (69, my emphasis).

To the extent that nature (*phusis*) is what moves us and contributes motion to desire, it seems that nature cannot be separated from norm-enforcing language, from convention and, hence, from linguistic convention as well. In this way, Aristotle anticipates the more contemporary view according to which desire is considered inseparable from language, an inseparability that makes every effort to write about desire an exemplification of the relation it seeks to portray. Moreover, a recourse to purely natural desire would be quite difficult within these Aristotelian terms, for nature subjected to ethos is a kind of second nature, one which is thoroughly embedded in culture.

DESIRE AND THE COSTS OF LINGUISTIC RECOGNITION

Aristotle situates desire as a culturally produced activity, one that takes place in relation to norms, and one that is related to how to make deliberate choices in the midst of ethical life. Spinoza will later claim that desire (*conatus*) is the passion in human beings from which all emotions are derived, and that basic to all human striving is a "desire to persist in one's own being." For liberal political theorists such as Hobbes, this formulation will turn into a view of desire as acquisitiveness or human selfishness. But there is a critical distance between a self-acquisitive desire (as a sign of selfishness) and self-preservative desire (as a sign of life-affirmation) in Spinoza's view, and later in Nietzsche's.

For Spinoza, desire will seek to enhance itself through reflections of the world that establish its internal harmony with that world. And the thesis of harmony, invoked by Diotima as the sign of the divine, will control the discourse on desire through the work of Hegel. But with Hegel, a persistent question arises whether desire is to be figured as an effort at self-duplication or as an effort to exceed, or even contest, the purview of the subject itself. This question presupposes the question of sexual difference, and we may suppose that that question is present in the discourse on the structure and aims of desire, even when—or most emphatically when—it remains unspoken or unspeakable.

Hegel's *Phenomenology of Spirit* introduces the notion of desire (*Begierde*) as the very movement by which consciousness redoubles itself as self-consciousness: "self-consciousness is Desire in general" (Hegel, par. 167). The possibility of having oneself reflected back to oneself is the inaugurating lure of desire; the lure of reflexivity, of mimetic reflection, initiates desire but immediately precipitates desire into a life and death struggle. For the Other, who will reflect back the subject's desire and whom, therefore, the subject desires (precisely as the reflection she or he promises), will inadvertently reflect back the subject's own duplicatability, exchangeability, nonsingularity, and will, with this very power of reflection, threaten the singularity of the subject. Irigaray will imagine this scene of reflexive redoubling as the ruse by which a masculine subject achieves self-confirmation for its universality, a desire for oneself as a universal "man," which is gratified at the prospect of the subject's (endless) reduplication. For Hegel, however, this prospect appears less gratifying. The redoubling of consciousness produces a desire for reciprocal recognition (*Anerkennung*), only then swiftly to transform this very desire into an effort to destroy the Other. The desire for destruction is thwarted by the sudden realization that the Other, who mirrors the subject, wields the power to destroy him in return.

Figured first as consumption, and then as recognition through reduplication, desire seeks to "negate" or overcome what is different or unassimilable in the Other. In Hegel's terms, the Other is paradoxically preserved and negated, and the subject can at once recognize himself in that Other without vanquishing the Other. Such a Hegelian resolution proves impossible for those such as Jacques Lacan, who will claim that the subject can never recognize himself in an Other but remains in a permanent relation of *mis*recognition. In this sense, the "negativity" that marks the Other, the not-me in Hegel, remains insuperable for Lacan and returns him to a thwarted Platonism: as much as desire seeks to recollect or recover one's origins in an effort to achieve a metaphysical oneness, it is thwarted from that recovery by a primary separation or loss. In the place of that return, desire acquires an imaginary trajectory.

The primary separation or loss figured in Lacan recalls the loss of the wings in Plato, the loss that inaugurates embodied desire. And such a founding separation, a structuring lack, can be found as well in the Aristophanic myth introduced in the *Symposium*. An originally hermaphroditic figure, the "third sex" in Plato provides the mythic justification for heterosexual copulation. To tame the arrogance of these spherical hermaphrodites (with their genitals on the outside), Zeus sunders them into separate and insufficient halves; their desire for one another emerges on the condition of their separation from one another. Although the Aristophanic myth implies that desire emerges on the condition of division, it also imagines all manner of sexual arrangements resulting from this ontological separation.

Within some versions of contemporary structuralist psychoanalysis, however, this original separateness is reconceived as the division into two sexes in need of each other, and desire is rendered as a function of sexual difference. Indeed, some critics have claimed that there can be no writing without sexual difference, and that sexual difference is the paradigm for understanding all differentiations within language. The production of the subject, the speaking "I," requires a repudiation of the maternal or of an original pleasure that precedes language itself. The "I" emerges only in relation to a "you," a "he," or a "she" who one is not; hence, the speaking subject emerges as part of the linguistic chain of intelligibility by virtue of this founding differentiation. All further efforts to signify within language thus presuppose that this speaking being is originally and permanently separated from its origin in pleasure. If one accepts that linguistic meanings are produced by virtue of linguistic differentiations (substitutions, metonymy), then it appears that the very possibility of linguistic intelligibility is to be derived from sexual difference as a founding difference.

Desire thus emerges in language, of language, precisely to the extent that the subject is foreclosed from a more original pleasure, one that can be posited as a phantasmatic beginning only retroactively by a subject in language. The effort of language to recapture this lost origin (a psychoanalytic version of Plato's doctrine of recollection) marks (and mars) every effort at referentiality within language. Desire is thus defined as displacement, but also as an endless chain of substitutions. Lacan refers to desire as a "ferret," figuring its status as driven, furtive or subterranean, and persistent. By identifying desire with metonymy, he implies that desire does not repeat with the regularity of metaphor, that it does not simply or fully substitute one object for another. As a movement that works through displacement, its objects recall the lost origin, but only in part, and through juxtaposition (or association), but not necessarily by semblance. In this way the aims of desire are not transparently represented in the objects or Others which it seeks; indeed, its aims are cloaked or displaced in such a way that what one desires is radically other than what one appears to seek. That desire is not what it appears to be, that it remains irreducible to appearance, implies that it emerges (or, rather, fails to emerge) as an opacity in language. Desire designates that opacity without which language cannot work.

If desire is irreducible to appearance, then it is also true that however desire appears to the subject is not necessarily the true aim and trajectory of desire. That true aim is, by definition, foreclosed. The subject may well be the last to know, if he or she ever does, what it is that he or she desires. The subject is constituted in the dislocation of desire. Prior to the splitting off of the subject from its *jouissance* (which is the fissure by which the subject is inaugurated), there is only this unbounded and differentiated pleasure (or so we imagine from a point of view in language closed off from the possibility of recourse to that experience). With the individuation of the subject (which takes place first through the mirroring production of the imaginary "ego"), desire emerges, but only in relation to need (which cannot appear in language) and to demand (the symbolic

effort to order the subject according to law). Desire is the site in which demand
and need are never reconciled, and this makes of desire a permanently vexed
affair. Further, desire is never fulfilled, for its fulfillment would entail a full return
to that primary pleasure, and that return would dissolve the very subject which
is the condition of desire itself. Hence, the fulfillment of desire would be its
radical self-cancellation. Desire thus emerges at an infinite distance from pleasure, indeed, always at the cost of pleasure, but also always at the cost of a conformity to the symbolic law.

This pursuit and failure of recollection as well as recognition marks the quandary of desire in language, for if language is based on the foreclosure of satisfaction, then the desire for satisfaction disrupts the very premise of language, eroding language from within. In Marguerite Duras's *The Ravishing of Lol Stein,* each
lover loves the other through an inarticulable set of memories, and the irrecover-
ability of those prior loves enables and vanquishes every contemporary instance
of love. The circuit of desire pushes the text toward the limits of language in
which the name names nothing or, rather, where the speaking of the name can
do nothing but evoke the site of permanent loss. Thus, Duras's male narrator,
Jack Hold, whose very name figures both embrace and deferral, finds that desire
evacuates the name of its referent and evokes the person as void:

> She shakes her head, murmurs my name.
> "Jack Hold."
> Lol's virginity uttering that name! Who except her, Lol Stein,
> the so-called Lol Stein, had noticed the inconsistency of the belief
> in that person so named. A dazzling discovery of the name the
> others have abandoned, have failed to recognize, which was invis-
> ible, an inanity shared by all the men of South Tahla, as much a
> part of myself as the course of my blood through my veins. She
> has plucked me, taken me from the next. For the first name, my
> name pronounced, names nothing." (Duras, 103)

Here it is not simply desire but its inevitable displacement through an Other,
or a series of Others, that renders it elusive, contests its "apparent" aim, derails
it from intentionality. The subject, understood as a center of intention, is temporarily vanquished; the subject, strictly speaking, does not desire; it is decentered
and dissolved through the force of desire. Lol wants to be Tatiana Karl, wants
to be desired as Tatiana Karl, wants to vanquish her, be vanquished by her, and
there is no desire without this triangulation in which displacement works as a
threat and incitement. Lacan's formulation that "desire is for the desire of the
Other" works in at least two ways: the desire for the Other's desire, to be its
object, but also to mime its ways and, in miming, to assume an identity other
than one's own.

The pursuit of her own vanquishing by Tatiana, the voluptuous return to the

scene of betrayal, is a pursuit of that dead end in which language might finally
fail—and where desire might have its chance. For Jack Hold it is impossible to
name or fix the singularity of the one he desires or to be named in return; this
perpetual misrecognition leads to a linguistic incapacity that approximates that
loss that cannot be named, that erodes the referential capacity of every name:

> The void is Tatiana naked beneath her dark hair, the fact. It is
> transformed, poured out lavishly, the fact no longer contains the
> fact, Tatiana emerges from herself, spills through the open win-
> dows out over the town, the roads, mire liquid, tide of nudity.
> Here she is, Tatiana Karl, suddenly naked beneath her hair, be-
> tween Lol Stein and me. The sentence has just faded away, I can
> no longer hear any sound, only silence, the sentence is dead at
> Lol's feet, Tatiana is back in her place. I reach out and touch and
> fail to recognize anything I have already touched. (106)

Although the sentence is said to fail, another sentence, the sentence of narration,
manages to get written. For Duras, paradoxically, the force of this putative void
is alleviated by its narration. In this sense, *The Ravishing of Lol Stein* is a text that
narrates the very void that is said to disrupt the possibility of narration. In a
sense, desire is temporarily resolved into narration, but in a language which seeks
to undo itself into its constitutive desire, but which returns to reenact the loss
that afflicts every such linguistic effort.

But what is desire finally for? And whom does Lol want, and can it be decided?
If the lost object of Lacanian psychoanalysis does not compel as a sufficient explanation for the trajectory of desire, what might?

Psychoanalytic Triangles and Their Critics

In a distinctive departure from psychoanalytic accounts of desire, mimesis, and
jealousy, René Girard writes in *Deceit, Desire, and the Novel* that the novel articulates the triangular structure of all desire, that all desire is mediated through a
third, a mediator, and that what appears to be a desire for the Other is, in fact,
a concealed way of desiring the mediator. This is a desire not simply to possess
the mediator, but to assume the place of the mediator, to vanquish the intermedi-
ary through a mimetic appropriation. In a theory which maintains some resonance with the notion of aggressive incorporation advanced by Melanie Klein,
Girard argues that the subject seeks to vanquish the mediator, who is also a rival,
through an aggressive mimeticism. The desire for the Other is the concealed
condition for a mimetic desire, the desire to be in the place of the mediator, the
one who is conjured as occupying the position of desire. In this way, desire is
born through the imitation of the conjured subject of desire. But because this
conjured subject of desire reveals the "void gnawing at himself . . . Nothing is

worse for the desiring subject than to see his own imitation brought into the open" (73).

For Girard, there is no desire prior to rivalry. As opposed to Lacan, for whom desire emerges from a primary splitting or repudiation, Girard insists that desire is the consequence of the triangularity of all social structure, and maintains that it is only as a consequence of the mimetic appropriation of the Other that desire is engendered at all.

Duras's novel thus traces these efforts at desirous and aggressive mimesis, but it also engages the reader in precisely such an ambivalent engagement. How would we understand the obsession of Lol Stein with Tatiana Karl, this desirous redoubling, in Girardian terms? Is the desire for Tatiana, or is it for Jack Hold, for Michael Richardson? And is the desire to imitate, to acquire desire through imitation, or is it to possess and vanquish the mediator, and would that mediator be Jack or Tatiana? Is there a way to answer these questions for sure, or are they finally undecidable? If Lol can desire them both, and desire each of them through the other, in addition to the lost Michael Richardson, then does the triangular structure remain in place, or does its very redoubling suggest that the map of power exceeds the triangular constraint? And is it possible to speak of the desire that underwrites the author/narrator relation, of Duras's mimetic relation to Jack Hold, as yet another articulation of desire as displacement, mimesis, and vanquishing?

For Lacan, who found Duras's text to be resonant with his own views on originary trauma, memory, and desire, language itself is structured as desire. Linguistic reference fails in the same way that desire is structured by failure: if language were to reach the object it desires, it would undo itself as language. For Girard, and in the recent work of Borsch-Jacobsen, desire fails not because of an originary foreclosure of the possibility of satisfaction, but because, quite simply, there is always someone else in the way, someone whose place cannot be fully appropriated. The "others" who disrupt Jack's hold on Lol (and who also facilitate it) are permanently there: there is no way of restricting the domain of alterity to just those two — despite the persistence of that fantasy.

Eve Kosofsky Sedgwick invokes Girard in her influential work, *Between Men: English Literature and Male Homosocial Desire,* to suggest that the apparent heterosexuality presupposed by so many narratives of desire is mediated by the rival, and that the rival is the concealed and essential object of desire. Whereas the Lacanian scheme appears to consecrate the heterosexualization of desire, the Girardian scheme in Sedgwick casts doubt on the sanctified pathos of heterosexual difference as a condition of desire. To what extent is the desire to move the rival out of the way a desire for the rival him/herself? And is identification merely an identification with the rival as object of desire, or can identification itself be a deflected sign of desire?

Irigaray will enter this scene of critical rejoinders to Lacan with the remark that "the subject is always already masculine." Is desire, then, a masculine problematic? Is it nothing other than the pathos of that failed return to a maternal origin, a return which, were it possible, would undo the subject in its masculinity, threaten his sense of temporary mastery, and enter him into a domain of threatening femininity? For Lacan, the subject is structured by the Other, which is to say that for the subject to remain the subject, it must *repudiate* the Other, and that its desire will nevertheless remain for that Other, the very sign of his potential undoing. This ambivalence suggests that there can be no desire without a prior repudiation, and that desire seeks a recovery of a lost Other that it simultaneously resists.

Lacan writes in "The Mirror Stage" of the "dehiscence" at the heart of man, the split, the divide that is "his" beginning. This "dehiscence" is understood as the founding and originating "bar" that establishes sexual difference along the ambivalent axis of repudiation and desire — the masculine version of heterosexual pathos. In an effort to debunk this institutionalization of sexual difference along the lines of this ambivalence, Monique Wittig (1985, 6) seeks recourse, paradoxically, to Plato and to a monistic conception of Being prior to sexual difference. "Being as being is not divided," she writes, but gender "tries to accomplish the division of Being." And though it may seem equally improbable to return to a metaphysics of plenitude, Wittig's radical speculation suggests that there may be other metaphysical scenes from which to conjecture the relation between language, desire, and sexual difference.

Although some feminist scholars have lauded the Lacanian contribution to psychoanalysis because it insists that sexual difference is at the foundation of language itself, it has become increasingly important in the context of contemporary lesbian and gay scholarship to ask *which version* of sexual difference is presupposed as the immutable foundation of language, and *at what cost?* The "scene" of founding repudiation and subsequent desire installs heterosexual pathos as the structuring erotics of language. Is this installation based on an unarticulated set of "repudiations" and "foreclosures" of its own? Why this scene rather than some other? Is it true that this is a scene that we cannot refuse because it structures us, forms us, in advance, as Lacanian scholars wryly note, or is it a scene privileged as the origin story for the purposes of valorizing the "inevitable" character of heterosexual desire?

Partly in response to the limitations of this position, Barthes sought to reclaim pleasure as the production and proliferation of a polysemous textuality that contests the univocal constraints on conceptual language. And toward the end of *The History of Sexuality,* volume 1, Foucault wrote that it was time to shift our theoretical concern from the discourse on desire (understood as a privileged term of psychoanalysis) to bodies and pleasures. And yet, by the time Foucault wrote the preface to volume 2 of that same work, he concedes the theoretical necessity of returning to the topic of the subject of desire: how is it produced, and how is desire installed as the essential activity of the subject?

In an effort to redeploy the Lacanian scheme toward a more expansive conception of desire and language, Kristeva sought to illuminate the "semiotic" dimension of language, in which a corporeal set of signs — sound, rhythm, and pulsation — undermines the possibility of communicative speech governed by the symbolic law. In *Anti-Oedipus* (1977), Gilles Deleuze and Felix Guattari question why desire must be figured as a "lack" at all, and seek recourse to Spinoza and Nietzsche to offer an alternative view of desire as primarily excessive and productive in its effects.

Where Lacan figured desire as that which might *subvert* the subject, reveal its decenteredness, reverse its intentionality, critics such as Leo Bersani have taken an even more radical view, suggesting the possibility of a "shattering" of the subject through the erotic force of desire, and of a masochism that has as its end the dissolution of the subject itself.

Although both Lacan and Girard postulate originary social structures, repression and rivalry, in which desire emerges, it appears more plausible, and perhaps less metaphysical, to assume that those founding scenarios are more variable and complex. What does it mean to speak about "the impossible desire to return" within the context of geopolitical displacements of various kinds? Is there a social or cultural unconscious to desire, and how are we to describe the complex intertwining of those racial and gendered imaginaries by which desire acquires its political valence?

If sexual difference is no longer credible as foundational to desire, then what possibilities exist for opening up the homosexual imaginary? And will the problematic relation of desire and language continue to haunt these more contemporary inquiries? If the terms by which we desire recognition are given in a discourse that precedes us, and that moves us in much the way the "soul" was once said to move us, to what extent are we moved by desires whose aims we neither originate nor fully know? And to the extent that we seek to recollect ourselves in the aims of such desires, are we not blocked from that recovery precisely because the discourses through which our desires are formed are never fully ours to own? In this strange reformulation of Aristotelian wisdom, it may be that precisely by virtue of the historicity and sociality of those desire-producing discourses that we are, in words, never fully recoverable to ourselves.

Such a predicament undermines the possibility of finding ourselves in what we read, in owning the very terms on which our very desire depends. Such a structuring misrecognition wrought through the uneasy relation of language and desire suggests that to desire is to err, but to err necessarily and, perhaps, never fully with intention or guilt.

Suggested Readings

Bersani, Leo. 1986. *The Freudian Body: Psychoanalysis and Art.*

Deleuze, Gilles, and Felix Guattari. 1977. *Anti-Oedipus.*

Foucault, Michel. 1990. *The History of Sexuality,* Volume 1.

Girard, René. 1965. *Deceit, Desire, and the Novel: Self and Other in Literary Structure.*

Halperin, David M., John J. Winkler, and Froma I. Zeitlin, eds. 1990. *Before Sexuality: The Construction of Erotic Experience in the Ancient Greek World.*

Kristeva, Julia. 1980. *Desire in Language: A Semiotic Approach to Literature and Art.*

Lacan, Jacques. 1992. *The Ethics of Psychoanalysis 1959–60.*

Sedgwick, Eve Kosofsky. 1985. *Between Men: English Literature and Male Homosocial Desire.*

Winkler, John J. 1990. *The Constraints of Desire: The Anthropology of Sex and Gender in Ancient Greece.*

27

Ethics

Geoffrey Galt Harpham

1. Ethics in Our Time

F OR MOST of the Theoretical Era (c. 1968–87), ethics, the discourse of "respect for the law," had no respect. All the critical schools that arose or
redefined themselves during this era—semiotics, deconstruction, feminism,
Marxism, and psychoanalysis, to name the most prominent—took as their
founding premise the radical inadequacy of such Enlightenment leftovers as "the
universal subject," the "subject of humanism," the "sovereign subject," the "traditional concept of the self"; and in the assessment of the various crimes and mis-
demeanors committed by or on behalf of this subject, ethics was seen to be heavily implicated. For it was in the discourse of ethics—was it not?—that the
subject, grossly flourishing in all its pretheoretical arrogance, claimed an undis-
turbed mastery over itself and indeed the entire world by claiming to base its
judgments and actions on the dictates of universal law. According to this account, whenever someone claimed to be acting on "the ethical imperative" or
"the moral law," they were in fact rendering mystical and grand their own private
interests or desires. Making claims of this sort, one might even persuade oneself
that one's interests were somehow globally necessary: ethics could be the particular way in which people preserved a good conscience while overriding or delegi-
timating the claims of others. Ethics thus became for many the proper name of
power, hypocrisy, and unreality. As the Marxist critic Fredric Jameson charged,
it was "ethics itself" that had arranged the binary oppositions such as self and
other, good and evil, to which the Western mind has become so disastrously
attached; and ethics itself that served as "the ideological vehicle and the legitimation of concrete structures of power and domination" (1981, 114).

Others echoed and varied this charge. "Women, stop trying," the French feminist Luce Irigaray wrote; "Do what comes to mind, do what you like: without
'reasons,' without 'valid motives,' without 'justification.' You don't have to raise
your impulses to the lofty status of categorical imperatives" (1985, 203). Irigaray
and others denounced one specific conceptual form of the "concrete structures
of power and domination" that Jameson noted, the way in which the presumably

unsexed subject of morality, the subject who was subject to categorical imperatives, was tacitly assumed to be male. As when one (male) philosopher, arguing
for a liberal pluralism, stated that "there are many different ends that men may
seek, and still be fully rational, fully men" (Berlin 1988, 14); or when another
contended that the "classic tradition" he would like to revive involves "one central functional concept, the concept of *man* understood as having an essential
nature and an essential purpose or function" (MacIntyre 1981, 56); or when a
third reflected on "that sense of freedom which men take to be peculiar to themselves," and meditated on "the intrinsic character of thought," which is "self-
correcting, when thinking reaches a first stage of complexity, as it does in adult
men" (Hampshire 1983, 78, 54). Somehow, ethical discourse, which ought to
concern itself exclusively with Reason, Freedom, Value, or the Good, still insistently constructs a particular sexual scenario, casting "man" in all the lead roles:
the Hero of Duty, the Prince of Reflection, the Knight of Temptation, the Sovereign of Freedom, the General Exemplum of Humanity.

Such sinister and silent collusion between particular, concrete arrangements
of power and an abstract and "universal" style of representation seemed to many
to be the peculiar specialty of ethics, and provoked the accusation that, in its
worldly work, ethics was predicated not on "respect" but rather on what Jacques
Derrida called "nonrespect," and not just for women. The mighty complex of
ideas and prejudices that Derrida titled "logocentrism" works tirelessly to neutralize or marginalize the qualities of "absence, dissimulation, detour, différance,
writing," and gets ethics to do the dirty work. The bias in favor of "presence"
that Derrida says characterizes all Western thought works by holding up speech
rather than writing as the more natural, fundamental, primary — in a word, ethical — form of language. "The ethic of the living word," Derrida writes, "would
be as respectable as respect itself if it did not live on a delusion and a nonrespect
for its own condition of origin, if it did not dream in speech of a presence denied
to writing, denied by writing. The ethic of speech is the *delusion* of a presence
mastered" (1978a, 139). Like Jameson and Irigaray, Derrida warned that a discourse that encouraged submission to a general or universal law lent itself to
projects of mastery whose agendas were not universal, just unvoiced or unacknowledged. In ethical discourse, it was widely believed, values and practices
with no special claim to worthiness became normative.

Thus, virtually all the leading voices of the Theoretical Era (an era conspicuous
for its deification of "leading voices") organized their critiques of humanism as
exposés of ethics, revelations of the transgressive, rebellious, or subversive energies that ethics had effectively masked and suppressed. And virtually all joined
Derrida in seeing ethics as a combination of mastery *and* delusion. For Jameson,
the focus of ethics on the individual confronting a moment of moral choice
obscured the deep currents of collective, historical life; for Jacques Lacan, the
Kantian ethic of rational self-legislation masked the kernel of desire that ulti-

mately aligns ethics with masochistic enjoyment, and Kant with de Sade; for Paul de Man, ethics had "nothing to do with the will (thwarted or free) of a subject," and was best considered a "language aporia," a "linguistic confusion," a "discursive mode among others" (1979, 206); for Michel Foucault, ethics was a typical humanistic soap bubble whose reality was the relentlessly productive force of various discursive and disciplinary regimes. For all of them, the truth of ethics was announced by Nietzsche: "a mere fabrication for purposes of gulling: at best, an artistic fiction; at worst, an outrageous imposture" (1956, 10).

Then, something happened.

On or about December 1, 1987, the nature of literary theory changed. When the *New York Times* reported the discovery of a large number of articles written by the youthful Paul de Man in a Belgian collaborationist newspaper in 1941–42, virtually everything about literary theory and criticism as practiced in the United States underwent a transformation as violent and radical as that which had been wrought a generation earlier by the advent of "theory" itself. A profession that had just accustomed itself to the tenuring of theoreticians was subjected to the spectacle of their dethroning; heated but still decorous debates about the nature of literary language, the role of metaphor in the discourses of rationality, the functioning of discursive regimes, the relevance of philosophy to literary study, the dominance of "Western metaphysics," abruptly gave way to charges of personal immorality, collaboration in the Holocaust, opportunism, and deception. The stakes and temperature of critical discourse rose appreciably. And as Jimmy Durante used to say, everybody wanted to get into the act. In the wild controversy that ensued, every possible position, it seemed, was attacked or defended by somebody. By his enemies, de Man was bluntly accused of complicity in Nazi savagery, while his friends and allies claimed to discern even in the most incriminating of the newly discovered articles signs that a rhetorically hypersubtle de Man was only appearing to collaborate while actually resisting. The later work also came in for reassessment. Some saw in the "impersonal" austerity of his literary criticism a mere continuation of his youthful enthusiasms; but to others, the stress de Man placed in his last years on linguistic "inhumanity" seemed a heroic attempt to imagine a language unstained by human criminality, as well as a warning to others of the errors into which he had fallen as a young man. Deconstructionists, who had been attempting to outlast and outpublish the feminist, Marxist, and historicist scholars who had been attacking them for their principled indifference to history, the material base, justice, and value, suffered their heaviest blow since the death of de Man himself in 1983. Deconstruction's dominance had discouraged any ethical evaluation of the author; but now that that dominance was rapidly proving to be delusory, the repressed—ethics, which had been repressed, ironically enough, because it was seen as an *agent* of repression—was returning in force, and the American academy gave itself over to a glut of judgment. Many antitheorists seemed simply astonished at their good fortune in finding de Man and deconstruction vulnerable on ethical grounds, just when they had nearly given up hope of victory on other grounds. When the last incontrovertible point was made, one thing, and perhaps only one, was clear: ethics was on the agenda.

The effect on deconstruction was traumatic. De Man's work suddenly switched genres, being read now not as literary criticism but as a coded testimony. The template of the wartime journalism disclosed in de Man's often curious and impacted phrasings patterns of obsessive worry about exposure, proleptic self-defense, meditations on the uselessness of confession, signals for help, as when he introduced, in the last year of his life, a second edition of his first book, *Blindness and Insight,* by noting, "I am not given to retrospective self-examination and mercifully forget what I have written with the same alacrity I forget bad movies—although, as with bad movies, certain scenes or phrases return at times to embarrass and haunt me like a guilty conscience" (1983, xii). The timing of the discovery had an unfortunate effect on J. Hillis Miller's *The Ethics of Reading* (1986), which had placed de Man in the succession of Kant: whereas Kant had evacuated the ethical subject of every feeling but "respect for the law," de Man had erased from the reading subject every concern but respect for the text. A properly respectful or ethical reading, Miller had argued, lingered in the apprehension of textual "undecidability"; and now, when the response to the wartime journalism began to assume threatening proportions, Miller charged de Man's enemies with a failure to *read*. It was noted by some that, measured against the virtually infinite prolongation Miller had envisioned, any definite judgment could seem premature, or "unethical." Although mounted with considerable energy and commitment, the argument that de Man's ethics could only be judged in de Man's terms was not universally persuasive.

Perhaps the most complex and productive effect of the de Man affair was on the work of Derrida. Painful though it was, the controversy seems actually to have stimulated Derrida not only to expand and deepen a meditation on ethics that was, as we have seen, present in his work from the very beginning, but to move his general critique in a new direction, his formidable style becoming in the process much more flexible and accessible. His long and deeply personal essay, "Like the Sound of the Sea Deep within a Shell: Paul de Man's War," proceeded through the newly discovered texts according to reading procedures he had established twenty years earlier, citing evidence for (*on the one hand*) active collaboration in the anti-Semitic project of the Reich, and (*on the other hand*) for an elusive, indeed fugitive critique of what de Man had referred to in one piece as "vulgar anti-Semitism," and, possibly, of all anti-Semitism inasmuch as it was vulgar. With excruciating attention to textual detail—an attention that, by itself, seemed to some violently inappropriate considering the context—Derrida "read" de Man, registering both the full, appalling force of the shock and, with a grim fidelity to principle, the scant but, he insisted, definite possibility that things were not as bad as they seemed — an argument that, to those persuaded otherwise, was reminiscent of Mark Twain's comment that Wagner's music was not as bad as it sounded. Derrida's essay drew the fire of those who wanted for once an unambivalent statement; they got what they wanted, but in the form of an unequivocally scathing criticism of themselves in a text that was at once Derrida's most intimate and most violent, a freeswinging diatribe entitled "Biodegradables."

This, clearly, was not Derrida's chosen battlefield. Unlike many other eminent philosophers or academics, Derrida never sought to use his position to make pronouncements, ethical or otherwise. But the crisis of the moment tested the strength of his principles and methods, and perhaps fortified him to undertake a general defense of deconstruction on ethical grounds. He reiterated arguments to the effect that, far from representing a principle of frivolity, deconstruction actually entailed a higher level of readerly and political responsibility by identifying the fissures and instabilities in what had seemed to be thoroughly grounded structures. And he systematized the ethical commitments of deconstruction in a 1988 essay, "Afterword: Toward an Ethic of Discussion," where he outlined a normative process of deconstructive reading in which a "layer or moment" of "doubling commentary" establishing the "minimal consensus" on the "relatively stable" meaning of a text and its relevant contexts was to be followed by a second, "productive" layer or moment of "interpretation." Derrida seemed to envision a structural relationship between these aspects of reading and what Kant defined as the antinomies of pure practical reason, necessity, and freedom. Stating that deconstruction began with the humble and disinterested reproduction of fact, Derrida was also claiming that the interpretive "freeplay" of his own texts constituted the full realization of traditional scholarship, the ripened completion of critical understanding. So far from licensing indifference or neutrality, Derrida said, he was trying to determine the conditions under which a reading became truly responsible by identifying a phase of undecidability through which reading must pass, a phase in which conclusions that had been taken for granted become subject to disinterested questioning. Why, Derrida asks at the end of this essay, "have I always hesitated to characterize [the unconditionality that prescribes deconstruction] in Kantian terms . . . when that would have been so easy and would have enabled me to avoid so much criticism, itself all too facile as well? Because such characterizations seemed to me essentially associated with philosophemes that themselves call for deconstructive questions" (1988, 153). The difference between Kant's discourse and his own is not that one is ethical and the other critical, for Derrida claims ethical value for deconstructive criticism. It is that Kant still believes in the subject and related "philosophemes," and so must be deconstructed — according to the ethical imperative that he himself glimpsed, but only glimpsed.

While Kant's particular formulations can be deconstructed, the imperative to deconstruct has become categorical, i.e., Kantian and ethical. At the same time (the late '80s), Derrida was turning to such concepts as law, justice, and responsibility, solidifying the image of deconstruction as a discourse of what might be called imperativity in general. Even "the subject" reappears in a 1989 interview in which Derrida speaks of the linking of "the ego" to an inhuman other, "and above all to the law, as subject subjected to the law, subject to the law in its very autonomy, to ethical or juridical law, to political law or power, to order (symbolic or not) . . ." (1991, 99). The subject can "return" on the condition that it be transformed and modernized—no longer the self-identical, self-regulating subject of humanism, but rather a subject inmixed with otherness. This otherness, Derrida said, would consist not only of the obligation that all people owe to other people, but also of the iron laws, the internal othernesses, which we, as speaking animals, harbor within our living consciousness: "the mark in general," "the trace," "iterability," "*différance*," othernesses that *are themselves not only human*" (116).

I have dwelt at some length on Derrida's account of the terms on which a return of the subject might be admissible or conceivable because it marks both a decisive emphasis in his recent work and a consensus emerging within various schools of thought about the role of such factors as necessity, law, and obligation in the formation of a subject—a subject that must be ethical. In fact, the date of December 1, 1987, does not mark the moment when ethics abruptly returned from its exile in a predeconstructive wilderness, but rather the approximate time when the large fact that all sorts of thinkers had for some time been heavily invested in ethics became inescapable. For it was not only Derrida who could claim to have been ethical all along. As North American readers now began to realize, a persistent strain of ethical concern had for some time troubled the margins of critical discourse, even in the work of those who had been thought to be most rigorously antihumanistic.

Marx, for example, was taken by Jameson as the authority for an antiethical campaign to "[transcend] the 'ethical' in the direction of the political and the collective" (1981: 60). But Philip J. Kain's *Marx and Ethics* (1988) argued that Marx himself rejected ethics only for a brief period in the mid-1840s and was a decisively ethical thinker both before and after. And as a number of readers noticed, Jameson's own polemic borrowed from the rhetoric of ethics: indeed, he began one book by announcing a "transhistorical" and "absolute" commandment—"Always historicize!"—as "the moral of *The Political Unconscious*" (9). Similarly, psychoanalytic criticism had for the most part sustained Freud's dismissive attitude toward any claims to ethical transcendence or grounding; but a 1986 volume called *Pragmatism's Freud: The Moral Disposition of Psychoanalysis* awakened suspicions that Freud might have underestimated or failed to appreciate his own ethical commitments. In the same year, Jacques Lacan's 1959–60 seminar *Ethique de la psychanalyse* appeared, crystallizing the complex and unorthodox ethics that had hitherto appeared in his work primarily in the form of cryptic comments such as "The status of the unconscious is ethical." If Lacan had been perceived by readers of *Ecrits* and *The Four Fundamental Concepts of Psychoanalysis* as a debunker of ethics, he now emerged as an ethical thinker in his own right with the claim that psychoanalysis did in fact have a law, if only one: that one must not "give way as to one's desire." The psychoanalytically informed French feminists who, in one mood, rejected the very idea of ethics often proposed as a replacement another ethic. In an early article, Julia Kristeva, for example, noted the dominance in linguistics of the concept of structure, and thus of values of regularity and systematicity that were, she claimed, drawn from "social contract" ethics. As a corrective, Kristeva sought to restore to its rightful place the notion of language as a signifying practice with revolutionary potential, in which the speaking subject was allowed to sense the "rhythm of the body as well as the upheavals of history." "Linguistic ethics," she wrote "consists in following the resurgence of an 'I'" (1980, 34). And Luce Irigaray, whom we last saw denouncing Kantian ethics, argued that feminine difference compelled not a rejection of ethics *tout court,* but rather a different ethic, an ethic of difference, or, as she put it in a 1984 book, *An Ethics of Sexual Difference.*

Even postmodernist theory, which originally defined itself in opposition to such aspects of "modernity" as Jürgen Habermas's neo-Kantian "discourse ethics," subsequently advanced its own ethic. While Habermas and Jean-François Lyotard, postmodernism's leading theoretician, disagreed on many issues, they held one key position in common — that the emphasis on language so central to contemporary self-understanding yielded a positive ethic. For Habermas, this ethic embraced the values implicit in transparent, undistorted, and open communication, a normative equality that was "counterfactually" immanent in all utterances whatsoever, no matter how duplicitous, inept, or mendacious. Lyotard, who had seemed to many readers an opponent of all norms, ideals, regulations, and even — given the density and obscurity of some of his texts — of transparent communication, argued against Habermas by defining a counterethic specific to postmodernity. Lyotard praised Levinas for completing the work Kant had begun, absolutely severing "the language game of prescription" from any connection with the "ontological discourse" cultivated by the knowledge-obsessed Greeks, and creating a perfect "emptiness" of the commandment to obey. "Obligation without normativity" — this was an ethic consistent with postmodernity's emphasis on heterodoxy and dissemination and also, interestingly enough, with the secret essence of modernity itself, which was beginning to be understood by Lacanians, Derrideans, and Foucauldians as the ethos of ungrounded commands, of necessity "suspended over an abyss."

It was, however, the late work of Foucault that represented the most decisive marker of the emergence of ethics. In the second and third volumes of the History of Sexuality series, and in a number of late essays and interviews — all of

which appeared in translation in the mid- 1980s — Foucault attempted a complicated series of rapprochements with the Enlightenment, with antiquity, with the
asceticism of early Christianity, with the notion of self-fashioning — in a word,
with ethics. The title of one of his several "final interviews," "The Ethic of Care
for the Self as a Practice of Freedom," indicates the direction of his thinking in
the last few years of his life, and suggests, too, the new clarity or "innocence" of
his last style. Having flamboyantly announced the obliteration of Man in his
earlier work, Foucault now, by a logic that continues to excite wonder, underwent a conversion to ethical humanism.

The massive and general consequence of (1) the de Man controversy, (2) the
rapidly accumulating evidence of a powerful interest in ethics among "literary"
theoreticians (theoreticians whose work influenced students of literature), and
(3) the appearance of several notable philosophical texts on ethics that drew
heavily on the formal and conceptual resources of literature — among which were
Alasdair MacIntyre's *After Virtue* (1981), Martha Nussbaum's *The Fragility of
Goodness* (1986), and Richard Rorty's *Contingency, Irony, and Solidarity* (1989) —
was a fundamental reorientation of literary theory through a convergence on the
question, the issue, the problem, the status of ethics.

2. ETHICS ITSELF

What might have escaped notice in this convergence was the curious fact that
ethics had been clearly understood in radically antithetical ways, as the agent of
repression *and* as the repressed itself, as the essence of classical humanism *and* of
postmodern antihumanism, as the discourse of the integrated and self-mastering
subject *and* of the fissured or overdetermined subject, as the locus of forthright
worthiness *and* of self-disguising power. Such a paradox compels the fundamental question: What *is* ethics?

The answers to this simple inquiry are complexity itself, for they take us
straight to the decentered center of ethics, its concern for "the other." Ethics is
the arena in which the claims of otherness — the moral law, the human other,
cultural norms, the Good-in-itself, etc. — are articulated and negotiated. In the
domain of ethics, "selfish" or "narrow" considerations are subjected to cancellation, negation, crossing by principles represented as "deeper," "higher," or "more
fundamental." Ethics is the ultimate trump card; to say, as did the President's
Commission on Medical Ethics in 1983, that "ending a patient's life intentionally is absolutely forbidden on moral grounds" is to attempt to end the life of
that particular dispute, for no claim can be advanced that would properly override the moral one. The elementary fact that ethics stands over and against other
kinds of claims only begins, however, to indicate the role of otherness in ethical
discourse. Considered as a Foucauldian "discursive regime," ethical discourse be-
trays an extraordinary regularity owing to its structural obsession with the relations between apparently opposed terms. In the field of ethics, philosophers con-

sider questions of self and other, interest and principle, fact and value, "is" and "ought," the "hypothetical" and the "categorical," *Moralität* and *Sittlichkeit,* rules and cultural norms, virtues and principles, the "view from nowhere" and the contingent position of the subject, meta-ethics and normative ethics. And the history of ethics is a history of debates: Hume v. Kant, Kant v. Hegel, Kant v. Nietzsche, emotivism v. rationalism, phallocentrism v. feminism, universalism v. communitarianism, deontology v. consequentialism. The real paradox of ethics is that a discourse that seems to promise answers is so obsessed with questions.

Moreover, the two questions that dominate ethical inquiry — How ought one live? and What ought I to do? — suggest incommensurable points of view. The first reflects the distanced perspective of some de-individualized and ideal being free to consider laws and norms as such; the second, the particular perspective of a real person confronting an actual situation. The consequence of this incommensurability has escaped the attention of many philosophers: it is that the controversies that structure the history of ethics can never be settled, for obedience to one kind of imperative alone would be — unethical. To consider only the point of view of "one," for example, would be to make oneself inhuman, a brain in a vat; while the absolute refusal to consider that point of view, to think only through the "I," would suggest a personality almost inconceivably self-absorbed and even mentally handicapped, powerless to generalize. Thus, despite the incoherence that would seem to be entailed by the overdetermination of action by different principles, both are necessary; for each, by itself, is radically unworthy if not simply impossible. The contentious history of ethics itself constitutes powerful evidence that ethics can never hope to resolve its internal difficulties and offer itself to the world as a guide to the perplexed. Articulating perplexity, rather than guiding, is what ethics is all about.

What makes the fact of overdetermination truly interesting is that ethical reasoning appears to be, in Stuart Hampshire's phrase, "underdetermined by the arguments," predicated on norms and ideals that stand beyond reasons and must simply be accepted or rejected (1983, 42). This feature of ethical thinking structures the one indispensable word in ethics, *ought*. Ethical discourse zeroes in on the *ought* by depriving it of any support in the form of appeals to fears, desires, or immediate interests that might distract from its peculiar force. The ethical *ought* is the *ought* in and of itself, reduced to its tautological essence: you ought to because you ought to. And yet, the stark *ought* of ethics is not empty; rather, it constitutes a compromise formation, proclaiming the law to a creature who is presumed to be free to follow it or not. If human beings were not free, there would be no need for urging, but if they were not in fact bound by the law, there would be nothing to urge. In the structure of the *ought,* we see, then, the style or strategy of ethical reasoning generally — apparently underdetermined but actually overdetermined.

While the apparent underdetermination of the *ought* suggests that we can simply choose right over wrong, its actual overdetermination confirms a gathering suspicion that can now be stated directly, that ethical choice is never a matter of selecting the right over the wrong, the good over the evil, and that a choice is "ethical" insofar as *both* options available for choosing embody principles that can be considered worthy. In other words, an ethical choice to do X rather than Y—to poison one's tormentor rather than permitting him to ruin one's life, to vote for Democrats on principle, to cut the kid some slack, to shoot doctors who perform abortions, etc.—is never merely a decision to act on principle rather than just acting any way one pleases. An ethical choice of actions follows a prior, often silent and even unacknowledged *choice of principles*. "To end a patient's life intentionally" may be absolutely forbidden on moral grounds, but the same could be said about "exposing a patient and his family to pointless suffering," and we will choose what to do based on which principle we think overrides the other. Do we decide to parole the convicted rapist? We can say we have chosen an "ethic of mercy" over an "ethic of retribution." Do we bomb the abortion clinic? The judge may differ, but we can tell our children that our choice was not "to bomb or not to bomb" but rather to pursue "an ethic of life" as opposed to other, less caring alternatives.

But while ethical choice is always a choice between ethics, the apparent underdetermination of the *ought* actively discourages an inquiry into this prior choice. The fact that the poor, bare, forked *ought* of ethics stands alone, without reasons, effectively masks the complicated interior determinations and weightings, the "feel" for the situation that eventually issues in decisions and acts. The discourse of practical ethics makes a fetish of a choice that is in some respects no choice at all, the (non)decision to act according to principle, according to a law that is given rather than invented for the occasion or crafted to rationalize our pursuit of self-interest. For since either option could be represented as exemplary of some principle or other, we could not have failed to act on principle; this is in fact one sense in which the imperative to act on principle could be "categorical." Practical ethical discourse thus misses the mark—and misses it, as it were, purposely—insofar as it focuses on the decision to "act ethically" or "obey the ethical law." Representing our actions in this way virtually invites some aggressive skeptic to come along and perform a triumphant "genealogy of morals," demonstrating how our choice was in fact driven by motives of interest, power, pleasure, self-aggrandizement, motives of which we might not even have been conscious. Skeptical genealogies can be performed with considerable guarantee of success because, in a terminal paradox, the fact that any choice can be reconciled with "principle" also means that any choice can also be shown to be *in*compatible with principle or *un*ethical because it violates some other, entirely credible principle. Thus every "ethical" decision violates some law or other, and violates it precisely because it is "ethical."

We have arrived in the vicinity of another distinctive feature of ethical dis-

course, the internal distinction philosophers have drawn within ethics in order
to segregate what Bernard Williams calls the "special system" of "morality." In
Ethics and the Limits of Philosophy (1985), Williams regrets the fact that morality—
which, he says, stresses the idea of obligation, works by the mechanism of blame,
overrates the importance of individual agency and pure rationality, and draws an
implausibly bright line between right and wrong—enjoys a nearly synonymic
relation with ethics. "We would be better off without it," Williams says of morality—and yet there it is, "irremovably, one name" for ethics as a whole (174, 6).
In the history of ethical discourse, the precise content of the terms "ethics" and
"morality" varies, sometimes indicating the general field of inquiry as opposed
to the particular rules one must follow, or right action itself as opposed to right
action for the right motive, or cultural norms as opposed to the iron law of
reason. But the gesture of drawing a kind of dotted line between phases or aspects of ethics remains remarkably constant.

Wishing to preserve the intuition behind this gesture, I would suggest that
we extend Williams's distinction, but try to overcome his fastidious distaste for
morality's violence and crudity. Morality represents, I would argue, a particular
moment of ethics, when all but one of the available alternatives are excluded,
chosen against, regardless of their claims. At the moment of morality, the circumstance of choice that defines and is defined by ethics is closed off by a decision that crushes all opposition in its drive to self-actualization. The injunction
not to decide on a final interpretation of a text may qualify as an "ethics of reading," but it is definitely not a morality; morality does not shrink from such tasks
but welcomes them as its proper responsibility. Morality is the "rigor" of ethical
thought, where the rubber of a definite principle meets the road of reality. Ethics
constitutes a general imperative to "act on principle"; morality constitutes a further imperative nested within the ethical that commands us to act now and on
the right principle, that is, the one we want to stand *as* principle. If morality is
stigmatized in the eyes of some who would prefer beveled to sharp edges, it is
because moral decision is on easy terms with desire and force, two factors that
embarrass those whose thought runs to piety. Also, as the moment when
thought ceases, morality has little defense against the suspicion that it stands for
nothing more than the fatigue, the impatience, the indifference, the compla-
cency, the death drive of ethical thought. The moral moment is irremovable,
however, not just because decisions must be made, but also because mere choice
has, by itself, no ethical value whatsoever; without decision, ethics would be
condemned to dithering. It is morality that realizes ethics, making it ethical. At
the same time, however, morality negates ethics, and needs ethics in order to be
moral. Decisions achieved without a passage through what Derrida would call
undecidability and what a more traditional account would call the circumstance
of free choice represent mere blindness and brutality. Ethics places imperatives,
principles, alternatives on a balanced scale, sustaining an august reticence, a prin-

cipled irresolution to which, nevertheless, the limited and precise prescriptions of morality must refer for their authority. So while, once again, neither ethics nor morality has any claim on our respect, their incoherent union is respect itself.

To illustrate some of the ways in which this network of othernesses might work in a particular case, we can track the argument of a recent book, Virginia Held's *Feminist Morality: Transforming Culture, Society, and Politics* (1993). Held is one of those who, in the wake of Carol Gilligan's claim for the specificity of female moral development, are seeking social "transformation" by renovating rather than rejecting ethics. The target is not ethics as such, but rather, as with Kristeva, "social contract" or "rational choice" theory, in which those kinds of activities in which men have, in advanced cultures, been historically dominant are advanced as universal norms. In contrast to Kristeva, however, Held argues not for anarchic upheaval but for the quieter virtues of "being" over those of "doing," family relations over contractual relations, and affect over abstract reason. A male-dominated society has, she contends, contrived to define the virtues and the principles of obligation in such a way as to distribute most of the rewards to men while representing women as sub-moral specialists in the "natural." Held argues in response that "feminist" values and practices such as relationships, shared values, mothering, and trust are matters of genuinely ethical import. Held thus offers a critique and a remedy. She seeks to provide a deepened historical understanding of the strategic uses of ethics in a phallocentric society by disclosing the *free choices,* and therefore purposive agency, at work in determining a human norm in a certain way. And she suggests that equally free choices can now be made to define, as Held puts it, "our own moral concerns as women" (48).

So far so good. But the rule is that every (moral) choice in an ethical situation chooses against other alternatives with comparable claims. In this case, the unselected alternatives include not only Kristeva's ethic of upheaval but also what might be called an ethic of equality. Many women may well wish to refuse any attribution of ethical "difference" as a losing game, dignify it how you will. They may be troubled by a self-proclaimed "feminist morality" that displays a residual attachment to traditional roles that they might feel constitute not genuine endowments but rather historical damage. And they may be unimpressed by an "ethic" invented, as it were, for the occasion, to meet the self-esteem needs of a certain group. Absent the strict neutrality of Kantian formulations (act only on universalizable maxims; people should be treated as ends and not only as means; etc.), a group-specific ethic may actually undermine the ethical credentials of ethics itself. With its promotion of "more intimate forms of interaction" based on "idealized models of the family and friendship groups" (228), Held's ethic in particular is vulnerable to the charge that it merely reinscribes the original problem. The family is, after all, the defining institution of the patriarchy; and some of the worst abuses in the public sphere, from a feminist perspective, have been committed by men acting as if they were members not of a society of law but of a "friendship group," i.e., an old-boy network, a locker room, a bar, a fraternity, a secret club. And even the argument that the family might be a more proper locus of ethical concern than the corporation might simply confirm, for some, the prejudice that women ought not to be allowed into business at any level higher than the secretarial.

Held seems partly aware of the problems inevitably created by the attempt to define a group-friendly set of principles, an ethic that is substantial rather than "abstract" and "formal." For the sketchiest and most tentative part of her book is the brief section at the end where she offers a "satisfactorily worked-out feminist and moral point of view." The new emphases include "different" "levels of caring and trust," common access to "universal emotions" and "universally shared concerns," a commitment to governmental help in "meeting needs," concern for the welfare of children, "changes in prevailing relationships between 'man' and 'nature,'" closer interpersonal relations, "an openness to new possibilities, and a deep sense of responsibility for living children, future generations, and global well-being." Such a list—drawn, it seems, from some Toastmaster's Guide to Ethical Bromides—says so little because it tries to say so much, to include every possible desideratum as a way of warding off the accusation of special pleading.

Because it posits an "overriding" imperative, ethics is a grievous offense to those who are overridden, and a mighty temptation to those who wish to override. But ethics, the general injunction to act on principle, cannot plausibly be advanced as the warrant for particular values or practices. The extreme generality of Held's ethic reflects, perhaps, her apprehension of the fact that the very notion of ethics cuts against the grain of feminism as a political movement with certain definite goals and projects. Still, not even the most abstract ethic can altogether get quit of the charge that it merely fronts for such goals and projects. Kant's very formalism has been seen as a natural expression of his own class (those with the leisure to think of themselves and the world from the formal point of view), a notion that would undoubtedly have astonished him. What we are beginning to understand is that ethics has, or is, two general and incommensurable functions. An ethical critique consists of an analysis of the free choices made by certain groups in the constitution of a given norm. All ethical systems can be shown by determined critics to be driven by a machinery of interest, and those who wish to transform culture, society, and politics often approach their project as Held does, through a critique of ethics, a project whose motto is: "Where monolithic necessity was, there shall freedom be." The revelation of freedom can be used to encourage both skepticism toward some norms and optimism about the prospects for achieving the second function of ethics, articulating and defending different norms. But here's the rub: the demonstration that a particular ethical system is politically, economically, or otherwise determined makes ethics in general look bad, and this makes it hard to propose an alternative ethic without exciting the same suspicions about its origins. The motto of properly ethical norms is "Where freedom was, there shall necessity be." Such norms just are, and those who follow them accept constraint as a law of their being, not as a mere preference. So while ethical critique must debunk the very notion of ethics as a precondition of its effectiveness, ethical norms, if they are to function as norms, must "forget" or "repress" their own genealogy. Held's dilemma—that her ethic is both too feminist and not feminist enough; or to put it another way, that it is too feminist to be ethical and too ethical to be feminist—exemplifies the general circumstance of ethics as a "critical term": that it is critical above all of itself.

3. ETHICS AND LITERATURE

Ethics has traditionally been a powerful critical term "for literary study." Literature, especially narrative, is said to "be ethical" in a number of ways. As a representation of life in which we are not directly engaged, literature lends itself well to the indispensable pedagogical activity of asking the classical philosophical questions: What obligations do I owe my fellow creature? What are the chief virtues and how should they be ranked? How can I negotiate conflicting claims? How can one know the good? Ethics also provides the general format for the classical kinds of literary questions: What insights does Quentin Compson achieve about the nature of historical responsibility? How does Huck mature over the course of the book? Was it right for Dorothea Brooke to marry Casaubon? Should Hamlet have killed the king immediately? Literature contributes to "ethical" understanding by showing motivations, revealing the ends of action, holding the mirror up to the community and the individual so they can judge themselves, promoting explanatory models that help make sense of the diversity of life, and imaging the "unity" that might be desirable in a human life. Such questions and concerns, typical of plot- and character-centered analysis, enjoy a codependency relationship with traditional humanism. For this reason, the ethical approach to literature, which is "theoretical" in the sense of being a kind of rehearsal or model of life, has been opposed to theory itself by MacIntyre, Rorty, Nussbaum, Iris Murdoch, and others. When such critics use the term "theory," they mean theory of two kinds, ethical theory exemplified by Kant, and literary theory exemplified by Derrida and deconstruction. With its referential specificity, human voice, and uncertain form, narrative—the argument goes—subverts both kinds of theory. As Eve Kosofsky Sedgwick writes, narrative, especially narrative "of a directly personal sort," can "disarm the categorical imperative that seems to do so much to promote cant and mystification about motives in the world of politically correct academia" (1990, 60). Martha Nussbaum reports that in Derrida's work, "the ethical vanishes more or less altogether," leaving her with "a certain hunger for blood," a craving she satisfies by blowing the dust off volumes by Aristotle and Henry James (1990, 170, 171). For a significant number of critics, the ethical approach to literature represents a highly effective "resistance to theory."

This is a bad mistake.

Ethics is, rather, the point at which literature intersects with theory, the point at which literature becomes conceptually interesting and theory becomes humanized. Within ethical theory, narrative serves as the necessary "example," with all the possibilities of servility, deflection, deformation, and insubordination that role implies. Take the moment when Kant defends his statement that all lies violate the categorical imperative against the objection that in certain cases one has a "right to lie" to protect others. In a little essay "On a Supposed Right to Lie Because of Philanthropic Concerns," Kant repeats his argument that lies erode the force of statements and contracts in general, thus vitiating "the very source of right"; but, aware that theory cannot defend itself without seeming dogmatic, he utters the inevitable words "for example." For example, if a man plotting a murder asks you whether his intended victim is in a certain house, you are still obligated to tell the truth, because — but let's let Kant, a masterly raconteur, tell the story:

> . . . it is indeed possible that after you have honestly answered Yes to the murderer's question . . . the [intended victim] went out unobserved and thus eluded the murderer, so that the deed would not have come about. However, if you told a lie and said that the intended victim was not in the house, and he has actually (though unbeknownst to you) gone out, with the result that by so doing he has been met by the murderer and thus the deed has been perpetrated, then in this case you may be justly accused as having caused his death. For if you had told the truth as best you knew it, then the murderer might perhaps have been caught by neighbors who came running while he was searching the house for his intended victim, and thus the deed might have been prevented. (Kant 1993, 65)

Lying does not necessarily solve the man's problem, and may well create problems for you as well as for "mankind in general"; but if you tell the truth, then, as Kant says, "public justice cannot lay a hand on you." The point in the present context is that the example, though necessary, creates certain problems for Kant. For while a strict formalism in theory might give the impression of an admirable rigor, the same formalist approach to an emergency in real life seems repugnant and inhuman. While public justice may be unable to punish you, your other friends, the murdered man's family, and the community in general may well choose to regard you as a pious monster, zealously protecting your own morality even at the expense of other people's lives. Theory requires examples, but the difference in kind between theory and example will always create an opportunity for the unpredictable subversion of the theory by the example enlisted to support it.

Narrative does not just exemplify (or fail to exemplify) theory; it excites it. William Styron's *Sophie's Choice* has stimulated a considerable amount of philosophical rumination because its central incident seems to provide a challenge to the theory of distributive justice. An officer in a German concentration camp demands that Sophie choose which of her two children will be sent to the gas chamber, threatening that if she refuses to choose, both will be sent. Sophie's choice causes a kind of theoretical nausea among those who believe, with John Rawls and others, that a noncontingent "justice" should prevail over any utilitarian determination of "the good." While utilitarian logic might tell us that it is "rational" to put some innocent people to death so that others may be spared, those holding the "antiutilitarian liberal standpoint" would defend the right of the individual not to be wronged. But as Slavoj Žižek explains it, in "Sophie's choice," "nobody is less harmed if she refuses the choice: in this case, both of the children die." Even the sacrificed child would have to accept the sacrifice, since he loses nothing by it that he had not already lost. So Sophie must choose, since choosing is preferable to not choosing on both utilitarian and anti-utilitarian grounds; yet, Žižek notes, "our ethical intuition tells us unmistakably that there is something wrong with it," and Sophie eventually commits suicide (1992, 72).

In both instances, Kant's and Styron's, narrative engages with theory in a process of reciprocal probing and stressing that tests the capacity of theory to comprehend and regulate practice, and the power of "actual life"—albeit in a highly exotic, speculative, and "theoretical" form—to elude or deform theory. Beginning with a dispute in philosophy, we find ourselves suddenly in a city full of intrigue and violence, with murderers stalking the streets, victims leaving home without a care in the world, neighbors rushing to the rescue, public tribunals, grieving families, whispering citizens; and from the appalling choice faced by a mother in a concentration camp, we move immediately to arguments about distributive justice, rationality, utilitarianism, political liberalism. The name for this mutual stimulation of theory and example, this fundamental instance of the relation of consciousness to life, is ethics: it is "in ethics" that theory becomes literary and literature becomes theoretical.

One of the most obdurate problems in literary theory is narrative form, the study of which seems to have stalled since Aristotle's statement that the plot of tragedy proceeds toward a moment of reversal, followed by recognition, and ending in a dénouement. The Russian formalists, the Chicago School of neo-Aristotelian formalism, and the more recent discipline of structural narratology have chosen to emphasize other aspects of narrative—its "grammar," "functions," "motifs," "logic," "indices," as well as its handling of temporality, point of view, narration, and so forth. But the attempt to define further the basic form of narrative has been virtually abandoned, defeated by the apparent shapelessness and singularity of extended narratives. Efforts such as those by Gerald Prince to define the "minimal story" — a state of affairs, followed by an action that brings about a new state that is the inverse of the first — have been criticized for being both too minimal, i.e., reductive, and not minimal enough in that it contains numerous elements. As Wallace Martin writes in *Recent Theories of Narrative*, "there is little hope of discovering an underlying set of structural principles in texts that so obviously confute our zeal for regularity," and so "the quest for a rigorous theory of narrative must end without closure" (83, 606). But lamentation or celebration may be premature. Perhaps theoretical closure can be achieved if we think of narrative in ethical terms. For one general but nonreductive way of characterizing all narratives from the simplest to the most complex is to remind ourselves of the antinomies of pure practical reason.

We can, for example, conceive of narrative form in a way that builds on Prince's basic insight by thinking of narrative as a representational structure that negotiates the relation, cultivated by ethical philosophers since Hume, of *is* and *ought*. Philosophers want to decide the question one way or the other, arguing either that there can be no determinate relation between the two kinds of propositions, or that there are (in such special cases as promises or contracts), various ways in which the two are bound together. But narrative has its own way of addressing the question, through plot. The most general and adequate conception of a narrative plot is that it moves from an unstable inaugural condition, a condition that *is* but *ought not* — a severance of the two — through a process of sifting and exploration in search of an unknown but retrospectively inevitable condition that *is* and truly *ought-to-be*. Narrative cannot posit a static *is;* this function, according to Gérard Genette, is allocated to "description," which inhabits narrative like a cyst. Nor can it prescribe an unresisted *ought:* this is the business of sermons. What it can — indeed what it must — do is to figure a process of rejecting disjunction in favor of ultimate union. Narrative plot thus provides what philosophy cannot, a principle of formal necessity immanent in recognizable worldly and contingent events that governs a movement toward the eventual identity of *is* and *ought*.

Another antinomy can be enlisted to address not the logic but the location of narrative form. As students of the scholarship on narrative form know, the concept of plot underwent a mighty shift during the 1970s, mutating from a formal property of the text to a kind of readerly phantasm or construction. The shift is virtually visible in the work of Peter Brooks, who oscillates in his important book *Reading for the Plot* between "plot" and "plotting"; and in that of Paul Ricoeur, who moved from a rigorously formalist position in an article on "Narrative Time" in 1980 to a far more readerly position in *Time and Narrative,* published a few years later. "To make up a plot," Ricoeur says in the later text, "is already to make the intelligible spring from the accidental, the universal from the singular" (1984, 41). Through a sustained rhetorical indecision, Ricoeur leaves open the question of whose "making"—the text's, the author's, or the reader's—is involved. Both Brooks and Ricoeur register the pressure exerted on formalism during this period, but neither is willing to surrender the idea of plot as formal feature. To hand the plot over to an all-licensed, plotting reader would be to make a dog's breakfast of narrative theory, which could no longer count on even the most minimal understanding of its central component. The text would be permanently disheveled, deprived of the structure that secured its coherence; empirical study would lie vanquished while the feckless reader frolicked.

Enter ethics, whose speciality is articulating the relation between freedom and necessity, desire and the law. An "ethical" approach to the dilemma of narrative theory would begin by conceding the strength of both formalist and reader-centered positions, and making of these apparently incompatible claims the cornerstone of its understanding. Plot is a construction of a particular narrative that uses only materials in that text. In one sense external to the narrative, plot is also deeply internal. In a word, plot is the law of the narrative, arising from within and yet not precisely as its own, since the narrative is regulated *by* the plot. Interestingly, this account also describes the reader. The reader is free and autonomous, and responsible for his or her construction of the text; but in order to make a plot at all, readers must believe that they "perceive" it; they must submit to the text and try to understand it "on its own terms." Readers thus construct the law of the text freely, but construct it as the law *of* the text. The text binds the reader, who binds the text. Where, then, is the law? In both, that is, in the relation between the two: the relation of reader to narrative text provides a compelling instance of the free submission of the subject to the law. Understanding the plot of a narrative, we enter into ethics.

How to think of ethics? *Can* one think of ethics? As the locus of otherness, ethics seems to lack integrity "in itself," and perhaps ought to be considered a matrix, a hub from which various discourses, concepts, terms, energies, fan out, and at which they meet, crossing out of themselves to encounter the other, all the others. Ethics is where thought itself experiences an obligation to form a relation with its other—not only other thoughts, but other-*than*-thought. Ethics is the *ought* in thought. And if the battles of literary theory are won on the playing fields of ethics, this is because literary theory, as a kind of oxymoron, has always already accepted the responsibility of otherness, just as literature itself bears the burden of managing the encounter between language and the world. Ethics will always be at the flashpoint of conflicts and struggles because such encounters never run smooth; that is what otherness is all about. No matter what settlement is reached with some other or other, there will always be some *other* other demanding our attention. Ethics does not solve problems, it structures them. And yet the durability of ethics, the fact that we continue to have what Žižek calls "ethical intuitions," suggests an ongoing commitment to the task, a commitment that is barely, but fairly, begun by the application of critical terms to literary study.

SUGGESTED READINGS

Booth, Wayne. 1988. *The Company We Keep: An Ethics of Fiction.*
Frazer, Elizabeth, Jennifer Hornsby, and Sabina Lovibond, eds. 1992. *Ethics: A Feminist Reader.*
Harpham, Geoffrey Galt. 1992. *Getting It Right: Language, Literature, and Ethics.*
Siebers, Tobin. 1988. *The Ethics of Criticism.*

28

Class

Daniel T. O'Hara

INTRODUCTION

THE MODERN literary critical use of "class" follows Marx's transformation of the term (about which more shortly) and the much later appearance of a "leftist" literary intellectual agenda in the 1930s. Although much is often made of the class theme in the literary criticism of that time, in America especially, none of the promising social critics of the 1930s goes on to develop a general theory of class fully adequate for literary study in the contemporary world. Such critics as Lionel Trilling in *The Liberal Imagination* (1950), Edmund Wilson in *Patriotic Gore* (1962), and Kenneth Burke in *The Grammar of Motives* (1945) and his subsequent theoretical texts, assimilate their local insights into the class realities of literary representation to larger moral, cultural, and philosophical concerns — the ethics of social manners, the history of national identity — formations, and to the symbolic grammar of human action, respectively. Class in America gets incorporated, after the 1930s, into the practice of cultural criticism or theory without further thought; much as in the case of the neo-Marxist Frankfurt School of such critical theorists as Theodore Adorno and Walter Benjamin and their later followers Fredric Jameson and Terry Eagleton, "class" is subsumed by the intense interest in the relation of avant-garde or experimental artforms to ideology. The work of Raymond Williams and a few other English social critics and postcolonial critics such as C. L. R. James has been taken seriously by more people only recently.

Consequently, despite today's rote invocations of "class" in the catchphrase "race, class, and gender," American criticism in particular has generally not kept in contact with the subsequent revisions in the theory of class, made in response to better empirical and logical analyses, within the relevant disciplines — the post-Marxist wing of analytic philosophy, radical social theory, and the materialist critique of political economy. These are the important heirs of the discourses whose matrix of concepts first made "class" possible as a serious term for Marx and any subsequent mode of intellectual study.[1] In what follows, then, I am attempting to reestablish that lost contact in a way which also addresses both the present function of American literary criticism and one major representative example of the past literature it still can profitably study. For reasons of space and my American focus, I leave implicit in my argument its debts to Gramsci, Bourdieu, Althusser, and other continental social thinkers (see the Marshall entry in Suggested Readings for references).

Specifically, here, I will discuss "class" in three interrelated ways. First, I will describe the present scene in the university teaching of literature in economically material terms to disclose the academic institution's newly representative class structure. I choose the American academy as my site of class analysis because I know it best. It is where I live and work, for the most part. And, in my experience and in that of the other faculty I know at my university and at other places around the country, the natural readership of *Critical Terms for Literary Study* — a standard text in required introductory courses in criticism for literature majors and graduate students — should find the situation in the academy of interest, if not of concern. But more importantly, I pick the academy because it mirrors in a markedly hypocritical fashion the harsh economic truths operating at large. That this is the case is, or should be, felt as a scandal. For the academy has always claimed to be a place largely free of such material constraints on its ideas and ideals, so that it could function as a separate critical sphere of adversarial culture, on the model, ultimately, of Socrates playing gadfly to the citizens of Athens. That the academy cannot do so, especially now, tells us a great deal about the real limits — past and present — of all so-called oppositional criticism. This painful lesson is particularly pertinent to the point of contemporary literary study, as well as extremely relevant to any possible theory of class that one might want to entertain for the purpose of developing an effectively radical critique of society.

The ultimate reason, however, why the academy is an instructive site for class analysis lies in its being a microcosm representative of economic developments in the larger world, such as the downsizing of the workforce, the increasing reliance on computer technology innovation, the selective privileging of a global multicultural perspective (so as to penetrate different "markets" here and around the world), and the practice of making token celebrities of a few members of

---

[1] As Mary Poovey has recently shown (see Suggested Readings), the history of the term "class" before Marx links it with the emergence of those natural, life, and social sciences such as chemistry, biology, and political economy (among others) for which thinking by means of tables, graphs, schemas — what Foucault sees as the theoretical grids of modern scientific rationality — is a habitual representational practice. (See the "discourse" entry in this volume.) That is, the mapping of nature's body in the periodic table of chemical elements, of the human body in medical anatomy, and of the social body in class analysis are interlinked activities in the emerging discourse of instrumental reason. Prior to the nineteenth century, the sense of class distinctions appeared embodied in literature via the principle of decorum; how one spoke marked one's social and even moral status.

"oppressed" or "marginalized" groups. The ultimate irony of these general developments, as they appear in the academy, just may lie in the grand spectacle of
(unwitting?) hypocrisy that results. Picture this: Stanley Fish, Edward W. Said,
or Cornel West are once again making an appearance on *The MacNeil-Lehrer
News Hour,* or *This Week with David Brinkley,* or *Firing Line.* The media take them
as spokespersons for an academy ostensibly "liberal" or even "radical" in its orientation, when actually the academy these critics speak for is, as they probably
know, a class-divided workplace of the few critical "stars" and the mass of intellectual drones, all of whom, "stars" and "drones" alike, are encouraged, ironically
enough, by these new circumstances, to embrace a "leftish" ideology of radical
liberation while using the latest instruments — PCs, e-mail, the Internet — of a
global capitalist rationality and in the latest style of the world media with its
increasingly tabloid tastes and ethics. This makes for a scene of instruction with
a vengeance.

The second way I will discuss class, then, will be in the context of Jon Elster's
post-Marxist social analysis. This theory, I believe, can shed light on the academic
situation, does possess a flexible coherence in itself, and may contain broader
implications for radical change. Finally, I will exemplify Elster's theory of class,
elaborated in light of current circumstances, professional and otherwise, by analyzing a 1903 novella by Henry James, *The Birthplace,* which, as James fully expected, no journal editor of his time dared to accept. This story, as we'll see,
delineates how class realities relate to the questions of truth and personal authenticity in what I take to be a prototypical postmodern setting of radical contingency and heterogeneous identities. What I mean by these last phrases Vaclav
Havel has memorably captured in his speech on receiving the Liberty Medal at
Independence Hall in Philadelphia on July 4, 1994. He observes early on that
"a symbol of that [postmodern] state [of mind] is a Bedouin mounted on a
camel and clad in traditional robes under which he is wearing jeans, with a tran-
sistor radio in his hands and an ad for Coca-Cola on the camel's back."[2] And
Havel concludes apropos such unreal scenes that "we live in [this] postmodern
world, where everything is possible and almost nothing is certain." What follows
here is my attempt to make "class" a little more possible for such an uncertain
world.

1. THE TWO PROFESSIONS: MULTICULTURAL PROLES AND POWERBOOK RADICALS

Looking around the profession these days sobers the mind. For 1993–94, English literature departments produced 1,082 new Ph.D.'s, a figure approximately
the same for each of the previous four years. For this same year, 1993–94, English literature departments advertised in the Modern Language Association's

[2] Vaclav Havel, "Our Troubled Quest for Meaning in a Postmodern World," *The Philadelphia
Inquirer,* Wednesday, July 6, 1994, A7.

Job Information List for 1,054 positions. The bad news is that only 60 percent of the advertised positions were tenure-track: the rest were adjunct, non-tenure-track positions. These figures for job production are also typical for recent years. Not only did English literature departments, for the year 1993–94, produce twenty-eight more Ph.D.'s than the total number of positions available, they also produced approximately 450 more Ph.D.'s than the available tenure-track positions, which was 632. This year's situation gets much worse when you add in the unemployed and underemployed Ph.D.'s from the previous four years. These are Ph.D.'s either unable to get any kind of college or university teaching position at all, a figure as high as 12 percent, and those Ph.D.'s teaching at an institution or a series of different institutions, on a one-year, usually renewable, adjunct basis. These adjunct positions are renewable for only up to five years, because of long-standing tenure policies. Finally, the number of Ph.D.'s from the last few years who are doing part-time teaching at a salary rate of $1,500 to $2,000 per course—that is, who do not even have a visiting or adjunct appointment, with a full course load at a somewhat decent salary—has been as high as 15 percent of the Ph.D. pool for the last four years.

What this means is that in 1993–94 the number of new and recent Ph.D.'s looking for one of the 632 tenure-track positions may have been as high as five thousand. And among this number of Ph.D.'s in the market, there are representatives of all schools and graduate programs, including the most prestigious institutions, such as Duke, Columbia, Princeton, or Harvard, with the most famous celebrity names for faculty, such as Fish, Said, or West. Despite the spate of actual and anticipated retirements, which as predicted has been accelerating at an ever faster rate, hiring lines come in a ratio of one replacement position for every four or five positions lost to retirement, illness, or death. This is, of course, due to the chronic financial woes in higher education, much of them caused by now institutionalized conservative fiscal and social agendas.

To make matters worse, immediate prospects for university and college enrollments, overall, look to be steady-state. But the best demographic projections for the long run strongly suggest that enrollments will drop precipitously, at least among the traditional college age population of eighteen-year-old students. Consequently, given this entire situation, schools are making do by adopting a fourfold policy of survival: (1) making occasional and highly selective or "target" tenure-track hires; (2) raising faculty productivity by increasing course loads and class sizes; (3) shifting resources from expensive graduate programs to less expensive, in fact, profitable undergraduate programs, with their extensive "service-course" components; and (4) appointing adjuncts and part-timers to these basic required writing and introductory courses, which "service" the university's general student body by teaching a bare-bones verbal and cultural literacy. As many as 40 percent of any department's total number of courses are staffed by non–tenure-track faculty, and at some schools the percentage is as high as 60 percent. To speak of a crisis in the profession in this general context is to risk euphemism.[3]

I rehearse all these statistics because they outline the stark material conditions in current literary study for faculty and would-be faculty alike. Naturally, the kinds of hires made in these conditions acquire a powerful instructive status for all concerned. Whatever the anchoring subspeciality — Renaissance (or "Early Modern," as it is now called), Critical Theory, or Composition and Rhetoric — the primary specialty marking these rare hires nowadays is a multicultural distinction of some kind: African American studies, gender studies, cultural studies, or postcolonialist studies.

I don't think this is simply political correctness at work. Such a hiring pattern is part of a continuing sincere effort to make the professoriate more representative and more responsive to the heterogeneous constituent groups of students it serves. Nonetheless, in some instances, and perhaps in a growing number, these hiring practices represent a reflex response on the part of administrators to the setting of implicit affirmative action "targets." University and college affirmative action officers scrutinize all the paperwork for any proposed hire in light of the number of women and minority candidates, first in the original pool of applicants, then in the group whose credentials are selected for review, and then among the finalists actually interviewed. Ideally, a department will land a woman or a minority candidate, virtually all of whom, for reasons I'll analyze, now embrace a multiculturalist identity politics; but at the least a department will have good overall numbers for the selection process, even if it finally hires as the product purchased, a white male doing gay studies or queer theory, or even if it must settle for a straight white male doing neo-Marxist critiques of popular culture.

This hiring scenario constitutes a powerful scene of instruction for new Ph.D.'s, struggling graduate students, and literature majors. The ethos of multiculturalism, its mind-set, which celebrates the emergence of excluded identities upon the professional and world historical stages, appeals, for more than fashionable reasons, to those facing the loss of the full intellectual life due to permanent professional non- or underemployment. Multiculturalism has, in this scene, an inspirational or edifying function. In such a bad labor market, it is truly the ideology of the oppressed. As already noted, however, multiculturalism as a cultural ethos of the profession gains in formative power by being reinforced at the material level of the institution, with this depression-styled labor market. This hiring pattern then takes on an indelible weight especially as graduate programs shrink, reduce their course requirements to speed fewer people to the degree, and also diversify their offerings even further — all of which things many graduate programs are now doing to "downsize" into "lean and mean" professional-making machines.

[3] Patricia Meyer Spacks, "The Academic Marketplace: Who Pays the Costs?" *MLA Newsletter,* 26, 2 (Summer 1994), 3.

The way graduate students and those English majors geared-up for graduate school speak of this endemic situation in the profession should truly become instructive for professors. For students now speak of a "choice" in "professional styles" between "the archival dig" and "the cookie-cutter take." The former style of work entails a lot of library research, a lot of time sifting evidence, considerable thinking, and many rewrites to get everything about one's argument—the evidence, the thesis, the genealogy of theoretical concepts—just right. "The archival dig" is something students speak of with a resentful nostalgia for the unknown, as a critical luxury which they have only heard about and which they associate with the profession up to the death of Foucault, this scholarly style's finest exemplar. Students cannot know "the archival dig" firsthand because they must always already be doing papers for conferences, getting essays circulated and published, and generally networking and promoting their names. Consequently, the "cookie-cutter take" is the only style of criticism they can afford to practice. It consists in the quick-fix fabrication of a distinctive-sounding framework, out of the latest detritus of incompatible multicultural positions (the amorphous "intersectionality" of race-class-gender subject-positions is the current rallying cry), whose sole purpose is to put one's marketable stamp on the object of analysis, whatever it may be: text, film, current event, and so on. The "cookie-cutter take" is the critical equivalent of a Robin Williams comic improvisation: "speed-ball" "word-salads" for a postmodern profession. To put it schematically, "the archival dig" is traditionally historical, documentary, theoretical, and text-centered; "the cookie-cutter take" is criticism in the present tense, free-floating (like anxiety), cynically pragmatic, and indiscriminately omnivorous. Any object can become the material for receiving the stylish cut, which makes everything one does look the same, like designer-named fashions.

This class of adjuncts and graduate students I call "multicultural proles" because they are, for the most part, a professional generation condemned to the worst conditions ever in the U.S. academy, even as they espouse, for mixed motives, the multicultural line. "Proles" they certainly are; whether they are, as a class, that multicultural in fact (as opposed to in theory) remains to be seen. The very few who do succeed in obtaining tenure-track positions, and the very, very few who, best exemplifying this line, actually ascend to the heights of professional stardom, can only act in ways that must secure and extend the current situation well into the foreseeable future. In the rare but spectacular successes of multicultural stars, multicultural proles—gypsy-scholars and soon-to-be gypsy-scholars—ruefully see their own alienated majesties returning to them.

It used to be the promise of higher education, and particularly of literary study, that students, whatever their familial and national identities and circumstances, could assume with the proper work professional and larger cultural identities of their own imaginative choice and revisionary devising. However initially alienating this practice of education may have been, students now see that if they possess the politically correct "original" identity, or can cleverly appropriate or opportunistically affiliate themselves with one or another such identity—that of some so-called or actually oppressed or marginalized group—then they at least have a chance of selling themselves in the job market and so can enter the distinctive hierarchy of the academy, a situation remarkably akin to those of other professions. Often, those few who will not or cannot perform in this fashion end up, in the academy, teaching in "Intellectual Heritage" or "Great Books" humanities programs where multicultural texts and politically correct attitudes are usually less prominent and rather less in demand than they are in departments of English and other literatures. To teach Plato and the Bible and Shakespeare for most of a semester is, to these few adjunct instructors, worth the addition of a week or two on the Koran, and certainly better than a semester of teaching the new *Heath Anthology of American Literature,* with its many bloated entries for writers whose works may be fashionable but the aesthetic value of which leave something to be desired for such recalcitrant adjuncts.

I call the rising multicultural stars of "the cookie-cutter take" critical style "powerbook radicals" (after the laptop computer) because it is among these newer members of the changing professional elite that I observe the greatest reliance upon Mac's, PCs and the Internet and the related emergence of a new theoretical posture of globalism in cultural matters. This theoretical globism, of the professional "left," ironically enough, aligns itself, wittingly or not, with the new postliterate global economy of sensational media images dominated by the multinational corporations. "Powerbook radicals," as they aspire to represent the world at large in some diversifying sense, will prove to be either the postmodern reincarnations of the renaissance genius, or, in their ersatz cosmopolitanism, the first instances of the institutionalization of the global dilettante as the latest figure for the oppositional critic. With little or no training in any other discipline or knowledge of other cultures, powerbook radicals use the latest technology to speak authoritatively about the new world order, to rail against this system, and to envision utopian alternatives to it in the virtual worlds of their computer terminals, even as their usage of these new machines of instrumental reason fosters the extension and profitability of the very global economic system they claim we should all desire to overcome.

Two dangers facing the multicultural proles should be glaringly evident, but a couple of anecdotes will spell them out conclusively. One is the danger of students' sacrificing the quest for knowledge to expediency. A brilliant graduate student I know, a young gay man who does queer theory, among several other things, asked me recently should he "commodify" himself solely as a queer theorist, since there was a steadily growing demand for this intellectual commodity in the job market. Shouldn't he worry about "learning anything else" he continued, until after he secured a position on this, he confessed, potentially constraining basis of pure identity politics. What could I say? I listened as he decided to go, as he put it, "the commodity route." Given the general state of affairs, I could not realistically advise him to do otherwise. Similarly, I was at a loss with another student, although a little less of a loss, as it turned out. The other danger represented for this second student, a black woman from the Caribbean, has to do with the wholesale appropriation of another people's cultural experience — an academic imperialism committed, perhaps sincerely, perhaps opportunisti- cally, in the name of global liberation, but often committed ignorantly in any event. This student from the Caribbean lamented recently that when she went to the Modern Language Association of America convention sessions on Caribbean writers, all the speakers were, as she characterized it with bitter irony, "young white women in short black leather skirts" — feminists who reduced Carribean women's texts to generalizations about the necessary destruction of patriarchy everywhere. After listening to her story, I suggested that she revise for publica- tion her paper on the positive cultural work of oral narratives, performed at ritual festivals in Trinidad, which tell of the desired return of authoritative male figures, in the historically specific context of a society whose family-structures had been virtually annihilated by slavery and its long aftermath. This paper had at least a chance of doing some important corrective work, if it ever does get a fair hearing. It may be that the professional strategies this student witnessed at the MLA convention will always be with us, but I believe that the present situation in literary study typifies a contemporary mind-set of cynical rationality, one the academy always used to say it tried to oppose, and may yet again. That the pres- ent class structure of the profession need not persist I hope to demonstrate in what follows.

2. Toward a Postmarxist Theory of Class

Traditionally, in Marxist and related strains of theoretical analysis, there are five distinct classes in modern society. The three primary classes are the "aristocracy," which represents the vestigial past, the "bourgeoisie," which represents the po- tent if soon-to-pass-away present, and the "proletariat," which represents the promise of the future. The two other classes, "the petty bourgeoisie" and the "lumpenproletariat," are liminal hybrids and have often puzzling links to the primary classes. I will discuss all five of these classes, briefly, in their order of priority as primary and secondary phenomena. (For the standard view of this topic, see the entry by Draper in the Suggested Readings.) Marx, by the way, defines a class pragmatically via what means of production, material or mental, its members own.

The aristocracy is the original land-owning class, the so-called "nobility" whose forebears conquered the lands their heirs inherit as huge estates by right of the laws they instituted often over the stifled objections of the native inhabit- ants who "lost" the lands. The bourgeoisie is the class owning the commercial, financial, and manufacturing means of production. This class attempts to assimilate all forms of labor—manual, artisan, and intellectual—to the standards and practices of one or another mode of its means of production. This is the notorious "bottom-line" mind-set. The bourgeoisie profits by driving down the costs of production, which includes paying workers the least amount their mere subsistence requires. It also profits by then extracting for itself the savings gained by cost-cutting, more efficiently organized labor forces, and technical innovation. This is the surplus value of labor since this profit is beyond a fair return on investment, and is ultimately had at the expense of the exploited and alienated workers who must sell their creative power to these "others" just barely to live. The bourgeoisie appropriates this surplus value of labor for its exclusive use, either in reinvestment or in the accumulation of luxury items. Marx derives his analysis here from the late eighteenth-century English political economist, David Ricardo. (For further discussion of "the surplus value theory," see the entries by Elster in the Suggested Readings.)

The proletariat is the class whose members own nothing but their physical labor-power, which they must sell individually to the bourgeois capitalists for subsistence wages, even as their bosses tend to act together (as a monopoly, if possible) to drive prices for goods up as much as possible, as much as the market can bear. But the proletariat, as workers on the frontlines of technical change, must receive instruction on the latest advances in order to maximize efficiency, and this means they must be made literate to begin with. By also being associated in large groups in the workplaces and cities and by necessarily participating in the circulation of information for the distribution and sale of products in a consumer society, the workers naturally grow in knowledge, technical and professional expertise, and communicational and organizational skills. Their capitalist "masters" thus breed ironically in their proletarian "slaves" the basis for their own eventual undoing. For once the proletariat can recognize itself as a class and starts to unionize and agitate for political change, that is, once the workers, too, choose to act in concert, then they pursue their own interests passionately. But since the proletariat constitutes the vast majority of people within the capitalist world system, and is on the cutting edge of technological change, it represents, as a class, especially through its intellectual vanguard, the promise of a better, more just future for all, once private property is abolished and exploitation has been replaced by mutual recognition, respect, and communal cooperation, after the inevitable bloody revolution occurs.

The petty bourgeoisie is the class of small self-employed farmers, businesspeople, and professional service-providers, such as teachers, nurses, journalists, and government employees. These people believe in and try to practice the ideology of radical individualism and the self-made man, and tend to side in political disputes with any one of the primary classes, depending upon their pragmatic estimate of the advantages to them of doing so. And the lumpenproletariat, what

Marx calls "the scum of the earth" (as opposed to the proletarian "salt"), is the class of totally alienated, unemployed and unemployable street-people, the deranged or chronically malcontent rabble who provide the raw materials for molding by the demagogic authoritarian populists from Napoleon to Hitler into counterrevolutionary tools and dupes, urban armies of thugs and would-be assassins, the protofascist motherlode.

This traditional Marxist theory of class presents several problems. First, it is time-bound. It can persuasively appear to account for human history, on the basis of class warfare, up to its own period—from the middle of the nineteenth century to the early twentieth. At this point and even more so subsequently its class categories and characterizations can too easily become fixed stereotypes, especially in the context of the incredible fluidity and radical contingency of a postmodern world. Second, as a grand narrative of humanity's past, present, and future, this time-bound theory aspires to explain everything totally, and, as such, like all other time-bound grand narratives, religious or secular, it sounds suspiciously like a coercive myth. (On this subject, see the entry by Fredric Jameson in the Suggested Readings.) Third, as a collapse of virtually all Marxist societies and the simultaneous embrace of liberal democracy and/or authoritarian populism by all classes apparently everywhere makes clear, the predictive power of this traditional Marxist theory of class leaves something to be desired, to say the least. Fourth, this theory also leaves uncertain the exact relationships between its general assumption of historical necessity and its specific strategic reliance on individual and collective free choice. Fifth, even sympathetic Marxist political economists and social theorists from Ernst Mandel to Jon Elster now seriously question Marx's use of Ricardo's surplus value theory of labor. Since the details of this critique are highly technical and mathematical, and not really to our purpose here, I will refer interested readers to the Suggested Readings (see, especially, the entries for Elster). Last, the way Marx uses class in different historical and cultural contexts makes it hard to distinguish a class from a "caste," an "estate," a "guild," a "status-group," or a "profession." Since this criticism, too, is highly technical, I'll once again refer interested readers to the appropriate Suggested Readings (see, especially, the entries by and on Oliver Cox).

In this context, then, the best theoretical definition of class that I've discovered appears in Jon Elster's *Making Sense of Marx* (1985): "A class is a group of people who by virtue of what they possess are compelled to engage in the same activities if they want to make the best use of their endowments" (331).[4] For example, when capitalists each act to keep costs down and also act in concert to drive prices up, despite antitrust laws against monopolies, they are acting as a class in this situation; that is, they are constituting by their action a collective agent or

[4] Jon Elster, *Making Sense of Marx: Studies in Marxism and Social Theory* (Cambridge and New York: Cambridge University Press, 1985), p. 331.

actor on the historical stage, with a prescribed script or scenario, which does allow for tactical improvisations, if necessary. Elster's definition suggests that "class" is an ever emergent albeit repeatable phenomenon. For a class emerges as a collective actor on the historical scene because the people forming membership in the class possess the same or very similar "endowments" — a broadly conceived term for their material and symbolic property or "capital," their "knowhow" and/or power-position in society. These individuals perceive, whatever their differences and rivalries in the short term, long-term common interests, and they believe and act upon this belief, in response to historical conditions, because certain courses of action will preserve and/or maximally enhance their holdings and positions. This sense of class as a repeatably emerging phenomenon makes it particularly appropriate for a postmodern world economy and the improvisatory cultural logic of late capitalism. Its "downsizing" — sudden, radical, destructive — is a pervasive phenomenon we see in the profession of literary study now all the time. Elster's flexible empirical sense of class, which evades Marx's more abstract and static structural formulations and stereotypes, is a major reason in favor of Elster's definition.

Another reason is equally important. Elster's "methodological individualism" makes the empirical assumption that groups are composed by individuals who are rational and self-interested. They act accordingly by making rational choices among available options when faced by historical necessity. As he moves from the individual level of agents (or "actors") and events to the always provisional but also always emerging collective level of historical action, Elster maintains this principle of "rational choice" theory and argues that individuals in groups are persuadable with respect to the perception of both their real personal interests and their commonality of interest with others. Rhetorical persuasion, precisely because all identities in a postmodern world are heterogeneous and constructed, is central for Elster to the formation of any collective agency.

In addition, given his definition's invocation of the "best use of their endowments," Elster can also discuss the making of value judgments — practical, aesthetic, ethical — insofar as all these kinds of value judgments implicate standards and criteria engaging a full array of cognitive, cultural, and political assumptions and beliefs, which function as reasons for making this or that choice. Elster's versatile post-Marxist theory of class sees a group ever in formation and reformation, whose members are rational and self-interested agents who can choose among different options when responding to perceived historical conditions and in light of both short-term satisfactions and long-term individual and collective interests. In light of my earlier analysis of literary study, this highly nuanced sense of class makes Elster's definition particularly useful for understanding the profession, as I'll try to show shortly in this section, as well as in this essay's last section.

A class, when analytically conceived, appears then as a collective actor on the historical scene. This appearance arises by virtue of its members' "endowments." These are what people possess or own: some means of economic and/or cultural production and reproduction, such as: general knowledge, technical expertise, physical labor-power or the machinery of capital formation, circulation, and distribution. Signs of privileged class position — the right clothing, a good house, a luxury car, and so on — are just that: signs of power, but not the power itself, of course, which lies in the capacity to produce socially valuable goods and services. As a result of how a group of people have to act in concert to make the best use of their endowments when facing particular historical circumstances, a class emerges to select one of several real options in a symbolic setting in which its members reciprocally recognize their rational, self-interested, and necessarily mutually respectful because overlapping intentions to keep possession of and/or significantly enhance their "endowments." This symbolic setting or recognition scene is the story, the narrative, that the members of a class tell and repeat, with revisions, about themselves and their group-in-(re-)formation. Class in this fashion promotes strategic critical recognitions and at least a wary respect. It thereby has an educative civilizing function, ironically enough, even as the class in question plays its part in the social war for more power, better position, and greater influence.

To summarize: Elster's "rational-choice," post-Marxist approach to the idea of social class — an idea he traces from Marx through Weber into later writers — assumes that social situations, as Anglo-American philosophers like to say, are rule-governed "games" with their own conventions, in which the presumption is that the participants in a game think themselves to be rational agents seeking to maximize their interests vis-à-vis each other, but who can and also do act in concert when they are persuaded to see that their interests overlap and are threatened or can be maximized by cooperation. This "rational-choice" model thus begins with the empirical experience of individuals who, whatever their circumstances and positions, act as if they are intelligent free agents. This analysis then moves to the more general level of ever-emergent collective agents also acting to freely choose from a contingent range of possible courses that they are forced to confront by specific historical developments, among which not least in importance are the consequences of past actions.

The greatest advantage of Elster's making sense of class inheres in how it frees us from thinking about classes as fixed and selectively privileged as the symbolic capital of Marxist intellectuals. Micropolitically, via Elster's revision of Marx, we can define individuals and the groups they strategically form and repeatedly renew in terms of what particular possessions or endowments are concerned in any particular context. No endowment, however comparatively small in the grand scheme of things, can be beside the point of discussion, negotiation, and care, if only for tactical purposes. Yet at the same time, macropolitically, we need never lose sight of the large-scale and historically institutionalized structures of

endowments striating a changing social scene. For example, the connections between employment practices in the academy with those in other professions and
in the corporate world stand out in this broader horizon. In short, we can use
the old names for classes strategically, pragmatically, with a certain ironic, even
(self-)parodic lightness, if the need arises.

Let's look, in this light, at my opening analysis of "multicultural proles" and
"powerbook radicals." Strictly speaking, from a conventional Marxist perspective, both of these groups should be seen as parts of the same whole, the class
of professional intellectual workers, a crossbreed of the petty bourgeoisie who
are, in theory anyway, self-employed service providers — teachers — who contract
to sell to the university their expertise for its use, and many of whom have organic ties to and/or ideological affiliations with repressed or marginalized
peoples. But in fact, as I've already stressed, only the former group, "multicultural proles," are in the position of acting like intellectual workers in this mixed-
breed or hybrid sense, whereas the latter group, "powerbook radicals," are in
the position of acting like an official "outlaw" caste. These critics compose a
professionally elite version of the old lumpenproletariat, as shaped by the demagogic forms and norms of the current academic celebrity machine and our sensa-
tionalistic corporate media culture. One of the markers of "postmodern" society
is precisely this substitution of impersonal machinelike or semiautomatic systems
of cultural (re-)production for the personal relationships of professional mentor-
ships and the wholesale social pathologies of "the leader" and "the cult of personality." This substitution of impersonal mechanisms of popular media images for
more personal modes of literate cultural transmission — celebrity icons instead
of personal masters — is the hallmark for what Wlad Godzich in *The Culture
of Literacy* (1994) considers our "postliterate state" beyond a now clearly passé
modernity.[5]

However this may be, the most important consequence of Elster's making
sense of Marx on class lies in the threefold diagnostic question his new definition
entails: What are the specific set of circumstances, the historical scene, in which
collective actors can make their appearances as distinctively recognizable figures?
How can this phenomenon be most convincingly analyzed in a creditable account of those circumstances when they do arise — that is, how can one most
usefully tell their story? And, finally, what can one do, if anyone wants to do so,
to promote most effectively the wedding of these collective actors to these stories
about them, with respect especially to improving the prospects of radical change?
In short, Elster on class encourages us to think of ourselves — intellectuals or
otherwise — as the real "authors" of such possible visions of radical change. In
this way, each of us may come to join one another in a mutual act of revisionary telling.

---

[5] Wlad Godzich, *The Culture of Literacy* (Cambridge, MA: Harvard University Press, 1994), p. 22.

If the emergence of "multicultural proles" and "powerbook radicals" constitutes an opportunity for such collective authorships, perhaps what needs to be envisioned in this case, in order to promote radical change, is a scenario in which adjunct faculty and graduate students are successfully unionized by strategically proposing to them the goal of abolishing current tenure practices. If we mean the most radical change of all, the abolition of tenure itself, such a move could establish a new free-for-all competition for positions based on market standards. This would tend to proletarianize in appearance and in fact the entire profession, and so destroy the present system of academic hierarchical distinction. One class of truly miserable intellectual workers would result. They could then act perhaps better in concert as one collective agent with and among other such collective agents in the world at large, perhaps even in the long-term interests of most people. This is a familiar vision, originally renewed for literary study in Frank Lentricchia's *Criticism and Social Change* (1983).

The "powerbook radicals," masters of the Internet and the Information Superhighway in my scenario, could then play the role of international organizers and global communication experts rather than, as now, merely the role of our ever-returning alienated majesties, those professionalized puppets of the celebrity image-making mill. Of course, we could choose to envision less radical change with respect to tenure practices, such as de-emphasizing sheer quantity of written productivity, including experimental collective work via the Internet, and re-emphasizing teaching effectiveness. I prefer the more radical vision, the abolition of tenure, since I do not believe it works to protect "free speech," whatever that may be, but I do see how it works to sustain an outmoded academic hierarchy of purely invidious distinctions. But this is just one man's opinion.

Since, as intellectuals, our "endowments" are various "knowledges," and since what we "possess" or "own" is professional expertise in the production, circulation, and regulation of cultural or symbolic capital, including certain socially accrediting discursive practices such as reading, writing, and critical thinking, we could be properly "compelled," in the light of my visionary scenario and by virtue of such "endowments," finally "to engage in the same actions," for the radical benefit of all. If we "want to make the best use" of our powers, we must begin to see what's there to be seen, necessities and possibilities alike. Or so I prefer to think.

3. "The Biggest Show on Earth": The Case of *The Birthplace*

The Birthplace (1903), by Henry James, tells the story of Morris and Isabel Gedge, a long-suffering, not very financially successful, British married couple. As Mrs. Gedge pointedly remarks, they have "'no social position'" (111).[6] In fact, from a classical Marxist perspective, they are generally self-employed, pro-

---

[6] Henry James, "The Birthplace" in Roger Gard, ed. *The Jolly Corner and Other Tales* (London and New York: Penguin, 1990), p. 111. Hereafter all citations from this work will be given in my text.

fessional service providers, or intellectual petty bourgeoisie. From Elster's perspective, they have not yet found their other class members, as such. That is, they do indeed have "no social position."

For a brief period they ran "a small private school of the order known as preparatory" (109). One of their pupils, Mr. Grant-Jackson's only son, had once fallen ill, had been near death, and the Gedges, especially Mrs. Gedge, had nursed the boy back to full health, while his parents were traveling in America. As this late tale opens, years have passed since this incident, and Mr. Gedge has failed at a series of practical enterprises. He has ended up "in charge of the grey town-library of Blackport-on-Dwindle," a provincial library the Jamesian narrator characterizes archly as "all granite, fog and female fiction" (110). I suppose, in good dialectical fashion, the latter sublates the granite and the fog in its stony amorphousness.

However that may be, in a romantic development as if drawn from this very predetermined female sentimental fiction, James's story has Mr. Grant-Jackson, now so many years after the fact, suddenly intervene to repay the debt to the Gedges. He does so by using his influence to get them appointed as the caretakers or "wardens" (110) for the cottage museum and birthplace, "the early home of the supreme poet, the Mecca of the English-speaking race" (110). Although, in characteristically late Jamesian fashion, the tale never mentions the names of Stratford-on-Avon or Shakespeare, these real if spectral presences, among others, loom over its telling.

Thanks to Mr. Grant-Jackson's belated influence, Mr. Gedge will no longer sell his labor power and intellectual resources to service provincial tastes. Now he, along with Isabel, will sell their labor, for only slightly more total income (but with the rent-free use of an adjoining cottage), to service "the Mecca of the English-speaking race." To this birthplace of pure genius itself come "types, classes, nationalities," expressive of "manners, diversities of behavior, modes of seeing, feeling" (125) unknown to Blackport-on-Dwindle, and so this fabulous spectacle constitutes the mode of mental travel for Mr. Gedge, "an untravelled man" (125).

To this traditional center of an imperial culture, from provincial, colonial, and even, as we'll see, postcolonial margins and peripheries, come these hoards, all of which the Gedges are to teach and delight as they uncritically retail the antiquarian details of the monumental genius and his humble, antiquarianly preserved birthplace. Ironically enough, as in the case of a certain Mr. and Mrs. B. D. Hayes, a young couple key to the tale's crisis, most of the pilgrims to the shrine are indeed postcolonials — Americans — because they can most afford to indulge their curiosity. Indeed, these Americans combine with their curiosity an ignorance of class and its constraints on free expression that make, for the Hayeses at least, Morris Gedge's position as the caretaker of genius and the warden of the birthplace, an interesting case.

But an acute problem has arisen for Morris Gedge by the time he meets the Hayeses. He has begun to realize that "the Body" or "the Committee" (as it is also called), which runs and oversees the birthplace and for which Mr. Grant-Jackson acts as mouthpiece, has expected him and his wife to play only one role. They are to enthusiastically give the vast anonymous numbers of "They" who visit the birthplace the same glorious legend of sublime genius amid the details of everyday life, all of which details are, as all concerned know, most likely founded upon absolutely "Nothing" (125) at all. This professional requirement for the Gedges to misrepresent, to lie, affects them differently, which complicates and increasingly exacerbates Morris Gedge's problem. Mrs. Gedge reasons, self-interestedly, that since next to nothing really is or can ever be known for certain about the genius of the English-speaking race — note, by the way, how race here is principally a linguistic being, and not a biological fact — Mrs. Gedge then speculates that nothing can ever be known for certain. Consequently, she concludes, any and perhaps all the details that she and her husband spout for the crowds may perhaps be contingently, accidentally true after all. Mr. Gedge, however, cannot accept his wife's casuistry, her pragmatist reasoning, and fledgling contingent theorizing. Instead, he grows more irritable, restless, and resentful. No negative capability for him! During the days he recounts to the gaping public, with rising sarcasm punctuated by knife-thick, more and more prolonged silences, the phony details of the legend. During the nights he haunts the birthplace to feel the authentic absence of genius all the more palpably, and so be in better possession of the truth he does know.

This growing double split between the Gedges and within Morris Gedge, between the public performance demanded by the profession of caretaker and the private sensibility, one in his case which had never been uniformly whole, clearly represents the unhappy consciousness of alienated labor, the alienated being of the worker: "One of the halves, or perhaps even, since the split [in Morris Gedge] promised to be rather unequal, one of the quarters, was the keeper, the showman, the priest of the idol; the other piece was the poor unsuccessful honest man he had always been" (127). Gedge calls the former public and professional part of the self interchangeably "the showman" and "the priest," and what this part performs he usually perceives as being the master of ceremonies role in "the Biggest Show on Earth" (144), a circus- or carnival-huckstering role of routinely retailing the legend to the masses. He calls the latter private and resentful part of the self "this primary character" (127), since whatever its original, constructed, and social origins it has indeed come first and has in fact lasted the longest. What Morris Gedge both desires and dreads is "this primary character's revenge, some supreme assertion of its identity" (127), the idea of which makes him shake in his shoes. His wife insistently cautions him to be politic.

Why all this fuss? I think the reason for the difference in Morris Gedge now lies in his change from being simply a cultural worker (schoolmaster, provincial librarian) to his being also a cultural investor or unwilling symbolic speculator. For Gedge not only sells his labor-power and expertise in certain discursive practices, just as he had done before, so as to purchase basic commodities of existence such as food, clothing, and shelter; he also must now speculate, according to a conventional corporate design, in the genius-legend market, actually performing and professionally investing in the commodified formulas and ritualized forms of this genius-legend's "facts" and museum souvenirs. He thus spends the symbolic capital of his discursive intelligence, such as it is, in order to sell the commodity of genius and its ersatz and fetishized birthplace, all for the purpose of bringing in more and more receipts. In legal and contractual terms, as an agent for his principal, the corporate "Body" or "Committee," Gedge administers, as curator, the cultural capital of the symbolic myth of romantic genius for profit. In this fashion, Gedge has been transformed by his new profession from an intellectual petty bourgeois into a representative disciplined subject of speculative or modern consumer culture. As such, Gedge appears to have only two choices: follow his wife's advice and example and mouth the profit-making if absurd pieties, or leave his new position in this cultural capitalist class and return to his petty bourgeois status.

When, as part of "some supreme assertion of his identity," Gedge does revolt, and tells the truth about the birthplace as he sees it to the apparently sympathetic Hayeses, he feels he has finally found, among this small circle of friends, the core of "the good society" (140). Here's where Elster's definition of class comes in most handy. The idea of a new class improvising itself into existence in this fashion is something his revision of Marxist categories allows us to credit, even as his perspective allows us to use the traditional Marxist categories, such as petty bourgeoisie and so on, with more allegorical versatility.

It is now that Mr. Grant-Jackson, on the Body's behalf, dramatically reappears, and warns Gedge that his prolonged and sullen silences during his wife's dutifully enthusiastic performances of the legend have been remarked by the public. These pointed silences would have brought their dismissal this time if he hadn't intervened, once again, in their interest, for old time's sake. As a result of this visitation, Gedge launches upon a new course of action, one which may help to form the core of a new society, although whether it should be christened "good" remains to be seen.

Gedge's new chosen course of action is to embellish the legend with an inventive vengeance that could have made the late Oscar Wilde of "The Decay of Lying" mighty proud, or at least laugh out loud in his grave. Gedge even risks going over the top with his new act:

> It was ever his practice to stop still at a certain spot in the room and, after having secured attention by look and gesture, suddenly shoot off: "Here!" They always understood, the good people — he could fairly love them now for it; they always said, breathlessly

and unanimously, "There?" and stared down at the designated point quite as if some trace of the grand event [of the genius' birth-struggles] were still to be made out. This movement produced, he again looked round. "Consider it well: *the* spot of earth—!" "Oh, but it isn't *earth*!" the boldest spirit—there was always a boldest—would generally pipe out. Then the guardian of the Birthplace would be truly superior—as if the unfortunate had figured the Immortal coming up, like a potato, through the soil. "I'm not suggesting that He was born on the bare ground. He was born *here*!"—with an uncompromising dig of his heel . . . Mr. and Mrs. Hayes were at first left dumb by [this rehearsal of his now standard performance]. They had uttered no word while he kept the game up, and . . . he could yet stand triumphant before them after he had finished with his flourish (151).

The Hayeses have now returned, two years later, after he has perfected his act, to warn Gedge that his wonderful reputation for improvising, elaborating, and ritualizing all these new "facts" has reached America, where his name in cultural circles is now all the rage, and so he may become perceived by "the Body" of suspiciously laying it on too thick. But they have also returned to witness, given his sudden rapid transition from one extreme—truth-telling—to its polar opposite—radical parody of the pieties of the genius discourse, the perfection of what the Hayeses hope is "a true case-study": "the case with an ideal completeness" (154). Gedge now understands that this "good society" of sympathetic friends depends upon this purely and selfishly aesthetic interest in him as "a case." Such an aesthetic motive of the spectator means, for Gedge at this moment, that the Hayes may not be real friends after all, since the "Gedge" as the potential preparator of a novel scandal due to this ironic emergence of his "critical sense" (144) is not his "true" self but merely his self-parodically revolting mask—or so Gedge still believes. (On "radical parody," see the entry by O'Hara in the Suggested Readings.)

Just at this final crisis-point, Mr. Grant-Jackson does indeed return with another message from "the Body." But although Mr. and Mrs. Hayes, Mrs. Gedge, and Morris Gedge himself now fear the worst, that his radical parody has been seen through, the questions of "real" knowledge, intention, and authenticity on all sides become purely moot. One may as well believe in free agency as not believe in it. What matters the most to "the Body" and so to Mr. Grant-Jackson, whatever they may or may not suspect, and so, as well, ultimately to the Gedges and to those aesthetically curious young Americans, the Hayeses, is the good news about the greatly increased receipts that, thanks to its priest's greatest-show-on-earth performances, this "carny" church of genius, with its sublime side-show, is now bringing in. And it is the receipts, as Morris Gedge delights in drawing suspensefully out Mr. Grant-Jackson's point for them all, "The receipts, it appears, speak — Well, volumes . . . They tell the truth" (159). Oh, *they* at least do?" Mrs. Hayes pointedly responds. So powerfully, in fact, do these receipts speak the truth that, as Mr. Grant-Jackson has just announced in private to Morris, the Gedges have received a substantial raise in their stipend. "They double us?" asks Isabel Gedge, with full dramatic irony. "Well — call it that," her husband responds. "In recognition," he concludes (160). The sentence from his lips, "There you are" (160) and its slight variation, "And there *you* are" (160), sounds a pointed refrain, as the tale ends.

The moral of this story could not be clearer: Direct critique will not be counte- nanced by the powers that be, and indirect critique, via parodic ridicule of con- ventional discourse practices, will be supported, even encouraged, whether fully understood as such or not, so long as the status of the receipts in question speaks the only "truth" now known, their always potentially infinite because purely speculative increase.

Three formal features of *The Birthplace* bring home its prototypically late capi- talist or postmodern "truth." The language of religion and its rituals — "shrine," "idol," "priest," "the Body" — in combination with the language of the modern international corporation, of business — "the committee," "souvenirs," "selling," "receipts" — constitute a broad range of topical, historical, literary, romantic allu- sion. All this composes an ironic allegory, a tale of truth-telling becoming radical parody, the circus of genius that represents James's own rueful fantasy about the fate, as a "genius" in his small way, awaiting him after his death. Given the poor receipts his later work did receive at the time of this tale (1903), and his long- ruminated twofold design for what became the New York Edition of the Col- lected Works (1907–1909) — for it to enshrine his reputation and to increase his writing revenues (it never did the latter) — this stylistic overdetermination of *The Birthplace* evokes more and more poignant resonances.

Similarly, the restricted point of view — the Jamesian narrator largely effacing himself in favor of the perceptions and the verbal habits of his protagonist, Mor- ris Gedge — acts to produce a systematic structure of ever contingent, socially symbolic ambiguities. To take one major example: Gedge first sees Mr. and Mrs. Hayes sentimentally as representing, with him, in miniature, the utopian idea of the "good society" of sympathetic friends; then, in disillusionment with their aestheticism, he sees them cynically as the merely curious spectators of the ideal case-study his story makes as he races perfectly from one polar opposite, truth- telling, to another, parody-lying. How are we as readers to credit his shifting point of view in this or any other instance of such a complex tale? Do we instead form our more independent, if still sympathetic, judgment of all these characters and their situation based on the presence in the text of suggestions of more complicated patterns of motivation? Like the stylistic overdetermination, this structural ambiguity of restricted point of view precludes any facile conclusion that *The Birthplace* is merely a despairing revelation, however blackly comic, of a genteel sensibility's defeat by crude commercialism.

Finally, the insistent refrain, with its elegant variation, uttered by Gedge literally as the tale's last words—"There you are" and then "And there *you* are!" (160); the subtly cruel manner in which Gedge creates and sustains for as long as possible the Hitchcockian suspense of the other characters; how he orchestrates the final scene of revelation about the truth of the receipts, the raise, and the general ironic reversal of expected tragic fortune; and the infectious nature of the turn-about for any and all spectators—"And there *you* are!"—as if we all are somehow intimately implicated in the truth the receipts speak volumes about: All these formal matters suggest that in the end Gedge discards his role of defeated if still "revolting" protagonist and assumes the more creative role of "authoring"—or, if you prefer, "co-authoring"—this final scene of aesthetic and moral judgment in *The Birthplace*.

Supporting this perhaps innovative-sounding conclusion is the pervasive, even contagious pattern of formal, specular doubling in the tale. The Hayeses are an ideal version of the Gedges, as Morris Gedge would wish himself and his wife to be. His former jobs as schoolmaster and librarian are matched by his new profession as the instructive caretaker for the genius of the English-speaking race. Even "the Body" has another name: "the Committee." The church of genius is also the circus. As we have seen, Gedge himself is split and at least doubled by his changing responses to his new role, a process which his wife's final questions apropos their salary raise—"They double us" (160)—resonates with ever widening implications. And, most significantly, Gedge at the last does assume, albeit in a minor mode, the master's role of the suspenseful tale-teller. Morris Gedge, as radical parodist and especially as improviser of this final scene, thus mirrors and is mirrored by his (and our) author, James himself.

In terms of Elster's post-Marxist theory of class, *The Birthplace* thereby demonstrates the emergence of a new if ironic collective aesthetic recognizing this new historical truth of receipts being the end-all and be-all, of being all in all. Such a truth subjects to critique all romantic idealism about genius, to be sure, as well as any sentimentally utopian notions of the good society of sympathetic friends, both of which positions depend on a practice of aesthetic spectatorship, of being above the fray of market conditions, which this story reveals is now impossible, even for beautiful, young, rich Americans. To confront his select, genteel audience of Anglo-American readers with this new reality destructive of aesthetic distance, critical disinterestedness, and mere Ivory Towerism, in a tale that both practices truthfully and parodies radically these very "virtues"—such is James's considerable achievement in *The Birthplace*. (For a divergent reading of late James, see the entry by Freedman in the Suggested Readings.)

The self-destructive form of this tale, which implicates characters, author, and

readers (then and now) in its mordantly comic "truth" suggests the initial emergence of both a new reality — the total penetration of culture by capitalistic standards of value — and a new class consciousness — among nouveau riche cultured
dilettantes, professional intellectual workers, and culture-starved masses from
around the globe. All stand discovered together here, ready to tell each other
our stories.

Elster's theory of class can help us to recognize this conflicted collective self-
discovery of a new class of speculative culture producer-consumers, a new class
of intellectuals now grown older and yet facing another painful birth in the place
where, for better or worse, "multicultural proles" and "powerbook radicals" currently play their assigned roles — the postmodern American university. "Types,
classes, nationalities, manners, diversities of behavior, modes of seeing, feeling,
of expression, would pass before him and become for him, after a fashion, the
experience of an untravelled man. His journeys had been short and saving, but
poetic justice again seemed inclined to work for him in placing him just at the
point in all Europe perhaps where the confluence of races was thickest." (125)
Perhaps, as poetic justice would now have it, we are at the point in all the world,
the American academy, where such an opportunity now is the greatest, an opportunity that includes our refusal of merely assigned roles, and entails our assumption of the new role of a collective self-authorship — to take *The Birthplace*'s creative intention one step beyond itself — which will be performed by subjects as
riven, mobile, and provocatively improvisatory as any of James's best: "So Gedge
had the last word. 'And there *you* are!'" (160).

Suggested Readings

Carver, Terrell, ed. 1991. *The Cambridge Companion to Marx.*
Cox, Oliver C. 1970. *Caste, Class, and Race: A Study in Social Dynamics.*
Draper, Hal. 1978. *Karl Marx's Theory of Revolution, Volume II: The Politics of So-
cial Classes.*
Elster, Jon, ed. 1986. *Karl Marx: A Reader.*
———. 1993. *Political Psychology.*
Freedman, Jonathan. 1990. *Professions of Taste: Henry James, British Aestheticism,
and Commodity Culture.*
Guillory, John. 1993. *Cultural Capital: The Problem of Literary Canon Formation.*
Hunter, Herbert and Sameer Y. Abraham, eds. 1987. *Race, Class, and the World
System: The Sociology of Oliver C. Cox.*
James, C. L. R. 1992. *The C. L. R. James Reader.* Edited by Anna Grimshaw.
James, Henry. 1990. "The Birthplace." In *The Jolly Corner and Other Tales.* Edited
by Roger Gard.
Jameson, Fredric. 1992. *Postmodernism, Or, The Cultural Logic of Late Capitalism.*
Lentricchia, Frank. 1983. *Criticism and Social Change.*
Marshall, Donald G. 1993. *Contemporary Critical Theory: A Selective Bibliography.*

O'Hara, Daniel T. 1992. *Radical Parody: American Culture and Critical Agency After Foucault.*

Poovey, Mary. 1994. "The Social Constitution of 'Class': Toward a History of Classificatory Thinking." In Dimock, Wai Chee and Michael Gilmore, eds. *Rethinking Class: Literary Studies and Social Formations.*

Williams, Raymond. 1973. *The Country and the City.*

———. 1958. *Culture and Society, 1780–1950.*

———. 1976. *Keywords: A Vocabulary of Culture and Society.*

In Place of an Afterword—
Someone Reading

Frank Lentricchia

THERE'S a little story once told by Wallace Stevens that I have to replot as I retell it. The story (Stevens's and mine) is actually an "anecdote": from the Greek, *anekdota,* meaning unpublished items. More familiarly, in English, a small gossipy narrative generally of an amusing, biographical incident in the life of a famous person whose biography's broad outline has long been a matter of public record. And more: this biography is often—when the famous person is also exemplary—a concentrated representation of the idealized story that a culture would like to tell about itself. Like all anecdotes, then, the one I have in mind can't work as an anecdote unless it somehow tells a story beyond the one it tells. So: an unpublished little story, funny and biographical, apparently stands in for a bigger story, a socially pivotal and pervasive biography which it illuminates—in an anecdotal flash the small story reveals the essence of the larger story and in that very moment becomes exegesis of a public text; the hitherto unpublished items become published. The teller of anecdotes has to presume the cultural currency of that large, containing biographical narrative which he draws upon for the sharp point he would give his anecdote, whose effect is ultimately political: to trigger a narrative sense of community that the anecdote evokes by evoking the master biography. In evoking the master biography, anecdote helps us to remember. And remembrance, so triggered, is the power which sustains, by retrieving, our basic cultural fiction.

One day, when he was a little boy, George Washington chopped down a cherry tree in his father's orchard. Americans usually get the point in a hurry; we hardly need to finish the story and deliver its famous moral punchline: the relationship of government and the people who elect it is transparent, sincere because the origin of the USA was honest. The father of our country, and our first president, could not tell a lie. No hidden motives, no secret plots. No need to be paranoid, we are a government of, by, and for the people. Here is another anecdote (fiction, story, lie): One day, my grandfather, my mother's father, at age seventy-nine, while rocking and smoking (but not inhaling) on his front porch in Utica, New York, in mid-August heat (which he disrecognized by wearing his long

429

johns), directed his grandson's attention (who was then about thirteen) to the
man sitting on *his* front porch across the street: not rocking or smoking but
huddled into himself, as if it were cold, age eighty. Gesturing with cigarette in
hand toward "this American," as he called him (in Italian he inserted between
"this" and "American" a salty adjective which is difficult to translate), all the
while nodding, and in a tone that I recognized only later as much crafted, he
said: *La vecchiáia è 'na carógna*. A story of biographical incident, maybe funny as
it stands, for sure funny if you can translate the Italian, but representative? Probably only in the mind of yours truly. You don't, because through no fault of your
own you probably can't, get the point (what really is this an anecdote *of*?),
though some in my family would—as would many first-generation Italian
Americans, some fewer of the second generation, and fewer yet of my generation. My mother's father is dead and those who remember him (and immigrants
like him) in the right way, with necessary specificity, where do I find them? Soon
this will be an anecdote for me alone because soon it will have no claim whatsoever to being what all we anecdotalists want our stories to be—a social form
which instigates cultural memory: the act of narrative renewal and the reinstate-
ment of social cohesion. I doubt that Stevens's story is any more accessible than
the one I just told about my grandfather. There is no Italian to trouble us in
Stevens's story but its language is equally foreign and its power to represent
equally in peril.

So when the relation of the teller of anecdotes to a potential audience ceases
to be unified by a single myth, anecdotes will lose their rhetorical power. The
anecdote will become (alas!) autonomous, a story for itself alone, not a literary
form whose genealogy, in parable and fable, underwrites an equation of literary
and social forms as forms of instruction. If anecdotes had minds of their own
they'd probably say, we don't like modern literary theories of aesthetic self-
sufficiency; restore us, good reader, to the way we were. The anecdotes about
George Washington are of course ceaselessly renewed by the political process of
American history, though in post-Watergate America the one about the cherry
tree may have lost much credibility. But who will renew my grandfather's cultural story? For whom can my grandfather's biography be important? What
might it mediate? Who, anyway, makes an anecdote work—its first author or its
cultural authorizer (who is rarely the first author), who by providing us with its
mediations thereby both binds and activates us collectively with its cultural
power?

The curious thing is that anecdotes, though they appear by their very nature
to depend on stable outside narrative, given and known, in fact—and most dramatically in their written, high literary style—work at critical turning points of
cultural crisis when the outside narrative seems to be slipping away and its binding power is almost extinguished. The anecdotalist's role (or desire) is to represent community by way of retrieving and re-creating the community's basic

story. To tell us what we think we already know is an effect of the genial style (trick) of his rhetoric—a literary bonding proleptic, he hopes, for the social and historical bonding that he wants to resuscitate and whose absence is the trigger for his little storytelling. The anecdotalist's act of memory is generative, critical, and cautionary: his implication is always let us remember together, take it to heart, see the bigger picture. The anecdotalist is therefore a deliberately cryptic teacher; he knows that what he wants he can't achieve alone; his largest hope is to engender an engaged readership whose cohesion will lie in a common commitment to a social project, the sustaining of life in collective narrative.

So here's the little story that I promised at the beginning as it was originally told by Wallace Stevens:

> Anecdote of the Jar
> I placed a jar in Tennessee,
> And round it was, upon a hill.
> It made the slovenly wilderness
> Surround that hill.
>
> The wilderness rose up to it,
> And sprawled around, no longer wild.
> The jar was round upon the ground
> And tall and of a port in air.
>
> It took dominion everywhere.
> The jar was gray and bare.
> It did not give of bird or bush,
> Like nothing else in Tennessee.

The advantage of beginning with this odd little genre of anecdotal lyric in the practice of Wallace Stevens is that we are forced at the outset into confronting the inadequacy of the modern literary theory of aesthetic autonomy (inadequate but possessed of many more than nine lives) and its corollary critical stance of trying to situate and constrain all commentary on texts within a text's formal boundaries. In its own most deeply felt metaphor, the classic formalist reading is a "close" reading—a desire for textual intimacy whose logic implies the end of reading in self-effacement, all the while, against this logic, elaborating itself in complex performances more complex, say the detractors of formalism, than the text being read. The American New Criticism, the critical movement which made formalism famous in this country, and whose death has been periodically announced ever since the late 1950s, remains in force as the basis (what goes without saying) of undergraduate literary pedagogy, so that, having passed into the realm of common sense, the ideological effect of the New Criticism in the United States is to sustain, under conditions of mass higher education, the romantic cult of genius by dispossessing younger readers of their active participation in the shaping of a culture and a society "of and for the people"—by stripping those readers of their right to think of themselves as culturally central storytellers: an extraordinary irony for a critical method whose initial effect was entirely democratic—to make the reading of classics available to all, even to those of us whose early cultural formation did not equip us to read Shakespeare and Milton, but a predictable irony, in retrospect, when we remember that new critical formalist reading at the same time defined and valued itself as secondary reading of explication. So while the New Criticism taught us to read, it simultaneously taught us how to subordinate our reading powers and humble ourselves before the "creative" authority of a superior primary writing.

At the very moment of formal engagement, which cryptically crafted, riddle-like anecdotes (like this one of Wallace Stevens) force us into with all possible zeal for close reading, we are led beyond the isolationist assumptions of formalism. The anecdotal lyric is (at best) a marginal and eccentric literary type, but its eccentricity may bring all the way forward what is most typical about literary form—the resistance of literary form (as literary form) to formalist desire for closure: there is always something outside the text. As a meta-literary phenomenon, anecdotal form is a concentrated instance of the radical involvement of the literary structure called "genre" in the organization of social life. The title of Stevens's poem and the first line urge us to imagine an extraliterary scene: "I placed a jar in Tennessee," but this is not an anecdote about a jar: it is an anecdote of *the* jar. However stylized for the purposes of anecdotal point making, however absurd if thought about through the norms of realism, the act described in the first line must nevertheless be imagined *as if* it were typical. The little action of this little story begins when someone places a single object some specific place (upon "*that* hill"), but the poem asks us in its title to conceive of the particular act and the particular object placed by this particular "I" as an instance of what can't be perceived and what isn't and can't be directly written about: a generic act, a generic object, a generic "I." Moreover, this is an anecdote that does not, apparently, centrally involve the human actor who places the jar and without whom presumably the jar could not be placed (since jars cannot place themselves). This is an anecdote about the jar itself, not jar placing: a fragment from the *jar's* biography. The larger narrative of which this poem is an unpublished item has to do with the jar's ideal form, its *jarness* not its *thisness*. Apparently the ideal character of the jar is the larger narrative text of which this specific jar that was placed in Tennessee is an example. In this light, the preposition in the title ("of") means not "about" but something like "belonging to," as if the jar could speak, as if the poem were really a story that a jar might tell about itself.

But if we learn anything from Plato about ideal things we learn that there is no time in them or for them: ideal entities are part of no story. In anecdote, however, we can't do without narrative and the temporal dimension, and this specific anecdote of Stevens does not disappoint us: it unfolds initially as the description of an action and the effects or consequences of that action—not as the description of a jar (and not as *the consequences of a jar:* absurd phrasing for an absurd but importantly mystifying idea). The connection of jar and human subject is unavoidable in Stevens's poem (for a while); this is a poem (or so it appears in the first line) about the consequences of jar placing. The devout formalist critic can notice but not respond (as a formalist) to questions of an economic sort that begin to press upon him at this point; nothing would seem to be further from the literary texture of this poem's mode and content than the phenomenon of capitalist culture that Marx characterized as "commodity fetishism," a formalist economics, as it were, a fascination with the commodity in itself, in isolation from the human process that brought it into existence. Can the consequences of jars be conceived apart form the intentional human process which produces and manipulates them? Puts them, for example, on hills in Tennessee? How can any inert product of human labor ever be spoken of as having in itself consequences, as if the thing had intentions of its own? These questions are precisely questions that the poem forces us to ask because the "I" who does the initial act of placing gets lost after the first line. The human actor becomes a panoramic onlooker, a distant voice, an innocent bystander: the jar takes on, somehow, an intentional life of its own. "I placed" but "It made" and "It took" and "It did not give." The jar did it. This jar, and the character of being possessed by any jar, are necessarily implicated with human activity, yet that fact is what is shunted aside after this poem's first line. The formalist critic, forced to talk about content, and Stevens's form gives him no choice, will be tempted to move at this point to the humanist reader's favorite sort of generalization: the generic activity of jar placing becomes an archetypal human act, not a socially determinate one, and the anecdote/parable/fable called "Anecdote of the Jar" concerns the consequences of the type of human activity (what shall it be called?) best particularized and named by qualities possessed by a jar, and not just any jar but the sort signaled by the modifications of grayness and bareness. This story is getting curiouser and curiouser: a human act that is like a gray, bare jar?

The act of jar placing is contextualized, almost literally—it is surrounded by wilderness—and its consequences are illuminated by the natural setting within which the act is said to take place. At the point in our formalist moment at which we notice *that,* we are tempted to step outside the formalist idea of literature as a collection of discreet, self-sustaining monads—single, isolated texts—and into another idea of literature, made current in the 1950s by Northrop Frye, who proposed it as an alternative to formalist criticism: the idea that all literary texts, rather than being peculiar autonomous entities, are representative instances of literary modes or genres that are historically ever-present, and which, taken all together, imply (this is Frye's greatest contribution to literary theory) a closed, self-sustaining verbal universe of literary structures, myths, and character types. Literature is generated by literature. Within that sort of assumption, we quickly translate "jar" and "wilderness" into the generative structural opposition of art and nature always present to the pastoral mode, though this move from the closed, atemporal world of the isolated text to the closed atemporal world of the autonomous literary universe will be made with a clean conscience only if the critic making that jump can ignore the word "Tennessee": a political designation, out of the lexicon of sovereignty, social order placed in the wild. Jar placing, then, is a second placing and second ordering whose action is an echo and repetition of a politically original act of state placing? Our formalism, which couldn't help but also be a humanism, now seems poised to serve the historicist interests of American studies.

It's hard to get through our formalist moment to whatever it is that is supposed to be outside the text: the textual woods is so lovely, dark and deep. Wanting to get on with it, see the thing whole, we find it hard to get out of the first stanza. The transpositions come easily, maybe too easily: jar vs. wilderness, as art vs. nature, as culture vs. nature. But a *slovenly* nature? This eye-catching and provocative little breakdown in decorum, firmly foregrounded by the only significant metrical substitution in the poem, sends us off into etymological research (Stevens was mad for etymologies) where we find not only what we expect ("untidy especially in dress or person, largely slipshod") but also, in close company, *sloven,* a noun in Flemish signifying a woman of low character; in adjectival form, "uncultivated, undeveloped" (in a social as well as agricultural sense). So: culture vs. nature as well-bred vs. vulgar as masculine vs. feminine? Mother nature as low-class slut? Is *that* somehow being said in this poem? We'd better look harder at point of view: mainly panoramic, but at two crucial spots limited. In the first stanza, we see the world for a moment according to a jar, refusing to keep its proud sense of its own well-formed self to itself, smugly taking itself as the distributing point of order and sole topographical coordinate; we see wilderness forced out of itself into order: "It made the slovenly wilderness / Surround that hill"; and in the third and last stanza we experience the point of view of the wilderness in the sense that the panoramic speaker takes the side of the wilderness. An old point of controversy about this poem—is the poet on the side of art or on the side of nature?—disappears when we note that Stevens lets nature get the last word in by characterizing the autonomous jar of art, at the end of the poem, as an absence of nature. Nature: maternal, creative, pliant; the jar: a receptacle that doesn't receive and from which nothing emerges—inflexible, hard, and possessed by a classic case of womb envy. "It did not give of bird or bush, / Like nothing else in Tennessee."

Formalists must all sooner or later come to the grievous conclusion about "Anecdote of the Jar" that the aged Ezra Pound came to about his *Cantos:* it will not cohere. And things only get worse: the imposing jar is also a "port" (haven? gate? but for whom?). The original structural opposition of "jar" and "wilderness," an opposition of nouns as substances, modulates into an opposition of verbs or actions: jars "take," the wilderness "gives." Jars take power—"dominion" (supreme authority, sovereignty, absolute ownership). Who is responsible for this power? Certainly not "I"; the jar did it. No longer can we avoid the question of tone; the postulate of the literary universe will not help us now, no amount of knowledge—not even Frye's—about literary structure will help us here to hear. Structuralists, by definition, cannot attend to nonrepeatable, unique textures of voice; structuralists, by definition, are tone-deaf. So what are we to make of the reiterated sounds of jar music, in the major key of "round"? A whole lot of "round" for such a short poem: surround, around, round (twice), ground. "Round": an insidiously invasive sound which evokes at this poem's aural level all of the big thematic points condensed in the key word of the poem: "dominion." Dominion "everywhere"—"everywhere"/"air"/"bare"—this triplet, in a poem otherwise devoid of rhyme, is unavoidable to the ear: a saturating totality, a faceless totality of authority. The jar is into every damn thing. In the world according to the jar, this aural imperialist, there is barely, just barely, one letter's worth of ground: mainly, in this world, there is "g-round." This madly incisive and potentially scary jabberwockian sense is the decisive entry to the poet's panoramic point of view, his presiding tonality: detached, above it all, neither for jars nor for nature, he writes in playful self-possession (whatever else you can say about him he's certainly not frightened of anything) this line, best read in the manner of W. C. Fields: "The jar was round upon the ground."

Northrop Frye's structuralist postulate of a literary universe of forms, always and simultaneously present to literary choice, encourages us to see Stevens's poem as a variant of traditional pastoral, and Stevens himself as on the side of nature and spontaneity (against art, culture, and systematic literariness). But the key to interpretation is not really *in* the genre that he's working with. It's in the peculiar, particular, and surprising tonal textures—in the mockery of the jar on its own aural terms ("round" being the sound which echoes the jar's essential formal property), in the individual talent over whom no literary tradition takes dominion. Having come to that conclusion, however, we are not much closer to answering the most pressing question of form that this poem poses: what, really, is this an anecdote *of,* what cautionary tale is embedded in the last line ("Like nothing else in Tennessee"), which is beginning to sound more and more like a finger-wagging warning to all us actual and would-be jar placers. If the tonal posture of this poem could not possibly be predicted, no matter how much we know about the structural oppositions of pastoral poetry, if this vocal feature seems original with this poet's handling of the genre, then maybe we need to look more deeply into this poet. And suddenly the next interpretive move virtually presents itself to us as our most enticing option yet. It seems so necessary: what is the place of "Anecdote of the Jar" within Stevens's corpus, the literary universe that inheres peculiarly in his writings taken as a totality? Not as texts written over a period of years but as texts present to one another as if they had been written all at once, in a single expressive act, bearing the poet's vision as if that vision were somehow wholly and always present to its constitutive texts, as their shaping presence.

"Anecdote of the Jar" has two contexts in Stevens's corpus. In the first, its occasion of publication, in Harriet Monroe's *Poetry,* in 1919, the poem appeared as part of an ensemble. After this original ensemble of fourteen poems was accepted, but not yet published, Stevens made several substitutions: one of them was "Anecdote of the Jar," and another he called a "trifle" whose title, "The Indigo Glass in the Grass," will make us hear once again the aural joke "The jar was round upon the ground." In "Anecdote of the Jar" Stevens's self-deprecating decadent idea of the poem as "trifle," as his inconsequential toy, reaches through itself, in trifling play, to something more than play. The odd harmony of the ensemble consists of a blending of the tones of playfulness and dead seriousness—a blend that "Anecdote of the Jar," better than any poem in the ensemble, perfectly concentrates. In the poetic corpus as a whole, the other context or occasion, Stevens's jar poem joins several other early poems with the formal term "anecdote" as part of their title, and, then, in his middle and later years, joins a continuing and troubled meditative strain present to virtually everything that he wrote. In this context the jar finds essential kinship with various artifacts like glasses, bowls, poetic images, thought itself, even poems, and with large conceptions, in his middle and later career, of the "hero" and "major man": all expressions of systematic endeavor; all the creation of structure, systems, reasons; all effects—in a word ambivalently dear to Stevens—of "abstraction." But:

> It was when I said,
> "There is no such thing as the truth,"
> That the grapes seemed fatter.
> The fox ran out of his hole.
>
> . . . .
> It is posed and it is posed
> But in nature it merely grows.
>
> . . . .
> You must become an ignorant man again
> And see the sun again with an ignorant eye. . . .
>
> . . . .
> How clean the sun when seen in its idea,
> Washed in the remotest cleanliness of a heaven
> That has expelled us and our images. . .

That last ellipsis is not mine; it belongs most originally to Wallace Stevens: a subtle signifier of the awe that motivates the words preceding it but which can't ever be put in words, imaged, or conceived. The ellipsis: not words left out, but words impossible. In 1913, in the midst of modernist revolution in poetry and philosophy, Josiah Royce replayed George Santayana's attack on Whitman as poet of barbarism by characterizing the yearning for pure perception—for the unposed, for the fattest grapes, for the sun utterly clean—as a sign of the modernist times: perception as a final moment of consciousness, with perceiver ("us") and perceived ("the sun") unified in an isolated fulfillment of seeing. This unspeakable moment represented by the ellipsis, this radical desire for the first perception, prior to reason, would wipe out representation—our history and our tradition ("us and our images") and all that we are accustomed to thinking of as human, everything that gets between us and the sun in itself. Perception, the image, the attack on reason, and the interest in the primitive in writers and artists like Stevens, Picasso, T. S. Eliot, and D. H. Lawrence are all code terms for the literary and artistic modernisms whose solidarity consists in the hatred of what sociologists call modernization. Modernist desire is for radical reduction to a condition barely human where we would become translated—were it possible—out of the sickness of our modernization and into mediums for vision, mere mediums. "Barbaric"—Santayana's description of modern writers who hated modernity—is fair as far as it goes. What it does not do justice to is the modernist's nostalgia for the barbarous, his feeling of being out of place ("You must become an ignorant man again"): his willingness to suspend social relations, not because he's antisocial but because the society he finds himself in seems to have designs upon his health.

So jars are Stevens's stand-ins (representations) for the world that fortunate Westerners call modern; jars get in the way, they mediate; they represent everything that makes it difficult to live a life that doesn't feel artificial ("modernized"). To live a modern life, for writers like Stevens and Eliot, is hard to distinguish from a living death. Jars are like the bowl in Stevens's "The Poems of Our Climate": cold, a cold porcelain, low and round . . . a bowl brilliant in its clarity and in whose ambience the day becomes a bowl of white and the world itself a world of white, perfect, inhuman. We don't want that world because the imperfect is our paradise:

> It was when the trees were leafless first in November
> And their blackness became apparent, that one first
> Knew the eccentric to be the base of design.

If the "eccentric," or uncentered, is the foundation of "design," then Stevens is here redefining "design" against the grain to mean something like intention without prior conception, purpose, plan, project, scheme, plot: uncontrolled intention, intention somehow unintended. And if the eccentric, or uncentered, is also the subversive foundation of "design" understood in its usual sense as "structure" (shape, pattern), then it is design or pattern without classic structurality—structure unstructured yet still, somehow, structured. The eccentric is the base of *design*. Design, from the Latin *designare,* and *signare* from *signum* (a mark or sign). Eccentric signs would be signs unplotted, surprising, even random. Eccentric design would be a thing both necessary and spontaneous; a form of determination, yet free. Jars—they're not that kind of design; they're products of coldest intention; they have structural centers. And what's more they seem to have designs upon power. They take dominion, they can even make something as unmanageable as a wilderness shape up, imitate their structural roundedness. A jar can make a wilderness surround itself; a jar can make the very ground into its mirror. Jars are humorless narcissists who think they are ungrounded. And they are involved in a secret, undercover narrative (a "plot"): What is it?

To move, as I just have, from the single poem as closed, isolate, verbal system, a world unto itself, to the poem as microcosmic fragment of a poetic corpus, is to move, in a sense, not at all: for the corpus, so conceived, as a timeless whole, is likewise closed and isolate. And to invoke an agent called "the poet" as creator of a corpus is to invoke a subject who always contained and expressed it all, so that those temporal distinctions of career that I've made ("early," "middle," and "late") are truly gratuitous—they make no difference. Not even "career," in this interpretive context, makes much sense since the term suggests a determinate act of will to shape a life, to set an ordered narrative in motion and thereby bring your life into control (into art) by making it a story. To so read either the single poem or the corpus, as I have, is to read *for* (look for, read on behalf of, from the perspective of) self-sufficient system. To invoke "the poet" in this context is not to invoke a human being who needs to be differentiated by categories of, say, class, or gender, or race (or all three) and who would need to be historically located; it is to invoke an agent whose function is to trigger a verbal agency which, once triggered, mysteriously operates itself as a rule-bound machine. In either instance, single poem or corpus, the verbal system must be treated as if it were its own magnificent cause of being. "The poet" so invoked as an originator is a necessary fiction (we have to invoke an individual at some point), yet at some other level he must be real ("Wallace Stevens" after all is the name of a person who was born, went to Harvard, liked his mother better than his father, married, worked for an insurance company and loved it, often took vacations to Florida without his wife, listened to the Saturday afternoon broadcasts from the Metropolitan Opera House, did not get divorced, made a lot of money, died of cancer, and maybe converted on his deathbed if you want to believe the nuns who attended him at the end, which I do.) Wallace Stevens, "the poet," is not subject to those modifications. For devout critics of system—all structuralists by deed if not by name—he is a verbal operator who functions in an ideal space.

But to pose the question about narratives, secret or otherwise, as I have throughout, is to move to history, or at least to be poised (or seem to be poised) at the brink of concerted historical reading. Even the devoutest formalist critic cheats; history makes them do it. I'm not devout; I've cheated two or three times to this point, I'm not quite sure how many, contaminating formal purity by mentioning Tennessee and American studies, and it could have been worse. I held back mentioning that Tennessee is an englishing of a Cherokee place name—a Cherokee village named Tanasi. And no use getting too sentimental about Indians and the wilderness. It was here first, apparently, I mean the wilderness, then the Indians, who "our forefathers" (*whose* forefathers?) slaughtered. Tennessee eventually took dominion over Tanasi, but the Indians did a little political placing of their own; they engaged frequently in their own territorial wars with considerable intensity. They set their cultures in the wilderness first; then we placed ours over theirs: we supplanted them, plowed them under. Jar placing, then, is a third-order placing? A representation of a repetitive action of domination, hard to separate from the course of American history?

I also brought in Josiah Royce and what he thought of modernism—he didn't like it but he knew what it was—and I wrote down dates, 1913, when Royce published the statements I alluded to, and 1919, when Stevens published "Anecdote of the Jar." Nineteen-nineteen becomes a readable fact for interpretation within the historical horizon of avant-garde modernist upheaval; that is the poem's immediate cultural context; its date of publication makes that context surround the poem. "Tennessee" is more difficult. It is surely a term for interpretation but one that resists formal reading, though not altogether if we can count, as "reading," formalist forgetting ("jarring") of its ground, a covering of the ground not unlike the way Tennessee sonically covers Tanasi. "Tennessee" looks like a determinate historical and political term in Stevens's poem, looks like an unambiguous invitation to do the work of historicizing this poem, but probably "gap" is better than "term." What are the limits of the historical horizon within which we would situate "Tennessee"? How far back does it go? To the Cherokee Indians? How far forward? Maybe all the way to Vietnam.

In its immediate literary culture Stevens's critique of artifice joins the general critique, at the center of the imagist movement and polemically (and entrepreneurially) urged in the criticism of Ezra Pound, of what was passing for "literature." It was a critique not of literature *tout court* but of official poetic practice in the 1890s and early years of this century, when those who would become the chief modernists were growing up and beginning to read what was being honored as "contemporary" poetry—an exercise, or so it seemed to Pound, Robert Frost, and others, in ever-increasing poetic vagueness inversely proportioned to the ever-increasing particularity (often of a harsh sort) in the language of realist fiction; frightened literariness, withdrawal into genteel hermitage. As Frost tirelessly pointed out, it was a language that never was, except in books: real people, at any rate—Frost meant those not born to high cultural privilege—don't talk *that* way. In this light, poetic modernism is round 2 of English romanticism, especially in its Wordsworthian phase. Pound's revisions of W. B. Yeats' early poems are in the mode of Wordsworth's legendary attacks on Thomas Gray in the preface to *Lyrical Ballads,* as is Stevens's late meditation in *Notes toward a Supreme Fiction,* when he evokes and then one-ups Wordsworth's attack on

Gray's use of archaic language. Stevens writes, "the sun must bear no name," not even the name "sun," which is just as artificial as "Phoebus"—the mythological object of Wordsworth's literary and social revolutionary scorn. The sun must simply be, let be, "in the difficulty of what it is to be." Words are like jars: Shelley thought the truth to be imageless; Stevens, immoralist of modernist lyric, appeared to think it altogether silent.

Wordsworth's critique of Gray is part of the larger romantic injunction: to "strip the evil of familiarity" from the world. Not to make the world strange but to see the strangeness that is there: a radically realist epistemological project replayed in the theoretical premises of imagism in Pound and T. E. Hulme. ("Could reality come into direct contact with sense and consciousness, art would be useless," Hulme wrote, "or rather we should all be artists." Or as Pound urged the project of the image: "Direct treatment of the 'thing,' whether subjective or objective.") A radically realist project, epistemologically, and an ethical and political project as well. Wordsworth's attack, like Frost's later on mannered language, is also an attack on the manners (social and poetic) of a class. Wordsworth argues, on behalf of a newly emergent ("slovenly") class (of which Frost may be the great American modernist representative), that the poetry of privilege speaks nothing like the language spoken by real men in a state of nature, who work farms, or the language of the new urban worker sunk into "savage torpor" by the self-alienating nature of his labor. The poetry of privilege—Frost is especially strong on this point—does not *speak;* it has no aural referent in the various worlds of communication (not even in the world of the privileged). Stevens, who had none of Frost's vocal sentiments, makes critical allusion to the issue by surrounding the pompous and empty "port" (comportment, carriage, syntax) of jar-speak ("of a port in air") with plain-speaking syntax ("I placed a jar in Tennessee"). A new poetry would presumably clear our consciousness—"wash" it "clean" of artifice and a contaminating social discourse and bring us into contact with (help us to see again, re-cognize) a social outside, a "ground" ruled and exploited by the class represented by Gray, the social outside now seen in an act of sympathy which a new poetry would encourage. The social and socialist implications of Wordsworth's theory of the poet (an instigator of radical community, he "binds together by passion and knowledge the vast empire of human society, as it is spread over the whole earth"; he does "not write for poets alone, but for men"), these implications were drawn out by Shelley: "The great secret of morals is love; or a going out of our own nature, and an identification of ourselves with [a] person not our own. A man, to be greatly good, must imagine intensely and comprehensively; he must put himself in the place of another and of many others." As a figure for the poetry opposed (not for the same reasons and on behalf of different goals) by Wordsworth, Frost, and Pound, the jar shows kinship with the letter that kills (jars do not "give of bird or bush"). Jars are representations not of the spirit of love but of the spirit of abstraction. In the romantic lexicon, from Wordsworth to Stevens, "artifice" and "abstraction" are synonyms and key coded words in a political anecdote of struggle.

Stevens's is an American jar, plain, bare, and gray, not Thomas Gray-like and not richly worked and elaborated, like Keats' Grecian urn, but something of a commentary on Keats' most famous ode and on Keats himself: commentary not in anxiety and competitiveness but in self-definition and political critique very close to home. This is a jar that provokes in Stevens no Keatsian desire for the death of identification and therefore no Keatsian pulling back from self-extinguishment, no Keatsian shock of awareness that the urn's life is dead life, no need to say "cold pastoral." And Stevens's jar is not tempting for another reason. It represents nothing like Keats' double-edged Western cultural heritage maybe worth being embarrassed by because maybe (for Keats) worth recuperating, sustaining, being engaged with. Nor is Stevens replaying Henry James's criticism of American culture as too thin to support really "fine" writing. Stevens's formation is close to that of Keats, but its American ground kept him from wishing to die out of his unprivileged class into the class of a precapitalist landed aristocracy (except in the South, and here very little, there is no American memory for this) which bears the burden of tradition. Keats' desire to die, reread from Stevens's perspective, is a desire for social death and rebirth: to become not a sod or a nightingale but a gentleman.

Stevens's poem, in this double focus of literary and social history, is an American poem which at once works as a metapoem, an anecdote of the wider cultural story of romantic and early modernist poetics, an antipoetics urging a literature against official literature, and a critical evaluation of the wider story. The literary criticism which Stevens called "Anecdote of the Jar" is a criticism not of Grecian urns and Thomas Gray's poetry but of plain old democratic American jars which he insists we see as figuring a work of oppression that cannot be explained in classic European terms of class relations (in classic Marxist terms). Wordsworth and Keats had the griefs and consolations of English society at a moment of decisive social change—they might have said: "The jar is them." Stevens, who has some of Wordsworth's and Frost's feeling for ordinary people, who celebrated ignorance in his poems as the pure access to the real, who once said of himself, in self-congratulation, that he had been working like an immigrant Italian, who never wanted to write in the language of real men and, like Shelley, never did, has no sentimentality for democratic myths. He forces us to say: "The jar is us." Whatever "Anecdote of the Jar" is an anecdote *of,* one thing is sure: unlike the anecdote about the father of our country who presumably could not tell a lie, this one doesn't seem calculated to make us feel good about ourselves.

Had Wallace Stevens lived through our Vietnam period he might have had the right answer to the question posed by Norman Mailer in 1967: *Why Are We in Vietnam?* Had he forgotten what he knew, long before our military intervention in Southeast Asia, he would have (had he lived so long) been reminded by Michael Herr who at the end of his book *Dispatches* (1970) wrote: "Vietnam Vietnam Vietnam, we've all been there." Herr maybe in part knew what he knew because he had read Stevens, who taught him about where we've all been, all along: "Once it was all locked in place, Khe Sanh became like the planted jar in Wallace Stevens's poem. It took dominion everywhere." Herr's perversely perfect mixed metaphor of the "planted jar," if it might have struck Stevens as an incisive reading of his poem, might also have awakened in him an obscure memory of one of the powerful philosophical presences of his Harvard days, William James, writing out of the bitterness of his political awakening, writing on 1 March 1899 in the *Boston Transcript* against our first imperial incursion in the Orient: "We are destroying down to the root every germ of a healthy national life in these unfortunate people. . . . We must sow our ideals, plant our order, impose our God." James might have ended his letter: "The Philippines the Philippines the Philippines, we've all been there."

The hypothetical "ifs" and subjunctive "mights" which fairly pepper my preceding paragraph may represent something like the lure of bad-faith political criticism: the desire for objective laws of historical force to offer themselves to a reader like myself who then need only record them as the true causes of texts like "Anecdote of the Jar" and *Dispatches*. James and Stevens, of course, did not read Herr; Herr did read Stevens, but I see no reason to think that he read James. Herr, Stevens, and James can be constellated as a single discursive body only because I've read them in a certain way; I name the constellation, I give it a shape: "can be constellated," a deluded construction; its passivity obscures what goes on in the act of interpretation. So my hypotheticals and subjunctives may be taken in another way, as an indication of where we always stand in the interpretive act: not on the realist's terra firma but in active ideological contest to shape our culture's sense of its own history. I offer Herr, Stevens, and James (in that order, reading backward, which is the way reading typically takes place: through our cultural formation) as three voices from a tradition of American anti-imperialist writing (a unified cultural practice) that cuts through the boundaries of philosophy, poetry, and journalism, a discourse of political criticism.

Stevens's poem is an anecdote of that political story, but to reach for American anti-imperialism and isolationism in the first two decades of this century, when he was coming of age as a writer, as the political cause of his poem is absurd, yet no more absurd perhaps than to reach for objective laws of historical influence. In either instance what is longed for is direct reflection of political reality in a literary text, a vulgar form of historicism, periodically practiced in Marxist circles (though hardly limited to those), in which the "time" of the literary text is treated as one and the same with political "time," as if the episode in the Philippines gave rise to the poem. The varieties of vulgar formalism are more useful;

they at least put the stress where it belongs, on the strange differences; it is easier to believe in literary causalities of literary texts, as if literature were self-originating. For the text in question, these causalities might be: Stevens's verbal play, the generic history of pastoral, the inner imperatives of Stevens's unfolding corpus, the literary-historical forces of romanticism, the first surge of modernist literary polemic, manifesto, and experiment (the ethical imperative of imagism). As an "effect" of such "causes," "Anecdote of the Jar" partakes of the time of literature whose integrity seems impervious to "outside" pressures. But it isn't: cultural practices are neither autonomous nor homogeneous. With all differences respected, they sometimes are made to stand in relation by acts of reading, acts of retelling or cultural constellating like Herr's remembering of Stevens in Vietnam, like my remembering of Herr's and James's anti-imperialist efforts; like my placing of Stevens as a writer "between" James and Herr and "between" our first intervention in Cuba, 21 April 1898, and our second intervention in Cuba, 21 April 1961. The storyteller's most powerful effect comes when he convinces us that what is particular, integrated, and different in a cultural practice (like the writing of rarefied high modernist poetry) is part of a cultural plot that makes coherent sense of all cultural practices as a totality: not a totality that is there, waiting for us to acknowledge its presence, but a totality fashioned when the storyteller convinces us to see it his way. I think we most believe in plots when they are hard to see; and a conspiracy that includes James, Michael Herr, and Stevens had better be hard to see.

Contemporary styles of literary theory and practice resemble nothing so much as Don DeLillo's funny anecdotal personification (in *Ratner's Star*) of a terrible fear not really separable from the modernist dream. Consider DeLillo's "Supreme Abstract Commander": one Chester Greylag Dent, "unaffiliated and stateless," who lives in a nuclear-powered submarine, thirty-five thousand feet under the sea ("just idling there in the dark and cold . . . the quietest place on earth"), attended by a eunuch who talks of an international cartel interested in "abstract economic power" and named ACRONYM (a "combination of letters formed to represent the idea of a combination of letters"); who is so old as to verge on transparency; who has been awarded a Nobel Prize in literature for his books on mathematics and logic, "handblocked in a style best described as undiscourageably diffuse"; who says in response to the question, What do you do? "I think of myself as the Supreme Abstract Commander. That's what I do"; who considers us mortals "not as a collection of races and nationalities but as a group that shows the same taxonomic classification, that of Earth-planet extant"; who never laughs but instead, when moved to such spontaneous expression, says, "Hilarious," or "Extremely mirth-provoking"—Chester Greylag Dent, who believes that the reason that he has been referred to "more than a few times as the greatest man in the world" has to do with "the life choice I've made. To suspend myself in the ocean zone of perpetual darkness. To inhabit an environment composed almost solely of tiny sightless feeble-minded creatures palpitating in the ooze"; who when asked about his shawls says he buys them from "this man in Sausalito."

When he wants to, DeLillo can evoke the horrors of abstraction, not impotently removed, but actively engaged in a deadly work of the sort which Herr describes in the work of MACV (an acronym representing Military Assistance Command, Vietnam), or in the cartographic work of reinscribing Vietnam as a military arena "which made for clear communication, at least among members of the Mission and the many components of . . . the fabulous MACV." And "fabulous" is just right: of a fable, not Vietnamese, generating and imposing a fable not Vietnamese: "Since most of the journalism from the war was framed in that language [MACV, I Corps, II Corps, DMZ] it would be as impossible to know what Vietnam looked like from reading most newspaper stories as it would be to know how it smelled." Like Stevens's and like DeLillo's, Herr's writing aims to be a counterdiscourse, working to undermine discourses of abstraction and domination—Supreme Abstract Commanders, whether they are called jars, the ruling class, Khe Sanh, or MACV, or imperialism. These counterdiscourses imply (rarely state) their deepest alternative values in desires for particularity; in the way it looked and smelled; in little scraps of dialogue about "this man in Sausalito." For life in the small things, "birds and bushes," which ought to be but are not invulnerable to imperial imposition.

The object of DeLillo's unmasking humor is captured in other stories which are not funny, told with great penetration by William James and Michel Foucault in reaction to their nightmares of system and discipline: the horrific political accompaniments of modernization. Foucault's disciplinary society and James's systematic life are the outcomes of a historical process and are twin accounts insofar as they take the price of our modernity to be the loss of self-determination in the normalizing actions of institutional life that James, long before Foucault, excoriated for "branding, licensing and degree-giving, authorizing and appointing, and in general regulating and administering by system the lives of human beings." James, writing before the paranoid age of surveillance and computer information banks, had his hopes: "I am against all bigness and greatness in all their forms, and with the invisible molecular forces that work from individual to individual, stealing in through the crannies of the world like so many soft rootlets, or like the capillary oozing of water, and yet rending the hardest monuments of man's pride, if you give them time." James believed that somehow the Supreme Abstract Commanders would lose and that history would finally come around to putting the individual on top.

Foucault is not sanguine about the survival of the individual. Discipline insidiously invades the ground of individuality in order to master it. Discipline takes us all through the gate of modernization, into safe port, where our individuality is studied so much the better to be controlled. Foucault's antidote is writing: not as a space for the preservation of identity and the assertion of voice, but as a labyrinth into which he can escape, to "lose myself," and, there, in the labyrinth, never have to be a self (a self, an identifiable principle of continuity, is a dangerous thing to be)—write yourself off, as it were, "write in order to have no face." Give no target to discipline: "Do not ask who I am and do not ask me to remain the same: leave it to our bureaucrats and our police to see that our papers are in order. At least spare us their morality when we write." If for James "individuality" translates into a philosophical positive—a given of liberalism—a hold-out in freedom and the site of the personal and of "full ideality," then for Foucault undisciplined and anarchic individuality may be precisely the unintended effect of a system which would produce individuality as an object of its knowledge and power (the disciplinary appropriation of biography), but which instead, and ironically, inside its safe, normalized subject, instigates the move to the underground where a deviant selfhood may nurture sullen schemes of resistance to a world in which paranoia is reason, not madness.

Stevens inhabits the world of James and Foucault; he is wary of system and surveillance and of the police in all their contemporary and protean guises. But Prospero-like he called upon his Ariel and Ariel rarely failed to respond, sometimes bearing unexpected gifts. After the jars, glasses, bowls, designs of various sorts, and images, after the (male) hero and (male) major man—all of them "must be abstract"—comes the fat girl. Who is she? Definitely no "central man" who, "cold and numbered," "sums us up," no canonical man "admired by all men"—those major men, they may be seated in cafés, but we will never see them. Instead we will see the "dish of country cheese / And a pineapple on the table." If we're lucky, we'll hear someone—could it possibly be the major man?—talk about "this man in Sausalito" who makes beautiful shawls. Coming late, after all his anecdotal portraits, so allegorical in intent, the fat girl seems real: not a literary device, not what anyone wants her to be—she's a fulfillment that can be wished for, as Stevens wishes for her in some of the most moving of his lyric lines, but what his writing itself cannot grant; what no writing can grant.

In the key verbs of "Anecdote of the Jar," the fat girl gives but she cannot be taken. Refusing to show herself in anecodotal lyric, she awaits, instead, the purer romantic lyricist. In "Anecdote of the Jar" Stevens tells a story whose most cryptically encoded lesson is the necessity of forsaking action, and the genre of action—storytelling—in favor of aesthesis, praise's ultimate awestruck medium. Stevens's story against story represents a longing for lyric itself and its imperative: a politics of lyricism which in James, Stevens, Herr, and Foucault amounts to a directive not to set molecular individuals into social system, not even into

literary systems of narrative; not to reencode Vietnam in the coordinates of
American imperial cartography. To find the fat girl is not to impose a plot upon
her—it is to find a "moving contour," unfixed and incomplete because alive, and
moving because we are moved. She appears:

> Fat girl, terrestrial, my summer, my night,
> How is it I find you in difference, see you there
> In a moving contour, a change not quite completed? . . .
> Bent over work, anxious, content, alone,
> You remain the more than natural figure. You
> Become the soft-footed phantom. . . .

References

Abel, Elizabeth. 1980. "[E]merging Identities: The Dynamics of Female Friendship in Contemporary Fiction by Women." *Signs* 6.

———, ed. 1982. *Writing and Sexual Difference*. Chicago: University of Chicago Press.

ABM Treaty Interpretation Dispute: Hearing before the Subcommittee on Arms Control, International Security and Science of the Committee on Foreign Affairs, House of Representatives. 1986. 99th Cong., 1st sess.

Abrams, M. H. 1977. *The Mirror and the Lamp: Romantic Theory and the Critical Tradition*. New York: Oxford University Press.

Adams, Hazard, ed. 1971. *Critical Theory since Plato*. New York: Harcourt Brace Jovanovich.

Adams, Henry. 1973. *The Education of Henry Adams*, edited by Ernest Samuels. Boston: Houghton Mifflin.

[Adorno, Theodor W., Max Horkheimer, et al.] 1941. "Research Project on Anti-Semitism." *Zeitschrift für Sozialforschung/Studies in Philosophy and Social Science* 9.

Adorno, Theodor and Max Horkheimer. 1972. *Dialectic of Enlightenment*, translated by John Cumming. New York: Herder & Herder (first published 1944).

Ahmad, Aijaz. 1993. *In Theory: Nations, Classes, Literatures*. London: Verso.

Aiken, H. D. 1955. "The Aesthetic Relevance of Artists' Intentions." *Journal of Philosophy* 52.

Althusser, Louis. 1970. "Marxism and Humanism." In *For Marx*. New York: Vintage.

———. 1971. "Ideology and Ideological State Apparatuses." In *Lenin and Philosophy*. New York: Monthly Review Press.

Althusser, Louis, and Etienne Balibar. 1970. *Reading "Capital."* London: New Left Books.

Anderson, Benedict. 1983. *Imagined Communities: Reflections on the Origins and Spread of Nationalism*. London: Verso.

Anderson, Laurie. 1984. *United States*. New York: Harper and Row.

Andrews, William L. 1986. *To Tell a Free Story: The First Century of Afro-American Autobiography, 1760–1865*. Urbana: University of Illinois Press.

Anscombe, G. E. M. 1957. *Intention*. Ithaca: Cornell University Press.

Antin, David. 1984. *Tuning*. New York: New Directions.

Antin, Mary. 1912. *The Promised Land*. Boston: Houghton Mifflin.

Arac, Jonathan. 1979. *Commissioned Spirits*. New Brunswick: Rutgers University Press.

———. 1987. *Critical Genealogies*. New York: Columbia University Press.

———, ed. 1988. *After Foucault*. New Brunswick: Rutgers University Press.

Archard, David. 1984. *Consciousness and the Unconscious.* Lasalle, Ill.: Open Court.

Arendt, Hannah. 1944. "Race Thinking before Racism." *Review of Politics* 6.

———. 1951. *The Burden of Our Time.* London: Secker & Warburg.

———. 1977. "What Is Authority?" In *Between Past and Present: Eight Exercises in Political Thought.* New York: Penguin Books.

Aristotle. 1907. *Theory of Poetry and Fine Art,* translated by S. H. Butcher. New York: Dover.

———. 1927. *Poetics,* translated by W. Hamilton Fyfe. Cambridge: Harvard University Press.

———. 1946. *The Works of Aristotle.* Vol. 11. Translated by W. Rhys Roberts. Oxford: Oxford University Press.

Armstrong, Nancy. 1987. *Desire and Domestic Fiction.* New York: Oxford University Press.

Auerbach, Erich. 1953. *Mimesis: The Representation of Reality in Western Literature,* translated by Willard Trask. Princeton: Princeton University Press.

Austin, J. L. 1962. *How to Do Things with Words.* Cambridge: Harvard University Press.

Bahro, Rudolph. 1978. *The Alternative in Eastern Europe,* translated by David Fernbach. London: New Left Books.

Bahti, Timothy. 1986. "Ambiguity and Indeterminacy: The Juncture." *Comparative Literature* 38.

Bakhtin, Mikhail. 1968. *Rabelais and His World,* translated by Hélène Iswolsky. Cambridge: MIT Press.

———. 1981. *The Dialogic Imagination,* edited by Michael Holquist, and translated by Caryl Emerson and Michael Holquist. Austin: University of Texas Press Slavic Series, no. 1.

Baldick, Chris. 1983. *The Social Mission of English Criticism, 1848–1932.* Oxford: Clarendon Press.

Ball, Charles. 1836. *Slavery in the United States: A Narrative of the Life and Adventures of Charles Ball, a Black Man.* Lewiston, Pa.: Shugert.

Barth, Fredrik. 1969. *Ethnic Groups and Boundaries: The Social Organization of Culture Difference.* Boston: Little, Brown.

Barthes, Roland. 1967. *Writing Degree Zero,* translated by Annette Lavers and Colin Smith. New York: Hill and Wang.

———. 1972. "The Structural Activity." In *Critical Essays,* translated by Richard Howard. New York: Hill and Wang.

———. 1974. *S/Z,* translated by Richard Miller. London: Jonathan Cape.

———. 1975. *The Pleasure of the Text,* translated by Richard Miller. New York: Hill and Wang.

———. 1977. *Image, Music, Text,* translated by Stephen Heath. New York: Hill and Wang.

———. 1979. "From Work to Text." In *Textual Strategies,* edited by Josue V. Harari. Ithaca: Cornell University Press.

Bate, Walter Jackson, 1970. *The Burden of the Past and the English Poet.* Cambridge: Harvard University Press.

Baudrillard, Jean. 1981. *For a Critique of the Political Economy of the Sign.* St. Louis: Telos Press.

Baudry, J-L. 1974. "Writing, Fiction, Ideology." *Afterimage* no. 5.

Baym, Nina. 1978. *Women's Fiction: A Guide to Novels by and about Women.* Ithaca: Cornell University Press.

Beardsley, Monroe. 1958. *Aesthetics: Problems in the Philosophy of Criticism.* New York: Harcourt, Brace and World.

Belsey, Catherine. 1980. *Critical Practice*. London: Methuen.

Benamou, Michel, and Charles Caramello, eds. 1977. *Performance in Postmodern Culture*. Madison: Coda Press and the Center for Twentieth Century Studies, University of Wisconsin-Milwaukee.

Benjamin, Walter. 1968. *Illuminations,* edited by Hannah Arendt, translated by Harry Zohn. New York: Harcourt, Brace and World.

———. 1973. "The Author as Producer." In *Understanding Brecht*. London: New Left Books.

———. 1977. *The Origin of Germanic Tragic Drama,* translated by John Osborne. London: New Left Books.

Berlin, Sir Isaiah. 1988. "On the Pursuit of the Ideal." *New York Review of Books* 35.

Bersini, Leo. 1986. *The Freudian Body: Psychoanalysis and Art*. New York: Columbia University Press.

Berthoff, Warner. 1981. *The Ferment of Realism: American Literature, 1884–1919*. Cambridge: Harvard University Press.

Bhabha, Homi. 1994. *The Location of Culture*. London and New York: Routledge.

Blackmur, R. P. 1952. *Language as Gesture*. New York: Harcourt Brace.

———. 1955. *The Lion and the Honeycomb*. New York: Harcourt Brace.

Blassingame, John W. 1985. "Using the Testimony of Ex-Slaves: Approaches and Problems." *The Slave's Narrative,* edited by Charles T. Davis and Henry Louis Gates. New York: Oxford University Press.

Bloom, Harold. 1973. *The Anxiety of Influence*. New York: Oxford University Press.

———. 1975a. *Kabbalah and Criticism*. New York: Seabury Press.

———. 1975b. *A Map of Misreading*. New York: Oxford University Press.

———. 1976. *Poetry and Repression: Revisionism from Blake to Stevens*. New Haven: Yale University Press.

———. 1989. *Ruin the Sacred Truths: Poetry and Belief from the Bible to the Present*. Cambridge: Harvard University Press.

Bongie, Chris. 1991. "Conrad and the New Imperialism." In *Macropolitics of Nineteenth Century Literature: Nationalism, Exoticism, Imperialism,* edited by Jonathan Arac and Harriet Ritvo. Philadelphia: University of Pennsylvania Press.

Booth, Wayne, C. 1961. *The Rhetoric of Fiction*. 2d ed. Chicago: University of Chicago Press.

———. 1974. *A Rhetoric of Irony*. Chicago: University of Chicago Press.

Borsch-Jacobsen, Michel. 1988. *The Freudian Subject,* translated by Catharine Porter. Stanford: Stanford University Press.

Boswell, James. [1799] 1960. *Boswell's Life of Johnson*. London: Oxford University Press.

Bourdieu, Pierre. 1984. *Distinction: A Social Critique of the Judgement of Taste,* translated by Richard Nice. Cambridge: Harvard University Press.

Bourne, Randolph S. 1977. *The Radical Will: Randolph Bourne — Selected Writings, 1911–1918,* edited by Olaf Hansen. New York: Urizen.

Bové, Paul A. 1986. "Agriculture and Academe: America's Southern Question." *Boundary* 2.

———. 1986. *Intellectuals in Power: A Genealogy of Critical Humanism*. New York: Columbia University Press.

———. 1988. "The Foucault Phenomenon." Introduction to Gilles Deleuze, *Foucault*. Minneapolis: University of Minnesota Press.

Brennan, William J., Jr. 1985. "The Constitution of the United States: Contemporary Ratification." Speech Delivered at Georgetown University, Washington, D.C., 12 October 1985.

Brooks, Cleanth. 1947. *The Well Wrought Urn*. New York: Reynal and Hitchcock.

Brooks, Peter. 1984. *Reading for the Plot*. New York: Alfred A. Knopf.

Brown, William Wells. 1853. *Clotel; or, The President's Daughter*. London.

Bullis, Jerald. 1986. "Up The Creek." *Boston Review* 11.

Buttrick, George A., et al., eds. 1952. *The Interpreter's Bible*. Vol. 6. New York: Abingdon.

Bynum, Caroline. 1987. *Holy Feast and Holy Fast: The Religious Significance of Food to Medieval Women*. Berkeley and Los Angeles: University of California Press.

Cahan, Abraham. 1986. *Grandma Never Lived in America*, edited by Moses Rischin. Indianapolis: Indiana University Press.

Canguilhem, Georges. 1978. *On the Normal and the Pathological*, translated by Carolyn R. Fawcett. Dordrecht: D. Reidel.

Cavell, Stanley. 1979. *The World Viewed: Reflections on the Ontology of Film*. Enl. ed. Cambridge: Harvard University Press.

Chicago, Judy. 1977. *Through the Flower: My Struggle as a Woman Artist*. Garden City: Anchor Books.

Christian, Barbara, ed. 1985. *Black Feminist Criticism*. New York: Pergamon Press.

Cioffi, Frank. 1976. "Intention and Interpretation." In *On Literary Intention*, edited by David Newton-de Molina.

Close, A. J. 1976. "*Don Quixote* and the 'Intentionalist Fallacy.'" In *On Literary Intention*, edited by David Newton-de Molina.

Cohen, Abner. 1974. "Introduction: The Lesson of Ethnicity." In *Urban Ethnicity*. London: Tavistock.

Coward, R., and J. Ellis. 1977. *Language and Materialism*. London: Routledge and Kegan Paul.

Culler, Jonathan. 1975. *Structuralist Poetics: Structuralism, Linguistics, and the Study of Literature*. Ithaca: Cornell University Press.

———. 1981. *The Pursuit of Signs: Semiotics, Literature, Deconstruction*. Ithaca: Cornell University Press.

Cunningham, Roger. 1987. *Apples on the Flood: The Southern Mountain Experience*. Knoxville: University of Tennessee Press.

Curtius, Ernst Robert. 1953. *European Literature and the Latin Middle Ages*, translated by Willard Trask. New York: Harper and Row.

De George, Richard and Fernande, eds. 1972. *The Structuralists: From Marx to Lévi-Strauss*. Garden City: Doubleday.

de Lauretis, Theresa, ed. 1986. *Feminist Studies, Critical Studies*. Bloomington: Indiana University Press.

Deleuze, Gilles. 1983. *Nietzsche and Philosophy*, translated by Hugh Tomlinson. New York: Columbia University Press.

———. 1988. *Foucault*, translated by Sean Hand. Minneapolis: University of Minnesota Press.

Deleuze, Gilles and Felix Guattari. 1977. *Anti-Oedipus*. New York: Viking.

———. 1992. *A Thousand Plateaus: Capitalism and Schizophrenia*. London: The Athlone Press. First published in 1988.

DeLillo, Don. 1976. *Ratner's Star*. New York: Alfred A. Knopf.

de Man, Paul. 1979a. "Semiology and Rhetoric." In *Allegories of Reading: Figural Language in Rousseau, Nietzsche, Rilke, and Proust*. New Haven: Yale University Press.

———. 1979b. *Allegories of Reading: Figural Language in Rousseau, Nietzsche, Rilke, and Proust*. New Haven and London: Yale University press.

———. 1982. "Epistemology of Metaphor." In *On Metaphor*, edited by Sheldon Sacks. Chicago: University of Chicago Press.

———. 1983a. "Review of Harold Bloom's *Anxiety of Influence*." In *Blindness and Insight: Essays in the Rhetoric of Contemporary Criticism*. 2d ed. Minneapolis: University of Minnesota Press.

———. 1983b. *Blindness and Insight: Essays in the Rhetoric of Contemporary Criticism*. 2d ed. Theory and History of Literature, vol 7. Minneapolis: University of Minnesota Press.

Derrida, Jacques. 1973. *Speech and Phenomena — and Other Essays on Husserl's Theory of Signs*, translated by David B. Allison. Evanston: Northwestern University Press. Originally published as *La Voix et le Phénomène* (Paris: Presses Universitaires de France, 1967).

———. 1977. "Signature Event Context." *Glyph* 1.

———. 1978a. *Of Grammatology*, translated by Gayatri Spivak. Baltimore: Johns Hopkins University Press. Originally published as *De la grammatologie* (Paris: Seuil, 1967).

———. 1978b. *Writing and Difference*, translated by Alan Bass. Chicago: University of Chicago Press. Originally published as *L'écriture et la différence* (Paris: Seuil, 1967).

———. 1978c. "Violence and Metaphysics: An Essay on the Thought of Emmanuel Levinas." In Derrida 1978b.

———. 1981. *Positions*. Chicago: University of Chicago Press.

———. 1982. "White Mythology: Metaphor in the Text of Philosophy." In *Margins of Philosophy*, translated by Alan Bass. Chicago: University of Chicago Press.

———. 1988a. "Afterward: Toward an Ethic of Discussion." In *Limited Inc.*, translated by Samuel Weber and Jeffrey Mehlman. Evanston: Northwestern University Press.

———. 1988b. "Like the Sound of the Sea Deep within a Shell: Paul de Man's War." *Critical Inquiry* 14.

———. 1989. "Biodegradables: Seven Diary Fragments," translated by Peggy Kamuf. *Critical Inquiry* 15.

———. 1991. "'Eating Well,' or the Calculation of the Subject: An Interview with Jacques Derrida." In *Who Comes after the Subject?* ed. Eduardo Cadava, Peter Connor, and Jean-luc Nancy. New York and London: Routledge.

Devereux, George. 1975. "Ethnic Identity: Its Logical Foundations and Its Dysfunctions." In *Ethnica Identity: Cultural Continuities and Change*, edited by George de Vos and Lola Romanucci-Ross. Palo Alto: Mayfield.

Devereux, George, and Edwin M. Loeb. 1943. "Antagonistic Acculturation." *American Sociological Review* 7.

Dixon, Peter. 1971. *Rhetoric*. London: Methuen.

Donoghue, Denis. 1984. *Ferocious Alphabets*. New York: Columbia University Press.

Doran, Madeleine. 1963. *Endeavors of Art: A Study of Form in Elizabethan Drama*. Madison: University of Wisconsin Press.

Douglass, Frederick. [1845] 1968. *Narrative of the Life of Frederick Douglass*. New York: Signet.

Dreyfus, Hubert L., and Paul Rabinow. 1983. *Michel Foucault*. Chicago: University of Chicago Press.

Ducrot, O., and T. Todorov. 1972. *Dictionnaire encyclopédique des sciences du langage*. Paris: Editions du Seuil.

Duras, Marguerite. 1966. *The Ravishing of Lol Stein*, translated by Richard Seaver. New York: Pantheon.

Eagleton, Terry. 1981. *Walter Benjamin: or, Towards a Revolutionary Criticism*. London: Verso Editions.

——. 1983. *Literary Theory: An Introduction*. Minneapolis: University of Minnesota Press.

——. 1976a. *Criticism and Ideology*. London: New Left Books.

——. 1976b. *Marxism and Literary Criticism*. Berkeley and Los Angeles: University of California Press.

Eco, Umberto. 1976. *A Theory of Semiotics*. Bloomington: Indiana University Press.

Eichenbaum, Boris. 1965. "The Theory of the 'Formal Method'." In *Russian Formalist Criticism: Four Essays*, edited by Lee T. Lemon and Marion J. Reis. Lincoln: University of Nebraska Press.

Elias, Norbert. 1982. *The Civilizing Process*. Pantheon.

Ellis, Havelock. 1893. "The Ancestry of Genius." *Atlantic Monthly* 71.

Ellis, J. 1978. "Art, Culture and Quality." *Screen* 19, no. 3.

Ellison, Ralph. 1964. "The World and the Jug." In *Shadow and Act*. Reprint. 1966. New York: Signet.

Emerson, Ralph Waldo. 1957. "Self-Reliance." In *Selections from Ralph Waldo Emerson: An Organic Anthology*, edited by Stephen E. Whicher. Cambridge: Riverside Press.

Empson, William. n.d. *The Structure of Complex Words*. Norfolk: New Directions.

Fiedler, Leslie, and Houston Baker, eds. 1981. *Opening up the Canon: Selected Papers from the English Institute*. Baltimore: Johns Hopkins University Press.

Fiscal Year 1985 Arms Control Impact Statements. Submitted to the Congress by the President Pursuant to Section 36 of the Arms Control and Disarmament Act (March 1984).

Foucault, Michel. 1971. *L'ordre du discours*. Paris: Gallimard.

——. 1972. *The Archeology of Knowledge and the Discourse on Language*, translated by A. M. Sheridan Smith. New York: Harper and Row.

——. 1977a. *Discipline and Punish: The Birth of the Prison*. Translated by Alan Sheridan. New York: Pantheon.

——. 1977b. "Intellectuals and Power." In *Language, Counter-Memory, Practice*, translated by Sherry Simon and edited by Donald F. Bouchard. Ithaca: Cornell University Press.

——. 1977c. "Nietzsche, Genealogy, History." In *Language, Counter-Memory, Practice*, translated by Sherry Simon and edited by Donald F. Bouchard. Ithaca: Cornell University Press.

——. 1977d. *The Order of Things*. London: Tavistock.

——. 1977e. "What Is an Author?" In *Language, Counter-Memory, Practice*, translated by Sherry Simon and edited by Donald F. Bouchard. Ithaca: Cornell University Press.

——. 1978. *The History of Sexuality*. Volume 1, *An Introduction*, translated by Robert Hurley. New York: Pantheon.

——. 1980. *Power/Knowledge: Selected Interviews and Other Writings, 1972–1977*, edited by Colin Gordon. New York: Pantheon.

——. 1983. "The Subject and Power." Translated by Leslie Sawyer. In *Michel Foucault: Beyond Structuralism and Hermeneutics*, edited by Hubert L. Dreyfus and Paul Rabinow. 2d ed. Chicago: University of Chicago Press.

——. 1985. *The History of Sexuality*. Volume 2. *The Use of Pleasure*, translated by Robert Hurley. New York: Pantheon.

——. 1986. *The History of Sexuality*. Volume 3. *The Care of the Self*, translated by Robert Hurley. New York: Pantheon.

Foucault, Michel. 1987. "The Ethic of Care for the Self as a Practice of Freedom." Interview with Raul Fornet-Betancourt, Helmut Becker, and Alfredo Gomez-Müller (January 20, 1983). In *The Final Foucault,* ed. James Bernauer and David Rasmussen. Cambridge, MA, and London: MIT Press.

————. 1988a. *Politics, Philosophy, Culture: Interviews and Other Writings, 1977–1984,* edited by Lawrence D. Kritzman. New York: Routledge.

————. 1988b. *Technologies of the Self: A Seminar with Michel Foucault,* edited by Luther H. Martin et al. Amherst: University of Massachusetts Press.

Franklin, Bruce. 1972. "The Teaching of Literature in the Highest Academies of the Empire." In *The Politics of Literature: Dissenting Essays in the Teaching of English,* edited by Louis Kampf and Paul Lauter. New York: Pantheon.

Freud, Sigmund. [1895] 1951. "Project for a Scientific Psychology." In *The Standard Edition of the Complete Psychological Works of Sigmund Freud,* translated and edited by James Strachey. Vol. 1. London: Hogarth Press and the Institute of Psychoanalysis.

————. 1957. *The Interpretation of Dreams.* London: Hogarth Press and the Institute of Psychoanalysis.

————. 1977. "Fetishism." In *On Sexuality.* Harmondsworth: Penguin.

————. [1912] 1958. "A Note on the Unconscious in Psychoanalysis." In *The Standard Edition of the Complete Psychological Works of Sigmund Freud,* translated and edited by James Strachey. Vol. 12. London: Hogarth Press and the Institute of Psychoanalysis.

————. [1915] 1957. "Repression." In *The Standard Edition of the Complete Psychological Works of Sigmund Freud,* translated and edited by James Strachey. Vol. 14 London: Hogarth Press and the Institute of Psychoanalysis.

————. [1919] 1957. "The Unconscious." In *The Standard Edition of the Complete Psychological Works of Sigmund Freud,* translated and edited by James Strachey. Vol. 14. London: Hogarth Press and the Institute of Psychoanalysis.

Frye, Northrop. 1963. "Literature as Context: Milton's Lycidas." In *Fables of Identity: Studies in Poetic Mythology.* New York: Harcourt, Brace and World.

————. 1957. *Anatomy of Criticism: Four Essays.* New York: Atheneum.

————. 1971. *The Critical Path: An Essay on the Social Context of Literary Criticism.* Bloomington: Indiana University Press.

Gans, Herbert J. 1979. "Symbolic Ethnicity: The Future of Ethnic Groups and Cultures in America." In *On the Making of Americans: Essays in Honor of David Riesman.* Philadelphia: University of Pennsylvania Press.

Gardiner, S. R., ed. 1877. *Documents Relating to the Proceedings against William Prynne.* London. Reprint. 1965. Camden Society Publications, n.s., vol. 18. New York: Johnson Reprint Corporation.

Gates, Henry Louis, Jr., ed. 1986. *"Race," Writing and Difference.* Chicago: University of Chicago Press.

Gayle, Addison, Jr. 1972. *The Black Aesthetic.* Garden City: Doubleday, Anchor Books.

Geertz, Clifford. 1973. *The Interpretation of Cultures.* New York: Basic Books.

————. 1980. "Blurred Genres: The Refiguration of Social Thought." *The American Scholar* 49.

Genette, G. 1972. *Figures III.* Paris: Editions du Seuil.

Gilbert, Sandra M., and Susan Gubar. 1979. *The Madwoman in the Attic: The Woman Writer and the Nineteenth-Century Literary Imagination.* New Haven: Yale University Press.

Gillman, Susan. 1989. *Dark Twins: Imposture and Identity in Mark Twain's America.* Chicago: University of Chicago Press.

Girard, René. 1965. *Deceit, Desire, and the Novel: Self and Other in Literary Structure,* translated by Yvonne Freccero. Baltimore: The Johns Hopkins University Press.

Glare, P. G. W., ed. 1982. *Oxford Latin Dictionary.* Oxford: Oxford University Press.

Goldberg, RoseLee. 1979. *Performance: Live Art, 1909 to the Present.* New York: Abrams.

Goodman, Nelson. 1976. *The Languages of Art.* Indianapolis: Hackett.

Gordon, Robert. 1982. *The Politics of Law.* New York: Pantheon.

Gramsci, Antonio. 1971. *Selections from the Prison Notebooks,* edited and translated by Quintin Hoare and Geoffrey Nowell Smith. New York: International Publishers.

———. 1973. *Letters from Prison,* edited and translated by Lynne Lawner. New York: Harper and Row.

Greenblatt, Stephen. 1980. *Renaissance Self-Fashioning: From More to Shakespeare.* Chicago: University of Chicago Press.

———. 1986. "Loudun and London." *Critical Inquiry* 12.

Guthrie, W. 1971. *The Sophists.* Cambridge: Cambridge University Press.

Habermas, Jürgen. 1975. *Legitimation Crisis.* Boston: Beacon Press.

———. 1979. *Communication and the Evolution of Society.* Boston: Beacon Press.

Halperin, David M., John J. Winkler, and Froma I. Zeitlin, eds. 1990. *Before Sexuality: The Construction of Erotic Experience in the Ancient Greek World.* Princeton: Princeton University Press.

Hampshire, Stuart. 1983. *Morality and Conflict.* Cambridge, MA: Harvard University Press.

Hartman, Geoffrey H. 1975. "War in Heaven." In *The Fate of Reading and Other Essays.* Chicago: University of Chicago Press.

Heath, Stephen. 1972. *The Nouveau Roman: A Study in the Practice of Writing.* London: Elek Books.

———. 1976. "Narrative Space." *Screen* 17, no. 3.

Hegel, G. W. 1977. *Hegel's Phenemenology of Spirit,* translated by A. V. Miller. New York: Oxford University Press.

Held, Virginia. 1993. *Feminist Morality: Transforming Culture, Society, and Politics.* Chicago and London: University of Chicago Press.

Herr, Michael. 1978. *Dispatches.* New York: Avon.

Highet, Gilbert. 1957. *The Classical Tradition: Greek and Roman Influences on Western Literature.* New York: Oxford University Press.

Hirsch, E. D. 1967. "Objective Interpretation." In *Validity in Interpretation.* New Haven: Yale University Press.

Hirst, P. 1976. "Althusser and the Theory of Ideology." *Economy and Society* 5.

Horsman, Reginald. 1981. *Race and Manifest Destiny: The Origins of American Racial Anglo-Saxonism.* Cambridge: Harvard University Press.

Hourani, Albert. 1991. *A History of the Arab Peoples.* Cambridge, MA: Harvard University Press.

Howard, Roy J. 1982. *Three Faces of Hermeneutics.* Berkeley and Los Angeles: University of California Press.

Howell, John. 1976. "Acting/Non-acting." *Performance Art* 2.

Howell, W. S. 1956. *Logic and Rhetoric in England, 1500–1700.* Princeton: Princeton University Press.

———. 1971. *Eighteenth-Century British Logic and Rhetoric.* Princeton: Princeton University Press.

Hoy, David Couzens, ed. 1986. *Michel Foucault: A Critical Reader.* Oxford: Basil Blackwell.

Huizinga, Johan. 1959. "The Task of Cultural History." In *Men and Ideas*, translated by James S. Holms and Hans van Marle. New York: Meridian Books.

Hull, Gloria T., Patricia Bell Scott, and Barbara Smith, eds. 1982. *All the Women Are White, All the Blacks Are Men, But Some of Us Are Brave: Black Women's Studies.* Old Westbury: Feminist Press.

Hulme, T. E. 1924. *Speculations.* New York: Harcourt, Brace.

Hungerland, Isabel C. 1955. "The Concept of Intention in Art Criticism." *Journal of Philosophy* 52.

Hunter, George K. 1978. *Dramatic Identities and Cultural Tradition: Studies in Shakespeare and His Contemporaries.* Liverpool: Liverpool University Press.

Irigaray, Luce. 1985. *Speculum of the Other Woman*, translated by Gillian C. Gill. Ithaca: Cornell University Press.

———. 1985. *This Sex Which Is Not One*, translated by Catherine Porter with Carolyn Burke. Ithaca: Cornell University Press.

———. 1993. *An Ethics of Sexual Difference*, translated by Carolyn Burke and Gillian C. Gill. Ithaca: Cornell University Press.

Iser, Wolfgang. 1974. *The Implied Reader.* Baltimore: Johns Hopkins University Press.

Isocrates. 1962. "Antidosis." In *Isocrates*, edited and translated by George Norlin. Vol. 2. Cambridge: Harvard University Press.

Jakobson, Roman. 1956. "Two Aspects of Language and Two Types of Aphasic Disturbances." In *Fundamentals of Language*. The Hague: Mouton.

———. 1960. "Linguistics and Poetics." In *Style in Language*, edited by Thomas A. Sebeok. Cambridge: MIT Press.

———. 1963. *Essais de linguistique générale.* Paris: Editions de Minuit.

———. 1971a. "The Metaphoric and Metonymic Poles." In *Critical Theory since Plato*, edited by Hazard Adams. New York: Harcourt, Brace, Jovanovich.

———. 1971b. *Selected Writings.* The Hague: Mouton.

Jameson, Fredric. 1972. *The Prison-House of Language: A Critical Account of Structuralism and Russian Formalism.* Princeton: Princeton University Press.

———. 1976. "The Ideology of the Text." *Salamagundi*, nos. 31–32.

———. 1981. *The Political Unconscious: Narrative as a Socially Symbolic Act.* Ithaca: Cornell University Press.

Jardine, Alice. 1985. *Gynesis.* Ithaca: Cornell University Press.

Johnson, Thomas H., ed. 1955. *The Poems of Emily Dickinson.* 3 vols. Cambridge: Harvard University Press.

Jones, Ernest. 1954. *Hamlet and Oedipus: A Classic Study in the Psychoanalysis of Literature.* New York: Anchor Books.

Joyce, James. 1968. *A Portrait of the Artist as a Young Man*, edited by Chester G. Anderson. New York: Viking Critical Text.

Juhl, P. D. 1980. *Interpretation.* Princeton: Princeton University Press.

Kain, Philip J. 1988. *Marx and Ethics.* Oxford: Clarendon Press.

Kant, Immanuel. 1993. "On a Supposed Right to Lie because of Philanthropic Concerns." In *Grounding for the Metaphysics of Morals*, translated by James W. Ellington. Indianapolis: Hacket Publishing Co.

Kavanagh, James H. 1985. "Shakespeare in Ideology." In *Alternative Shakespeares*. London: Methuen.

———. 1982. "Marxism's Althusser: Toward a Politics of Literary Theory." *Diacritics* 12, no. 1.

Kennedy, George. 1963. *The Art of Persuasion in Greece.* Princeton: Princeton University Press.

———. 1972. *The Art of Persuasion in the Roman World (300 BC-AD 300)*. Princeton: Princeton University Press.

Keohane, Nannerl O., Michelle Z. Rosaldo, Barbara G. Gelpi, eds. 1982. *Feminist Theory: A Critique of Ideology*. Chicago: University of Chicago Press.

Kermode, Frank. 1983. *The Art of Telling: Essays on Fiction*. Cambridge: Harvard University Press.

Kernan, Alvin. 1959. *The Cankered Muse: Satire of the English Renaissance*. New Haven: Yale University Press.

Kerrigan, William, ed. 1983. *Pragmatism's Freud: The Moral Disposition of Psychoanalysis*. Baltimore and London: The Johns Hopkins University Press.

Kirschner, Judith Russi. 1980. *Vito Acconci: A Retrospective, 1969 to 1980*. Chicago: Museum of Contemporary Art.

Kohn, Hans. 1967. *The Idea of Nationalism*. New York: Collier Books.

Kolodny, Annette. 1980. "A Map for Rereading: or, Gender and the Interpretation of Literary Texts." In *New Literary History* 11.

Kott, Jan. 1974. *Shakespeare Our Contemporary*. New York: Norton.

Kristeva, Julia. 1980. *Desire in Language: A Semiotic Approach to Literature and Art*, edited by Leon S. Roudiez, translated by Thomas Gora, Alice Jardine, and Leon S. Roudiez. New York: Columbia University Press.

Kuhn, Thomas. 1962. *The Structure of Scientific Revolutions*. Chicago: University of Chicago Press.

Lacan, Jacques. 1977a. "The Agency of the Letter in the Unconscious, or Reason since Freud." In *Ecrits: A Selection*, translated by Alan Sheridan. New York: W. W. Norton. Originally published as *Ecrits* (Paris: Seuil, 1966).

———. 1977b. "The Direction of Treatment and the Principles of Its Power." In *Ecrits: A Selection*, translated by Alan Sheridan. New York: W. W. Norton. Originally published as *Ecrits* (Paris: Seuil, 1966).

———. 1978. "The Unconscious and Repetition." In *The Four Fundamental Concepts of Psychoanalysis*, translated by Alan Sheridan. New York: W. W. Norton.

———. 1992. *The Ethics of Psychoanalysis 1959–60*, translated by Dennis Porter. New York: Norton. Originally published as *Ethique de la psychanalyse*, 1986.

Lakoff, George, and Mark Johnson. 1980. *Metaphors We Live By*. Chicago: University of Chicago Press.

Langbaum, Robert. 1972. *The Poetry of Experience: The Dramatic Monologue of Experience in Modern Literary Tradition*. Chicago: University of Chicago Press.

Lanham, Richard. 1976. *The Motives of Eloquence*. New Haven: Yale University Press.

Laplanche, J., and J. B. Pontalis. 1973. *The Language of Psychoanalysis*. London: Hogarth Press.

Large, Andrew. 1985. *The Artificial Language Movement*. London: Basil Blackwell.

Lawson, John. 1972. *Lectures Concerning Oratory*, edited by E. N. Claussen and K. R. Wallace. Carbondale: Southern Illinois University Press.

Leavis, F. R. 1962. *The Common Pursuit*. London: Peregrine Books.

Leitch, Vincent B. 1983. *Deconstructive Criticism: An Advanced Introduction*. New York: Columbia University Press.

Lemon, Lee T., and Marion J. Reis, eds. 1965. *Russian Formalist Criticism: Four Essays*. Lincoln: University of Nebraska Press.

Lentricchia, Frank. 1980. *After the New Criticism*. Chicago: University of Chicago Press.

———. 1987. *Ariel and the Police*. Madison: University of Wisconsin Press.

Levinson, Sanford, and Steven Mailloux, eds. 1988. *Interpreting Law and Literature: A Hermeneutic Reader*. Evanston: Northwestern University Press.

Lévi-Strauss, Claude. 1968. *Structural Anthropology,* translated by C. Jacobson and B. G. Shoepf. Vol. 1. London: Allen Lane.

——. 1977. *Tristes Tropiques,* translated by John and Doreen Weightman. New York: Pocket Books. Originally published as *Tristes Tropiques* (Paris: Plon, 1955).

Lévi-Strauss, Claude, and Roman Jakobson. 1962. "Charles Baudelaire's 'Les Chats'." *L'Homme.*

Lewis, C. S. 1954. *English Literature of the Sixteenth Century, Excluding Drama.* Oxford: Clarendon Press.

Leyda, Jay. 1960. *The Years and Hours of Emily Dickinson.* Vol. 2. New Haven: Yale University Press.

Lipking, Lawrence. 1981. *The Life of the Poet: Beginning and Ending Poetic Careers.* Chicago: University of Chicago Press.

Lloyd, David. 1993. *Anomalous States: Irish Writing and the Post-Colonial Moment.* Dublin: Lilliput Press.

Locke, Alain. 1925. *The New Negro.* New York: Boni.

Loeffler, Carl E. 1980. *Performance Anthology: Source Book for a Decade of California Performance Art.* San Francisco: Contemporary Arts Press.

Lukács, George. 1971. *History and Class Consciousness: Studies in Marxist Dialectics.* Translated by Rodney Livingstone. Cambridge: MIT Press.

McCloskey, Donald. 1985. *The Rhetoric of Economics.* Madison: University of Wisconsin Press.

McKeon, Richard, ed. 1941. *The Basic Works of Aristotle.* New York: Random House.

MacDougall, Hugh B. 1982. *Racial Myth in English History: Trojans, Teutons, and Anglo-Saxons.* Montreal: Harvest House; Hanover: University Press of New England.

MacIntyre, Alasdair. 1981. *After Virtue.* Notre Dame: University of Notre Dame Press.

Macherey, Pierre. 1978. *A Theory of Literary Production,* translated by Geoffrey Wall. London: Routledge and Kegan Paul.

Macherey, Pierre, and Etienne Balibar. 1981. "Literature as an Ideological Form: Some Marxist Propositions." *Praxis* 5.

Macksey, R., and E. Donato, eds. 1970. *The Structuralist Controversy.* Baltimore: Johns Hopkins University Press.

Mailloux, Steven. 1982. *Interpretive Conventions: The Reader in the Study of American Fiction.* Ithaca: Cornell University Press.

——. 1985. "Rhetorical Hermeneutics." *Critical Inquiry* 11.

Mann, Thomas. 1963. *Death in Venice,* translated by H. T. Lowe Porter. New York: Random House.

Mannheim, Karl. 1964. *Ideology and Utopia.* New York: Harvest.

Marks, Elaine, and Isabelle de Courtivron, eds. 1980. *New French Feminisms.* New York: Schocken.

Marotti, Arthur. 1986. *John Donne, Coterie Poet.* Madison: University of Wisconsin Press.

Martin, Wallace. 1986. *Recent Theories of Narrative.* Ithaca and London: Cornell University Press.

Marx, Karl. 1963. *The Eighteenth Brumaire of Louis Bonaparte.* New York: International Publications.

——. 1977. *Capital,* vol. 1. New York: Vintage.

Marx, Karl, and Friedrich Engels. 1970. *The German Ideology.* New York: International Publications.

Matthiessen, F. O. 1960. *The James Family.* New York: Alfred A. Knopf.

Meltzer, Françoise. 1987. *Salome and the Dance of Writing: Portraits of Mimesis in Literature.* Chicago: University of Chicago Press.

Metz, C. 1974. *Film Language: A Semiotics of the Cinema.* New York: Oxford University Press.

Meyer, Ursula. 1972. *Conceptual Art.* New York: Dutton.

Michaels, Walter Benn. 1987. *The Gold Standard and the Logic of Naturalism.* Berkeley and Los Angeles: University of California Press.

Miller, J. Hillis. 1987. *The Ethics of Reading: Kant, de Man, Eliot, Trollope, James, and Benjamin.* New York: Columbia University Press.

Miller, Nancy, ed. 1987. *The Poetics of Gender.* New York: Columbia University Press.

Minnis, A. J. 1984. *Medieval Theory of Authorship.* London: Scolar Press.

Mitchell, W. J. T., ed. 1983. *The Politics of Interpretation.* Chicago: University of Chicago Press.

———. 1985. *Against Theory: Literary Studies and the New Pragmatism.* Chicago: University of Chicago Press.

———. 1986. *Iconology: Image, Text, Ideology.* Chicago: University of Chicago Press.

Montrose, Louis Adrian. 1983. "'Shaping Fantasies': Figurations of Gender and Power in Elizabethan Culture." *Representations* 2.

Motherwell, Robert, ed. 1951. *The Dada Painters and Poets: An Anthology.* New York: Wittenborn.

Mukařovský, Jan. 1970. *Aesthetic Function, Norm and Value as Social Facts,* translated by Mark Suino. Ann Arbor: University of Michigan Department of Slavic Languages and Literature.

Murdoch, Iris. 1993. *Metaphysics as a Guide to Morals.* New York: Allen Lane.

Murphy, J. J. 1966. *Rhetoric in the Middle Ages.* Berkeley and Los Angeles: University of California Press.

Murray, Albert. 1973. *The Hero and the Blues.* Columbia: University of Missouri Press.

Nelson, John S., Allan Megill, and Donald N. McCloskey. 1987. *The Rhetoric of the Human Sciences: Language and Argument in Scholarship and Public Affairs.* Madison: University of Wisconsin Press.

Newton, Judith. 1988. "History as Usual? Feminism and the 'New Historicism'." *Cultural Critique* 9.

Newton-de Molina, David, ed. 1976. *On Literary Intention.* Edinburgh: Edinburgh University Press.

Nietzsche, Friedrich. 1956. "A Critical Backward Glance." In *The Birth of Tragedy and the Genealogy of Morals,* translated by Francis Golffing. Garden City, NY: Doubleday Anchor Books.

Nolte, Ernst. 1987. "Zwischen Geschichtslegende und Revisionismus? Das Dritte Reich im Blickwinkel des Jahres 1980." In *"Historikerstreit:" Die Dokumentation der Kontroverse um die Einzigartigkeit der nationalsozialistischen Judenvernichtung.* Munich and Zurich: Piper.

Norbrook, David. 1984. *Poetry and Politics in the English Renaissance.* London: Routledge and Kegan Paul.

Nussbaum, Martha Craven. 1986. *The Fragility of Goodness.* Cambridge: Cambridge University Press.

———. 1990. *Love's Knowledge: Essays on Philosophy and Literature.* New York: Oxford University Press.

Oberdorfer, Don. 1985. "ABM Reinterpretation: A Quick Study." *Washington Post,* 22 October.

O'Hara, Daniel T. 1985. *The Romance of Interpretation.* New York: Columbia University Press.

Ohmann, Richard. 1971. "Speech Acts and the Definition of Literature." *Philosophy and Rhetoric* 4.

Ong, Walter S. 1958. *Ramus, Method, and the Decay of Dialogue.* Cambridge: Harvard University Press.

————. 1982. *Orality and Literacy.* London: Methuen.

Owens, Craig. 1983. "The Discourse of Others: Feminists and Postmodernism." In *The Anti-Aesthetic: Essays on Postmodern Culture,* edited by Hal Foster. Port Townsend, Wash.: Bay Press.

Palmer, Richard E. 1969. *Hermeneutics: Interpretation Theory in Schleiermacher, Dilthey, Heidegger, and Gadamer.* Evanston: Northwestern University Press.

Patterson, Lee. 1987. *Negotiating the Past: The Historical Understanding of Medieval Literature.* Madison: University of Wisconsin Press.

Peirce, Charles Sanders. 1931–58. "The Icon, Index, and Symbol." In *Collected Works,* edited by Charles Hartshorne and Paul Weiss. Vol. 2. Cambridge: Harvard University Press.

Perelman, Chaim, and Lucy Olbrechts-Tyteca. 1969. *The New Rhetoric: A Treatise on Argument.* Notre Dame: University of Notre Dame Press.

Pitkin, Hanna. 1967. *The Concept of Representation.* Berkeley and Los Angeles: University of California Press.

Placido, Beniamino. 1978. *Interpretazioni di Twain.* Edited by Alessandro Portelli. Rome: Saveli.

Plato. 1935. *Republic,* translated by Paul Shorey. Cambridge: Harvard University Press.

————. 1952. *Gorgias,* edited and translated by W. C. Helmbold. Indianapolis: Bobbs-Merrill.

————. 1956a. *Phaedrus,* edited and translated by W. C. Helmbold and W. G. Rabinowitz. Indianapolis: Bobbs-Merrill.

————. 1956b. The Works of Plato, Jowett translation, edited by Irwin Edman. New York: Modern Library.

Poe, Edgar Allen, 1985. "Eureka." In *Edgar Allan Poe: Poetry and Tales.* New York: The Library of America.

Poirier, Richard. 1971. *The Performing Self: Compositions and Decompositions in the Languages of Contemporary Life.* New York: Oxford University Press.

Pope, Alexander. 1979. "An Essay on Criticism." In *The Norton Anthology of English Literature I,* edited by Meyer Abrams, E. Talbot Donaldson, et al. Fourth edition. New York: W. W. Norton.

Pound, Ezra. 1968. *Literary Essays of Ezra Pound.* New York: New Directions.

Poussin, Guillaume T. 1843. *De la Puissance Américaine.* Paris.

Pratt, Mary Louise. 1992. *Imperial Eyes: Travel Writing and Transculturation.* London and New York: Routledge.

Price, Martin. 1964. *To the Palace of Wisdom: Order and Energy in Eighteenth-Century Literature.* New York: Doubleday.

Prince, Gerald. 1973. *A Grammar of Stories.* The Hague: Mouton.

Princeton Encyclopedia of Poetry and Poetics. 1965. Edited by Alex Preminger, Frank J. Warnke, and O. B. Hardison. Princeton: Princeton University Press.

Propp, Vladimir. 1970. *Morphology of the Folk Tale,* translated by Laurence Scott. Austin: University of Texas Press.

Puttenham, George. [1589] 1970. *The Arte of English Poesie.* Cambridge: Cambridge University Press.

Rabinow, Paul, and William M. Sullivan, eds. 1979. *Interpretive Social Science: A Reader.* Berkeley and Los Angeles: University of California Press.

Ray, William. 1984. *Literary Meaning.* Oxford: Oxford University Press.

Reichert, John. 1980. *Making Sense of Literature.* Chicago: University of Chicago Press.

Rich, Adrienne. 1979. *On Lies, Secrets, and Silence.* New York: W. W. Norton.

Ricoeur, Paul. 1974. "Consciousness and the Unconscious." In *The Conflict of Interpretations: Essays in Hermeneutics,* edited by Don Ihde. Evanston: Northwestern University Press.

———. 1981. "Narrative Time." In *On Narrative,* edited by W. J. T. Mitchell. Chicago and London: University of Chicago Press.

———. 1984–88. *Time and Narrative,* translated by Kathleen McLaughlin and David Pellauer. 3 vols. Chicago: University of Chicago Press.

Riell, Peter Hanns. 1975. *The German Enlightenment and the Rise of Historicism.* Berkeley and Los Angeles: University of California Press.

Robbins, Bruce. 1986. *The Servant's Hand.* New York: Columbia University Press.

Robbins, Derek. 1991. *The Work of Pierre Bourdieu: Recognizing Society.* Milton Keynes: Open University Press.

Rorty, Richard. 1982. *The Consequences of Pragmatism.* Minneapolis: University of Minnesota Press.

———. 1986. "Foucault and Epistemology." In David Couzens Hoy, ed., *Michel Foucault: A Critical Reader.*

———. 1989. *Contingency, Irony, and Solidarity.* Cambridge and New York: Cambridge University Press.

Roth, Moira. 1983. *The Amazing Decade: Women and Performance Art in America, 1970–1980.* Los Angeles: Astro Artz.

Royce, Josiah. 1968. *The Problem of Christianity.* Chicago: University of Chicago Press.

Sacks, Peter. 1986. *The English Elegy.* Baltimore: Johns Hopkins University Press.

Sacks, Sheldon, ed. 1979. *On Metaphor.* Chicago: University of Chicago Press.

Sahlins, Marshall. 1976. *Culture and Practical Reason.* Chicago: University of Chicago Press.

Said, Edward W. 1975. *Beginnings.* New York: Basic Books.

———. 1978. *Orientalism.* New York: Pantheon.

———. 1983. *The World, the Text, and the Critic.* Cambridge: Harvard University Press.

Sammons, Jeffrey L. 1977. *Literary Sociology and Practical Criticism.* Bloomington: Indiana University Press.

Santayana, George. 1957. *Interpretation of Poetry and Religion.* New York: Harper and Row.

de Saussure, Ferdinand. 1959. *Course in General Linguistics,* translated by Wade Baskin. New York: The Philosophical Library.

Schechner, Richard. 1969. "Containment Is the Enemy." Interview with Judith Malina and Julian Beck. *Drama Review* 13.

———. 1977. *Essays on Performance Theory, 1970–1976.* New York: Drama Book Specialists.

Scheffler, Israel. 1967. *Science and Subjectivity.* Indianapolis: Bobbs-Merrill.

Scholes, Robert. 1985. *Textual Power.* New Haven: Yale University Press.

Sedgwick, Eve Kosofsky. 1985. *Between Men: English Literature and Male Homosocial Desire.* New York: Columbia University Press.

———. 1990. *The Epistemology of the Closet.* Berkeley and Los Angeles: University of California Press.

Shelley, Percy Bysshe. 1840. *A Defence of Poetry.*

Sherwin, Paul S. 1977. *Precious Bane: Collins and the Miltonic Legacy.* Austin: University of Texas Press.

Shklovsky, Victor. 1965. "Sterne's *Tristram Shandy:* Stylistic Commentary." In *Russian Formalist Criticism: Four Essays,* edited by Lee T. Lemon and Marion J. Reis. Lincoln: University of Nebraska Press.

Showalter, Elaine, ed. 1985. *Feminist Criticism: Essays on Women, Literature, Theory.* New York: Pantheon.

Shultz, George. "Arms Control, Strategic Stability, and Global Security." Address before the 31st Annual Session of the North Atlantic Assembly, San Francisco, 14 October, 1985. *Department of State Bulletin* 85, no. 2105.

Sidney, Sir Philip. 1965. *An Apology for Poetry,* edited by Geoffrey Shepherd. London: Nelson.

Simpson, David. 1988. "Literary Criticism and the Return to 'History.'" *Critical Inquiry* 14.

Skinner, Quentin. 1976. "Motives, Intentions, and the Interpretation of Texts." In *On Literary Intention,* edited by David Newton-de Molina.

Sloane, Thomas. 1985. *Donne, Milton, and the End of Humanist Rhetoric.* Berkeley and Los Angeles: University of California Press.

Smart, Barry. 1983. *Foucault, Marxism, and Critique.* London: Routledge and Kegan Paul.

Smith, Barbara Herrnstein. 1983. "Contingencies of Value." *Critical Inquiry* 10, no. 1. In Robert van Hallberg, ed., *Canons.*

———. 1988. *Contingencies of Value: Alternative Perspectives for Critical Theory.* Cambridge: Harvard University Press.

Smith, Henry Nash. 1836. *Slavery in the United States: A Narrative of the Life and Adventures of Charles Ball, a Black Man.* Lewistown, Pa: Shugert.

———. 1958. Introduction to *The Adventures of Huckleberry Finn.* Boston: Riverside Press.

Sonneck, Oscar George Theodore. 1909. *Report on "The Star-Spangled Banner," "Hail Columbia," "America," "Yankee Doodle."* Washington, D.C.: Government Printing Office.

Spitzer, Leo. 1962. "*Explication de Texte* Applied to Walt Whitman's Poem 'Out of the Cradle Endlessly Rocking.'" In *Essays on English and American Literature,* edited by Anna Hatcher. Princeton: Princeton University Press.

Spivak, Gayatri. 1987. *In Other Worlds.* New York: Routledge and Kegan Paul.

Spurr, David. 1993. *The Rhetoric of Empire: Colonial Discourse in Journalism, Travel Writing, and Imperial Administration.* Durham and London: Duke University Press.

Stallman, R. W. 1950. *Critic's Notebook.* Minneapolis: University of Minnesota Press.

Starobinski, Jean. 1971. *Les mots sous les mots: Les anagrammes de Ferdinand de Saussure.* Paris: Gallimard.

Stein, Gertrude. 1957. *Lectures in America.* Boston: Beacon Press.

Stowe, Harriet Beecher. 1852. *Uncle Tom's Cabin; or, Life Among the Lowly.* Boston: Jewett.

Summers, David. 1985. "Intentions in the History of Art." *New Literary History* 17.

Taine, Hippolyte A. 1897. *History of English Literature,* translated by H. Van Laun. London: Chatto and Windus.

Taussig, Michael. 1993. *Mimesis and Alterity: A Particular History of the Senses.* New York and London: Routledge.

Thomas, William I. 1973. "Life History." *American Journal of Sociology* 79.

Thoreau, Henry David. 1985. *Walden.* In *Henry David Thoreau.* New York: The Library of America.

Tillyard, E. M. W. 1944. *The Elizabethan World Picture.* New York: Macmillan.

Tomkins, Calvin. 1976. "Ridiculous." *New Yorker* 52.

Tompkins, Jane P. 1985. *Sensational Designs: The Cultural Work of American Fiction, 1790–1860.* New York: Oxford University Press.

———, ed. 1980. *Reader-Response Criticism: From Formalism to Post-Structuralism.* Baltimore: John Hopkins University Press.

Tuve, Rosemond. 1947. *Elizabethan and Metaphysical Imagery: Renaissance Poetic and Twentieth-Century Critics.* Chicago: University of Chicago Press.

Twain, Mark. [1889] 1982. *A Connecticut Yankee in King Arthur's Court,* edited by Allison R. Ensor. New York: Norton.

———. 1979. *Mark Twain's Notebooks and Journals. Vol. 3, 1883–1891,* edited by Robert Pack Browning, Michael B. Frank, and Lin Salamo. Berkeley and Los Angeles: University of California Press.

———. 1984. *Life on the Mississippi,* edited and introduced by James M. Cox. New York: Penguin American Library.

———. 1985. *Adventures of Huckleberry Finn,* edited by Walter Blair and Victor Fischer. Berkeley and Los Angeles: University of California Press.

Vail, R. W. G. 1937. "Yankee Doodle." *Collections of the Rhode Island Historical Society* 30, no. 2.

Vickers, Brian. 1988. *In Defence of Rhetoric.* Oxford: Clarendon Press.

Vincent, Stephen, and Ellen Zweig. 1981. *The Poetry Reading: A Contemporary Compendium on Language and Performance.* San Francisco: Momo's Press.

von Hallberg, Robert, ed. 1984. *Canons.* Chicago: University of Chicago Press.

Wellek, René. 1982. "The Fall of Literary History." In *The Attack on Literature and Other Essays.* Chapel Hill: University of North Carolina Press.

White, Hayden. 1973. *Metahistory: The Historical Imagination in Nineteenth-Century Europe.* Baltimore: Johns Hopkins University Press.

———. 1988. *The Content of the Form.* Baltimore: Johns Hopkins University Press.

White, Robin. 1979. "Interview with Vito Acconci." *View.* Oakland: Crown Point Press.

Wilden, Anthony. 1972. *System and Structure: Essays in Communication and Exchange.* London: Tavistock Publications.

Williams, Bernard. 1985. *Ethics and the Limits of Philosophy.* Cambridge, MA: Harvard University Press.

Williams, Raymond. 1958. *Culture and Society, 1780–1950.* London: Chatto and Windus.

———. 1977. *Marxism and Literature.* Oxford: Oxford University Press.

———. 1979. *Politics and Letters.* London: New Left Books.

———. 1983. "Structural." In *Keywords: A Vocabulary of Culture and Society.* Rev. ed. New York: Oxford University Press.

Wimsatt, W. K. 1954. *The Verbal Icon: Studies in the Meaning of Poetry.* Lexington: University of Kentucky Press.

Wimsatt, W. K., and Monroe C. Beardsley, 1946. "The Intentional Fallacy." *Sewanee Review.* In David Newton-de Molina, *On Literary Intention.*

Winkler, John J. 1990. *The Constraints of Desire: The Anthropology of Sex and Gender in Ancient Greece.* New York: Routledge.

Wittig, Monique. 1985. "The Mark of Gender." *Feminist Issues* 5.

Wolff, Janet. 1984. *The Social Production of Art.* New York: New York University Press.

Woolf, Rosemary. 1968. *English Religious Lyric in the Middle Ages.* Oxford: Clarendon Press.

Wordsworth, William. 1800. Preface to the Second Edition of *Lyrical Ballads.*

Young, Robert, ed. 1981. *Untying the Text: A Poststructuralist Reader.* Boston: Routledge and Kegan Paul.

Zetzel, James E. G. 1984. "Re-creating the Canon: Augustan Poetry and the Alexandrean Past." In *Canons,* edited by Robert von Hallberg. Chicago: University of Chicago Press.

Žižek, Slavoj. 1992. *Enjoy Your Symptom! Jacques Lacan in Hollywood and Out.* London and New York: Routledge.

Contributors

Kwame Anthony Appiah is professor of Afro-American studies and philosophy at Harvard University. He is the author of *Assertion and Conditionals, For Truth in Semantics,* and *In My Father's House: Africa in the Philosophy of Culture.*

Paul A. Bové is professor of English at the University of Pittsburgh. He is the editor of *boundary 2,* an international journal of literature and culture, and author of *Intellectuals in Power: A Genealogy of Critical Humanism, In the Wake of Theory,* and *Mastering Discourse.* He is writing books on Henry Adams, Edmund Wilson, and fundamentalism in America.

Judith Butler is professor of rhetoric and comparative literature at the University of California, Berkeley. She is the author of *Subjects of Desire: Hegelian Reflections in Twentieth-Century France; Gender Trouble: Feminism and the Subversion of Identity;* and *Bodies that Matter: On the Discursive Limits of "Sex."* She is currently at work on a book concerning injurious language.

Seamus Deane, formerly professor of modern English and American literature at University College, Dublin, is now the Keough Professor of Irish Studies at the University of Notre Dame, Indiana. He is the author of three critical works, most recently of *The French Revolution and Enlighten-ment in England, 1789–1832;* the editor of eight books, most recently of the introduction and notes to the Penguin Classics edition of James Joyce's *Portrait of the Artist As a Young Man;* and the author of four books of poetry.

Stanley Fish is Arts and Sciences Professor of English and professor of law at Duke University, and the executive director of Duke University Press. His books include *Surprised by Sin: The Reader in Paradise Lost; Self-Consuming Artifacts; Is There a Text in This Class?; Doing What Comes Naturally: Change, Rhetoric, and the Practice of Theory in Literary and Legal Studies;* and *There's No Such Thing As Free Speech: And It's a Good Thing, Too.*

John Fiske is professor of communication arts at the University of Wisconsin—Madison. He is the author or co-author of nine books, most recently of *Media Matters: Everyday Culture and Political Change.*

Gerald Graff is the George M. Pullman Professor of English and Education at the University of Chicago. He is the author of several books, most recently *Professing Literature: An Institutional History* and *Beyond the Culture Wars: How Teaching the Conflicts Can Revitalize American Education,* and co-editor (with James Phelan) of a forthcoming edition of *The Adventures of Huckleberry Finn.*

465

Stephen Greenblatt is The Class of 1932 Professor of English Literature at the University of California, Berkeley. He is the editor of the journal *Representations* and the author, most recently, of *Renaissance Self-Fashioning: From More to Shakespeare*, *Shakespearean Negotiations: The Circulation of Social Energy in Renaissance England*, and *Marvelous Possessions: The Wonder of the New World*.

John Guillory is professor of English at The Johns Hopkins University and the author of *Cultural Capital: The Problem of Literary Canon-Formation*.

Geoffrey Galt Harpham is professor of English and director of the Program in Literary Theory at Tulane University. He is the author of three books, including *The Ascetic Imperative in Culture and Criticism* and *Getting It Right: Language, Literature, and Ethics*, both published by the University of Chicago Press.

Myra Jehlen is professor of English at Rutgers University. She is the author of *Class and Character in Faulkner's South* and *American Incarnation: The Individual, the Nation, and the Continent*.

Barbara Johnson is professor of romance and comparative literatures and Mellon Professor of the Humanities at Harvard University. She is the author of *The Critical Difference: Essays in the Contemporary Rhetoric of Reading*, *A World of Difference*, and *The Wake of Deconstruction*, and the translator of Jacques Derrida's *Dissemination*.

James H. Kavanagh is visiting associate professor of English at Wesleyan University. He is the author of *Emily Brontë* and has published other essays on ideology and culture in *Alternative Shakespeares* and *Alien Zone*.

Frank Lentricchia is professor of English at Duke University. His books include *After the New Criticism*; *Criticism and Social Change*; *Ariel and the Police:*

Michel Foucault, William James, Wallace Stevens; *The Edge of Night*; and *Modernist Quartet*.

Thomas McLaughlin, professor of English at Appalachian State University, is the author of the textbook *Literature: The Power of Language* and co-editor of *Reading for Difference: Texts on Gender, Race, and Class*.

Steven Mailloux is professor of English at Syracuse University. He is the author of *Interpretive Conventions: The Reader in the Study of American Fiction* and *Rhetorical Power*, and co-editor, with Sanford Levinson, of *Interpreting Law and Literature: A Hermeneutic Reader*.

Françoise Meltzer teaches literary theory at the University of Chicago, where she is professor of comparative literature. She is the author of *Salome and the Dance of Writing: Portraits of Mimesis in Literature* and *Hot Property: The Stakes and Claims of Literary Originality*, and the editor of *The Trial(s) of Psychoanalysis*.

Louis Menand is professor of English at the Graduate Center of the City University of New York and contributing editor of the *New York Review of Books*. He is the author of *Discovering Modernism: T. S. Eliot and His Context* and editor of a forthcoming volume entitled *The Future of Academic Freedom*.

J. Hillis Miller is Distinguished Professor of English and Comparative Literature at the University of California, Irvine. His most recent books include *Ariadne's Thread*, *Illustration*, and *Topographies*.

W. J. T. Mitchell is the Gaylord Donnelley Distinguished Service Professor in the Department of English Language and Literature and the Department of Art at the University of Chicago. He is editor of the journal *Critical Inquiry* and the author, most recently, of *Picture Theory: Essays on Verbal and Visual Representation*.

Daniel T. O'Hara is professor of English

at Temple University. He is the author of four books, most recently of *Radical Parody: American Culture and Critical Agency after Foucault*. He is the editor of *Why Nietzsche Now?*, co-editor (with William Spanos and Paul Bové) of *The Question of Textuality: Strategies of Reading in Contemporary American Criticism,* and review editor of the journal *boundary 2*.

Annabel Patterson, the Karl Young Professor of English at Yale University, is the author of *Hermogenes and the Renaissance: Seven Ideas of Style, Marvell and the Civic Crown, Censorship and Interpretation: The Conditions of Writing and Reading in Early Modern England, Pastoral and Ideology: Virgil to Valéry, Shakespeare and the Popular Voice, Reading between the Lines,* and *Reading Holinshed's* Chronicles.

Lee Patterson is professor of English at Yale University. He is the author of *Negotiating the Past: The Historical Understanding of Medieval Literature* and *Chaucer and the Subject of History.*

Donald E. Pease is the Ted and Helen Geisel Professor of Humanities at Dartmouth College. He is the author of *Visionary Compacts: American Renaissance Writings in Cultural Context* and editor of Duke University Press' New Americanists series.

Louis A. Renza is professor of English at Dartmouth College and the author of *"A White Heron" and the Question of Minor Literature.*

John Carlos Rowe is professor of English at the University of California, Irvine, and the author of *Henry Adams and Henry James: The Emergence of a Modern Consciousness, Through the Custom House: Nineteenth-Century American Literature and Modern Theory, The Theoretical Dimensions of Henry James,* and, forthcoming, *At Emerson's Tomb: The Politics of American Literary Modernism.*

Henry M. Sayre is professor of art at Oregon State University. He is the author of *The Object of Performance: The American Avant-Garde since 1970,* and *A World of Art.*

Barbara Herrnstein Smith is Braxton Craven Professor of Comparative Literature and English at Duke University. Her books include *Poetic Closure: A Study of How Poems End, On the Margins of Discourse: The Relation of Literature to Language,* and *Contingencies of Value: Alternative Perspectives for Critical Theory.*

Werner Sollors is professor of American literature and language and of Afro-American studies at Harvard University. He is the author of *Beyond Ethnicity: Consent and Descent in American Culture* and the editor of *The Invention of Ethnicity,* and *The Return of Thematic Criticism.*

Index

Abel, Elizabeth, 198
Abel, Karl, 23
Aboriginals, Australian, 327, 332
Abraham, 275
Abraham, Nicholas, 67
Absalom, Absalom! (Faulkner), 74
Acconci, Vito, 93–94
Adam and Eve, 275
Adams, Hazard, 33
Adams, Henry, 199, 201
Adonis, 186
Adorno, Theodor W., 294, 357, 406
Adventures of Huckleberry Finn, The (Twain), 69, 125–27, 265–73, 291, 298
Advertising, 16, 66, 88–89
Aeneid (Virgil), 231
Aesthetics, 11–12, 32, 179–80, 236, 334
"Affective Fallacy, The" (Wimsatt and Beardsley), 33
Afro-American literary criticism, 285–87
After the New Criticism (Lentricchia), 34
After Virtue (MacIntyre), 394
"Afterword: Toward an Ethic of Discussion" (Derrida), 391
Ahmad, Aijaz, 361
Algeria, 360
Alice in Wonderland (Carroll), 302
Allegories of Reading (de Man), 145
Allegory, 106, 107, 123–25, 369–70
Althusser, Louis, 143, 310, 313, 314
Ambiguity, 164–65
American Revolution, 21, 137, 283, 289
Anatomy of Criticism (Frye), 34, 36, 255
Anderson, Benedict, 289
Anderson, Laurie, 99–101
"Anecdote of the Jar" (Stevens), 7–8, 428–45
Anglo-Saxon (journal), 274

Anglo-Saxonism, 274, 279–80, 282–86
"Anglo-Saxon Race, The" (Tupper), 274–79, 285, 287
Anglo-Saxons, 364
Anonymous discourse, 143–44
Anscombe, Elizabeth, 137–38
Anthropology, 34, 229; and concept of culture, 325; and literary history, 260–61; and race, 277, 282; structural, 30–31, 33, 36, 40, 72–73. *See also* Culture
Anti-Ballistic Missile (ABM) Treaty, 128–34
Antidosis (Isocrates), 207
Antin, David, 100–103
Antin, Mary, 297
Anti-Oedipus (Deleuze), 385
Apophrades, 188, 191
Apostrophe, 83
Aquinas, St. Thomas, 148
Archaeology of Knowledge (Foucault), 53, 143–44
Arendt, Hannah, 193, 195, 197, 294
Ariosto, 229
Aristocracy, 413
Aristotle, 28, 106, 138, 148, 236; on desire, 376–78; on narrative, 66–69, 71, 72; on representation, 11, 13, 15; on rhetoric, 206–8, 220
Armstrong, Nancy, 260
Arnold, Matthew, 295, 323, 324, 338
Arthur (the king), 283
Articulation, 35–36
Askesis, 188, 191–94, 198
Astronomy, 106, 207
As You Like It (Shakespeare), 69, 227–28
Auctor, 105–10
Augustine, St., 148
Austen, Jane, 238

Austin, J. L., 138, 212–14
Australian Aboriginals, 327, 332
Author, 5, 105–16; and discourse, 62–63. *See also* Intention; Writing
Autonomy, textual. *See* Formalism; New Criticism

Babenco, Hector, 315
Bachelard, Gaston, 55, 145
Bahro, Rudolph, 61
Bahti, Timothy, 165
Bakhtin, Mikhail, 26, 67, 220
Ball, Charles, 298–99
Balzac, Honoré de, 93
Barber, C. L., 33–34
Barth, Fredrik, 299
Barth, John, 97–98
Barthes, Roland, 1, 67, 161, 220; on author, 62, 106, 112–16; on language and pleasure, 384; on readerly and writerly texts, 93; on structure, 35, 36; on writing, 39–40
Bate, Walter Jackson, 187, 193, 200
Baudelaire, Charles, 33
Baudrillard, Jean, 29–30, 36
Beardsley, Monroe C., 33, 111, 140–43
Beautiful, the, 373
Beauty, 179–80, 258
Beck, Julian, 96
Beethoven, Ludwig van, 91–92
Being, 384
Bellamy, Edward, 295
Belshazzar, 122–24
Benjamin, Walter, 216, 365
Benson, Sir Frank Robert, 279
Bentham, Jeremy, 337
Benveniste, Emile, 27–28
Beowulf, 285
Bersani, Leo, 385
Berthoff, Warner, 255
Betrayed by Rita Hayworth (film), 315
Bettelheim, Bruno, 28
Between Men: English Literature and Male Homosocial Desire (Sedgwick), 383
Bible, 106, 187, 275; Belshazzar's feast in, 122–23; as canon, 233, 237, 239
Binary differences, 31
"Biodegradables" (Derrida), 391
Biology and race, 277, 282, 286
Birthplace, The (James), 408, 419–26
Black Aesthetic movement, 286
"Black Betty" (Leadbelly), 93
Black Boy (Wright), 352
"Black Cat, The" (Poe), 190–91

Blackmur, R. P., 64, 67
Blacks: and Afro-American literary criticism, 285–87; in American colleges, 343–44; and canon-formation, 234–35, 258; in Cooper, 281–82; in Elizabethan literature, 277–79; and medievalism metaphor, 297; as race, 277, 278, 289; Twain on, 125–26, 266, 267, 270, 291, 297–99. *See also* Race; Slavery
Blake, William, 4, 80–86
Blassingame, John W., 299
Bleich, David, 220
Blindness and Insight (de Man), 390
Bloom, Alan, 220
Bloom, Harold, 186–201
Bloomfield, Leonard, 27–28
Bodily ego, 372
Body, the, 371–72
Boileau, Nicolas, 4
Booth, Wayne, 67, 220, 221
Borges, Jorge Luis, 17, 39, 97–98
Bork, Robert, 306
Borsch-Jacobsen, Michel, 383
Boston Sunday Herald, 296–97
Boston Transcript, 441
Boswell, James, 263–64
Boundary, ethnic, 299–303
Bourdieu, Pierre, 360
Bourgeoisie, 289, 291, 413–14
Bourne, Randolph S., 297, 346
Bové, Paul A., 51, 64
Brawne, Fanny, 173
Brecht, Bertold, 326
Brennan, William, 136–37, 141, 143
Britain. *See* Great Britain
British Council, 362
British Empire, 359, 363
Brontë, Charlotte, 180–83
Brooks, Cleanth, 32, 164, 247
Brooks, Peter, 68, 403
Brown, William Wells, 298
Browne, Sir Thomas, 256
Browning, Robert, 17–21
Bruitism, 95
Bullis, Jerald, 196
Burke, Kenneth, 64, 67, 196, 220, 406
Buttrick, George A., 123
Bynum, Caroline, 260–61
Byron, Lord, 252

Cage, John, 96
Cahan, Abraham, 297
Cambridge School of English, 338
Camus, Albert, 360

Canguilhem, Georges, 55
Cankered Muse: Satire of the English Renaissance, The (Kernan), 255
Canon, 5, 233–49, 257–58, 265; criterion for, 343; great books, 43, 342, 343, 346, 412; and multiculturalism, 347; and race, 285–87. *See also* Value/evaluation
"Canonization, The" (Donne), 244–48
Canterbury Tales (Chaucer), 295
Cantos (Pound), 433
Capitalism, 258, 260, 297, 432; the bourgeoisie, 289, 291, 413–14; capitalists as a class, 415; and commodification of culture, 324; cultural studies critique of, 325; exchange value in, 29–30; and ideology, 308, 310, 319; and nationalism, 360; New Criticism on, 51
Capital punishment, 137
Carlyle, Thomas, 256, 284, 295
Cassirer, Ernst, 25
Castration, 153, 271
Castro, Fidel, 306
Catcher in the Rye, The (Salinger), 242
Catharsis, 67
Celts, 364
Cézanne, Paul, 139
Character, 5
"Charles Baudelaire's 'Les Chats'" (Lévi-Strauss and Jakobson), 33
Chase, Cynthia, 73
Chaucer, Geoffrey, 285, 295
Chiasmus, 76
Chicago, Judy, 98–99
Chicago literary school, 67, 402
Chomsky, Noam, 27–28, 55, 205, 219
Christ, 76, 81–83
Christianity, 233, 237, 280
Christie, Agatha, 70–71, 189, 196
Chroniques algériennes (Camus), 360
Cicero, 106, 207, 216
Civic culture, 346
Civil War, U.S., 70, 259, 297–98
Cixous, Hélène, 47
Class, 7, 272, 406–27; aristocracy, 413; bourgeoisie, 289, 291, 413–14; and canon-formation, 242; as a collective actor, 416–17; Conant on, 341; Elster's definition of, 415; and gender, 264, 267, 272; history of term before Marx, 407n; and ideology, 308–14, 319; and language, 323; lumpenproletariat, 413, 414–15, 418; Marx on, 406, 413; Marxist theory of, 413–15; middle class, 323; and multiculturalism, 346, 347; and nationalism, 360;

petty bourgeoisie, 413, 414, 418; post-Marxist theory of, 413–19; proletariat, 413, 414
Classification, 182
Clinamen, 188–89, 198
Clocks, The (Christie), 189, 196
Closing of the American Mind, The (Bloom), 220
Codes, 13–14
Cohen, Abner, 293
Cold War, 339–40, 345
Coleridge, Samuel Taylor, 148, 190, 246
Colonialism, 278–79, 281, 354, 355
Columbia University, 342
Columbus, Christopher, 296
Comanches, 296
Committee on the Present Danger, 340
Commodification of culture, 324
Computers, 32, 37, 205, 412
Conant, James B., 340
Concepts, 87
Connecticut Yankee in King Arthur's Court, A (Twain), 290–304
Conrad, Joseph, 355–56
Consciousness: and unconscious, 148–52, 156–58
Constative utterances, 212–14
Constitution: English, 282; U.S., 135–37
Context, 166–67, 173, 174
Contingency, Irony, and Solidarity (Rorty), 394
Conventions, 13–14
Cooper, James Fenimore, 281
Corneille, Pierre, 4
Count of Monte Cristo, The (Dumas), 295
Course in General Linguistics (Saussure), 26, 40, 159, 256–57
Crane, R. S., 67
Crane, Stephen, 259
Critical Legal Studies movement, 218
Critical self-consciousness, 218
Criticism, literary. *See* Literary criticism
Criticism and Social Change (Lentricchia), 419
Critique of Judgment (Kant), 179–80
Croce, Benedetto, 141
Cromwell, Oliver, 227
Crosby, Alfred W., 354
Crosby, Bing, 291
Cuba, 442
Culler, Jonathan, 173–74
Cultural Literacy (Hirsch), 220
Cultural nationalism, 358, 361, 363, 365
Cultural pluralism, 346
Cultural relativism, 346
Cultural studies, 325

Culture, 4–7, 225–32; anthropology and concept of, 325; author's relationship to, 107–16; civic culture, 346; and gender, 264–66; and ideology, 307, 309; industrialization of, 324–25; literary production as form of, 260–61; in modern life, 349–50, 352; monogenealogy of, 356; and narrative, 69–73; and nationalism, 360–62; and nature, 29–31; and power, 361, 368; racially based concept of, 364. *See also* Anthropology; High culture; Mass culture; Popular culture

Culture and Anarchy (Arnold), 323

Culture and Society (Williams), 326

Culture of Literacy, The (Godzich), 418

Cunningham, Roger, 297

Curtius, Ernst Robert, 193, 241

Cushing, Frank Hamilton, 297

Cybernetics, 31–32

Czerny, Karl, 92

Dada, 92–95

Daemonization, 188, 190–91, 194

Dakota Indians, 297

Danes, 283, 285

Daniel, Book of, 122–24, 127

Dante, 187, 193, 295

Darwin, Charles, 279

Darwinism, 359; Social Darwinism, 279

Death, 87

Death instinct, 151

Death in Venice (Mann), 374–75

"Death of the Author, The" (Barthes), 106, 112–16

Declaration of Independence, 187, 188

Deconstruction, 1, 34; on ambiguity, 165, 169, 173–74; and decolonization, 356–57; and de Man's Nazi association, 389–90; Derrida on, 391–92; on ethics, 387; on intention, 144–45; on literary history, 256–60; on narrative, 67, 76–77; on rhetoric, 214–18; on value/evaluation, 178. *See also* Poststructuralism

Deep structure, 30–31, 160

Deerslayer, The (Cooper), 281

Defence of Poetry (Shelley), 138–39

Defense of Poesie, The (Sidney), 314

Dehiscence, 384

De la grammatologie (Derrida), 144

Deleuze, Gilles, 51, 56, 385

DeLillo, Don, 442–43

de Man, Paul, 161, 196, 165, 200; on concepts as tropes, 87; on deconstructive act, 215–16; Derrida on, 390–91; on ethics, 389; on intention, 145; on narrative, 67, 76–78; Nazi association, 389–91

Democracy, 61, 235, 243, 431, 440

Demons II (film), 317

Derrida, Jacques, 5, 31, 67, 161, 165; on author's death, 62; on deconstruction, 391–92; on de Man, 390–91; on ethics, 388; on influence, 196, 200–201; on intention, 144; Kant compared to, 391–92; Nussbaum on, 400; on psychoanalysis, 154; on truth and rhetoric, 214–15, 217, 257, 259; on writing, 39, 42–48, 359

Descartes, René, 148, 151

Desire, 369–86; Aristotle on, 376–78; and the costs of linguistic recognition, 378–82; feminist theory of, 377–78; Hegel on, 378–79; Lacan on, 157, 159–60, 370, 379, 380, 381, 383, 385; and language, 369, 370, 380, 381, 383, 385; and masculinity, 377, 384; and metonymy, 380; as never fulfilled, 381; Nietzsche, 378, 385; Plato on, 369, 370, 371–74, 379; psychoanalysis on, 382–85; and sexual difference, homoeroticism, and mastery, 374–78, 380, 385; Spinoza on, 378, 385; and the subject who desires, 376; triangular structure of, 382

Desire and Domestic Fiction (Armstrong), 260

Desire, Deceit, and the Novel (Girard), 382–83

Determinacy/indeterminacy, 5, 163–75

Devereux, Georges, 288, 289

Dewey, John, 346

Diachronic linguistics, 27, 40

Dialogical narrative theory, 67

Dickens, Charles, 69, 229

Dickinson, Emily, 122–24, 126, 127, 238

Didisheim, Peter, 130

Différance, 43–45

Dilthey, Wilhelm, 143

Diotima, 372, 373, 374, 378

Discourse, 5, 50–64; anonymous, 143–44; ethical discourse, 394, 396; in performance art, 101–3

Discourse ethics, 393

Dispatches (Herr), 440–42

Displacement: in dreams, 87

Dissection, 35–36

Distance, 333–34

Distributive justice, 402

Diversity, 336–53; in American colleges, 343–45; in Harvard report, 343; and meritocracy, 344, 345; and multiculturalism, 336–37, 345–49; paradox of, 347

Divine Comedy (Dante), 187, 193, 295

Dixon, Peter, 206
Donne, John, 244–48, 252
Donoghue, Denis, 197
Doran, Madeleine, 92
Douglass, Frederick, 48
Downsizing, 410, 416
Doyle, Sir Arthur Conan, 189, 196
Drama, representation in, 14
Dramatism, 220
Dreams, 46, 66; displacement in, 87; figurative in, 87; and unconscious, 41–42, 149, 151, 153, 155
DuBois, W. E. B., 286
Duchamp, Marcel, 94–96
Dukakis, Michael, 319
Duke University, 344
Duras, Marguerite, 381–82, 383

Eagleton, Terry, 188, 197, 216–17, 406
Earle, Ralph, 131–32
Ecological Imperialism (Crosby), 354
Economics, 209–10
Ecrits (Lacan), 41, 393
Education, 430–31; and canon-formation, 238–44, 246–47; general education, 341–43; and ideology, 311; and race, 285; standardized tests, 340. *See also* Universities
Educational Testing Service, 340
Ego, 151–52, 156–57, 372, 392
Ego and the Id, The (Freud), 372
Egoist, The (Meredith), 69–70
Ego psychology, 152, 157
Eichenbaum, Boris, 67, 251, 255
Eighteenth Brumaire of Louis Napoleon, The (Marx), 256
Einstein, Albert, 23
Eliot, George, 75, 229
Eliot, T. S., 50–52, 142–43; and Bloom's theory of influence, 198; on the canon, 246; criticism of Western rationality, 358; Ellison influenced by, 350, 351; and high culture, 337–39; and modernism, 329; *The Waste Land*, 142, 256, 350
Elizabethan literature, 92; race in, 277–79
Elizabethan World Picture (Tillyard), 251
Ellis, Havelock, 303
Ellison, Ralph, 350–51, 352
Elster, Jon, 408, 415–18
Embarrassment, 329–30
Emerson, Ralph Waldo, 188, 191, 192, 201
Empson, William, 77
Endeavors of Art (Doran), 92
Engels, Friedrich, 307, 309–10
England, 264; metaphysical poetry in,

245–48; Prynne trial in, 135; race in, 274, 276–79, 282–85, 286. *See also* Great Britain
English, Standard, 241–42, 246
English departments, 338, 408–10
English Elegy, The (Sacks), 255
English Religious Lyric in the Middle Ages (Woolf), 255
Enlightenment, the, 209, 280, 286; and ethics, 387; and imperialism, 357; poetic influence in, 188, 196, 197, 200
Epistemology, 307, 347
"Epistle to Doctor Arbuthnot" (Pope), 227
Esperanto, 205
Essay on Criticism (Pope), 142, 186–87
"Ethic of Care for the Self as a Practice of Freedom" (Foucault), 394
Ethics, 387–405; discourse ethics, 393; ethics itself, 394–400; is and ought, 403; and language, 393; and literature, 400–404; morality, 397; the ought, 395, 396, 404; of the Theoretical Era, 387–94; and value, 179
Ethics and the Limits of Philosophy (Williams), 397
Ethics of Reading, The (Miller), 390
Ethics of Sexual Difference, An (Irigaray), 393
Ethiopians, 275
Ethique de la psychanalyse (Lacan), 392
Ethnicity, 285, 288–304, 311, 348. *See also* Race
Ethnomethodology, 220
Ethos (habit), 378
Etiological myths, 72
Eureka (Poe), 192
European Literature and the Latin Middle Ages (Curtius), 241
Evaluation. *See* Value/evaluation
Exchange value, 29–30, 37, 178
Exile, 367
Expressionism, 15–16, 139

Faber Book of America, The, 348
Faerie Queen, The (Spenser), 228
Family, the, 398–99
Family resemblances, 55–56, 60
Family values, 335
Fanon, Frantz, 360
Fathers, The (Tate), 50
Faulkner, William, 52, 74, 98
Faust (Goethe), 153
Femininity, 263, 377
Feminism, 1, 167; on author, 111, 112; on desire, 377–78; on ethics, 387, 393, 398–

Feminism (*continued*)
400; feminist responses to *New Newlywed Game,* 327, 328; on gender, 265; on ideology, 311; and influence, 198; on Lacan's theory of desire and language, 384; and performance, 97–99; on rhetoric, 220, 221; on value/evaluation, 177

Feminist Morality: Transforming Culture, Society, and Politics (Held), 398

Ferment of Realism: American Literature, 1884–1919, The (Berthoff), 255

Fetishism, 16

Feudalism. *See* Middle Ages

Fields, W. C., 434

Figurative language, 6, 80–90, 152, 156. *See also* Metaphor(s); Tropes

Films, 14; and ideology, 312–18

Finnegans Wake (Joyce), 50, 366, 367

Fiscal Year 1985 Arms Control Impact Statement, 128

Fish, Stanley, 408

Flaubert, Gustave, 40, 281

Fliess, Wilhelm, 153

Ford, Ford Madox, 358

Form: and matter, 377; structure versus, 25–30, 32

Formalism, 6, 25–26, 146; on influence, 198–99; on interpretation, 123, 124, 129–30; and literary history concept, 251–55; and narrative form, 402; performance art versus, 97–98; on representation, 15–16; Russian, 26, 32, 34, 67, 71, 251–55, 402; and Stevens's "Anecdote of the Jar," 430–33, 441–42. *See also* New Criticism

"Formalist School of Poetry and Marxism, The" (Trotsky), 26

Forman, H. B., 172

Foucault, Michel, 5, 209, 161, 261, 407n; archival digging by, 411; on author, 62–63, 106, 113–16, 143; on desire, 369; on discourse, 51, 53–64; on ethics, 389, 393–94; on intention, 143–45; on language and pleasure, 384; on modernity, 443–45

Foundationalist theory: of interpretation 123, 129–30, 133–34; of rhetoric, 206, 207, 220

Fountain (Duchamp), 94–96

Four Fundamental Concepts of Psychoanalysis, The (Lacan), 393

4' 33" (Cage), 96

Fragility of Goodness, The (Nussbaum), 394

France, 55; French Empire, 359; French Revolution, 289, 294, 295; literary theory in, 39–41, 47; nationalism, 362; political events of 1960s in, 39, 41, 61–62; and race, 281, 284, 287; Reign of Terror, 294, 302

Frankfurt School, 111, 324, 406

Franklin, Benjamin, 293, 301, 302

Franklin, Bruce, 309

"French and the Comanches, The" (Twain), 296

French Empire, 359

French Revolution, 289, 294, 295

Freud, Sigmund, 23, 46, 67, 113, 143, 221; on bodily ego, 372; on desire, 377; on dream mechanisms, 87; on ethics, 392; Lacan on theories of, 28, 41–42, 156–61; and literary influence, 196; Oedipus complex of, 74, 152–55, 161; on unconscious, 139, 147–46. *See also* Psychoanalysis

Frost, Robert, 438–440

Frye, Northrop, 50, 186, 196, 255; on literary structure, 34, 36, 255; on literary universe of forms, 432, 434

Futurism, 92–93, 139

Gadamer, Hans-Georg, 143

Galileo, 26

Gans, Herbert, 292

Garcia Marquez, Gabriel, 368

Gardiner, S. R., 135

Garfinkel, Harold, 220

Gates, Henry Louis, Jr., 47

Geertz, Clifford, 220–21

Gender, 4–7, 263–73; and canon-formation, 234–35, 238–39, 242; femininity, 263, 377; and ideology, 311, 319; and influence, 197, 198; and literature, 258, 260; and multiculturalism, 346, 347; and nationalism, 360; and popular culture, 321, 322, 323; and psychosexual development, 152–53; responses to *New Newlywed Game,* 328; and textual indeterminacy, 167, 168; and value/evaluation, 177, 184; and writing, 47. *See also* Feminism; Masculinity; Women

Genealogy of discourse, 56–64

General education, 341–43

General Education in a Free Society (1945), 341–43, 347

Genesis, Book of, 187, 275

Genetic fallacy, 192

Genette, Gérard, 67, 403
Genius, 164, 254, 276, 430; author as, 108–12, 115–16
Genre, 50–52, 431. *See also* Discourse
Geoffrey of Monmouth, 283
Geometry, 207
German Ideology, The (Marx and Engels), 307
Germany, 251, 316; race and ethnicity in, 282, 283, 285, 286, 290
GI Bill, 341
Gilbert, Sandra M., 47, 197, 198
Gilligan, Carol, 398
Giotto, 146
Girard, René, 381–82, 385
Glare, P. G. W., 121
Glasnost, 61
Gnosticism, 196, 233
Godzich, Wlad, 418
Goethe, Johann Wolfgang von, 141, 148, 153, 303
Gogh, Vincent van, 139, 146
Gold Standard and the Logic of Naturalism, The (Michaels), 260
Gorbachev, Mikhail, 61
Gordon, Robert, 218
Gorgias, 204
Gorgias (Plato), 204
Governability, 61
Grammar, 27–28, 241
Grammar of Motives, The (Burke), 406
Gramsci, Antonio, 53, 59, 61–62
Gray, Thomas, 438–40
Great books, 43, 342, 343, 346, 412
Great Britain, 289; British Empire, 359, 363; nationalist ideology, 362; Standard English in, 241; in Twain's *Connecticut Yankee,* 291–303. *See also* England
Great Expectations (Dickens), 69, 229
Greece, ancient, 15, 240–41, 275, 276, 285. *See also* Aristotle; Plato; Socrates
Greeley, Horace, 296
Greenberg, Clement, 97
Greenblatt, Stephen, 208, 260
Greimas, A. J., 67
Grimm brothers, 290
Grimmelshausen, Hans Jacob Christoph von, 290
"Grizzly Bear, The" (Housman), 74–78
Grotowski, Jerzy, 96
Guattari, Felix, 385
Gubar, Susan, 47, 197, 198
Gutenberg, Johannes, 295, 302

Guthrie, Peter, 207
Gynesis, 46–47

Habermas, Jürgen, 205, 218–19, 393
Habit (*ethos*), 378
Halperin, David, 377
Hamilton, Lee, 131
Hamlet (Shakespeare), 74, 91, 94, 96, 97, 99, 168, 193–96, 264–65
Hampshire, Stuart, 395
Harris, Joel Chandler, 298
Hartman, Geoffrey H., 201
Hartmann, Eduard von, 148
Harvard report (*General Education in a Free Society*), 341–43
Harvard University, 340
Havel, Vaclav, 408
Heart of Darkness (Conrad), 355
Hebrews, 233, 275–76
Hegel, Georg Wilhelm Friedrich: critiques of, 55; on desire, 378–79; Foucault on, 64; and intention, 144; on master-slave relationship, 157–58; philosophy of history, 355; and structure, 28; and the unconscious, 148
Heidegger, Martin, 143
He Knew He Was Right (Trollope), 76–77
Held, Virginia, 398–400
Hellenistic Age, 240–41
Henry, O., 242
Herder, Johann Gottfried, 283–84, 286, 290
Hermeneutic narrative theory, 67
Herr, Michael, 440–45
Heterosexuality: and desire, 370, 384
Hierarchy of taste, 330
High culture: Eliot on, 337, 338; Frankfurt School on, 324–25; mass culture compared to, 326; popular culture compared to, 331–35
Highet, Gilbert, 194
High Modernism, 358
Hippias, 204
Hippocrates, 275
Hirsch, E. D., 142–43, 163, 169, 220, 346
Historicism, 36, 137; on author, 111, 113; formalism as, 433, 441; and literary history concept, 250–51, 258–61
History, 3–4, 6, 220, 437; and canon-formation, 238–45, 248; and gender, 264; and imperialism, 355; intention in, 144; literary, as critical term, 250–62; literary study versus study of, 230–31; as narrative, 68; poststructuralism on, 55, 60; structur-

History (*continued*)
    alist view of, 25, 27, 28, 34, 41; in Twain's
    Connecticut Yankee, 395. *See also* Histor-
    icism
History of English Literature (Taine), 251,
    284–85
History of the Kings of Britain (Geoffrey of
    Monmouth), 283
History of the Royal Society of London (Spratt),
    256
History of Sexuality, The (Foucault), 384, 393
Histriomastix (Prynne), 135
Hobbes, Thomas, 109–10, 378
Hoffmann, E. T. A., 154–55
Hoggart, Richard, 326
Holland, 284–85
Holland, Norman, 220
Homer, 153–54, 186, 236, 275
Homme, L', 33
Homosexuality (homoeroticism): and aca-
    demic hiring, 410; and desire, 374–78,
    384, 385; and ideology, 315, 316; and liter-
    ary history, 258, 260
Horkheimer, Max, 357
Horney, Karen, 152–53
Housman, A. E., 74–78
"How Bigger Was Born" (Wright), 352
Howell, John, 96–97, 99, 100
Howells, William Dean, 291, 296
How to Do Things with Words (Austin), 138,
    212–14
Hoy, David Couzens, 194
Huizinga, Johan, 261–62
Hulme, T. E., 439
Humanism, 433; Bloom on, 199–200; cri-
    tiques of, 388; and imperialism, 359; and
    literary history, 254; and literary influence,
    186; and rhetoric, 207
Human nature, 208–9, 282
Hume, David, 286
Hunter-Gault, Charlayne, 344
Husserl, Edmund, 26, 137, 143
Hyde, Henry, 130, 133
Hypnosis, 151

Icon, 14, 15
Id, 151–52, 156
Idea, 87
Idealism: German, 186; and ideology, 310;
    on intention, 138–39; on representation,
    15; repression of signifier by, 41; and struc-
    turalism, 25–26, 29; transcendental, 149
Ideal speech situation, 218–29
Identification: in dreams, 87

Identities, social, 322
Identity politics, 346
Ideology, 5–6, 225, 306–20; and canon-
    formation, 234, 237, 243; of gender, 264,
    269–73; and rhetoric, 216–17. *See also* Pol-
    itics
Idolatry, 15, 16
Iliad (Homer), 153–54, 275
Imagism, 438–39, 442
Imitation, 14, 68–69. *See also* Representation
Imperialism, 354–68; colonialism compared
    to, 354, 355; and nationalism, 360, 363;
    naturalizing its own history, 357; New Im-
    perialism, 355, 362
Incest, 72–73
Incommensurability thesis, 346
Indeterminacy. *See* Determinacy/indeter-
    minacy
Index, 14
Indians, American, 281–82, 296–97, 299
"Indigo Glass in the Grass, The" (Stevens),
    435
Influence, 186–201
Information Superhighway, 419
Information theory, 31–32
Infrastructure. *See* Deep structure
Ingarden, Roman, 67
Insel Felsenburg, Die (Schnabel), 290
Intellectuals, 418–19
Intention, 5, 135–46, 166. *See also* Author;
    Interpretation
Intention (Anscombe), 137–38
"Intentional Fallacy, The" (Wimsatt and
    Beardsley), 111, 140–43
Intentionalist theory of interpretation, 123,
    124, 129–30
Internet, 412, 419
Interpretation, 6–7, 121–34, 254, 259; and
    evaluation, 185; historical context as
    ground of, 244–45; and influence, 188. *See
    also* Determinacy/indeterminacy; Intention;
    Performance; Reading
Interracial marriage, 348
Inventione, De (Cicero), 207
Invisible Man (Ellison), 350–51
Ion (Plato), 163
Ireland, 358, 363–68
Irigaray, Luce: on desire, 375–76, 377, 379,
    383–84; on ethics, 387, 393; on female
    writing, 47
Irish Literary Revival, 366
"Irony as a Principle of Structure" (Brooks),
    32
Irving, Washington, 296

Is and ought, 403
Iser, Wolfgang, 67, 220
Isle of Pines (Neville), 290
Isocrates, 207, 216
Ivanhoe (Scott), 279–82

Jackson, Jesse, 319
Jacob, 275
Jakobson, Roman, 26, 33, 158–60, 251–53, 258
James, C. L. R., 406
James, Henry, 76–77, 440; *The Birthplace,* 408, 419–26
James, William, 441–45
Jameson, Fredric: and class, 406; on deconstruction, 258–59; and discourse, 50–51; on ethics, 387, 388; on history as textual, 220, 221; Lacan's influence on, 161; on Marx and ethics, 392; and narrative, 67
Jane Eyre (Brontë), 180–83
Jardine, Alice, 46–47
Jauss, Hans Robert, 67, 220
Jefferson, Thomas, 187, 188, 281, 283, 286
Jesus Christ, 76, 81–83
Jew of Malta, The (Marlowe), 277–78
Jews, 277–78, 281–82, 285, 316
John Donne, Coterie Poet (Marotti), 247–48
Johnson, Samuel, 263–64
Jokes, 66
Jones, Ernest, 195
Jouissance, 1, 220
Joyce, James, 50, 138–39, 186, 236; and Irish nationalism, 363, 364, 365–68
Jungle Book (Kipling), 72
Justice, distributive, 402

Kabbalah, 196
Kafka, Franz, 78
Kain, Philip J., 392
Kallen, Horace M., 346
Kant, Immanuel, 149, 179–80, 286; de Man compared to, 390; Derrida compared to, 391–92; on ethics, 388–89, 398, 399, 400; and structure, 23, 25, 28, 29, 33
Keats, John, 66, 172–75, 440
Kennedy, George, 206
Kenosis, 188, 190, 198, 199
Kernan, Alvin, 255
Keywords (Williams), 3, 24–25
King Lear (Shakespeare), 230
Kinship, 229–30
Kipling, Rudyard, 72
Kirshner, Judith Russi, 93, 94
Kissinger, Henry, 98

Kiss of the Spider Woman (film), 314–18
Klein, Melanie, 152–53, 382
Kolodny, Annette, 198
Kott, Jan, 167
Kristeva, Julia, 2, 42, 161, 385, 393, 398
Kuhn, Thomas, 210–12, 221, 257
Kyd, Thomas, 194

Lacan, Jacques, 2, 28, 45, 67; on the body, 372; on desire, 157, 159–60, 370, 379, 380, 381, 383, 385; on ethics, 392–93; on Kantian ethics, 388–89; on signifying chain, 41–42; on unconscious, 152, 156–61
"Lamb, The" (Blake), 80–86
Langbaum, Robert, 21
Language: and canon-formation, 240–43; and class, 323; and culture, 230; and desire, 369, 370, 380, 381, 383, 385; Esperanto, 205; and ethics, 393; figurative, 6, 80–90; indeterminacy in, 166, 170–72, 175; Latin, 121, 241; and literary theory, 1–7; literature as, 252–53; narrative as, 71; and nationalism, 282–84, 290; norm-enforcing language, 378; philology, 27, 28, 216; and pleasure, 384; representation in, 13–14; rhetoric as form of, 205, 219; and sexual difference, 380, 384, 385; Standard English, 241–42, 246; structuralist theory of, 25–31, 34, 35, 37; and unconscious, 152, 159–61. *See also* Discourse; Poststructuralism; Structuralism
Lanham, Richard, 208–9
Large, Andrew, 205
Latin, 121, 241
Latin America, 315
Law, 34, 135–37, 218
Lawrence, D. H., 329, 358
Lawson, John, 207
Leadbelly, 93
Learning Piece (Acconci), 93
"Leatherstocking Tales" (Cooper), 281
Leitch, Vincent B., 198
Lentricchia, Frank, 7–8, 34, 196–98, 216, 419
Levinas, Emmanuel, 392, 393
Lévi-Strauss, Claude, 40, 48, 67, 160; on incest, 72–73; and structure, 30–31, 33–36
Lewis, C. S., 255
Lewis, R. W. B., 33
Lewis, Wyndham, 358
Leyda, Jay, 123
Liberal Imagination, The (Trilling), 406
Life on the Mississippi (Twain), 190

"Like the Sound of the Sea Deep within a Shell: Paul de Man's War" (Derrida), 390
Limericks, 70
Linguistics. *See* Language; Structuralism
Lipking, Lawrence, 172–73
Literary criticism: author, 105–16; canon, 233–49; culture, 225–32; and de Man's Nazi association, 389; determinacy/indeterminacy, 163–75; discourse, 50–64; distance in, 333–34; and diversity, 336; ethnicity, 288–304; figurative language, 80–90; gender, 263–73; ideology, 306–20; influence, 186–201; intention, 135–46; interpretation, 121–34; literary history, 250–62; narrative, 66–79; performance, 91–103; race, 274–87; representation, 11–21; rhetoric, 203–22; structure, 23–37; terms used in, 3–8; unconscious, 147–62; value/evaluation, 177–85; writing, 39–49. *See also* Literary theory; New Criticism; *and specific terms*
Literary history, 250–62. *See also* History
Literary theory: and de Man's Nazi association, 389; and ethics, 400–403; importance of, 1–3. *See also* Literary criticism
Literary Theory: An Introduction (Eagleton), 216–17
Literature: concept of, 40, 112, 255–56; and diversity, 336–53; Elizabethan, 92, 277–79; English departments, 338, 408–10; and ethics, 400–404; literature as literature, 339, 343; magic narrative, 368; and multiculturalism, 347, 349; narrative, 6, 66–79, 155–56, 370, 400, 402–4; plot, 5, 66, 71, 403; as representation, 11; and society, 242; value of, 6. *See also* Canon; Literary criticism; Literary theory; Novel(s); Poetry
Literature and Revolution (Trotsky), 26
Literaturgeschichte der deutschen Stämme und Landschaften (Nadler), 290
Living Theater, 96
Locke, Alain, 297, 346
Locke, John, 109–10
Logic, 205
Logocentrism, 43–48, 388
Longinus, 163
Looking Backward: 2000–1887 (Bellamy), 295
Lord Jim (Conrad), 355
Lothrop, C. D., 123, 124
Love, 69, 373
Lowes, John Livingston, 186
Lucan, 193
Ludlum, Charles, 97

Lukács, Georg, 61, 67
Lumpenproletariat, 413, 414–15, 418
"Lycidas" (Milton), 186
Lying, 401
Lyotard, Jean-François, 393
Lyrical Ballads (Wordsworth), 438–40

Mabou Mines, 96
McCloskey, Donald, 209–10
McDonald's Corporation, 88–89
McFarlane, Robert, 128
MacIntyre, Alasdair, 394, 400
McNamara, Robert, 98
Madwoman in the Attic (Gilbert and Gubar), 47
Magic narrative, 368
Maieutic, 148
Mailer, Norman, 440
Mailloux, Steven, 186
Making of the English Working Class, The (Thompson), 325
Making Sense of Marx (Elster), 415
Maleczech, Ruth, 96–97
Malinowski, Bronislaw, 30
Mallarmé, Stéphane, 40, 45–46
Malory, Thomas, 292, 295
Man, Paul de. *See* de Man, Paul
Manet, Édouard, 139
Mann, Thomas, 374–75
Mannheim, Karl, 309
Marcos, Imelda, 309
Marlowe, Christopher, 277–78, 285
Marotti, Arthur, 247–48
Marriage, interracial, 348
Marriage of Heaven and Hell (Blake), 4
Martin, Wallace, 403
Marvell, Andrew, 227
Marx, Karl, 29, 256, 432; as author, 113; on class, 406, 413; on ethics, 392; on ideology, 307, 309–10; on the individual, 143. *See also* Marxism
Marx, Leo, 33
Marx and Ethics (Kain), 392
Marxism, 1, 441; on author, 111, 112; on class, 413–15; on ethics, 387; on ideology, 307–14; on narratives, 67; on nationalism, 362; poststructuralism versus, 54, 56, 59–61; on value/evaluation, 177; and writing theory, 40–41
Marxism and Literature (Williams), 3
Masculinity: and desire, 377, 384; gender, 263; patriarchal construction of, 327–28
Mass culture: failure rate of products of, 326–27; high culture compared to, 326;

popular culture compared to, 325, 326, 331

Mass media, 16; and ideology, 306–8, 312–19; and multiculturalism, 348

Mastery, 374–78, 388

Materialism, 41

Mathematics, 205

Matter and form, 377

Matthew, St., 233, 278

Meaning. *See* Interpretation; Value/evaluation

Media. *See* Mass media

Meditation 6 (Taylor), 43–45

Meeker, Leonard, 130

Meese, Edwin, 136

Merchant of Venice, The (Shakespeare), 277–78

Meredith, George, 69–71

Meritocracy, 341, 344, 345

Merleau-Ponty, Maurice, 26

Metalepsis, 191

"Metamorphosis, The" (Kafka), 78

Metaphor(s), 80, 216; and ambiguity in poetry, 164; defined, 83–84; metaphysical conceit as, 44; and unconscious, 150, 152, 156, 159–60

Metaphysical conceit, 44

Metaphysical poetry, 245–48

Metaphysics: and desire, 370

Metonymy, 80, 216; defined, 83–84; desire as, 380; and influence, 190; and unconscious, 159–60

Meyer, Ursula, 93

Michaels, Walter Benn, 260

Middle Ages, 193, 242, 260, 283; author in, 106–8; in Twain's *Connecticut Yankee,* 291–303

Middle class, 323

Middlemarch (Eliot), 75, 229

Midsummer Night's Dream, A (Shakespeare), 260

Miller, J. Hillis, 390

Milton, John, 186, 187, 191, 203–4, 431

Mimesis, 14, 16

Mind, 25–26, 28–29, 63, 148. *See also* Psyche; Reason

Minimalism, 139

Minnis, A. J., 106

Minstrelsy of the Scottish Border (Scott), 284

"Mirror Stage, The" (Lacan), 384

Modernism, 140–41; exile of modernist writers, 367; High Modernism, 358; and imperialism and nationalism, 363; in Joyce, 365; in poetry, 246, 435–42; repressed primitive in, 357–58. *See also* New Criticism; Postmodernism

Modernity, 337–38, 341–42, 364, 365, 443–45

Modern Language Association, 339, 349, 408, 413

Moholy-Nagy, László, 95

Molière, 263, 264, 273

Monet, Claude, 139

Monroe, Harriet, 435

Montrose, Louis, 260

Moors, 277

Morality, 397. *See also* Ethics

Morphology, 27, 71

Morphology of the Folk Tale (Propp), 71

Morte d'Arthur (Malory), 292, 295

Moses, 39

Motherwell, Robert, 95

Mots et les choses, Les (Foucault), 113

Mukarovsky, Jan, 26–33

Multiculturalism: and academic hiring, 410, 411–12; and diversity, 336–37, 338, 345–49

Mumford, Lewis, 33–34

Murder of Roger Ackroyd, The (Christie), 70–71

Murdoch, Iris, 97–98, 400

Museums, 358

Music, 16, 179; performance of, 91–92, 95–96

"My Last Duchess" (Browning), 17–21

Mystery stories, 70–71

Myth(s), 186, 261, 429, 432; criticism of, 33–34; etiological, 72

Nadler, Josef, 290, 303–4

Narrative, 6, 66–79, 155–56, 370, 400, 402–4

"Narrative and Plot" (Ricoeur), 403

Narrative of the Life of Frederick Douglass (Douglass), 48

Nashe, Thomas, 194

Nationalism, 359–68; cultural nationalism, 358, 361, 363, 364; and culture, 360–62; and ethnicity, 289–90; European, 362; and imperialism, 360, 363; and language, 282–84, 290; and literary history, 251; and poetry, 284; and race, 282–87, 360; socialist opposition to, 362; South American nationalist revolutions, 361–62

Native Son (Wright), 351

Natural History (Pliny), 138

Nature, 29–31; *phusis,* 377–78

Nature (Emerson), 192

Negativity, 379

Nero, 135

Neutral principles theories, 124, 129–30
Neville, Henry, 290
New Criticism, 6, 64; on ambiguity, 164–65; on author, 111–12, 116; and Bloom's influence theory, 196, 199; and canon-information, 246–47; and cult of genius, 430–31; on discourse, 50–52; on ideology, 306; on intention, 140, 142, 144; on literary history, 253–54; on narrative, 67; on structure, 32–34; on unity, 4. See also Formalism
"New Developments in Legal Theory" (Gordon), 218
New Imperialism, 355, 362
New Negro, The (anthology), 297
New Newlywed Game, 321, 322, 327–35
New Rhetoric: A Treatise on Argumentation, The (Perelman and Olbrechts-Tyteca), 220
Newton, Isaac, 26
New World discoveries, 107–10
Nietzsche, Friedrich: on desire, 378, 385; on ethics, 389; on the modern condition as weightlessness, 349; and poststructuralism, 56; and rhetoric, 216, 217; on the will, 148
Nitze, Paul, 131
Nixon, Richard, 98, 100
Noah, 275
Nolte, Ernst, 294
Normans, 279–80, 283
Norton Anthology of English Literature, 238, 241
Nostromo (Conrad), 355–56
"Note on the Unconscious in Psycho-Analysis, A" (Freud), 149–50
Notes toward a Supreme Fiction (Stevens), 438–39
Nous, 25, 28–29
Novel(s), 220, 239, 253, 260, 289; culture in, 229; discourses of, 50; influence in, 187; narrative in, 68, 69; representation in, 14, 16
Nussbaum, Martha, 394, 400

Oberdorfer, Don, 128
"Ode to a Nightingale" (Keats), 66
"Ode to Joy" (Schiller), 337
Odyssey, The (Homer), 186
Oedipus complex, 74, 152–55, 161, 188–97, 200
Oedipus Rex (Sophocles), 72–74, 152–55, 194
Of Grammatology (Derrida), 43
Olbrechts-Tyteca, L., 220

Oliver, Ariadne, 196
Oliveros, Pauline, 102, 103
Olivier, Sir Laurence, 11–12, 96
Omar Khayyám, 39
"On a Supposed Right to Lie Because of Philanthropic Concerns" (Kant), 401
On Lies, Secrets, and Silence (Rich), 47
On the New German Literature: Fragments (Herder), 283–84
On Truth and Lie (Nietzsche), 216
Ordeal of Richard Feverel, The (Meredith), 70–71
Ordre du discours, L' (Foucault), 53
Orientalism (Said), 47
Origin of Species (Darwin), 279
Othello (Shakespeare), 277–78
Otherness (the Other): and desire, 379, 381, 382, 384; and ethics, 392, 394, 404; and imperialism, 356, 357; Lacan on, 157–58
Ought, the, 395, 396, 403, 404
"Out of the Cradle Endlessly Rocking" (Whitman), 186
Owens, Craig, 100
Oxford English Dictionary, 27, 121, 178, 204, 279

Paine, Tom, 293
Painting, 32, 97
Panegyric, 226
Paradigms in science, 211, 257
Paradise Lost (Milton), 203–4
Paradise Now (theater piece), 96
Patriarchy: construction of masculinity, 327–28
Patriotic Gore (Wilson), 406
Paul, St., 233
Penis envy, 152–53
People, the, 322–25
Perception, 137; role of language in, 87, 89; yearning for pure, 435–36
Perelman, Chaim, 220
Performance, 91–103; narrative as, 69–74, 78. See also Interpretation
Performative utterances, 212–15
Performing Self, The (Poirier), 97–98
Personification, 75–80, 83
Petty bourgeoisie, 413, 414, 418
Phaedrus (Plato), 43, 46, 204, 373, 375
Pharmakon, 46
Phelan, James, 168–69
Phenomenology, 26, 67, 112, 137
Phenomenology of Knowledge, The (Cassirer), 25
Phenomenology of Spirit (Hegel), 157, 378–79
Philippines, 309, 441

Philology, 27, 28, 216

Philosophy: aesthetics, 11–12, 32, 179–80, 236, 334; Being, 384; binary oppositions in, 43; epistemology, 307, 347; figurative language in, 86–87; on form, 25–26, 28–29; and ideology, 307; on intention, 137–38; and literature, 167–68, 257; logic, 205; materialism, 41; and modernism, 435–36; phenomenology, 26, 67, 112, 137; positivism, 250–51; pragmatism, 60; realism, 15, 311; as rhetoric, 204–7, 211–13; Sophists, 204, 206, 207, 275; on unconscious, 147–48; value in, 177, 178. *See also* Ethics; Idealism

Philosophy of Symbolic Forms (Cassirer), 25

Philosophy of the Unconscious (Hartmann), 148

Phonemics, 27

Phonetics, 27

Photorealism, 16

Phusis (nature), 377–78

Physics (Aristotle), 377

Picasso, Pablo, 329

Pioneers, The (Cooper), 281

Pixote (film), 315

Placido, Beniamino, 297

Plato, 138, 148, 236, 431; on Being, 384; on desire, 369, 370, 371–74, 379; *nous* of, 25, 28–29; *Phaedrus,* 43, 46, 204, 373, 375; on poets, 163; on representation, 11, 14–15; on rhetoric, 204, 209, 218; *Symposium,* 372–73, 379

Pleasure, 384

Pliny, 138

Plot, 5, 66, 71, 403. *See also* Narrative

Plotinus, 148

Pluralism, cultural, 346

Poe, Edgar Allan, 39, 155, 192, 201; "Black Cat," 190–91; "Purloined Letter," 42, 160–61

"Poems of Our Climate, The" (Stevens), 329

Poetics (Aristotle), 66–69, 71, 72

Poetry, 289; Bentham on, 337; determinacy/indeterminacy in, 163–65; Eliot on, 338; figurative language in, 80–86, 89–90; formalism on, 253; influence in, 186–201; intention in, 141–42, 145; interpretation of, 122–24, 127; metaphysical, 245–48; modernist, 246, 435–42; as narrative, 74–79; and nationalism, 284; performance art as, 95–96, 100–103; prose versus, 50, 52; representation in, 14, 16–21; Richards on, 339; signifier/signified in, 42–45; of Stevens, 428–45; structure in, 33

Poetry (Monroe), 435

Point of view, 5

Poirier, Richard, 97–98

Politics, 7, 167–68; and discourse, 56–64; and ideology, 307, 312–20; and influence, 197–98; of interpretation, 126–34; and literary history, 258, 260; in metaphysical poetry, 247–48; representation in theory of, 11–12; of rhetoric, 216–17; and Steven's "Anecdote of the Jar," 440–42; and writing, 46–48. *See also* History; Ideology

Pollock, Jackson, 146

Poovey, Mary, 407n

Pope, Alexander, 142, 186–87, 227

"Popular and the Realistic, The" (Brecht), 326

Popular culture, 321–35; defined, 322–23; high culture compared to, 331–35; mass culture compared to, 325, 326, 331; sensationalism of, 328

Pornography, 15

Portrait of the Artist as a Young Man, A (Joyce), 138–39

Positivism, 250–51

Postmodernism: and Bloom's influence theory, 199; and decolonization, 356–57; on ethics, 393–94; on exile, 367; on intention, 143–46; in Joyce, 365; on representation, 16–17; and structure, 29–30, 35–37; supermarkets and museums as characteristic institutions of, 358

Poststructuralism: on author, 113–16; and Bloom's influence theory, 200–201; on discourse, 50–64; on narratives, 67; on rhetoric, 215–16; on structure, 31–37

Poulet, Georges, 67

Pound, Ezra, 143, 198, 358, 433, 438–39

Power, 260, 261, 312; authorial, 107; and culture, 361, 368; and discourse, 51, 54, 57–64; rhetoric of, 207. *See also* Politics

Pragmatism, 60

Pragmatism's Freud: The Moral Disposition of Psychoanalysis, 392

Prague linguistic school, 26, 33

Prelude, The (Wordsworth), 186

Price, Martin, 255

Prince, Gerald, 403

Princess Casamassima, The (James), 76–77

Princeton Encyclopedia of Poetry and Poetics, 140–43

Procreation, 372–73

Progress, 355

Proletariat, 413, 414

Promised Land, The (Antin), 297

Propp, Vladimir, 67, 71

Prose versus poetry, 50, 52
Prosopopoeia, 75, 76
Protagoras, 204
Protogenes, 138
Proust, Marcel, 145
Prynne, William, 135–36, 141
Psyche, 57, 60, 63. *See also* Mind
Psychoanalysis, 1, 28, 171; on author, 112; on desire, 382–85; on ethics, 387, 392–93; and Marxist ideology theory, 310, 313, 314; on narrative, 67; poststructuralism versus, 54, 60; on sexual difference, 379–80; on unconscious, 147–62; on value/evaluation, 178; and writing theory, 40–42. *See also* Freud, Sigmund; Oedipus complex
Psychobiology, 31–32
Psychology, 34, 148. *See also* Psychoanalysis
Puig, Manuel, 315
Punishment, 60,137
Puns, 122–24, 149, 151, 156
"Purloined Letter, The" (Poe), 42, 160–61
Pynchon, Thomas, 186

Quintilian, 207, 216

Race, 4–7, 274–87, and canon-formation, 234–35; and ethnicity, 289, 294, 303; and gender, 264, 272; German, 290; and ideology, 311, 319; and imperialism, 355; interracial marriage, 348; and multiculturalism, 346; and nationalism, 282–87, 360; in popular culture, 333; racially based concept of culture, 364; in Twain, 125–26, 266, 267, 270, 271, 291, 297–99. *See also* Blacks; Ethnicity
Rambo, 327, 332
Rational choice theory, 398, 416, 417
Rationality of women, 377
Ratner's Star (DeLillo), 442–43
Ravishing of Lol Stein, The (Duras), 381–82, 383
Raw/cooked distinction, 31
Rawls, John, 402
Ray, William, 216
Readerly texts, 93
Reader-response theory, 1, 67
Reading: against the grain, 171, 175; and canon-formation, 239–42, 246–48; Lacan's theory of, 45–46; of Steven's poetry, 428–45. *See also* Interpretation; Performance
Reading for the Plot (Brooks), 403
Reagan, Ronald, 11–12, 128, 131, 133, 318–19, 332

Realism, 15, 311
Reason, 209, 257, 280, 286; the Enlightenment and imperialism, 357–58; rationality of women, 377. *See also* Mind
Recent Theories of Narrative (Martin), 403
Reception theory, 178
Red Badge of Courage, The (Crane), 259
Reed, John, 295
Reign of Terror, 294, 302
Relationships, social, 322
Relativism, cultural, 346
Relativity, 186
Religio Medici (Browne), 256
Religion, 34, 163–64, 209, 260; and ideology, 309–11; intention in, 137–38; and race, 275–76; and unconscious, 147
Renaissance, 33–34, 139, 168, 230, 242, 264; author in, 107, 109; and literary history, 193, 194; and literary influence, 252, 257, 260
Repetition in narratives, 70, 75–76
Representation, 11–21, 32, 37, 356–57
Repression, 357
Republic of Letters, 110
Restitution of Decayed Intelligence (Verstegen), 283
Rhetoric, 5, 7, 203–22, 257; and indeterminacy, 170–71, 175; of interpretation, 126–34; as study of figurative language, 83, 87–88; of unconscious, 160
Rhetoric (Aristotle), 206
Rhetoric of Economics, The (McCloskey), 209–10
Rhetoric of Fiction, The (Booth), 220, 221
Rhetoric of Irony, A (Booth), 221
Rhinelander, John, 130, 132
Ricardo, David, 414, 415
Rich, Adrienne, 47
Richards, I. A., 337–39, 340
Richard the Lionheart, 280
Ricoeur, Paul, 67–68, 148–49, 403
Riell, Peter Hanns, 251
Road to Xanadu, The (Lowes), 186
Robinson, Edwin Arlington, 242
Rob Roy (Scott), 281
Rogers, Will, 291
Romanticism, 252; English, 438–40, 442; German, 290; and influence, 187, 190–92, 197; on intention, 138–39; and metaphysical poets, 246; and nonrational, 148, 164; on the people, 324; unity in, 4
Rome, ancient, 241, 243, 285
Rorty, Richard, 60, 221, 394, 400
Rousseau, Jean-Jacques, 39, 148

Royce, Josiah, 435–36, 438
Ruin the Sacred Truths (Bloom), 192–93
Rusk, Dean, 98
Russian formalism, 26, 32, 34, 67, 71, 251–55, 402
Russian Revolution, 295

Sacks, Peter, 255
Sacks, Sheldon, 87
Sahlins, Marshall, 261
Said, Edward W., 47, 55, 64, 365, 408
Salammbô (Flaubert), 281
Salinger, J. D., 242
"Sandman, The" (Hoffmann), 154–55
Santayana, George, 435–46
"Sarrasine" (Balzac), 93
Sartor Resartus (Carlyle), 256
Satire, 226, 291
Saussure, Ferdinand de, 143; and literary history, 256–57; sign theory of, 40–43, 158–61; and structuralism, 26–31, 36, 40. *See also* Signs, theory of; Structuralism
Schechner, Richard, 96
Scheffler, Israel, 211
Schelling, Friedrich Wilhelm Joseph von, 148
Schiller, Friedrich von, 337
Schleiermacher, Friedrich, 143
Schnabel, Johann Gottfried, 290
Scholes, Robert, 219–21
Schopenhauer, Arthur, 148
Schwitters, Kurt, 95
Science: figurative language in, 86–87; French critics on history of, 55–56; and ideology, 310; and literary historicism, 250–51; literature as opposite of, 164, 175; paradigms in, 211, 257; and race, 276–77, 280; rhetoric versus, 209–11
Scotland, 284, 286
Scott, Sir Walter, 70, 279–82, 284
Scritti Pollitti, 1
Searle, John, 214
"Second Coming is at Hand, The" (Yeats), 364–65
Secret Agent, The (Conrad), 355
Sedgwick, Eve Kosofsky, 383, 400
Selfishness, 378, 394
Semiotics, 1, 216; on ethics, 387; on narratives, 67, 71; representation in, 11–12; and structure, 31, 34–35
Seneca, 194
Serious/nonserious utterances, 213–14
Sexual difference, 374–78, 380, 384, 385
Sexuality, 57, 58; heterosexuality, 370, 384; incest, 72–73; Plato's third sex, 379; procre-ation, 372–73; in psychoanalysis, 148–49, 152–55. *See also* Gender; Homosexuality; Oedipus complex
Sexual orientation, 346
Shakespeare, William, 92, 167, 214, 240, 285, 431; *As You Like It,* 69, 227–28; and culture, 227–29; *Hamlet,* 74, 91, 94, 96, 97, 99, 168, 193–96, 264–65; *King Lear,* 230; and literary influence, 193–96; *Merchant of Venice,* 277–78; *Midsummer Night's Dream,* 260; *Othello,* 277–78; race in, 277–79; *Tempest,* 231–32, 278–79
Shakespeare Our Contemporary (Kott), 167
Shapiro, Miriam, 98
Shaw, George Bernard, 363, 365
Shelley, Percy Bysshe, 138–39, 439, 440
Sherwin, Paul S., 196
Shklovsky, Victor, 253
Shultz, George, 128–29
Sibilants, 27
Sidney, Sir Philip, 257–314
Signified/signifier. *See* Signs, theory of
Signs, theory of, 26–27, 29, 31; and unconscious, 159–61; and writing, 40–44
Simile, 80, 83, 156
Simon, Paul, 121
Sklovskij, Viktor, 67
Slavery, 137, 266, 278, 286; Hegel on, 157–58; Twain on, 297–99, 301–2; and writing, 48
Slavery in the United States (Ball), 298–99
Slavic formalism. *See* Russian formalism
Sloane, Thomas, 208
"Slumber Did My Spirit Seal, A" (Wordsworth), 74–79, 168–69, 174–75
Smart, Barry, 59
Smith, Barbara Herrnstein, 198, 220
Smith, Gerard, 131, 133
Smith, Henry Nash, 33–34, 265, 298
Social contract theory, 398
Social Darwinism, 279
Social identities, 322
Socialism, 61, 362. *See also* Marxism
Social relationships, 322
Sociological narrative theory, 67
Socrates: on desire, 372–73, 374, 375; and rhetoric, 204, 209; on the unconscious, 148; on writing, 43
Sofaer, Abraham, 129–32
Sollers, Philippe, 39
"Song of Myself" (Whitman), 186
Songs of Innocence (Blake), 81
Sonneck, Oscar George Theodore, 289
Sophie's Choice (Styron), 402

Sophists, 204, 206, 207, 275
Sophocles, 72–74, 153–55, 194
South America, 361–62
Soviet Union, 128, 307–8
Space, 23–24
Speech: criterion of correct, 241, 242; writing versus, 43–48, 388
Speech-act theory, 138
Speech and Phenomena (Derrida), 43
Spenser, Edmund, 191, 228, 229
Spinoza, Benedict, 378
Spitzer, Leo, 186
Sprachgeist, 284
Spratt, Thomas, 256
Springfield Republican, 123
Springsteen, Bruce, 318–19
Stage Blood (play), 97
Stallman, R. W., 140–42
Standard English, 241–42, 246
Standardized tests, 340
Standpoint epistemology, 346
Star Chamber, 135
Starobinski, Jean, 42
Stein, Gertrude, 103
Sterne, Laurence, 253
Stevens, Wallace, 191; "Anecdote of the Jar," 7–8, 428–45
Stowe, Harriet Beecher, 298
Strassburg, Gottfried von, 290
Strategic Defense Initiative (SDI), 128
"Structural Activity, The" (Barthes), 35, 36
Structuralism, 1; on individual, 143; and literary history, 256–57; on narratives, 67, 71; and Stevens's "Anecdote of the Jar," 434–38; on structure, 25–34; on writing, 40–41. *See also* Poststructuralism
Structure, 23–37
Structure of Scientific Revolutions, The (Kuhn), 210–12
Style, 63, 141
Styron, William, 402
Subject: of desire, 376; in ethics, 392; Lacan on, 157–58
Sublime, the, 374
Super-ego, 151–52, 156
Supermarkets, 358
Supplément, 45
Supreme Court, U.S., 136–37
Surplus value, 414, 415
Symbol, 5, 14, 15
Symbolic ethnicity, 292
Symposium (Plato), 372–73, 379
Synchronic linguistics, 26–27, 40
Synecdoche, 189, 190

Synge, John Millington, 363, 366
Syntagmatics, 27
System, 24–25, 31, 40
Systems analysis, 31–32
S/Z (Barthes), 93

Tacitus, 283, 285
Taine, Hippolyte, 251, 252, 284–85
Tale of Two Cities, A (Dickens), 295
Tasso, Torquato, 229
Taste, hierarchy of, 330
Tate, Allen, 50, 52
Taylor, Edward, 43–45
Television, 88, 312–13
Tel Quel, 39, 40
Tempest, The (Shakespeare), 231–32, 278–79
Tenure (academic), 409, 419
Tessera, 188–90, 198, 199
Tests, standardized, 340
Text, the: in high and popular culture, 331–35; readerly texts, 93; undecidability of, 390; writerly texts, 93
Textuality, concept of, 40
Textual Power (Scholes), 219–21
Theater of the Ridiculous, 97
Theology, 34. *See also* Religion
Theoretical Era, 387, 388
Theory, literary. *See* Literary theory
Third sex, 379
Third World, 258, 260
Thomas, William I., 297
Thompson, E. P., 325–27
Thoreau, Henry David, 187, 188, 252
Through the Flower: My Struggle as a Woman Artist (Chicago), 98–99
Tillyard, E. M. W., 251
Time, 23–24
Time and Narrative (Ricoeur), 403
Todorov, Tzvetan, 67
Tolstoy, Leo, 75
Tomkins, Calvin, 97
Tompkins, Jane, 178
Toscanini, Arturo, 92
Totalitarianism, 357, 362
Totem and Taboo (Freud), 196
To the Place of Wisdom: Order and Energy in Eighteenth-Century Literature (Price), 255
Tradition, 361, 364
Tragedy, 67, 72
Transformational grammar, 28
Translation, 121–22
Transumption, 191
Travel writing, 359
Treaties, interpretation of, 127–34

Trilling, Lionel, 406
Tristes Tropiques (Lévi-Strauss), 48
Tristram Shandy (Sterne), 253
Trollope, Anthony, 70, 76–77
Tropes, 80–90; in narratives, 75–79. *See also*
  Figurative language
Tropological narrative theory, 67
Trotsky, Leon, 26
Trump, Donald, 309
Truth: linguistic concept of, 55–57, 59, 257;
  and rhetoric, 205–21
Tudor, David, 96
tuning (Antin), 101–3
Tupper, Martin, 274–79, 285, 287
Turkey, 359–60
Tuskegee Institute, 350
Twain, Mark, 190, 289; *Connecticut Yankee,*
  290–304; *Huckleberry Finn,* 69, 125–27,
  265–73, 291, 298
Tylor, Edward B., 225, 227

Ulysses (Joyce), 186
"Uncanny, The" (Freud), 154–55
Uncle Tom's Cabin (Stowe), 298
Uncle Tom's Children (Wright), 351
Unconscious, 139–40, 147–62; figurative in,
  87; and ideology, 310; and influence, 188;
  structure of, 28, 41–42
Under Western Eyes (Conrad), 355
Union of Concerned Scientists, 130
United States: ABM Treaty of, as interpreta-
  tion example, 128–33; black nationalism
  in, 285–87; foreign interventions by,
  440–42; ideology in, 307–8, 313, 317–19;
  and race, 281–83, 289; in Twain's *Connecti-
  cut Yankee,* 291–303
United States, Parts 1–4 (Anderson), 99–101
Unity, 4
Universal Pragmatics, 219
Universities, 345, 407–8; English depart-
  ments, 338, 408–10; tenure, 409, 419
University of Chicago, 342
University of Georgia, 344
University of Virginia, 283
Ursonate (Schwitters), 95
Uses of Literacy, The (Hoggart), 326

Validity in Interpretation (Hirsch), 142–43
Vallee, Rudy, 291
Value/evaluation, 6–7, 57, 177–85; and ethics, 179, 395; exchange, 29–30, 37, 178;
  family values, 335; surplus value, 414, 415.
  See also Canon
van Gogh, Vincent, 139, 146

Vargas Llosa, Mario, 368
Verstegen, Richard, 283
Vico, Giambattista, 55, 209
Vietnam, 97, 98, 100, 438, 440–45
Virgil, 187, 193, 231
Voltaire, 286

Wagner, Richard, 91–92
Waiting for Godot (Beckett), 99
Walden (Thoreau), 187, 188
Walker, Alice, 39
War and Peace (Tolstoy), 75
Washington, Booker T., 300, 350, 351
Washington, George, 428, 431
Waste Land, The (Eliot), 142, 256, 350
Weber, Max, 337, 349
Webster's New World Dictionary, 263n
Wellek, René, 254
Well Wrought Urn, The (Brooks), 247
West, Cornell, 408
"What Is an Author?" (Foucault), 106,
  113–16
Wheatley, Phillis, 286
Whiggism, 60
White, Hayden, 67–68, 220, 257
White, Robin, 93
Whitman, Walt, 186, 191, 435–36
Why Are We in Vietnam? (Mailer), 440
Wilde, Oscar, 363
Wilden, Anthony, 32
Wilkins, Bishop, 205
Will, 148, 389
Will, George, 318–19
Williams, Bernard, 397
Williams, James D., 296, 298–99
Williams, Raymond, 3–4, 24–25, 258, 325,
  326, 406
Williams, William Carlos, 94
William the Conqueror, 279–80
Wilson, Edmund, 406
Wimsatt, W. K., 33, 111, 140–43, 253
Winkler, John J., 377
Wittgenstein, Ludwig, 55, 145
Wittig, Monique, 384
Womanhouse, 98, 100
Women: and academic hiring, 410; in Ameri-
  can colleges, 344; and ethics, 387; female
  writing, 47; femininity, 263, 377; and hier-
  archy of taste, 330; and literature, 258; in
  Mann's fantastic logic, 375; passivity of,
  377; psychoanalysis on, 152–53; rational-
  ity of, 377; responses to *New Newlywed
  Game,* 327, 328; responsibility for emo-
  tional management by, 330; works by in

Women (*continued*)
    the canon, 234, 238, 242. *See also* Femi-
    nism; Gender
Woolf, Rosemary, 255
Word: complex, 77; functions of, 29
Wordsworth, William, 39, 186, 438–40; "A
    Slumber Did My Spirit Seal," 74–79, 168–
    69, 174–75
Wright, Richard, 351–52
Writerly texts, 93
Writing, 5, 6, 39–49; and canon-formation,
    239–42; deconstructivist theory of,
    257–59; Derrida on, 39, 42–48, 359; and

desire, 374; and influence, 201; and sexual
    difference, 380; and slavery, 48; speech ver-
    sus, 43–48, 388; travel writing, 359. *See
    also* Literature
Writing and Difference (Derrida), 43, 45–46
Writing Degree Zero (Barthes), 40

"Yankee Doodle" (song), 289
Yeats, W. B., 358, 363, 364–65, 366, 438

Žižek, Slavoj, 402, 404
Zuni Indians, 297